More information about this series at http://www.springer.com/series/8165

European Yearbook of International Economic Law

Marc Bungenberg • Markus Krajewski •
Christian J. Tams • Jörg Philipp Terhechte •
Andreas R. Ziegler

Editors

European Yearbook of International Economic Law 2019

 Springer

Editors

Marc Bungenberg
Faculty of Law
Saarland University
Saarbrücken, Germany

Markus Krajewski
Faculty of Law
University of Erlangen-Nuremberg
Erlangen, Germany

Christian J. Tams
School of Law
University of Glasgow
Glasgow, UK

Jörg Philipp Terhechte
Competition and Regulation Institute
Leuphana University Lüneburg
Lüneburg, Germany

Andreas R. Ziegler
Faculty of Law and Criminal Sciences
University of Lausanne
Lausanne, Switzerland

ISSN 2364-8392 ISSN 2364-8406 (electronic)
European Yearbook of International Economic Law
ISBN 978-3-030-22484-4 ISBN 978-3-030-22485-1 (eBook)
https://doi.org/10.1007/978-3-030-22485-1

This Springer imprint is published by the registered company Springer Nature Switzerland AG.
The registered company address is: Gewerbestrasse 11, 6330 Cham, Switzerland

Editorial EYIEL 10 (2019)

The signing of the Treaty of Versailles in June 1919 not only marked the formal ending of World War I but also established the International Labour Organization (ILO): a key feature of the inter-war order, alongside the League of Nations. Thus, 2019 is the ILO's centenary year, which makes the ILO one of the oldest international organisations in today's United Nations family. The editors of the European Yearbook of International Economic Law seized this opportunity to devote the special section of EYIEL 10 to the ILO and international labour law in general and their relationship with international economic law. The contributions to this volume highlight the close connection of international labour law and international economic law and invite readers to appreciate the common grounds of, as well as fundamental differences between, the two subfields of international law. We also hope that this volume provides a future research agenda that avoids treating international labour and economic law as entirely separate entities.

The special section is opened by former Director of the Office of Legal Services of the ILO *Anne Trebilcock* who offers a consideration of the ILO as an actor in international economic law in the past and the future. In her chapter, *Trebilcock* traces the evolution of the ILO's mission and means of action in relation to international economic law. She highlights key markers along the road towards the goal of achieving social justice, from the ILO's constitutional origins to major ILO Declarations to the recent ILO Centenary Initiatives. *Trebilcock* laments the divergent paths taken by international economic law and transnational labour law and identifies avenues to bring them closer in order to achieve decent work for all on a sustainable planet.

Emilios Christodoulidis reflects on the ILO's centennial anniversary by discussing the shift to a pragmatic "common sense" approach in the ILO context. Taking his cue from Alain Supiot's important defence of the "spirit of Philadelphia", *Christodoulidis* argues that the Philadelphia Declaration of 1944 renewed and deepened the commitments on which the ILO was built in 1919 and seeks a firm theoretical footing in Supiot's defence of the law's "dogmatic" foundations. The chapter then goes on to track a "double mutation", firstly away from political-constitutionalist protection of work towards a form of human rights protection and secondly away from "hard" institutional processes to "soft" aspirational standards. *Christodoulidis* claims that this separation misreads and undercuts the integrity of international labour law, which depends on holding together its organising principles and their instantiations.

Working relations in global supply chains are not the first, but certainly one of the most important intersections between international labour and international economic law. *Valentina Grado* addresses this intersection as she maps the ILO's work concerning decent work in global supply chains (GSCs). Although GSCs create millions of jobs and opportunities for economic and social development, they often seriously disregard core labour standards and pose significant challenges to decent work. The chapter illustrates and critically analyses the work of the (2016) 105th Session of the International Labour Conference dealing with GSCs. In addition, *Grado* describes and discusses further significant instruments adopted by the Governing Body to ensure decent work in GSCs, including respect for international labour standards. Finally, she evaluates the adequacy of the recent ILO initiatives in the field of GSCs in delivering better labour conditions for workers within them.

In a similar vein, *Shin-ichi Ago* assesses if and how the supervision of international labour standards can contribute to the implementation of the UN Guiding Principles on Business and Human Rights which were adopted by the UN Human Rights Council in 2011. *Ago* recalls that some specialised agencies of the UN and regional organisations responded to the recommendation of the Human Rights Council and contributed to the implementation of Guiding Principles. In this respect, *Ago* analyses activities of the ILO and concludes that, in the area of labour and social rights, the ILO supervision mechanism also plays an important role in the implementation of the UNGP. However, he highlights the limiting factor that observance of international labour standards is a matter for governments and that enterprises are not directly accountable to the ILO standards. *Ago* also refers to the ILO's own instrument of corporate accountability, the ILO Tripartite Declaration of Principles concerning Multinational Enterprises and Social Policy, which may serve as an additional tool to implement a part of the UN Guiding Principles and which is discussed in greater length by *Jernej Letnar Cernic* in this volume.

The next two chapters address the relationship between international labour law and labour standards on the one hand and specific subfields of international economic law on the other. While *Franz Christian Ebert* addresses international financial institutions (IFIs), *Henner Gött* looks at trade and investment agreements.

Asking about the potential labour safeguards of IFIs to prevent violations of ILO Core Labour Standards, *Ebert* looks at the safeguards' legal design, reviews the normative content of selected IFI labour safeguards and assesses their relationship with relevant ILO instruments. *Ebert* also scrutinises the scope of relevant labour safeguards and shows several loopholes, which could allow borrowers to avoid many of the requirements by adjusting the project structure. Furthermore, *Ebert* assesses the safeguards' practical implications and examines the mechanisms established by several IFIs to prevent and provide remedy for violations of the safeguards' requirements. *Ebert* concludes by emphasising the need for more comprehensive protections of workers with regard to IFI activities.

Gött addresses a core topic linking trade and labour law and assesses the linkages of trade, investment and labour in Preferential Trade Agreements (PTAs). The chapter examines the scope and content of contemporary trade-labour and investment-labour linkages in some of the major latest-generation PTAs, analysing both substantive provisions and institutional mechanisms for their implementation. *Gött* argues that the examined substantive provisions have considerable potential for the protection and promotion of labour standards in the context of trade and investment liberalisation. However, whether this potential can be tapped largely depends on how they are implemented. A recurring issue in this respect is that the pertinent implementation mechanisms for labour provisions suffer from a lack of sufficient and necessary structures that persist even in latest-generation PTAs. Against this background, there is a need for a systematic and structural revision of PTA labour provisions.

The last two chapters return to issues closer to international labour law, but with significant implications on international economic relations. *Reingard Zimmer* addresses International Framework Agreements (IFAs) and transnational collective bargaining while *Jernej Letnar Cernic* looks at the ILO Tripartite Declaration on Multinational Enterprises (MNEs).

As the necessity of responses from the workers' side to the internationalisation of business became more and more evident, global trade union federations started to negotiate and sign global agreements with transnational companies. *Zimmer* assesses these International Framework Agreements and the more recent transnational collective agreements. She suggests that as the agreements are the product of social dialogue they are thus a form of collective bargaining. However, *Zimmer* notes the content of agreements with European scope differs significantly from the content of international agreements. While the latter primarily deals with minimum social standards, European agreements cover a wide range of subjects, restructuring being the main topic. The chapter also refers to the Bangladesh Accord on Fire and Building Safety, which contains not only a stronger mechanism of enforcement but also a legally binding dispute resolution mechanism. In summary, *Zimmer* suggests that the development of transnational collective agreements can be characterised as a step towards the internationalisation of industrial relations.

Cernic concludes the special section commemorating the 100th anniversary of the ILO with an analysis of the ILO Tripartite Declaration of Principles concerning Multinational Enterprises and Social Policy as revised in 2017. *Cernic* argues that the ILO Governing Body should rephrase the vague and conditional language of the Tripartite Declaration and improve its implementation tools, particularly the interpretation procedures by opening it to individual claimants. In this way, it would enable the rights-holders to enforce the core labour rights included in the declaration against adverse corporate conduct.

Part II of this Yearbook is devoted to regional issues and focuses on recent developments in North America and the EU.

Steve Charnovitz analyses the recent trade strategy of the USA vis-à-vis China and finds that many complaints against China involve behaviour that is contrary to WTO rules, even though the USA lodged only two WTO cases against that behaviour. He argues that this suggests that the current US Administration prefers to confront China with power-based measures in the form of unilateral tariffs. *Jean-Michel Marcoux* assesses the renegotiation of NAFTA in the form of the United States–Mexico–Canada Agreement (USMCA). He suggests that, despite some notable exceptions, several changes included in USMCA reflect the current political landscape in which the renegotiation was held and are hardly reconcilable with the characterisation of the agreement as the most advanced existing trade deal. *Marcoux* also questions the innovation and sophistication of the Agreement by pointing out that several provisions reflect a bilateral approach, either which can potentially restrict trade or partially replicate the language of other free trade agreements.

Maryna Rabinovych and *Luke Tattersall* address European topics. *Rabynovich* analyses the promotion of the rule of law through EU Free Trade Agreements. She explores the foundational ("framework") foreign policy and legal prerequisites behind the EU's promotion of the rule of law through FTAs and discusses the example of administrative cooperation and public procurement chapters of three categories of EU FTAs. *Tattersall* looks at the challenges to international investment law in the EU in light of the Judgement of the European Court of Justice in the so-called *Achmea* case.

Part III of the Yearbook focusses on institutions with a contribution on the rule of law in International Monetary and Financial Law by *Marcin J. Menkes*, an analysis of the Appellate Body of the WTO by *Fernando Dias Simões* and the assessment of the WTO case law in 2017 by *Kholofelo Kugler, Faith Tigere-Pittet* and *Saweria Mwangi*.

Finally, Part IV (which concludes this Yearbook) brings together reviews of recent books; these reflect the breadth and diversity of international economic law, from mega-regional trade agreements to the calculation of damages.

The editorial reforms introduced in Volume 9 of the EYIEL are proving to be successful: Online-first publication is now a standard feature of the Yearbook. Our Assistant Editor *Judith Crämer* has taken up most of the managerial tasks and responsibilities of collecting and editing the contributions to this volume. Without her tremendous commitment and enthusiasm, EYIEL 10 would not have been possible; the editors are therefore most grateful to her. *Judith Crämer* was supported by *Athene Richford* at the University of Glasgow. Finally, we are grateful to *Anja Trautmann* at Springer for her continuing support of EYIEL.

Saarbrücken, Germany   Marc Bungenberg
Erlangen, Germany   Markus Krajewski
Glasgow, UK   Christian J. Tams
Lüneburg, Germany   Jörg Philipp Terhechte
Lausanne, Switzerland   Andreas R. Ziegler
September 2019

Contents

Editors and Contributors

About the Editors

Marc Bungenberg Faculty of Law, Saarland University, Saarbrücken, Germany

Markus Krajewski Faculty of Law, University of Erlangen-Nuremberg, Erlangen, Germany

Christian J. Tams School of Law, University of Glasgow, Glasgow, UK

Jörg Philipp Terhechte Competition and Regulation Institute, Leuphana University Lüneburg, Lüneburg, Germany

Andreas R. Ziegler Faculty of Law and Criminal Sciences, University of Lausanne, Lausanne, Switzerland

Contributors

Shin-ichi Ago Ritsumeikan University, Kyoto, Japan

Jernej Letnar Černič Faculty of Government and European Studies, Nova univerza, Ljubljana, Slovenia

Steve Charnovitz George Washington University Law School, Washington, DC, USA

Emilios Christodoulidis University of Glasgow, Glasgow, UK

Franz Christian Ebert Max Planck Institute for Comparative Public Law and International Law, Heidelberg, Germany

Henner Gött Institute of International and European Law, Jean Monnet Chair for European Union and Global Sustainable Development Through Law, Göttingen, Germany
Department of International Economic and Environmental Law, Georg-August-University Göttingen, Göttingen, Germany

Valentina Grado University of Naples L'Orientale, Naples, Italy

Winfried Huck Ostfalia University of Applied Sciences, Brunswick European Law School (BELS), Wolfenbüttel, Germany

Kholofelo Kugler Advisory Centre on WTO Law, Geneva, Switzerland

Maria Laura Marceddu King's College London, London, UK

Jean-Michel Marcoux McGill University, Faculty of Law, Montreal, QC, Canada

Marcin J. Menkes Warsaw School of Economics, Warsaw, Poland

Eleni Methymaki University of Oxford, St. Catherine's College, Oxford, UK

Saweria Mwangi World Trade Organization, Geneva, Switzerland

Faith Pittet Tutwa Consulting Group, Johannesburg, South Africa

Jens Hillebrand Pohl Maastricht University, Maastricht, The Netherlands

Maryna Rabinovych University of Hamburg, Hamburg, Germany

Gianpaolo Maria Ruotolo University of Foggia, Foggia, Italy

Fernando Dias Simões Chinese University of Hong Kong, Hong Kong, PR China

Luke Tattersall Essex Court Chambers, London, UK

Anne Trebilcock Labour Law Institute, Georg-August University, Göttingen, Germany

Reingard Zimmer Berlin School of Economics and Law, Berlin, Germany

Part I
100 Years International Labour Organization

The ILO as an Actor in International Economic Law: Looking Back, Gazing Ahead

Anne Trebilcock

Contents

1 Introduction

The 100th anniversary of the founding of the International Labour Organization (ILO) in 1919 presents an opportune moment to reflect on its past and its possible future as an actor in international economic law (IEL). Yet most texts on IEL do not even mention the body of international law that governs many labour issues, whether

A. Trebilcock (✉)
Labour Law Institute, Georg-August University, Göttingen, Germany

© Springer Nature Switzerland AG 2019
M. Bungenberg et al. (eds.), *European Yearbook of International Economic Law 2019*,
European Yearbook of International Economic Law (2020) 10: 3–34,
https://doi.org/10.1007/8165_2019_25, Published online: 17 September 2019

in the form of classic international labour law[1] or of the more broadly conceived transnational labour law.[2] Today, international economic law is most often thought of as encompassing fields dealing with international trade, foreign investment, monetary issues, often intellectual property, and sometimes international development.[3] While a few authors, notably Petersmann,[4] have taken a more inclusive view of IEL to embrace its normative aspects, the bulk of writing in the field has focused on more specific and often highly technical issues, without any reference to possibly relevant elements of the ILO's work. Using harsher terms, Chimni argues that since international labour law is not viewed by mainstream international economic law to be part of that body of law, the latter does not treat "the exploitation of those directly involved in wealth creation" as a central concern.[5] In light of globalization, Arthurs goes so far as to suggest the possible absorption of labour law into "the law of economic subordination and resistance" to "super-ordinate economic power".[6]

Definitions of IEL vary in amplitude and depth,[7] but for present purposes, a brief one will suffice: "the Public International Law analysis of the economic phenomena of international concern".[8] Surely standards setting minimum conditions at work and in social protection as part of a country's international competitiveness and development strategy fall within that scope. As do rules governing migration of workers as labour market actors. While such standards can lay down ground rules for the respect for human dignity in a globalized economy, at the same time an economy's functioning directly affects society. The impact of international economic, financial and trade policy and practices can be severe, from job creation or displacement traceable to international trade to erosion of collective bargaining.[9] In short, there is a continuing interplay between macroeconomic policy and frameworks for addressing labour and social protection issues, including their relationship to the major challenge of today: coming to grips with climate change.

On balance, the ILO's work has been met with both praise (e.g. Charnovitz, Helfer, Jenks, Sinclair) and critique (Langille, Maupain).[10] Will the organization be nimble enough to confront the challenges of its second century? It will certainly be put to the test. This essay traces the ILO's concern with IEL over time, before looking at possible pathways to greater convergence between the ILO's mission and macroeconomic policy frameworks. Space constraints unfortunately do not permit

---

[1]For an overview of international labour law, see e.g. Servais (2017) and Thouvenin and Trebilcock (2013).

[2]Blackett and Trebilcock (2015) and Trebilcock (2017).

[3]Qureshi (1999).

[4]Petersmann (2002, 2012).

[5]Chimni (2013), p. 253.

[6]Arthurs (2014), pp. 138 and 141.

[7]See Charnovitz (2011).

[8]Qureshi (1999), p. 11.

[9]Compa (2014) and Rittich (2015).

[10]Charnovitz (2000), Helfer (2006), Langille (2010, 2015), Maupain (2019) and Sinclair (2018).

examining regional dimensions of the situation, such as the interplay between the ILO and the European Union, but this does not imply their lack of importance alongside initiatives taken at the global level.

2 The ILO's Concern with International Economic Law

2.1 Preamble to the ILO Constitution

Highlights on the ILO's century timeline reveal the Organization's consistent concern with economic factors as both influences on and means of achievement of the ILO's mission: social justice. Established through Chapter XIII of the Treaty of Versailles, the ILO has a constitution whose preamble states in part:

> [...] whereas conditions of labour exist involving such injustice, hardship and privation to large numbers of people as to produce unrest so great that the peace and harmony of the world are imperilled; and an improvement of those conditions is urgently required [...].

Written in 1919, these words unfortunately still resonate a century later. As do the preamble's concerns with "the regulation of labour supply," "the provision of an adequate living wage," "equal remuneration for work of equal value," "protection of the interests of workers when employed in countries other than their own [...]" and more. Yet it is the so-called comparative advantage paragraph of the preamble that has been cited more often in recent years: "the failure of any nation to adopt humane conditions of labour is an obstacle in the way of other nations which desire to improve the conditions in their own countries." Drawing on the work of Sen and Nussbaum, Langille has pointed out that the preamble as a whole, linking social justice and the maintenance of peace, sees social justice "as the very point of development and its necessary precondition."[11] The ILO's construct based on social dialogue also set out an alternative to what international bolshevism had on offer, with article 427 of the Versailles treaty proclaiming that "labour should not be regarded merely as a commodity or article of commerce".

2.2 Constitutional Framework

With pre-World War I antecedents that aimed at harmonization of labour legislation,[12] the ILO was given several unique constitutional features, sketched here in summary form. It is a tripartite organization in which representatives of governments, employers and workers share, on a 2:1:1 basis in plenary sessions, decision-

---

[11]Langille (2009), Sen (1999, 2000) and Nussbaum (1999, 2000).
[12]Servais (2017), pp. 21–24.

making power in the International Labour Conference (ILC) and in the Governing Body.[13] This competence extends to taking financial and operational measures for the functioning of the institution; adopting international conventions, which are treaties, and recommendations, which provide guidance; making decisions in relation to complaints of a state's failure to give effect to a ratified convention[14]; and directing the work of the secretariat (the International Labour Office). The Secretariat in turn may undertake research and statistical work and advise member states in line with decisions taken at the annual ILC. The Constitution provides the basis for the Secretariat to engage in technical cooperation carried out in a number of the ILO's 187 member states and for the Organization to conclude agreements with them as well as with other international and regional organizations.[15]

As the prominent international jurist C Wilfred Jenks (ILO Legal Adviser and later Director-General of the Organization) observed, the ILO had always employed "a dynamic interpretation" of its Constitution.[16] The ultimate arbitrator of its meaning, and of that of ILO Conventions, lies with the International Court of Justice (ICJ), although the ILO is also empowered under Article 37(2) of the Constitution to set up its own tribunal for this purpose. (The ICJ's predecessor, the Permanent Court of International Justice, was called upon six times to interpret the ILO Constitution or an international labour convention.) Many key elements of the system set up to supervise the effect given to ILO Conventions and Recommendations, as well as of freedom of association principles, are not mentioned in the Constitution, but rather grew out of decisions taken by the annual Conference or by the Governing Body. A number of such ILO innovations were later adopted by other international organizations.[17]

2.3   Early ILO Positions on IEL

Before the outbreak of the Second World War led to the dissolution of the League of Nations, the ILO was structurally linked to it. In that period, some of the work of the secretariat and several resolutions adopted by the International Labour Conference evidenced the Organization's early concern with selected economic issues.[18] ILO

---

[13]For details, see the Standing Orders of the International Labour Conference and the Rules of the ILO Governing Body. Publications and official documents of the ILO may be found on its website, www.ilo.org.

[14]For descriptions of the process of adoption of Conventions and Recommendations and the various supervisory procedures and complaint mechanisms, see International Labour Office (2019).

[15]See Articles 10 (on functions of the International Labour Office) and 12 (on cooperation with other public international organizations).

[16]Sinclair (2018), p. 105; Trebilcock (2018).

[17]Sinclair (2018) and Charnovitz (2000).

[18]For instance, the Resolution concerning the effect of rationalization and international industrial agreements upon the conditions of labour (1928), the Resolution concerning measures to be taken in the economic sphere to remedy the international crisis in the coal industry (1931), Resolution

officials participated in diplomatic discussions of monetary policy at the Genoa Conference in 1922.[19] Five years later, the ILO was a co-convener, with the League of Nations and the International Management Institute, of the World Economic Conference. As the economic depression of the 1930s deepened, "it became evident that the ILO's traditional standard-setting activities were no longer an adequate response" to the crisis.[20] In 1932, the ILO Conference called on states to lay the foundations for a stable international monetary system, and with the most representative organizations of employers and workers to examine "the problems of production and international trade."[21] In 1933, the ILO drew the attention of the forthcoming Monetary and Economic Conference to a need for restoration of stable monetary conditions, with a system to avoid future price-level fluctuations, cessation of economic warfare through trade, increase in purchasing power, and adoption of [employment-generating] public works.[22] After that Conference failed to reach agreement on these issues, the ILO appealed to the League of Nations to ensure that national economic measures should take account of those points.[23] Serious statistical and economic research work backed up ILO positions on such topics.[24]

Furthermore, aside from the notable ambivalence about the exploitation of resources (including human) in colonies of major member states,[25] the ILO's first decades were also a period of sowing the seeds of basic human rights principles such as freedom of association,[26] the abolition of forced labour[27] and protection of children from economic exploitation.[28] At the same time, much of the ILO's work in this period focused on technical issues such as hours of work, minimum wage-fixing, health and safety at work, labour inspection, maternity protection, and minimum labour conditions for seafarers. In the early years of the ILO, restrictions

---

concerning the gold truce (1932), Resolution concerning measures to overcome the economic crisis (1934).

[19]Sinclair (2018), p. 44.

[20]Id., p. 95.

[21]Resolution concerning action to be taken to remedy the present crisis, adopted by the International Labour Conference, 16th Session, Record of Proceedings (1932), pp. 839–840.

[22]Resolution addressed to the World Monetary and Economic Conference, adopted by the International Labour Conference, 17th Session, Record of Proceedings (1933), p. 686.

[23]Resolution concerning measures to overcome the economic crisis, adopted by the International Labour Conference, 18th Session, Record of Proceedings (1934), p. 662.

[24]Rodgers et al. (2009), pp. 172–176.

[25]Maul (2012), p. 11.

[26]Right of Association (Agriculture) Convention 1921 (No. 11).

[27]Forced Labour Convention, 1930 (No. 29), which was adopted as a corollary to the Slavery Convention (1926), originally had the dual aim of prohibiting forced labour while in the meantime improving conditions endured by workers in colonies of major powers (background documents from this time displayed racist stereotypes that make the modern reader cringe).

[28]Such as the Night Work of Young Persons (Industry) Convention, 1919 (No. 6). This and other minimum age instruments were later displaced by the Minimum Age Convention, 1973 (No. 138) and the Worst Forms of Child Labour Convention, 1999 (No. 182), which are two of the ILO's core labour Conventions (see Sect. 2.8).

were also placed on women's work in certain fields and at certain hours, topics on which various women's movement networks had divergent views.[29] These instruments were later replaced by ones aimed at equality of opportunity.[30] The 1919 Women's Labour Congress (which convened in parallel to the first International Labour Conference of the ILO and influenced its agenda) highlighted both the direct contribution (as labour market participants) and indirect contribution (as enablers for others to participate in the labour market) of women to national economies.[31] The Global Commission on the Future of Work (see Sect. 3.3.1) recently returned to the question of recognizing unpaid as well as paid work in economic terms.

2.4   The Declaration of Philadelphia and the New Impetus for Employment Promotion

After arranging the wartime relocation of its headquarters to Canada, the ILO adopted what is known as "the Declaration of Philadelphia" at a conference held in that city in 1944. The Declaration reoriented the ILO's work in important ways.[32] It reaffirmed in Para. I that "(a) labour is not a commodity; (b) freedom of expression and of association are essential to sustained progress; (c) poverty anywhere constitutes a danger to prosperity everywhere; (d) the war against want requires [...] continuous and concerted international efforts [...]".[33] The Declaration explicitly empowered the Organization to further programmes to achieve more specific goals, including in Para. III(d) "policies in regard to wages and earnings, hours and other conditions of work calculated to ensure a just share of the fruits of progress to all, and a minimum living wage to all employed and in need of such protection." "[T]he collaboration of workers and employers in the preparation and application of social and economic measures" was also foreseen in Para. III(e).

Later incorporated into the Organization's Constitution, the Declaration proclaims, in Para. II(d), a "responsibility" of the ILO "to examine and consider all international economic and financial policies and measures in the light of [the] fundamental objective" of lasting peace based on social justice. The Declaration of Philadelphia and the 1948 Havana Charter arising out of the UN Conference on Trade and Employment together would have anchored an institutionalized role for

---

[29]Boris et al. (2018).

[30]Equal Remuneration Convention, 1951 (No. 100) and Discrimination (Employment and Occupation) Convention, 1958 (No. 111), which are fundamental labour Conventions. See also the gender-neutral Workers with Family Responsibilities Convention, 1981 (No. 156) and the Night Work Convention, 1991 (No. 171). Maternity protection instruments were also later revised; the up-to-date treaty is the Maternity Protection Convention, 2000 (No. 183).

[31]Boris et al. (2018).

[32]Blackett (2018), Ghebali (1989), Jenks (1970), Maupain (2013) and Supiot (2012).

[33]Declaration concerning the aims and purposes of the International Labour Organisation, Annex to the ILO Constitution, para. I.

the ILO in relation to trade. Since the Charter never entered into force, the connection with the ILO was left unmade.[34] Instead, the Bretton Woods institutions, initially the International Monetary Fund and the International Bank for Reconstruction and Development (the World Bank), were set up. Their work later significantly challenged the ILO's approach towards labour standards and social protection (see Sect. 2.5). This was in part because much of IEL has remained philosophically resistant to suggestions for redistribution, although some cracks are appearing[35] in light of growing awareness of the corrosiveness of stark inequalities within and between nations.

Shortly after the United Nations was established in 1945, the ILO reached an agreement with it, which recognized the ILO as a specialized agency responsible for taking action under its basic instrument to accomplish its purposes.[36] However, once the Economic and Social Council of the United Nations was up and running, the ILO did not have the impact on broader policies it had hoped.[37] It did, however, convince ECOSOC to endorse the importance of national and international policies for the attainment of full employment, a leitmotif of the ILO's work in line with Keynesian economics. The emergence of development economics in the 1950s extended the ILO's work on employment and working conditions in the context of decolonization as from the end of that decade.[38] In 1964, the ILO adopted the Employment Policy Convention (No. 122), which requires ratifying states to declare and pursue policies to promote full, productive and freely chosen employment, and to consult employer and worker organizations in the process. It reflected an approach of state-centred development, which was also pursued by the World Bank at the time.[39] In the same year, the ILO established its International Training Centre in Turin for what it termed agents of development.

Also in 1964, the ILO Conference adopted its first Declaration concerning the Policy of Apartheid in South Africa, relying on the Declaration of Philadelphia in its rationale. Among other elements, the Declaration appealed to governments, employers and workers in all ILO member countries to "apply all appropriate measures to lead South Africa to renounce apartheid". In "ILO-speak," this acknowledged economic measures such as divestment, boycotts and sanctions being called for by anti-apartheid activists. Annual discussion of reports under this Declaration, revised twice, kept up the pressure even though the country had withdrawn from the ILO (it remained bound by conventions it had ratified). The ILO also engaged in technical cooperation and training in front line states, and worked intensively with South Africa once it had abandoned apartheid and rejoined the Organization.[40]

---

[34]Charnovitz (2000), p. 178; Stoll (2018), pp. 18–19.

[35]Ratner (2017), pp. 754–756 and 772–774.

[36]Agreement between the International Labour Organisation and the United Nations (1945), Article I.

[37]Alcock (1971).

[38]Maul (2012).

[39]Sinclair (2018), pp. 243–244.

[40]Maul (2012), pp. 238–245; Rodgers et al. (2009), pp. 54–56. For further detail, see Rubin (2008).

The launch of the World Employment Programme in 1969 spurred ILO research in a number of countries to challenge received notions about the post-colonial development process,[41] including its gender dimension.[42] One track explored pursuing development through "redistribution with growth," an idea endorsed at the World Employment Conference in 1976. That meeting also highlighted the role of international economic reforms and cooperation in meeting the basic needs of the poor.[43] Another major thread put the focus on rural workers, especially women, producing work that later informed debate on the informal economy.

By the end of the 1960s, it had become more than clear that the power wielded by multinational corporations could rival the capacity of a number of states. Global production systems came to replace much nationally-based industry. Such developments led the Organisation for Economic Co-operation and Development (OECD) to adopt its Declaration for Multinational Enterprises in 1976. Under that Declaration, OECD National Contact Points began to play an active role in vindicating labour and social rights.[44] A year later, the ILO Governing Body adopted the Tripartite Declaration of Principles concerning Multinational Enterprises and Social Policy (MNE Declaration). However, since the complaint procedure atrophied after a stalemate in the early years, the ILO MNE Declaration has been used chiefly as a promotional tool, providing guidance on labour standards to firms (now done through a "Help Desk"). Both the OECD and ILO instruments have been revised, the ILO MNE Declaration most recently in 2017.[45]

At the other end of the economic spectrum, the informal economy—first known as the informal sector—posed some apparent dilemmas for ILO constituents.[46] Much of traditional labour law centred around the formal employment relationship, and few workers in the informal economy were organized. With the ILO's increasing focus on poverty, however, debate in the Organization moved from calls to stamp out the informal economy to seeing a need to upgrade it and forge links with formal enterprises. This took the Organization as a whole some time to absorb, finally adopting a Conference resolution on the topic in 2002 that helped pave the way for the adoption of the Transition from the Informal to the Formal Economy Recommendation, 2015 (No. 201). This Recommendation served as a reaffirmation that the ILO's mandate covers all workers. The new instrument called for an integrated framework, including inter alia a comprehensive employment policy framework that might include "pro-employment macroeconomic policies that support aggregate

---

[41]Rodgers et al. (2009), pp. 185–188.

[42]Britwun (2018), pp. 307–308.

[43]Rodgers et al. (2009), pp. 193–194.

[44]Bonucci and Kessedjian (2017).

[45]For a detailed discussion see the contribution by Jernej Letnar Cernic in this volume.

[46]La Hovary (2015).

demand, productive investment and structure transformation [...] and trade, industrial, tax, sectoral and infrastructure policies that promote employment, enhance productivity and facilitate structural transformation processes".[47]

Another huge group of largely forgotten workers, those engaged in domestic work in private households, finally achieved comprehensive recognition of their rights in the Decent Work for Domestic Workers Convention (No. 189) and Recommendation (No. 203), 2011. The background work and the instruments themselves reflect the important transnational migration aspects of this large economic sector, a source of remittances for many sending states.[48]

2.5   The Challenge of the "Washington Consensus"

Back to the 1970s. A push by many emerging countries for a "New International Economic Order" to adapt rules of the global economy more towards development proved highly contentious, including in the ILO.[49] While the ILO was continuing to rally around various means of employment promotion with emphasis on government action, a shadow fell over its time line. This was the emergence of the so-called Washington consensus, in which neoliberal economists stressed private enterprise, property rights, freer markets and smaller government. This thinking was to gain the upper hand as guidance for economic development, thereby marginalizing much of the ILO's normative and advisory work, and challenging trade unions and their members as "insiders" or even as "rent seekers". The neoliberal school of thought saw national labour regulation such as minimum wages, severance pay and social security schemes only as market distortions, raising the cost of labour, and as contributing to, rather than combatting, poverty.[50] Beginning in the 1980s, structural adjustment programs linking loans or financial support to policy reforms pushed by the World Bank and the IMF led to widespread retrenchment in the civil service of many countries, often alongside a scaling back of social benefits, a relaxation of legislative labour protections, a weakening of labour inspection through decentralization and reduced resources, as well as the dismantling of peak level collective bargaining. While civil society groups and trade unions voiced opposition to such measures, employer representatives largely took the view that the international finance institutions' (IFI) approach involved purely macroeconomic issues that fell outside the ILO's mandate.

It was difficult for the ILO, with its vastly lower level of human and financial resources, to counter neoliberal narratives effectively, but it tried. Clashes in the streets of some countries over trade liberalization and IFI-imposed reform made the

---

[47]Recommendation No. 2014, para. IV.15.

[48]Blackett (2019).

[49]Stoll (2018), pp. 20–22; Rodgers et al. (2009), pp. 212–214.

[50]Deakin (2011, 2016); Rodgers et al. (2009), pp. 104 and 195–196; Berg and Kucera (2008). See also Leimgruber (2013).

ILO's emphasis on social dialogue look more attractive. The clear divergence of approaches between the ILO and the IFIs also led to some outreach, such as informal agreement in the mid-1990s between the ILO, the IMF and the World Bank to exchange drafts of their flagship reports for comment prior to publication.[51] In the late 1990s, the Bank began to pursue a milder, more participatory "Post-Washington Consensus".[52]

By the beginning of the twenty-first century, the Bank was also placing greater emphasis on quantification and indicators, including on "voice" (defined much more loosely than freedom of association and collective bargaining), "regulatory burden" and "rule of law".[53] Some of this work has been sharply criticized on various grounds. For instance that, "[...] the widely used datasets of the work Bank [...] focus on 'costs to business' in a narrow and literal sense of firms' compliance costs. This omits consideration of the costs to employers of the absence of labour law rules, which might take the form of lack of access to skilled labour, weak domestic demand for goods, and weak governance.".[54] For example, the World Bank's Doing Business Index, before its revision in light of serious questioning of its methodology, viewed a country's repeal of laws preventing unfair termination of employment as a positive factor in its rankings.[55] This applied regardless of whether the relevant ILO Convention had been ratified or not, suggesting a rather selective approach to an otherwise broad support for the rule of law by the IFIs.

Eventually, however, the IFIs joined the growing consensus that respect for core labour standards was part and parcel of "good governance" (see Sect. 2.6). The International Finance Corporation (IFC) adopted its Policy and Performance Standards on Social and Environmental Sustainability in 2006, a step followed and enhanced by the European Bank for Reconstruction and Development in 2008.[56] The World Bank also followed suit, albeit less vigorously. Although such developments have certainly marked victories for ILO principles, debate continues over the role of labour market institutions in tackling inequality not only of opportunity, but inequality of outcomes as well.[57]

2.6   Trade Liberalization and the "Social Clause" Debate

Part of the rule of law involves adherence to the fundamental principle of freedom of association. The ILO's longstanding insistence on this freedom for all workers gave

---

[51]Rodgers et al. (2009), p. 201.

[52]Charnovitz (2000); for ILO arguments, see e.g. Sengenberger (2005).

[53]Sinclair (2018), p. 278.

[54]Deakin (2016), p. 55.

[55]See e.g. Berg (2015), pp. 9–10.

[56]Novitz (2010).

[57]Berg (2015), p. 2.

crucial support to the *Solidarnoscz* trade union in Poland, which lit the spark that eventually led most countries in the former Soviet bloc to opt for political democracy and market economies.[58] After the fall of the Berlin Wall in 1989, however, the lead role in those countries' transitions fell to the World Bank, IMF and the OECD, not the ILO. Deep reforms, pursued quickly, were accompanied by growing inequality that later engendered populist movements. The financial institutions' advocacy of privatization and liberalization of trade, exchange rates, capital accounts and the labour market all at once led to major disruption in many people's lives. Although the need for step-by-step action, accompanying measures and greater participation in such transitions has since become well recognized,[59] the ILO's call to cushion the blows of the 1990s transitions (through supportive institutions, social protection systems and industrial relations systems to handle conflict based on freedom of association and collective bargaining) went largely unheeded.

This was also the period in which an ever greater share of production was moving from economically developed to emerging economies, many of which were showing high growth rates. More open markets and trade liberalization were seen as bringing risks as well as benefits, however. As the development debate on the issue of child labour continued, calls for its elimination intensified[60]; the ILO launched its major International Programme for the Elimination of Child Labour in 1992. Some countries in the North began to link trade and respect for workers' rights, at least on paper, as from the mid-1980s, and later many trade agreements added a social dimension.[61] By the 1990s, it had become more than clear that globalization had wrought fundamental change in a number of sectors. Methods of production increasingly relied on global supply chains. As the ILO's 75th anniversary (1994) approached, the Organization embarked on a reflection about its role in a transformed post-Cold War and increasingly globalized world. The Director-General's report to the Conference contained a frank assessment of the ILO's so far limited ability to fulfil the role foreseen for it in the Declaration of Philadelphia.[62]

Just after that session of the Conference, the ILO Governing Body set up an open-ended Working Party on the Social Dimensions of the Liberalization of International Trade (later renamed the Working Party on the Social Dimension of Globalization). In a rather extraordinary exercise of self-censorship, this forum agreed not to mention linking trade and labour standards through trade sanctions (the so-called "social clause" debate). This did not make the issue go away. Indeed, it spilled over to derail the OECD's efforts in the mid-1990s to gain an agreement on multilateral investment rules and coloured meetings of the General Agreement on Tariffs and Trade (GATT) and its successor, the World Trade Organization (WTO).[63]

---

[58]Rodgers et al. (2009), p. 51.
[59]Trebilcock (2014) and Fenwick and Novitz (2010).
[60]Nesi et al. (2008).
[61]International Labour Office/International Institute of Labour Studies (2013).
[62]International Labour Office (1994), pp. 91–94.
[63]Compa (1998). See also Hepple (2005) and Kaufmann (2007).

2.7   World Summit for Social Development and the WTO Singapore Declaration

In the meantime, the 1995 World Summit for Social Development sought common ground, and its outcome document called for simultaneous progress on the economic, environmental and social fronts. Consensus began to build around the idea of core labour standards. At the end of 1996 delegates to the first Ministerial Meeting of the WTO adopted the Singapore Declaration, which recalled countries' commitments to "internationally recognized core labour standards."[64] The Singapore Declaration also recognized that the ILO was the competent body to set and deal with these standards, and that economic growth, development and further trade liberalization contribute to the promotion of these standards. Largely in response to emerging economies' concerns, the Declaration rejected the use of standards for protectionist purposes.[65] In the same period, an influential OECD study on core workers' rights and international trade provided support for examining a range of mechanisms for the mutual reinforcement of core labour standards and trade.[66] In addition, the Asian financial crisis (1997) cast serious doubt on the pretension that economic success depended upon weak labour market institutions and "rights free" space. Indeed, the IMF even came out in favour of ratification of core labour standards in several of the countries affected.

2.8   ILO Declaration on Fundamental Principles and Right at Work

Within the ILO, the debate was basically resolved through the adoption of the Declaration on Fundamental Principles and Rights at Work in June 1998. Its rationale, similar to that of the Declaration of Philadelphia, is enabling people "to claim freely and on the basis of equality of opportunity their fair share of the wealth which they have helped to generate, and to achieve fully their human potential." The Declaration highlights principles and rights that enable people, with equal opportunity, to enjoy their childhoods without exploitation and to shape their own destinies, freely building their own occupational organizations to bargain on their behalf.[67] It can be seen as stating a development goal to be achieved through political liberalism, with an assumption that this approach will lead to more equitable distribution.

---

[64]World Trade Organization (1996), Singapore Ministerial Declaration, WTO Ministerial Conference, Singapore, 9–13 Dec. 1996, WT/MIN(96)/DEC/W, 13 December 1996.

[65]See para. 5 of the 1998 ILO Declaration; see also Hesterman (2014).

[66]Organisation for Economic Co-operation and Development (1996).

[67]Trebilcock (2004), p. 350.

The principles and rights identified in the Declaration are freedom of association and recognition of the right to collective bargaining, prohibition of forced labour, elimination of discrimination in employment or occupation, and the effective abolition of child labour. Eight Conventions designated as core or fundamental correspond to these principles. This departure of singling out some from a large body of legally equivalent instruments generated heated academic debate,[68] but over time, the Declaration has become generally viewed as having well proved its worth.[69] The fundamental principles have been taken up in numerous other influential instruments and policy documents, such as the UN Global Compact (1999), the UN Guiding Principles on Business and Human Rights (2011), and the OECD Guidelines for Multinational Enterprises (1976, as revised), to name only a few.

Based on constitutional principles, the Declaration applies to all member states whether or not they have ratified the corresponding ILO Conventions. One of the effects of the Declaration was to encourage their ratification, and it succeeded spectacularly by leading to almost universal ratifications of most of these instruments. But a significant portion of the world population lives in large countries that have not yet ratified all of them, particularly the Conventions on freedom of association and collective bargaining. One aspect of the ILO's centenary celebration is to push for missing ratifications and to encourage ratification of the Protocol to the Forced Labour Convention, 1930 (No. 29), adopted in 2014 in the wake of concerns over "modern slavery" and trafficking in persons.

An equally important aspect of the 1998 Declaration was the support pledged by the ILO to member states seeking to make progress in relation to fundamental rights at work. Identification of their needs was informed by the requirement that non-ratifying countries supply annual reports, as foreseen in the follow-up to the Declaration. In addition, the follow-up mandated the ILO secretariat to prepare global reports on one or more of the principles, "to provide a dynamic global picture," and to serve as a basis for assessing effectiveness of the support provided. While the annual reports have since waned in their importance, the initial global reports set the stage for major new technical cooperation programs, most notably on combatting forced labour. Recent global reports have covered all of the fundamental principles at the same time, charting gaps as well as noting progress.

2.9 The Decent Work Agenda and the 2008 Declaration on Social Justice for a Fair Globalization

Beginning in 1999, the ILO rebranded its social justice mission under the phrase "Decent Work". This concept embraced all forms of work, not just formal employment, and adopted an integrated approach involving rights at work, employment

---

[68] Alston (2004), Fudge (2007), Langille (2005) and Maupain (2005).

[69] Reynaud (2018).

generation, social protection and social dialogue, all to be cross-cut by a gender dimension. The Decent Work Agenda focused on "creating opportunities for women and men to obtain decent and productive work, in conditions of freedom, dignity, security and human dignity."[70] This became converted into the following pillars: employment and enterprise development, social protection, standards and rights at work, and governance and social dialogue—a framework endorsed by the UN Chief Executives Board in 2007.

One of the inevitable conclusions of the "social clause" debate and its sequelae was a renewed call for greater policy coherence. In light of this, the ILO set up a World Commission on the Social Dimension of Globalization in 2003. A year later, its report, A Fair Globalization, made a case for reformed global governance, including "fair rules for trade, finance and investment, measures to strengthen respect for core labour standards, and a coherent framework for the cross-border movement of people".[71] The ILO has continued to pursue greater policy coherence in its active engagement with the G7, the G20 and in other fora such as the World Economic Forum.

Through the Declaration on Social Justice for a Fair Globalization, adopted in June 2008, the International Labour Conference transposed the Decent Work approach more fully into how the ILO itself is to function.[72] Picking up on ideas put forward by the World Commission, the 2008 Declaration also reinforced the Organization's determination to engage other international actors more fully toward achieving its goals, while leaving it for each State to determine its national needs and priorities, subject to existing international obligations.[73] This instrument also nuanced the statement in the 1998 Declaration concerning comparative advantage and protectionist trade purposes. The 2008 Declaration affirmed that "the violation of fundamental principles and rights at work cannot be invoked or otherwise used as a legitimate comparative advantage and that labour standards should not be used for protective purposes."[74] In relation to trade, the vast literature on its relationship to respect for labour rights can only be briefly touched upon here. Suffice it to say that while calls for a labour rights conditionality clause in the WTO framework have never gained wide support and are unlikely to do so,[75] a number of regional and bilateral trade and investment treaties do contain labour rights clauses of varying importance.[76] While these can have positive effects on respect for workers' rights

---

[70]International Labour Conference (1999), 87th Session, Decent Work—Report of the Director General, p. 3.

[71]World Commission on the Social Dimension of Globalization (2004), p. 143.

[72]Maupain (2013) and Trebilcock (2010b).

[73]See paras. I.C and II.B of the 2008 ILO Declaration.

[74]ILO 2008 Declaration, para. I.A(iv).

[75]Joseph (2011), pp. 130–137; Hestermeyer (2014).

[76]Atleson et al. (2008), Gött (2018) and ILO/IILS (2013).

and poverty reduction, context and pacing very much matter, as do a range of policy interventions.[77]

2.10 From the 2008 Financial Crisis to the Social Development Goals

Only months after adoption of the 2008 Declaration, the financial crisis hit, throwing millions out of work and rocking faith in monetary and financial policy as pursued up to then. In June 2009, the Conference adopted a document entitled Recovering from the Crisis: The Global Jobs Pact. It put employment and social protection at the heart of crisis response. The Pact included calls for a shift to a low-carbon, environment friendly economy and reiterated appeals for stronger policy coherence among multilateral institutions in support of development. It further stressed the need for building a gender dimension into crisis response.

The ILO ended up with invitations to sit at the head table with the major financial institutions at G20 meetings. In later years, meetings involving only Ministers of Labour and Social Affairs deepened discussions, but were side events. Statements adopted at various G20 sessions have been supportive of the Decent Work Agenda and greater policy coherence. On the ground, however, this has not always been translated into advice given or conditionalities imposed.[78]

What the ILO has not be able to influence ex ante does not escape its grasp, however. The ILO supervisory bodies may well be called upon to examine whether economic policy measures taken by governments, willingly or under pressure, are compatible with their giving effect to ratified ILO Conventions. Comments of the independent and well-respected ILO Committee of Experts on the Application of Conventions and Recommendations (CEACR) directed to Greece, for example, also had the IMF, the European Commission and the European Central Bank in their cross-hairs. This was because those institutions had, as part of the drastic measures to address the meltdown of the Greek economy, insisted on legislative changes that effectively dismantled centralized collective bargaining in the country. As the CEACR pointed out, under the Right to Organize and Collective Bargaining Convention, 1949 (No. 98), the organizations of employers and of workers must remain free to determine the level at which they choose to bargain.

In relation to Convention No. 98's companion Convention, the Freedom of Association and Protection of the Right to Organise Convention, 1948 (No. 87), in 2012 the employers in the ILO governing structures reasserted objections raised some 20 years earlier in relation to the right to strike (which is not explicitly

---

[77]See e.g. European Parliamentary Research Service, The Generalised Scheme of Preferences Regulation (No 978/2012), European Implementation Assessment, PE 627.134, December 2018; Trebilcock (2014).

[78]Bohoslavsky and Ebert (2018) and Ebert (2015).

mentioned in the instrument). Long recognized by the ILO Governing Body's Committee on Freedom of Association (and external human rights bodies, as well as explicitly in Article 8 of the International Covenant on Economic, Social and Cultural Rights) as inherent to the exercise of freedom of association, the right to strike was also seen by the CEACR as being protected by the Convention. The debate escalated to questioning the role of that body in relation to determining the meaning of ILO Conventions. The CEACR has clarified its overall approach to the exercise of its mandate but not backed down on this issue. Although there seems to be a tacit accord to agree to disagree, the dispute between ILO constituents has unnecessarily weakened the institution.[79]

2.11   Business and Labour Rights to the Fore

A more positive development for the ILO involved the adoption of the UN Guiding Principles on Business and Human Rights in June 2011. The "protect, respect and remedy" framework gave fresh impetus to core labour standards enshrined in the labour rights in the 1998 Declaration and in the labour articles of the International Covenant on Economic, Social and Cultural Rights.[80] The processes put into motion by the Guidelines provide opportunities for deepening understanding of effective measures for enhancing respect for labour rights in firms.[81]

Several high-profile industrial disasters also occurred in this period, with factory fires and building collapses claiming the lives of over 1600 workers in Bangladesh and Pakistan between 2012 and 2013 alone. Following the largest of these, the Rana Plaza disaster, the ILO used its roles as convenor and as neutral broker to facilitate arrangements for setting up a multi-stakeholder scheme for country-wide factory inspections and handling complaints.[82] The ILO also drew on the principles of an earlier technical international labour standard, the Employment Injury Benefits Convention, 1964 (No. 121), as the basis for serving as trustee for an orderly handling of the many compensation claims.[83] These actions represented creative uses of the ILO's mandate and standards in the aftermath of this preventable tragedy.

Such incidents also spurred discussion of global supply chains, known as well as global value chains. In a resolution adopted in 2016, the Conference highlighted the importance of policy coherence among all multilateral initiatives related to decent

---

[79]Bellace (2014), La Hovary (2015), Maupain (2019) and Swepston (2013).

[80]Trebilcock (2015) and Zandvliet and van der Heijden (2015).

[81]See e.g. Zandvliet and van der Heijden (2015).

[82]See e.g. Reinecke and Donaghey (2015).

[83]However, there are also fears that the new paradigm represented by the Accord could risk courts' deferral to a new type of private ordering; see Salminen (2018).

work in global supply chains, and made some specific suggestions in this direction.[84] It also reiterated a long-standing appeal to remove exclusions of the application of labour legislation in export processing zones. From the post-Rana Plaza response to more classic ILO approaches of using pressure to push member states to effect change (such as in Myanmar or Qatar in relation to forced labour[85]), the ILO has resorted to a wide range of strategies to nudge countries towards compliance with universal norms.

2.12   Addressing the Future of Work

In the run up to the ILO's 90th anniversary, the ILO Century Project began filling some gaps in the ILO's history.[86] In 2017 the ILO turned its gaze to its Future of Work Centenary Initiatives on the future of work, an end to poverty, women at work, green growth and jobs, standards, enterprises and (mostly internal) governance. Within this framework, the standards initiative has several aspects, a major one involving a stepped up review of much of the body of ILO standards. This is being pursued by the ILO Governing Body's Standards Review Mechanism (SRM), one response to some critiques that the ILO body of standards is too large and, in some instances, not up to date.[87] The tripartite SRM has been proceeding cautiously, and the results cannot be predicted. Clear candidates for standards that are obsolete are already being declared so by the International Labour Conference under the 1997 amendment to the ILO Constitution that entered into force in 2015.

As the centenary approached, the ILO organized national and regional future of work dialogues in more than 110 states and set up the Commission on the Future of Work, co-chaired by two Heads of State. Drawing on research as well as consultations, the Commission's report of early 2019 highlighted the unprecedented changes faced by the world of work in relation to technology and artificial intelligence, demographics, climate change, and globalization. While predicting a massive realignment of jobs, it struck a positive note about the opportunities also created, such as major investment and innovation opportunities in renewable energy and environmentally sustainable construction.[88] The Commission's recommendations touched upon skills, transformative and measurable gender equality, a universal social protection floor (already the subject of the Social Protection Floor Recommendation, 2012 (No. 202)), harnessing and managing technology for decent work, and collective representation though social dialogue as a public good. The group

---

[84]ILO (2016), Resolution concerning decent work in global supply chains, International Labour Conference, 105th session, 2016, paras. 16(m) and 23(e).

[85]See e.g. Tapiola and Swepston (2010); Graham (2018); but see Langille (2015).

[86]See e.g. Kott and Droux (2013), Maul (2012) and Rodgers et al. (2009).

[87]Langille (2010) and Maupain (2013).

[88]Global Commission on the Future of Work (2019), p. 10.

pointed out the usefulness of collective bargaining, but strangely did not mention their global corollary, international framework agreements.[89] The Commission laid out the contours of a Universal Labour Guarantee, to apply regardless of employment status, that would encompass fundamental workers' rights, an adequate living wage, limits on and flexibility in working hours, and protection of safety and health at work. It stressed that this would apply to all workers, including those in digitally mediated work in the platform economy.[90]

Furthermore, the Commission encouraged incentives to promote investments in key areas for decent and sustainable work.[91] It urged reshaping business incentive structures for longer-term investment approaches and exploring supplementary indicators of human development and well-being. This would incorporate a measure of unpaid work performed in the service of households and communities. Finally, noting that "there are strong, complex and crucial links between trade, financial, economic and social policies," the Commission called for more systematic and substantive working relations among the WTO, the Bretton Woods institutions and the ILO.[92] Related to this idea is the Commission's suggested new indicator or indicators "to measure the distributional and equity dimensions of economic growth [...]."[93]

With a nod to the critical role of the private sector, the Commission suggested that enterprises account for the impact of their activities on the environment and on communities.[94] The ILO had shown a long-standing interest in environmental issues both inside and outside workplaces, and the Rio Declaration on Sustainable Development (1992) had formed the basis for a special ILO programme on work and the environment in the 1990s. With the current debate on climate change, it has returned to the topic, and the Global Commission has underscored the importance of such a reorientation.

2.13 A Few Elephants in the Room

One issue that the Global Commission mentioned rather in passing was migration. The very mention of the "protection of the interests of workers when employed in countries other than their own" in the Preamble to the ILO Constitution had already signaled an opening up from a staunch position of state sovereignty in relation to this controversial topic. The ILO has adopted a number of instruments on the topic, ranging from equal treatment between nationals and non-nationals in social security,

---

[89]See the contribution by Reingard Zimmer in this volume.

[90]Global Commission on the Future of Work (2019), pp. 38–39 and 43–44.

[91]Id., pp. 46–51.

[92]Id., p. 14.

[93]Id., p. 50.

[94]Id., p. 49.

including acquired rights, to more comprehensive instruments. The Migration for Employment Convention (Revised), 1949 (No. 97) and the Migrant Workers (Supplementary Provisions) Convention (No. 143) and its accompanying Recommendation influenced the United Nations Convention on the Rights of All Migrant Workers and Members of their Families (adopted in 1990, entry into force 2003). The relatively low level of ratifications of these instruments led ILO constituents to adopt the ILO's Non-Binding Multilateral Framework on Migration (2006). This document, together with conclusions of an ILO Conference discussion on the subject in 2017,[95] became reflected in the Global Pact for Safe, Orderly and Regular Migration, adopted by the UN General Assembly in December 2018.[96] Given the differing perspectives of sending and receiving countries, however, none of these texts has seriously tackled the root issue of the fundamental imbalance of having expanded freedom of movement of capital, goods and services, but not of labour, in the world economy. The issue is not going to go away, and indeed the Global Pact cites climate change as one of the drivers of migration. These two areas yell out for integrated, sensible approaches and concrete action, beginning at the international level. On top of these factors comes a shift in geopolitics in a reshuffled, multipolar world that leaves many uncertainties about future adherence to human rights values. Perhaps a deeper examination of the underlying moral assumptions could help arrive at understanding in relation to IEL.[97]

3 Pathways to Convergence?

3.1 Back to Basics for Avoiding Conflict

The divergence of the paths taken by transnational labour law and IEL has impoverished both fields. The side-lining of social issues has contributed to populist backlash against trade liberalization and necessary restructuring measures. It need not have been so. The missions of the IMF, the WB and the WTO are, to quote the Global Commission, "complementary and compatible objectives".[98] The WTO, for instance, was set up with the aim of "raising standards of living, ensuring full employment and a large and steadily growing volume of real income." And yet it often seems as if expansion of trade or adherence to certain monetary policies have become ends in themselves, divorced from a raison d'être that shares much with the ILO's aim of peace based on social justice, with full and productive work front and centre.

---

[95]The discussion was based on the CEACR's General Survey on Conventions Nos. 97 and 143, and the latter's accompanying Recommendation, No. 151.
[96]UN General Assembly Res/73/195, 11 January 2019 (adopted 19 December 2018).
[97]Ratner (2017).
[98]Global Commission on the Future of Work (2019), p. 56.

3.1.1 International Law Devices

As several authors have suggested, there are a number of means for avoiding a conflict of norms. The most obvious is coordination ex ante.[99] Consultations are already foreseen in the ILO standard setting regime, at least in relation to UN bodies, when a draft ILO Convention or Recommendation "affects the activities of such organization".[100] In addition, the ILO has a number of institutional cooperation agreements with non-UN organizations, such as with the Organisation for Economic Development and Co-operation, but not yet with the IMF, the WTO or the World Bank. Promising appears to be the idea of mutual supportiveness.[101] The Better Work programmes undertaken by the International Finance Corporation together with the ILO in a number of countries have drawn much praise for linking improvement of working conditions and expanded market access in selected sectors.[102]

Pauwelyn cautions about having clarity about the nature of an apparent (or real) conflict before selecting a possible device, such as reference to other relevant rules of international law.[103] "There is no need to expand the mandate of the WTO as an international organization for the WTO to take account of other trade concerns [. . .]. The fact that the WTO is part of international law should suffice."[104] Further support comes from references in the preamble to the WTO's founding instrument to "raising standards of living, [and] ensuring full employment [. . .]." Analysis of public procurement regulatory regimes and labour rights also illustrates how a careful reading of the processes involved reveals openings for achieving both economic and social goals.[105]

Other devices for avoiding a norm conflict include systemic integration through conflict avoidance by reliance on Art. 31(1)(c) of the Vienna Convention on the Law of Treaties.[106] The ILO's own approach to treaty law has reflected both leaning towards an evolutionary approach in interpretation while moderating this by greater reference to preparatory works than is normally the case.[107] In some but not all cases, the doctrine of lex specialis will help resolve the issue.[108] Similarly, a close look at the terms of a particular instrument may reveal that there is in fact no conflict and/or that multiple objectives may be given effect simultaneously.[109] Many of the criticisms of ILO standards as being "too one size fits all" or "too prescriptive" fail to

---

[99]Pauwelyn (2003), pp. 237–240.

[100]Standing Orders of the International Labour Conference, Article 39bis.

[101]Finke (2014), pp. 435–437.

[102]Maupain (2019), Langille (2015) and Rossi et al. (2014).

[103]Pauwelyn (2003), pp. 253–256.

[104]Id., 492; see also Hesterman (2014), pp. 281–285.

[105]Corvaglia (2017) and Hassel and Helmerich (2016).

[106]Finke (2014), pp. 431–435; Karamanian (2012), p. 270; Pauwelyn (2003), pp. 263–268.

[107]Trebilcock (2018), pp. 855 and 871–873.

[108]Finke (2014), pp. 427–431.

[109]Karamanian (2012), p. 271.

take into account the broad consultation that occurs prior to their adoption as well as of the many flexibility devices used in such instruments, not to mention the substance of their texts (Trebilcock 2010a). A more difficult scenario emerges when ILO Conventions are simply ignored, such as in law-making in the area of insolvency law by the UN Commission on International Trade Law (UNCITRAL).[110]

3.1.2 Data, Research and Reports

Other ways to facilitate greater coherence involve reliance on data, research and major reports. Although the use of indicators in relation to respect for international labour standards is controversial, it is incontestable that for economists, what can be counted counts. Since 1923, the ILO has convened a periodic International Conference of Labour Statisticians. Its decisions and recommendations have guided policy makers over decades on a range of issues, such as consumer price indices, real wages, statistics on employment injuries and occupational diseases, social protection coverage and more. Recent action by this forum, and the ILO secretariat work that supports it, have been significant in two respects. Firstly, progress has been made in connection with developing Decent Work Indicators and statistical methods that will be used to feed into the SDG process (see Sect. 3.2). Secondly, it has responded to the challenge of capturing the many different forms of work, not just formal employment.

ILO statistical work is also used to inform ILO research reports and flagship reports. A yearly research conference brings labour economists and lawyers together around a decent work theme.[111] The annual World Employment and Social Outlook focuses on changing themes, with recent attention given to green jobs and sustainable enterprises and jobs. In addition, the Global Wage Report uses data to draw policy conclusions, such as the 2018/2019 publication on closing the gender wage gap. The biannual World Social Protection Report tracks trends and new developments. Each of these flagship reports provides opportunities for collaboration or at least discussion with other multilateral organizations. Moreover, since the early days of the ILO, the periodical International Labour Review has published articles by leading economists alongside authors from other disciplines.

In recent years, the ILO and the WTO secretariats have done joint studies on trade and employment, and the ILO and the World Bank have collaborated in highlighting good practices in the area of training. More such endeavours would serve to enhance deeper understanding between the institutions involved, and help support greater

---

[110]This was not surprising, since the ILO did not put much effort into convincing the multiple actors involved in these negotiations of the need to respect provisions of the Protection of Workers' Claims (Insolvency of the Employer) Convention, 1992 (No. 173); see Block-Lieb and Halliday (2017), p. 287.

[111]See its outputs such as Berg (2015), Rossi et al. (2014) and Berg and Kucera (2008).

policy coherence. For a critical challenge still lies in shifting the narrative around the relationship between labour markets, labour standards and economic growth.[112]

3.2   Could the SDGs Enhance Social and Economic Policy Coherence?

Another avenue worth pursuing runs through the Social Development Goals (SDGs), adopted by the UN General Assembly in 2015. The tracking of progress towards achieving the SDGs by 2030 may offer a way to move forward towards achieving the aims of the 2008 and the Philadelphia Declarations. As the CEACR recently recalled, "[t]he Decent Work Agenda, and the international labour standards benchmarking it, suffuse the 17 Sustainable Development Goals (SDGs) adopted by the UN General Assembly."[113] The targets and indicators adopted permit tracking progress towards the Goals.[114] The ILO is the custodian of 17 of the indicators and recently issued a guidebook that explores them in more depth.[115]

The 2030 Agenda reflects an understanding that "decent work is both a means and an end to sustainable development."[116] The Agenda "commits to fostering a dynamic business sector and protecting labour rights and environmental and health standards in accordance with international instruments, including ILO standards and the UN Guiding Principles on Business and Human Rights."[117] Yet as before, the challenge will be to translate this into reality.

Under SDG 8 ("Promote sustained, inclusive and sustainable economic growth, full and productive employment and decent work for all"), Indicator 8.8.2 is the "increase in national compliance of labour rights (freedom of association and collective bargaining) based on International Labour Organization (ILO) textual sources and national legislation, by sex and migrant status". The "textual sources" include CEACR reports, and a resolution adopted by the ICLS will assist on methodology.[118] Several other SDG indicators refer to legislation and policies that

---

[112]Arthurs (2014); Rittich (2015); and Sengenberger (2005).

[113]Committee of Experts on the Application of Conventions and Recommendations (2019), General Report, International Labour Conference, 108th Session, General Report, p. 14, citing ILO (2016).

[114]The Goals and Indicators appear in UN General Assembly (2015), Transforming our World: the 2030 Agenda for Sustainable Development, Resolution adopted by the General Assembly on 25 September 2015, UNGA Res. A/RES/70/1, 21 October 2015, pp. 14/35–27/35.

[115]ILO (2018), Decent Work and the Sustainable Development Goals: A Guidebook on SDG Labour Market Indicators.

[116]International Labour Office (2016), para. 10.

[117]Id., para. 52.

[118]20th International Conference of Labour Statisticians (ICLS), Geneva, 10–19 October 2018, Resolution concerning the methodology of SDG indicator 8.8.2 on labour rights (ICLS/20/2018/ Resolution II).

fall within the domain of many ratified ILO Conventions. For instance, SDG 8.7 aims at ending forced labour and child labour. SDG 8.5 pledges achieving "full and productive employment and decent work for all women and men, including for young people and persons with disabilities, and equal pay for work of equal value." Under Goal 5 ("Achieve gender equality and empower all women and girls"), Indicator 5.5.1 is "whether or not legal frameworks are in place to promote, enforce and monitor equality and non-discrimination on the basis of sex". In addition, SDG 10 envisages "an assault on discrimination and implementation of reinforced pro-equality measures, especially fiscal, wage and social protection policies".[119] Detail-rich CEACR reports could inform the work of the High-level Political Forum on Sustainable Development's annual review.

SDG 17 addresses issues, which include enhanced global macroeconomic stability and policy coherence, investment promotion and trade. Indicator 17.14 is on enhancement of policy coherence for sustainable development, but no data are specified in this respect. This could provide an opening for the ILO to seize. The Global Commission has also suggested a new indicator "to measure the distributional and equity dimensions of economic growth".[120] The logic of the 1998 and 2008 Declarations implies that these goals should not be allowed to be seen in isolation from core labour standards and well-functioning labour market institutions. In the ILO's view, "a strong and distinctive feature of the Agenda is that it stresses enhanced global economic governance aimed at providing an enabling international economic environment for sustainable development, and commits to the pursuit of policy coherence as a key means of implementation."[121]

SDG Goal 12 concerns ensuring sustainable consumption and production patterns. Target 12.7, to promote sustainable public procurement practices, offers considerable scope for building in social and environmental as well as economic criteria. Without delving into the intricacies of this under various regimes, it can be said that, "the different international regulations on public procurement offer – in both their negotiating and reform processes – the possibility of including social and labour concerns in the conduct of the procurement process[...]"[122]

The aspiration to decouple economic growth from environmental degradation reflects the attention given to climate change under SDG 13. "The ILO tripartite 'Guidelines for a just transition towards environmentally sustainable economies and societies for all' can play a vital role in this respect."[123] The ILO's work on green growth and green jobs is likely to accelerate, providing new opportunities for cooperation on macroeconomic issues. Like other international organizations, the ILO has recognized the "urgent action required to safeguard the future of the

---

[119]International Labour Office (2016), para. 41.

[120]Global Commission on the Future of Work (2019), p. 50.

[121]International Labour Office (2016), para. 64.

[122]Corvaglia (2017), p. 233.

[123]International Labour Office (2018); International Labour Office (2016), para. 30.

planet."[124] The Global Commission on the Future of Work has highlighted the importance of involving employer and worker organizations closely in the many transitions that will be required.

With periodic reporting on progress to the General Assembly, there is guaranteed attention to them through 2030. The SDG process is thus likely to be helpful in bringing social, environmental, and economic policy onto the same page. The fly in the ointment, however, is that like the ILO's, a UN process based on regular reporting by states—albeit it with much civil society input along the way—is not going to be a game-changer. Yet, no one seems to be calling for making dispute resolution mechanisms stronger, to bring them more into line with the systems in place for trade and investment.

3.3   Additional Proposals

3.3.1   Global Commission Proposals

The Global Commission on the Future of Work has made some additional recommendations that, if pursued, could also have important economic implications. One is to abandon companies' quarterly earnings reports in order to give them space to pursue longer-term strategies. Another is to include the cost of externalities in business decision-making, calling on firms to calculate in costs of clean-up and of medical care when environmental and social harm results from their activities.

While pushing for greater coherence in the work of the various multilateral institutions, the Global Commission put several ideas to the 2019 International Labour Conference to consider about the ILO's own future role. It recommended that the ILO put in place institutional arrangements for it to be the focal point in the international system for the development and comparative policy analysis of national future of work strategies, drawing on a deepened understanding of how processes of digitalization and automation are affecting the world of work.[125] The Commission further urged evaluating ILO standards to make sure they are "up to date, relevant and subject to adequate supervision,"[126] a process already underway. In stressing the universality of the ILO's mandate while calling for innovative action to address the growing diversity of situations in which work is performed, the Commission expressed faith in the ILO's mandate and involvement of employers and workers alongside governments as equipping it well for these tasks.[127] Whether and how the International Labour Conference intends to follow these and other recommendations will start to be known as from June 2019.

---

[124]Id., para. 82.
[125]Global Commission on the Future of Work (2019), p. 55.
[126]Id.
[127]Id., p. 57.

3.3.2 Individuals' Proposals

Several ILO observers, both those with insider knowledge and relatively detached academics, have put forward ideas for reinvigorating the ILO to make it better fit for purpose in the years to come. A few are highlighted here; it is likely that more ideas will emerge from the impetus given by the centenary. The planned publications from the recent ILO's Law for Social Justice conference and the McGill Law course on Transnational Futures of International Labour Law look quite promising in this respect.

Former ILO Legal Adviser and Adviser to various Director-Generals, Francis Maupain, who played a pivotal role in relation to both the 1998 and the 2008 Declarations, holds out hope for the SDGs as a force for greater coherence. He argues that "in a sense, [the ILO's] comparative advantage may have to do more with the blind spots in the 2030 strategy, as regards the 'enabling' policies and institutions that will become necessary to make the adjustments implied by the simultaneous pursuit of these goals acceptable and effective."[128] To operationalize this, he suggests that the ILO could put in place a regular tripartite discussion with representatives of international financial institutions at the annual ILO conference, to heighten awareness of the impact of their policies on employers and workers. This is an idea worth pursuing. Another proposal of his, for the ILO to grant a "decent work" label to multinational enterprises that make a commitment to offer all workers along the supply chain some fundamental guarantees consistent with ILO standards,[129] is much more problematic. It ignores the complexity of corporate law and business strategy that strive to limit liability along supply chains; it would also run the risk of a charge of "bluewashing" that was made earlier against the UN Global Compact. All the same, Maupain usefully reminds us of the space and opportunity created by the ILO's tripartite structure, anchoring it in the real economy, and by the wording of its Constitution.

Steve Charnovitz tips his hat to the ILO's influence on the progressive development of human rights over the last century, and notes that now "a key task will be to similarly influence the progressive development of international economic law."[130] Recalling the responsibility laid on the ILO in the Declaration of Philadelphia to examine all international economic and financial policies in light of the Organization's fundamental objectives, he urges it to "rise to that challenge." (id.) As one means to do so, he suggests that the ILO should prepare an annual "social justice impact statement" examining the actions of organizations such as the WTO or the World Bank.[131] This would indeed put flesh on the bones of the Declaration of Philadelphia. He endorses Maupain's proposals for stepping up ILO work on

---

[128]Maupain (2019), p. 38.

[129]Id., pp. 47–49.

[130]Charnovitz (2000), p. 184; see also Charnovitz (2006).

[131]Charnovitz (2015), p. 93; Supiot (2012).

employment, but has reservations about the earlier idea of a social labelling system that would be government-based.

Brian Langille also advocates the ILO moving away from setting and supervising formal standards, and towards expansion of the Better Work initiatives.[132] The late Bob Hepple (Sir Bob) made several proposals to "reinvent transnational labour regulation," including replacing non-core conventions and recommendations by a few framework conventions supplemented by codes of practice and methods of coordination of national policy along the lines of the European Union's Open Method of Coordination.[133] He also supported use of sanctions in extreme cases, and expansion of positive conditionality in granting trade preferences.[134] Former ILO official Jean-Michel Servais has intimated that European Directives in the areas of civil and commercial law, as well as on accessibility to information, should be a source of inspiration for international labour law.[135] While this may be feasible, it is unlikely to work well in regions with much less economic integration than the EU, however.

Another former ILO official, Janelle Diller, also proposes enhanced cooperation between the ILO and World Bank institutions, with the necessary adjustments in how the ILO itself works.[136] She lauds the legally original approach taken by the ILO's consolidated Maritime Labour Convention, 1986, as a model built on publicly-authorized certificates of compliance undertaken at industry initiative. How transferable this would be to other sectors without such a strong tradition of social dialogue remains unclear, however. On the other hand, there are many insights to be drawn from the innovative ways in which the ILO has served as neutral chair and trustee in the post-Rana Plaza disaster processes, in which she was directly involved.

Drawing on a notion of shared responsibility for remedying the unjust conditions of labour that goes beyond states, Axel Marx, Jan Wouters, Glenn Rayp, and Laura Beke have argued for "sweeping reform of the entire ILO operational and institutional structure".[137] This would entail incorporating a conception of shared responsibility into the very structure of the ILO, which the authors themselves admit is aspirational. Yossi Dahan, Hanna Lerner and Faina Milman-Sivan explore how the ILO could play a more active role in relation to corporate social responsibility.[138] Their proposals also foresee a wider range of actors involved in formulating standards, and of the means of reporting and examining complaints. Some aspects would require a structural opening up of tripartism. While tripartism is certainly a strength in comparison to purely inter-governmental organizations, the institution is being

---

[132]Langille (2010).

[133]Hepple (2006), pp. 273–274.

[134]Id., p. 274.

[135]Servais (2017), p. 362.

[136]Diller (2013), pp. 146–147.

[137]Marx et al. (2015), p. 304.

[138]Dahan et al. (2016).

increasingly challenged by processes that involve more actors or indeed by the waning force of the traditional ones.[139]

On top of this comes the entrepreneurship of private law entities vying to influence market rules through various means, from codes of conduct to initiatives of the International Organisation for Standardization, which has increasingly encroached on traditional ILO territory. Since the ILO's founding, the world has moved away from an almost entirely state-based system to a situation in which public and private norms and enforcement mechanisms interact.[140] Zandvliet and van der Heijden argue for mechanisms to stimulate greater synergy between public and private orders in the international labour field.[141] The potential for outreach by the ILO in shaping and diffusion of its norms is indeed huge. At the same time, however, the ILO's constitutional safeguards of legitimacy against regulatory capture by non-labour-market actors need to be maintained. Perhaps a hybrid form of "tripartism plus" permitting greater engagement for civil society organizations[142] will emerge alongside the ILO's tripartite core.

4 Conclusion

With tectonic changes looming in the world of work and beyond, significant new directions in IEL and transnational labour law are inevitable. Will they mean greater or lesser respect for dignity at work and for encouragement of responsible entrepreneurism in a fair globalization? Words marking the ILO's 75th anniversary ring as well today: "The future role and influence of the ILO will depend in part on developments and decisions [...] over which it may not be able to exert much control. But they will also depend on the readiness and the capacity of the ILO to play such as a role [...]. It must be prepared to take risks [...]"[143] () and have the support of decision makers to do so. The hard work will involve how to overcome resistance to more root-and-branch solutions both among the ILO's tripartite constituents and, within them, the member states that do not necessarily pursue coherent positions across various multilateral organizations.[144] Other multilateral institutions will need to change in tandem. As Compa reminds us, "social justice for working

---

[139]Arthurs (2014), Block-Lieb and Halliday (2017) and La Hovary (2018).

[140]Hassel and Helmerich (2016), p. 259.

[141]Zandvliet and van der Heijden (2015).

[142]Under the Standing Orders of the International Labour Conference, non-governmental organizations can already apply to be observers, and many of their representatives are present among the average of 5000 persons attending the conference each year.

[143]ILO (1994), pp. 100–101.

[144]See e.g. Hesterman (2014), pp. 284–285.

people is not a by-product of economic growth. Policy makers have to choose it and build it into the architecture of trade and investment systems."[145]

There is no single path to social justice; it will take a variety of approaches and the mobilization of many actors to achieve. Just societies will be possible only with macroeconomic policies that support well-designed labour market institutions and job creation.[146] The latter will be significantly challenged by the expansion of artificial intelligence. Maupain observed that it has been crises that have pushed the ILO to take its own major institutional initiatives.[147] Today's looming crisis of climate change may not be a world war, but it threatens to be even more devastating. At the same time, the AI and climate challenges harbour opportunities. The ILO has long been well aware of the crucial interplay among economic, financial and labour/social issues. In its second century, the institution will surely continue to push for still badly needed policy coherence towards social justice and peace on a sustainable planet.

References

Alcock A (1971) History of the International Labour Organisation. Macmillan, London

Alston P (2004) Core labour standards and the transformation of the international labour rights regime. Eur J Int Law 15:457–521

Arthurs H (2014) Making bricks without straw: the creation of a transnational labour regime. In: de Búrca G, Kilpatrick C, Scott J (eds) Critical legal perspectives on global governance. Hart, Oxford, pp 129–142

Atleson J, Compa L, Rittich K, Sharpe C, Weiss M (2008) International labor law: cases and materials on workers' rights in the global economy (with documentary supplement). West Law Publishers, Eagan

Bellace J (2014) The need for definitional coherence in the global governance system. Int J Comp Labour Law Ind Relat 30(2):175–198

Berg J (ed) (2015) Labour markets, institutions and inequality. Edward Elgar, Cheltenham

Berg J, Kucera D (eds) (2008) In defence of labour market institutions. Palgrave/Macmillan, Basingstoke

Blackett A (2018) This is hallowed ground. In: Fitzgerald OE, Hughes V, Jewett M (eds) Reflections on Canada's past, present and future in international law. Centre for International Governance Innovation, pp 409–423

Blackett A (2019) Everyday transgressions: domestic workers' transnational challenge to international labour law. ILR Press, Cornell

Blackett A, Trebilcock A (eds) (2015) Research handbook on transnational labour law. Edward Elgar, Cheltenham

Block-Lieb S, Halliday TC (2017) Global lawmakers: international organizations in the crafting of world markets. Cambridge University Press, Cambridge

---

[145]Compa (2014), p. 15.

[146]See e.g. Berg (2015), pp. 30–31.

[147]Maupain (2019), pp. 49–51.

Bohoslavsky JP, Ebert FC (2018) Debt crises, economic adjustment and labour standards. In: Bantekas I, Lumina C (eds) Sovereign debt and human rights. Oxford University Press, Oxford, pp 284–302

Bonucci N, Kessedjian C (eds) (2017) 40 years of the OECD guidelines for multinational enterprises. OCED, Paris

Boris E, Hoehtker D, Zimmermann S (eds) (2018) Women's ILO: transnational networks, global labour standards and gender equity, 1919 to present. ILO/Brill, Leiden

Britwun AO (2018) Organizing rural women in Ghana since the 1980s: trade union efforts and ILO standards. In: Boris E et al (eds) Women's ILO: transnational networks, global labour standards and gender equity, 1919 to present. ILO/Brill, Leiden, pp 300–317

Charnovitz S (2000) The International Labour Organization in its second century. Max Planck Yearbook of United Nations Law, pp 147–184

Charnovitz S (2006) The (neglected) employment dimension of the World Trade Organization. In: Leary VA, Warner D (eds) Social issues, globalisation and international institutions. Martinus Nijhoff, Leiden, pp 125–155

Charnovitz S (2011) What is international economic law? J Int Econ Law 14(1):3–22

Charnovitz S (2015) Reinventing the ILO. Int Labour Rev 154(1):91–96

Chimni BS (2013) Critical theory and international economic law: a Third World Approach to International Law (TWAIL) perspective. In: Linarelli J (ed) Research handbook on global justice and international economic law. Edward Elgar, Cheltenham, pp 251–273

Compa L (1998) The multilateral agreement on investment and labor rights: a failed connection. Cornell Int Law J 31:683–712

Compa L (2014) Re-planting a field: international labour law for the twenty-first century. Cornell University LR School Digital Commons, Ithaca

Corvaglia MA (2017) Public procurement and labour rights: towards coherence in International Instruments of Procurement Regulation. Hart, Oxford

Dahan Y, Lerner H, Milman-Sivan F (eds) (2016) Global justice and international labour rights. Cambridge University Press, Cambridge

Deakin S (2011) The contribution of labour law to economic and human development. In: Davidov G, Langille B (eds) The idea of labour law. Oxford University Press, Oxford

Deakin S (2016) Labour law and development in the long run. In: Marshall S, Fenwick C (eds) Labour regulation and development: socio-legal perspectives. Edward Elgar, Cheltenham, pp 33–59

Diller J (2013) International labour law and the challenge of pluralism in the international order. Manchester J Int Econ Law 10(2):128–147

Ebert FC (2015) International financial institutions' approaches to labour law: the case of the International Monetary Fund. In: Blackett A, Trebilcock A (eds) Research handbook on transnational labour law. Edward Elgar, Cheltenham

Fenwick C, Novitz T (2010) Human rights at work: perspectives on law and regulation. Hart, Oxford

Finke J (2014) Regime-collisions: tensions between treaties (and how to solve them). In: Tams CJ, Tzanakopoulos A, Zimmermann A, Richford A (eds) Research handbook on the law of treaties. Edward Elgar, Cheltenham, pp 415–446

Fudge J (2007) The new discourse of labour rights: from social to fundamental rights? Comp Labor Law Policy J 29:29

Ghebali V-Y (1989) The International Labour Organisation: a case study on the evolution of U.N. specialised agencies. Martinus Nijhoff, Dordrecht

Global Commission on the Future of Work (2019) Work for a brighter future. International Labour Office, Geneva

Gött H (2018) Labour standards in international economic law. Springer, Cham

Graham M (2018) Qatar World Cup: lessons for embedding fundamental labor rights in sport. Int Labor Rights Case Law 4:205–211

Hassel A, Helmerich N (2016) Institutional change in transnational labor governance: implementing social standards in public procurement and export credit guarantees. In: Dahan Y, Lerner H, Milman-Sivan F (eds) Cambridge University Press, Cambridge, pp 239–265

Helfer L (2006) Understanding change in international organizations: globalization and innovation in the ILO. Vanderbilt Law Rev 59(3):650–726

Hepple B (2005) Labour laws and global trade. Hart, Oxford

Hepple B (2006) Rights at work. In: Ghai D (ed) Decent work: objectives and strategies. ILO, Geneva

Hesterman HP (2014) Economic, social, and cultural rights in the World Trade Organization. In: Riedel E, Giacca G, Golay C (eds) Economic, social and cultural rights in international law: contemporary issues and challenges. Oxford University Press, Oxford, pp 260–285

International Labour Office (1994) Defending values, promoting change: social justice in a global economy – an ILO agenda. International Labour Office, Geneva

International Labour Office (2016) The end to poverty initiative: the ILO and the 2030 agenda

International Labour Office (2018) World Employment and Social Outlook 2018: greening with jobs

International Labour Office (2019) Rules of the game: an introduction to the standards-related work of the International Labour Organization

International Labour Office/International Institute of Labour Studies (2013) Social dimensions of free trade agreements. ILO, Geneva

Jenks CW (1970) Social justice in the law of nations: the ILO impact after 50 years. Oxford University Press, London

Joseph S (2011) Blame it on the WTO. Oxford University Press, Oxford

Karamanian SL (2012) Human rights dimensions of investment law. In: de Wet E, Vidmar J (eds) Hierarchy in international law: the place of human rights. Oxford University Press, Oxford, pp 236–271

Kaufmann C (2007) Globalisation and labour rights: the conflict between core labour rights and international economic law. Hart, Oxford

Kott S, Droux J (2013) Globalizing social rights: the International Labour Organization and beyond. Palgrave Macmillan, Basingstoke

La Hovary C (2015) The informal economy and the ILO: a legal perspective. Int J Comp Labour Law Ind Relat 30(4):391–412

La Hovary C (2018) The ILO's mandate and capacity: creating, proliferating and supervising labour standards for a globalized economy. In: Gött H (ed) Labour standards in international economic law. Springer, Cham, pp 37–65

Langille B (2005) Core labour rights – the true story (reply to Alston). Eur J Int Law 16:409–437

Langille B (2009) Re-reading the Preamble to the 1919 ILO Constitution in light of recent data on FDI and worker rights. Columbia J Transl Law 42(1):87–99

Langille B (2010) Imagining post 'Geneva Consensus' labor law for post 'Washington consensus' development. Comp Labour Law Policy J 31:523–552

Langille B (2015) The curious incident of the ILO, Myanmar and Forced Labour. In: Blackett A, Trebilcock A (eds) Research handbook on transnational labour law. Edward Elgar, Cheltenham, pp 509–522

Leimgruber M (2013) The embattled standard-bearer of social insurance and its challenger: the ILO, The OECD and the 'Crisis of the Welfare State', 1975–1985. In: Kott S, Droux J (eds) Globalizing social rights: the International Labour Organization and beyond. Palgrave Macmillan, Basingstoke, pp 293–309

Marx A, Wouters J, Rayp G, Beke L (2015) Global governance of labour rights: assessing the effectiveness of transnational public and private policy initiatives. Edward Elgar, Cheltenham

Maul D (2012) Human rights, development and decolonization: the International Labour Organization, 1940–1970. Palgrave Macmillan, Basingstoke

Maupain F (2005) Revitalization not retreat: the real potential of the 1998 ILO declaration for the universal protection of workers' rights. Eur J Int Law 16:439–465

Maupain F (2013) The future of the International Labour Organization in the global economy. Hart, Portland

Maupain F (2019) A second century for what? The ILO at a regulatory crossroad. Int Organ Law Rev 16:1–53

Nesi G, Nogler L, Pertile M (eds) (2008) Child labour in a globalized world: a legal analysis of ILO action. Ashgate, Aldershot

Novitz T (2010) Core labour standards conditionality: a means by which to achieve sustainable development? In: Faundez J, Tan C (eds) International economic law, globalization and developing countries. Edward Elgar, Cheltenham

Nussbaum M (1999) Women and equality: the capabilities approach. Int Labour Rev 138 (3):227–245

Nussbaum M (2000) Women and human development: the capabilities approach. Cambridge University Press, Cambridge

Organisation for Economic Co-operation and Development (1996) Trade, employment and labour standards: a study of core workers' rights and international trade. OECD, Paris

Pauwelyn J (2003) Conflict of norms in public international law: how WTO law relates to other rules of international law

Petersmann U (2002) Time for a United Nations 'Global Compact' for integrating human rights into the law of worldwide organizations: lessons from European Integration. Eur J Int Law 13:621

Petersmann U (2012) International economic law in the 21st century: constitutional pluralism and multilevel governance of interdependent public goods. Hart, Oxford

Qureshi AH (1999) International economic law. Sweet and Maxwell, London

Ratner SR (2017) International investment law through the lens of global justice. J Int Econ Law 20 (4):747–775

Reinecke J, Donaghey J (2015) The 'Accord for Fire and Building Safety in Bangladesh' in response to the Rana Plaza Disaster. In: Marx A et al (eds) Global governance of labour rights: assessing the effectiveness of transnational public and private policy initiatives. Edward Elgar, Cheltenham, pp 257–277

Reynaud E (2018) The International Labour Organization and globalization: fundamental rights, decent work and social justice. ILO research paper no. 21, International Labour Office, Geneva

Rittich K (2015) The ILO: challenges in time of crisis. Int Labour Rev 154(1):85–90

Rodgers G, Lee E, Swepston L, van Daele J (2009) The ILO and the quest for social justice, 1919–2009. ILO, Geneva

Rossi A, Luinstra A, Pickles J (eds) (2014) Towards better work: understanding labour apparel global value chains. Palgrave/Macmillan, Basingstoke

Rubin N (2008) From pressure principle to measured militancy – the ILO in campaign against apartheid, paper prepared for the ILO Century Project. ILO, Geneva

Salminen J (2018) The Accord on fire and building safety in Bangladesh: a new paradigm for limiting buyers' liability in global supply chains? Am J Comp Law 66:411–451

Sen A (1999) Development as freedom. Anchor Books, New York

Sen A (2000) Work and rights. Int Labour Rev 139(2):119–128

Sengenberger W (2005) Globalization and social progress: the role and impact of international labour standards. Friedrich Ebert Stiftung, Bonn

Servais J-M (2017) International labour law, 5th edn. Wolters Kluwer, Alphen aan den Rijn

Sinclair GF (2018) To reform the world: international organizations and the making of modern states. Oxford University Press, Oxford

Stoll PT (2018) International economic and social dimensions: divided or connected? In: Gött H (ed) Labour standards in international economic law. Springer, Cham, pp 11–35

Supiot A (2012) The spirit of Philadelphia: Social Justice vs the Total Market. Verso, Brooklyn

Swepston L (2013) Crisis in the ILO Supervisory System: dispute over the right to strike. Int J Comp Labour Law Ind Relat 29(2):199–218

Tapiola K, Swepston L (2010) The ILO and the impact of labor standards: work on the ground after an ILO Commission of Inquiry. Stanf Law Policy Rev 21(3):513–526

Thouvenin JM, Trebilcock A (eds) (2013) Droit international social (2 vols)

Trebilcock A (2004) Do global players need global rules? In: Hönekopp E, Jungnickel R, Straubherr T (eds) Internationalisierung der Arbeitsmärkte, Bundesagentur für Arbeit, BeitrAB 282, 347–358

Trebilcock A (2010a) Putting the record straight about International Labor Standard setting. Comp Labor Law Policy J 31(3):553–570

Trebilcock A (2010b) From social justice to decent work: is the shift in the ILO significant for international law? In: Ruiz Fabri H, Wolfrum R, Goglin J (eds) Select proceedings of the European Society of International Law, vol 2. 2008, pp 697–716

Trebilcock M (2014) Dealing with losers: the political economy of policy transitions. Oxford University Press, Oxford

Trebilcock A (2015) Due diligence on labour issues – opportunities and limits of the UN guiding principles on business and human rights. In: Blackett A, Trebilcock A (eds) Research handbook on transnational labour law. Edward Elgar, Cheltenham, pp 97–107

Trebilcock A (2017) Why the shift from international to transnational law is important for labour standards. In: Gött H (ed) Labour standards in international economic law. Springer, Cham, pp 57–65

Trebilcock A (2018) International Labour Organization. In: Bowman MJ, Kritsiotis D (eds) Conceptual and contextual perspectives on the modern law of treaties. Cambridge University Press, Cambridge, pp 848–880

World Commission on the Social Dimension of Globalization (2004) A fair globalization: creating opportunities for all. International Labour Office, Geneva

Zandvliet R, van der Heijden P (2015) The rapprochement of ILO standards and CSR mechanisms: towards a positive understanding of the 'Privatization' of international labour standards. In: Marx A et al (eds) Global governance of labour rights: assessing the effectiveness of transnational public and private policy initiatives. Edward Elgar, Cheltenham

Anne Trebilcock is former Legal Adviser and Director of Legal Services, International Labour Organization (the UN Specialized Agency). She is affiliated with the Labour Law Institute, Georg-August-Universität, Göttingen, and is a Member of the Asian Development Bank Administrative Tribunal. She holds a JD from the University of California, Berkeley and a BA from Wellesley College, and is a member of the Michigan State Bar. She has served as the neutral chair of internal dispute resolution bodies in several international organizations, as well as a lecturer at universities in Europe and North America.

The ILO and the New 'Common Sense': Reflections on a Centenary

Emilios Christodoulidis

Contents

1   The New 'Common Sense'

The centenary of the ILO gives us an opportunity to reflect on a regression, as perplexing as it is incontestable. Perplexing because the ILO was the first international organisation to be instituted, marking, symbolically, the priority afforded by the international community to the protection of work. It is not just the priority given to the dignity of work that was remarkable; also remarkable was the institution of a process of decision-making by a tripartite body comprising governments, employers, and workers which makes the ILO the only international organization within the UN system that allows for the active participation of non-governmental actors in the decision-making process.[1] *Dignity* and *democracy*: the two commitments that in 1919 marked a unique achievement in the theory of international organisations, a moment of political *intervention* in the field of the political economy with a view to protecting the producers of value across the globe. If one hundred years later we stand before the accelerated erosion of both ideals – of dignity in the rampant

---

[1]On the 'tripartite' structure of the ILO and its novelty see Tikriti (1982) and Lahovary (in this volume).

E. Christodoulidis (✉)
University of Glasgow, Glasgow, UK
e-mail: emilios.christodoulidis@glasgow.ac.uk

© Springer Nature Switzerland AG 2019   35
M. Bungenberg et al. (eds.), *European Yearbook of International Economic Law 2019*,
European Yearbook of International Economic Law (2020) 10: 35–52,
https://doi.org/10.1007/8165_2019_43, Published online: 7 September 2019

commodification of labour, and of democracy in the multiple facets of collective disempowerment – we should pause to contemplate when and why a new *common sense* came to install itself *at the expense of* the commitment to bringing dignity and democracy to working lives; and to face up to the political and juridical responsibility of too easy a surrender to the false necessities of market thinking.

The erosion has been so comprehensive as to have shifted the coordinates of what can be taken as reasonable and possible in the field of international labour protection, and it is this readjustment of normative expectations that is captured by the 'new common sense'. This paper offers suggestions at the level of theory-construction rather than institutional analysis, and questions how certain contingent developments and features have entrenched themselves as structural, and therefore equipped with a formative power that forecloses issues and thematics, and sets operational dynamics and developments on seemingly unquestionable trajectories. Theory as *critical* undertaking, in the sense in which Marx reads Hegel, is not the *ex post* rationalisation of real processes; instead its task is to hold up those processes to the power of reason.[2] The stakes of critical theory construction are explicitly and self-consciously political, and political thinking is crucially the struggle over the terms of the description of reality, over the describability of alternatives, the struggle, in other words, to put to question what becomes vested with self-evidence as 'common sense'. This requires us to re-assess what are necessary and what are contingent conditions of the action-choices that lie ahead of us. But it also involves looking to the past to discern what decisions, at what junctures, did send us along the paths we travelled. We typically reserve the term 'genealogy' for the latter, for the enterprise, that is, that addresses the gathering work that explanatory frameworks and contexts have performed for us in delivering our understanding of our past, with their specific forces of rationalisation at play.[3] Only in this way will the *fore*closing of options be resisted, and an enhanced reflexivity restored to the present in a way that equips it to revisit the distinction between necessity and contingency outwith the seemingly intractable path-dependencies that hold the present captive to the kind of market distributions and allocations of value that have come to define labour protection today.

We will return to the theoretical issue later. For now, let us take a concrete example. The High Level Mission that visited Greece in 2011 on behalf of the ILO reported on the 'exponential' rise in the use of part time and 'rotation' contracts, as well as the emergence of large numbers of 'discouraged' workers.[4] New

---

[2]On this sense of critical theory see Christodoulidis (2019) and Christodoulidis and van der Walt (2018).

[3]Rationalisation would include here the range of classifications, causalities, imputations, and the array of techniques of selection through which the past is rendered operative for the present. We understand '*genealogy*' as the critical intervention that addresses (following Foucault) the conditions of possibility of the formation of knowledge. See Foucault (1977).

[4]See Ewing (2012) and the useful post on the Institute of employment Rights website (http://www.ier.org.uk/news/troika-imposing-illegal-terms-greece) More generally see Countouris and Freedland (2013).

contractual arrangements had seen wages and pensions fall by over a third of their value. The concern was not only that wages established by collective agreements have been slashed. Also, employers had now won the right not to pay collectively agreed wage rates, if they could secure the 'agreement' of workers to accept less and to sign away minimum terms and conditions of employment. Commenting on Greek measures aimed at decentralizing collective bargaining, the Mission concluded that these were 'likely to have a significant – and *potentially devastating* – impact on the industrial relations system in the country'; that 'the entire foundation of collective bargaining in the country may be vulnerable to collapse under [the] new framework'.[5] Far from acting to reverse the changes in light of the ILO's conclusions, however, an unperturbed Troika and the indebted Greek government have forced through a series of proposals to further restrict labour rights, especially rights to protection against unfair dismissal and to take collective action.[6] The gulf between the legal obligations that were established at Philadelphia and the destruction of labour protection and degradation of worker dignity is staggering in all this, but whether the latter will 'no doubt eventually be fully confronted with a day of reckoning in the courts' as Keith Ewing hopefully puts it,[7] very much depends on how far the 'new common sense' becomes realigned to the new market exigencies of austerity politics.

The Greek political economy is one of many casualties of austerity politics, notable perhaps most for the *speed* of the unravelling of the fragile achievement of its Social State and the destruction of labour protection. Over the past decades, we have been witnessing a progressive dismantling of labour protection as an unavoidable effect of the *global* organisation of trade that circumvents any possible *municipal* safeguards. At the global level, and as a result of the economic freedom afforded to capital to circumvent the national systems of social protection by relocating to cheaper sites, systems of social and labour protection have been thrown into the vicious circle of competitive alignment, with the slashing of the welfare budget and the diminution of social protection as the principal adjustment factor. The effects that the 'race to the bottom' has had on labour protection and on social rights more generally have been devastating. The *social constitution* entrusted with the redress of the worse effects of market integration has typically only be mobilized at the extreme end of the released social devastation, as *ultimum refugium* at the most basic level of guaranteeing the needs of biological existence, and remains otherwise inoperative in regard of the majority of the effects of the erosion of social protection.[8]

---

[5]ILO, 101st Session, *Report of the Committee of Experts on the Application of Conventions and Recommendations* (Geneva: ILO, 2012) (Greece), my emphasis. See Supiot 'Solidarity and work: what are the prospects for Greece?' Discussion with Emilios Christodoulidis, Open Democracy, 17 May 2015. At: https://www.opendemocracy.net/can-europe-make-it/solidarity-and-work-what-are-prospects-for-greece.

[6]For an early account see Koukiadaki and Kretsos (2012).

[7]See Ewing (2012).

[8]The Greek Conceil d'Etat examined the constitutionality of the austerity measures in *Koufaki and Adedy v. Greece*. In its judgment of 20 February 2012 (Decision 668/2012 of the Council of State

This is all well known, and what is most striking about these developments is their assumed *un*-remarkability. It has become commonplace in times of economic crisis for business to make a case against regulation and the imposition of labour standards, on the grounds that economic survival depends on reducing labour costs, passing risks on to employees and curbing the power of work groups and trade unions. The constant refrain from politicians on the political Right (and the supposedly pragmatic 'third way' Left) is that legislative burdens on businesses must be removed. Why, and when, the question arises – or *should* arise – did this devastating impoverishment of our ability to act on these contingent arrangements, and against the entrenchment of the distribution of advantages they effect, come to occupy the position of the new *common sense*? A common sense now buttressed by the unrelenting dismissal of alternatives as *philosophically naïve, politically destabilizing* and – as intentionally undercutting the competitiveness of national states – also *unpatriotic*.

The constitution of the ILO is a good place to begin our short genealogical venture, proclaiming as it does that 'labour is not a commodity.' (Article I) And there is no better interlocutor to do this than Alain Supiot, and his recent insightful, stubborn defence of the *'spirit of Philadelphia'*.[9] The next section involves an account of his analysis of what the Philadelphia Declaration of 1944 established in its renewal and deepening of the commitments on which the ILO was set up in 1919, and Sect. 3 seeks a firmer theoretical footing in Supiot's theoretical defence of the law's 'dogmatic' foundations. Sections 4 and 5 track a double mutation, firstly away from the political dimension of the protection of labour and toward a form of human rights protection, and secondly away from 'hard' institutional processes to 'soft' aspirational standards. This gradual migration allows a certain decisive separation to install itself and organise the field, a break between a pragmatic common sense on the one hand, and on the other an aspirational, if not utopian, discourse. The last section argues that this disjuncture misunderstands the integrity of law that depends on holding together its organising principles and their instantiations, and is therefore installed to the detriment of, and as a violation of, legality.

(Plenary Assembly)) it rejected several arguments based on the alleged breach of the principle of proportionality by the disputed measures was justified because the aim was not merely to remedy the immediate acute budgetary problem but also to strengthen the country's financial stability in the long term. In addition the Court observed that the applicants had not claimed in so many words that their situation had deteriorated to such an extent that *their very subsistence was in jeopardy*. The case was taken to the European Court of Human Rights in 2013 where it was dismissed as inadmissible as 'manifestly unfounded'. (Decision of the ECHR dated 7th May 2013 (Case Koufaki and Adedy v. Greece)). Proceeding to the proportionality test, the Court, underlined that the financial crisis constitutes an element which is seriously taken into account when examining salary cuts, and concluded that the measures were not disproportionate.

[9]Supiot (2010).

2   The Spirit of Philadelphia

Adopted at the 26th Conference of the ILO in Philadelphia in 1944, the *Declaration of Philadelphia* sought to adapt the guiding principles of the ILO to the new realities and aspirations of an international society that was emerging out of the wreckage of the World War. The document preceded the creation of the UN and its Declaration of 1948, a precedence that arguably positioned, at that stage, the ILO as the economic counterpart of the emerging world-political institution. The important monograph celebrating the spirit of that re-founding, Alain Supiot's *L' Ésprit de la Philadelphie* analyses the constitutional protection of the relationship of work above all as a human relationship, not a market exchange. Humanism is the constant that runs through this work that argues that there is no defensible theory of value production other than adapting the economy to the needs of human beings. Supiot's is a fully-fledged normative theory of a constitutional-social hermeneutic, reaching down to include, decisively, unapologetically and crucially, what has come to be known as the 'social question', the question of social and labour protection. For Supiot the human condition is constitutively tied to the dignity of labour.

Supiot draws a number of key principles from the Declaration of Philadelphia. Here is a summary account of how they link up[10]:

The Declaration neither revealed nor invented fundamental principles but affirmed them. It is an affirmation that is explicitly 'dogmatique' – in the way 'dogma' carries an axiological reference to the integrity of legal reason (and under-lies the anthropological function of law).[11]

The affirmation constitutes an act of reason. Its rationale: no durable peace can be established except on the basis of social justice.[12]

The organization of the economy is subordinate to social justice; a subordination that Supiot argues was already present in the 1919 constitution of the ILO in linking durable peace to social justice. Nevertheless, the Declaration of Philadelphia enhances this in two directions. First, it gives it global reach in affirming that all human beings enjoy the protection of liberty, dignity, economic security and equal opportunities' (Art. IIa). Second it makes the realization of social justice thus understood as the 'central aim of all national and international politics.'[13]

---

[10]Supiot (2010), pp. 21–25.

[11]The 'anthropological function' of law is analysed in Supiot's major theoretical work *Homo Juridicus* (2007).

[12]Supiot (2010), p. 24: 'un paix durable ne peut être établie que sur la base de la justice sociale.'

[13]Supiot (2010), p. 24: 'To this end it is important to renew two imperatives declared in the Declaration of Philadelphia. The first of these is the objective of social justice, which must be re-established as the unit of measure of the soundness of the juridical order in the following sense: that 'all national and international policies and measures, in particular those of an economic and financial character, should be judged in this light and accepted only in so far as they may be held to promote and not to hinder the achievement of this fundamental objective' (Declaration of Phila-delphia art II, c). The second is the imperative of social democracy, which allows us to found this evaluation in the diversity of experiences, and which requires that 'the representatives of workers

The Declaration establishes as foundational the concept of dignity. The Declaration 'erects' dignity as the fundamental principle that subtends (informs and rationalizes) all other principles and rights. To breach it, breaches the entire juridical order.[14] At stake is nothing short of the 'reification' of man. It is dignity – as supreme – that informs and makes sense of the articulation of the principles of liberty and security, not the other way round. It is dignity that ensures the proper balance between the two subordinate principles. As such, it underlies the following four commitments:

to resisting the commodification of labour

to the freedom of association

to solidarity – as tied also explicitly to the redress of poverty[15]

to social democracy, linked directly to the redress of need.

And with this we come to Supiot's central claim: that it is the inverse perspective of what the Declaration sought to affirm that currently dominates the actual processes of globalization.[16] The objective of social justice has given way to the free circulation of capital and commodities. The priority of ends to means has been reversed. And instead of indexing the economy to human needs and finance to the economy, the economy has been indexed to finance and people – as 'human capital' – to the service of the economy.[17] Also under strain have come the 'legal constructions that brought together the 'economic' and the 'social' dimensions of work under the aegis of the State. The deregulation of labour law and the generalization of statutory social protection can be seen as two sides of the same coin: labour can be freely bought and sold, stripped of its relation to the person, who only appears when there is a 'need' so great that society as a whole can no longer ignore it. The policies of international financial institutions reveal this process even more clearly: on the one hand, in the name of free competition they encourage the demolition of systems of solidarity, while on the other hand, they finance programmes to fight poverty, in the name of 'human development.'[18]

The stated objective of Supiot's book is to track the great inversion that appears to have abolished the lessons of the period of 1914–1945. And the normative point to argue that despite this collapse and inversion 'the spirit [of Philadelphia] retains all its pertinence',[19] disappointed, one might add, but not discredited. *It is this*

---

and employers ... [participate] in free discussion and democratic decision with a view to the promotion of the common welfare' (ibid., art I, d).

[14]'La dignité humaine est un principe sur lequel on ne peut pas transiger sans remettre en cause l'ordre juridique tout entire.' Supiot (2010), p. 22.

[15]Supiot (2010), p. 23: 'La pauvreté, où qu'elle existe, constitue un danger pour la prosperité de tous.'

[16]Supiot (2010), ch. 1 ('Le grand retournement') pp. 29 ff.

[17]Supiot (2010), p. 25.

[18]Supiot (2010), p. 101.

[19]Supiot (2010), p. 25.

affirmation that sustains the work. Because alongside the uncompromising attack on the market enthusiasts, fundamentalists, commissars and 'law and economics' apologists, Supiot's work never gives up the faith that law still possesses the resources to reclaim its humanising function. 'While the context within which the market function has changed it still rests *on dogmatic foundations*. If we need to be reminded of this today it is because the dominant economic *doxa* has fallen into the trap of the legal fictions on which it is based.'[20] Inherent tensions and resistances to marketisation abound: 'certain things resist their transformation into commodities, because they retain, e.g. the mark of the person who created them.'[21] Or the trade in 'human resources' inherent in the institution of the labour market contradicts the separation of persons and things on which the market system rests. Finally the hollowing-out of contract generates compensatory gestures, however transitory: 'Special domains of law have developed (labour law, social security law, [etc.]) in order to accommodate the elements that fall outside the sphere of the calculation of individual interests'[22] and rational utility maximization. However, the resistance is forever under threat: 'These special areas of law prop up an ordinary law of contract that is less and less capable of mastering the complexity of the phenomenon of contractualisation. The effectiveness of such props is, moreover, constantly diminished by the progress of free trade and the opening up of national frontiers to the circulation of capital, goods and services, which obliges States to reduce these props or adapt them accordingly.'[23]

What does Supiot mean when he insists that the humanizing function of law, as captured and expressed in the 'spirit of Philadelphia', 'rests on *dogmatic* foundations'? And what does it mean to hold on to the concepts of dignity and *solidarity* as the counter of 'commodification' and the inspiration behind the spirit of Philadelphia as dogmatic resources? It is to these questions that we turn now.

3   Solidarity and Dignity as *Dogmatic* Resources

The defence of the 'spirit' of Philadelphia as sustaining rather than merely overlaying international labour protection requires us to take a brief look at Supiot's legal theory and in particular his use of the concept of 'dogma'. The most obvious way in which his theory connects to the analysis of the ILO is in the emphasis he places on the notion that the Declaration of Philadelphia did not *enact* fundamental principles but *affirmed* them. It is an affirmation that is explicitly 'dogmatique', for Supiot, in the way 'dogma' carries an axiological reference to the integrity of legal reason. To understand this we need to look at the two facets of the dogmatic, the function of

---

[20]Supiot (2010), p. 94.

[21]Supiot (2010), p. 97.

[22]Supiot (2010), p. 100.

[23]Supiot (2010), p. 100.

'interdiction' and 'judgement' that characterize it. Supiot will go as far as to say that 'la question dogmatique de l'interdit ne pouvait être évacuée sans évacuer ce qui fonde la raison chez l'homme.'[24]

The dogmatic dimension is what supports, for Supiot, the function of law as a *critical* social hermeneutic. There is, to be sure, a prima facie tension in bringing together dogma and critique. Ordinarily we take *dogmatic* to mean what resists questioning; and what is taken for granted signifies and achieves closure; not the openness we associate with the critical attitude. And yet, for Supiot, it is precisely the unquestionability that attaches to the dogmatic that allows it to harbour critique. His attention here is to the kind of pre-understandings that attach to the juridical – to the ratio juris we might say – that set in place the conditions for interpretation as proper to the law. Dogma, that is, does the work of sustaining a discursive space proper for legal interpretation. The 'unquestionability' that dogma imports is at the root of the very autonomy of juridical reason. Supiot's priority is thus with the resources of interpretation that the dogmatic sustains: The dogmatic sets the limit points that sustain the symbolic order; to question them comes at the cost of it coming undone, of collapsing the achievement that is law. Where dogma does the work of sustaining the discursive space by setting in place the non-negotiable mainstays of the common, the work of legal hermeneutics is to unfold the dogmatic resources *as interdiction and as judgement.*

Take the two terms *interdiction* and *judgement* severally and in their combination. *Interdiction* is a wonderful term for the equivocation it carries: on the one hand it *resists, stems and interrupts* and on the other it mediates: *inter-dicts.*[25] On the one hand it refers to the sense of 'diction' that *mediates* by carrying meanings 'between' ('*inter*') registers; on the other hand to the sense of *preventing* (stemming, interrupting) the subjection of the logic of one medium (law or politics) to that of another (economics). There is something profoundly urgent in this latter function of interdiction. The *non-negotiability* of the fundamental values of dignity and solidarity that underlie what it means to *belong* in a world, are vested with the unquestionability that make them conditions rather than object of question, pre-understandings, pre-dispositions, guiding orientation, however, we might describe the hermeneutic enterprise of calling them forth our culture's symbolic resources in renewed acts of interpretation-cum-determination. It is at the level of this renewed instantiation that one must understand the exercise of *judgement.* Judgement fulfils the function of specification, concretisation, or instantiation, of the abstract value resources in specific, particular, occasions. In their combination interdiction and judgement attach a very particular meaning to critique understood as the *recuperation* of law as dogma that is instantiated rather than re-invented, *affirmed* – remember – was Supiot's term, in its critical invocation in judgement. A productive tension now installs itself at the juncture of closure and under-determination, calling forth the interpretative practices that enjoin us in community.

---

[24]Supiot (2010), p. 88.

[25]Supiot (2010), p. 88.

In the interstice that opens up between legal dogma and its productive deployment in interpretation, Supiot sets the opportunity-structure of legality as both limit and occasion. As he puts it in the earlier *Homo Juridicus*: 'The law hedges in every new beginning and at the same time assures its freedom of movement.'[26] If hermeneutics always depends on a horizon that cannot be transcended, the notion of the dogmatic as origin and limit is rolled out in every new interpretation. Juridical reason is therefore deployed within the set of values it enacts as fundamental presuppositions to it.

If the above analysis of interdiction and judgement appears somewhat removed from the analysis of the Declaration of Philadelphia, it is nonetheless what gives Supiot's defence of its 'spirit' its foundation and its élan. What he is able to draw from the dogmatic is an argument to resist 'liquider toute espèce d'interdit au nom de la liberté économique'; in other words to resist the slippage from the juridical to the market mindset that makes possible – and *sensible* – the erosion of judicial protection in the name of economic exigency. Interdiction is the term for the *non-negotiability* of these values and judgement the term for how they are deployed and mobilized in interpretation. In constitutional jurisprudence, we refer to *'rationalisation'* as the process of imbuing meaning to decisions by drawing on constitutional principle. Constitutional interpretations that are supposed instantiations of general principles and yet give the lie to those principles are deficient laws, to be righted as unconstitutional. Where the relation between principles and their instantiations is eroded and the dialectic is broken, any possibility of making sense of the law as a rational enterprise disappears with it.

Let us look more concretely at how interdiction and judgement operate to sustain the spirit of Philadelphia. The protection of work draws its essential rationale from the interdiction that 'labour is not a commodity'. As such it is, in principle, distinguished from the circulation of commodities and the regulation of that circulation, and constitutively tied instead to the constitutional protection of *dignity* (of the worker) and of *solidarity*, the ideal that undergirds and informs the whole category of social rights. That is why Supiot answers the constitutional question over the aspiration of *do justice to labour* as, above all else, a question of dignity and solidarity. Regarding the former, there is a developing constitutional jurisprudence of dignity and it would be dogmatically wrong and strategically imprudent to ignore its growing significance. This is not just a question of strategy, though it is undoubtedly that too, but crucially a question of the very foundation of law. As fundamental constitutional aspiration and dogmatic resource, the protection of human dignity sets a standard against which all interpretation of law must measure itself.

The other key dogmatic resource of the Philadelphia Declaration is *solidarity*. Supiot reminds us that in its original juridical sense – that dates from Roman law – solidarity was the term for what was effectively a technique of holding co-responsible all those who played a role in the generation of a certain risk.[27]

---

[26]Supiot (2007), p. 58.
[27]Supiot (2013), p. 99.

This meaning was generalised with the advent of the Social State which introduced the pooling of the risks of existence and gave solidarity the organisational form of social security and public services, to which one contributed according to one's resources and benefited according to one's needs. For the purposes of this founding of social rights constitutionalism on solidarity as legal-constitutional foundation, it is important to identify the key function that *solidarity* performs as *constitutional value*. If *social rights* (social protection and capacity to act) give institutional form to solidarity, the fact that they receive sanction as constitutional rights, means a political-constitutional commitment that underwrites social and labour protection and the obligation of social security. To understand solidarity as the foundation of the Social State and the founding commitment to mutualise the risks of existence through the provision of social protection, is to appreciate the gesture that understands societal valorisation as irreducibly collective, where even those less exposed to risks bear a duty of responsibility given that they partake as beneficiaries of the totality of social production (in both the formal and the informal economy). If today we are exposed to a radical withdrawal of the protection afforded to labour, the effect of this withdrawal, as Mark Freedland and Nicola Countouris have pointed out, is the 'demutualisation' of personal work relations, turning the individual worker into the sole bearer of risks formerly mutualised between workers and employing enterprises.'[28]

We might conclude with this: to conceptualise the principles of Philadelphia as the constitutionalisation of labour protection in the international field, to treat them as a *constitutional* accomplishment, means two things. It means first that, at the level of constitutional content, dignity and solidarity are affirmed as fundamental and irreducible values, tied to the deep dogmatic resources of juridical thinking; and second that, at the level of form, they are the sources of the rationalization of law, or in more mundane terms, they are what inform the interpretation of law. In this function, they are not constitutional directives, but standards for the protection of work. In the final section, we will see what difference this makes.

4   International Labour Protection as Human Rights

In the grand symphony of globalization, economic science has thus won pride of place as founding discourse for the universal order, leaving law the role of second fiddle: human rights.[29]

We began our account with a question over a regression, perplexing it was suggested given the novelty and significance of the ILO's mission. The weakening of the protection afforded to work internationally, the covert or blatant disregard for the principles enshrined in the Constitution and the Declaration, has been often visited

---

[28]Freedland and Kountouris (2011), p. 233.

[29]Supiot (2013), p. 86, my emphasis.

and typically treated as an outcome of the radical differentiation of a globalising economy re-launched as a 'total market', on the one hand, and the political-legal means to regulate its operation, on the other. At the root *of this emergent 'common-sensical' disregard for the principles of dignity and solidarity of work* lies a concession to 'pragmatism', the recognition of a certain asymmetry, as crucial as it is inevitable: While labour protection is predominantly the province of states, the capacity of states to protect labour has been crucially undercut by the global organisation of the economy. Globalisation involves the maximisation of the rates of return for capital circulating globally as effected through the circumvention of state systems of labour protection. The motor of profit extraction *is* the weakening of social and labour protection. For our pragmatists, and the new common sense that they offer, these are not hypothetical connections but objective conditions underlying the performance of national economies that are caught up in wage competition and the race to the bottom.

The above is, I would suggest, an analysis that, with variations of course, is widely conceded and celebrated (from the left and the right respectively) as the 'reality' of globalisation. But those who oppose the staggering inequality and degradation of work that it carries in its wake, assuage us that the recognition need not lead to abandoning the aspiration to protect work, so long as we appreciate that labour protection need not be enshrined in national constitutional orders and municipal systems of social security alone, and that it can find expression and support in international labour rights. Taken for granted certain assumptions about what can be protected nationally given the weakening of state capacity, the *grand compensatory gesture* involves the migration of labour protection to the international level. The development plays out at both theoretical and institutional levels. Re the latter: in 1998, in the wake of the Singapore summit, the WTO 'washed its hands' of any involvement in labour disputes, and thereby *relieved* the regulation of international trade of its effects on the world's producers.[30] In the subsequent 'division of labour', as it were, the ILO now with exclusive jurisdiction over the protection of labourers internationally, adopted the Declaration on Fundamental Principles and Rights at Work,[31] elevating four freedoms (freedom of association, the prohibition of forced labour, the effective abolition of child labour, and the elimination of discrimination in employment) to the position of 'core' principles, that is, binding on members of the ILO irrespective of ratification.

The new jurisdictional divide is devastating. As Supiot puts it pointedly, employment and unemployment levels depend much more on the organisation of international trade than on the policies of national governments, which, he argues, paradoxically makes the effectiveness of the protection of collective rights inversely proportionate to job security: those who need them most are effectively

---

[30]Hughes and Wilkinson (1998), p. 375.

[31]*ILO Declaration on Fundamental Principles and Rights at Work and its Follow-up*, adopted by the International Labour Conference at its 86th Session, Geneva, 18 June 1998.

deprived of any recourse to them (the 'Matthew effect' he calls it).[32] The 'division of labour' between the institutions, the artificial separation it effects in the field of production, is the first step in the drawn-out disempowerment of labour. The question that remains key to this whole development from our point of view, is whether a meaningful continuity might connect the new ILO Declaration (on Fundamental Principles and Rights at Work) with the Declaration of Philadelphia; or whether we are faced instead with a hollowing out of the standards of the protection of work to the status of aspirations or directives rather than actionable principles of law. We will take up this question in the next, final, section. For now let us look at the question whether labour rights are well protected as human rights.

Naturally, the literature on the question is rich and has yielded important insights and debates[33]; I certainly do not want to imply that there are no dividends to be had by the migration of labour protection to core human rights. For some commentators it represented a positive move towards ensuring the continued relevance of the ILO and international labour standards in a globalized world,[34] and the question of the symbolic value of this 'elevation' cannot be dismissed out of hand. Keith Ewing, for whom 'to a very large extent the reliance on human rights [to defend work] is a reflection of the failure of the promise of democracy, and of the capture of democracy by economic power'[35] recently, expressed a cautious optimism about certain developments in the wake of the ECtHR's use of the freedom of association to protect the right to strike in the 2008 Turkish cases of *Demir and Baykara*.[36] At a 'more practical level,' he concedes, 'human rights instruments provide an opportunity for workers to fight back, at a time when democracy has failed them, and when human rights courts appear at the moment to be responsive to the claim that workers' rights are human rights.'[37] Note the caveats, the references to the 'practical' and the 'timely' of the conjuncture, and the resigned admission that the moment may indeed be fleeting, or have flown.

In an interesting rejoinder to Patrick Macklem's *The Sovereignty of Human Rights*, Ruth Dukes makes the important point that Macklem's defence of international labour rights overestimates the capacity of international human rights to guard against the danger, or to mitigate the consequences, of the liberalisation of trade and finance on the lives of workers. For Macklem, she says, international human rights are understood to represent 'reasons that social, political and legal actors rely on in

---

[32]Supiot (2013), pp. 112, 110.

[33]Amongst the earlier and best collections, Alston (2005) With a special focus on the ILO see Fenwick and Novitz (2010).

[34]Langille (2005), p. 409.

[35]Ewing (2010), p. x.

[36]Demir and Baykara v Turkey [2008] ECHR 1345.

[37]Ibid., xiv–xv.

international arenas to advocate interfering in the internal affairs of a State and to provide assistance to States to promote their protection.'[38] Instead

> [i]t is quite clear that the capacity of international labour rights to fulfil these aims is limited. As drafted in the form of Conventions or Recommendations, international labour rights are intended for incorporation by nation states into their own individual domestic legal systems. They are not addressed to private or non-state actors – transnational corporations, banks and other financial institutions, supranational regulatory bodies – and do not, of themselves, create duties binding upon such actors. Their potential reach is coextensive with the – separate – jurisdictions of those Member States which are bound to incorporate them, and limited just as those jurisdictions are limited.[39]

In discussing, earlier, the asymmetry between markets going global and labour protection remaining state-bound, we identified a key 'architectonic' aspect of the organisation of production harnessed to the logic of profit extraction at the price of devaluing labour. But, it is not just the differential between the global and the national that inhibits the capacity of states to place limits on the economic power of global actors; the powerlessness is further compounded by obligations actually assumed by, or imposed on states. For Dukes,

> in the process of signing free trade agreements, nation states may surrender elements of their sovereignty, voluntarily restricting their ability to raise labour standards or even maintain and enforce existing standards. They do this not only by creating economic conditions which may encourage a race-to-the-bottom, but also by legally binding themselves to dismantle barriers to trade and market freedoms, even if such barriers take the form of labour rights or long-established practices of collective bargaining.[40]

This puts Macklem's rationale for the endorsement of international human rights – remember 'to provide assistance to States to promote their protection' – in a rather more sobering light. And it is here perhaps that we may most clearly appreciate the creeping consensus around a new common sense of human rights protection, which does in fact, despite the exalted tones that accompany it, mark a surrender of the constitutional dimension of labour protection. Whatever the limited dividends of defending labour rights as human rights, the migration of labour protection to the language of human rights leaves it vulnerable to the sources of private power, replaces collective and corporate descriptors and determinations for individual ones, and most importantly undercuts the constitutional function of labour law.[41] To appreciate the latter in its international dimension, in the light, that is, of the principles of the Constitution of the ILO as renewed through the Declaration of Philadelphia, we turn now to an argument about the unity of international labour law.

---

[38]Macklem (2015), p. 13.

[39]Dukes (2017), p. 559.

[40]Dukes (2017), p. 560.

[41]See Dukes (2014).

5 Principles and Their Instantiations: An Argument About the Unity of Law

Any discussion of the unity of International Labour Law has to confront the growing gap between organising principle and actual practice, in which interstice the new 'common sense' has come to install itself and redeem. This common sense involves, as we have argued above, the surrender of political will to the exasperated concession that a global market makes a nonsense of any attempt to institutionalise, let alone constitutionalise, labour protection. In the face of the disarticulation between the principles – the protection of solidarity and dignity of work – and the reality of the competitive race that is global economic practice, the principles need to be seen at best as *aspirations*.

A plea for the unity of law is an argument that this disarticulation *misreads* the law. There is a descriptive and normative side to it. On the *descriptive* side, the argument is that the best way to make rational sense of the system of international labour law, like any system, is to see it in terms of the unity of general principle and individual statute and decision. *Normatively* unity requires us to hold up current practices to the principles they instantiate. Or at least so I will argue.

Underlying the unity of International Labour Law are those principles that Philadelphia enshrined, and that we visited, with Supiot, in Sect. 2 above. The first established priority was that the organisation of the economy was subordinate to *social justice*, and what this meant at the level of constitutional principle the affirmation that all human beings enjoy the protection of 'liberty, dignity, economic security and equal opportunities' (Art. IIa); that the realisation of social justice was the 'central aim of all national and international politics.'. The second was the elevation of the concept of *dignity* to a fundamental principle. To breach it, Supiot had suggested, breaches the entire juridical order.[42] And it was dignity that informed the articulation of liberty and security, and served to support the Constitution's key commitments (1) to resisting the commodification of labour, (2) to the freedom of association, (3) to solidarity and, (4) to social democracy. We discussed this above; now let us note how these principles allow us to conceptualise the unity of international labour law.

If what has been proclaimed at the level of founding principle is in fact subverted at the level of legal practice, the question of unity throws open the question of the rationality of international labour law. A disjunction arises between the principle and its instantiation such that undercuts the rationality of law. After all, a standard cannot be *rationally* subverted in *its* own instantiation. To avoid this obvious injunction the distinction has typically been deployed between 'hard' and 'soft' law, relegating the principles to the sphere of 'soft' law, imperfectly supporting the hard realities of legal practice and settlement of labour disputes. But it is one thing to acknowledge that current legal practice is (still) only an imperfect realisation of its stated

---

[42]"La dignité humaine est un principe sur lequel on ne peut pas transiger sans remettre en cause l'ordre juridique tout entire." Supiot (2010), p. 22.

principles. It is quite another to rationalise the violation of (or non-compliance to) principles in terms of a distinction between hard and soft law, where principles are relegated to soft law against the 'realities' of, say, the fast-tracking of 'hard' economic freedoms. The problem arises when these two are conflated. Then the arguments that no instantiation ever fully realises its aspiration, and that general principles make possible a certain variety of concrete interpretations, are collapsed into a quite different one: that declaratory principles are to be contrasted with *jus cogens*. They become 'less prescriptive'; 'they lack effectiveness'; 'they fail to establish themselves as real recognised standards'; 'their aspirations have abated'[43]; etc. *But general principles are not deficient norms.* They are valid norms and they underlie real practices. If the practices don't stand up to the principles, then they are mistakes. And it is the job of observers of legal practice to identify those mistakes and of judges to right them.

The reference to fundamental principles of Labour law as 'soft law' thus belies the importance of what is at stake., their entrenchment elevates social policy priorities above economic interests (Because, of course, there lurks here a further disturbing symmetry between two sets of distinctions: built into the very idea of soft law as 'soft', is a subordination of social policy priorities to the non-negotiable (hard) imperatives of economic policy coordination.) Instead we need to remind ourselves that the validity of the constitutional principles of labour protection makes them prescriptive, and their generality imports an important 'element of reflexivity' into the process. The operation of all law (including that of 'soft law') depends on the allocation of the code values 'legal' and 'illegal' to real situations awaiting regulation. This allocation is guided by programmes,[44] some at quite concrete levels some at more general levels. Of course the allocation of legality and illegality is simpler when the programming is more concrete. And of course general principles, are in contrast poorly selective: their guidance value in terms of precise individual legal decisions is more limited. But at whatever level of generality programming occurs (regulation, directives, statutes, general principles) it nonetheless gains its quality as legal through its contribution in allocating, *in the last instance*, law's code values to events in the world. The trick in relegating these principles to 'soft law' is to confuse what is poorly selective with what is invalid. Such relegation breaks the articulation of levels of legal decision-making that alone makes sense of the unity of the law, by placing its organising principles outside the sphere of validity, and thus turning them into an irrelevance as mechanisms of redress of the disempowerment and dispossession suffered by the world's labourers.

Law's civilizing mission requires that the forces of global capital be met with international labour standards, and forging the unity of labour law at the supra-

---

[43] In the European context, 'formally, the [2000] Charter is merely a solemn proclamation by the European Parliament, Council and Commission. It was at one point hoped that, although the instrument is not as yet legally binding, it could provide a new source of reference for the courts in the exercise of its [sic] fundamental rights jurisprudence. This aspiration has abated...' Novitz (2005), p. 228.

[44] See Luhmann (2010) on the distinction between 'coding' and 'programming' in the legal system.

national level is a distinct possibility, even if that political will has been absent so far. The problem with relying on the ILO as the institution 'competent to devise and enforce these standards' writes Hugh Collins, is that while 'it was useful for capitalist countries to assert international labour standards in their ideological battle with communism,' they never intended this ideological weapon to become an effective instrument of labour legislation.'[45] Whether this 'represents the triumph of hope over experience'[46] depends on how seriously we take the transformative opportunities that law itself makes available against the 'false necessity' of economic imperatives. To understand this transformative opportunity as immanent to international labour law depends on restoring the rationality of a system by re-aligning its practices to its stated values, against the erosion of its autonomy, its subsumption to the logic of capitalism and the more extreme pathologies attendant to the rampant commodification of labour.

What I have argued is that unity requires us to hold our practices up to scrutiny in terms of the principles they are meant to be instantiations for. I have argued that there is a dialectic here, that operates between the setting of the standards and interpreting the minimum requirements that those standards set, a distinction similar to that between 'aspiration' and 'duty' wonderfully deployed by Lon Fuller[47] to set the basis of any understanding of the law warranting the name. There is a crucial distinction here that unity alerts us to: that between the limits of the tension that maintains the interplay between aspiration and standard, on the one hand, and, on the other, instantiations that give the lie to the principles that underlie them. In the former case, the tension is productive, and commands a constant attentiveness to standards that by their very nature exceed what can in each concrete case be actualised. But this is a tension that is crucially not a contradiction, such as that we encounter in practice, in instantiations that belie the guiding principles, and which is replicated at the level of theory and redeemed through the conflations that plague many discussions of soft law. In the case where instantiations belie the principles, the dialectic is broken and with it the unity of the law goes under. And with it, also, goes under any possibility of making sense of the law as a rational enterprise that depends for its rationality on holding together principles and their instantiations. Of course any intelligent discussion of unity will accept that the temporal dimension makes it impossible to ascribe any static meaning to fundamental principles: their non-negotiability, as underpinned by their *dogmatic* status (see above) does not mean that there will be no variation of what dignity, solidarity, etc., mean and demand. But just as there is a significant distinction to be drawn between relative truths and outright lies, there is one too between the variability of instantiations, and those that give the lie to the principles of democratic empowerment, social justice and the protection of dignity that undergird our constitution of international labour law, as established in 1919 and renewed in 1944, to redress the

---

[45]Collins (2005), p. 883.
[46]Collins (2005), p. 883.
[47]In the first chapter of Fuller (1969).

fundamental injustice of the subsumption of labour to capital, the collapse of the *political* economy into its market form, and the manifest injuries inflicted on the labouring classes of the globe. To return to those principles in not anachronistic as the new 'common sense' would have it; it is not a case of arresting history or turning our back to the present; it is instead to recover a different continuity that might allow us, to quote Supiot one final time, 'de trouver dans l'intelligence du passé les moyens de comprendre le present et de se projeter dans l'avenir.'[48]

References

Alston P (2005) Facing up to the complexities of the ILO's core labour standards Agenda. Eur J Int Law 16(3):467–480

Christodoulidis E (2019) Critical theory and the law. In: Christodoulidis E, Dukes R, Goldoni M (eds) Research handbook on critical legal theory. Edward Elgar

Christodoulidis E, van der Walt J (2018) Critical legal studies: Europe. In: Dubber MD, Tomlins C (eds) The Oxford handbook of legal history. Oxford University Press

Collins H (2005) Review. In: Barnard C, Deakin S, Morris GS (eds) The future of labour law: Liber Amicorum Sir Bob Hepple QC. Hart, Oxford, 2004

Countouris N, Freedland M (eds) (2013) Resocialising Europe in a time of crisis. Cambridge University Press, Cambridge

Dukes R (2014) The labour constitution: the enduring idea of labour law. Oxford University Press, Oxford

Dukes R (2017) International labour rights: legitimizing the international legal order? Univ Toronto Law J 67:544–568

Ewing K (2010) Foreword. In: Fenwick C, Novitz T (eds) Human rights at work: perspectives on law and regulation. Bloomsbury Publishing

Ewing K (2012) A Crisis of Legality accessible at: https://www.ucl.ac.uk/labour-rights/resocialising-europe-time-crisis-project-conference-book

Fenwick C, Novitz T (eds) (2010) Human rights at work: perspectives on law and regulation. Bloomsbury Publishing, London

Foucault M (1977) Language, counter-memory, practice: selected essays and interviews. Cornell University Press

Freedland M, Kountouris N (2011) 'Conclusion' in the legal construction of personal work relations. Oxford University Press, Oxford

Fuller LL (1969) The morality of law. Yale University Press

Hughes S, Wilkinson R (1998) International labour standards and world trade: no role for the world trade organization? New Polit Econ 3:375–389

Koukiadaki A, Kretsos L (2012) Opening Pandora's box: the sovereign debt crisis and labour market regulation in Greece. Ind Law J 41:276–304

Langille B (2005) Core labour rights – the true story. Eur J Int Law 16:409–437

Luhmann N (2010) Law as a social system. Oxford University Press, Oxford

Macklem P (2015) The sovereignty of human rights. Oxford University Press

Novitz T (2005) The European Union and international labour standards: the dynamics of dialogue between the EU and the ILO. In: Alston P (ed) Labour rights as human rights. Oxford University Press, Oxford

---

[48]Supiot (2010), p. 88 ['to find in the intelligence of the past the means to understand the present and to project a future.'].

Supiot A (2007) Homo Juridicus. Verso, London
Supiot A (2010) L'Esprit de Philadelphie. La justice sociale face au marché total. Seuil, Paris
Supiot A (2013) Grandeur and misery of the social state. New Left Rev 82:99–113
Tikriti A-K (1982) Tripartism and the International Labour Organisation. A study of the legal concept, its origins, function and evolution in the law of nations. Almqvist & Wiksell, Stockholm

Emilios Christodoulidis holds the Chair of Jurisprudence at the University of Glasgow. He is also Docent of the University of Helsinki and member of the Executive Committee of the IVR (International Association for Social and Legal Philosophy). His research interests lie in Legal Philosophy and Social and Political Theory.

Decent Work in Global Supply Chains: Mapping the Work of the International Labour Organization

Valentina Grado

Contents

1   Introduction

Notoriously, economic globalisation has led to a shift in the way business is conducted. Originally it was largely confined within the borders of individual states; then it assumed the form of multinational enterprises (MNEs), with mother

The author wishes to thank Concetta Maria Pontecorvo (*Professore Associato* of International Law, University of Naples Federico II) for her stimulating comments on earlier drafts of this chapter.

V. Grado (✉)
University of Naples L'Orientale, Naples, Italy
e-mail: vgrado@unior.it

© Springer Nature Switzerland AG 2019   53
M. Bungenberg et al. (eds.), *European Yearbook of International Economic Law 2019*,
European Yearbook of International Economic Law (2020) 10: 53–86,
https://doi.org/10.1007/8165_2019_26, Published online: 1 October 2019

companies located mostly in the Global North (the so-called *home* states) and their subsidiaries operating mostly in the Global South (the so-called *host* states); ultimately, it became large, fragmented global supply chains (GSCs), that is transnational networks of companies operating in several different countries. The latter encompass a broad range of commercial activities—such as conception, production and distribution of goods and services—often coordinated by (home) lead firms (brand-name MNEs, and global retailers), who, in turn, have business relationships with hundreds of corporations mainly domiciled in host states and acting as suppliers, contractors, and other business partners. In 2015, the International Labour Organization (ILO) noted that "the number of GSC-related jobs has increased rapidly over the past decades...[o]ut of 40 countries with available data to which methodology could be applied, 453 million people where employed in GSCs in 2013, compared with 296 million in 1995". It further observed that "[m]ost of the overall increase is driven by emerging economies, where GSC-related jobs grew by an estimated 116 million. Overall, GSC-related jobs represent 20.6 per cent of total employment among the countries analysed, compared with 16.4 per cent in 1995".[1] While GSCs have created in fact millions of jobs and opportunities for economic and social development, at the same time they have been however in the public spotlight due to both their several and serious disregards of labour standards and the significant decent work challenges they pose.

Against this backdrop, this chapter deals with the so far done ILO's work on the crucial topic of decent work in GSCs. Our discussion proceeds in several stages, as follows. Section 2 first highlights the main reason of the Organization's long inaction on the phenomenon of GSCs. Section 3 describes the work of the (2016) 105th Session of the International Labour Conference (ILC) dealing with this issue, by critically analysing—respectively—the ILO Office pre-conference report on ILC's agenda item IV; the debate on it during the ILC 15th Session; the conclusions achieved by the ILC on the topic; and the merits and demerits of these conclusions. Sections 4–6 will then illustrate and discuss the further significant work recently undertaken by the ILO Governing Body, namely by: the adoption of the (2017) Programme of Action and the Roadmap on decent work in GSCs; the new (2017) version of the ILO Tripartite Declaration of Principles concerning Multinational Enterprises and Social Policy (ILO MNE Declaration) and, finally, by its action on specific segments of GSCs that are represented by *export processing zones* (EPZs). Section 7 concludes by discussing the adequacy of the recent and foreseen ILO's initiatives in the field of GSCs in delivering better labour conditions for workers within them.

---

[1]ILO (2015), p. 132.

2   The Main Reason for ILO's Inaction on International Supply Chains Till 2016

Within the ILO's framework, its tripartite executive body, the Governing Body, has the task of setting items for discussion by the ILC. In March 2006, the workers' representatives in the Governing Body proposed to put on the agenda of the ILC the issue of decent work in GSCs.[2] As it is well known, the decent work concept was formulated in 1999 by the ILO's constituents as a means to identify the Organization's main purpose. Since then the primary goal of the ILO has become the promotion of opportunities for women and men to obtain decent and productive work, in conditions of freedom, equity, security and human dignity. Decent work should be achieved through the implementation of the ILO's four strategic objectives, that is: promoting—respectively—employment, social protection, and social dialogue as well as promoting, respecting, and realising the fundamental principles and rights at work.[3] For the purpose of this chapter it is important to remember that the latter objective incorporates the 1998 ILO Declaration on Fundamental Principles and Rights at Work, which identifies four core labour standards (CLS), i.e.: (a) freedom of association and the effective recognition of the right to collective bargaining; (b) the elimination of all forms of forced or compulsory labour; (c) the effective abolition of child labour; and (d) the elimination of discrimination in respect of employment and occupation.

The 2006 workers' aforementioned proposal was supported only by a handful of governments and not by the employers, who underlined that the ILO international labour standards covered all possible situations and relationships in the world of work; therefore, in their opinion, the important thing was not so much to develop new general standards, but rather to ensure the more effectively application of the existing standards.[4] Even if the workers' representatives continued to support the item on decent work in GSCs at *every* subsequent meeting of the Governing Body,[5] it was only after the Rana Plaza disaster in Bangladesh in April 2013 and the first strategic report of ILO Director-General (Guy Ryder) that the Governing Body decided, in October 2013, to place on the agenda of the (2016) 105th ILC's Session an item for general discussion on decent work in GSCs. It is worth noting that in his first strategic report Ryder acknowledges the ILO's inadequacy in attending to the contemporary realities of the world of work. A distinctive feature of these realities is the fragmentation of production processes along increasingly complex and dispersed production chains, which may cover several countries or even regions.[6] According to the report, the urgent need for the ILO to engage with private enterprises is due to

---

[2]ILO (2006), par. 9.

[3]ILO (2008). On decent work see e.g. ILO (1999) and Nizami and Prasad (2017).

[4]ILO (2006), par. 5.

[5]Thomas and Turnbull (2018), p. 546.

[6]ILO (2013), para. 74.

both the serious abuses occurring within GSCs and the Organization's weak response to those violations.[7] Most importantly, on the issue of how the ILO could address the matter of labour practices along international chains, the report acknowledges the importance of the responsibilities of member states to apply ratified conventions but—at the same time—it wonders whether this purely state-centric approach is sufficient. In the light of the fact that private actors are the drivers of the constantly shifting supply chains or production networks, it indicates that additional opportunities for the ILO to promote decent work in their operations should be considered.[8] In other words, the report seems to recommend the development of a system of labour governance based not only on the traditional (horizontal) territorial approach (states bearing responsibility towards workers within their jurisdiction) but also on vertical labour governance along the supply chain (transnational corporations also responsible for enforcing labour rights within their chains of production).

3 The (2016) 105th Session of the International Labour Conference: Agenda Item IV—Decent Work in Global Supply Chains

On April 2016, the Office published a pre-conference report (Sect. 3.1). This was followed by a debate on it in June 2016 (Sect. 3.2). Finally, in June 2016 the ILC agreed on a set of conclusions on the fourth item on the agenda of its 105th Session (Sect. 3.3), characterised—as we will discuss—by several merits and demerits (Sect. 3.4).

3.1 The Pre-conference Report of the ILO Office

The Office background report (*Decent work in global supply chains*), consisting of five chapters and an appendix, aims to provide evidence regarding employment, working conditions and labour rights in GSCs.[9]

Its first chapter (*Introduction: Setting the stage*)[10] underlines the growing importance of GSCs as a common way of organising investment, production and trade in the global economy. It recognises that GSCs are complex, diverse, fragmented, dynamic and evolving organizational structures and defines them as "the cross-border organization of the activities required to produce goods or services and the process of bringing them to consumers through inputs and various phases of

---

[7]Ibid., para. 141.
[8]Ibid., para. 75.
[9]ILO (2016a).
[10]Ibid., pp. 1–4.

development, production and delivery".[11] In addition, this chapter discusses GSCs' major features, which are analysed more in detail in chapter two. It further recognises that, on the one hand, GSCs have contributed to job creation (particularly in developing countries), technology transfer, higher-value activities and skills development. On the other hand, the practice of cross-border sourcing of goods and services places significant downward pressure on wages, working conditions and the respect for fundamental rights of workers participating in the chains. Finally, this chapter highlights the existence of governance gaps and the difficulties created by cross-border sourcing versus national level legislation, regulation and jurisdiction.

The report's second chapter (*Global supply chains and the world of work*)[12] describes the GSCs' main drivers (telecommunications, technologies, logistics and trade agreements) and their various forms within two main types of intra- and inter-enterprise relationships, i.e.: (1) foreign direct investment (FDI) by MNEs with direct ownership of their overseas subsidiaries; and (2) the increasingly predominant model of international outsourcing, where lead firms do not have ownership or a direct contractual relationship, except with first-tier suppliers and intermediaries. Importantly, it defines the lead firm (mostly based in developed countries) as "the company that controls the global supply chain and sets the parameters with which other firms in the chain must comply, and is typically responsible for the final sale of the product".[13] This chapter further describes the typical typologies of GSCs that is producer-driven or buyer-driven. Producer-driven supply chains refer to those chains in which producer enterprises have the most significant influence over the production process, with wholly owned subsidiaries worldwide. Instead, in buyer-driven chains, lead firms (retailers and brand-name companies) make decisions with which supplier companies must comply. Within this second type of GSCs there is an asymmetrical power between the global buyer and the supplying companies and the pressure of the former on producer prices and standards of production may generate negative impacts on working conditions and fundamental rights of the workers participating in the chains. This global pressure can further encourage supplier firms to further subcontract parts of their production to suppliers in subcontracted tiers who use forms of employment which may not comply with labour standards, in some extreme cases resorting to forced and child labour. This chapter also describes the major production, trade and investment trends and the scale and quality of employment in GSCs. Data, statistics and case studies are presented on these topics. The studies cited on quality of employment show both positive and negative results, the latter being violations of labour standards, frequently in lower tiers. As far as wages and working time are concerned, the chapter recognises that the existence of low wages remains a source of concern; women are paid at the low end of the scale; wage structures do not reward skills; productivity gains are not shared with workers; low prices paid to suppliers create pressure down

---

[11]Ibid., p. 1.
[12]Ibid., pp. 5–26.
[13]Ibid., p. 5.

the supply chain to reduce costs, which may lead to downward pressure on wages; statutory minimum wages are often too low and this contributes to excessive overtime work, which in turn raises concerns about occupational safety and unhealthy working conditions. On the subject of non-standard forms of employment, their use by suppliers presents significant regulatory challenges. With regard to migrant workers, the latter are often found in non-standard forms of employment; moreover, the increasing cross-border flows of workers have also resulted in a greater risk of forced labour and trafficking in persons. In this chapter there is also a brief section on EPZs, describing their growth, exemptions from national labour laws in some countries, lack of enforcement of labour legislation and mixed records both in economic and social terms.

Chapter three of the background report (*Upgrading for decent work in global supply chains*)[14] explores the process through which the employment created by GSCs may attain decent work (*upgrading*). Particularly, it explores two forms of upgrading in GSCs: economic upgrading (that is, the process of suppliers moving from low-value to high-value activities in global chains) and social upgrading (that is, the process of achieving decent work conditions in GSCs), underling that to achieve decent work and desired developmental outcome social upgrading must accompany economic upgrading. Importantly, it specifies that social upgrading concerns the qualitative aspects of employment and does not condone the violation of applicable national laws and international labour standards, including the four CLS which must be respected everywhere, at all times and under all circumstances. However, it underlines the existence of challenges for social upgrading with respect to all four CLS. It also illustrates examples of the positive and negative combination of economic and social upgrading, with the conclusion that the link between economic and social upgrading is not automatic. Therefore, it calls for a clear role and need for governance mechanisms that support and promote integrated and mutually reinforcing economic and social upgrading.

The report's chapter four (*Governance in global supply chain*)[15] recognises the governance deficit in GSCs, partly because of a lack by governments of host countries of the institutional capacities to regulate and enforce labour standards and partly because of the cross-border nature of supply chains. It considers the different programmes and structures that have evolved to govern particular aspects of global supply operations, by categorising them into four types: public governance, private governance, social partners' and multilateral initiatives.

Public governance describes the state's duty to enforce national labour laws and regulations and to implement ratified international labour conventions.[16] This includes labour administration, inspection and enforcement functions, such as dispute resolution and prosecution of violators. The report highlights the challenges particularly applicable to GSCs as related to: (1) weak laws and law enforcement

---

[14]Ibid., pp. 27–37.

[15]Ibid., pp. 39–64.

[16]Ibid., pp. 41–47.

mechanisms in host states; (2) lack of jurisdiction, respectively, of the host states (to eventually hold foreign lead firms accountable) and of the home states (to regulate the extraterritorial conduct of corporations headquartered within their own jurisdiction); (3) the twin doctrine of separate corporate personality and limited liability, allowing MNEs to minimise legal liability for labour violations committed by their subsidiaries and/or suppliers; and (4) recent national legislative initiatives aimed at improving transparency in supply chains by lead firms, even if their impact on sustainable workplace compliance cannot be determined yet. This part of the report further describes some policies that have been developed to increase labour compliance, such as labour provisions in trade agreements, public lending and public procurement policies. These all have potential but their overall impact is not significant enough.

Private governance[17] is led by companies, employers' organizations or industry associations through private compliance initiatives, such as codes of conduct and social auditing; certification initiatives or other self-reporting mechanisms; sectoral initiatives and social labelling initiatives. According to the report such instruments have many shortcomings, including: their limitation to upper-tier supplies; their weakness in detect violations of enabling rights, such as freedom of association and the right to collective bargaining; inadequate accountability; and their failure to address the root causes of non-compliance.

Social partners' initiatives take place at the enterprise, sectoral, national or international levels.[18] These mechanisms require negotiation between workers and the employer. Examples of such governance include social dialogue, collective bargaining, multi-stakeholder initiatives (in which NGOs are often included) and international framework agreements between MNEs and global union federations. Although social partners are crucial to the effective implementation and enforcement of national labour laws, inclusiveness may be limited due to the lack of participation of: (1) lead firms at the national level; (2) small and medium-sized enterprises (SMEs) at the local level, and (3) union affiliates in workplaces (with regard to international framework agreements).

Multilateral initiatives include international regulatory mechanisms set up by international organizations.[19] The most relevant to this respect are the ILO MNE Declaration; the OECD Guidelines for Multinational Enterprises; the UN Global Compact, and the UN Guiding Principles on Business and Human Rights (UN Guiding Principles). Although these multilateral initiatives may require reporting, monitoring activities or complaints processes, the report underlines that they have limited capacity to enforce their standards directly.

The second section of background document's chapter four[20] indicates that, in order to close the governance gap in GSCs, there is a need to reinforce the layers of

---

[17]Ibid., pp. 47–52.

[18]Ibid., pp. 52–58.

[19]Ibid., pp. 58–61.

[20]Ibid., pp. 61–64.

governance and strengthen public capacity and social dialogue. It also describes three examples of how improved governance could be applied to promote decent work, such as the comprehensive programme to combat forced labour in Brazil; the ILO-IFC Better Work programme; and the ILO Maritime Labour Convention (2006).

The report's last chapter (*The way forward*)[21] focuses on the need to use a holistic approach to promote decent work in GSCs. It underlines, in particular, the role of the ILO in bringing together the main actors and stakeholders responsible to bridge governance gaps; the need to promote international labour standards and to assess whether additional guidance or *standard* (the last word in ILO-language meaning a *convention*) are needed to effectively promote decent work in GSCs; closing governance gaps by the coordination and combination of different and complementary compliance mechanisms; promoting inclusive and effective social dialogue at different levels including cross-border; strengthening development cooperation programmes; deepening the value of existing processes; strengthening labour administration systems; closing the knowledge gap and improving statistics; and, promoting partnerships and improving coherence and coordination between regional and multilateral organizations with mandates in closely related fields.

Under the perspective of a thorough evaluation of the content and actual relevance of the pre-conference report, it should be recognised that—although providing a complete and up-to-date assessment on the situation of decent work in GSCs—it presents two major limitations. The first one relates to the structure and functioning of these chains (examined in chapter two). According to the report, global buyers—as lead firms—control their supply chains and can, through their market power, dictate prices and the details of production which negatively affect wages, working conditions and the respect of CLS of the workers within the chains. In other words, the report highlights some of the ways in which MNEs may *contribute* to violations of labour standards by their *own activities*, occurring—for example—in case the buyer demands significant last-minute changes in product specifications without adjusting price or delivery dates, thus creating strong incentives for suppliers to breach international labour standards. This first scenario may happen in supply chains with a captive or even hierarchical governance structure, which are characterised by a group of small suppliers that are dependent on one or a few MNEs in their resource and market access.[22] However, as already pointed out by scholars, there are also other forms of GSCs governance, for example the modular chain governance, where major suppliers are able to operate independently of the lead firms and the latter does not control the supply chain.[23] In this second scenario the MNE is *not contributing* to the abuses by its own activities, but nevertheless it is implicated by its *link* to the goods or services it procures, e.g. suppliers use child labour to manufacture a product for the contracting enterprise (the buyer), without

---

[21]Ibid., pp. 65–68.

[22]Gereffi et al. (2005), p. 84.

[23]Ibid.

any pressure (contribution) from this enterprise to do so. As we will see below, a *different responsibility* of the MNE is attached to this second scenario according to the UN Guiding Principles.

The second major limitation relates to the governance gaps, as the report rightly acknowledges. To this respect, as already mentioned, chapter four reviews existing regulatory approaches to promote decent work in GSCs and it underlines their many shortcomings in the field of public governance, private governance, social partners' and multilateral initiatives. However, taking into account that the second section on "closing the governance gaps" only describes three example of improved governance and that the first two of them belong to the traditional (horizontal) territorial approach of labour governance, the report seems—in our opinion—to discuss not sufficiently how existing governance gaps could be close; for example, by the adoption of a new ILO convention on GSCs.

3.2   The Debate on Agenda Item IV at the ILC

As foreseeable, during the debate on agenda item IV at the 2016 Session of the ILC, the employers' and the workers' representatives were sharply divided on issues such as whether GSCs determine opportunities and/or challenges for the realisation of decent work, whether there is a governance gap at the international level; and, if so, whether a new standard (that is a convention) on GSCs should be adopted.

The employers highlighted that GSCs have stimulated growth, created jobs and contributed to productive employment and decent work. They argued that, while there are decent work deficits in some GSCs, these deficits are not unique to cross-border supply chains, but rather reflect the challenges in the general economy, such as a high prevalence of informality, ineffective labour inspections and legal systems, and inadequately developed social protection systems. For example, referring to the Rana Plaza tragedy, they stressed that the root cause was the lack of capacity of the government to implement and enforce its laws, including issuing of building permits and conducting building safety inspections. According to them, there was no evidence of a governance gap at the international level caused by cross-border supply chains, rather only a lack of implementation and enforcement of governance at national level. In addition to ratified international labour standards, the ILO Declaration on Fundamental Principles and Rights at Work, and the UN Guiding Principles were considered by the employers fully adequate to address decent work issues in all circumstances, including cross-border supply chains; what was needed was more effective implementation of national laws and regulations. Therefore, according to them no new standard setting on supply chains was required. Furthermore, the employers' representatives disagreed with the inference in the pre-conference report that lead firms always held control over the GSCs, for instance to dictate prices and the details of production in the supply chains, and as such contribute to the violations of labour standards committed by their overseas subsidiaries and/or suppliers.[24]

In contrast, the workers' representatives underlined the unequal power between lead firms and subcontractors which place a significant downward pressure on wages, working conditions, and the respect of CLS of workers within the chains. In their opinion, the subcontracting to SMEs abroad, which is characteristic for the business model in GSCs, had contributed to decent work deficits. One cause of such deficits is the lack of local legislation and its enforcement, made difficult by the cross-border nature of the production; the other is the weak coordination and the lack of enforceable instruments to hold governments and business accountable. On the latter point, it was highlighted that currently the responsibility of MNEs for the acts of their subsidiaries or suppliers abroad is governed largely by voluntary guidelines such as the ILO MNE Declaration, the OECD Guidelines for Multinational Enterprises, and the UN Guiding Principles; however, those guidelines have not succeeded in changing practices. In addition, a major problem in workers' opinion is the lack of adequate remedy when their rights are violated. Local suppliers where the violations occur are unlikely to face indeed accountability, often because of weak, under-resourced or corrupt administrative and judicial processes. At the same time, lead firms are often de facto immune from legal accountability, as there might be no course of legal action or jurisdiction in the host or home country when a violation is caused by their suppliers or subsidiaries. To address gaps in governance, the workers' representatives asked for a revision of the ILO MNE Declaration; the creation of a reporting mechanism whereby breaches of the ILO MNE Declaration could be addressed effectively and the adoption of a convention on decent work in GSCs. Central to this convention should be the obligation of states to pass laws aimed at regulating the conduct of enterprises under their respective jurisdiction, wherever the alleged harms may occur. Another component of the instrument should be mandatory due diligence, with respect to international labour standards, and an obligation for transparency of supply chains; guarantees for freedom of association and the right to collective bargaining at all levels of the supply chain; minimum wage setting mechanisms to ensure living wages; the promotion of industry-wide and cross-border bargaining and the promotion of secure employment relationships in GSCs. The convention should include, finally, further guidance on how to ensure the implementation of existing standards, bring together the provisions in existing conventions relevant to GSCs, and provide an integrated framework applicable throughout the chain.[25]

A few considerations are worth to be made with regard to the polarised views of employers' and workers' representatives. Beginning with the former, their position on the foremost responsibility of governments to ratify and implement ILO conventions and, especially, to enforce national regulations is certainly sharable, in the light of the fact that labour rights violations in GSCs are often linked to governance gaps

---

[24]ILO (2016b), e.g. paras. 12–19.
[25]Ibid., e.g. paras. 20–21, 69 and 129–132.

in host countries which allow local companies to act in contravention of national laws and/or international labour standards. Thus, reliance on effective host country regulation and remedies is, on the one hand, critically important for ensuring observance of workers' rights but, on the other hand, it remains a long-term proposition due to—inter alia—the enormous pressure put on these countries by MNEs which threat the withdrawal of business if strong protective standards are enforced (the so-called *race to the bottom* phenomenon). Second, the employers' argument that the existing regulatory framework (that is, national-level enforcement of labour standards and the UN Guiding Principles) is an adequate response to serious abuses of labour standards in GSCs is—instead—in our opinion *at least* doubtful, in the light—respectively—of the transnational nature of some business operations and the limitations (discussed in what follows) of the currently international standards on business and human rights, such as the UN Guiding Principles.

Turning to the workers' position, their proposal for a new convention based— inter alia—on (home) states' regulations of the extraterritorial conduct of enterprises within their jurisdiction and on mandatory due diligence for companies throughout their cross-border supply chains is, certainly per se, commendable; but, admittedly, it also raises many questions, such as on the legality under customary international law of these (home) regulations with extraterritorial reach (as we will see below), on the potential effectiveness of a convention and—especially—on the actual feasibility of such a convention.

During the 2016 ILC debate, with a clear divide between employers and workers, the position of governments' representatives became crucial; and several of them— especially from the European and the African continents—shared the workers' views on the existence of governance gaps[26]; the need for a new binding international regulation or, at least, to assess whether current ILO instruments are sufficient to promote decent work in GSCs or whether there is a need for new ones.[27]

3.3   The Outcomes of the 105th ILC Session on Agenda Item IV

After many heated debates and several late-night negotiating sessions, a set of conclusions was finally agreed by the ILC.[28] In what follows, a brief illustration of their very relevance and actual scope seems useful to the end of this study.

On the subject of the opportunities emerged from GSCs for the realisation of decent work,[29] the ILC conclusions—after having highlighted that GSCs are complex, diverse and fragmented—recognise that those chains have contributed to

---

[26]Ibid., e.g. paras. 27, 29, 79, 83, 140 and 175.

[27]Ibid., e.g. paras. 45, 147, 156 and 161.

[28]ILO (2016c).

[29]Ibid., paras. 1–2.

economic growth, job creation, poverty reduction and can contribute to a transition from the informal to the formal economy. In addition, GSCs are considered being a possible engine of development by promoting technology transfer, adopting new production practices and moving into higher value-added activities, which would enhance skills development, productivity and competitiveness.

With regard to the challenges for the realisation of decent work,[30] the conclusions indicate that failures at all levels within GSCs have contributed to decent work deficits in the areas of occupational safety and health, wages, and working time. Such failures have also contributed to: (1) the undermining of labour rights, particularly freedom of association and collective bargaining; (2) informality and non-standard forms of employment; (3) the acute presence of child labour and forced labour in the lower segments of some GSCs; and (4) the presence of migrant workers and homeworkers that may face various forms of discrimination. In addition, there is the presence of women who are disproportionately represented in low-wage jobs in the chain's lower tiers and they are too often subject to discrimination and various forms of workplace violence. Furthermore, there are decent work deficits in a significant number of EPZs linked to GSCs. Finally, the conclusions recognise that governments may have limited capacity and resources to effectively enforce compliance with national laws and, most importantly, that these governance gaps have being exacerbated by the expansion of GSCs.

As far as the past interventions are concerned,[31] the conclusions recognise that despite a wide range of policies, actions and programmes have been put in place by the Office, ILO constituents and other stakeholders, decent work deficits and governance gaps continue to exist.

On the subject of the appropriate future interventions,[32] the conclusions refer to the UN Guiding Principles which are grounded in the recognition of: (a) states' existing obligations to respect, protect and fulfil human rights; (b) the role of business enterprises, required to comply with all applicable laws and to respect human rights; and (c) the need of access to effective remedies for victims. In addition, the conclusions underline that the ILO, due to its global mandate, expertise and experience in the world of work, is best placed to lead global action for decent work in GSCs. More in detail, the conclusions state that governments, business and social partners have different but complementary responsibilities in promoting decent work in GSCs.

As to states,[33] they have in particular—according to the ILC conclusions—the duty to adopt, implement and enforce national laws and regulations, and to ensure that CLS and ratified labour conventions protect and are applied to all workers. Governments should specifically: (a) strengthen labour administration and inspection systems in order to ensure full compliance with laws and regulations and access

---

[30]Ibid., paras. 3–7.

[31]Ibid., paras. 8–12.

[32]Ibid., paras. 13–14.

[33]Ibid., paras. 15–16.

to effective remedy; (b) actively promote social dialogue and CLS, including in EPZs; (c) use public procurement to promote CLS; (d) where appropriate, require enterprises owned or controlled by the state to implement due diligence procedures; (e) create an enabling environment to help enterprises to identify sector-specific risks and implement due diligence procedures in their management systems and, in addition, clearly communicate on what they expect from enterprises with respect to responsible business conduct; (f) stimulate transparency and encourage, and, where appropriate, require that enterprises report on due diligence within their supply chains to communicate how they address their human rights impacts; (g) fight corruption, including by protection of whistle-blowers; (h) consider to include CLS in trade agreements; (i) set out clearly the expectation that all business enterprises domiciled in their territory and/or jurisdiction respect human rights throughout their operations; (j) implement measures to improve working conditions for all workers, including in GSCs; (k) target specific measures at SMEs to increase their productivity and promote decent work; (l) provide guidance and support to employers and business to take effective measures to identify, prevent, mitigate and account for how they address the risks of forced or compulsory labour in their supply chains; (m) implement policies to facilitate the transition from the informal to the formal economy; and (n) cooperate through regional bodies to harmonise laws and practices.

With specific regard to businesses,[34] according to the conclusions they have a responsibility to respect human and labour rights in their supply chains consistently with the UN Guiding Principles, and to comply with national law wherever they do business. In particular, enterprises should carry out human rights due diligence in order to identify, prevent, mitigate and account for how they address their adverse human rights impacts.

As far as the social partners are concerned,[35] they should jointly promote decent work and CLS, including in GSCs, through sectoral initiatives, collective agreements, cross-border social dialogue and international framework agreements, where appropriate.

Finally, with regard to the ILO action,[36] the conclusions call upon the Organization to develop a specific programme of action to address decent work in GSCs based—inter alia—on some ILO Declarations, all relevant international labour standards, and various conclusions adopted by the ILC. In particular, under the programme of action the ILO should, first of all, promote the ratification and implementation of the ILO standards relevant to decent work in GSCs. Second, it should strengthen capacity building and provide technical assistance to member states on labour administration and inspection systems, including in EPZs. Third, the ILO should promote effective national and cross-border social dialogue, thereby respecting the autonomy of the social partners. Fourth, the Organization should

---

[34]Ibid., paras. 15 and 18.
[35]Ibid., para. 17.
[36]Ibid., paras. 22–23.

assess the impact and scalability of development cooperation programmes, and develop sectoral and other approaches to address decent work challenges in GSCs. Fifth, the ILO should provide leadership to drive policy coherence among all multilateral initiatives and processes related to decent work in GSCs and work in partnership with international organizations and forums (e.g. UN, OECD, G7 and G20), and take into account international frameworks such as the UN Guiding Principles, and the OECD Guidelines for Multinational Enterprises. Sixth, the Organization should strengthen its capacity to give guidance to enterprises on the application of labour standards within their supply chains and make information available on specific country situations, laws and regulations, including on the implementation of labour rights due diligence in coherence with already existing international frameworks. Seventh, the ILO should consider adopting an action plan to promote decent work and protection of CLS for workers in EPZs. Eighth, it should take a proactive role in generating and making accessible reliable data on decent work in GSCs, in cooperation with all relevant organizations and forums, to create synergies in statistics and research. Finally, the Organization should carry out further research and analysis to better understand how supply chains work in practice, how they vary by industry, and what their impact is on decent work and CLS.

The conclusions further remember[37] that the ILO MNE Declaration is the Organization's framework supported by all tripartite constituents that aims at maximising positive impacts of MNEs and resolve possible negative impacts. Within the review process of this instrument, the Governing Body should consider the setting up of mechanisms to address disputes.

Most importantly, in their last paragraph[38] the conclusions recognise that current ILO standards may not fit for the purpose to achieve decent work in GSCs. Therefore, the ILO should review this issue and convene, as soon as appropriate, by decision of the Governing Body, a tripartite meeting to: (a) assess the failures which led to decent work deficits in GSCs; (b) identify the salient challenges of governance to achieving decent work in GSCs; and (c) consider what guidance, programmes, measures, initiatives or standards are needed to promote decent work and/or facilitate reducing decent work deficits in GSCs.

3.4   Merits and Demerits of the 2016 ILC Conclusions on Agenda Item IV

In the light of the above, the concluding text agreed by the 2016 ILC on decent work in GSCs seems to show many merits but also several pitfalls, which are worth of a closer comment on.

---

[37]Ibid., paras. 24 and 23(e).

[38]Ibid., para. 25.

Beginning with the former, it is clear that—by affirming that GSCs are complex, diverse and fragmented—the conclusions recognise first of all the existence of *different structures* of GSCs (captive or modular, simple or complex) and, therefore, the *different ways* MNEs (or lead firms) may be involved with negative impacts occurring in the group or network. Second, the text highlights in a balanced way the many *benefits* brought about by GSCs but, at the same time, the numerous decent work *deficits* created by them. Third, by underling the existence of failures *at all levels* within GSCs, the conclusions—again in a balanced way—underline that *both* MNEs (lead firms) and their suppliers may be responsible for social irresponsible behaviours. Fourth, the text clearly acknowledges the role of GSCs in *exacerbating governance gaps*, finally settling a question that was initially denied by the employers' representatives during the debate. Fifth, the conclusions admit the *insufficient* interventions (by the Office, ILO constituents, and other stakeholders) put in place in the past, the *current* existence of decent work deficits and governance gaps; and the need to *address* these challenges. Finally, in order to ensure an improvement of the conditions of workers within GSCs, the text emphasises that governments, business and social partners have *complementary* but *different* responsibilities. Significantly in this respect the conclusions *fully rely on* the UN Guiding Principles in order to define the different responsibilities of states and business enterprises for achieving decent work on GSCs. Thereby, they embrace a normative framework that, although has become a common reference point in the area of business and human rights, is characterised by strengths as well as limitations and pitfalls. Being clearly impossible to examine here in detail all these issues, we will limit our discussion on some key positive/critical aspects of the UN Guiding Principles most linked to the protection of international labour standards in GSCs.

As widely known, the UN Guiding Principles—endorsed by the UN Human Rights Council in 2011 and developed by the Special Representative of the Secretary-General on the issue of human rights and transnational corporations and other business enterprises (Professor John Ruggie)—are not legally binding and do not create new international law obligations.[39] They aim to operationalise the former UN "Protect, Respect and Remedy" Framework developed in 2008 and based on three distinct but interlocked pillars: (a) the duty of states to *protect* human rights against abuses by third parties, including business enterprises; (b) the corporate responsibility to *respect* human rights; and (c) access to effective *remedy* for those who are harmed.[40]

As far as the Framework's first pillar is concerned, UN Guiding Principle 1 reiterates that the state's international human rights obligations require, inter alia, the duty to protect against corporate-related human rights abuses within its territory and/or jurisdiction by adopting appropriate steps to prevent, investigate, punish and redress such abuses through effective policies, legislation, regulations

---

[39]UN Human Rights Council (2011). For a comment see e.g. Mares (2012); Wetzel (2016), pp. 183–192.
[40]UN Human Rights Council (2008).

and adjudication. Thus, the UN Guiding Principles *as well as the 2016 ILC conclusions* recognise the (non-controversial) obligation of *host* States to protect worker's rights violations committed by local suppliers as well as subsidiaries of MNEs based on their territory. Further recommendations address by both texts to states vis-à-vis enterprises are: (a) where appropriate, require corporations owned or controlled by the state to implement due diligence procedures; (b) provide guidance on responsible business conduct; (c) encourage and (where appropriate) require self-reporting on due diligence and how enterprises address their human rights impacts; and, (d) set up clearly the expectation that all business enterprises domiciled in their territory and/or jurisdiction respect human rights throughout their operations.[41] With regard to this last invitation, the Commentary to UN Guiding Principle 2 explains: "[a]t present states are not generally required under international human rights law to regulate the extraterritorial activities of businesses domiciled in their territory and/or jurisdiction. Nor are they generally prohibited from doing so, provided there is a recognized jurisdictional basis". Therefore, according to the UN Guiding Principles *home* states are not obliged to prevent human rights violations overseas by corporations domiciled in their territory and/or jurisdiction but they are permitted to do so provided two conditions are met: there needs to be a recognised basis of jurisdiction, and the actions of home states need to meet an overall reasonableness test, which includes non-intervention in internal affairs of other States.[42] Although this approach notoriously does not reflect increasing international recognition—by UN treaty bodies and some scholars—of the *legal obligation* of (home) states to regulate their transnational business activities,[43] we will confine our brief analysis on the legality under customary international law of the workers' proposed (home) states legislation that mandates due diligence (concerning international labour standards in the supply chain) by MNEs operating in their territories.

Before dealing with this issue, it is important to highlight the implications of mandatory due diligence concerning supply chains (which we will discuss again later on). Domestic supply chain-related law is an avenue by which home states (can) impose human- and labour-related norms *directly* on lead firms (mother companies of MNEs or global buyers) based on their territory and *indirectly* on their foreign subsidiaries and/or suppliers. Because the former has a legal responsibility to seek that the latter act in a responsible way, home states' lead firms are required to influence the conduct of their subsidiaries/suppliers in other countries and to impose due diligence requirements upstream in supply chain.[44] As a result, home states supply chain-related regulations (can) impose *indirect* obligations outside their

---

[41]UN Human Rights Council (2011), UN Guiding Principles 3–4 and their Commentaries; ILO (2016c), para. 16.

[42]UN Human Rights Council (2008), para 19.

[43]See, *ex multis*, Skogly (2017) and Krajewski (2018).

[44]For the potentialities and challenges posed by domestic laws regulating GSCs with respect to human rights and labour practices, whereby companies are not only regulated entities but also serve as regulators themselves (imposing standards on their suppliers in other countries) see e.g. Sarfaty (2015), pp. 421–422.

territory on foreign upstream companies and *indirectly* force them to comply with these rules. Therefore, self-evidently, these regulations raise two main questions: those of their legality in the light of—respectively—the rules of sovereignty and international jurisdiction and the principle of non-intervention in internal affairs.

Starting with the first issue, it could be argued that the aforementioned laws interfere with the host country's sovereign right under international law to regulate activities occurring within its jurisdiction and therefore produce extraterritorial effects by prescribing the adoption of a conduct outside the territory of the regulating state. However, it is important to underline that many domestic regulations may indeed have some effect beyond the territory of the regulating state, but not all of them will be considered as being applied extraterritorially. This is particularly the case of national supply chain-related laws address to corporations (with foreign activities) which are domiciled in the regulating (home) state. Indeed, they are in line with the rules on prescriptive jurisdiction; moreover—being enforced within the territory of the regulating (home) state—they seem also to be consistent with the rules on enforcement jurisdiction. Turning to the question on whether those national supply chain-related laws constitute a violation of the non-intervention norm by inducing changes in the host country's internal regulatory regime, it must be underlined that an intervention is prohibited only if it relates to a matter that concerns the *domestic affairs* of the target state. The workers' proposed (home) states regulations of transnational business activities, being aimed at producing compliance by local companies of domestic laws adopted after the ratification of the new ILO *convention*, would not constitute an unlawful intervention in the *internal affairs* of host states. This is because respect for existing laws does not negatively affect the political, economic or (importantly) the social system of (host) states which *freely* decided to be part of a new (labour) convention.

In the light of the above, it is possible to underline that the UN Guiding Principles *as well as the 2016 ILC conclusions*—by recognising only host states' obligations to protect as well as by giving a significant margin of appreciation to home states—take a rather *weak* approach to the role governments should play in achieving decent work in GSCs. It is also clear that the barriers to regulating corporate activity abroad are political rather than legal, in the light of the fact that customary international law does not prevent home states to act in this direction.

Turning to the Framework's second pillar, the UN Guiding Principles 11–24 set out the responsibility of business enterprises to respect human rights, the latter understood as a social expectation towards companies to avoid infringing upon the rights of others and to address adverse human rights impacts with which they are involved. According to them, this responsibility exists independently of states' abilities to meet their own human rights obligations; it applies to all enterprises, regardless of their size, sector, operational context, ownership and structure and it extends (over and above compliance with national laws) to all internationally recognised human rights.[45] Companies are expected "to avoid causing or contributing to adverse human rights impacts through their own activities", but also "to seek to prevent or mitigate adverse human rights impacts that are directly linked to their operations, products or services by their business relationships, even if they have not contributed to those impacts".[46] In order to meet the responsibility to respect, UN Guiding Principles 15–22 concretely require enterprises to have in place policies and processes, including: (a) a "policy commitment" on human rights compliance; (b) a "human rights due diligence" process to identify, prevent, mitigate and account for how they address their human rights impacts; and (c) processes to enable the remediation of any adverse human rights impacts they have caused or contributed to. With regard to the human rights due diligence process, it involves: (1) assessing actual and potential human rights impacts; (2) integrating and acting upon the findings; (3) tracking responses; and (4) communicating how impacts are addressed. This process should also draw on internal and/or independent external human rights expertise, and involve meaningful consultation with potentially affected groups and other relevant stakeholders, as appropriate to the size of the enterprise and the nature and context of the operation.[47]

In light of this brief illustration, the Framework's second pillar provides some useful elements in order to qualify the corporate responsibility to respect human rights but—at the same time—it is characterised by several shortcomings.

Beginning with the former, it should be first mentioned the fact that the corporate responsibility to respect extends to *all internationally recognised human rights* understood, at a minimum, as those expressed in the Universal Declaration of Human Rights, the International Covenant on Civil and Political Rights, the International Covenant on Economic, Social and Cultural Rights, and the principles concerning fundamental rights in the eight ILO core conventions as set out in the 1998 ILO Declaration on Fundamental Principles and Rights at Work.[48] As a result, the responsibility to respect applies to the *four CLS as defined in the eight fundamental ILO conventions*[49]; as well as to *labour-related human rights* mentioned in the main human rights treaties, such as the right to, respectively, a fair and sufficient remuneration, safe and healthy working conditions, equal opportunity for promotion, and rest, leisure, reasonable limitation of working hours and holidays with pay.[50]

Moreover, the second pillar distinguishes between *three* levels of business' involvement with negative impacts on human rights, as: (a) a company may cause adverse impacts through its own activities (e.g. by employing itself child labour); (b) a company may contribute to such an impact through its own activities (e.g. through purchasing decisions which create strong incentives for a supplier to

---

[45]UN Human Rights Council (2011), UN Guiding Principles 11, 12 and 14 and their Commentaries.

[46]Ibid., UN Guiding Principle 13.

[47]Ibid., UN Guiding Principles 17–21 and their Commentaries.

[48]Ibid., Commentary to UN Guiding Principle 12.

[49]Bellace (2014), p. 185.

[50]On these labour-related human rights see e.g. MacNaughton and Frey (2016), pp. 626–628.

breach international labour standards); and (c) a company may be directly linked to adverse impacts through its business relationships yet without contribution on its part (e.g. without any pressure from the global buyer, the product contains components which are manufactured by suppliers using child labour). A different responsibility is attached to each scenario.[51] Where the company causes an adverse impact, it should take steps to cease the impact and engage in remediation. In turn, *contribution* and *linkage* are particularly relevant in the context of (domestic or global) supply chains. Where the enterprise is contributing to the abuse by its own activities, it should take appropriate steps to address those contributions (inter alia, termination and remediation). Finally, where the enterprise is implicated in the abuse solely by the direct link to its operations, goods or services through its supply chain relationships at whatever tier, appropriate action will depend on a number of factors such as the "enterprise's leverage over the entity concerned"; "how crucial the relationship is to the enterprise, the severity of the abuse, and whether terminating the relationship with the entity itself would have adverse human rights consequences".[52] The combination of these variables will yield different conclusions as to what action should be taken. Appropriate responses by an enterprise may include: mitigating the risk that the adverse impact continues/recurs (when the enterprise possesses the leverage); seeking ways to increase the leverage to enable mitigation (when the enterprise lacks the leverage); and considering ending the relationship either where the enterprise lacks the leverage or where it is unable to increase its leverage. Therefore, the UN Guiding Principles incorporate an *extended corporate responsibility* with respect to its supply chain, which does not stop with the company's own activities, but also includes those adverse impacts that are directly linked to its products by its business relationships even beyond the first-tier relationships.[53]

Lastly, the second pillar introduces an innovative concept—*human rights due diligence*—as the means through which an enterprise can operationalise its responsibility to respect human rights in its own activities and supply chains. More in detail, UN Guiding Principle 17 defines the parameters for human rights due diligence: it should cover both the impacts that the business may cause (or contribute to) through its own activities and those that may be directly linked to an enterprise's operations, products or services through its business relationships. With regard to the nature and extent of the human rights due diligence, it should be commensurate with the severity (and probability) of the actual and potential adverse impacts; the nature and context of the enterprise's operations; and its size. Lastly, the timeframe of human rights due diligence should be ongoing, because risks may change over time as the enterprise's operations and operating context evolve.

---

[51]UN Human Rights Council (2011), UN Guiding Principle 19 and its Commentary.

[52]Ibid. Leverage is considered to exist where the enterprise has the ability to effect change in the wrongful practices of the entity that causes a harm.

[53]Commentary to UN Guiding Principle 17 acknowledges that a supply chain may have so many numbers of entities that a reasonable approach to human rights due diligence in such a context would warrant prioritisation for assessment of general areas (e.g. suppliers' operating context, operations, products or services involved) where the risk of adverse human rights impact is highest.

Therefore, human rights due diligence goes *beyond* corporate due diligence (that is, processes to manage enterprises' own risks), being primarily aimed at protecting actual and potential victims of negative human and labour rights impacts.[54] Moreover, in addition of being a *process* which help ensure that the expectations placed on business are both reasonable and feasible in the light of the circumstances, human rights due diligence has started to be used as a basis for attaching *legal liability* to lead firms throughout their group or network.[55]

Turning to the limitations of the second pillar, the most significant one is the voluntary and non-binding nature of the requirements for corporate business (domestic or transnational) operations. In this respect, it is sufficient to underline that according to the 2018 report of the UN Working Group on the issue of human rights and transnational corporations and other business enterprises—the body mandated inter alia to promote good practices and lessons learned on the implementation of the UN Guiding Principles—only a small number of committed enterprises, mainly large companies, have made progress on due diligence. The majority of companies—both large and small—still need to embrace their human rights responsibilities, including through an effective, efficient and inclusive due diligence process.[56]

Another important pitfall concerns the specific issue of *corporate respect in the supply chain*. As already mentioned, this pillar uses two concepts in relation to the attribution of responsibility to the enterprise. The first is *contribution to harm*, occurring for example where a decision or action taken by a global buyer creates strong incentives for a foreign supplier to breach international labour standards. Self-evidently, in this scenario the responsibility to respect is grounded in the enterprise's *own* impacts. The second concept is the enterprise's responsibility to act in order to seek to *mitigate* the occurrence of negative impacts caused by its direct suppliers or even sub-tier suppliers, even if it has neither caused not contributed to harm. In this second crucial scenario—as it has been reported by the Office, serious labour abuses often occur in the *periphery* of transnational groups or networks—a sound foundation justifying the lead firm's responsibility to act (from using leverage to minimise impacts to termination of the relationship) is missing.

Further shortcomings relate, lastly, to the fact that this pillar articulates the concept of human rights due diligence at a high level of abstraction. As a result, by employing an ambiguous and imprecise language, it leaves many critical questions unanswered, such as: what *labour rights adverse impacts* are (for example, related to the right to just conditions of work); what the scope of adequate *labour rights due diligence* should be; how *labour rights risks* should be measured; how the concept of *leverage* should be applied and what exactly constitutes *severe* labour rights abuses.[57]

---

[54]See e.g. Muchlinski (2015), pp. 334–339; McCorquodale et al. (2017), pp. 198–201.

[55]See, *ex multis*, Cossart et al. (2017); Grado (2018b), pp. 244–250.

[56]UN Human Rights Council (2018), paras. 25 and 27.

[57]For further critical analysis of this concept see e.g. Deva (2013), pp. 93–103; Trebilcock (2015).

The limits of the UN Framework's second pillar further confirm that the governance labour systems pinpointed in the 2016 ILC conclusions may *not* be adequate for the purpose to achieve decent work in GSCs.

4 The (2017) ILO Programme of Action and the Roadmap on Decent Work in GSCs

In March 2017, the Governing Body adopted a Programme of Action and a Roadmap specifically aimed to address decent work in GSCs through a comprehensive and coordinated framework.

The former, anchored in the core pillars of the ILO Decent Work Agenda and started in 2017, is finalised to create change in a number of critical areas over a period of 5 years (2017–2021).[58] It has five areas of action that it will pursue, including: (1) *knowledge generation and dissemination* (for timely and effective generation of evidence-based knowledge and the establishment of a knowledge and research capacity to support and promote strategies to achieve decent work): (2) *capacity building* (in order to improve capacity of tripartite constituents and enterprises to engage in successful sustained efforts at the national, sectoral, regional and international levels to advance decent work in GSCs); (3) *effective advocacy for decent work in GSCs* (that is focused advocacy for advance decent work in supply chains at national, sectoral, regional and international levels, with the core of these key advocacy messages being the promotion of ratification and implementation of key international labour standards); (4) *policy advise and technical assistance* (that is strategic and coherent policy advise and technical support by the Office to enable governments, business and social partners to develop and implement a target mix of policies for reducing decent work deficits and governance gaps): and (5) *partnership and policy coherence* (that is the intensification of ILO's work with UN agencies, multilateral institutions, other international forums and GSCs actors to develop and promote policies that advance decent work in GSCs).

Additionally, the Programme endorses the nine ILO technical areas of action suggested by the 2016 ILC conclusions. For each of these technical areas, specific deliverables and a timetable for action are provided; each deliverable, in turn, is linked to one of the five aforementioned areas of action.[59]

Furthermore, the Programme is expected to be coherent with the UN Guiding Principles, paying close attention to those of them related to the (already explained) different responsibilities of lead firms in their GSCs.

Finally, the Programme of Action also foresees three further significant meetings (already called for by the Governing Body in November 2016): (1) in 2017, a tripartite Meeting of Experts to identify possible action to promote decent work

---

[58] ILO (2017a).

[59] Ibid., Appendix.

and CLS in EPZs; (2) in 2018, a meeting on cross-border social dialogue, as called for in the 2013 ILC conclusions on the recurrent discussion on social dialogue, to address decent work in GSCs, including human rights due diligence; and (3) in 2019, a meeting—following a midterm report by the Office—on the three elements indicated in the last paragraph of the 2016 ILC conclusions.

As to the Roadmap, it was developed in order to identify concrete and prioritised areas of action.[60] For the period 2017–2018 the Office was tasked: (1) to prioritise the first two areas of action (knowledge generation and dissemination and capacity building); (2) to start with selected elements from the other three areas of action in order to ensure smooth progress over 5 years; and (3) to ensure logical sequencing among all five areas of action. With respect to the Roadmap for 2019–2021, the specific steps it includes are: (1) midterm stocktaking and continued implementation of all five areas of action; (2) preparation of a midterm report and its presentation to the Governing Body in November 2019; (3) final consolidated assessment of progress of the Programme of Action, last 3 months of 2021; and (4) preparation of a final report and its presentation to the Government Body in October 2022.

5   The (2017) Revised Tripartite Declaration of Principles Concerning Multinational Enterprises and Social Policy

A further relevant development within the Government Body's initiatives on decent work in GSCs took place in March 2017, when it adopted a new ILO MNE Declaration text with two annexes.[61] Being this instrument analysed in another chapter of this volume, we will confine our comment on the main positive/critical elements which were introduced in the 2017 version.[62] As widely known, the ILO MNE Declaration is the only Organization's instrument that provides direct guidance—inter alia—to MNEs on a broad range of issues, such as employment promotion, non-discrimination, security of employment, training, conditions of work and life, and industrial relations. However, it is important to underline that the pre-2017 version covered only the hierarchical form of GSC's governance; did not address the responsibilities of entities within the corporate group and did not include a dispute resolution procedure.

The recent revision has added (only a few) principles (addressed to MNEs) related to specific decent work issues, such as the elimination of forced or compulsory labour; wages, benefits and conditions of work; and, remedies for abuses of human rights. More importantly, by outlining the fact that on the issue of human rights states and enterprises have different roles, the revised text refers to the

---

[60]ILO (2017b).

[61]ILO (2017c).

[62]See also Grado (2018a), pp. 223–230 for a detail analysis and the contribution by Jernej Letnar Černič in this volume.

corporate responsibility to respect as called by the UN Guiding Principles.[63] However, it must be also highlighted in this regard that the corporate's responsibility to respect is not perfectly aligned with the UN Guiding Principles related to the Framework's second pillar. First of all, this is because by affirming that MNEs should respect CLS *throughout their operations*,[64] the responsibility seems to be limited to the violations committed by their overseas subsidiaries. Second, because the new text states that MNEs should use their leverage to *encourage* their business partners to provide effective remediation for abuses of internationally recognised human rights.[65] This is in line with UN Guiding Principle 22 according to which when adverse impacts are solely directly linked to the enterprise's operations, products or services by a business relationship, the responsibility to respect human rights does not require that the enterprise itself provide for remediation, *though it may take a role in doing so*. However, the same UN Guiding Principle clearly states that when a corporation is *contributing* to harm, it should *provide* for remediation.

The last significant limitation of the 2017 version relates to the fact that, contrary to the invitation of the 2016 ILC conclusions, it does not establish mechanisms or instruments to mediate, settle and/or provide remedy for disputes between MNEs and workers' organizations. Significantly in this respect, Annex II (*Operational Tools*) only includes: a regional follow-up mechanism; the Declaration's promotion by tripartite appointed national focal points; its promotion by the Office; company-union dialogue; and an interpretation procedure. Therefore, it is evident that the focus remains on *promotion* of the *voluntary* principles envisaged in this instrument.

6 Decent Work and Protection of Fundamental Principles and Rights at Work in *Export Processing Zones* (EPZs)

As to the first technical Meeting of Experts on EPZs, in March 2017 the Governing Body established its agenda charging significantly and specifically with: (a) discussing possible action to promote decent work and CLS for workers in EPZs; and (b) adopting conclusions which will provide guidance on the content and modalities for an action plan on EPZs as called for in the 2016 ILC conclusions on decent work in GSCs.[66] Against this backdrop, on November 2017 the Office published a background report (Sect. 6.1) that was followed by the adoption of a set of conclusions (Sect. 6.2); finally, on March 2018 the Governing Body adopted follow-up action (Sect. 6.3).

---

[63]ILO (2017c), para. 10.

[64]Ibid., paras. 25, 27, 30 and 47.

[65]Ibid., para. 65.

[66]ILO (2017d), para. 405.

6.1   The Background Report of the ILO Office

The Office report, consisting of a background and four chapters, is worth here of a short analysis and comment in the light of specific situations in EPZs, where decent work deficits are widespread.[67]

First of all, its background[68] underlines that—though the ILO has a long history of examining and discussing employment, labour rights and social issues in relation to EPZs—since 2008 there is however a gap in knowledge on how EPZs affect decent work.

The report's first chapter (*EPZs: Purpose, how they work and estimated numbers*)[69] starts by highlighting that estimates of the number of EPZs are few and far between. In 2006, the ILO counted 3500 EPZs (or similar zones); since then, no comprehensive survey on the phenomenon is available. However, the United Nations Conference on Trade and Development (UNCTAD), in turn referring to an article in The Economist, suggested that as of 2015, there were over 4500 EPZs, over 3000 more than 20 years previously.[70] On the issues of variety and evolution of EPZs, this chapter underlines that discussions over EPZs have been impeded by the fact that they have been defines in various ways. The ILO, for example, defines them as "industrial zones set up to attract foreign investors, in which imported materials undergo some degree of processing before being exported again".[71] However, it highlights that a common characteristic in all definitions used by different international institutions is that a zone is an enclave, both in terms of its geography and its exceptional regulatory and institutional features, even if it has interactions with the economy outside the special zone. These enclaves are created by government policy to promote FDI and exports and have become increasingly common among countries seeking export-led economic growth. With regard to the objectives of EPZs policies, they are numerous: attraction of foreign exchange earnings, which can be used to import crucial capital and materials for production; spur industrialisation; participation in global economies; technology transfers; address other development issues (such as tackling unemployment); and creating employments for workers, whose earnings can further stimulate economic development. The main incentives offered to attract foreign investors to EPZs are fiscal exemptions but also weak protection of workers' rights as well as exemptions or derogations from national labour rights.

The report's second chapter (*Impact of EPZs on fundamental principles and rights at work*)[72] describes the challenges and deficits posed by these zones on CLS. On the issues of freedom of association and collective bargaining, it confirms

---

[67]ILO (2017e).

[68]Ibid., pp. 1–2.

[69]Ibid., pp. 3–17.

[70]UNCTAD (2015), p. 4.

[71]ILO (1998b), p. 3.

[72]ILO (2017e), pp. 19–27.

that violations of these rights in EPZs are common in developing countries. With regard to discrimination in EPZs, the most prevalent challenge relates to gender discrimination. Finally, with regard to child labour and forced labour, this chapter underlines that the former is more likely to occur upstream in the production chain while the latter may appear in EPZs link to migrant workers who are required to pay recruitment fees and transportation before they are allowed to leave their jobs.

The report's third chapter (*Other elements of decent work in EPZs*)[73] focuses, respectively, on employment creation, job stability, skill development, hours of work, wages, occupational safety and health (OSH), social protection, labour inspection and social dialogue.

With regard to employment creation, EPZs generate direct employment, but the latter varies significantly between countries and has often been disappointing. On the issue of stability of employment, EPZs tend to have a high rate of turnover of workers, due to the use of fixed-term contracts and the intensive nature of the work. As skill development is concerned, despite progress in many EPZs, it still lags behind in many countries. With regard to wages, different studies indicate that EPZs pay higher wages, but without implying that they are decent or liveable wages. On the issue of hours of work, in EPZs they tend to be long, exceeding legal limits, due to—on the demand side—poor supply chain management and—on the supply side—the low wages paid to workers. With regard to OSH in EPZs, violations of OSH legal requirements have been documented in many countries. Additionally, the repetitive manual labour involved in EPZs work exposes workers to significantly higher risks of serious injury. As far as social protection is concerned, workers in EPZs in developing countries are more likely to have social protection such as health care and social security than non-EPZ workers; however, social protection in law does not always materialise in practice. On the issue of labour inspection, even if national labour law includes EPZs within its scope, these laws are often not enforced in the majority of countries. Frequently, the problem lies in the labour inspectorates as a whole: in many countries, they are under-resourced in terms of staff levels, transportation and materials. Finally, with regard to social dialogue, the report underlines that it can help to improve decent work outcomes in EPZs.

The report's last chapter (*Conclusions and suggested points for discussion*)[74] affirms that EPZs present a mixed picture. On the one hand, they have generated exports and foreign exchange as well as created jobs and employment opportunities for certain groups, young women in particular. On the other hand, EPZs are characterised by problems in the protection of especially the first two CLS and workers' rights concerning hours of work and OSH. Therefore, the chapter highlights the role that the ILO could play in providing assistance to tripartite constituents in countries operating EPZs to better promote decent work and protect CLS, for example by means of its decent work country programmes or by developing comprehensive guidelines.

---

[73]Ibid., pp. 29–40.
[74]Ibid., pp. 41–42.

In the light of the above, the report—admittedly—provides for interesting reading on labour rights and working conditions in some EPZs which are often the result of the unwillingness of host countries to implement their own labour law. However, by considering EPZs *exclusively* within their national context, it does not provide an analysis on the linkages between those zones and GSCs, that is on the relationship between (home) lead firms' actions and omissions and the violations of international labour standards by their foreign subsidiaries and/or suppliers operating in (host states') EPZs. This is in our opinion a missed opportunity, especially in the light of previous ILO studies on the subject. Indeed, in 1998 the latter already recognised that "changes in production chains are clearly beyond the control of a zone-operating country and its social partners" and therefore recommended ILO research activities "on the practices of transnational enterprises, in view of the particular relevance of this subject for EPZs".[75]

6.2   The Achievements of the Tripartite Meeting of Experts on EPZs

The tripartite Meeting of Experts was convened from 21 to 23 November 2017; it reviewed the report prepared by the Office; and, by consensus, adopted a set of conclusions as well as recommendations for follow-up.[76] Being EPZs a key segment of GSCs, a brief illustration of and comment on the Meeting's final text seem to be very relevant to the end of our study.

The conclusions start by underlining that there are limited recent empirical studies on EPZs in general, on decent work impacts of EPZs and on the protection of CLS for workers in EPZs. Although there seems to be a general trend towards an increase in the number of EPZs and the countries using them since the last ILO count in 2006, the conclusions add that the approximately 10-year gap in knowledge underscore the need for up-to-date information and counsel against a one-size-fits-all approach.[77]

On the issue of opportunities offered by EPZs,[78] according to the conclusions the latter have helped to, respectively, attract foreign exchange earnings; stimulate domestic enterprises to move up in the value chain; create formal employment especially for young women; and, give workers higher wages as well as include them in social protection schemes.

With regard to the challenges and deficits in realising fundamental rights and decent work,[79] the conclusions underline their presence in many EPZs. More in detail, (a) workers commonly face barriers to exercising their right to organize and

---

[75]ILO (1998b), p. 15; ILO (1998a), para. 32.

[76]ILO (2017f).

[77]Ibid., para. 3.

[78]Ibid., para. 4.

[79]Ibid., para. 5.

union may face barriers and discrimination; (b) collective bargaining remains rare; (c) women workers are at risk of harassment and discrimination in the workplace; (d) in some cases workers face delays in payment or non-payment of wages due upon dismissal, and social protections in law do not always materialise in practice; (e) hours of work tend to be too long, putting workers at greater risk of accidents and injuries; (f) forced overtime can also exist; and (g) migrant workers are particular vulnerable.

On the additional actions that governments should take to further promote decent work and protection of CLS in EPZs, the conclusions elaborate many recommendations.[80] In particular, (a) government EPZ policies should ensure that worker's rights are protected and that, at a minimum, CLS are not compromised in any policy to attract investors to EPZs; (b) where appropriate, access to incentives in EPZs should be conditioned on a commitment to upholding decent work; (c) governments should place a high priority on strengthening labour inspection systems in both EPZs and the broader economy in countries where they are currently inadequate to fully protect workers' rights; (d) access to remedy should be speedy and fines for violations of worker's rights should be sufficiently dissuasive; (e) governments should ratify conventions and apply the provisions of ratified conventions in law and practice to the whole of the country, including EPZs; and (f) they should promote collective bargaining and ensure an enabling environment for sustainable industrial relations; improve working conditions and social protection; and support enterprises to undertake due diligence.

As far as enterprises are concerned,[81] the conclusions highlight that because EPZs are often linked to GSCs, their strategies for sourcing may also impact the rights of workers in EPZs in significant ways. Therefore, all companies are called to respect workers' rights and use their leverage to take steps to ensure that the rights of workers in their supply chains are also respected and that workers have access to remedy when their rights are violated, as advocated for in the UN Guiding Principles and the ILO MNE Declaration.

On the role of employers' organizations,[82] they should encourage and support enterprises to respect CLS and promote decent work; abide by national law; support public labour inspections in EPZs; carry out due diligence; and use their leverage with business partners in their value chains to advance CLS and decent work. Employers' organizations should also engage in social dialogue concerning policies to promote decent work in EPZs.

On the role of workers' organizations,[83] they should provide targeted support to workers in EPZs (in particular women, youth, migrant workers and refugees) and also engage in social dialogue at all levels.

---

[80]Ibid., paras. 8–10 and 12–14.

[81]Ibid., para. 11.

[82]Ibid., para. 15.

[83]Ibid., para. 16.

On the role of the multilateral system,[84] the conclusions recognise its possible contribution to strengthen governance in EPZs and promote policy coherence at global levels in areas impacting EPZ development, such as policies on inclusive and sustainable growth, trade and investment policies, industrialisation and SME development strategies, and protection of human rights.

Finally, the conclusions suggest that the ILO could provide support to tripartite constituents in countries operating EPZs to better promote decent work and CLS.[85] Support could include the following: (a) improve the knowledge base to obtain up-to-date information and a more holistic picture of the nature of EPZs; (b) strengthen the capacity of national labour inspection systems, including inspections in EPZs; (c) promote and expand the Enabling Environment for Sustainable Enterprises programme to include EPZs; (d) provide technical assistance to tripartite constituents; (e) advocate for ratification and implementation of the fundamental conventions, as well as relevant standards on OSH and social protection; (f) support the social partners to engage in industrial relations and broader social dialogue to reduce labour deficits in EPZs; (g) build capacity of employers' and workers' organizations, and through them, enterprises and workers operating in EPZs; (h) address shortages of skilled labour, including in EPZs; (i) provide technical assistance to governments and social partners in mainstreaming CLS and decent work in EPZs; (j) document good practices by governments, social partners and enterprises in realising CLS in EPZs and share these experiences more broadly; and (k) support the development of social dialogue at all levels. In addition, with regard to the multilateral system,[86] the ILO should: (a) intensify the collaboration with international organizations to ensure better understanding of the role of EPZs in the context of the 2030 Agenda for Sustainable Development; (b) cooperate with international financial institutions and regional banks to further promote decent work and respect of CLS in EPZs; (c) work with the G20, taking into account its recent commitment to promote sustainable GSCs; and (d) engage in UN Development Assistance Frameworks and with the World Association of Investment Promotion Agencies to increase the effectiveness, sustainability and alignment of EPZs with the Sustainable Development Goals and the Decent Work Agenda.

Finally, the conclusions suggest that the above actions should be concrete and aligned with existing ILO programmes e.g. the Programme of Action on decent work in GSCs.[87]

The concluding text is welcomed for several reasons. First of all, in the light of limited recent empirical studies on EPZs, it recommends the updating of the ILO's knowledge base and the development of a more *holistic* picture of the nature of EPZs which—in our opinion—should include zones' linkages with *domestic* producers but also with *foreign* lead firms. Second, in a balanced way the conclusions highlight

---

[84]Ibid., para. 17.

[85]Ibid., para. 18.

[86]Ibid., para. 19.

[87]Ibid., para. 20.

both *positive* and *negative* aspects of EPZs related to decent work and CLS. Third, they underline the importance of *protecting* freedom of association and collective bargaining for workers in EPZs as well as promoting social dialogue. Fourth, the conclusions recognise the *special* role to be played by (host) governments which are often undermining their duty to protect labour standards in EPZs. Finally, and in contrast to the pre-meeting report of the Office, they also recognise the *responsibilities* of all companies to *respect* worker's rights in EPZs. On this last point and pending the publication of the full report of the Meeting's proceedings, it is difficult to understand why the conclusions refer only to the responsibilities of corporations to *use their leverage* to take steps to ensure that the workers' rights in their supply chains are respected, without mentioning that the indecent working conditions in EPZs may be in part also driven by *demand* from lead firms operating outside national borders.

6.3   The (2018) Decision of the ILO Governing Body on the Follow-Up Action on EPZs

On February 2018, the Director-General elaborated the first supplementary report.[88] It refers to the main recommendations addressed to the constituents and to all ILO supportive actions elaborated by the Meeting of Experts for follow-up; the latter, if adopted by the Governing Body, would form the basis for an action plan on EPZs, as called for in the 2016 ILC conclusions on decent work in GSCs. However, during the 332nd Session of the Governing Body (March 2018) the employers' representatives expressed great concern about the creation of a stand-alone action plan on EPZs, because it could duplicate efforts and would be based on outdated information; instead they suggested to incorporate all the recommendations addressed to the ILO into existing initiatives and action plans.[89] This proposal was shared by many governments' representatives.[90] Therefore, at the end of the discussion, the Governing Body took note of the outcome of the Meeting of Experts, endorsed its conclusions and requested the Director-General to include the recommended follow-up action in the implementation of subsequent programmes and budgets. Self-evidently, this decision is a missed opportunity because an action plan—as proposed by workers' representatives—could have assessed *specific* EPZs with decent work deficits and the role of *all* stakeholders, including the responsibility of leads firms for those deficits.[91]

---

[88]ILO (2018a).

[89]ILO (2018b), paras. 311–312.

[90]Ibid., paras. 314–315.

[91]Ibid., para. 308.

7 Concluding Remarks

As already mentioned, the 2016 ILC concluding text on decent work in GSCs is very significant for several reasons. First of all, for the first time in the 100-year history of the ILO, it addresses what has become one of the key features of economic globalization. Second, the conclusions recognise the potential of GSCs in advancing the prospects of decent work conditions for millions of workers across the globe but, also, the dangers posed by this complex transnational production model and its significant impact on workers' rights. Third, they expand the role of the ILO itself in working on GSCs' issues, by mandating the Organization to use its traditional means such as technical cooperation, research, information and communication, promotion of social dialogue, coordination with other international organizations and—most *importantly* (even though only *eventually*)—*standards-setting* activities. Finally, the concluding text emphasises that the responsibility to implement effective and efficient legal labour regimes lies primarily with the state (which must act in collaboration with workers' and employers' organizations). However, it also suggests that effective governance of GSCs involves a role for the private sector as well. Significantly in this respect the conclusions refer many times to the businesses' responsibility to respect human rights in their supply chains and the due diligence processes aimed at reducing or eliminating their negative impacts on—inter alia—labour-related human rights. Admittedly, however, the introduction of the concept of *labour rights due diligence* and especially its possible *hardening* into national regulatory frameworks via a new ILO convention led—as foreseeable—the employers' representatives to develop a defensive strategy to ensure that any progress on that concept would be painstakingly small. On this last point it is worth underlining, first of all, that according to the Programme of Action on decent work in GSCs the ILO Helpdesk for Business on International Labour Standards has the task of providing enterprises with information on specific country situations, laws and regulations, including on the implementation of labour rights due diligence.[92] The latter, being a free and *confidential* service of the Office that provides answers to individual questions,[93] has no mandate to develop guidance on what the concept of labour right due diligence requires and, self-evidently, is not intended to adjudge enterprises' compliance with international labour standards. Similarly, the new (2017) version of the ILO MNE Declaration, by only referring in one paragraph to the corporate responsibility to respect human rights, does not clarify—in fact—the ambiguities of the labour rights due diligence concept. Additionally, this instrument is still characterised by the lack of any oversight mechanism. Last but not least, the follow-up action on EPZs endorsed by the Governing Body in 2018 calls on employers' organizations for encouragement and support enterprises to respect CLS and carry out due diligence, without any involvement of ILO's bodies or services.

---

[92]ILO (2017a), para. 27.

[93]ILO (2017c), Annex II, para. 1.c.

In the light of the above, the perspective of the ILO's reframing of global labour governance through public vertical regulation becomes very tenuous, depending on the position that the governments' representatives will assume in the future. Hopefully, therefore, the next two tripartite meetings—respectively—on cross-border dialogue and human rights due diligence (scheduled for the end of 2018 but postponed in 2019) and on the adequacy of ILO's instruments to govern GSCs (scheduled for 2019) will suggest, at least, the adoption of a guidance on how the due diligence process applies to labour rights. The latter, by limiting enterprises' ability to selectively interpret and apply labour-related human rights, is—in our opinion— an essential element of any effective and legitimate public labour rights due diligence regulatory initiative. Without this intervention by the ILO, its efforts to promote decent work in GSCs are likely to be seen as the elephant that gave birth to a mouse.

References

Bellace JR (2014) Human rights at work: the need for definitional coherence in the global governance system. Int J Comp Labour Law Ind Relat 30(2):175–198

Cossart S, Chaplier J, Beau De Lomenie T (2017) The French law on duty of care: a historic step towards making globalization work for all. Bus Hum Rights J 2(2):317–323

Deva S (2013) Treating human rights lightly: a critique of the consensus rhetoric and the language employed by the guiding principles. In: Deva S, Bilchitz D (eds) Human rights obligations of business: beyond the corporate responsibility to respect? Cambridge University Press, Cambridge, pp 78–104

Gereffi G, Humphrey J, Sturgeon T (2005) The governance of global supply chains. Rev Int Polit Econ 12(1):78–104

Grado V (2018a) La revisione della Dichiarazione tripartita di principi sulle imprese multinazionali e la politica sociale: *business as usual*? Diritto pubblico comparato ed europeo 20(1):199–236

Grado V (2018b) The EU "conflict minerals regulation": potentialities and limits in the light of the international standards on responsible sourcing. In: The Italian yearbook of international law, vol XXVII. Brill Nijhoff, Leiden, pp 235–257

ILO (1998a) Note on the proceedings, Tripartite meeting of export processing zones-operating countries. ILO, Geneva

ILO (1998b) Labour and social issues relating to export processing zones. ILO, Geneva

ILO (1999) Decent work. ILC, 87th Session. ILO, Geneva

ILO (2006) Minutes of the 297th Session, Governing Body. GB.297/PV. ILO, Geneva

ILO (2008) Declaration on social justice for a fair globalization. ILC, 97th Session. ILO, Geneva

ILO (2013) Towards the ILO centenary: realities, renewal and tripartite commitment. ILC, 102nd Session. ILO, Geneva

ILO (2015) World employment and social outlook 2015: the changing nature of jobs. ILO, Geneva

ILO (2016a) Report IV, Decent work in global supply chains. ILC, 105th Session. ILO, Geneva

ILO (2016b) Reports of the committee on decent work in global supply chains. ILC, 105th Session. ILO, Geneva

ILO (2016c) Resolution and conclusions concerning decent work in global supply chains. ILC, 105th Session. ILO, Geneva

ILO (2017a) Follow-up to the resolution concerning decent work in global supply chains (general discussion): revised ILO programme of action 2017–21, Governing Body. GB.328/INS/5/1 (Add.1). ILO, Geneva

ILO (2017b) Follow-up to the resolution concerning decent work in global supply chains: roadmap for the programme of action, Governing Body. GB.329/INS/3/2. ILO, Geneva

ILO (2017c) Tripartite declaration of principles concerning multinational enterprises and social policy. ILO, Geneva

ILO (2017d) Minutes of the 329th Session, Governing Body. GB.329/PV. ILO, Geneva

ILO (2017e) Promoting decent work and protecting fundamental principles and rights at work in export processing zones. ILO, Geneva

ILO (2017f) Conclusions to promote decent work and protection of fundamental principles and rights at work for workers in EPZs. ILO, Geneva

ILO (2018a) First supplementary report: report of the meeting of experts to promote decent work and protecting fundamental principles and rights at work in export processing zones. GB.332/INS/14/1. ILO, Geneva

ILO (2018b) Minutes of the 332nd Session, Governing Body. GB.332/INS/PV. ILO, Geneva

Krajewski M (2018) The state duty to protect against human rights violations through transnational business activities. Deakin Law Rev 23:13–39

MacNaughton G, Frey DF (2016) Decent work, human rights and the sustainable development goals. Georgetown J Int Law 47(2):607–663

Mares R (ed) (2012) The UN guiding principles on business and human rights: foundations and implementation. Martinus Nijhoff, Leiden

McCorquodale R, Smit L, Neely S, Brooks R (2017) Human rights due diligence in law and practice: good practices and challenges for business enterprises. Bus Hum Rights J 2 (2):195–224

Muchlinski P (2015) Operationalising the UN business and human rights framework: the corporate responsibility to respect human rights and due diligence. In: Lundan S (ed) Transnational corporations and transnational governance: the costs of crossing borders in the global economy. Palgrave Macmillan, Cham, pp 325–353

Nizami N, Prasad N (2017) Decent work: concept, theory and measurement. Palgrave Macmillan, Cham

Sarfaty GA (2015) Shining light on global supply chains. Harv Int Law J 56(2):419–463

Skogly S (2017) Extraterritorial obligations and the obligation to protect. In: Kuijer M, Werner W (eds) Netherlands yearbook of international law, vol 47. T.M.C. Asser Press, The Hague, pp 217–244

Thomas H, Turnbull P (2018) From horizontal to vertical labour governance: the International Labour Organization (ILO) and decent work in global supply chains. Hum Relat 71(4):536–559

Trebilcock A (2015) Due diligence on labour issues – opportunities and limits of the UN guiding principles on business and human rights. In: Blackett A, Trebilcock A (eds) Research handbook on transnational labour law. Edward Elgar, Cheltenham, pp 93–107

UN Human Rights Council (2008) Protect, respect and remedy: a framework for business and human rights. UN Doc. A/HRC/8/5

UN Human Rights Council (2011) Guiding principles on business and human rights: implementing the United Nations "protect, respect, remedy" framework. UN Doc. A/HRC/17/31

UN Human Rights Council (2018) Corporate human rights due diligence: emerging practices, challenges and ways forward. UN Doc. A/73/163

UNCTAD (2015) Enhancing the contribution of expert processing zones to the sustainable development goals: an analysis of 100 EPZs and a framework for sustainable economic zones. UN, Geneva

Wetzel JRH (2016) Human rights in transnational business: translating human rights obligations into compliance procedures. Springer, Cham

Valentina Grado is Professor of International Law at the University of Naples L'Orientale, Italy, where she teaches International Law and the Law of International Organizations. Valentina holds a PhD in International Law from the University of Naples Federico II, Italy. She has been several times visiting scholar at the Max Planck Institute for Comparative Law and International Law of Heidelberg, Germany. Her research interests focus, inter alia, on international law and the governance of natural resources in conflict and post-conflict situations as well as on business and human rights. Valentina is a member of the Italian Society of International and European Law.

Supervision of International Labour Standards as a Means of Implementing the Guiding Principles on Business and Human Rights

Shin-ichi Ago

Contents

1 Introduction

According to Para. 25 of the Foundational Principle (on remediation) of the UN Guiding Principles on Business and Human Rights[1] (hereinafter referred to as UNGP): "As part of their duty to protect against business-related human rights abuse, States must take appropriate steps to ensure, through judicial, administrative, legislative or other appropriate means, that when such abuses occur within their territory and/or jurisdiction those affected have access to effective remedy." In the

---

[1] UN Doc. A/HRC/17/31 endorsed by the Resolution of the Human Rights Council 17/4 of 16 June 2011. This document is sometimes cited as Ruggie Principles, named after the comprehensive report submitted by the Special Representative of the Secretary General of the UN, John Ruggie, who formulated this set of principles after a long, laborious effort. See Ruggie (2013).

S. Ago (✉)
Ritsumeikan University, Kyoto, Japan
e-mail: ago-law@fc.ritsumei.ac.jp

© Springer Nature Switzerland AG 2019   87
M. Bungenberg et al. (eds.), *European Yearbook of International Economic Law 2019*,
European Yearbook of International Economic Law (2020) 10: 87–106,
https://doi.org/10.1007/8165_2019_27, Published online: 26 July 2019

subsequent "Operational Principles", the UNGP mentions "State-based judicial mechanisms", "State-based non-judicial grievance mechanisms" and "Non-State-based grievance mechanisms". Para. 28 states: "Another category comprises regional and international human rights bodies. These have dealt most often with alleged violations by States of their obligations to respect human rights. However, some have also dealt with the failure of a State to meet its duty to protect against human rights abuse by business enterprises. . .. States can play a helpful role in raising awareness of, or otherwise facilitating access to, such options, alongside the mechanisms provided by States themselves."

The UNGP do not mention concrete examples of the "Non-State-based grievance mechanisms". It is, however, almost certain that treaty bodies, such as the Human Rights Committee of the ICCPR, are self-explanatorily included in this group of mechanisms. The Inspection Panel of the World Bank and similar arrangements in other regional development banks could also be mentioned in this context. The ILO's supervisory mechanisms would also fall into this group, while it is not clear whether the Special Representative of the Secretary General had considered this. Specialists in human rights law sometimes forget that most labour rights, if not all of them, are human rights. Some text books on international human rights law have completely neglected the existence of the ILO in describing the history of international protection of human rights, although the ILO under the Versailles Treaty system functioned as a human rights arm of the League of Nations, long before the UN started working out various human rights instruments under the auspices of the Economic and Social Council, the Commission of Human Rights, in particular.

We should not forget the role played by the ILO in the international protection of human rights, to which the Organization has contributed since almost a century ago. The ILO, therefore, plays a significant role also in providing a remedy mechanism in the implementation of the UNGP.

2 ILO's Traditional Supervision of International Labour Standards as a Remedy Mechanism in Cases of Infringements of UNGP Labour-Related Human Rights Principles

Supervision of the implementation of international legal norms is usually performed by organs of inter-governmental institutions. It is, therefore, not a judicial process, but it is an international administrative act. While a remedy for infringements of human rights is normally entrusted to judicial mechanisms, administrative processes can play a significant role, too. In public international law, unlike in the domestic legal system, an administrative act is often deprived of legally binding force. However, supervisory functions of various UN treaty bodies, such as the Human Rights Committee of the International Covenant on Civil and Political Rights or the organs of the ILO discussed below, are equipped with a strong persuasive power, so that the member-States cannot easily dismiss the recommendations. The ILO's historical supervisory organs are particularly important, because their recommendations are seriously considered by the Member states. They can, therefore, perform a remedial function in cases where labour rights are infringed.

The following sections will illustrate how the ILO's supervisory mechanism may contribute to protecting the rights of its constituents, especially with regard to the fundamental labour rights of workers.

It must be noted that the examples given for each procedure described below do not necessarily illustrate cases, in which actual remedies were obtained. There are no records of the final outcome of the recommendations made by the supervisory bodies. The only record, so to say, can be found in the Reports of the Committee of Experts on the Application of Conventions and Recommendations (hereafter CEACR) referred to below (Sect. 2.3.1). Each year the CEACR puts the number of "Cases of progress" in its General Report. For instance, in its latest report published in February 2019, it indicated that there were 18 cases of progress.[2] It further noted that 3077 cases of progress were found by the Committee of Experts since it had started counting the number of those cases since 1964.[3] The importance is that there are ways to seek remedies.

2.1 Representation Under Article 24 of the ILO Constitution

Article 24 of the ILO Constitution provides for a mechanism, under which an industrial organization can lodge a representation ("réclamation" in French) before the ILO's Governing Body, alleging a member State has not fulfilled the obligation set forth in a Convention, which it had ratified. The Governing Body would establish a committee to look into the representation and normally within a year it arrives at a finding, which would be presented before the Governing Body to be adopted as its final conclusion. The Governing Body's conclusion is a recommendation and not legally binding, but it can help the situation to be addressed.

2.1.1 Examples

A few cases are shown below to demonstrate how the Article 24 procedure can be used and to what extent a breach of labour rights by an enterprise, fundamental labour rights in particular, can be remedied.

In 1988, a trade union of airline pilots in Greece lodged a representation to the ILO, alleging the non-observance by Greece of forced labour Conventions, Nos.

---

[2] Report of the Committee of Experts on the Application of Conventions and Recommendations, ILC.108/III(A), ILO Geneva 2019, p. 24.

[3] Ibid, p. 25.

29 and 105. The tri-partite committee set up by the Governing Body of the ILO to examine the case concluded that the call-up of the pilots and flight engineers of Olympic Airways took place under conditions contrary to the provisions specified of Conventions Nos. 29 and 105, and recommended the government "to (i) ensure that the relevant legislation is brought into line with the forced labour Conventions [and] (ii) to ensure that no judicial or administrative action be pursued which might involve the imposition of the penalties on those concerned."[4]

In 1995, a Brazilian trade union referred to a situation of many workers, in various sectors of the rural economy, who were subjected to forced labour and debt bondage. Their poverty was due to an expanding foreign investment by big multinational enterprises, facilitated by generous tax incentives by the government and financed by various national banks. The Committee set up to examine the representation reached the conclusion that the allegations that thousands of workers, including minors, in certain regions and types of enterprise, were subjected to forced labour by means of debt bondage were well-founded and that this situation was in violation of Conventions Nos. 29 and 105 ratified by Brazil. The Committee called on the Government of Brazil to take the necessary steps "(i) to reinforce the inspection system and to ensure the systematic and diligent investigation of com-plaints of forced labour; (ii) to ensure the enforcement of national penal legislation against placing people in a situation analogous to slavery and against the illegal transfer of workers from one part of the national territory to another, and compliance with inspection arrangements in rural areas; (iii) to ensure the rapidity of the pro-ceedings initiated and the strict application of the penalties imposed; [and] (iv) to ensure coordination of the activities of the various government bodies, trade unions, Church organizations and civil bodies in the campaign for the complete elimination of forced labour".[5]

In 1998, a trade union in Bosnia and Herzegovina submitted a representation, alleging non-observance of Convention No. 111 on discrimination in employment and occupation. The representation referred to a large number of workers of an aluminium company, who were dismissed solely on the ground of their nationality. The Committee considered that the situation constituted a violation of Convention No. 111, since the type of discrimination described in the representation was of the kind prohibited by Article 1, paragraph (a), of that instrument, in that it involved an exclusion based solely on national extraction or religious belief which had the effect of destroying equality of opportunity and treatment in employment and occupation between workers of Croatian extraction and workers of Bosnian or Serbian extrac-tion employed by the aluminium company's undertakings. The Committee invited the government of Bosnia and Herzegovina to take the necessary measures to ensure

---

[4]Report of the Committee set up to examine the representation made by the Hellenic Airline Pilots Association (HALPA) under article 24 of the ILO Constitution alleging non-observance by Greece of the Forced Labour Convention, 1930 (No. 29), and the Abolition of Forced Labour Convention, 1957 (No. 105) (*Official Bulletin*, Vol. LXXI, 1988, Series B, Supplement 1).

[5]ILO Governing Body 1995, GB.264/16/7.

that workers dismissed from the aluminium factories solely on the grounds of their Bosnian or Serbian extraction or their religion, "(i) receive adequate compensation for the damage that they have sustained; (ii) receive payment of any wage arrears and any other benefits to which they would be entitled if they had not been dismissed; and (iii) are as far as possible reinstated in their posts without losing length of service entitlements".[6]

Concerning the same Convention, in 2009 a Japanese trade union submitted a representation alleging non-observance by the Japanese government and the Committee's report was adopted by the Governing Body in 2011.[7] The complainant union pointed at discriminatory wages paid between man and men and women workers in its company and criticized several court judgments, which did not see discrimination in the application of Article 4 of the (Japanese) Labour Standards Law, while they constituted a breach of international obligations. The Committee concluded that "it does not appear that a broad scope of comparison, going beyond the same job duties, type of jobs and employment management categories, is being applied generally in practice, in the implementation of the legislation in force" (Labour Standards Law and Equal Employment Opportunity Law). Hence, the situation is not in full conformity with the Convention. It invited the Government to take due note of the matters raised in the conclusions of the Committee's report and to include detailed information thereon in its next report under Article 22 in respect of the Equal Remuneration Convention, 1951 (No. 100) and entrusted the Committee of Experts on the Application of Conventions and Recommendations with following up the matters raised in this report with respect to the application of the Equal Remuneration Convention, 1951 (No. 100).[8]

2.1.2 Characteristics of Article 24 Representation

As of December 2018, over 170 Article 24 representations were recorded, among which some had not be declared receivable. An interesting phenomenon is that in the first 50 years of the procedure, fewer than 10 cases were registered, while there was a remarkable increase in number of representations in the recent decades. Not all of them relate to infringements of fundamental labour rights, such as forced labour or discrimination, by specific private companies, but a significant number of cases aim

---

[6]ILO Governing Body 1999 GB.274/15/3, GB.276/16/4.

[7]ILO Governing Body 2011 GB.312/INS/15/3.

[8]The Committee is of the view that the interpretation by Japanese national courts of Article 4 of the Labour Standards Law may be correct in and as of itself, but from the perspective of the ILO Convention, it does not fully cover the obligations under international law. The Committee implicitly suggests that the judiciary, as a State organ, should pay attention to the State's international obligations. Article 98, para 2 of the Constitution of Japan makes it clear that international treaties are valid in the national legal system. It is established jurisprudence that customary international law and ratified treaties supersede the laws of the land, although they are not above the Constitution.

at remedying human rights abuses of companies. It is again noted here that the procedure does not directly address the companies breaching the labour rights, but it recommends the governments to ensure that the treaty obligation is met, thereby indirectly forcing the companies to abide by Committee reports. The case cited above on Bosnia and Herzegovina is a clear situation which shows limits in the effective remedy of infringements of principles enshrined in the Guiding Principles. Another characteristic of the Article 24 representation is that many of the Committee's conclusions refer to the Committee of Experts' follow up. This is because the Committee's conclusions are final. Apart from publicizing in the ILO's official documents, there is no appeal envisaged in case of non-observance of the conclusions. The Committee of Experts, on the other hand, in its exercise of Article 22 examinations of governmental reports, can endlessly pursue a matter until satisfactory results are achieved. The small number of cases recorded in the first 60–70 years of the history of Article 24 representation can be attributed to the fact that complainant organizations preferred to achieve their goals by referring to the Committee of Experts' regular supervision under Article 22 of the Constitution, rather than the one-year procedure under Article 24 which is definitive. The reason why there was an influx of cases recently is not easy to find, but it is possible that the Article 24 procedure has suddenly become better known among the social partners or the complainant organizations have wished more publicity of their claims, such as press coverage when representation procedures are employed.

2.2   Complaints Under Article 26 of the ILO Constitution

Article 26 of the ILO Constitution provides for a complaint, which can be lodged by a member State against another member State, or by the motion of the Governing Body itself, or even by a delegate of the International Labour Conference, against any member State, which is allegedly breaching obligations set forth in a Convention. (In the case of a complaint by a member State against another, both States must have ratified the Convention.) Unlike in the case of Article 24 representation procedures, the complaint procedure under Article 26 provides for details of the procedure from Articles 27 to 34 of the ILO Constitution. It is important to note that Article 33 provides for an action envisaged in the case of non-observance after the conclusion of the Commission of Inquiry set up by the procedure.[9]

---

[9]Article 33: "In the event of any Member failing to carry out within the time specified the recommendations, if any, contained in the report of the Commission of Inquiry, or in the decision of the International Court of Justice, as the case may be, the Governing Body may recommend to the Conference such action as it may deem wise and expedient to secure compliance therewith." An action taken by the Conference may involve economic sanctions, which are rare but did happen in a relatively recent case against Myanmar.

2.2.1 Examples

Taking into consideration that the Article 26 procedure is designed to accommodate allegations of non-compliance basically made by governments against other governments, with an exception that delegates of the International Labour Conference are also entitled to lodge complaints, it is not surprising that there are not many complaints under this scheme, in which companies are directly or indirectly made accountable. The following case, however, shows how rights of individuals were explicitly mentioned and their remedy was sought.

In 1989, a number of worker delegates of the International Labour Conference submitted a complaint under Article 26, alleging Romania was not observing the obligations under Convention No. 111 on Discrimination (Employment and Occupation). In 1991, the Commission of Inquiry appointed under this scheme found, among other things, that Romania had not complied with the requirements under Convention No. 111 in law and practice and recommended, *inter alia*, to put "an end to the effect of discriminatory measures in employment and restoring equal opportunity and treatment which was suspended or altered to the persons concerned (for example Mr. [I] of Craiova and Mr. [P] of Cluj)."[10] The Conference delegates' allegation was far-reaching, mentioning that a "significant minority of Romanian citizens of Hungarian origin (more than 2 million persons, or 9.5 per cent of the population) are subjected to particular discrimination in the political, cultural, social and employment spheres" and concrete cases were not always mentioned. However, in some instances, concrete names and situations were depicted and their solutions were recommended. The case of Mr. I and Mr. P is one of these. Neither of them had submitted the complaint by themselves, but many other workers who suffered discrimination in Romania could be construed as being represented by the worker delegates of the Conference.

2.2.2 Particularity of Article 26 Procedure

As of today, there have been 32 Complaints recorded since the ILO's establishment, the very first one being in 1923, a complaint lodged by an Indian worker delegate at the Conference alleging non-observance by India of Hours of Work (industry) Convention No. 1.[11] Among them, there are 18 cases in which the Commission of Inquiry was not established, because of various reasons, such as withdrawal by the complainant, satisfactory solution, ILO's technical assistance sought, referral to Committee on Freedom of Association or the Committee of Experts on the

---

[10]Report of The Commission of Inquiry appointed under article 26 of the Constitution of the International Labour Organisation to examine the observance by Romania of the Discrimination (Employment and Occupation) Convention, 1958 (No. 111), Vol. LXXIV, 1991, Series B, Supplement 3. (Mr I was employed in a railway company in Craiova and Mr P in an electric engineering company in Cluj.)

[11]O.B. Vol. XX, No. 1, 1935, p. 15. This complaint was not pursued.

Application of Conventions and Recommendations. Six cases were lodged by governments against other governments, 23 by employer or worker delegates of the International Labour Conference (in one case by both employer and worker delegates jointly) and in 3 cases, the Governing Body itself initiated the procedure. The great majority of cases are lodged by delegates to the Conference, which enable some of individual cases of infringements of labour rights to be possibly addressed. Even in a complaint of a collective nature, the eventual adoption of the reports of the Commission of Inquiry might provide remedy to the victims of labour rights infringements.

2.3   Remedy by Regular Supervision

2.3.1   The Committee of Experts on the Application of Conventions and Recommendations

Regular examination of governmental reports submitted by member States in accordance with Article 22 of the ILO Constitution forms the most fundamental basis of the ILO's supervision. Unlike the above mentioned two procedures, this Article 22 activity takes place without any specific infringements of ILO Conventions being alleged (complained) by ILO constituents. Like labour inspections in a national legal system, the ILO's supervisory organ checks member States' compliance with ILO instruments *ex officio* regardless of any representation or complaints and recommends changes to laws and practices of a State, which in the eyes of the ILO, do not comply with their international legal obligation to observe the ratified Convention.

While the regular supervision of ratified Conventions is not clearly mentioned in the ILO's Constitution, ILO's competence in regularly supervising the conduct of member States can be based on Article 22 of the Constitution and its mechanism, particularly the examination of the CEACR, which has continued over 90 years since its establishment, has become a basis for all the ILO's supervisory activities.

The examination by CEACR takes place basically on written reports and accompanied documents by the member governments, but it heavily relies on observations sent to it, either together with governmental reports or separately, by industrial organizations, i.e. trade unions or employer associations. An individual worker or employer cannot send an observation, but their specific allegations and pleas for a remedy can be relayed by industrial associations to which they are related.

2.3.2   Examples

In an Observation of CEACR adopted in 2013 (published for the 103rd session of ILC in 2014) concerning the application of Indigenous and Tribal Peoples Convention, 1989 (No. 169) by Costa Rica (Ratification: 1993), the Committee "invite [d] the Government to include in its next report information on the activities of the forum for dialogue and the result of the studies conducted in the context of the El Diquís hydroelectric project", that may have a bearing on Articles 6, 7(3), 15 and 16 of the Convention. The Committee's comment was inspired by an *amparo* (protection of constitutional rights) action brought against the Costa Rican Electricity Institute (ICE) for breach of Article 6 of the Convention. As the Constitutional Chamber of the Supreme Court of Justice found the action to be premature on grounds of factual uncertainty because, being in its initial, feasibility stage, the project pertained to the future, the Committee wished to continue to supervise the development.

In 2018, CEACR published an observation, referring to submissions made by a number of Japanese trade unions. It pointed out that the Equal Remuneration Convention, 1951 (No. 100), ratified by Japan in 1967, had not been fully complied with and made the following recommendations, among others: "Given that the wage disparity between men and women narrowed only very slightly between 2012 and 2015 with a remaining wage gap of 26.3 per cent, the Committee once again urges the Government to take immediate and concrete action to ensure the existence of a legislative framework clearly establishing the right to equal remuneration for men and women for work of equal value."[12]

2.3.3 Discussion at the Conference Committee on the Application of Standards

The Committee on the Application of Standards (hereinafter referred to as the Conference Committee) is a standing committee set up by the International Labour Conference a few years after the ILO's establishment, which meets every year and is composed of tripartite members of the Conference. It picks up some important cases from the CEACR reports and enters into an active dialogue with the governmental delegates to the Conference, against which allegations of non-observance had been made. Usually, cases of special gravity are selected for the discussion at this Committee, so that when a case comes to this level, the non-observance or breach of a treaty obligation is highly suspected and the government representatives appearing before this Committee find their task of defending their positions very challenging.

2.3.4 Examples

In 1988 the Conference Committee on the Application of Standards discussed the question of non-observance by India of the Indigenous and Tribal Populations Convention, 1957 (No. 107), ratified by India in 1958. The Committee noted "the

---

[12]Report of the Committee of Experts on the Application of Conventions and Recommendations, International Labour Conference, 107th Session, 2018 Report III (Part A), p. 382.

very important human issues raised in the observation of the Committee of Experts which referred to comments received from the International Federation of Plantation, Agricultural and Allied Workers, and also to the real and considerable efforts made by the Government to alleviate the effects of displacement and settlement on the tribal populations affected by the dam project" and it hoped "that the Government will continue to supply information on measures taken with a view to ensuring the full application of the Convention in respect of all the points raised, taking into account the views and needs of the populations concerned and the comments received from the International Federation of Plantation, Agricultural and Allied Workers."[13]

In 2016, the Conference Committee discussed application of Discrimination (Employment and Occupation) Convention, 1958 (No. 111) ratified by Qatar in 1976. The Committee "expressed concern that discrimination in employment is not prohibited in law and in practice and that the Government has failed to take the necessary measures to guarantee non-discrimination consistent with Convention No. 111", and, in part, urged the Government to:

– comply, in both law and practice, by 2017, with the conclusions adopted by the ILO Governing Body in June 2015 in relation to the representation under article 24 of the ILO Constitution concerning Convention No. 111;
– ensure that legislation covers all recognized prohibited grounds of discrimination set out in Article 1(1)(a) of the Convention, in both direct and indirect forms, and undertake measures to ensure that discrimination in employment and occupation is prohibited in law and practice; [and]
– ensure that domestic workers are included in the protection of anti-discrimination law.[14]

2.3.5   Common Features of the Regular Supervision

This procedure has, as do all other ILO mechanisms, its limits both in the *locus standi* and the way remedies are materialized (i.e., no individual, be it a worker deprived of his/her labour rights or a person belonging to an indigenous people who has been discriminated in employment, can directly use it and the ultimate addressee of the findings of the ILO's supervisory bodies are governments, and not enterprises). The former limit can be largely cured by the fact that individual workers or an indigenous people can ask a trade union to represent their interests. The latter limit is more substantive, in that the remedy can only be ensured by governmental

---

[13]Individual Case (CAS)—Discussion: 1988, Publication: 75th ILC session (1988), Indigenous and Tribal Populations Convention, 1957 (No. 107)—India (Ratification: 1958), drawn from ILO website: https://www.ilo.org/dyn/normlex/en/f?p=1000:13100:0::NO:13100:P13100_COM MENT_ID:2554333.
[14]Record of Proceedings, ILC 2017, Part II, p. 144.

actions, which include in some cases legislative initiative that again calls for another state body, the legislature, to come in.

However, the greatest advantage in the regular supervision is found in the fact that it is continuous, as it can follow up the case until the supervisory body is satisfied that the relevant international labour standard is observed and the labour rights are protected.

2.4 Freedom of Association Complaints

2.4.1 "Special" Nature of the Freedom of Association Procedure

Complaints procedure before the Committee on Freedom of Association (hereinafter referred to as CFA) has have a very unique character. Its basis is neither provided for in the constitutional instrument nor in Conventions adopted by the ILO. It is a very special procedure, which has emanated from a practice, originally designed in a collaboration between the United Nations Economic Social Council and the ILO, by establishing a Fact-finding and Conciliation Commission for Freedom of Association.[15] The requirement of acceptance by the government concerned on the establishment of such a commission was a bottleneck that made this procedure very underutilized. In order to overcome this bottleneck, the ILO's Governing Body, which had initially been entrusted with the task of screening complaints lodged for submission to the Fact-finding Commission, turned to become a body to look into the substance of the complaints. As of 2018, more than 3000 cases have been dealt with by this special procedure and it occupies an important role in the ILO's supervisory activities, though limited to cases of alleged infringements of freedom of association rights. Another important benefit of this procedure is that a complaint can be lodged even if a government has not ratified Conventions 87 or 98.

2.4.2 Examples

The Federation of United Workers (FTU) alleged anti-union practices by Chue Wing & Co. Ltd (ABC Foods) against the Syndicat des Travailleurs des Etablissements Privés (STEP) in Mauritius, including intimidation to withdraw from the trade union, anti-union campaigns, a prohibition of trade union meetings, surveillance arrangements and refusal by the management of professional assistance to union members. While acknowledging the intervention of the Government to solve the issues raised by the FTU by means of various tripartite meetings, the CFA recommended

---

[15]The development of this process is described in many publications, such as Valticos and von Potobsky (1995), pp. 295–299.

harmonious industrial relations between Chue Wing & Co. Ltd and the STEP in observance of the principles of freedom of association.[16]

In 2003 the General Secretary of the Niger Electricity Workers' Union (SYNTRAVE) was allegedly dismissed from the Niger Electricity Company (NIGELEC) for reasons of anti-union discrimination, in violation of national legislation protecting the workers' representatives and allegations were made to the effect that SYNTRAVE's legitimate trade union activities, specifically by opposing the freedom of workers to join the union and by discriminating against it, were hampered. The CFA in 2005 recommended, *inter alia*, that, "the Government issue appropriate instructions rapidly to the management of NIGELEC to respect the legislative provisions designed to guarantee equal treatment of trade union organizations legally present within an enterprise, and not to discriminate against SYNTRAVE."[17]

In 2006 a complaint was lodged before the CFA alleging that PT Securicor Indonesia, in the context of a merger with Group 4 Falck, refused to enter into negotiations, committed several acts of anti-union discrimination and harassment, including the dismissal of 308 union officials and members and refused to reinstate them in spite of several court orders to that effect. The CFA in its recommendations of 2006, *inter alia*, recalled that, "no one should be penalized for carrying out or attempting to carry out a legitimate strike", and requested, "the Government to specify the circumstances under which only 24 out of 308 workers were finally reinstated pursuant to their dismissal for having participated in the strike which began on 25 April 2005".[18]

2.4.3 Advantage and Limits of the CFA Procedure

As the huge number of cases shows, this special procedure has become the most frequently utilised means of seeking remedies in the overall ILO's complaint based supervisory activities. It has a great advantage in making possible for the trade unionists, whose rights were infringed, to come before the ILO even if Convention Nos. 87 or 98 are not applicable in their jurisdictions. The fact that it is a Governing Body's committee, which meets three times a year, makes it also easier to come to a quicker conclusion. On the other hand, especially from the point of view of the implementation of the UNGP, it has a limit of restricting the complaint only to freedom of association cases and the usual restriction of *locus standi* of the complainants.

---

[16]CFA Report No 364, June 2012, Case No 2901 (Mauritius).

[17]CFA Report No 340, March 2006, Case No 2429 (Niger).

[18]Report No 348, November 2007, Case No 2494 (Indonesia).

3 ILO's Tripartite Declaration on Multinational Enterprises

3.1 A Peculiar Legal Instrument

The ILO's traditional supervision, we have seen above, has the obvious limits of providing remedies, which are to be materialized by governments, and it does not directly address enterprises. Possible human rights infringements of an enterprise can only be rectified by legislative or governmental actions. The bringing up of complaints (representations, complaints, or observations, as the case may be) is also restricted to industrial associations (employers' associations or trade union organizations) and not to individuals or groups of non-employer or non-worker organizations. It is therefore necessary to briefly look at a different ILO instrument, which is neither an ILO Convention nor an ILO Recommendation, but which could possibly play a role in the remedy part of the UNGP, as it addresses enterprises directly, along with their social partners (i.e., governments, employers' and workers' associations).

The Tripartite Declaration of Principles concerning Multinational Enterprises and Social Policy (hereinafter referred to as the Tripartite Declaration) was adopted in 1977, a year after the OECD adopted a similar instrument, with a wider coverage.[19] As it is stated in Para. 4, the "principles set out in this Declaration are commended to the governments, the employers' and workers' organizations of home and host countries and to the multinational enterprises themselves." Para. 5 further states: "These principles are intended to guide the governments, the employers' and workers' organizations and the multinational enterprises in taking such measures and actions and adopting such social policies, including those based on the principles laid down in the Constitution and the relevant Conventions and Recommendations of the ILO, as would further social progress." Para. 4 is clear in addressing employers' and workers' organizations, as well as enterprises themselves. This was made possible by the use of a declaration adopted by the Governing Body. If it were a regular ILO Convention or a Recommendation, enterprises would not be made directly accountable because international treaties usually address States or international institutions, and not always bind an individual.

3.2 "Enforcement" of the Tripartite Declaration

The Tripartite Declaration is a legally non-binding instrument. However, like the OECD Guidelines, it is more than just a policy statement of an inter-governmental institution. It also has a follow-up machinery attached to the substantive provisions. The follow-up is conducted in the form of periodic reports requested by the

---

[19]See also the contribution by Jernej Letnar Černič in this volume.

Governing Body and by "interpretation by the ILO", a procedure approved by the Governing Body in 1980 and revised in 1986 and most recently and substantially in 2017.[20]

The 2017 revision is of a substantial nature, which differs from former revisions in 2000 and 2006. Previous revisions were basically to update the Declaration by adding newly adopted Conventions and Recommendations into the reference. The 2017 revision not only updated the Conventions and Recommendations, but added new elements, thus increasing the total number of paragraphs from 59 (the original 1977 Declaration had 58 paragraphs) to 69 and, more importantly, added an Annex entitled "Operational Tool". From our perspective, it is remarkable to note that Para. 10 makes an explicit reference to the UNGP by partly citing it.[21]

3.2.1 The Periodical Survey

A reporting exercise began when the Governing Body at its 205th (February-March 1978) Session invited governments to report periodically on the effect given to the Declaration after full consultation with the national employers' and workers' organizations.[22] The action taken by the Governing Body was confirmed and reinforced in a resolution adopted at the 65th Session of the International Labour Conference in June 1979.[23] Consequently, the first such reports, for the years 1978 and 1979, were examined in September 1980 by an ad hoc committee of the Governing Body. The Committee recommended, in particular, a second round of government reports covering the years 1980, 1981 and 1982, the creation of a standing Governing Body Committee on Multinational Enterprises entrusted with the follow-up, a procedure for the examination of disputes concerning the application of the Tripartite Declaration (also referred to as the interpretation procedure) and a series of studies which the Office would undertake in areas specifically relevant to it. The Governing Body endorsed the above proposals at its 214th (November 1980)

---

[20]Procedure for the examination of disputes concerning the application of the Tripartite Declaration of Principles concerning Multinational Enterprises and Social Policy by means of interpretation of its Provisions. Official Bulletin (Geneva, ILO), 1986, Vol. LXIX, Series A, No. 3, pp. 196–197 (to replace Part IV of the Procedures adopted by the Governing Body at its 214th Session (November 1980)). See Official Bulletin, 1981, Vol. LXIV, Series A, No. 1, pp. 89–90. Most recently at the 329th (March 2017) Session of the Governing Body. *Tripartite Declaration of Principles concerning Multinational Enterprises and Social Policy,* ILO Geneva 2017 GB.329/POL/7, pp. 18–19.

[21]Para. 10, (b)(c)(d), in particular. Ibid. p. 4. It is, however, confusing to see the way how the UNGP is referred to here. Sub-paragraphs (b), (c) and (d) are almost full citations, while (e) is drafted from the perspective of the ILO Declaration.

[22]GB.205/10/2, para. 9 and GB.205/PV(Rev.), p. VI/4.

[23]"Resolution concerning follow-up to the World Employment Conference", International Labour Conference, 65th Session, Record of Proceedings (Geneva, International Labour Office, 1979), section on multinational enterprises, XCV–XCVI.

Session.[24] The second government reports on the Declaration were examined by the Committee on Multinational Enterprises and its report was approved by the Governing Body during its 224th (November 1983) Session.[25] In 1984, the Governing Body[26] decided that the third round of government reports should cover 1983, 1984 and 1985 and that the next full-scale report (fourth survey) on the Declaration should be undertaken for 1986, 1987 and 1988. The fifth and sixth reports (1980–1982; 1983–1985; 1986–1988; 1989–1991; and 1992–1994) and Seventh and Eighth Surveys for years 1996–1999 and 2000–2004 followed.[27] This reporting exercise continued until 2006, when the Governing Body decided to postpone it, in view of concern about the low rate of response to the Eighth Survey, as well as the lack of detail contained in the responses.[28]

After postponing the discussion of the form of periodical survey for a number of years, the ILO Governing Body, at its 320th session in March 2014, adopted a new follow-up mechanism on the Tripartite Declaration, comprised of promotional activities and an information gathering mechanism, thus practically abandoning the periodical review exercise conducted over the previous 30 years. As part of the information gathering process, the Office would collect prior to each ILO Regional Meeting country-level experiences on harnessing opportunities and addressing challenges related to foreign direct investment (FDI) and activities of multinational enterprises as well as on the promotion of the principles of the Tripartite Declaration. This information gathering would be done through a short questionnaire addressed to governments, employers' and workers' organizations of the region. The input received through the questionnaire would inform a report that then forms the basis for a discussion by the tripartite constituents during the Regional Meetings. After four regional meetings, a global report would be presented to the ILO Governing Body that would allow for the identification of lessons learned and good practices as well as for an assessment of the ILO member States' needs and the effectiveness of promotional activities related to the Tripartite Declaration. The 2017 revision of the Declaration continued to avail itself of this information gathering activity prior to regional meetings: The Regional follow-up.[29]

The 2017 revision introduced a novelty in the succeeding paragraph of the same Annex: "(b) Promotion at the national level/promotion by tripartite appointed national focal points". The phrase "national contact points" resembles that of the OECD Guidelines, but it is meant for the promotion of the Declaration and not for conciliation envisaged under the former. On the other hand, the mandate of the national contact points is not clearly defined, and perhaps can eventually develop

---

[24]GB.214/6/3, para. 85; GB.214/PV(Rev.), p IV/11.

[25]GB.224/17/30.

[26]GB.228/19/24, paras 12 and 14.

[27]Para. 7 of the GB.301/MNE/4 301st Session 2008.

[28]Report of the Subcommittee on Multinational Enterprises GB.294/10 (Rev.) p. 2 paras 6 and 7.

[29]GB.329/POL/7, Annex II, Operational tools, 1 Promotion, (a) Regional follow-up.

into a role played by the OECD's organ of the same name. We do not know at this stage, however, how this will develop.

All of these promotional measures are important, but when it comes to a possible mechanism of remedy for the purpose of the UNGP, they have no immediate effect in remedying infringements. This aspect of the ILO Declaration was already critically analysed by Jerney Černič 10 years ago.[30]

3.2.2 Interpretation Procedure

The "Procedure for the Examination of Disputes Concerning the Application of the Tripartite Declaration of Principles Concerning Multinational Enterprises and Social Policy by Means of Interpretation of its Provisions", adopted by the Governing Body in March 1986, which did not exist when the original instrument was adopted in 1977, provided for the submission of requests for interpretation in cases of a dispute on the meaning and application of its provisions. The importance of this procedure lies in its ability to contribute to the harmonious development of labour relations, either by its use or by its availability, the latter of which may encourage disputants to confront their difficulties and to gain a perspective capable of mutual accommodation. It was not designed to solve conflicts or determine findings or provide recommendations. It was not a supervision like the examination by CEACR, which concludes with findings and even suggests (recommends) amendment to, or abolition of, legislative texts, to make the member-States abide by their obligations under the ILO instruments. On the other hand, the Interpretation Procedure of the Tripartite Declaration was designed to function, at least, as a sort of supervision without explicitly calling it so. If there had been a consensus to regard it as a quasi-supervisory procedure, the system would have worked. However, unlike in the case of the OECD Guidelines, the ILO's procedure has not been fully utilized. To date, there have only been five cases in which the Governing Body of the ILO issued "official" interpretations of the relevant provisions of the Tripartite Declaration. Nonetheless, a "successful" conclusion was reported in one case, where paragraph 26 of the Declaration was "interpreted" as to the duties of a multinational enterprise to give reasonable prior notice of changes, which would have major employment effects. The ILO (Governing Body), referring to the Termination of Employment Convention, 1982 (No. 158) as a guide, maintained that paragraph 26 requires reasonable prior notice of intended changes in operations to be given to the workers' representatives and their organizations, where such organizations are identifiable under national law and practice, and if such representatives and organizations exist, it is insufficient to inform the workers affected on an individual basis.[31]

---

[30]Černič (2009), pp. 29–30.

[31]Web information: Interpretation Procedure at Work: BIFU Case (1984–1985), Multi: Multinational Enterprise and Social Policy, at: http://www.ilo.org/public/english/employment/multi/tripar tite/cases.htm. However, this URL was recently removed from the ILO's website.

The fact that no more cases are reported in the ILO's website on multinational enterprises suggests that the procedure had not been particularly successful. Many ILO Conventions are now referred to in the OECD Guidelines and the latter appears to have overtaken the ILO's function in materializing the aims of the non-binding instrument. The ILO appeared to have shifted the emphasis on promotional activities rather than sticking to the "interpretation" method to make the Tripartite Declaration apply. However, the 2017 revision revived the procedure: Annex II, 3 "Procedures for the examination of disputes concerning the application of the Tripartite Declaration of Principles concerning Multinational Enterprises and Social Policy by means of interpretation of its provisions".

However, from the point of view of the UNGP, it is regrettable that the contents of the Interpretation Procedure have not changed from the original version. That is to say, there is a significant number of restrictions left intact as to the scope of the subject matters and the complainant organizations, thereby making the use of the procedure difficult. The restrictive manner of its application, such as limiting the initiator of the interpretation only to the traditional tripartite constituents of the ILO[32] and making receivable such requests only when all other means are not employed, has made the Tripartite Declaration not user-friendly.[33]

3.3 Difference Between the OECD Guidelines and the ILO Tripartite Declaration

The idea was unique, in 1977, to adopt an instrument as a declaration of the Governing Body to address the issue of multinational enterprises in a non-conventional manner. However, despite its existence over 30 years, the instrument has apparently not achieved its basic objective. The periodic review process

---

[32]Para 5 of the Procedure: "Requests for interpretation may be addressed to the Office: (a) as a rule by the government of a member State acting either on its own initiative or at the request of a national organization of employers or workers; (b) by a national organization of employers or workers, which is representative at the national and/or sectoral level, subject to the conditions set out in paragraph 6. Such requests should normally be channelled through the central organizations in the country concerned; (c) by an international organization of employers or workers on behalf of a representative national affiliate."

[33]Para 2, of the Procedure: "The procedure should in no way duplicate or conflict with existing national or ILO procedures. Thus, it cannot be invoked: (a) in respect of national law and practice; (b) in respect of international labour Conventions and Recommendations; (c) in respect of matters falling under the freedom of association procedure. The above means that questions regarding national law and practice should be considered through appropriate national machinery; that questions regarding international labour Conventions and Recommendations should be examined through the various procedures provided for in articles 19, 22, 24 and 26 of the Constitution of the ILO, or through government requests to the Office for informal interpretation; and that questions concerning freedom of association should be considered through the special ILO procedures applicable to that area."

may have achieved better results and the "interpretation" procedure might have created a working system of supervision, if it had been more frequently utilized.

The greatest difference between the relatively successful record of the application of the OECD Guidelines and that of the ILO Tripartite Declaration appears to lie in the composition of the bodies that look into the cases. In the case of the ILO, it is the Office (Secretariat), which will "prepare a draft reply in consultation with the Officers of the Committee on Multinational Enterprises".[34] In the case of the OECD, it will be a National Contact Point, which looks into the question and suggests a solution. The fact that a secretariat of an international organization (ILO) is the body to propose eventual changes to the activities of multinational enterprises makes the weight of the product lighter. The NCP, on the other hand, is a body authorized by the OECD Guidelines to follow-up the original instrument and it can be assimilated as a "treaty body", such as the Human Rights Committee established by the ICCPR. The OECD Guidelines are, obviously, not an international treaty,[35] but the OECD has endeavoured to make it closer to a treaty,[36] by using a treaty-like procedure, such as "adherence" to the Guidelines, which is similar to "ratification" of a convention, and created a supervisory mechanism with an international administrative function.

The difference between the ILO's instrument and the OECD's is found in its difference of the follow-up mechanisms, but that difference is based on the fundamental difference in the degree of consensus at the time of the adoption of the instrument. The ILO Governing Body was clear in its decision not to adopt a legally binding instrument. Hence, it is outside the ambit of the regular supervisory mechanism of ILO. It is, therefore, understandable that the reporting exercise has not been rigorously pursued, nor the "interpretation" machinery frequently relied on. The OECD, on the other hand, while being fully aware that it was not adopting a treaty, tried as much as possible to assimilate it to a binding instrument as we have seen above.

---

[34]Para 7 of the Procedure [n 20].

[35]The OECD had adopted treaties, such as the Anti-Bribery Convention or the Model Tax Convention, but in the case of multinational enterprises, it did not choose to adopt the Guidelines as a treaty.

[36]"The Guidelines provide voluntary principles and standards for responsible business conduct consistent with applicable laws and internationally recognized standards. However, the countries adhering to the Guidelines make a binding commitment to implement them in accordance with the Decision of the OECD Council on the OECD Guidelines for Multinational Enterprises." (OECD Guidelines, Preamble, para. 1).

4   Conclusion

The UNGP have been adopted as a non-legally binding instrument. As the name indicates they set out guidelines which UN member-States, as well as business entities, should endeavour to follow. They are also an instrument of a principle-setting nature lacking in self-executing provisions. In order to materialize its goals, a vigorous follow-up is required. The Working Group on Business and Human Rights is instrumental in achieving the goals and it has been organizing the Global Forum every year, *inter alia*, which has become a true forum to face the stakeholders and promote the implementation of various principles set forth in the UNGP. Efforts being made by the Inter-governmental Working Group to try to formulate a legally binding treaty are, while its future is not so clear, are also noteworthy.[37]

However, there are various existing tools with which the principles can be put into motion. The existing machineries in institutions, such as the OECD, UN human rights bodies, international financial institutions and the ILO, are readymade tools to achieve concrete results. The ILO's machineries, in particular, with its history-strengthened supervisory functions, can serve, and are already serving, for the endeavour to materialize the principles set out in the UNGP.

Obviously, the ILO's machineries have their limitations in terms of the coverage of human rights principles, in that they can only deal with labour-related human rights, as well as *locus standi*. However, the former limitation can be, to some extent, overcome by the fact that some of the ILO Conventions can cover basic human rights in general, such as non-discrimination principles and the freedom of expression. The latter limitation is largely cured by the fact that industrial organizations, both trade unions and employers associations, can represent the interests of individual persons whose human rights have been infringed. Some of the examples shown above have illustrated that infringements as to the principles of freedom of association and protection of indigenous peoples can be remedied by the 90-year-old supervisory machineries of the 100-year-old organization.

References

Černič JL (2009) Corporate responsibility for human rights: analyzing the ILO Tripartite Declaration of Principles concerning multinational enterprises and social policy. Miskolc J Int Law 6 (1):24–34
Ruggie JG (2013) Just business. W. W. Norton & Company, New York
Valticos N, von Potobsky G (1995) International labour law. Kluwer Law and Taxation, Deventer

---

[37]Report on the fourth session of the open-ended intergovernmental working group on transnational corporations and other business enterprises with respect to human rights, A/HRC/40/48, 2 January 2019, pp. 1–27.

Shin-ichi Ago is Professor of Law at Ritsumeikan University, Kyoto and Professor Emeritus of Kyushu University, Fukuoka. He received both his LL.B. and LL.M. from the University of Tokyo, and obtained his Doctorat ès Sciences Politiques from the University of Geneva (IUHEI), specializing in public international law. He is Judge at the Asian Development Bank Administrative Tribunal since 2013 and from 2015, he is member of the ILO's Committee of Experts on the Application of Conventions and Recommendations.

Labour Safeguards of International Financial Institutions: Can They Help to Avoid Violations of ILO Core Labour Standards?

Franz Christian Ebert

Contents

1 Introduction

The relationship between labour standards and International Financial Institutions (IFIs) is an uneasy one.[1] On the one hand, many IFIs have recognized the ILO's Core Labour Standards[2] and have occasionally used their institutional influence to

---

This article further develops research published in Ebert (2018) and partly draws on Ebert (2014).

---

[1] For the purpose of this article, a broad understanding of the term "international financial institution" is adopted, comprising international organisations providing financial services to public or private actors. This includes institutions at the global level, the regional level, and the sub-regional level. For a similar definition see Ragazzi (2012a), para. 1.

[2] See, for example, Fischer (1999); ADB, Social Protection Strategy (2001), pp. 15–16. The World Bank endorsed this concept only after some hesitation due to concerns relating to the economic impact of trade union rights; see in this regard Anner and Caraway (2010), pp. 156–159.

F. C. Ebert (✉)
Max Planck Institute for Comparative Public Law and International Law, Heidelberg, Germany
e-mail: ebert@mpil.de

© Springer Nature Switzerland AG 2019   107
M. Bungenberg et al. (eds.), *European Yearbook of International Economic Law 2019*,
European Yearbook of International Economic Law (2020) 10: 107–132,
https://doi.org/10.1007/8165_2019_45, Published online: 31 October 2019

promote basic workers' rights.[3] On the other, by means of labour-related condition-ality in financial assistance programmes[4] as well as other devices such as the World Bank's Doing Business Reports,[5] IFIs have exercised significant pressure on states to deregulate domestic labour standards.[6] This has entailed adverse effects on workers' rights, including on those relating to the ILO's Core Labour Standards,[7] and on the workers' share of domestic income,[8] among others.

An important matter of concern pertains to the investment projects financed by certain IFIs.[9] For some time, a debate has been going on as to what measures IFIs should take in order to avoid contributing to labour standards violations in the course of investment projects supported by them.[10] Ranging from local business endeav-ours to transnational infrastructure projects, these projects frequently involve a sizeable workforce. Often taking place in countries with weak governance structures, a variety of projects financed by IFIs have allegedly involved severe labour rights violations.[11] At the same time, in part responding to external criticism from civil society actors, numerous IFIs have adopted policies to prevent or remedy labour standards violations in the course of the projects they support.[12] This gives rise to the question of whether these safeguards actually entail positive effects for the protec-tion of workers rather than merely providing a marketing tool for IFIs.

This chapter tackles this question focussing on the potential of IFI safeguards to protect ILO Core Labour Standards in the course of the investment projects financed by these institutions. Set out in the ILO's 1998 Declaration on Fundamental Princi-ples and Rights at Work and further specified in the ILO's Fundamental Conven-tions, the Core Labour Standards constitute a key set of internationally protected workers' rights.[13] They concern, more specifically, the prohibition and eradication of

---

[3]For an example concerning the IMF from the 1990s, relating to trade union rights, see Darrow (2003), p. 183.

[4]See, e.g., Ebert (2015), pp. 129–132.

[5]See, for a review of the labour law implications of this instrument, Bakvis (2009), pp. 426–428. For a critique of the methodology of Doing Business' labour component see, e.g., Berg and Cazes (2008), especially at pp. 364–371.

[6]For an overview see Bohoslavsky and Ebert (2018), pp. 285–286.

[7]See Abouharb and Cingranelli (2007), pp. 196, 199–200; Blanton et al. (2015), p. 332.

[8]See O'Brien (2014), p. 158.

[9]The IMF does not carry out such investment projects and is therefore not included in this analysis.

[10]See, e.g., Bakvis and McCoy (2008), pp. 5–6.

[11]See e.g. ITUC (2011), pp. 19–26; Human Rights Watch (2014) World Bank: Investigate Uzbekistan's Forced Labor. Inspection Panel Should Ensure Funds Not Used for Abuses. Washington. Available at: https://www.hrw.org/news/2014/12/17/world-bank-investigate-uzbekistans-forced-labor and Connel T (2016) Uzbekistan Forced Labor Linked to World Bank Loan, available at: https://www.solidaritycenter.org/uzbekistan-forced-labor-victim-files-worldbank-complaint/, highlighting, among others, instances of forced labour in projects in the cotton sector of Uzbekistan and child labour in a project in the Ugandan telecommunication sector, respectively, financed by the World Bank and the IFC, respectively.

[12]See, e.g., Yifeng (2018), pp. 111–114; Murphy (2014), pp. 401 and 418–424.

[13]See further La Hovary (2009), pp. 49–51.

forced labour and child labour, freedom of association and the right to collective bargaining, as well as employment-related non-discrimination.[14] The institutions analysed include, in particular, the World Bank[15] and its sister organisations dealing with the private sector, the International Finance Corporations (IFC) and the Multilateral Investment Guarantee Agency (MIGA).[16] In addition, the labour safeguards of two IFIs at the regional level are analysed in depth, namely the African Development Bank Group (AfDB)[17] and the European Bank for Reconstruction and Development (EBRD).[18] Moreover, several other IFIs are considered, including sub-regional institutions, e.g. the Black Sea Trade and Development Bank,[19] and cross-regional institutions, such as the New Development Bank.[20]

The contribution proceeds in three steps. Section 2 looks at the safeguards' legal design. Its first part reviews the normative content of selected IFI labour safeguards

---

[14]ILO Declaration on Fundamental Principles and Rights at Work and its Follow-up, adopted 18 June 1998, para. 2. The relevant conventions are Forced Labour Convention, 1930 (No. 29); Abolition of Forced Labour Convention, 1957 (No. 105); Minimum Age Convention, 1973 (No. 138); Worst Forms of Child Labour Convention, 1999 (No. 182); Equal Remuneration Convention, 1951 (No. 100); Discrimination (Employment and Occupation) Convention, 1958 (No. 111); Freedom of Association and Protection of the Right to Organise Convention, 1948 (No. 87); Right to Organise and Collective Bargaining Convention, 1949 (No. 98).

[15]The World Bank is composed of two international organisations, the International Bank for Reconstruction and Development (IBRD) and the International Development Association (IDA). While IBRD mainly deals with middle-income countries, IDA focusses on the most impoverished countries. See further on the institutional setting of these two organisations; Schlemmer-Schulte (2012), especially paras. 1, 65, 97.

[16]All of these form part of the World Bank Group; see further Ragazzi (2012b), paras. 1–7. While the IFC offers a variety of financial and other services to private companies, MIGA mainly focusses on providing guarantees to investors undertaking business projects in developing countries. See Asrani and Dann (2012), paras. 11–14 and Schill (2012), paras. 20–29.

[17]The African Development Bank Group is made up of the African Development Bank as well as the African Development Fund and the Nigeria Trust Fund. Similarly to the World Bank's IDA, the African Development Fund provides finance on concessional terms to the low-income countries of the region. This is also the purpose of the Nigeria Trust Fund, which was established by means of an agreement between the African Development Bank and Nigeria and is funded by this country. See at: https://www.afdb.org/en/about-us/corporate-information/ and further Suzuki (2012), paras. 15 and 28.

[18]Established after the end of the Cold War, the EBRD was set up to deal with the countries of the former Soviet Union as well as with the countries of Eastern and Central Europe, see Suzuki (2012), para. 10.

[19]The Black Sea Trade and Development Bank was created in the context of the Black Sea Economic Cooperation (see further Tiroch 2012, para. 24). It provides funding for projects in the Bank's 11 member countries, which includes the countries bordering the Black Sea as well as some other countries from the region; see at https://www.bstdb.org/about-us/who-we-are.

[20]Created by Brazil, China, India, Russia, and South Africa, the New Development Bank, the New Development Bank aims to provide funding to BRICS countries and other countries from the Global South; see at: https://www.ndb.int/about-us/essence/mission-values/. Similarly to the Asian Infrastructure Investment Bank sponsored by China, the New Development Bank can arguably be understood as an effort to create additional alternatives to the World Bank that is often perceived as dominated by the United States; see Wang (2017), p. 114.

and assesses their relationship with relevant ILO instruments, arguing that coherence between the two is limited at best. The section's second part explores the scope of relevant labour safeguards and identifies several loopholes that may provide borrowers[21] with avenues to avoid many of the requirements by adjusting the project structure. Section 3 then turns to the operationalization of IFI labour safeguards in practice. To this end, it first examines the mechanisms established by several IFIs to prevent and remedy violations of the requirements embodied in the safeguards, highlighting the significant amount of discretion provided to the IFI and/or the borrower in this regard. The section then reviews evidence on the safeguards' application, highlighting positive outcomes in several cases despite an overall mixed picture. The concluding section points to some general caveats that may hamper the safeguards overall effectiveness and emphasises the need for more comprehensive mechanisms to protect workers with regard to IFI activities.

2 The Legal Design of IFI Labour Safeguards

2.1 Qualified Support for Core Labour Standards: The Content of IFI Labour Safeguards

2.1.1 Key Actors and Main Standards Covered

IFI safeguards aim at avoiding that activities financed by IFIs contribute to social or environmental harm. Typically, they consist of two key components: First, a set of substantive standards which must be observed in the course of the project financed and which are often addressing the borrowers directly. Second, the procedures to be put in place by the IFI and the borrower, respectively, through which the implementation of the aforementioned standards is to be ensured.[22] Some IFI safeguards additionally contain an exclusion list, which sets out areas in which the IFI concerned must not provide finance.[23] This section takes a comparative look at the scope and content of IFI labour safeguards.

In this regard, a leading role in the World Bank Group and beyond has been taken by the IFC. Already in the late 1990s, the IFC adopted guidelines precluding financial support for projects that involve forced labour and certain forms of child labour.[24] Following consultations with various stakeholders, the IFC adopted a more

---

[21]The term borrower is used here to describe all entities receiving funds from IFIs regardless of whether they are active in the public or private sector.

[22]Some also involve a general vision statement; see e.g. the World Bank, A Vision for Sustainable Development (2016) and AfDB, African Developments Bank Group's Integrated Safeguards System (ISS) (2013), p. 15.

[23]See, e.g., EBRD Environmental and Social Exclusion List, in EBRD, Environmental and Social Policy (2014), Appendix 1, p. 8.

[24]IFC (1998) Policy Statement on Forced Labor and Harmful Child Labor. Washington.

comprehensive labour safeguard as part of its "Sustainability Framework".[25] Adopted in 2006 and revised in 2012,[26] IFC's Sustainability Framework has inspired a number of investment policies by other actors in the public and private sector.[27] An almost identical policy was notably adopted by the MIGA in 2007[28] and aligned with the updated IFC safeguards 6 years later.[29] IFC's policies also served as a blueprint for the labour safeguard regarding the World Bank's public sector activities that was eventually adopted in 2016 in the context of its new "Environmental and Social Framework". In addition, a variety of regional development banks have integrated labour standards concerns into their investment project-related safeguards,[30] which may cover the public sector, the private sector or both.[31]

In this regard, two main approaches can be distinguished: Some IFIs have relied on a "succinct" approach.[32] Here, labour standards requirements are typically integrated in a general safeguard on environmental and social risk management and tend to address a relatively small set of issues in a rather broad manner.[33] For example, the New Development Bank includes some labour issues into its general safeguard on "Environmental and Social Assessment". Its requirements focus on the application of domestic law and ILO Conventions "applicable to the country" in addition to more detailed occupational health and safety requirements.[34] Similarly,

---

[25]The Sustainability Framework is composed of a Policy on Environmental and Social Sustainability, the Performance Standards on Environmental & Social Sustainability, and an Access to Information Policy. See IFC's dedicated website at: https://www.ifc.org/wps/wcm/connect/topics_ext_content/ifc_external_corporate_site/sustainability-at-ifc/policies-standards/sustainability+framework.

[26]IFC (2012) Performance Standards on Social & Environmental Sustainability.

[27]Among others, a number of private banks adopted the "Equator Principles" in 2003 which extensively draw on the IFC's Performance Standards. See further Sims E (2009) The promotion of respect for workers' rights in the banking sector: Current practice and future prospects, Employment Sector Employment Working Paper No. 26, https://www.ilo.org/wcmsp5/groups/public/@ed_emp/@emp_ent/@multi/documents/publication/wcms_125545.pdf, pp. 18–21. These Principles were revised in 2006 and updated in 2011 to incorporate the content of the IFC Performance Standards. See Equator Principles, Equator Principles, The Newly Revised IFC Performance Standards—Guidance on Implementation by EP Association Members from 1 January 2012, http://www.equator-principles.com/index.php/all-ep-association-news/254-revised-ps.

[28]See on this Murphy (2014), p. 409.

[29]MIGA (2013) Performance Standards on Environmental and Social Sustainability, Washington; MIGA (2013) Policy on Environmental and Social Sustainability, Washington (hereinafter MIGA Sustainability Policy), MIGA (2013) Access to Information Policy, Washington.

[30]Meanwhile, other major regional IFIs, such as the Asian Development Bank and the Inter-American Development Bank, as of now, do not seem to have adopted a labour safeguard.

[31]For example, the AfDB's safeguards apply to both the Bank's public and the private sector operations; see AfDB, Operational Safeguard 1—Environmental and Social Assessment (2013), p. 22.

[32]Yifeng (2018), p. 113 speaks of a "succinct version of an environmental and social policy [. . .] with a brief reference to labour standards".

[33]See Yifeng (2018), p. 113 on whose work this categorization is based.

[34]NDB, ESS1: Environmental and Social Assessment (2016), para. 22.

the Asian Infrastructure Investment Bank (AIIB) sets out requirements concerning occupational safety and health as well as forced labour and child labour, the latter of which are also part of the AIIB's exclusion list.[35] For its projects in the private sector, some additional requirements "consistent with relevant national law" apply, notably relating to working and employment conditions, retrenchment, non-discrimination as well as the establishment of a grievance mechanism.[36] Different labour issues are also addressed by some of the smaller IFIs, such as the Nordic Investment Bank (NIB)[37] and the Black Sea Trade and Development Bank.[38]

A more comprehensive approach is embodied in the safeguards of the World Bank, IFC/MIGA as well as of the EBRD and the AfDB.[39] All of those instruments deal to some extent with matters relating to the four ILO Core Labour Standards.[40] In addition, they contain detailed requirements relating to occupational safety and health,[41] with EBRD's Safeguards dealing with safety and health matters of workers and local communities jointly in a dedicated safeguard.[42] Some of these safeguards

---

[35] See AIIB, Environmental and Social Standard 1: Environmental and Social Assessment and Management (2016), section D and AIIB, Environmental and Social Exclusion List (2016).

[36] AIIB, Environmental and Social Standard 1: Environmental and Social Assessment and Management (2016), section D. Requirements regarding "workers' organizations and collective bargaining" concern exclusively the "compliance with national law"; ibid.

[37] NIB's safeguards state that "[r]espect for workers' rights and their freedom of association is part of good business", that NIB "does not accept discrimination", and that "workers' [. . .] safety and health s essential for the productivity and efficiency of the business". Further, this safeguard policy declares that "[u]se of forced labour is not accepted by NIB" and that "NIB requires the client to comply with international standards for the employment of minors". NIB, Sustainability Policy (2012), p. 2.

[38] BSTDB-financed projects must comply with relevant domestic and EU labour law; see BSTDB, Environmental and Social Policy (2014), p. 6. In addition, the BSTDB safeguards contain references to the ILO Core Labour Standards, ILO conventions regarding forced and child labour, and, somewhat obscurely, "the fundamental human rights for decent work and social justice", ibid., p. 3. Confusingly, the safeguards also consider "the right for decent work" and "respect for health and safety" as part of the ILO's Core Labour Standards, ibid., pp. 2–3. The safeguards make it clear though that these issues are dealt with "depending on their relevance on each particular case", ibid., p. 4. Further, financial intermediaries supported by BSTDB are required to ensure the application of relevant labour requirements vis-à-vis their sub-borrowers, ibid., p. 5.

[39] Similar standards are contained in the safeguards of the European Investment Bank (EIB); see EIB, EIB Environmental and Social Standard 8, Version 10.0 of 8 October 2018. Labour Standards. However, given that the EIB is, as an EU institution, rather than an IFI proper, it will not be considered in the following.

[40] See below Sect. 2.1.2.

[41] See World Bank, Environmental and Social Standard 2. Labor and Working Conditions (2016) (WB ESS2), paras. 24–30; IFC, Performance Standard 2. Labor and Working Conditions (2012) (IFC PS2), para. 23; MIGA Performance Standard 2. Labor and Working Conditions (2013) (MIGA PS2), para. 23.

[42] EBRD, EBRD Performance Requirement 4. Health and Safety (2014) (EBRD PR4).

furthermore address retrenchment concerns[43] and equal treatment for migrants.[44] Employment conditions are also addressed although relevant standards mostly refer to local conditions and applicable domestic law.[45] Finally, a grievance mechanism for project workers and, if applicable, their organizations is provided for.[46] Several of these IFI safeguards also expressly obligate borrowers to observe domestic labour laws.[47]

2.1.2   Coherence with ILO Standards?

A number of IFI labour safeguards refer to ILO Core Labour Standards, albeit in different ways.[48] Some IFIs also claim a certain degree of coherence of their safeguards with these ILO standards.[49] The question of the coherence of IFI safeguards with the relevant ILO instruments therefore deserves particular scrutiny.

EBRD is on the forefront in this regard by requiring that projects financed by it "comply, at a minimum, with [. . .] the fundamental principles and standards embodied in the ILO conventions".[50] Thereby, the normative content set out in the eight ILO Fundamental Conventions is directly incorporated into EBRD's labour safeguards. The specific reach of the obligations contained therein is, however, not exactly clear. While the relevant provision refers to a footnote listing the relevant

---

[43]See IFC PS2, paras. 18–19; MIGA PS2, paras. 18–19; AfDB, Operational Safeguard 5—Labour Conditions, Health and Safety (2013) (AfDB OS5), p. 50 as well as EBRD, Performance Requirement 2: Labour and Working Conditions (2014) (EBRD PR2), para. 19.

[44]See IFC PS2, para. 11; MIGA PS2, para. 11; EBRD PR2, para. 16. AfDB OS5, p. 49 speaks, more ambiguously, of "comparable terms and conditions".

[45]See WB ESS2, paras. 10–12; IFC PS2, para. 10; MIGA PS2, para. 10; EBRD PR2, para. 15; AfDB OS5, p. 49.

[46]See WB ESS2, paras. 21–23; IFC PS2, para. 20; MIGA PS2, para. 20; EBRD PR2, para. 20; AfDB OS5, p. 50.

[47]See notably IFC, Performance Standard 1. Assessment and Management of Environmental and Social Risks and Impacts (2012) (IFC PS1), para. 6; MIGA, Performance Standard 1. Assessment and Management of Environmental and Social Risks and Impacts (2013) (MIGA PS1), para. 6; EBRD PR2, para. 5.

[48]See IFC PS2, para. 2; MIGA PS2, para. 2 ("have been in part guided by", respectively). See also World Bank, Guidance Note for Borrowers. ESS2: Labor and Working Conditions (2018) (WB ESS GN2), para. 2.2 ("is in part informed by"); EBRD PR2, para. 2 (referring to the four ILO Fundamental Conventions), AfDB OS5, p. 49 (stating as a "specific objective" to "[a]lign Bank requirements with the ILO Core Labor Standards").

[49]See IFC, Guidance Note 2. Labor and Working Conditions (2012) (IFC GN2), para. 2 ("By applying Performance Standard 2, the client will be able to operate its business in a manner consistent with the four core ILO labour Conventions"); World Bank, Review and Update of the World Bank's Safeguard Policies Environmental and Social Framework (Proposed Third Draft). Strengthening the Effectiveness of our Safeguard Policies to Enhance the Development Outcomes of Bank Operations (August 2016), paras. 66 and 95 ("[a]ll core labor standards are reflected in the proposed labor provisions" and "[ESS2] reflects the core principles of ILO's Fundamental Principles and Rights at Work", respectively).

[50]EBRD PR2, para. 5.

ILO instruments,[51] the formulation "fundamental principles and standards" leaves it open whether borrowers would have to abide by all or only some of the requirements enshrined in these conventions.[52]

For most IFI safeguards, coherence with ILO instruments varies significantly depending on the specific Core Labour Standard at issue. With regard to forced labour, consistency with ILO standards is high for all five IFI safeguards analysed here. Notably, the definitions of the term "forced labour" used draw heavily on the definition contained in the ILO's Forced Labour Convention,[53] which is expressly referred to in IFC's Guidance Note on Performance Standard 2.[54]

As for child labour, the situation is mixed with regard to mandatory age limits. The highest degree of ILO coherence is attained by EBRD, which requires borrowers' compliance with "all relevant national laws or international labour standards regarding employment of minors, whichever provide a higher degree of protection for the child".[55] This is contrasted by AfDB's safeguards, which preclude harmful child labour and refers to relevant ILO conventions in this regard but are silent on minimum age matters.[56] With regard to IFC and MIGA, Performance Standard 2 on Labor and Working Conditions (PS2) only obligates borrowers to abide by the domestic law on the matter.[57] While the related Guidance Note[58] requires borrowers to follow the age limits as stipulated by the relevant ILO instruments,[59] this Note is non-binding in nature. The World Bank's Environmental and Social Standard 2 on Labor and Working Conditions (ESS2) establishes a minimum working age of 14 years in contrast with the ILO's Minimum Age Convention, which provides for 15 years as a general minimum age.[60]

---

[51]EBRD PR2, para. 5, footnote 4.

[52]For a similar point in relation to labour provisions in trade agreements see Agustí-Panareda et al. (2015), pp. 363–367.

[53]See, e.g., IFC PS2, para. 22; MIGA PS2, para. 22; WB ESS2, para. 20; EBRD PR2, para. 11; AfDB OS5, p. 50.

[54]IFC GN2, para. 67, footnote 15. IFC's Performance Standard 2 defines "forced labour" as "any work or service not voluntarily performed that is exacted from an individual under threat of force or penalty" (IFC PS2, para. 22). Meanwhile, Article 2 (1) of the ILO's Forced Labour Convention, 1930 (No. 29) sets out the following definition of this term: "all work or service which is exacted from any person under the menace of any penalty and for which the said person has not offered himself voluntarily".

[55]EBRD PR2, para. 9.

[56]AfDB OS5, p. 50.

[57]IFC PS2, para. 21. Only for "hazardous work," a minimum age is foreseen.

[58]MIGA expressly refers to the IFC's Guidance Note on the Performance Standards; see https://www.miga.org/guidelines-policy.

[59]IFC GN2, paras. 61, 62 and 64. The general age limit is set at 15 years. This age limit can for developing countries, however, be reduced to 14 years if certain conditions are met. Furthermore, children of at least 13 years can perform certain forms of light work. See Articles 2(3–5) and 7(1) of the ILO's Minimum Age Convention, 1973 (No. 138).

[60]Compare WB ESS2, Para. 17 to Article 2(3) of the ILO Minimum Age Convention, 1973 (No. 138).

The strongest inconsistency between the IFI safeguards and ILO standards concerns arguably the areas of non-discrimination and workers' freedom of association. Under most IFI labour safeguards, observance is not fully required where the borrowing state's domestic laws conflict with the relevant IFI standards[61]: With the exception of EBRD's safeguards,[62] the requirements on non-discrimination are watered down with regard to countries whose laws involve discrimination vis-à-vis certain groups.[63] For example, under the World Bank's ESF borrowers need in such cases only to "seek to carry out" the project "to the extent possible" in line with the relevant standards.[64] Hence, full observance of the ILO instruments in question is not mandatory.[65] A similar the situation exists—except for AfDB's safeguards[66]— concerning countries which apply restrictions on or ban trade union organizations.[67] Here, too, the borrower's compliance with the pertinent ILO standards[68] is not obligatory as borrowers are, in such scenarios, merely obliged to not bar workers from putting in place alternative mechanisms and to not perform "discriminat[ion] or retaliat[ion]" against workers that "participate, or seek to participate" in the aforesaid mechanisms.[69] Overall, the coherence of IFI safeguards with the Core Labour Standards as defined by the ILO is—perhaps with the exception of those of EBRD—subject to considerable limitations.

2.2 Leaving Borrowers an Exit Option: The Coverage of Labour Safeguards

2.2.1 Differentiating the Protection of Workers

Most of the requirements described above are not applicable to the entirety of the project workforce.[70] Covered by these requirements are typically only workers with

---

[61]See prominently WB ESS2, paras. 13 and 16. Regarding IFC's PS2, see further Ebert (2014), pp. 235–237.

[62]Cf. EBRD PR2, para. 12.

[63]See, e.g., IFC PS2, para. 16; MIGA PS2, para. 16; WB ESS2, para. 13; AfDB OS5, p. 50.

[64]WB ESS2, para. 13. For a similar provision see IFC PS2, para. 16; MIGA PS2, para. 16.

[65]See notably the ILO Equal Remuneration Convention, 1951 (No. 100) as well as the ILO Discrimination (Employment and Occupation) Convention, 1958 (No. 111).

[66]Cf. AfDB OS5, pp. 49–50.

[67]See, with regard to the World Bank, Van Den Meersche (2017), p. 171.

[68]See notably the ILO Freedom of Association and Protection of the Right to Organise Convention, 1948 (No. 87) as well as the ILO Right to Organise and Collective Bargaining Convention, 1949 (No. 98).

[69]WB ESS2, para 16; IFC PS2, para. 14; MIGA PS2, para. 14; EBRD PR2, para. 13. As concerns EBRD, it is unclear how the relevant provision relates to the requirement to comply with "the fundamental principles and standards" of the ILO Fundamental Conventions, two of which deal with trade union rights; EBRD PR2, para. 5.

[70]It should also be noted that some safeguards contain different standards for projects carried out through financial intermediaries. See, e.g., World Bank, Environmental and Social Standard 9. Financial Intermediaries (2016).

a direct contractual link with the borrowers in the context of the project ("direct workers", following the denomination of IFC, MIGA, and the World Bank).[71] In this regard, the formulation "directly engaged" used in IFC's, MIGA's and, in a slightly modified version, the World Bank's safeguards highlight that even persons qualified by domestic law as "self-employed" may be covered by the safeguards.[72] For its part, EBRD defines the term "worker" under its labour safeguard as covering "the employees of the client"[73] while the requirements set out in AfDB's safeguards apply mainly to the "employees" or "workers" of the borrower.[74]

From these definitions it is clear that numerous workers that are involved in the project will fall outside this category, for instance where project activities are outsourced to third parties.[75] For those workers, IFI labour safeguards establish additional categories, which involve different standards of protection. The main categories in this regard are (1) certain workers under a contractual relationship with a third party ("contracted workers") and (2) workers contracted by certain suppliers of the borrower ("supply chain workers").

The labour-related requirements applying to the aforementioned categories of workers are significantly lower than those applying to "direct workers" and some of them are characterized by a high degree of vagueness. With regard to contracted workers, borrowers typically do not need to ensure contractors' actual compliance with the relevant labour requirements but are only required to take certain preventive actions.[76] For example under IFC's, MIGA's and EBRD's labour safeguards, the borrower must make "reasonable efforts" to ensure that contractors are "reputable and legitimate enterprises" and possess management systems that allow them to observe the relevant requirements.[77] The borrower also needs to make arrangements

---

[71]IFC PS2 and MIGA PS2, para. 4 in conjunction with para. 5, respectively; WB ESS2, para. 3 (a) in conjunction with para. 4.

[72]IFC PS2, para. 4; MIGA PS2, para. 4; WB ESS2, para. 3 (a), the latter using the formulation "employed or engaged directly".

[73]EBRD PR2, para. 4. It is not entirely clear whether the term "employee" is to be understood as under the domestic law applicable to the project or whether an autonomous understanding could apply in certain cases. Furthermore, it should be noted though that EBRD's dedicated health and safety safeguard also comprises certain "non-employee workers engaged by the client through contractors or other intermediaries". EBRD PR4, para. 8. This is on the condition that they have been hired "to work on project sites or perform work directly related to the core functions of the project"; ibid.

[74]See AfDB OS5, pp. 49–51.

[75]Reportedly, workers directly hired by the borrower are oftentimes in the minority in projects financed by IFIs; see Government of Germany, German Comments on the World Bank Safeguards Review (April 2015), p. 3.

[76]See WB ESS2, para. 5 in conjunction with paras. 31–33; AfDB OS5, p. 51. Requirements on retrenchment embodied in IFC's, MIGA's and EBRD's safeguards do not apply to contracted workers; see IFC PS2, para. 24; MIGA PS2, para. 24; EBRD PR2, para. 21.

[77]See IFC PS2, para. 24; MIGA PS2, para. 24; EBRD PR2, para. 21. For similar wording see WB ESS2, para. 31. AfDB's safeguards formulate this obligation in a way that appears to impose a higher standard of conduct on the borrower ("the borrower or client ascertains"); AfDB OS5, p. 51.

to "manag[e] and monito[r]" the performance of its contractors through suitable processes and ensure that the contractors' workers have access to a grievance mechanism.[78] The World Bank and AfDB also require borrowers to include the labour safeguards' requirements into their contracts with their contractors,[79] while other IFI safeguards limit themselves to making "reasonable efforts" in this regard.[80]

A lower standard applies to "primary supply workers". In this regard, the borrower's obligations are largely confined to identifying cases of forced and child labour.[81] Under several IFI safeguards, this requires furthermore that a "high" or "significant" risk of child labour and forced labour is apparent in the first place.[82] If such practices are ascertained, the borrower must usually "take appropriate steps" to address the problem.[83] Often IFI labour safeguards also come with an obligation to monitor the relevant parts of the supply chain on a continuous basis.[84] Similarly, in cases of substantial occupational safety problems[85] or a "high" or "significant" risk thereof[86] the borrower has to put in place "procedures and mitigation measures" to deal with such risks.[87] Where the primary supplier cannot be brought into compliance, the borrower must adjust its supply chain to stop sourcing from the supplier concerned.[88]

Finally, under the World Bank's ESS2 also workers "providing community labor" ("community workers") are subject to a reduced set of requirements.[89] This concerns, among others, workers involved in "food for work programs and public

---

[78]See WB ESS2, paras. 32 and 33 (quote at para. 32); IFC PS2 and MIGA PS2, paras. 25 and 26 (quote at para. 25), respectively; EBRD PR2, paras. 22 and 23 (quote at para. 22). For similar wording, albeit without references to grievance mechanisms, see AfDB OS5, p. 51.

[79]See WB ESS2, para. 32; AfDB OS5, p. 51. AfDB also extends this requirement to "subcontractors and intermediaries"; AfDB OS5, p. 51. Similarly, the World Bank's ESS2 contains a requirement to ensure that contractors "include equivalent requirements and non-compliance remedies in their contractual agreements with subcontractors"; WB ESS2, para. 32.

[80]See, e.g., IFC PS2, para. 25; MIGA PS2, para. 25; EBRD PR2, para. 22.

[81]See, e.g., IFC PS2, para. 27; MIGA PS2, para. 27; EBRD PR2, para. 24; AfDB OS5, p. 51. The relevant provisions under the World Bank's ESF are slightly less demanding in this regard given that here the borrower merely has to "require" its supplier to detect such risks; WB ESS2, para. 40.

[82]IFC PS2, para. 27; MIGA PS2, para. 27; WB ESS2, para. 40; AfDB OS5, p. 51.

[83]IFC PS2, para. 27; MIGA PS2, para. 27; EBRD PR2, para. 25; AfDB OS5, p. 51. Under the ESF, the borrower only has to obligate the supplier to carry out these measures; WB ESS2, para. 40.

[84]IFC PS2, para. 27; MIGA PS2, para. 27; EBRD PR2, para. 25. The World Bank's ESF only provides that "[t]he labor management procedures [ ] set out roles and responsibilities" in this regard; WB ESS2, para. 40.

[85]See EBRD PR2, para. 25.

[86]IFC PS2, para. 28; MIGA PS2, para. 28; WB ESS2, para. 41; AfDB OS5, p. 51.

[87]WB ESS2, para. 41; EBRD PR2, para. 25. IFC PS2 and MIGA PS2, para. 28, respectively, limit the need for such preventive measures to the avoidance of "life-threatening situations" while AfDB OS5, p. 51 confines it to "imminent danger, death or serious harm to workers".

[88]See WB ESS2, para. 42; IFC PS2, para. 29; MIGA PS2, para. 29; AfDB OS5, p. 51; EBRD PR2, para. 25.

[89]WB ESS2, para. 3(d).

works as safety nets programs".[90] Most ESS2 requirements, in particular those pertaining to non-discrimination, employment conditions and occupational health and safety, are examined case-by-case.[91] Only the requirements concerning forced and child labour apply systematically to community labour.[92]

2.2.2 Avoiding Compliance by Outsourcing?

Two additional problems are apparent concerning the coverage of IFI labour safeguards. First, none of the IFI labour safeguards comes with guidance as to which parts of the project activities can or should not be outsourced to contractors or suppliers. Borrowers can, as a result, circumvent the requirements applying to "direct workers" through a simple modification of the project's structure. In the worst case, the less demanding set of requirements that applies to contracted workers and supply chain worker could even provide an incentive for the outsourcing of work to contractors or sub-contractors.

Second, a number of contracted and supply-chain workers run the risk of not being covered by any aspect of the IFI labour safeguards whatsoever. This is due to these categories often being defined in a relatively narrow manner. For example, under the World Bank's ESF as well as under IFC's and MIGA's Performance Standards the term "contracted worker" is defined as any worker hired[93] by a third party "to perform work related to core functions [IFC/MIGA: "core business processes] of the project".[94] The crucial component of this definition is the concept of the "core functions" or "core business processes" of the project. The relevant safeguards define them as "those production and/or service processes essential for a specific [. . .] activity without which the [relevant project would be unable to] continue".[95] Deciding which processes are "essential" for the project's continuation is, unsurprisingly, less than straightforward and hard to resolve in abstract terms. Given this lack of a clear definition—and in the absence of additional guidance[96]—it

---

[90]WB ESS2, para. 34 footnote 23.

[91]WB ESS2, para. 35. Whether the ESS2's requirements apply to community workers mainly depends on this being "proportionate" to "a) the nature and scope of the project; (b) the specific project activities in which the community workers are engaged; and (c) the nature of the potential risks and impacts to the community workers." Ibid.

[92]WB ESS2, para. 37.

[93]See IFC PS2, para. 4; MIGA PS2, para. 4; WB ESS2, para. 3 b).

[94]WB ESS2, para. 3 b; IFC PS2, para. 4; MIGA PS2, para. 4.

[95]WB ESS2, para. 3 b, footnote 4; IFC PS2 and MIGA PS2, para. 4, footnote 3, respectively.

[96]The Guidance Notes to both the IFC's Performance Standards and the World Bank's ESF do not further elucidate this aspect; cf. IFC GN2, paras. 11–12 and 84–92 and WB ESS GN2, paras. 3.5, 4.1, 7.1.

appears that borrowers will not find it difficult to argue that numerous processes are not included in the relevant labour safeguards.[97]

Comparable issues can be discerned as concerns the coverage of workers in the supply chain. The World Bank, IFC and MIGA define "primary suppliers" as "suppliers who, on an ongoing basis, provide directly to the project goods, and materials essential for the core functions [IFC/MIGA: core business processes] of the project".[98] Similar problems exist concerning EBRD's labour safeguards whose supply chain-related requirements apply to "the supply chain of goods and materials which are central to the core functions of the project".[99] AfDB's labour safeguards limit relevant requirements to the "primary supply chain", a term for which no definition is apparent.[100]

Generally speaking, the IFI's labour safeguards can be considered a step towards protecting labour standards in the context of IFI-funded projects. Given the drawbacks discussed above, this should, however, only be considered modest progress. Furthermore, much of the potential of these arrangements will hinge on their application in practice, some aspects of which will be addressed in the following section.

3　Putting IFI Labour Safeguards in Practice

3.1　The Implementation Mechanisms of Labour Safeguards

3.1.1　Due Diligence

The implementation of IFI safeguards relies primarily on "due diligence", which draws on the concepts of risk analysis and management common among private sector financial institutions.[101] This involves an assessment to be undertaken by the borrower through which compliance problems related to the project and possible avenues to address them can be identified.[102] Usually, also the IFI's staff is required

---

[97]This problem is partly avoided by EBRD's labour safeguards, which aside from "non-employee workers" "perform[ing] core functions of the project" also include those "work[ing] on project sites"; EBRD PR2, para. 21. A similar point can be made for AfDB's labour safeguards which includes all "workers procured by third parties to work directly on or support the project"; AfDB OS5, p. 51.

[98]WB ESS2, para. 3 c, footnote 5; IFC PS2 and MIGA PS2, para. 4, footnote 4, respectively.

[99]EBRD PR2, para. 24. See also EBRD PR2, para. 25 in conjunction with para. 24.

[100]AfDB OS5, p. 51.

[101]For a critical analysis in this regard see Sarfaty (2012), pp. 137–139.

[102]See IFC PS1, paras. 7–12; MIGA PS1, paras. 7–12; World Bank Environmental and Social Standard 1. Assessment and Management of Environmental and Social Risks and Impacts (2016) (WB ESS1), paras. 23–35; EBRD, Performance Requirement 1. Assessment and Management of Environmental and Social Impacts and Issues (2014), paras. 4, 7–9. Different rules apply usually if

to carry out their own risk assessments.[103] That being said, many IFI safeguards rely principally on the risk assessment of the project carried out by the borrower himself,[104] which requires in certain cases the involvement of "independent specialists".[105] The borrower must also undertake consultations with stakeholders relevant to the project.[106] The specific features of the due diligence exercise partly depend on the risk classification that the IFIs undertake for each project.[107]

The risk assessment typically serves as a basis for an action plan that is prepared by the borrower and submitted to the IFI.[108] These plans set out the measures, which the borrower must take within a given timeframe to address the problems identified.[109] Once the project agreement is concluded, the borrower as well as the IFI's staff must monitor the project with a view to ensuring compliance with the action plan and other relevant aspects of the agreement.[110] The borrower is also required to put in place a grievance mechanism for complaints pertaining to the project.[111]

In spite of the often detailed rules on due diligence contained in IFI safeguards, certain limitations remain. Among others, the emphasis on the project assessment by the borrower or the consultants hired by the borrower may undermine the independence of the due diligence process.[112] Borrowers may notably benefit from not discerning certain labour-related problems in order to minimize the costs of the project's implementation.[113] In addition, the relevant procedures involve consider-

---

the IFI's investment is made by means of financial intermediaries; see, e.g., EBRD, Environmental and Social Policy (2014) (EBRD ESP), para. 28.

[103]See IFC, Policy on Environmental and Social Sustainability (2012) (IFC Sustainability Policy), paras. 26 and 28; MIGA Sustainability Policy, paras. 26 and 28; World Bank, World Bank Environmental and Social Policy for Investment Project Financing (2016) (WB ESP), paras. 30–32; EBRD ESP, paras. 29–35.

[104]See, e.g., WB ESP, para. 32.

[105]WB ESS1, para. 25. See also EBRD PR1, para. 10, referring to "independent experts".

[106]See IFC PS1, paras. 25–28; MIGA PS1, paras. 25–28; WB ESP, para. 53; AfDB, Operational Safeguard 1. Environmental and Social Assessment (2013) (AfDB OS1), pp. 27–28; EBRD, PR1, para. 10.

[107]See IFC Sustainability Policy, para. 40; MIGA Sustainability Policy, para. 38; WB ESP, para. 20; AfDB OS1, pp. 24–25; EBRD PR1, para. 10–13.

[108]See, e.g., AfDB OS1, p. 23; EBRD PR1, para. 17–20.

[109]See, e.g., WB ESP, para. 46; EBRD PR1, paras. 17–19.

[110]See, e.g., IFC PS1, paras. 22–24; WB ESS1, paras. 40, 45–50; EBRD PR1, para. 24.

[111]See, e.g., IFC PS1, para. 35; MIGA PS1, para. 35; WB ESP, para. 60–61; AfDB OS1, p. 29; EBRD, Performance Requirement 10. Information Disclosure and Stakeholder Engagement (2014), para. 28.

[112]See on the IFC's Performance Standards McBeth (2010), p. 215 and ITUC (2011), p. 13.

[113]In the case of the World Bank's ESF, this is exacerbated by the strong reliance on the borrower country's laws and institutions, which can substitute for the Bank's Environmental and Social Standards if the Bank considers them "materially consistent" there with; WB ESP, para. 23. See further Van Den Meersche (2017), pp. 166–168.

able latitude as to how the due diligence is to be performed and through which measures the compliance problems identified are to be addressed.[114] Furthermore, the time limits relating to the implementation of the requirements often lack specificity.[115] As a result, IFI staff possess palpable discretion with regard to the implementation of the safeguards, which may lead to an uneven application of the labour safeguards at hand.

3.1.2 Complaint Mechanisms

The limitations of the due diligence procedures noted above underscore the importance of mechanisms through which complaints relating to specific projects can be filed. Two types of mechanisms can be distinguished: The first one consists of procedures that have been established within the departments of the IFIs. One example is IFC's Social and Environmental Development Department, which receives inquiries as well as complaints concerning IFC-funded projects by interested actors.[116] Furthermore, EBRD created a "Trade Union Communication Mechanism" in early 2019 through which the Bank's Environmental and Social Department is to provide a timely response to trade unions raising problems concerning the labour safeguards' implementation.[117]

Secondly, several IFIs have established quasi-judicial complaint mechanisms to provide persons affected by IFI-funded projects with a recourse against the institutions' operational management. The oldest and most widely known of these mechanisms is the World Bank's Inspection Panel. Consisting of three members and supported by a secretariat,[118] the Inspection Panel examines submissions by individuals and groups subject to certain eligibility criteria.[119] It reports to the World Bank's Board of Executive Directors,[120] thereby being autonomous from the Bank's

---

[114]WB ESS1 stipulates, for example that the borrower "will assess, manage and monitor the environmental and social risks and impacts of the project [...] so as to meet the requirements of the ESSs *in a manner and within a timeframe acceptable to the Bank*" (emphasis added). WB ESS1, para. 14.

[115]Among others, the World Bank's safeguards provide a "draft ESCP will be disclosed as early as possible, and before project appraisal", see WB ESP, para. 36. See further Dann and Riegner (2017), p. 11.

[116]See ITUC (2011), p. 19.

[117]See ITUC/Global Unions Washington Office, Trade Union Communication Mechanism for the European Bank for Reconstruction and Development (2019), p. 1.

[118]World Bank Inspection Panel Updated Operating Procedures (2014) (WBIP Procedures), paras. 7–8.

[119]For a submission to be eligible a party needs to demonstrate that "its interests have been or are likely to be directly affected by an action or omission of the Bank as a result of a failure of the Bank to follow its operational policies and procedures with respect to the design, appraisal and/or implementation of a project financed by the Bank". See IBRD and IDA (1993) The World Bank Inspection Panel Resolution (Res. No. IBRD 93-10, Res. No. IDA 93-6), para. 12.

[120]WBIP Procedures, para. 6.

staff and management. After an eligibility assessment, the process involves an investigation phase where the merits of the complaints are assessed.[121] Issuing injunctions to halt ongoing work or to grant compensation is not within the Panel's competences.[122] Instead, the Board of Executive Directors is in charge of following up on the Inspection Panel's reports.[123] This has usually involved an Action Plan devised by the World Bank's Management which have in most cases been accepted by the Board of Executive Directors.[124] That being said, in several cases the Board has required amendments to the action plan at stake. Furthermore, the Panel has sometimes asked the Bank's Management to prepare implementation reports and, albeit less frequently, has assigned the evaluation of the implementation of the required measures to the Panel itself.[125]

Similar recourse mechanisms exist for the labour safeguards adopted by several other IFIs. This includes, notably, the Compliance Advisor/Ombudsman (CAO) for the IFC and MIGA, the Project Complaint Mechanism for the EBRD, and the Independent Review Mechanism for the AfDB. These bodies are independent from the IFIs' operational activities[126] to the extent that they report to the IFI's senior management[127] or its board.[128] Typically, their competences comprise a dispute resolution component for complaints brought by interested parties, a compliance assessment component involving the investigation of alleged infringements of safeguard policies by the IFI staff, and partly also an advisory component directed at the IFI's management.[129] Any eligible complaint can be assessed by the recourse mechanism with a view to facilitating an amicable dispute settlement.[130] Where dispute settlement is deemed unfeasible or turns out to be unsuccessful, the procedure to carry out a compliance investigation can be activated.[131] In the case of the

---

[121] See further Naudé Fourie (2009), especially at pp. 177–181.

[122] See further Carrasco and Guernsey (2008), pp. 595–597.

[123] WBIP Procedures, para. 71.

[124] See Wong and Mayer (2015), p. 506.

[125] See ibid., pp. 506–507.

[126] See, for the CAO, Saper (2012), p. 1295 and, more generally Bradlow (2005), especially at p. 455.

[127] See, e.g., IFC/MIGA, CAO Operational Guidelines (2013) (CAO Guidelines), p. 4.

[128] See, e.g., African Development Bank/African Development Fund Board of Directors, Resolution B/BD/2015/03—F/BD/2010/04 concerning the Independent Review Mechanism (2015), p. 1.

[129] See CAO Guidelines, p. 5; EBRD, Project Complaint Mechanism (PCM). Rules of Procedure (2014) (EBRD PCM Procedure), p. 1. An advisory function is performed by the CAO and the AfDB's IRM but not by the EBRD's PCM; see AfDB, The Independent Review Mechanism. Operating Rules and Procedures (2015) (AfDB IRM Procedure), paras. 68–77; CAO Guidelines, pp. 28–29.

[130] See, e.g., CAO Guidelines, pp. 13–15, 18; AfDB IRM Procedure, para. 42; EBRD PCM Procedure, paras. 36–39.

[131] See CAO Guidelines, pp. 14, 16; AfDB IRM Procedure, para. 50; EBRD PCM Procedure, para. 40. In the case of the CAO, the compliance investigation is subject to a positive "compliance appraisal" by the CAO and can also be set in motion by MIGA's and IFC's senior management, the President of the World Bank Group, and the CAO itself. See CAO Guidelines, pp. 22–23.

CAO, for example, the investigation typically includes a "compliance panel" composed by experts from outside the World Bank Group[132] and leads to an "investigation report" which assesses the observance of relevant policies by the staff of IFC or MIGA.[133]

Notwithstanding their quasi-judicial features, the procedures of the IFI's recourse mechanisms are not free from political components. Notably, the criteria for determining whether to initiate a dispute resolution or compliance investigation are in many instances broad and provide the recourse mechanism with substantial discretion.[134] In some cases, the IFI's president or board must consent before the dispute settlement[135] or compliance function of the relevant mechanism[136] is activated. Besides, the recourse mechanism's findings do typically not entail any legal implications but depend on follow-up actions by the IFI's management[137] or Board of Directors.[138] This raises the question of what concrete practical effects these mechanisms can actually entail, which shall be examined in the following section.

3.2 The Potential Impact of Labour Safeguards: Insights from Prior Experiences

3.2.1 An Overview of the Evidence

In recent years, IFI safeguards have been relied upon for workers' rights purposes on a variety of occasions. For example, the International Transport Workers' Federation

---

[132]See CAO Guidelines, p. 24.

[133]CAO Guidelines, p. 25.

[134]The World Bank Inspection Panel can decline an investigation also if the submission fulfils the "technical eligibility criteria for an investigation", considering, for example, the severity of the "alleged harm and possible non-compliance by the Bank with its operational policies". World Bank Inspection Panel Updated Operating Procedures (2014), paras. 41 and 43 lit. a. On AfDB's dispute resolution procedure see AfDB IRM Procedure, para. 39. On the CAO's compliance procedure see CAO Guidelines, p. 23; Saper (2012), p. 1303.

[135]See EBRD PCM Procedure, para. 36. Here, the decision is with the President.

[136]With regard to the AfDB's recourse mechanism, the investigation is subject to the approval of the Group's Board or President; see AfDB IRM Procedure, paras. 53–55. In the case of the World Bank Inspection Panel, it is the Board that must authorise the initiation of the Panel's investigation; WBIP Procedures, para. 49. That being said, the Board normally grants the authorization without entering into a discussion of the request's merits. See ibid and World Bank Group, Clarification of the Board's Second Review of the Inspection Panel (1999), para. 9.

[137]See, e.g., CAO Guidelines, p. 4. Although the CAO's reports are usually public, the President of the World Bank Group can bar the compliance report from being published. See CAO Guidelines, p. 25.

[138]See, e.g., EBRD PCM Procedure, para. 46. In the case of AfDB, the decision rests with the President or the Board, depending on whom approved the project concerned; AfDB IRM Procedure, para. 65.

has invoked the EBRD's labour safeguards in relation to a conflict between the Polish trade union Solidarnosc and the Polish container company DCT Gdansk.[139] Furthermore, the World Bank Inspection Panel has scrutinized a case involving alleged child and forced labour in a World Bank-funded project in Uzbekistan.[140]

Most of the evidence concerning the application of IFI labour safeguards pertains to IFC's Performance Standards. The available research suggests that the Performance Standards—and related action by IFC's Social and Environmental Development Department—have helped on a number of occasions to address labour-related compliance problems. One case concerned a Brazilian airline, which allegedly was involved in anti-union activities. Further to complaints by trade unions, IFC raised the matter with the borrower, which, as union sources reported, contributed to halt these activities.[141] Another case involved a building enterprise active in Uganda, which allegedly had ignored a collective agreement it had concluded with a local trade union. Here, IFC's contacts with the company were reportedly instrumental in achieving the collective agreement's application.[142] Further, IFC's Performance Standards have in at least one instance, been used to improve the situation of contracted workers. A case in point concerned contractors of a cement company in Iraq, which was not abiding by the local legal requirements concerning employment conditions. In this case, the workers considered their reliance on the Performance Standards vis-à-vis the IFC's client company as a key factor that led the company to induce its contractors towards consulting with workers' organizations and improved the conditions of a significant number of workers.[143]

Having said that, other cases raised with the IFC led to only a marginal or no improvement at all with respect to the raised labour issues.[144] Trade unions have attributed this, depending on the case at hand, to weaknesses in IFC's investigations, IFC's failure to appropriately engage with the borrower, and the restrained disclosure of relevant information.[145] It is therefore unsurprising that a number of labour-related cases have been filed with the Compliance Advisor Ombudsman (CAO), which shall be analysed in the following.

---

[139]See International Transport Workers' Federation, Poland's largest container terminal bans dock union organisers, 11 March 2015, available at: https://www.itfglobal.org/en/news/polands-largest-container-terminal-bans-dock-union-organisers.

[140]See World Bank Inspection Panel (2013) Report and Recommendation, Republic of Uzbekistan: Second Rural Enterprise Support Project (P109126) and Additional Financing for Second Rural Enterprise Support Project (P126962) (Report No. 83254-UZ). This case had occurred even before the Bank had adopted its dedicated labour safeguard. See further Ebert (2018), pp. 296–297.

[141]See Bakvis and McCoy (2008), p. 6.

[142]See Murie (2009) BWI Strategies to Promote Decent Work Through Procurement: The Example of the Bujagali Dam Project in Uganda. GURN Discussion Paper; No. 9. ILO, Geneva, pp. 15–16.

[143]Bakvis, Behind the World Bank's projects in Iraq, Equal Times (19 July 2013), available at: https://www.equaltimes.org/behind-the-world-banks-projects-in-iraq#.XJqVXNh7mM_.

[144]See, e.g. ITUC (2011), pp. 19–21 and 25–26 for a description of relevant cases.

[145]ITUC (2011), pp. 21, 23 and 27.

3.2.2   The Case of the Compliance Advisor Ombudsman

Over the last two decades, the CAO has increasingly served as a forum for addressing labour concerns and hence provides ample material for analysis. Between 2001 and 2018, the CAO has dealt with more than 40 labour-related cases, more than half of which have been filed in the last 5 years of that period.[146] Most frequently, complaints have concerned wages and other employment conditions,[147] occupational safety and health,[148] as well as retrenchment and severance pay-related matters.[149] To a lesser extent, violations of trade union-related requirements have been alleged[150] while cases dealing with discrimination and sexual harassment[151] as well as forced and child labour are so far scarce.[152]

At the time of writing, about a fourth of the cases were pending at the dispute resolution or compliance stage.[153] Of those cases that had been concluded about a third had been terminated at the dispute resolution stage.[154] Most of the other cases were transferred to the compliance stage,[155] often after one or more parties had opposed a mediation effort by the CAO.[156]

Remarkably, of the cases that had been transferred to the CAO's compliance function more than half were found not to "warrant" a proper investigation and thus were dismissed after the compliance appraisal.[157] It is here where the CAO's discretion, provided for by its Operational Guidelines, plays out.[158] For example, the CAO has stated that "[a]bsent aggravating circumstances, disputes between an employer and individual employees around issues of pay and benefits will not raise substantial concerns regarding the E&S outcomes of an IFC investment such that would merit a CAO compliance investigation."[159] This approach excludes a number

---

[146]See the Annex of this chapter. Information on all cases is available on the CAO's website at http://www.cao-ombudsman.org/cases/.

[147]See Annex, Cases 3, 6, 10, 11, 15–20, 22, 23–27, 30, 37, 40, 41 and 43.

[148]See Annex, Cases 2, 6, 8, 11, 12, 14–17, 19, 28, 30, 32–35, 40, 42 and 43.

[149]See Annex, Cases 6–10, 18, 20, 24, 26, 27, 31, 32 and 37.

[150]See Annex, Cases 5, 6, 17, 21, 28, and 36, 38 and 39.

[151]See Annex, Cases 4 (dealing with sexual harassment), 6, 30, and 31 (dealing with discrimination matters).

[152]See Annex, Cases 1, 15 and 28 (dealing with child labour).

[153]See Annex, Cases 1, 19, 37 and 43 (dispute resolution stage) as well as Cases 4, 6, 8, 9, 12, 30, 33 and 34 (compliance stage).

[154]See Annex, Cases 1, 2, 7, 10, 22, 23, 26, 28, 38 and 39.

[155]The only exception appears to be Case 29 in the Annex.

[156]See Annex, Cases 4–8, 11–13, 20, 21, 24, 25, 27, 30–35, 41, and 43.

[157]E.g. CAO, Appraisal Report. AES Sonel (#11579) Cameroon, 26 June 2014, p. 10. See also Annex, Cases 3, 11, 13, 14, 20, 23–25, 27, 31, 32, 35 and 36.

[158]See Sect. 3.1.2 above.

[159]CAO, Compliance Appraisal Report. Appraisal of IFC investment in Harmon Hall, Mexico (IFC Project #29753). CAO complaints numbered: 02–06 and 08, April 8, 2015, p. 12; CAO, IFC investment in Plato, Compliance Appraisal: Summary of Results. Kyrgyzstan Project #32583 Complaint 01, July 29, 2015, p. 11.

of scenarios from the CAO's scrutiny while leaving it open what kind of "aggravating circumstances" would need to be adduced for such complaints to merit a compliance investigation.

That being said, in all the cases that did proceed to the compliance investigation stage the CAO has found some compliance deficits with regard to Performance Standard 2. In several instances, the CAO noted deficiencies concerning the review of environmental and social risks by the IFC.[160] Among others, in a case regarding a Colombian aviation company, the CAO found that "IFC did not adequately understand the PS2 (i.e. labour-related) risk attached to its investment prior to commitment".[161] Further, the CAO observed significant deficits in the way IFC performed its due diligence as concerns Performance Standard 2.[162] Similarly, in a report on three cases concerning a run-of-the-river power plant in Uganda the CAO held that the IFC's project assessment was not "commensurate to risk", partly because IFC had failed to obtain sufficient expertise in occupational health and safety matters.[163] The CAO has also criticized IFC for disbursing tranches of loans despite compliance deficits concerning labour-related requirements and a lack of sufficient remedial action.[164] Notably, in a case involving trade union rights issues in pulp and paper companies in Malaysia, the CAO observed that IFC did not only suspend the project's supervision "at the client's request" but also did not use contractual remedies even though it knew the client was not addressing the issues.[165] In some cases, the CAO has, moreover, directly challenged IFC's legal interpretations of the Performance Standards.[166] In one instance, it held that IFC had "erred in deciding that the Bujagali Energy-06 complainants were not covered by its E&S requirements".[167] Similarly, in another cases the CAO found itself "unable to support IFC's argument that disclosure is discretionary in cases where a client has contentious relationships with its workers or their union representatives."[168]

---

[160]See, e.g., CAO, CAO Investigation of IFC Environmental and Social Performance in Relation to: Amalgamated Plantations Private Limited (APPL), India, September 6, 2016, pp. 64–65; CAO, Compliance Investigation Report. IFC Investment in Bidco Bev. & Det. Kenya (Project #33385) Complaint 01 & 04, October 2, 2018, pp. 31–32.

[161]CAO, Complaint from Global Unions on behalf of unions representing employees of Avianca, Investigation of IFC Investment in Avianca S.A., Colombia, CAO Ref: C-I-R9-Y12-F165, April 27, 2015 (CAO, Avianca), p. 16.

[162]See ibid., pp. 16–17.

[163]CAO, CAO Investigation of IFC/MIGA Social and Environmental Performance in Relation to: Bujagali Energy Ltd and World Power Holdings, Uganda, November 3, 2017, p. 35.

[164]See, e.g., CAO, Avianca, pp. 17–19 and 22.

[165]CAO, Compliance Investigation. IFC Investment in Bilt Paper B.V. (Project #34602), Malaysia, April 13, 2018, p. 46.

[166]For an analysis concerning non-labour related CAO cases see Bradlow and Naudé Fourie (2013), p. 43.

[167]CAO, CAO Investigation of IFC/MIGA Social and Environmental Performance in Relation to: Bujagali Energy Ltd and World Power Holdings, Uganda, November 3, 2017, p. 35.

[168]See CAO, Avianca, p. 25.

Despite these findings, concrete practical outcomes of the CAO's compliance investigations are difficult to detect. Indeed, for none of the cases analysed was there clear evidence available suggesting that the workers' complaints had been addressed by the client further to the CAO's investigation report. A number of factors may contribute to this result. For one, in the absence of any binding effect of the CAO's investigation report on IFC's Management, IFC's action has in several cases been delayed. In some instances it is furthermore not entirely clear whether IFC will comply with the CAO's recommendations altogether.[169] For another, unlike in the dispute resolution phase the focus of the compliance investigation is not on the behaviour of the client company but on that of IFC or MIGA, as a result of which there are fewer avenues for redress for the victims. More importantly, the proceedings of some compliance investigations were excessively lengthy. Indeed, some cases took more than 4 years from the filing of the complaint to the adoption of the investigation report.[170] This increases the risk that by the time the CAO's investigation is concluded the project has already come to an end and IFC and MIGA will not have the capacity to leverage change in their client's practice. For example, in the Avianca case, the investigation report was issued about 4 years after the complaint had been filed with the CAO and close to 7 years after the original complaint had been brought to the attention of IFC.[171] By that time, the loan had already been repaid, which considerably diminished IFC's ability to influence Avianca's approach to trade unions.[172]

More palpable effects for complainants seem to have been achieved at the dispute resolution stage. In a number of cases, the CAO's mediation efforts resulted in agreements between the complainant(s) and the client company concerned that addressed the issues raised in the respective complaints. One example concerns a Turkish automobile supplier, Standard Profil, which was allegedly involved in infringements of workers' freedom of association, among other issues.[173] On the basis of an evaluation of the case the CAO proposed several measures, including labour-related capacity building and awareness raising as well as an independent labour audit.[174] In another case, involving outstanding wage and severance

---

[169]See, e.g., CAO, Compliance Monitoring Report. IFC Investment in Bujagali Energy Ltd, Uganda, IFC Projects #24408 and #39102, MIGA Project #6732, CAO Complaints -04, -06, -07 & -08, February 27, 2019, p. 9; CAO, Compliance Monitoring Report, IFC Investment in Amalgamated Plantations Private Limited (APPL), India, Project Numbers 25074 and 34562, January 23, 2019, p. 25.

[170]See, e.g., Annex, Cases 5 and 40.

[171]See CAO, Avianca, pp. 1–8.

[172]See further ITUC (2015) Avianca-Colombia: IFC Should Follow Ombudsman's Recommendations for Labour Standards Compliance, Say Unions. Press Release of 19 May 2015. Available at: http://www.ituc-csi.org/avianca-colombia-ifc-should-follow?lang=de.

[173]See further Arp (2012), pp. 37–38.

[174]CAO, Turkey/Standard Profil-01/Duzce. Ombudsman Conclusion Report—Standard Profil, Turkey, June 2012, p. 2. See also Berber Agtas (2009) Promoting Core Labour Standards through the Performance Standards of the IFC: The Case of Turkey, Global Union Research Network Discussion Paper No. 8, ILO, Geneva, pp. 38–89.

payments of a polyester company in Egypt, the CAO's dispute resolution efforts led to an agreement further to which the payments in questions were made by IFC's borrower.[175] Further, the CAO's mediation in a case concerning 93 labour-related disputes surrounding a power plant in Uganda led to an amicable settlement in 19 of these disputes while 67 others were resolved through other means.[176] In the same case, the CAO participated in the implementation of several structural measures, including the reinforcement of the local Medical Arbitration Board for settling occupational health and safety disputes, and a workshop for IFC staff aimed at "designing better grievance mechanisms".[177] Two other complaints, dealing with companies in Turkey and Mauritius, respectively, were resolved by IFC during the course of the dispute resolution stage.[178]

Overall, it would appear that the dispute resolution phase holds the largest potential for achieving concrete results for workers affected by IFC-funded projects. In the mid- and long-term, the compliance investigations could help to bring about change regarding IFC's processes and practices concerning the implementation of Performance Standard 2. This seems, however, too early to assess as the implementation of the CAO's recommendation by IFC is still pending in the bulk of the relevant cases.[179]

4 Conclusion

This chapter has analysed the labour safeguards of IFIs with regard to their potential to prevent or remedy violations of the ILO's Core Labour Standards in the context of projects financed by them. A variety of IFIs have adopted safeguards dealing with labour-related matters, of which the paper has considered the five most comprehensive ones in depth. These safeguards come with a due diligence procedure as well as with complaint mechanisms which can examine submissions from third parties. There is evidence, notably pertaining to the IFC Performance Standards, suggesting that IFI labour safeguards have entailed in some instances positive outcomes in terms of the ILO Core Labour Standards as well as with regard to certain other labour matters.

---

[175]CAO, CAO Assessment and Dispute Resolution Conclusion Report, Complaint Regarding IFC's Investment in Egyptian Indian Polyester Company—Sokhna (IFC Project #28878), May 2017, p. 7.

[176]CAO, CAO Ombudsman Conclusion Report: Uganda: Bujagali Energy-04/Bujagali, November 2013, p. 3.

[177]Ibid.

[178]See CAO, Assan Aluminyum Project. Complaint Conclusion Report, August 2010, p. 2; CAO, Ombudsman Assessment & Conclusion Report. Complaint Regarding the Africa Investco Project (Project #27819), September 2012, p. 6.

[179]See Annex, Cases 15–18, 21, 39–41.

That being said, a number of features constrain the potential of the IFI's labour safeguards. While the IFI safeguards analysed here address all four Core Labour Standards, in most cases coherence with them is imperfect. Moreover, IFIs tend to apply lower standards of protection to workers without a direct contractual link to the borrower, which renders it possible that borrowers circumvent the obligations under the labour safeguards by designing the structure of the project accordingly.

On the procedural side, several characteristics of the IFI policies may complicate the effective implementation of the labour safeguards. A key aspect involves the delegation of responsibility for impact assessments and monitoring to the IFIs' borrowers. Furthermore, the discretionary components in the safeguards' implementation procedures as well as in the procedures relating to the IFIs' complaint mechanisms reduce the labour safeguards' remedial potential. These aspects should be seen in the context of the increasing pressure on IFIs due to the growing availability of alternative sources of finance from the public[180] and the private side.[181] This provides borrowers with increasing leverage to advocate for flexible standards and leads to a somewhat paradox situation where the substantive scope of certain IFI safeguards is increased while at the same time new elements of flexibility are introduced, which may undermine their effective implementation.[182]

This notwithstanding, the aforesaid IFI labour safeguards mark an important step forward with regard to the protection of labour standards in IFI project finance activities. Going forward, a major challenge consists in translating the IFI labour safeguards into actual improvements on the ground through a better implementation of relevant requirements.[183] Furthermore, a need persists to devise similar policies for the IFI's non-project finance activities, which are not covered by any specific labour safeguard.[184] Ongoing scrutiny and advocacy by trade unions and other civil society actors will continue to be vital in this regard.

Annex: Table of Cases Filed with the Compliance Advisor/ Ombudsman[185]

1. Cambodia/VEIL II-01/Ratanakiri Province (February 10, 2014)
2. Cameroon/Chad-Cameroon Pipeline-02/Cameroon (May 16, 2011)
3. Cameroon/AES Sonel-02/Doula (February 21, 2013)
4. Chile/Alto Maipo-02/Cajon del Maipo (July 05, 2017)
5. Colombia/Avianca-01/Colombia (November 14, 2011)

---

[180]See also Bugalski (2016), pp. 3–4.

[181]See, e.g., Davis and Dadush (2010).

[182]See for a similar point on the World Bank, Passoni et al. (2016), p. 926.

[183]For a critical perspective concerning IFC's Performance Standards see Cradden et al. (2017).

[184]See further Ebert (2018), p. 299, focussing on the World Bank.

[185]Documentation for all cases is available at: http://www.cao-ombudsman.org/cases/.

6. Egypt/Alex Dev Ltd-01/Wadi al-Qamar (April 09, 2015)
7. Egypt/Egyptian Indian Polyester Company—Sokhna-01/India (October 27, 2016)
8. Egypt/Alex Dev Ltd-02/Beni Suef (February 13, 2017)
9. Egypt/Alex Dev Ltd-03/Beni Suef (May 10, 2017)
10. Egypt/Egyptian Indian Polyester Company—Sokhna-02/India (August 20, 2017)
11. Georgia/Trans-Anatolian Pipeline-01/Vale (March 29, 2017)
12. Ghana/MPS-01/Tema (February 26, 2018)
13. Guatemala/Guatemala: TCQ-01/Puerto Quetzal (March 20, 2014)
14. India/SN Power-01/CAO Vice President Request (December 01, 2008)
15. India/Tata Tea-01/CAO Vice President Request (May 01, 2012)
16. India/Tata Tea-02/Assam (February 02, 2013)
17. Kenya/Bidco Bev. & Det.-01/Thika (June 10, 2016)
18. Kenya/Bidco Bev. & Det.-04/Thika (May 23, 2017)
19. Kenya/Bridge International Academies-01/Kenya (June 15, 2018)
20. Kyrgyz Republic/Plato-01/Bishkek (April 07, 2015)
21. Malaysia/Bilt Paper-02/Sipitang (June 01, 2015)
22. Mauritius/Africa Investco-01 (March 28, 2012)
23. Mexico/Harmon Hall-01/Mexico (December 02, 2011)
24. Mexico/Harmon Hall-02/Puerto Vallarta (September 06, 2013)
25. Mexico/Harmon Hall-03-06/Puerto Vallarta and Merida Campestre (October 14, 2013)
26. Mexico/Harmon Hall-07/San Luis Potosi (March 04, 2014)
27. Mexico/Harmon Hall-08/Puerto Vallarta (March 14, 2014)
28. Nicaragua/Nicaragua Sugar Estates Limited-01/León and Chinandega (March 01, 2008)
29. Nigeria/Niger Delta Contractor Revolving Credit Facility-01/Niger Delta (June 01, 2001)
30. Nigeria/Eleme Fertilizer-01/Port Harcourt (April 11, 2018)
31. Pakistan/Pakistan: Bank Alfalah-01/Saddar Karachi (May 06, 2015)
32. Peru/Yanacocha-06/Cajamarca (February 06, 2014)
33. Peru/Yanacocha-09/Cajamarca (January 27, 2017)
34. Peru/Yanacocha-10/Cajamarca (May 10, 2017)
35. Peru/Yanacocha-11/Cajamarca (December 06, 2017)
36. South Africa/Lonmin-01/Vice President request (August 21, 2012)
37. Togo/Togo LCT-02/Lomé (February 16, 2018)
38. Turkey/Standard Profil-01/Duzce (September 01, 2008)
39. Turkey/Assan Aluminyum-01/Dilovasi (October 01, 2008)
40. Uganda/Bujagali Energy-04/Bujagali (March 21, 2011)
41. Uganda/Bujagali Energy-06/Bujagali (April 03, 2013)
42. Uganda/Bujagali Energy-08/Bujagali (June 06, 2017)
43. Ukraine/MHP-01/Vinnytsia (June 05, 2018)

References

Abouharb R, Cingranelli D (2007) Human rights and structural adjustment. CUP, Cambridge

Agustí-Panareda J, Ebert FC, LeClercq D (2015) ILO labor standards and trade agreements: a case for consistency. Comp Labor Law Policy J 36:347–380

Anner M, Caraway T (2010) International institutions and workers' rights: between labor standards and market flexibility. Stud Comp Int Dev 45:151–169

Arp B (2012) La integración de los derechos humanos en la labor del Banco Mundial: El caso del Ombudsman y Asesor en Materia de Observancia. Revista Española de Derecho Internacional 64:11–14

Asrani S, Dann P (2012) International Finance Corporation (IFC). In: Wolfrum R (ed) Max Planck Encyclopedia of Public International Law, vol V. OUP, Oxford, pp 793–896

Bakvis P (2009) The World Bank's doing business report: a last fling for the Washington Consensus? Transfer: Eur Rev Labour Res 15:419–438

Bakvis P, McCoy M (2008) Core labour standards and international organizations: what inroads has labour made? Friedrich Ebert Stiftung, Bonn

Berg J, Cazes S (2008) Policymaking gone awry: the labor market regulations of the doing business indicators. Comp Labor Law Policy J 29:349–381

Blanton RG, Blanton SL, Peksen D (2015) The impact of IMF and World Bank programs on labor rights. Polit Res Q 68:324–336

Bohoslavsky JP, Ebert FC (2018) Debt crises, economic adjustment, and labour standards. In: Bantekas I, Lumina C (eds) Sovereign debt and human rights, vol 2018. OUP, Oxford, pp 284–302

Bradlow D (2005) Private complainants and international organizations: a comparative study of the independent inspection mechanisms in International Financial Institutions. Georgetown J Int Law 36:403–494

Bradlow D, Naudé Fourie A (2013) The operational policies of the World Bank and the international finance corporation. Int Organ Law Rev 10:3–80

Bugalski N (2016) The demise of accountability at the World Bank? Am Univ Int Law Rev 31:1–56

Carrasco ER, Guernsey AK (2008) The World Bank's Inspection Panel: promoting true accountability through arbitration. Cornell Int Law J 41:577–629

Cradden C, Graz J-C, Pamingle L (2017) Governance by contract? The impact of the International Finance Corporation's social conditionality on worker organization and social dialogue. Working Paper Université de Lausanne/Swiss Network for International Studies. https://snis.ch/wp-content/uploads/2017/11/3296_final_wp_governancebycontract_final_working_paper_1.pdf

Dann P, Riegner M (2017) Safeguard-Review der Weltbankgruppe. Ein neuer Goldstandard für das globale Umwelt- und Sozialrecht? Deutsche Gesellschaft für Internationale Zusammenarbeit (GIZ), Bonn

Darrow M (2003) Between light and shadow: the World Bank, the International Monetary Fund and International Human Rights Law. Hart, Oxford

Davis KE, Dadush S (2010) The privatization of development assistance: symposium overview. N Y Univ J Int Law Polit 42:1079–1089

Ebert FC (2014) The integration of labour standards concerns into the environmental and social policy of the International Finance Corporation. Verfassung und Recht in Übersee 47:229–249

Ebert FC (2015) International Financial Institutions' approaches to labour law: the case of the International Monetary Fund. In: Blackett A, Trebilcock A (eds) Research handbook on transnational labour law. Edward Elgar, Cheltenham, pp 124–137

Ebert FC (2018) Labour standards and the World Bank. Analysing the potential of safeguard policies for protecting workers. In: Gött H (ed) Labour standards in international economic law. Springer, Cham, pp 273–304

Fischer S (1999) A role for labor standards in the new international economy? Opening and overview: International Architecture Reform, 29 October 1999 (Washington)

ITUC (2011) Labour standards in World Bank group lending. Lessons Learned and Next Steps, Washington

La Hovary C (2009) Les droits fondamentaux au travail. Origines, statut et impact en droit international. Presses Universitaire de France, Paris

McBeth A (2010) International economic actors and human rights. Routledge, London

Murphy H (2014) The World Bank and core labour standards: between flexibility and regulation. Rev Int Polit Econ 21:399–431

Naudé Fourie A (2009) The World Bank Inspection Panel and quasi-judicial oversight. In search of the 'Judicial Spirit' in public international law. Eleven International Publishing, Utrecht

O'Brien R (2014) Antagonism and accommodation: the labor-IMF/World Bank relationship. In: Kaasch A, Stubbs P (eds) Transformations in global and regional social policies. Springer, Heidelberg, pp 153–174

Passoni C, Rosenbaum A, Vermunt E (2016) Empowering the inspection panel: the impact of the World Bank's new environmental and social safeguards. N Y Univ J Int Law Polit 49:921–958

Ragazzi M (2012a) Financial institutions, international. In: Wolfrum R (ed) Max Planck Encyclopedia of Public International Law, vol IV. OUP, Oxford, pp 21–29

Ragazzi M (2012b) World Bank group. In: Wolfrum R (ed) Max Planck Encyclopedia of Public International Law, vol X. OUP, Oxford, pp 909–912

Saper B (2012) The International Financial Corporation's Compliance Advisor/Ombudsman (CAO): an examination of accountability and effectiveness from a global administrative law perspective. Int Law Polit 44:1279–1329

Sarfaty GA (2012) Values in translation. Human rights and the culture of the World Bank. Stanford University Press, Stanford

Schill SW (2012) Multilateral Investment Guarantee Agency (MIGA). In: Wolfrum R (ed) Max Planck Encyclopedia of Public International Law, vol VII. OUP, Oxford, pp 410–416

Schlemmer-Schulte S (2012) International Bank for Reconstruction and Development (IBRD). In: Wolfrum R (ed) Max Planck Encyclopedia of Public International Law, vol V. OUP, Oxford, pp 363–393

Suzuki E (2012) Regional development banks. In: Wolfrum R (ed) Max Planck Encyclopaedia of Public International Law, vol VIII. OUP, Oxford, pp 824–838

Tiroch K (2012) Black Sea. In: Wolfrum R (ed) Max Planck Encyclopaedia of Public International Law, vol I. OUP, Oxford, pp 949–956

Van Den Meersche D (2017) Accountability in international organisations: reviewing the World Bank's environmental and social framework. In: Sciso E (ed) Accountability, transparency and democracy in the functioning of Bretton Woods Institutions, pp 157–187

Wang H (2017) New multilateral development banks: opportunities and challenges for global governance. Global Policy 8:113–118

Wong Y, Mayer B (2015) The World Bank's Inspection Panel. A tool for accountability? World Bank Leg Rev 6:495–530

Yifeng C (2018) The making of global public authorities: the role of IFIs in setting International Labor Standards, AIIB Yearbook of International Law, pp 109–128

Franz Christian Ebert, LLM (Utrecht), is a research fellow at the Max Planck Institute for Comparative Public Law and International Law in Heidelberg. Previously, Franz worked as a research officer at the International Labour Organization's research branch in Geneva and was a visiting professional at the Inter-American Court of Human Rights in Costa Rica. Franz has advised and consulted for several NGOs, government agencies, and international organizations.

Linkages of Trade, Investment and Labour in Preferential Trade Agreements: Between Untapped Potential and Structural Insufficiencies

Henner Gött

Contents

I wish to express my gratitude to Anne Trebilcock, Till Patrik Holterhus, Franz Christian Ebert, Laura Wanner and Paul Thiessen.

H. Gött (✉)
Institute of International and European Law, Jean Monnet Chair for European Union and Global Sustainable Development Through Law, Göttingen, Germany

Department of International Economic and Environmental Law, Georg-August-University Göttingen, Göttingen, Germany
e-mail: hgoett@gwdg.de

© Springer Nature Switzerland AG 2019
M. Bungenberg et al. (eds.), *European Yearbook of International Economic Law 2019*,
European Yearbook of International Economic Law (2020) 10: 133–166,
https://doi.org/10.1007/8165_2019_28, Published online: 31 July 2019

1 Introduction

Labour provisions in preferential trade agreements (PTAs) are becoming increasingly common. 25 years after their first inception, several major economies regularly include 'trade-labour linkages' in their trade agreements. What is more, labour provisions have begun to 'spill over' into international investment law, mainly because a number of large-scale PTAs contain both labour and investment chapters and, thus, form what could be called an 'investment-labour linkage'.

However, while their proliferation continues, labour provisions have never truly become a success story. Their often painstakingly drafted substantive, institutional and procedural clauses have at best achieved modest results and arguably have never unfolded their full potential. This record of underperformance has persisted to date despite the fact that labour provisions have incrementally been developed further with every new generation of PTAs.

Against this background, this chapter will enquire into the scope and content of contemporary trade-labour and investment-labour linkages as they exist in some of the major latest-generation PTAs, in order to assess their prospects and potential. It will proceed as follows: After a short contextualization of PTA labour provisions (Sect. 2), it will examine trade-labour linkages (Sect. 3) and investment-labour linkages (Sect. 4) in contemporary PTAs, including their substantive clauses and their mechanisms for implementation and enforcement. The analysis will show that both linkages have noteworthy potential for protecting and promoting labour standards in the context of trade and investment liberalization. However, structural insufficiencies in their implementation and enforcement mechanisms may severely hamper the exploitation of this potential and may perpetuate labour provisions' low performance. As a consequence, this contribution argues that current reform debates, instead of incrementally developing particular provisions or choosing between different 'approaches' to labour provisions, should focus on these structural issues and should consider the inclusion of new, but arguably more effective mechanisms in future PTAs.

2 Contextualizing Labour Provisions in Contemporary PTAs

2.1 Implications of Trade and Investment Liberalization on Labour Standards

The liberalization of trade and investment has had a profound impact on labour topics. On the one hand, it has fostered economic growth and employment creation across the globe, and has contributed to the economic and social development of many countries. On the other hand, it has also played a role in the creation or aggravation of substantial challenges, such as high levels of unemployment and poverty, income inequality, the growth of the informal economy, and the accompanying rise of employment relations with low levels of worker protection.[1]

Being major drivers of liberalization, trade and investment agreements have played a vital role in these developments. The reduction or removal of customs and other barriers to trade in goods and services, as required under trade agreements, has allowed employers to relocate production to states with more business-friendly labour regulations, or to integrate local workplaces into global supply and production chains. This increase in transnational mobility in turn has in many cases increased their economic bargaining power vis-à-vis domestic trade unions and governments.

The liberalization of investment flows and the internationalization of investment protection, for their parts, have allowed foreign investors to become powerful actors in domestic labour relations of their host states, acting either as employers themselves or as financiers, creditors or major business partners of local employers. Moreover, investors have on several occasions made use of investor rights and investor-state dispute settlement mechanisms provided for in investment agreements to challenge their host states' labour regulations or policy.[2] It is noteworthy that in the majority of cases, investors' claims, at least insofar as they concerned labour issues, were unsuccessful. However, the low success rate must not be mistaken for a sign that labour standards are sufficiently resilient against adverse influence caused by investment law. For one part, many of the cases were rejected on case-specific grounds.[3] What is more, there have been other cases that more visibly illustrate the potential impact of investment protection on labour standards.[4] Beyond specific cases, the mere prospect of investment arbitration may induce host states to refrain from enforcing or increasing labour standards to begin with (so-called regulatory chill).

---

[1]ILO (2008), p. 5.

[2]For instance, in *Noble Ventures v. Romania* and in *Plama v. Bulgaria*, the investors claimed that their host states had violated its duty to provide full protection and security against allegedly unlawful strikes and blockades by local trade unions, ICSID, *Noble Ventures v. Romania*, ICSID Case No. ARB/01/11, 12 Oct 2005, para. 160 et seqq.; ICSID, *Plama Consortium Limited v. Bulgaria*, ICSID Case No. ARB/03/24, 27 Aug 2008, para. 236. In *Paushok v. Mongolia*, the investor claimed that a Mongolia's introduction of a new windfall tax due for every non-Mongolian worker hired in excess of a permissible limit of 10% of the investor's workforce constituted a violation of Mongolia's obligation to accord fair and equitable treatment, UNCITRAL, *Sergei Paushok, CJSC Golden East Company and CJSC Vostokneftegaz Company v. Mongolia*, Award on Jurisdiction and Liability, 28 April 2011, para. 353. In *Veolia v. Egypt*, the investor argued that an increase of the statutory minimum wage violated its rights under a stabilization contract it had concluded with Egypt under a prior government, ICSID, *Veolia Propreté v. Egypt*, ICSID Case No. ARB/12/15, 25 May 2018.

[3]In *Noble Ventures v Romania* and *Plama* for example, the investor's claims were dismissed as the investors were not able to provide sufficient proof, ICSID, *Noble Ventures v Romania*, ICSID Case No. ARB/01/11, 12 Oct 2005, para. 160; ICSID, *Plama Consortium Limited v. Bulgaria*, ICSID Case No. ARB/03/24, 27 Aug 2008, paras. 248–249.

[4]See e.g. *Piero Foresti, Laura de Carli & Others v. South Africa*, ICSID Case No. ARB(AF)/07/01, 4 August 2010.

2.2 The Emergence of Trade-Labour and Investment-Labour Linkages Through Labour Provisions in Preferential Trade Agreements

In response to these challenges, and to put up with increasing pressure from trade unions and other societal groups, leading economies began to include labour standards in their trade policies and instruments. The main idea was to enhance the protection and promotion of labour standards by either making them an ex ante condition for trade liberalization or by submitting their implementation and enforcement to ex post review, notably through international trade law's dispute settlement mechanisms with the possibility of 'hard' enforcement via suspension of trade benefits (often referred to as 'trade sanctions').[5] Unsuccessful attempts in the 1990s to create such a trade-labour linkage at WTO level gave a boost to including labour provisions in bilateral and regional preferential trade agreements (PTAs).[6] Today, labour provisions are an increasingly common sight in PTAs.[7] They are regularly included in PTAs by several major economies, including the USA, the EU or Canada, but also other countries, such as Chile or New Zealand.

The inclusion of labour provisions in PTAs has also had a noticeable side-effect on international investment law. In general, labour-related provisions in international investment agreements remain a rarity until today. Virtually no free-standing bilateral investment treaty (BIT) contains any such provisions.[8] By contrast, some of the economically and politically most important PTAs contain both labour provisions and rules on investment liberalization and in some cases also investor protection.[9] Unlike the overwhelming majority of BITs, these PTAs integrate investment and labour issues into one overarching treaty framework. They can therefore be regarded as trailblazers of an emerging investment-labour linkage. This investment-labour linkage largely presents itself as a 'by-product' of combining a broad range of topics within comprehensive PTA frameworks. Still, it must be considered an intended development, as many labour provisions explicitly mention both trade *and* investment.[10]

Investment-labour linkages are not yet as established components of PTAs as their trade counterparts. Moreover, it is unclear whether they will continue to exist, as future PTAs might not include investment chapters anymore. Following the recent surge of criticism against international investment protection, leading economies

---

[5]Ebert (2017), pp. 307 ff.; ILO, IILS (2013), pp. 31 ff.

[6]See Singapore Ministerial Declaration, 18 Dec 1996, WT/MIN(96)/DEC, para. 4; Maupain (2013a), pp. 178ff.

[7]According to a 2016 study, nearly half of trade agreements with labour provisions came into existence since 2008 and over 80% of agreements entering into force since 2013 included them. ILO (2016), p. 22.

[8]Gordon et al. (2014), pp. 10 ff.; VanDuzer (2016), pp. 171 f.

[9]E.g. CETA (Chapters 8 and 23), CPTPP (Chapters 9 and 19) or USMCA (Chapters 14 and 23).

[10]Gött and Holterhus (2018), pp. 237 f.

have begun to reconsider the inclusion of investment chapters in PTAs. The USMCA foresees a phase-out of investor-state dispute settlement (albeit not of investor protection as such) between Canada and the USA.[11] Moreover, the EU, Singapore and Vietnam outsourced investment protection and ISDS from their signed PTAs into separate BITs, and the European Commission announced that it will continue to negotiate such separate agreements in the future.[12] Against this background, the future role of PTAs in bringing investment and labour into one common treaty context has become more uncertain. That being said, investment-labour linkages continue to exist in a range of non-EU PTAs that have already entered into force or are currently under negotiation. What is more, given that both EU FTAs and EU BITs are explicitly intended to be integral parts of the EU's partnership and cooperation framework agreements with the respective state,[13] the 'European' investment-labour linkage might resurface in another shape.

2.3   Labour Provisions' Underperformance

Despite labour provisions becoming an increasingly regular element of PTAs, it appears to be an overall consented assessment that those provisions that have been existing and been put to practice have been underperforming.[14] They do not live up to expectations regarding the protection and promotion of labour standards in the context of trade and investment liberalization.

As with PTAs in general, it is inherently difficult to gather reliable empirical data on their performance.[15] What is more, some labour provisions are still new and still await to be thoroughly tested in practice. That being said, with some labour provisions being in force since way over two decades, and with labour provisions increasingly being included in PTAs, there is a steadily growing body of data and experience, and trends emerging from existing studies support the impression of underperformance.[16] Repeatedly, the parties have not or not sufficiently implemented and enforced labour standards, and labour rights violations continue to exist.[17] A particular issue is that the mechanisms foreseen to implement and enforce labour provisions are hardly ever activated, and if so, only in a markedly

---

[11]Art. 14.2(4) USMCA.

[12]This happened in response to the CJEU's 2017 advisory opinion on the EU-Singapore FTA, see CJEU, Opinion 2/15 *EU-Singapore FTA*, ECLI:EU:C:2017:376, see also Hainbach (2018), pp. 199 ff. Moreover, on the insistence of Japan, EUJEPA only provides for investment liberalization, but excludes investment protection and ISDS.

[13]See e.g. Art. 4.12(1) EU-Singapore Investment Protection Agreement.

[14]E.g. Dombois et al. (2004); Ebert and Posthuma (2011), pp. 20 ff.; ILO, IILS (2013); ILO (2017), pp. 50 ff.; Abel (2018a).

[15]In particular, there is a lack of systematic large-scale empirical research, ILO (2017), p. 14.

[16]Kamata (2015), p. 20.

[17]Marx and Soares (2015), pp. 158 ff. and 167 ff.

reluctant, occasional or non-systematic manner.[18] Against this background, enhancing the effectivity of labour provisions has become a top priority in debates on the future shape of PTA labour provisions.

3   Contemporary Trade-Labour Linkages

Labour provisions in each PTA resemble a unique conglomerate of established and new or experimental clauses, shaped by the PTA's own drafting history. Still, many elements are recurring, and some PTAs—usually the economically most important ones—are more influential for the further development of labour provisions than others. Therefore, this section will examine labour provisions in selected latest-generation PTAs, in order to provide an overview of where 'the' trade-labour linkage stands at present. The primary points of reference will be the Comprehensive Economic and Trade Agreement (CETA) between the EU and Canada, the EU free trade agreements with Singapore and Vietnam, the EU-Japan Economic Partnership Agreement (EUJEPA), the Comprehensive and Progressive Agreement for Trans-Pacific Partnership (CPTPP)[19] and the United States-Mexico-Canada Agreement (USMCA).

3.1   Substantive Clauses

Contemporary PTAs' labour provisions contain a range of widely differing substantive clauses that create international rights and obligations between the PTA parties. Some of them are closely related to trade law rules, either defining exceptions from trade disciplines (Sect. 3.1.1) or as provisions targeting the import of goods produced in violation of labour standards (Sect. 3.1.2). Other provisions seek to actively improve the situation in the parties, imposing obligations to effectively enforce labour laws and not to derogate from them (Sect. 3.1.3) or to pursue and achieve multilateral or bilaterally agreed labour standards (Sect. 3.1.4).

3.1.1   Preservation of Policy Space: Labour-Relevant Exceptions from Trade Disciplines

PTAs contain a vast array of obligations to liberalize and facilitate trade between the parties by removing customs and other trade barriers. In principle, the PTA parties

---

[18]Ebert (2017), pp. 307 ff.
[19]Incorporating by reference the earlier Trans-Pacific Partnership Agreement (TPP). For convenience, both TPP and CPTPP provisions will be cited as "CPTPP" here.

have to fulfill these obligations irrespective of whether their domestic labour laws and policies would be affected.[20] However, PTAs typically contain exception clauses preserving policy space for the parties by providing that the non-discriminatory adoption or enforcement of measures do not constitute a violation of the parties' obligations, provided that such measures pursue a policy goal mentioned in the clause.[21] Such exception clauses are inspired by Article XX GATT and Article XIV GATS and, in large parts, repeat or even incorporate these provisions.[22]

The issue whether and to what extent these exceptions cover trade-restricting measures of labour regulation has repeatedly flared up in debates.[23] The overall conclusion is that they only do so in a very limited manner. Exception clauses do not comprehensively exempt all measures pertaining to labour regulation. Instead, they enumerate an exhaustive list of permissible measures, some of which may be read to cover certain labour aspects, notably measures to protect public morals, human life or health, and measures relating to products of prison labour. Thus, measures taken by a party to protect or promote labour standards can only be justified if they fall within these exceptions.[24]

3.1.2 Importation Bans and Conditions for Goods Produced Under Illicit or Low Working Conditions

Some recent PTAs seek to exclude certain specified goods from preferential treatment if such goods were produced under illicit or low working conditions.

Firstly, Article 19.6 CPTPP obliges the parties to discourage the importation of goods produced by forced or compulsory labour. Article 23.6 USMCA goes even further and requires that such importations be prohibited by appropriate measures and to "establish cooperation for the identification and movement of goods [sic]" produced by forced labour. As a general matter, such measures are prone to conflict with WTO rules.[25] The CPTPP and the USMCA deal with this issue by footnotes to these provisions clarifying that the parties must still adhere to all their obligations under WTO law or other trade agreements.[26] While these clauses arguably prevent conflicts with WTO law, they may at the same time put a significant strain on the parties options to implement the envisaged importation barriers, because WTO law

---

[20]Pursuant to Art. 27 VCLT, the parties may not invoke domestic law as justification for the non-performance of a treaty.

[21]E.g. Art. 32.1 USMCA. Some of these clauses also apply to investment liberalization and non-discrimination of investors, e.g. Art. 28.3(1) CETA.

[22]E.g. Art. 32.1(1) and (2) USMCA.

[23]Addo (2015), pp. 135 ff.; Cottier (2018), pp. 85 ff.

[24]Blüthner (2004), pp. 312 ff.; Cottier (2018), pp. 85 ff.

[25]Read (2005), pp. 239 ff.

[26]Art. 19.6. CPTPP, explanatory footnote 6; Art. 23.6 USMCA, explanatory footnote 10.

significantly limits the parties' discretion for imposing importation bans or measures of equivalent effect. WTO law inter alia contains obligations to accord most-favoured nation treatment to all "like products" (Art. II(4) GATT) and prohibits non-tariff border restrictions (Art. IX GATT). What is more, the contours of these rules are notoriously unclear and have given rise to thorny issues.[27] The WTO dispute settlement bodies have not yet had a chance to clarify the application of WTO rules on importation restrictions in the context of labour standards.

Secondly, regarding the import of certain vehicles, the USMCA modifies trade disciplines in another interesting way: Instead of imposing importation bans, the USMCA provides that certain categories of vehicles only qualify as 'originating goods'—and thus only benefit from the USMCA's rules on preferential market access—if they have sufficient "labour value content". This is the case if a defined percentage of a vehicle was produced by workers earning a base wage of at least $16 per hour.[28] This required "labour value content" per vehicle is 30% upon the entry into force of the agreement and is successively rising to up to 40% for certain classes of vehicles over specified time periods.[29]

The aforesaid rules are unprecedented. Both their permissibility under WTO law[30] and their effects remain to be tested in practice. As to their effects, it is to be noted that they set an incentive for the parties (in this case notably Mexico) to create or increase wage floors, in order to keep vehicle producing companies in their territories. On the other hand, caution is warranted. Firstly, the USMCA does not oblige its parties to actually introduce or increase their minimum wage floors.[31] It is likely that flanking cooperative measures would be necessary to actually increase the minimum wage, which, however, would require voluntary engagements. Secondly, even if the rules should prove to be effective, the fixation of a concrete minimum wage and the limitation to one industry sector in the treaty text makes them inflexible, with future adjustments of the wage floor or expansion to other industries requiring treaty revisions or amendments.[32] At the same time, fixation in the treaty text concentrates the power to define and adjust the wage floor in the hands of the parties' governments, leaving it unclear whether there is a role for collective bargaining between workers and employers.

---

[27] See e.g. Howse (1999); Kaufmann (2007), pp. 134 ff.; Cottier (2018).

[28] Annex 4-B. Art. 7 (3) lit. a USMCA.

[29] Annex 4-B. Art. 7 (1) USMCA.

[30] Notably, given the considerable relevance of the automotive industry in the USMCA parties, the question has arisen whether the rules stand in the way of liberalizing 'substantially all trade' in the sense of Art. XXIV(8) lit. b GATT, Titievska and Pietsch (2018).

[31] Against this backdrop, it has been suggested that the main aim of the labour value content rules seems to be to incentivize production relocations to high-wage countries, i.e. from Mexico to the USA and Canada, Titievska and Pietsch (2018).

[32] Ebert and Villarreal (2018).

3.1.3   Obligations to Effectively Enforce and to Maintain Existing Standards

Instead of directly conditioning market access of goods and services, other clauses seek to ensure that the parties effectively enforce their existing labour laws, and that they do not waive or derogate from them as an incentive for trade. The overall objective of such provisions is to prevent the parties from engaging in a 'race to the bottom' to create a regulatory environment that is most appealing to businesses.

Since the 1994 North American Agreement on Labor Cooperation (NAALC; the NAFTA side-agreement on labour), PTAs have consistently obliged the parties to effectively enforce their domestic labour laws.[33] Lack of effective enforcement of labour laws is a frequent problem in many states. In principle, creating an international obligation to effectively enforce labour standards enables a party to hold another party accountable for such enforcement gaps. That being said, this obligation alone does not prevent the parties from altering their domestic labour laws.

A frequent further element of PTA labour provisions are so-called "non-lowering of standards" clauses (hereinafter: "NLS clauses"). For instance, pursuant to Article 16.2(2) EUJEPA,

> [t]he Parties shall not encourage trade or investment by relaxing or lowering the level of protection provided by their respective (. . .) labour laws and regulations. To that effect, the Parties shall not waive or otherwise derogate from those laws and regulations or fail to effectively enforce them through a sustained or recurring course of action or inaction in a manner affecting trade or investment between the Parties.[34]

NLS clauses supplement the obligation to effectively enforce existing labour laws through a non-derogation requirement. They thus address the important danger of circumvention of that obligation. That being said, NLS clauses typically employ (and combine) highly indeterminate phrases. In the *US-Guatemala* arbitration, phrases like "sustained or recurring course of action or inaction" or "in a manner affecting trade or investment between the parties" gave rise to considerable uncertainty and controversy.[35] Presumably in response thereto, Article 23.4 USMCA defines waivers or derogations "in a manner affecting trade or investment between the parties" as those involving:

> (1) a person or industry that produces goods or provides services traded between the Parties or has investment in the territory of the Party that has failed to comply with this obligation; or
> (2) a person or industry that produces goods or provides services that compete in the territory of a Party with goods or services of another Party.[36]

---

[33]Brooks (2018), p. 46. The obligation can either extent to the entirety of a party's labour laws and regulations or to specified parts of them, see e.g. the definition of 'labour laws' in Art. 19.1 CPTPP and Art. 23.1 USMCA. Some agreements also discipline the parties' discretion on how to allocate their enforcement resources, Art. 19.5(2) CPTPP; Art. 23.5(3) USMCA.

[34]In a similar manner, but limited to certain labour laws, Art. 19.4 CPTPP and Art. 23.4 USMCA.

[35]CAFTA-DR Arbitral Panel, *In the Matter of Guatemala – Issues Relating to the Obligations Under Article 16.2.1(a) of the CAFTA-DR*, final report, 14 June 2017, pp. 45–47 and 50–65.

[36]Art. 23.4 USMCA, explanatory footnote 7.

Such clarifications may help to shape the understanding of indeterminate phrases in NLS clauses. That being said, given the opulent breadth of the USMCA's clarification, one might ask if it makes sense to retain the 'in a manner affecting...' requirement at all.[37]

3.1.4 Obligations to Pursue and Achieve International Standards

Furthermore, many PTAs oblige the parties to pursue and achieve international labour standards. There are two principal kinds of clauses, which are often employed complementarily: On the one hand, PTAs increasingly refer to existing international standards, notably ILO instruments. On the other hand, many PTAs also contain genuine bilaterally agreed standards.

ILO Instruments and Other International Standards

A growing number of PTAs references existing ILO and other international instruments on labour standards.

The most common points of reference are legally non-binding but politically important international instruments. As to ILO instruments, the most typical reference is to the 1998 ILO Declaration on Fundamental Principles and Rights at Work and the core labour standards enshrined therein.[38] Some more recent agreements also reference the ILO's 2008 Declaration on Social Justice for a Fair Globalization.[39] Further referenced instruments are key declarations and resolutions pertaining to the UN Millennium Development and Sustainable Development agendas[40] and, in some instances, human rights instruments, notably the 1948 Universal Declaration of Human Rights.[41] As to the nature of the reference, the respective instruments are usually "recalled",[42] "affirmed"[43] or "reaffirmed".[44] The precise legal consequence of this language remains ambiguous. While recalled or (re)affirmed instruments may inform the interpretation and implementation of the PTA, it remains open whether and to what extent the PTA legally obliges the parties to adhere to them.

---

[37]Other FTAs require that the host state purports to encourage trade or investment, e.g. Art. 23.4 (2) CETA. Such regulatory intent is hard to isolate and to prove, not least because the host state's motivation for relaxing labour regulation will rest on several (and often interchangeable) motives.

[38]E.g. Art. 23.3(1) CETA; Art. 16.3(2) EUJEPA; Art. 23.3(1) USMCA.

[39]E.g. Art. 22.1(1) CETA.

[40]E.g. Art. 22.1(1) CETA; Art. 16.1(1) EUJEPA.

[41]CETA, preambular clause 4.

[42]E.g. Art. 22.1(1) CETA.

[43]E.g. Art. 23.3(1) CETA.

[44]E.g. the 1998 ILO Declaration on Fundamental Principles and Rights at Work (Art. 16.3(2) EUJEPA) or the 2006 ECOSOC Ministerial Declaration on Generating Full and Productive Employment and Decent Work for All (Art. 12.2(2) EU-Singapore FTA).

As to legally binding other instruments, some recent EU FTAs require the parties to effectively implement ratified ILO conventions,[45] and to make "continued and sustained efforts on their own initiative" to ratify fundamental ILO conventions insofar as they have not yet done so.[46] These obligations have the potential to strengthen and to reinforce the ILO's efforts to protect and promote labour standards. However, to what extent they actually do remains open. In this respect, it must be recalled that states are anyways under an obligation to implement ratified ILO conventions. Similarly, they are already required under the ILO Constitution to seek ratification of ILO conventions by their competent domestic bodies.[47] Whether and to what extent the obligation to make 'continued and sustained efforts' goes beyond these obligations remains subject to interpretation.

Bilaterally Agreed Labour Standards

Many PTAs define own labour standards that the parties must achieve and maintain. A classic example is the canon of so-called 'internationally recognized workers' rights' included especially in US FTAs that the parties commit to promote and implement.[48] Recent PTAs increasingly include standards on further issues, e.g. on working conditions, notably minimum wages, working hours, and occupational safety and health,[49] or on migrant workers.[50] In addition, they require the parties to maintain mechanisms for monitoring and labour inspection,[51] and to provide for appropriate administrative and judicial remedies against labour law violations.[52]

It is worth noting that for most of the topics covered by such bilaterally agreed standards, there already exist numerous international instruments, in particular ILO conventions and recommendations. Against this background, the inclusion of bilaterally agreed standards remains an ambiguous development. On the one hand, PTA-specific standards resemble an opportunity for states to progressively create new standards or to spell out existing labour standards in more detail between them than would be possible in multilateral fora. For instance, the USMCA explicitly

---

[45] Art. 16.3(5) EUJEPA.

[46] Art. 16.3(3) EUJEPA.

[47] Art. 19(5) lit. b ILO Constitution.

[48] On the development see Alston (2004), pp. 499 ff. These nowadays include freedom of association and the effective recognition of the right to collective bargaining, the elimination of all forms of forced or compulsory labour, the effective abolition of child labour, a prohibition on the worst forms of child labour, and other labour protections for children and minors, the elimination of discrimination in respect of employment and occupation, and acceptable conditions of work with respect to minimum wages, hours of work, and occupational safety and health (see e.g. Art. 23.1 USMCA).

[49] 19.3(2) CPTPP; Art. 23.3(2) USMCA.

[50] Art. 23.3(2) lit. c CETA; Art. 23.8 USMCA; ILO (2017), p. 15.

[51] Art. 23.5(1) lit. a CETA; Art. 23.5(2) USMCA.

[52] See e.g. Art. 23.5 CETA; Art. 19.8 CPTPP; Art. 23.10 USMCA.

recognizes the close interconnection between the right to strike and freedom of association[53] (whereas that interconnection has recently come under increasing pressure inside the ILO[54]). Moreover, bilaterally agreed standards can step in insofar as a PTA party has not ratified the relevant international instruments.[55]

On the other hand, given the available alternative of incorporating already existing international standards, the parties' choice to define their own bilateral standards bears the risk of relaxing, relativizing and even delegitimizing both the existing international standards and those institutions dealing with them, notably the ILO. A classic example in this regard is the inclusion of a canon of 'internationally recognized workers' rights' in lieu of references to the fundamental ILO conventions.[56] Recent PTAs contain further bilateral standards with an unclear relationship to their ILO counterparts. One example is Article 23.9 USMCA, concerning the implementation of policies against gender-based discrimination at the workplace.[57] While the provision contains some progressive language, no other grounds of discrimination are mentioned, such as race, colour, religion, political opinion or national origin. All of these other grounds already appear in the definition of discrimination under Article 1(1) lit. a ILO Convention No. 111 of 1958; one of the ILO's fundamental labour conventions.[58]

Eventually, what impact bilaterally agreed standards will have, and whether they will reinforce or compete with international standards, will crucially depend on their interpretation and application by the parties, in particular on the parties' readiness to align these standards to ILO instruments and practice.

3.1.5   Interim Conclusion

The analysis of contemporary trade-labour linkages has revealed a set of established clauses, complemented by some progressive elements. In some instances, there is a certain untested potential for conflict with the pertinent WTO rules on PTAs.[59]

---

[53] Art. 23.3 USMCA.

[54] On the employers' group's interventions and the ILO's post-2012 constitutional crisis, in which the question of the right to strike being an intrinsic corollary of freedom of association played a central role, see Maupain (2013b); La Hovary (2018), pp. 44 ff.

[55] For instance, Art. 23.7 USMCA explicitly obliges the parties to address cases of violence, threats or intimidation against workers. That governments are required to do so is laid down in ILO Conventions No. 87 and 98 and established in the practice of the ILO's supervisory bodies, see ILO (2006), paras. 44–60. However, the two ILO conventions have not been ratified by the USA.

[56] E.g. Art. 16.8 CAFTA-DR; Art. 23.1 USMCA; Alston (2004), pp. 499 ff.

[57] The formulations are rather weak, requiring each party to implement such policies it considers appropriate, and explicitly stating in a footnote that the USA does not have to take further action.

[58] In fact, a clarifying footnote even explicitly states that no amendments to Title VII of the US Civil Rights Act 1964 on equal employment opportunities are required.

[59] That being said, the emergence of PTA labour provisions has so far not been challenged within the WTO.

Above and all, however, while the examined clauses are legally binding, almost all of them leave considerable leeway for interpretation and application. Telling from their wording, many labour provisions have considerable potential for protecting and promoting labour standards in the PTA parties. Moreover, these provisions can become relevant aspects to take into account when interpreting a PTA's other provisions, leading e.g. to a 'labour-friendly' understanding of trade liberalization obligations or exception clauses.[60] That being said, whether this potential can be fully exploited will crucially depend on how these provisions will be interpreted and applied in practice.

3.2 Mechanisms for Implementation and Enforcement: Recurring Structural Insufficiencies

As the impact of labour provisions decisively depends on how they are interpreted and implemented in practice, it is necessary to turn to the principal modes (Sect. 3.2.1) and the institutional mechanisms (Sect. 3.2.2) for implementation and enforcement contained in contemporary PTAs' labour provisions.

3.2.1 The Principal Modes of Implementation

PTAs envisage several modes of implementation and enforcement. Some PTAs contain so-called ex ante conditionalities, i.e. they provide that the PTA will only enter into force once a party has fulfilled certain specified labour obligations. Ex ante conditionality uses the leverage created by the prospect of preferential treatment for trade and investment and has been among the most effective parts of PTAs' labour provisions.[61] On the other hand, they are a one-off tool that invariably do not cover issues the parties have not foreseen or could not settle during the negotiations.

Post-entry into force, three further modes can be distinguished:

The first modus is separate implementation by each party through their respective domestic organs and procedures.

The second is implementation through bilateral cooperative activities. PTAs usually foresee long catalogues of possible subject-matters or modes of bilateral cooperation.[62] Some PTAs further envisage bilateral technical assistance or capacity building.[63] A growing number of agreements also envisages (both joint and separate) monitoring and impact assessments.[64] This can broadly be circumscribed as a

---

[60]On this see e.g. VanDuzer (2016), pp. 147 ff.; Gött and Holterhus (2018), p. 242.

[61]Ebert (2017), pp. 310 f.; ILO, IILS (2013), pp. 38 ff.

[62]E.g. Art. 23.7 CETA.

[63]E.g. Art. 16.5 CAFTA-DR.

[64]Art. 16.11 EUJEPA.

'political' or administrative working method, in which common labour-related objectives are promoted either on a project basis or through cooperation at a more structural or systemic level.

The third way of implementation is dispute settlement, which comes to play retrospectively when a party fails to meet its obligations. Labour provisions typically contain special mechanisms for dispute settlement. As to their structure, these dispute settlement mechanisms vary considerably. Under some PTAs, dispute settlement takes place exclusively through intergovernmental consultations.[65] However, many PTAs define further stages, such as the insertion of an independent panel of experts[66] or inter-state arbitration.[67] Especially in those later stages, dispute settlement resembles a rather 'legal' working method, with a focus on alleged breaches of obligations and procedures, being highly formalized and of a quasi-adjudicatory nature.

3.2.2   Institutional Mechanisms

Contemporary PTAs typically establish two complementary institutional mechanisms for post-entry into force implementation. Firstly, they create an overarching committee structure and mechanisms for civil society participation. Secondly, they also establish special mechanisms for dispute settlement between the parties.

Committee Structure and Civil Society Participation

Most contemporary PTAs use an administrative framework in the form of a committee structure.[68] The committee structure usually has at least two levels. On the highest level, a main committee supervises the implementation of the entire agreement.[69] The main committee usually meets at ministerial level[70] and may inter alia adopt binding interpretations[71] or address the issue of treaty amendments.[72] The main committee is served by a number of topic- or chapter-specific subcommittees,

---

[65]E.g. under a range of Chilean FTAs, ILO (2017), p. 52. See also Art. 6(1) Hong Kong-EFTA Agreement on Labour.

[66]This has been the means of choice in recent EU agreements, see. e.g. Art. 23.10 CETA; Art. 16.18 EUJEPA.

[67]In particular in US and Canadian Agreements, Abel (2018a), pp. 153 ff.

[68]PTAs usually allow for a dynamic evolution of the committee structure. Main committees can create new (or dissolve existing) subcommittees and may modify the allocation of tasks. Furthermore, each (sub)committee retains wide discretion as to its own procedure.

[69]E.g. the Trans-Pacific Partnership Commission' (Art. 27.1 CPTPP), the CETA Joint Committee (Art. 26.1 CETA) or the Free Trade Commission (Art. 30.1 USMCA).

[70]Art. 22.1(3) EUJEPA.

[71]Art. 26.1 (5) (e) CETA; Art. 9.24 (3) CPTPP; Art. 23.14 USMCA.

[72]Art. 27.2(2) lit. c CPTPP; Art. 30.2(2) CETA.

including on different aspects of trade, investment, and labour or, in the case of EU agreements, on trade and sustainable development, including environmental and labour issues.[73] These subcommittees supervise the implementation and administration of the agreement within their respective scope of work. They can inter alia facilitate cooperation, evaluate provisions and their functioning, take a role in the settlement of disputes, or propose decisions to be taken by the main committee.[74]

Apart from these intergovernmental committees, a growing number of PTAs also contains institutionalized mechanisms for civil society participation. For instance, EU PTAs require each party to establish a Domestic Advisory Group (DAG) and to convene a bilateral annual Civil Society Forum.[75] Both the DAGs and the Forum are composed of trade union federations, business organizations, NGOs and other stakeholders "in a balanced and representative manner".[76] While the precise purpose of civil society participation remains somewhat ambiguous,[77] their main function in practice is to raise issues of interest or concern, facilitate civil society deliberation and provide views to the governmental committees and to the parties themselves.

The intergovernmental committees and the civil society participation mechanisms form a coherent institutional structure in which political, administrative or legal aspects of the trade-labour and investment-labour linkages can be dealt with.

Inter-State Dispute Settlement

PTAs contain dedicated mechanisms for dispute settlement between the parties. These special mechanisms preclude either party from reacting to treaty violations by taking measures foreseen under general international law, such as suspension or termination of the PTA (or some of its provisions) as a reaction to a material breach (Art. 60 VCLT) or countermeasures under the law of state responsibility. Some PTAs' labour provisions even explicitly provide that their dispute settlement mechanisms are exhaustive.[78]

Broadly speaking, three stages of dispute settlement can be distinguished:

On the first stage, each party can request bilateral intergovernmental consultations to settle the dispute.[79] Some agreements foresee as an additional step that the parties bring the matter before the agreement's main committee should bilateral consultations fail.[80]

---

[73]Art. 19.12 CPTPP; Arts. 22.4 and Art. 26.2.1 (g) CETA.

[74]Art. 26.2 CETA; Art. 27.2 (2) (a) CPTPP.

[75]E.g. Arts. 22.4 and Art. 23.8(3) CETA. For a non-EU example, see Art. 19.14(2) CPTPP.

[76]Art. 22.5(2) CETA.

[77]Orbie et al. (2018), pp. 135 ff.

[78]E.g. Art. 23.11(1) CETA.

[79]E.g. Art. 19.15 CPTPP.

[80]Art. 23.17(8) USMCA.

If the matter cannot be settled through consultations, each party can, on a second stage, bring it before an independent body for examination of the alleged violations. In US and Canadian agreements, this body is usually an arbitral tribunal, established either under the PTA's general rules or under special rules contained in the labour provisions, depending on the PTA at hand.[81] EU agreements foresee a panel of experts the establishment of which is specifically provided for in the pertinent labour- or sustainable development chapters.[82] In both cases, the body is made of independent and impartial experts on labour law and policy nominated by the parties. The body renders an interim and a definitive report indicating violations of labour provisions and may, under a range of PTAs, make recommendations on how to improve the situation or suggest a plan of action.[83]

On the third stage, cases of persistent non-compliance can be brought back before the independent body. Under some (mostly US and Canadian) agreements, the body may permit the temporary suspension of trade benefits ('trade sanctions') or order the payment of fines as an *ultima ratio* to enforce compliance.[84] Other (most prominently European) agreements foresee that cases of non-compliance be settled through further consultations instead.[85]

3.2.3 Structural Insufficiencies

Having examined the envisaged modes and institutional mechanisms for implementation and enforcement under contemporary PTAs, the question remains whether these mechanisms ensure a reasonably effective implementation of PTAs' labour provisions.

As to contemporary PTAs themselves, it is too early to make definitive findings. What can be done, however, is to assess the latest-generation labour provisions in the light of lessons learned from earlier agreements. In practice, labour provisions in new PTAs are heavily influenced by their predecessors in earlier agreements and by chapter templates used by major economies during the negotiations.

Responding to articulated needs and criticisms, many economies have incrementally developed and modified their labour provisions in order to make them more effective and more acceptable to stakeholders. However, reforms and modifications of labour provisions have usually addressed relatively confined issues of particular clauses or topics. By contrast, the main structural features of labour provisions have, for better or worse, largely remained the same over time. One consequence of this is that structural insufficiencies of early PTA labour provisions have 'survived' and now resurface in later agreements.

---

[81] See. e.g. Art. 19.15(12) CPTPP; Abel (2018a).
[82] E.g. Art. 23.10 CETA; Art. 16.18 EUJEPA.
[83] Art. 23.10(11) CETA.
[84] Abel (2018b), pp. 174 ff.
[85] E.g. Art. 16.8(6) EUJEPA.

While an exhaustive survey of such insufficiencies would exceed the limits of this chapter, two interrelated issues provide a lucid example: The central role of the parties' governments in the implementation and enforcement of labour provisions, and the resulting non-alignment of procedural means and genuine interest in implementation.

Governments' Central Role and the Problem of 'Over-Politicization'

As can be seen inter alia from PTAs' intergovernmental committees and the existence of inter-state dispute settlement mechanisms, implementation and enforcement of labour provisions is mostly designed as a government-driven process. The consequence of this design is that labour provisions' implementation and enforcement crucially depends on the will and capability of the parties. This has had a decisive impact on the performance of both cooperative implementation and dispute settlement.

As to cooperative activities, governments have initiated a range of initiatives under various agreements. Yet, whether and to what extent they did was heavily contingent on their respective political agendas and preferences, and how the latter could (or could not) be reconciled with those of the other party. Further relevant factors were the parties' internal allocation of competences between different departments[86] and the availability of sufficient resources.[87] Many activities occurred on a comparatively low scale, concerned only very specific or one-time engagements and often lacked a systematic plan or the necessary political or financial backing.[88]

The decisive importance of governments' preferences and ability is most visible in labour provisions' dispute settlement provisions. By their design, only governments can activate PTA labour dispute settlement procedures, and only governments can decide to carry a case further to one of the subsequent stages, e.g. to arbitration or before a panel of experts.[89] To a limited extent, governments have made use of this discretion.[90] In the overwhelming majority of cases, however, governments either refused to trigger dispute settlement mechanisms altogether or settled the case amicably on the first (consultation) stage.[91] The *US-Guatemala* arbitration was the only case so far in which a government chose to proceed to the second stage of dispute settlement.[92] The third (enforcement) stage, which under some agreements

---

[86]Harrison et al. (2018), pp. 9 f.

[87]Compa (2001), pp. 147 ff.; Finbow (2006), p. 232; Bolle (2016), pp. 5 f.

[88]ILO, IILS (2013), pp. 79 ff.

[89]Abel (2018b), p. 166; Gött (2018), p. 196.

[90]For example, the USA have initiated dispute settlement in some cases arising under the NAALC, the CAFTA-DR, the US-Bahrain FTA and others, Congressional Research Service (2018), p. 2; ILO (2016), pp. 44 f.

[91]Dombois et al. (2004); ILO, IILS (2013), pp. 84 ff.; Abel (2018a).

[92]Brooks (2018), p. 45.

can include the suspension of trade benefits, has never been launched under any PTA.

The crucial issue with this government-centred design is that governments are almost inevitably in a position in which they have to serve and reconcile many (and often contrary) interests at the same time. Firstly, they have to serve the interests of both 'their' workers and employers, which can be different from (and even conflict with) those of workers and employers in the other party. Secondly, governments are entangled in complex diplomatic relations with the other party, which they have an incentive to preserve and promote. And thirdly, they must be aware that any measure of enforcement they take against a non-compliant other party may result in that other party 'firing back' at a later point in time. As several studies conducted under earlier PTAs have indicated, this intricate interdependence resulted in an 'over-politicization' of dispute settlement. This over-politicization posed a strong incentive for governments not to take implementation measures at all (in particular measures of enforcement), or to find a *modus vivendi* with the other party on a 'common lowest denominator'.[93]

Under earlier agreements, governments' central role, combined with their manifold ties and constraints, can be seen as a major source for labour provisions' low performance rates. The issue is not that disputes over non-compliance were politically contentious as such. Rather, the problem lies in the parties' constraining the procedure based on considerations that were unrelated to the question of a possible breach of obligations in a given case.[94]

Non-alignment Between Interest and Capacities: The Sidelining of Stakeholders and 'Disappointment Trap'

By contrast, those actors with a genuine and 'unrestrained' interest in the implementation and enforcement of labour provisions are largely sidelined. This applies notably to trade unions and NGOs, but also to employers and their associations.[95]

In practice, non-governmental actors have played a decisive role in the implementation and enforcement of labour provisions. Insofar as parties undertook cooperative activities, they have involved non-governmental stakeholders, e.g. in periodic reviews and impact assessments.[96] The key role of non-governmental actors is even more visible in dispute settlement. In virtually all cases in which labour dispute settlement mechanisms were activated, non-governmental actors had proactively identified cases, gathered evidence, prepared submissions and brought them to

---

[93]Dombois et al. (2004), p. 293; Dombois (2006), p. 246.

[94]Dombois et al. (2004), p. 293; Dombois (2006), p. 246; Nolan Garcia (2009), p. 189; Greven (2012), p. 88; ILO, IILS (2013), p. 49.

[95]Under earlier PTAs, labour-related submissions have been made by all three groups, see Greven (2012), p. 89; ILO, IILS (2013), pp. 43 ff.

[96]ILO (2016), pp. 125 ff.

the attention of governments. They also supported pending cases with advocacy campaigns and followed up on submissions, which had a traceable impact on how the respective cases were perceived by governments.[97] Reversely, there are no reports of governments initiating dispute settlement procedures without being urged to do so by non-governmental actors.

Yet, both cooperative mechanisms and labour provisions' dispute settlement mechanisms are designed and applied in a manner putting non-governmental stakeholders in the position of mere petitioners. In cooperative activities, they may provide views and present matters to the parties, including through PTAs' domestic and bilateral civil society participation mechanisms, but there is hardly any mandatory follow-up. In cases of alleged violations of obligations, non-governmental actors may approach the parties with grievances and urge them to take action, but they have no procedural capacities on their own to initiate dispute settlement and to submit a case to independent examination, let alone enforcement.[98]

This sidelining of non-governmental actors has had a traceable impact on the performance of labour provisions. In a range of cases, grievances brought to the attention of governments were not followed up upon at all or only with significant delay.[99] In cases in which alleged violations were taken on by the parties, the subsequent dispute settlement procedure moved on a markedly slow pace, delaying the solution of a case for years.[100] In other cases, governments diverted or 'diluted' the initial submissions by altering the focus of enquiry or settling the dispute without addressing problems that the petitioners had brought forward.

Empirical studies suggest that the described treatment of cases by the parties led to perceptions that grievances were 'whitewashed' and issues were not taken seriously. This in turn resulted in non-governmental actors being discouraged to further engage in the implementation of labour provisions. This situation has aptly been referred to as a "disappointment trap",[101] which, given non-governmental actors' central factual role, contributed significantly to labour provisions' low performance rates.

3.2.4 Persistence of Structural Insufficiencies in Contemporary PTAs

Despite the continuous evolution of labour provisions, and despite the fact that recent major PTAs contain a range of innovative clauses, the aforesaid potentially insufficient structural features resurface in all latest-generation labour provisions.

---

[97]Gött (2018), pp. 189 f.

[98]Gött (2018), pp. 190 f.

[99]ILO, IILS (2013), p. 45.

[100]For instance, the US-Guatemala case took a total of 9 years, for an overview see ILO (2016), pp. 45 ff.

[101]Dombois et al. (2004), p. 267.

At the outset, it is worth noting that there have been certain improvements to implementation mechanisms under some recent agreements. For example, under the CPTPP and the USMCA, the public may make submissions which governments have to consider and respond to in a timely manner.[102] Moreover, the parties shall invite the views of unions, employers' associations and other stakeholders on potential areas of cooperation, and shall, where appropriate, provide for their participation.[103] Likewise, under the latest EU agreements, the parties have to administer and implement labour provisions in a transparent manner and provide opportunities for civil society participatory mechanisms and the public to comment.[104] Domestic Advisory Groups have the explicit right to meet on their own initiative and express their opinions independently and to submit those opinions to the parties.[105] Still, these provisions merely enable non-governmental actors to make statements and submissions and, as far as obligations to react exist, prevent them from being entirely ignored. By contrast, contemporary clauses do not oblige the parties to follow up or take further action on any comments received.

The situation is comparable regarding dispute settlement. Irrespective of whether a PTA adopts the 'US approach' (i.e. a model involving suspensions of trade benefits as a means to enforcement) or the 'EU approach', non-governmental actors continue to be confined to the position of petitioners. In EU-PTA dispute settlement, non-governmental actors may petition the parties to commence consultations, they will be informed about the final report of a panel of experts, and may submit observation as to its follow-up.[106] In between these steps, they are excluded from the procedure. Unlike the parties, they may not comment on a panel's interim reports.[107] The CPTPP's and USMCA's rules are similar.[108]

It is too early to assess with certainty whether the recurrence of the aforesaid structural flaws will affect the performance of newer PTAs' labour provisions in the same way as they did in older agreements. However, first experiences suggest that similar issues may arise. For example, under the EU-Korea FTA, in which civil society participation is foreseen through Domestic Advisory Groups and a bilateral Civil Society Forum, it took the EU almost 5 years to initiate formal consultations with Korea, counting from the day the EU's Domestic Advisory Group first urged the European Commission to do so.[109]

---

[102] Art. 19.8 CPTPP; Art. 23.11 USMCA.

[103] Art. 19.10(3) CPTPP; Art. 23.12(4) USMCA. See also Art. 19.14(1) CPTPP.

[104] Art. 16.10 EUJEPA. See also Art. 16.16(4) EUJEPA.

[105] Art. 16.15(3) EUJEPA.

[106] Art. 16.18(6) EUJEPA.

[107] *E contrario* Art. 16.18(4) EUJEPA.

[108] The final report of the arbitral panel is made public, see e.g. Art. 28.18 CPTPP.

[109] ILO (2017), p. 73.

3.3   Conclusion

Contemporary PTAs' trade-labour linkages feature a variety of both established and innovative substantive clauses. Many of these provisions have potential to improve the protection and promotion of labour standards. Whether this potential can be tapped depends on how these clauses are interpreted and applied through the pertinent mechanisms for implementation and enforcement. However, as seen, these mechanisms perpetuate structural deficits that have already surfaced under earlier PTAs. While this article has not conducted a comprehensive survey of all such structural insufficiencies, the discussed issues of a government-driven implementation and a corresponding sidelining of actors with a genuine interest in implementation suggests that the persisting structural insufficiencies will continue to put a strain on labour provisions' performance.

4   Contemporary Investment-Labour Linkages

As mentioned in the introduction, PTAs' investment-labour linkages emerged mainly as a 'by-product' of trade-labour linkages. As a result, investment-labour linkages are mainly built on the same clauses, the scope of which has merely been expanded to also cover investment-related issues. Hence, much of what has been said in the previous section applies *mutatis mutandis* in the context of contemporary investment-labour linkages.

That being said, as discussed in more detail in this section, they can become relevant not only between the PTA parties, but also in the context of investor rights. Depending on the particular clause at hand, they can e.g. serve to limit these rights, or they can influence their interpretation. This, alongside some further important peculiarities of investment-labour linkages, will now be addressed in turn.

4.1   Substantive Elements

4.1.1   Preservation of Policy Space: Reaffirmations of the Right to Regulate

Some recent PTA investment chapters (as well as some new-generation BITs) reaffirm the parties' so-called right to regulate, i.e.

> their right to adopt within their territories regulatory measures necessary to achieve legitimate policy objectives, such as the protection of public health, safety, the environment or public morals, social or consumer protection or the promotion and protection of cultural diversity.[110]

---

[110]Art. 8.1(2) EUJEPA.

The main purpose of such clauses is to preserve policy space for the host state. Originally drafted with a view to limit investor protection, the scope of the pertinent clauses has been expanded in the latest agreements to also limit PTA provisions on investors' market access or even trade in services in general.[111]

The scope, effect and use of right to regulate clauses remains to be tested in practice. On the one side, the protection and promotion of labour standards will qualify as a "legitimate policy objective".[112] Hence, it is conceivable that right to regulate clauses will facilitate striking a just balance of interests in labour-related trade in services or investment disputes, for example as an aspect guiding the interpretation of investor rights.[113] On the other hand, it is questionable if right to regulate clauses as they stand at present are sufficiently equipped to achieve such a balance. The rather rudimentary language ("legitimate policy objectives") leaves ample discretion to the interpreter. Some PTAs seek to enhance clarity by providing additional language. For example, Art. 8.9(2) CETA stipulates that,

> (...) the mere fact that a Party regulates (...) in a manner which negatively affects an investment or interferes with an investor's expectations (...), does not amount to a breach of an [investor right].[114]

However, by focusing on "the mere fact" that a party regulates, the clarification appears to miss the mark altogether. Experience shows that the issue in investment disputes is almost never "the mere fact" that a state regulates in a manner affecting the investment. Rather, disputes mostly arise about more intricate issues, such as whether a measure was sufficiently transparent, predictable and proportionate or struck a proper balance of interests in a concrete case. Most right to regulate clauses do not address these other issues at all.[115]

Besides, a further aspect deserves mention: Many agreements also mention the right to regulate in another context, namely as a limitation to the parties' labour obligations under the PTA. In this context, right to regulate clauses emphasize the parties' right to determine their own labour-related objectives, strategies, policies and priorities, to define their own levels of domestic protection, and to adopt or change their labour laws and policies accordingly.[116] Again, the precise impact of such clauses remains somewhat diffuse. However, in any event, they show that

---

[111]E.g. Art. 8.1(2) EU-Vietnam-FTA; Art. 8.1(2) EUJEPA.

[112]Gött and Holterhus (2018), p. 243.

[113]See e.g. UNCITRAL, *Saluka Investments v. Czech Republic*, Partial Award, 17 March 2006, paras. 305–306.

[114]Compare the slightly stricter wording of Art. 14.16 USMCA.

[115]For a rare exception, Art. 20 SADC Model-BIT, after reaffirming host states' right to regulate, provides that "[e]xcept where the rights of a Host State are expressly stated as an exception to the obligations of this Agreement, a Host State's pursuit of its rights to regulate shall be understood as embodied within a balance of the rights and obligations of Investors and Investments and Host States, as set out in this Agreement."

[116]Art. 13.2(1) EU-Vietnam-FTA; Art. 16.2 EUJEPA. Such reaffirmations have a long tradition, see already Art. 2 NAALC.

reaffirming a *right* to regulate primarily strengthens the parties' sovereignty to do so, leaving it to the state concerned whether and how to use it with regard to labour issues.

4.1.2 NLS Clauses in the Context of Investment

In order to attract new foreign investors (or in order to incite them to stay in the country), states have repeatedly resorted to waivers or derogations from their labour laws. Therefore, the abovementioned NLS clauses are of particular relevance in the investment context.

It has already been observed above that these clauses use markedly broad and ambiguous language that may substantially weaken their grip, depending on how they will be interpreted and applied. Besides, a further aspect becomes highly relevant in the context of investment: The obligation "not to waive or derogate" does not prohibit to *freeze* labour laws and standards on the level existing at a point in time. Therefore, a state remains entitled to promise not to increase its standards. Such a promise can e.g. be included in a so-called stabilization contract between a foreign investor and the host state, i.e. an agreement aiming at protecting the investor against regulatory changes that may have adverse effects on the investment. For a practical example, in *Veolia v. Egypt*, the investor reportedly invoked a stabilization contract to challenge a subsequent increase of statutory minimum wages by Egypt.[117] Freezing labour standards in this way would not violate an NLS clause and would only amount to a breach of the PTA insofar as it would violate the host state's obligation to achieve and maintain international labour standards or bilaterally agreed labour standards.

4.1.3 Regulation of Investor Conduct

Some contemporary PTAs go further and seek to ensure that not only the host state, but also the investors themselves comply with certain standards of protection. In this vein, recent PTAs focus on the promotion of codes of conduct and Corporate Social Responsibility (CSR), often in rather short provisions. In this manner, Article 19.7 CPTPP provides that:

---

[117]ICSID, *Veolia Propreté v. Egypt*, ICSID Case No. ARB/12/15, 25 Jun 2012, Zimmer (2018), p. 225. In *Goetz v. Burundi*, the investor brought a case because the host state repealed a prior derogation of its labour laws that had attracted the investor, ICSID, Antoine Goetz et al. v. Burundi, ICSID Case No. ARB/95/3, 10 Feb 1999. In *Paushok v. Mongolia*, the tribunal dismissed the investor's challenge against changes of labour regulation but indicated that the decision could have been different had the parties concluded a stabilization agreement, UNCITRAL, Sergei Paushok, CJSC Golden East Company and CJSC Vostokneftegaz Company v. Mongolia, Award on Jurisdiction and Liability, 28 Apr 2011, para. 370.

[e]ach Party shall endeavour to encourage enterprises to voluntarily adopt corporate social responsibility initiatives on labour issues that have been endorsed or are supported by that Party.

Some PTAs also reference existing CSR instruments, such as the OECD Guidelines for Multinational Enterprises or the ILO Tripartite Declaration of Principles concerning Multinational Enterprises and Social Policy.[118]

It has to be noted that, by addressing the host states rather than the investors themselves, the relevant clauses target investor conduct only indirectly. To be sure, creating international investor obligations that are directly enforceable by the host state through international investment arbitration, as sometimes demanded in public debate, is not necessarily a more promising alternative.[119] However, there are already existing examples in other BITs and BIT templates of more nuanced mechanisms to regulate investor conduct, e.g. by making the investor's adherence to certain standards a condition for access to investor-state arbitration,[120] or by allowing for reductions or off-setting of damages in case of misconduct.[121] The recent major PTAs fall short of such more innovative mechanisms.

Moreover, the respective clauses largely contain hortatory language: For example, under the CPTPP, the parties owe efforts to "endeavour to encourage"[122] the use of CSR schemes, but are not obliged to ensure in any way investors' (or other enterprises') conduct.[123] This does not prevent the parties from adopting a broad variety of measures that encourage (or even oblige) foreign investors to observe CSR schemes, e.g. in investment contracts or in applicable domestic civil or administrative law.[124] However, how and to what extent they do is placed at their discretion.

4.1.4 Conflict Rules Subordinating the Investment Chapter

Article 14.3(1) USMCA contains an explicit conflict rule subordinating its investment chapter to other parts of the agreement. It provides that

[i]n the event of any inconsistency between [the investment chapter] and another Chapter of this Agreement, the other Chapter shall prevail to the extent of the inconsistency.

---

[118]Art. 22.3(2) lit. b CETA; Art. 16.5 lit. e EUJEPA.

[119]Critical e.g. Abel (2018a).

[120]Art. 18(1) ECOWAS Supplementary Act on Investment.

[121]E.g. Art. 23 Dutch Model-BIT (regarding compliance with the 2011 UN Guiding Principles on Business and Human Rights and the OECD Guidelines for Multinational Enterprises); Art. 43(1) 2016 Draft Pan-African Investment Code. The 2016 Draft Pan-African Investment Code foresees a range of investor obligations, including on labour issues, e.g. in Arts. 19 et seqq. and Art. 34.

[122]Art. 19.7 CPTPP.

[123]A prominent (albeit rather unique) exception is Art. 72 EU-CARIFORUM, which obliges the parties to ensure that investors act in accordance with core labour standards.

[124]Gött and Holterhus (2018), p. 256.

Given its broad wording, the clause also applies to the USMCA's labour chapter. In principle, it could serve as a normative basis for interpreting investor rights in a 'labour-friendly' manner, to the effect that investors cannot claim compensation for adverse effects of the host state's labour regulations on its investment. That being said, the clause presupposes a reasonably clear understanding of the pertinent labour provisions. However, as seen above, many of these clauses leave ample leeway for interpretation in one or the other direction. Against this background, an actual "inconsistency" between the investment chapter and labour provisions is likely to be a rather rare phenomenon.

4.1.5 Interim Conclusion

Examination of investment-labour linkages in contemporary PTAs reveals that some important issues are left unaddressed, such as the question of freezing standards of protection via stabilization contracts. However, the foremost observation is, again, that the relevant clauses are open-worded and leave considerable latitude for inter-pretation and implementation in one or the other way. Depending on how they are understood, they could have a traceable impact on investment protection under the examined agreements. For instance, they could guide the interpretation of central contentious investment law terms—such as 'fair and equitable treatment', 'indirect expropriation' or 'legitimate expectation'—in a 'labour-friendly' way.[125] That being said, if this will happen crucially depends on how and by whom the pertinent clauses are interpreted and applied. Again, it is therefore warranted to examine the modes and mechanisms for implementation of investment-labour linkages.

4.2 Mechanisms for Implementation and Enforcement

Investment-labour linkages in contemporary PTAs largely employ the same modes and institutional mechanisms for implementation and enforcement as trade-labour linkages. Thus, in principle, investment-labour linkages can be applied and enforced through any of the aforesaid means, e.g. through cooperation in the committees, or via inter-state dispute settlement.

Nonetheless, some aspects deserve mention. Firstly, as far as investment-labour linkages are concerned, the existence of an overarching committee structure is in many respects an innovation. Traditional BITs usually do not foresee political or administrative committees. This correlates with the self-perception of international investment law as a means to de-politicize investment disputes.[126] The committee structure, aiming at enabling interaction on administrative or political questions,

---

[125]Gött and Holterhus (2018), pp. 248 ff.

[126]Shihata (1986), p. 4.

holds the latent potential to 're-politicize' investment law within an ordered bilateral institutional framework.[127]

Secondly, apart from dedicated labour dispute settlement mechanisms, it is conceivable that labour clauses will be indirectly enforced through investor-state dispute settlement. For this to happen, an investor must bring an arbitration against the host state, claiming that the latter has violated applicable labour provisions under the PTA. Practice in this respect is scarce, but not entirely absent. For instance, in *UPS v Canada*, the investor argued that a derogation from labour regulations in violation of the NAALC amounted to discriminatory treatment, because the derogation only benefited one of its competitors.[128] Those cases, however, are clearly exceptional. A central hurdle will be to establish that the investor has *locus standi*, i.e. the investor has to show why it can bring a claim based on a specific labour provision. Cases at hand may be e.g. certain labour standards protecting the interests of employers.

4.3 Similar Structural Insufficiencies and the Risk of Underperformance

Again, the question remains whether these mechanisms for implementation and enforcement are suitable for tapping the potential of the substantive clauses of investment-labour linkages. Comprehensive empirical research on investment-labour linkages is not yet available. Still, it is worth noting that there is a structurally similar situation as in the case of trade-labour linkages. There as here, there is a non-alignment of interest and procedural capacities to enforce investment-labour linkages.

As far as cooperation on investment and labour topics is concerned, the process is again government-driven and facilitated through direct intergovernmental contacts or the PTA's governmental committees, confining non-governmental actors the role of petitioners and commentators.

Investor-state dispute settlement, for its part, can exclusively be initiated by the investor against the host state. Whether and to what extent labour issues will be addressed thus depends first and foremost on the will and capacity of these actors. It is for the investor to determine the scope of the arbitration by tailoring its claims, and it is for the host state to decide whether to raise labour provisions as a defense or not. By contrast, other actors that have a genuine interest in implementing and enforcing investment-labour linkages, notably trade unions, NGOs (but potentially also domestic employers), will only be heard if they apply to be admitted as a third party or as *amici curiae*. To be sure, this is not to say that these other actors would be left entirely without voice. *Amicus curiae* submissions have been admitted in past

---

[127]Gött and Holterhus (2018), p. 260.

[128]ICSID, *United Parcel Service of America Inc. v. Canada*, ICSID Case No. UNCT/02/1.

labour-related arbitral practice,[129] and are explicitly envisaged under contemporary PTAs.[130] What is more, as seen, investors themselves have occasionally attempted to demand the proper implementation of labour provisions. However, structurally, other non-governmental actors remain sidelined. *Amicus curiae* submissions, even insofar as they are admitted, can be restricted and must not be considered by an arbitral tribunal.[131] In any event, investor-state dispute settlement does not provide any means for other non-governmental actors to proactively push for the implementation and enforcement of investment-labour linkages.

In consequence, there is a structural risk that the newly emerging investment-labour linkages will fall into the same 'disappointment trap' as their trade counterparts, leading to similarly low performances.

4.4   Conclusion

The findings with regard to contemporary investment-labour linkages are broadly similar to those concerning their trade counterparts. The pertinent substantive clauses leave ample leeway for interpreting and applying them in several directions. As to the mechanisms for implementation and enforcement, the structural issue of sidelining actors with a genuine interest in implementing labour provisions resurfaces, with key procedural capacities being concentrated in the hand of the parties' governments or, insofar as ISDS is concerned, of investors.

5   Towards a Systematic and Structural Revision of PTA Labour Provisions

As the preceding analysis has shown, a structural problem of contemporary labour provisions lies in the fact that they largely depend on the will and the capacity of actors to exhaust their potential, while placing pertinent mechanisms for implementation and enforcement in the 'wrong' hands. This leaves us with the question how the situation could be improved.

One option would be to create specific rules guiding the conclusion and interpretation of PTAs. For instance, the 2018 Zero Draft of a Legally Binding Instrument to Regulate, in International Human Rights Law, the Activities of Transnational Corporations and Other Business Enterprises provides that future trade or investment

---

[129]ICSID, *United Parcel Service of America v. Canada*, Decision on Petitions for Intervention and Participation as Amici Curiae, 17 Oct 2001, para. 73; ICSID, *Foresti et al. v. South Africa*, ICSID Case No. ARB(AF)/07/01, 5 Oct 2009.

[130]E.g. Art. 9.23(3) CPTPP; Art. 3-8(6) EU-Vietnam Investment Protection Agreement.

[131]See Art. 9.23(3) CPTPP.

agreements shall not contain provisions that would "conflict with the implementation" of the Draft.[132] Moreover, the Draft provides that

> existing and future trade and investment agreements shall be interpreted in a way that is least
> restrictive on their ability to respect and ensure their obligations under [the Draft], notwith-
> standing other conflicting rules of conflict resolution arising from customary international
> law or from existing trade and investment agreements.[133]

Despite the somewhat cumbersome wording, it is conceivable that such provisions—if eventually adopted—may reinforce the interpretation and implementation of PTA labour provisions in the future.[134] That being said, they pose questions
of interpretation of their own, and would in any event require separate ratification by
a PTA's parties.

A second option would be to specify the PTA's relevant substantive clauses.
More elaborate clauses may help to clarify the meaning and scope of PTAs' labour
provisions. Indeed, there have been a number of proposals as to how substantive
labour provisions could be amended or complemented,[135] and recent PTAs (as well
as published negotiating texts) show that states are increasingly willing to include
language going beyond core labour standards. However, more elaborate clauses also
tend to be more difficult to negotiate. Furthermore, it is likely that clauses still would
have to be modified at a later point to react to unforeseen future developments.
Against this background, keeping provisions' language open might even preserve
the necessary flexibility in certain cases.

Thus, in order to make better use of substantive labour clauses' potential, future
drafts will have to reconsider the mechanisms for implementation and enforcement.
A key challenge will be to achieve a better alignment between actors' interests and
procedural capacities. There is increasingly common ground that the procedural
rights of such actors, notably the right to initiate review procedures, must be
strengthened, although there remain differences about how insight should be translated into concrete treaty provisions. Some commentators have proposed to create
domestic procedures pursuant to which interested actors could force the PTA parties
to activate the PTA's labour-related dispute settlement mechanisms.[136] However,
this would arguably not sufficiently remedy the structural insufficiencies described
above. Petitioners could compel the government to react, but would subsequently
still remain bystanders, while governments would retain their current discretion to
delay the matter or settle the case on a diplomatic compromise. The issue of over-
politicization persists, and it may be asked if can be gained if governments that
refuse to address a case voluntarily are 'carried to the hunt'. Such structural problems

---

[132] Art. 13(6) Zero Draft.

[133] Art. 13(7) Zero Draft.

[134] Arguably, they would constitute an interpretation agreement in the sense of Art. 31(3) lit.
a VCLT.

[135] E.g. Harrison et al. (2018); Bronckers and Gruni (2018), pp. 4 ff.; Stoll et al. (2018).

[136] E.g. Bronckers and Gruni (2018), pp. 4 ff., who propose amending the EU's Trade Barrier
Regulation accordingly.

would be avoided by another proposal that is currently being discussed, namely to create a collective complaint procedure open to trade unions, employers and NGOs.[137] Such a procedure would ensure immediate access of these groups to an independent examination of alleged labour law violations, leading up to a binding declaration of non-compliance as well as, instead of 'trade sanctions', the possibility of compensation.

The task, though, is not 'just' to come up with creative innovations. Another major challenge will be to achieve a common understanding and acknowledgement of the fact that many insufficiencies are deeply rooted in the structure of PTAs' labour provisions, an insight that is still frequently missed in reform debates. For instance, in a 2017 non-paper forming the basis of public consultations on how to improve sustainable development chapters in EU PTAs, the European Commission essentially presented the way forward as a binary choice between the current 'EU approach' and the inclusion of 'trade sanctions' as provided for in the 'US approach'.[138] Given the underlying structural insufficiencies of both approaches, the choice presented by the Commission misframed the debate from the start. As was rightly emphasized in many responses the Commission received, there is a need for a 'third option' that, instead of picking approaches, examines and evaluates the root causes for underperformance in a systematic and comprehensive manner.[139]

But even insofar as a common understanding of the nature of the pertinent issues can be reached, a further challenge will lie in calling into question highly path-dependent conceptions on how the implementation and enforcement of a PTA and its different provisions should work. Government-driven implementation has been the traditional choice of means in international trade law, and bipolar investor-state dispute settlement (to the exclusion of other actors) has been the traditional implementation mechanism of international investment law. This trade/investment 'heritage' echoes in the abovementioned implementation mechanisms for PTA labour provisions. What is more, the strong orientation of new PTAs towards earlier ones has resulted in a considerable degree of continuity, resilience and longevity of substantive, procedural and institutional choices that were made in early PTAs' labour provisions. Accordingly, any attempt to overcome the aforesaid structural insufficiencies in order to achieve a better alignment of actors' interests and the necessary procedural capacities will have to surmount fundamental and well-established features of PTA labour provisions.[140]

---

[137]Gött (2015b); AK Europa (2017), p. 10; Foundation for European Progressive Studies (2018), pp. 20 f.; Gött (2018), for a textual proposal see, Stoll et al. (2018). Outside the labour context, the idea has also been promoted by consumer associations, VZBV (2017), p. 9; VZBV (2019), p. 23.

[138]European Commission (2017) pp. 1 ff.

[139]Harrison et al. (2018), pp. 1 ff.; AK Europa (2017), pp. 2 ff.

[140]This will be particularly challenging regarding investment-labour linkages, given that enhancing the procedural capacity of other non-governmental actors would almost inevitably call into question the bipolar structure of investment protection and investor-state dispute settlement in order to enhance an 'enforcement balance' among different economic actors, Gött (2015a); Gött (2018), p. 181; see also Stoll et al. (2017), pp. 202 f.; Stoll (2018), pp. 289 f.

Notwithstanding these considerable intricacies, it is submitted that a systematic and structural revision of PTA labour provisions should be attempted. Firstly, even imperfect labour provisions will most likely accommodate the impact of PTAs on labour standards better than omitting labour provisions altogether. Secondly, carefully revised labour provisions can help to integrate 'their' PTAs into regional and international development agendas and also to (better) interlink them with the ILO. Finally, well-drafted labour provisions that appropriately tackle the social downsides of economic globalization can reinforce the case for rule-based international cooperation vis-à-vis the resurgent tide of power politics, nationalism and unilateralism. Recent paradigmatic events such as the Brexit referendum or Donald Trump's election as US President provide lucid examples of how globalization-related labour issues can successfully be instrumentalized for nationalist agendas. Against this background, it becomes all the more important that future global-minded trade and investment treaty projects step up their efforts to convince those who are not per se opposed to international economic cooperation, but have been critical of existing trade and investment agreements because they desire globalization to be socially fair (er). In order not to lose these societal groups to fundamentally anti-globalist opposition, trade and investment policies are well-advised to embrace more wholeheartedly the social dimension of economic globalization and to integrate a 'socially acceptable offer' into future PTAs. Of course, well-designed and implemented labour provisions can only be one element of such an effort, and labour provisions are obviously no panacea. Nevertheless, their relevance should not be underestimated, considering that PTAs are widely understood and promoted as setting the tone for the future development of the global economic order.

References

Abel P (2018a) Comparative conclusions on arbitral dispute settlement in trade-labour matters under US FTAs. In: Gött H (ed) Labour standards in international economic law. Springer, Cham, pp 153–184

Abel P (2018b) Counterclaims based on International Human Rights Obligations of Investors in International Investment Arbitration. Brill Open Law 1(1)

Addo K (2015) Core labour standards and international trade – lessons from the regional context. Springer, Berlin

AK Europa (2017) Non-paper of the Commission services on Trade and Sustainable Development (TSD) chapters in EU Free Trade Agreements. AK Europa, Brussels

Alston P (2004) 'Core Labour Standards' and the transformation of the international labour rights regime. Eur J Int Law 15:457–521

Blüthner A (2004) Welthandel und Menschenrechte in der Arbeit: the compatibility of human rights at work with the WTO-System. Lang

Bolle M (2016) Overview of labor enforcement issues in free trade agreements. Congressional Research Service, Washington D.C.

Bronckers M, Gruni G (2018) Improving the enforcement of labour standards in the EU's Free Trade Agreements. In: Prévost D, Alexovicova I, Pohl J (eds) Restoring trust in trade: Liber Amicorum in honour of Peter Van den Bosche. Hart

Brooks T (2018) U.S.-Guatemala Arbitration Panel clarifies effective enforcement under labor provisions of free trade agreement. Int Labor Rights Case Law 4(1):45–51

Compa L (2001) NAFTA's Labour Side Agreement and International Labour Solidarity. In: Waterman P, Wills J (eds) Place, space and the new labour internationalisms. Antipode, pp 147–163

Congressional Research Service (2018) NAFTA and the Preliminary U.S.-Mexico Agreement, Washington D.C.

Cottier T (2018) The implications of EC – Seal products for the protection of core labour standards in WTO law. In: Gött H (ed) Labour standards in international economic law. Springer, Cham, pp 69–92

Dombois R (2006) Sozialklauseln im US-Freihandelsabkommen: ein wirksames Mittel internationaler Arbeitsregulierung? Industrielle Beziehungen 13:238–252

Dombois R, Hornberger E, Winter J (2004) Internationale Arbeitsregulierung in der Souveränitätsfalle – Das Lehrstück des North American Agreement on Labor Cooperation zwischen den USA Mexiko und Kanada. LIT, Münster

Ebert FC (2017) The Comprehensive Economic Trade Agreement (CETA): are existing arrangements sufficient to prevent adverse effects on labour standards? Int J Comp Labour Law Ind Relat 33(2):295–330

Ebert FC, Posthuma A (2011) Labour provisions in trade arrangements: current trends and perspectives. IILS discussion paper series, ILO, Geneva

Ebert FC, Villarreal P (2018) The renegotiated 'NAFTA': what is in it for labour rights? EJIL: Talk! 11 October 2018

European Commission (2017) Trade and Sustainable Development (TSD) chapters in EU Free Trade Agreements (FTAs). European Commission, Brussels

Finbow R (2006) The limits of regionalism: NAFTA's labour accord. Ashgate, Aldershot

Foundation for European Progressive Studies (2018) Towards a progressive model for international trade and investment. FEPS, Brussels

Gordon K, Pohl J, Bouchard M (2014) Investment treaty law, sustainable development and responsible business conduct: a fact finding survey. OECD working papers on international investment, 2014/01. OECD, Paris

Gött H (2015a) TTIP-Rechtsschutz zu Ende denken. Verfassungsblog, 22 September 2015

Gött H (2015b) Individual labour complaint procedures in future free trade agreements? Völkerrechtsblog, 13 November 2015

Gött H (2018) An individual labour complaint procedure for workers, trade unions, employers and NGOs in future free trade agreements. In: Gött H (ed) Labour standards in international economic law. Springer, Cham, pp 185–209

Gött H, Holterhus TP (2018) Mainstreaming investment-labour linkage through 'Mega-Regional' trade agreements. In: Gött H (ed) Labour standards in international economic law. Springer, Cham, pp 233–271

Greven T (2012) Anforderungen an Legitimität und Effektivität von Sozialklauseln in Handelsverträgen. In: Scherrer C, Hänlein A (eds) Sozialkapitel in Handelsabkommen – Begründungen und Vorschläge aus juristischer, ökonomischer und politologischer Sicht. Nomos, Baden-Baden, pp 83–102

Hainbach P (2018) The CJEU's Opinion 2/15 and the future of EU Investment Policy and Law-Making. Issues Econ Integr 45(2):199–209

Harrison J, Barbu M, Campling L, Ebert F (2018) Labour standards provisions in EU free trade agreements: reflections on the European Commission's reform agenda. World Trade Rev 2018:1–23

Howse R (1999) The World Trade Organization and the protection of workers' rights. J Small Emerging Bus Law 3:131–172

ILO (2006) Digest of decisions and principles of the freedom of Association Committee of the Governing Body of the ILO, 5th edn. ILO, Geneva

ILO (2008) Declaration of social justice for a fair globalization. ILO, Geneva

ILO (2016) Assessment of labour provisions in trade and investment agreements. ILO, Geneva

ILO (2017) Handbook on assessment of labour provision in trade and investment arrangements. ILO, Geneva

ILO, IILS (2013) Social dimensions of free trade agreements. ILO, Geneva

Kamata I (2015) Labor clauses in regional trade agreements and effects on labor conditions: an empirical analysis. Kyoto University, Japan

Kaufmann C (2007) Globalization and labour rights. Hart, Oxford

La Hovary C (2018) The ILO's mandate and capacity: creating, proliferating and supervising labour standards for a globalized economy. In: Gött H (ed) Labour standards in international economic law. Springer, Cham, pp 38–56

Marx A, Soares J (2015) Does integrating labour provisions in free trade agreements make difference? An exploratory analysis of freedom of association and collective bargaining rights in 13 EU trade partners. In: Wouters J, Marx A, Dylan G, Nates B (eds) Global governance through trade – EU policies and approaches. Edward Elgar, Cheltenham, pp 158–185

Maupain F (2013a) The future of the International Labour Organization in the globalized economy. Oxford

Maupain F (2013b) The ILO regular supervisory system: a model in crisis? Int Organ Law Rev 10:117–165

Nolan Garcia K (2009) Transnational advocacy and labor rights conditionality in the international trading order. University of New Mexico, Albuquerque

Orbie J, Putte L, Martens D (2018) Civil society meetings in EU free trade agreements: the purposes unravelled. In: Gött H (ed) Labour standards in international economic law. Springer, Cham, pp 135–152

Read R (2005) Process and production methods and the regulation of international trade. In: Read R, Perdikis N (eds) The WTO and the regulation of international trade: recent trade disputes between the European Union and the United States. Edward Elgar, Cheltenham, pp 239–266

Shihata IFI (1986) Towards a greater depoliticization of investment disputes: the roles of ICSID and MIGA. Foreign Invest Law J/ICSID Rev 1:1–25

Stoll P-T (2018) International investment law and the rule of law. Goettingen J Int Law 9 (1):267–289

Stoll P, Holterhus TP, Gött H (2017) Investitionsschutz und Verfassung. Mohr Siebeck, Tübingen

Stoll P-T, Gött H, Abel P (2018) A model labour chapter for future EU trade agreements. Friedrich-Ebert-Stiftung, Bonn

Titievska J, Pietsch M (2018) United States-Mexico-Canada Agreement (USMCA): potential impact on EU companies. European Parliamentary Research Service, European Union

VanDuzer J (2016) Sustainable development provisions in international trade treaties: what lessons for international investment agreements? In: Krajewski M, Hindelang S (eds) Shifting paradigms in international investment law, pp 142–176

VZBV (2017) Implementing and enforcing consumer rights in trade agreements – position paper of the Federation of German Consumer Organisations (vzbv). Verbraucherzentrale Bundesverband e.V., Berlin

VZBV (2019) Europe, keep working for consumers! For strong consumer rights and a fair single market. Guidelines for the 2019 European elections – consumer policy guidelines of the Federation of German Consumer Organisations (Verbraucherzentrale Bundesverband – vzbv) for the legislative period from 2019 to 2024. Verbraucherzentrale Bundesverband e.V., Berlin

Zimmer R (2018) Implications of CETA and TTIP on social standards. In: Gött H (ed) Labour standards in international economic law. Springer, Cham, pp 211–231

Henner Gött   is a senior research fellow at the Jean Monnet Chair for European Union and Global Sustainable Development Through Law (Prof. Dr. Peter-Tobias Stoll), Institute of International Law, University of Göttingen, Germany. He is a fully trained German lawyer, completed clerkships at the German Federal Foreign Office (department for UN politics), the German Federal Constitutional Court and two international law firms, holds a law degree from the University of Münster, an LL.M. from the University of Cambridge (Queens' College) and a PhD in law from the University of Göttingen. Henner researches, publishes and teaches in international economic and labour law, international institutional law, and European and German constitutional law. He has also advised governmental institutions and non-governmental organizations on various questions of international and European law, particularly in the area of trade and investment agreements and the international protection and promotion of labour standards.

From International Framework Agreements to Transnational Collective Bargaining

Reingard Zimmer

Contents

1   Introduction

Traditionally, law and policy with regard to collective agreements have been the preserve of individual nation states, not least because of the extreme diversity in their systems of industrial relations. Neither at global level nor at the level of the European Union or elsewhere a legal framework for the conclusion of transnational collective agreements has been established. However, as is well known, due to liberalized

R. Zimmer (✉)
Berlin School of Economics and Law, Berlin, Germany
e-mail: reingard.zimmer@hwr-berlin.de

© Springer Nature Switzerland AG 2019   167
M. Bungenberg et al. (eds.), *European Yearbook of International Economic Law 2019*,
European Yearbook of International Economic Law (2020) 10: 167–192,
https://doi.org/10.1007/8165_2019_29, Published online: 17 October 2019

financial markets, lowered transport costs and the rise of modern communication methods, transnational companies transferred production sites or outsourced production towards areas, where labour is cheaper and standards are lower. The internationalization of business thus has not been held back by national boundaries. It is therefore nothing new that important company decisions are no longer necessarily taken in the country where the measures are to be implemented but in the company or group headquarters, quite possibly even on a different continent.[1] Consequently, more than 20 years ago, in the early 1990s, global trade union federations (GUFs) of specific sectors and transnational companies started to negotiate and sign global agreements. Today, numerous international framework agreements (IFAs)[2] with the aim to protect social standards[3] are in place whose scope goes beyond national boundaries. The agreements developed over time and new agreements on European level emerged, although those are structurally rather different from the ones on international level, as will be explained below. Meanwhile, the development may be described as the beginning of transnational collective bargaining, as elaborated below.

2 Development of International Framework Agreements

The first four agreements were concluded from 1988 on between the global union federation IUF/IUL and the French food company BSN (Danone). It took 10 years until a confederation from another sector followed the example: in 1998, the Building and Woodworkers' International (BWI) signed their first IFA with the furniture company IKEA on social standards. The first IFA with a German company was agreed upon 1999[4] between BWI and Faber Castell[5]; the first agreement in the chemical sector is dated 2000 (between ICEM and the German company Freudenberg).[6] UNI global union started with the conclusion of IFAs 2001 (with the French retailer Carrefour); the first IFA in the metal sector was achieved in 2002 (between the former GUF IMF and the German car producer VW), followed by numerous others. It took until 2006 that the first IFA in the banking sector was concluded between UNI and the Australian Bank NAG. In the meanwhile, IFAs are to be found in all sectors including the service sector, most agreements are from the metal- and electronic industry[7] and were concluded by the GUF IndustriAll, which

---

[1]For an early analysis of this issue, see Fröbel et al. (1979), pp. 21 ff., 75 ff., and 115 f.

[2]Due to the global scope of application, the expression "global framework agreements" (GFAs) may also be found in literature.

[3]Cf. to take some examples out of many Telljohann et al. (2009); as well as Sobczak (2012), pp. 139 ff.; each with further citations.

[4]The agreement was renewed 2000 and 2008.

[5]Faber Castell is selling high quality office material.

[6]The IFA was revised 2008.

[7]Including the automobile sector and suppliers.

had been founded in 2012.[8] By now more than 140 agreements in all branches can be detected, around 87% of all concluded with European transnational companies.[9]

3 Characteristics and Content of Current International Framework Agreements

3.1 Characteristics of International Framework Agreements

Unlike unilateral codes of conduct, agreements between GUFs and transnational corporations are commitments between two parties. The settlements are usually called international (or global) framework agreements (IFAs), nevertheless expressions like "agreement", "joint opinion", "declaration", "charter", "convention" or "action program" are also used. The principles stipulated in a first agreement may be deepened in a follow-up and expand the existing frame. Some IFAs are concluded for a limited period, after the expiration reviewed and, if necessary, revised.[10] Unlike at national level, where in several countries industry-wide (sectoral) or national collective agreements continue to predominate, IFAs are exclusively group or company agreements.[11] Based on an IFA, transnational corporations confirm to adhere to the agreed standards and to implement the negotiated provisions. The commitment in the meanwhile also counts for subsidiary companies and suppliers, whereas the whole value chain is not always covered.

Although around 13% of the global agreements were concluded with companies based outside Europe,[12] IFAs are a rather European phenomenon that derived from European industrial relations.[13] In contrast to unilateral CSR instruments, international framework agreements are the product of negotiations[14] and thus an

---

[8]IndustriAll was founded 2012 by the unification of the global union federations International Metalworkers' Federation (IMF), International Federation of Chemical, Energy, Mine and General Workers' Unions (ICEM) and the International Textiles Garment and Leather Workers' Federation (ITGLWF).

[9]Own list: Zimmer (2008), p. 327 ff updated October 2018.

[10]This is the case e.g. for the IFAs with EDF, ISS, OTE, RAG, Telefónica and Sécuritas, for further information see Zimmer (2008), p. 159.

[11]In the following discussion, I will use the term "company" even though some agreements apply throughout the group of companies.

[12]These are the companies/groups: Ability (Brazil); Al Jazeera Media Network (Qatar); AngloGold (South Africa); Antara (Indonesia); Banco do Brasil (Brasil); Chiquita (USA); Felaban-Bancing Association (Argentine); Fonterra (New Zealand); Icomon (Brasil); Itaú-Banc (Brasil); Mizuno (Japan); NAG-Banc (Australia); Nampak (South Africa); Quebecor (Canada); Petrobas (Brasil); Shoprite (South Africa) and Takashimaya (Japan).

[13]Telljohann et al. (2009), pp. 22 and 83 ff., as well as Daugareilh (2006), p. 116.

[14]Krause (2012), p. 750.

instrument of industrial relations.[15] As the transnational company is accepting the trade union confederation with the conclusion of an IFA as a negotiating partner, a long-term relation between GUF and transnational company is created on global level.[16] Nevertheless, IFAs often have more than one contractual party. Whereas on the employer side mostly there's only the transnational company,[17] on the workers' side often not only the GUF, but also national trade unions or actors like the EWC are involved in negotiations and conclusion of the agreement. International framework agreements generally comprise the following basic characteristics[18]:

- a GUF is involved in the conclusion and negotiation of the agreement;
- the IFA is based upon rights which derive from ILO-standards;
- the agreement contains a mechanism to monitor the implementation.

The scope of more recent agreements mostly also includes suppliers.[19]

3.2   Content of International Framework Agreements

In general, the main topic of IFAs are social standards. Nevertheless, some agreements are limited to specific topics, like e.g. the agreement concluded between the global union confederation IUF/IUL with Danone (BSN) on equality of men and women (1989, renewed 2005), the agreement on skills training (1992, renewed 2005) or the IFA on the protection of occupational safety and health, concluded in 2014 between UNI global union and the French telecommunication company Orange, to name just a few examples. Whereas early agreements were fairly rudimentary and contained little more than ILO core labour standards; later, further standards were included, mostly also based upon ILO conventions. In the meantime the agreements developed further and now usually contain rules on implementation and monitoring, like e.g. complaints mechanisms; annual meetings of signatory parties, partly with an expanded circle; reporting of management & indicators for the reporting, as well as provisions on decentralized social dialogue or on training and education.[20] This development is partly described as a shift from a quantitative approach (conclusion of as many IFAs as possible) towards a more qualitative approach, bearing in mind an effective implementation.[21] Quite a number of IFAs

---

[15]Zimmer (2019b), para. 2; Zimmer (2012), p. 260.

[16]Drouin (2015), p. 222; Miller (2004), p. 216; Thomas (2011), p. 274; Zimmer (2019b), para. 2; similar IOE (2007), p. 1.

[17]There are a few agreements with multiple companies as contractual party on the employers' side, like e.g. the Bangladesh Accord or the Indonesian Freedom of Association Protocol.

[18]Drouin (2015), p. 218; Zimmer (2019b), para. 1.

[19]Whereas subcontractors are only exceptionally bound, e.g. in the IFA with Inditex.

[20]Zimmer (2013b), p. 252; Hadwiger (2017), p. 415.

[21]Müller et al. (2008), p. 9.

contain provisions on trade union rights, which derive from ILO-convention 135, e.g. the prohibition of any kind of discrimination of workers' representatives.[22] In addition, some IFAs contain provisions on access to premises, neutrality in case of organizing campaigns or even the ban of strike-breakers,[23] which can be described an "enabling rights".[24] Moreover, provisions which provide an individual entitlement to training measures for management and workers, can be found.[25]

3.3 Implementation and Monitoring of International Framework Agreements

Most IFAs contain provisions that demand the translation into (all local) languages, as well as the information of the workforce. Unlike in unilateral codes of conduct, workers' representatives play a central role in the implementation. Mostly the parties agree on the necessity to monitor the adherence to the agreement and quite often, the agreement foresees the creation of a committee on parity basis in charge of the implementation.[26] The signing parties often agree to meet periodically or upon necessity to exchange information on the implementation; partly the meeting of an existing body like the European works council (EWC) or the world works council[27] is used for the monitoring.[28] There's hardly any monitoring performed by external parties, the case of Umicore is an exception, where in addition to a monitoring committee (as described above), external auditors present their reports at the annual meeting of the monitoring committee.[29]

Most agreements don't foresee a dispute resolution mechanism, in 2017 only 10% of all IFAs contained provisions on dispute resolution (which would either include mediation or arbitration).[30] Furthermore, only few agreements are provided

---

[22]Research from 2008 had shown that around 54% of the IFAs contained the prohibition of the discrimination of workers' representatives, see Zimmer (2008), p. 170.

[23]Such a clause can be found in the IFA of IndustriAll with the Spanish textile and apparel company Inditex (2014), in the IFA between IndustriAll and Umicore, as well as in the IFA of IndustriAll and Tchibo from 2016.

[24]Thomas (2011), p. 273.

[25]See the IFA between the IMF (by now IndustriAll) and Brunel from 2007 or the IFA negotiated between Inditex and IndustriAll (in the revised version from 2014) or in Annex II (access to premises).

[26]Following research from 2017, 85% of all agreements foresee such a committee, see Hadwiger (2017), p. 413.

[27]This is a worldwide body of workers' representatives, which is orientated on the EWC and formed on a voluntary basis (in consent with the employer). Sometimes a different wording is used, e.g. World Employee Forum, etc.

[28]Zimmer (2019b), para. 15 f; see further: Welz (2011), pp. 39 f.

[29]See § 5.4 IFA between IndustriAll and Umicore from 2014.

[30]Hadwiger (2017), p. 409.

with a clause on the jurisdiction to apply in case of dispute. Regulations of the kind agreed with Arcelor and Umicore, that in case of a dispute, Luxembourg or Belgian law shall apply, are an exception.[31] The participating actors always emphasized, that the enforceability of agreements rests less on legal enforceability, but is rather a question of trade union strengths.[32] Implementation problems and violations were, in the first instance, supposed to be clarified internally as they arise, without striving for legal enforceability.[33]

Nevertheless, numerous case studies point out, that the content of IFAs often is not implemented along the value chain and sometimes even not implemented at all.[34] A central factor for the successful implementation of an agreement seems to be the integration of local actors. If the different trade unions from the countries involved are integrated into the process of negotiation and implementation, the chance is higher, that the agreement will be filled with life in practice, as for example practiced with the Indonesian Protocol on Freedom of Association. This is even more the case, if training measures for the trade unions at local level and for local management on the content and specifics of the IFA are carried out.[35] The ongoing discussion about the effectivity of the agreements increasingly involves the question of including stronger elaborated dispute resolution mechanisms[36] as well and the example of a binding mechanism as concluded in the Bangladesh Accord certainly has its effect on further negotiations of IFAs,[37] as will be elaborated below. Based upon this, the idea of a neutral instance like the ILO involved in the process of monitoring, mediation and dispute settlement of IFAs, as suggested by the Committee on Decent Work in Global Supply Chains at the 105th International Labour Conference (2016)[38] could be a thriving improvement.[39]

---

[31]More far-reachingly Blé (2011), p. 209; Zimmer (2013b), p. 252.

[32]Hadwiger (2017), p. 412; Sobczak (2012), pp. 140 f.

[33]Blé (2011), pp. 209 f; Jagodzinski (2012), p. 42; Sobczak (2012), pp. 140 f; Zimmer (2013b), pp. 252 f.

[34]Royle and Ortiz (2009), pp. 653 ff.; Stevis and Fichter (2012); Fichter et al. (2013).

[35]This conclusion is the result of interviews concluded with all actors around the agreement on the protection of trade union rights (Freedom of Association Protocol) between Indonesian trade unions and sportswear companies like Adidas, Nike, Puma, Pentland, as well as local suppliers in November/December 2018 by the author.

[36]Hadwiger (2017), pp. 411 ff.

[37]Zimmer (2016a), p. 5.

[38]ILO (2016); see also: ILO (2019), ILO Centenary Declaration for the future of work (IV. D.).

[39]This has been successfully practiced in the supervision of the Bangladesh Accord.

4   New Discourse: Transnational Collective Agreements

By the time, industrial relations within Europe were deepened and also European Framework Agreements (EFAs) increasingly concluded, although structurally quite different compared to IFAs. Nevertheless, more actors were on the scene and the terminology changed towards transnational collective agreements (TCAs).[40] With this development, the aspect that the agreements are the product a form of collective bargaining is stronger emphasized[41] and the development of TCAs is characterized as a step towards the internationalization of industrial relations.[42]

The European Commission labels those collective agreements as "transnational" that are concluded by employees' representatives with the representatives of transnational enterprises and whose scope encompasses several countries.[43] Besides trade union federations, the term "employees' representatives" also includes elected employee representative bodies like European works councils. International (collective) company agreements have a global scope, whereas the scope of European (collective) company agreements includes only European countries. In the meanwhile, 318 transnational company agreements all together (global and EU) have been identified in a database of the European Commission (in cooperation with the ILO).[44] Nevertheless, the characterization of the European Commission seems too narrow, since there exist agreements, which are applied only to one country, but were concluded by several global trade unions (or confederations)[45] with several transnational companies from several countries, like e.g. the Bangladesh Accord or the Indonesian Freedom of Association Protocol. Such agreements bear in mind the transnationalization of production and of the value chains and should also be categorized as "transnational". The debate on transnational collective agreements however, ignores the collective bargaining agreements (CBAs) of the International Transportworkers' Federation (ITF), which are not listed up in the database of the European Commission. The ITF in fact has been the pioneer of comprehensive international collective bargaining on behalf of the seafarers. Facing the flag of convenience policy of international ship-owners, the ITF has been concluding CBAs

---

[40]Cf. Rüb et al. (2011); Zimmer (2013b), pp. 248 ff.

[41]Schömann (2011), p. 29; Zimmer (2013b), pp. 248 f.

[42]Telljohann et al. (2009), pp. 11 f.

[43]Cf. European Commission (2008), p. 3.

[44]See list of all identified CBAs from September 2018 (some agreements are no longer in force), European Commission/ILO (2018). https://ec.europa.eu/social/main.jsp?catId=978&langId=en (download 18.1.2019).

[45]Or in the case of the Indonesian Protocol, negotiation and conclusion was at least supported by the respective GUF.

on wages, working-time and further working conditions for more than 30 years, mostly with one company covering one vessel.[46]

4.1 European Collective Agreements

Factors like the development of the European Social Dialogue (Art. 154, 155 TFEU) and of workers' representation through European works councils, which are granted information and consultation rights, among others, fostered the Europeanisation of industrial relations through the Europeanisation of the industrial relations actors.[47] In addition to social partner agreements reached in the framework of the social dialogue or agreements establishing a European Works Council (EWC),[48] further Europe-wide agreements on different topics have been concluded since the 2000er years at company level. Though these agreements were inspired by IFAs, they form a new category of transnational agreements on company/group level, as elaborated below. Currently 71 such agreements (still in force) are to be detected at the EU-database.[49]

4.1.1 Content of European Collective Agreements

The content of TCAs with European scope highly differs from the content of international agreements (IFAs). While the latter deal primarily with minimum social standards, European agreements cover a wide range of subjects. A 2009 study for the European Foundation identified restructuring as by far the most frequently addressed issue in European collective agreements. Other subjects include occupational health and safety, social dialogue, sub-contracting, equal opportunities, further training and labour mobility, as well as protection for non-smokers, minimum social standards and CSR.[50] Although there is some overlap, e.g. between non-discrimination as part of the core labour standards in IFAs and the topic equal opportunities which can be found in European agreements, the content of European agreements is much closer to the needs of everyday politics of workers' representatives in the EU-countries.

---

[46]Concerning the politics of the ITF and the international CBAs, see information on the webpage of the ITF. Concerning legal aspects: Däubler (1997); Lillie (2004), pp. 47 ff. as well as Zachert (2000), pp. 121 ff.; and Zimmer (2015), pp. 103 ff.

[47]Hoffmann et al. (2002), p. 45; Telljohann et al. (2009), p. 28.

[48]Both of these type of agreements are not part of this analysis.

[49]See list of all identified CBAs (European and international), European Commission/ILO (2018).

[50]Telljohann et al. (2009), pp. 28 ff.; similar and earlier Waddington (2006), p. 565.

4.1.2 Contracting Parties

The European agreements were concluded on the one hand, by European trade union federations at industry level, coalitions of national trade unions from several European countries with corporate representatives, many of them European Works Councils, and company representatives on the other. EWCs play a greater role in the initiation and conclusion of European agreements than in the negotiation of global agreements. Even in European agreements to which EWCs were not a signatory party, they were often involved in the initiation and implementation of the negotiations, as studies have shown.[51] In research (already) from 2006, Waddington noted that around a quarter of the EWCs surveyed had concluded a transnational agreement.[52] Over the years, an increasing number of EWCs developed internal working, communication and networking structures, transforming themselves from information and consultation bodies to pro-active institutions concluding agreements with central management on a wide range of issues.[53] Additionally, research in the metalworking sector shows that, a significant proportion of EWCs also reach informal agreements with central management.[54] This development can be explained not least by the fact that EWCs have access to the necessary resources. Meanwhile also the first SE-Works Councils[55] negotiate and conclude transnational agreements.[56] In contrast to EWC founding agreements, most of the SE founding agreements for the Works Council do contain the explicit authorization to negotiate and conclude agreements with management.[57]

4.2   Mandate for the Conclusion and Negotiation of Agreements

It has to be analysed, whether the actors, which are negotiating and concluding TCAs are legally legitimized for this.

---

[51]Hoek and Hendrickx (2009), p. 11; Rüb et al. (2011), p. 19; Carley (2001), pp. 13 ff.; Zimmer (2013c), p. 318.

[52]Waddington (2006), p. 565.

[53]See Rüb et al. (2011), p. 19; Telljohann et al. (2009), p. 57; Zimmer (2013a), p. 462; Zimmer (2013c), ELLJ, p. 318.

[54]Of the EWCs surveyed, some 26% reached agreements of that kind, see Müller et al. (2012), p. 461.

[55]Societas Europea.

[56]The Allianz SE Works Council for example, concluded Guidelines concerning Work Related Stress with Management (2011), the SE-Works Council from MAN produced a Declaration on Human Rights and Working Conditions with management (2012), Guidelines concerning Lifelong Learning were concluded by the Allianz SE Works Council (2012), just to mention some prominent examples.

[57]Zimmer (2013c), p. 319.

4.2.1   European Level

Agreements of European Works Councils do not devote themselves primarily to "soft" issues, but deal instead with topics like restructuring and financial participation. EWCs thus negotiate and conclude particularly agreements in areas, which in labour relations are the exclusive preserve of trade unions, even in a country with a dual system like Germany. It is therefore not astonishing, that trade unions are questioning the legitimization of EWCs as actors of collective bargaining. This is seen as the exclusive right of trade unions, who might (or might not) include EWCs in the process. The predecessor of IndustriAll Europe, the European Metalworkers federation (EMF) passed mandatory guidelines on the role of EWC in the conclusion of agreements as early as 1996. Rules governing the role of union coordinators were passed in the year 2000, principles on transnational restructuring adopted in 2005. In 2006, the EMF developed a mandating procedure for the negotiation of TCAs with European firms which have since been taken over by the other industry foundations.[58]

Trade unions base their argumentation that EWC are not legitimized to conclude TCAs on the fact that neither the EWC-Directive 2009/38/EC nor the national implementation acts do explicitly provide EWCs with a mandate to negotiate other than founding agreements. The same applies to Regulation 2157/2001/EC for SE-works councils.[59] Whether a legitimization could derive from the context of Directive 2009/38/EC or Regulation 2157/2001/EC and a mandate through the founding agreements could enable EWCs (or SEs) to conclude valid agreements, is controversially debated among legal scholars.[60]

Trade unions (or trade union confederations) derive "the right to negotiate and conclude collective agreements *at the appropriate levels*" from Art. 28 EU-Charter of Fundamental Rights (EU-CFR). In conjunction with Arts. 155(1) and 152 TFEU, this might be seen as a basis for authorization for trade unions (and trade union confederations) to conclude TCAs.[61] In general, trade union organizations are legitimised by their members and receive a mandate for collective bargaining from them. This is not just the case for trade union organizations on national level, but also for the sectoral confederations in the EU.[62]

---

[58]Cf. EMCEF-mandate procedure (dated 01.07.2010), see Zimmer (2013c), pp. 320 f.

[59]Council Regulation (EC) No. 2157/2001 of 8 October 2001 on the Statute for a European company (SE).

[60]See in more detail Zimmer (2013c), pp. 321 ff.; Zimmer (2013a), pp. 466 ff., both with further references.

[61]Zimmer (2013b), pp. 254 f.

[62]Collective bargaining and the conclusion of CBAs is defined as a central task in trade union statutes. Upon joining the trade union, members sign to accept the statutes and therefore mandate the organisation to bargain collectively on behalf of the member, see Zimmer (2016b), pp. 18 f.

4.2.2 International Level

On international level, there's no explicit basis for authorization for trade unions to conclude TCAs, but nevertheless the right to bargain collectively is guaranteed in all international conventions: Art. 4 ILO-Convention 98; Art. 6 European Social Charter, as well as Art. 11(1) of European Convention on Human Rights (ECHR), which also includes the right to collective bargaining since the decision of the European Court of Human Rights in the case of Demir & Baykara.[63] As trade union organizations are legitimized by their members and receive a mandate for collective bargaining from them,[64] the legitimization to negotiate and conclude TCAs can also be taken for granted at international level.

5 Stronger Mechanism of Enforcement in the Bangladesh Accord

New developments concerning TCAs can be highlighted with the conclusion of new agreements like the Accord on Fire and Building Safety in Bangladesh (Bangladesh Accord), which contains not just a stronger mechanism of enforcement, but a legally binding dispute resolution mechanism, which represents a qualitatively new development. Though it is disputed among scholars whether the Bangladesh Accord may be categorized as an IFA, since the scope of application is only Bangladesh and in contrast to classical IFAs, on the employer side a multitude of transnational companies belong to the contracting parties.[65] However, according to the view represented here, an IFA is concluded by a GUF, contentwise it is based upon rights which derive from ILO-standards and a mechanism to monitor the agreement is included (see Sect. 3.1). Since all criteria apply as described, there is just more than one GUF involved, which does not make a structural difference. The Bangladesh Accord is therefore classified as a specific IFA and does also fall under the definition of a TCA (see at Sect. 4).

---

[63]ECtHR, Demir and Beykara v. Turkey, Judgement of 12 November 2008—No. 34503/97.

[64]Collective bargaining and the conclusion of CBAs is defined as a central task in trade union statutes. Upon joining the trade union, members sign to accept the statutes and therefore mandate the organisation to bargain collectively on behalf of the member, Zimmer (2016b), pp. 18 f.

[65]E.g. at the conference Max Planck Institute for Comparative Public Law and International Law/University of Bristol/University of Oslo/SMART on Transnational Labour Law in an Era of Rising Nationalism: A New Role of Public Institutions for Sustainable Market Practices? 20/21 June 2018 in Heidelberg.

5.1   General Information on the Bangladesh Accord

The Bangladesh Accord is an agreement between more than 220 transnational brand companies and the global trade union confederations IndustriAll and UNI-Global Union,[66] as well as eight Bangladeshi trade unions[67] to improve health and safety in the workplace in Bangladesh.[68] It was signed after the building collapse of the Rana Plaza ready-made garment factory in Bangladesh on 24 April 2013, where 1133 workers were killed and thousands more severely injured. The agreement was first concluded in 2013 for a term of 5 years (ending on 12 May 2018) with a follow up agreement (2018 Transition Accord) for 3 more years (until 31 May 2021), which replaced the 2013 Accord and was signed by the two GUFs and over 190 brands and retailers.[69] The 2018 Transition Accord is a continuation of the 2013 Accord with some new provisions, based upon the initial agreement from 2013.

To improve health and safety at the workplace, comprehensive inspections of the signatory parties' suppliers were codified, as well as the elimination of any deficiencies that might be discovered by means of remediation programs. On top of this, there are training programs for local management and employees.[70] The signatory brand companies are to provide the funds required for the administration of the Accord, which is organized through an own office. The regulations underlying the factory inspections are based, on one hand, on national law (Bangladesh National Building Code), interacting with ILO-Conventions on occupational safety & health[71] and the national action plan of Bangladesh (National Tripartite Plan of Action).[72] The inspections were carried out under the supervision of the Accord office, but after a judgment of the Appellate Court in December 2018, debates to close down the Accord office operations in Bangladesh are taking place. In this case, the governmental Department of Inspections of Factories and Establishments (RCC-DIFE) would take over. Currently discussions between the steering committee

---

[66]In addition, four NGOs signed the agreement as witnesses (Workers Rights Consortium, International Labour Rights Forum, Clean Clothes Campaign and Maquila Solidarity Network); the list may be found online under http://bangladeshaccord.org/signatories/.

[67]The Bangladesh Textile and Garments Workers League; the Bangladesh Independent Garment Workers Union Federation; the Bangladesh Garments, Textile and Leather Workers Federation; the Bangladesh Garment and Industrial Workers Federation; the Bangladesh Revolutionary Garment Workers Federation; the National Garment Workers Federation; the United Federation of Garment Workers; and the IndustriAll Bangladesh Council (IBC).

[68]In addition, four NGOs signed the agreement as witnesses; the list of signatory parties may be found online here: http://bangladeshaccord.org/signatories/ (24.11.2018).

[69]See http://bangladeshaccord.org/about.

[70]For further details see Zimmer (2016a), p. 4.

[71]For further information on the ILO-Conventions on OSH, see: Zimmer (2019a), § 5, para. 187 ff.

[72]Zimmer (2016a), p. 3.

of the Accord with the Government of Bangladesh and the Bangladesh Garment Manufacturers and Exporters Association (BGMEA) are taking place.[73]

5.2   Mechanism of Implementation

The Accord contains comprehensive mechanisms of implementation, most of which were already agreed upon in the agreement from 2013. The information about the Accord is widely spread among the workers, including information regarding the complaint mechanism in place. Implementation includes, above all, capacity-building by means of training measures for workers, managers and security staff on fire and building safety by experts, as well as Accord-certified trade unions trainers, covering basic safety procedures and precautions (par. 12 b; par. 11 Transition Accord). A Health and Safety Committee has to be established at factory level (par. 12a). The complaint mechanism in place enables employees at factories producing for Accord company signatories to report safety problems on a hotline free of charge and if wished, they may stay anonymously. The number of 660 complaints raised in 2018 indicates, that the mechanism is working quite well.[74] Such mechanisms of action are characterised as proactive problem-solving strategies,[75] which supplement the so-called "command-and-control" action mechanisms based on traditional monitoring.[76]

Key decisions are taken in a steering committee with parity representation of management and trade union representatives; further input may be given by an advisory committee, consisting of delegates from the social partners and from NGOs. In contrast to the great number of IFAs with similar provisions, the Accord provides the steering committee with an ILO representative as a neutral chair (para. 1.2 Transition Accord). As research has shown, such a neutral and competent chair is a central factor for finding a solution in case the social partners are stuck with a problem.[77] Conflicts between the signatory parties are discussed first in the steering committee, if the dispute cannot be resolved, a court of arbitration may be appointed (as explained below).

---

[73]See: https://bangladeshaccord.org/updates/2019/02/14/statement-on-transition-discussions-with-government-of-bangladesh-bgmea.

[74]See   under   https://bangladeshaccord.org/updates/2019/01/24/update-safety-and-health-complaints.

[75]Ter Haar and Keune (2014), p. 14.

[76]Ter Haar and Keune (2014), p. 20.

[77]In-depth interviews with the signing parties of an agreement to protect trade union rights in Indonesia (the FoA-Protocol) at the end of 2018 have shown, that such a neutral chair would be necessary to prevent stagnation in the supervisory committee in cases of conflict.

5.3 Legal Enforceability of the Accord Through International Arbitration

If a conflict cannot be resolved in the steering committee, each party of the conflict may initiate an arbitration process. The arbitration takes place in The Hague and is administered by the Permanent Court of Arbitration (PCA)[78] which, is appointed in accordance with the UNCITRAL regulations for international commercial arbitration.[79] In case the parties fail to agree upon the presiding arbitrator, in accordance with the UNCITRAL rules the secretary-general of the PCA will be nominated as appointing authority. Initially it seemed that the mere threat of such a procedure would put sufficient pressure on the signing brands to foster compliance with the agreed standards,[80] nevertheless in 2016 two arbitration cases were initiated by the GUFs IndustriAll and UNI, which finally in 2018 did not end with arbitration awards, but were settled out of court.[81]

Due to the agreement (Art. 3.3 Transition Accord), arbitration awards based upon the Accord are legally enforceable in the country of the headquarters of the signatory company in accordance with the New York Convention.[82] As in the case of court decisions, in most legal orders the binding effect of arbitration awards are limited to the country where the arbitration took place. If the New York Convention applies,[83] written agreements due to which the parties are voluntarily undergoing arbitration procedures not only have to be recognized (Art. 2 New York Convention) but the award is also acknowledged and enforceable outside the national territory.[84]

As the Accord contains obligations on the contracting parties, it can be categorized as a (binding) contractual agreement.[85] It becomes clear, that in contrast to earlier TCAs, the signatory parties of the Accord wanted to create binding regulations in order to improve building safety and fire prevention in Bangladesh.[86] Due to the agreed dispute resolution mechanism the Bangladesh Accord can be categorised as a new model of cooperation between global purchasers and global trade union organisations regarding the implementation of social minimum standards.[87] This is not just a novelty, but the experience of the negotiating actors will rather have its

---

[78]Art. 3.3 Transition Accord (2018), this was a change compared to the Accord from 2013.

[79]Cf. United Nations Commission on International Trade Law (2013), UNCITRAL Arbitration Rules.

[80]Zimmer (2016a), p. 6.

[81]See online https://pcacases.com/web/sendAttach/2438.

[82]The Convention on the Recognition and Enforcement of Foreign Arbitral Awards (New York Convention) of 10 June 1958, online http://www.newyorkconvention.org/11165/web/files/original/1/5/15457.pdf.

[83]The New York Convention has 156 member states, see online http://www.newyorkconvention.org/list+of+contracting+states.

[84]International Council for Commercial Arbitration (2011), p. 32.

[85]With regard to IFAs: Krause (2012), p. 749.

[86]Evans (2015), p. 607; Zimmer (2016a), p. 6.

[87]Holdcroft (2015), p. 100; Rahmann (2014), pp. 73 f; Zimmer (2016a), p. 6.

impact on the negotiation of new transnational agreements. Furthermore, brand companies signing up to the Accord thereby acknowledge a liability for working conditions (at least with regard to building safety and fire prevention).[88] Nevertheless, the Accord was concluded in a specific situation, when the attention of world public opinion was directed towards the procurement policies of transnational brands in Bangladesh,[89] a constellation that is not so easily repeatable.

6 Legal Enforcement of Transnational Collective Agreements

Although numerous transnational company agreements have now been signed and notwithstanding the right to collective bargaining guaranteed in international conventions[90] and in the EU-Charter,[91] a legal framework governing such agreements neither exists at global nor at EU level. Existing agreements therefore operate in a legal grey area, with their legal nature and effect highly contested.[92] It remains to be analysed, how TCAs are legally enforceable without an out-of-court dispute settlement mechanism in place like in the case of the accord.

6.1 Applicable Law

The applicable law for TCAs derives from the statute for collective agreements.[93] In Germany, the German Flag Act acknowledges collective bargaining agreements (CBA) for the maritime sector with trade unions from other countries; the election of a statute for CBAs by the parties involved is admissible (Art. 21 para. 4 p. 2 *Flaggenrechtsgesetz*). Such a special provision doesn't exist for other sectors.[94] Rules might derive from International Private Law. According to Art. 1.1 Rome I Regulation[95] the rules of International Private Law are created for "contractual

---

[88]Evans (2015), p. 620.

[89]Zimmer (2016a), p. 6.

[90]Art. 4 ILO-Convention 98; Art. 6 ESC; Art. 11.1 ECHR, which also includes the right to collective bargaining since the decision of the European Court of Human Rights in the case of Demir & Baykara (ECtHR 11.12.2008—No. 34503/97).

[91]Art. 28 EU-Charter.

[92]On that debate, see: Krause (2012), pp. 758 ff.; Thüsing (2010), p. 91; Zimmer (2013b), pp. 252 ff.; Zimmer (2008), pp. 267 ff.; all with further references.

[93]Schlachter (2019), Art. 9, para. 32.

[94]Zimmer (2008), p. 270.

[95]Regulation 593/2008/EC of the European Parliament and of the Council of 17 June 2008 on the law applicable to contractual obligations (Rome I).

obligations". Some scholars are rejecting the application of the Rome I Regulation on collective agreements.[96] Bearing in mind the comprehensive guarantees of collective bargaining for the social partners in international (and European) law, including the conclusion of CBAs, this view is unreasonable.[97] Agreements, which contain obligations of the contracting parties, can be categorized as contractual agreements (*in personam* agreements)[98] and are described as expressions of the general principle of contractual freedom.[99] According to the general interpretation in literature, the Rome I Regulation is applicable to TCAs (like IFAs). Some authors argue for analogous application,[100] others opt for direct application, due to the characterization of IFAs as contractual obligations.[101] The main arguments are, that the concept of contractual obligations is interpreted widely and based upon a wide autonomous concept, according to which contractual obligations include all obligations of one party to another[102] and the rules of the Rome I Regulation therefore apply to TCAs.

According to Art. 3.1 Rome I Regulation, the parties may autonomously define by which legal system the agreement is governed.[103] Without a choice of law, (neither explicitly nor by implication) the agreement is subject to the law of the state with the closest connection (Art. 4.4 Rome I Regulation). Reference is to be made to the focus of the TCA,[104] whereby due to the worldwide application this might not be easily identified. Indications might be the chosen language, the seat of the contractual parties or the country with most employees.[105] Since often the trade union of the country is involved, where the headquarter of the company is based, in case of uncertainties the legal order of the country where the headquarter is based

---

[96]Löwisch and Rieble (2017), para. 392 ff.

[97]Zimmer (2019b), § 8, para. 20.

[98]With regard to IFAs: Krause (2012), p. 749.

[99]Hauch (2015), p. 100; Zimmer (2019a, b), § 8, para. 18.

[100]Däubler (2016), paras. 781 and 788; Kocher (2014), para. 45; Thüsing (2010), p. 91; Zimmer (2008), p. 270.

[101]Deinert (2013), § 15, para. 20; Schlachter (2019), Art. 9, para. 32; De Koster and van den Eynde (2009), pp. 135 ff.; Felkl (2010), pp. 207 ff.; Hoek and Hendrickx (2009), pp. 9 and 19; Krause (2012), p. 763; Seifert (2006), p. 221.

[102]Magnus (2011), para. 27 f; Hoek and Hendrickx (2009), p. 18; Krause (2012), p. 749; Meißner and Ritschel (2012), p. 62; Zimmer (2019b), § 8, para. 20; Zimmer (2013a), p. 470.

[103]Däubler (2016), paras. 781 ff.; Deinert (2013), § 15, para. 24; Drouin (2015), p. 227; Schlachter (2019), Art. 9, para. 7; Hoek and Hendrickx (2009), pp. 19 f and 22 f; Junker (1992), p. 423; Kocher (2014), para. 46; Krause (2012), p. 763; Meißner and Ritschel (2012), p. 63; Thorn (2019), para. 5; Seifert (2006), p. 221; Zimmer (2013b), p. 470.

[104]Deinert (2013), § 15, para. 25; Schlachter (2019), Art. 9, para. 32; Kocher (2014), para. 48; Krause (2012), p. 763; Thorn (2019), para. 5.

[105]Däubler (2016), para. 788; Schlachter (2019), Art. 9, para. 32; Krause (2012), p. 763; Thüsing (2010), p. 91.

might be a good point of reference.[106] The Rome I Regulation is only to be applied to agreements concluded since 17.12.2009 (Art. 28.1 Rome I Regulation).[107]

6.2   Country to File the Case

The country where the lawsuit has to be filed is determined by the Brussels Ia Regulation[108] (since 15.1.2015). The Brussels Ia Regulation applies according to Art. 1 for civil disputes, if the defendant is residing in the EU, Art. 4.1 Brüssel Ia Regulation.[109] Based on Art. 25.1 Brussels 1a Regulation, agreements on choice of forum are admissible; the parties of a TCA therefore may define, in which country the lawsuit has to be filed.[110] In the absence of such a clause, the general rule applies, whereupon an action has to be brought in the country where the defendant is domiciled.[111] A company (or legal person) is domiciled at the place of the statutory seat, the central administration or the principle place of business, Art. 63.1 Brussels 1a Regulation. Is the headquarter based outside Europe (e.g. in the USA), the Brussels 1a Regulation doesn't apply, but rather national law is applicable.[112] Rights out of an IFA concluded with a company based in Germany may thus be claimed in Germany, although the violation might have occurred in a country of the global south.[113]

6.3   Legal Framework for Transnational Collective Agreements

As there's no legal frame for TCAs, international, as well as European agreements legally operate in a grey area. For the EU the European Commission has been considering the establishment of a legal framework for voluntary Europe-wide

---

[106]Krause (2012), p. 763; Seifert (2006), p. 221; Thüsing (2010), p. 91; Zimmer (2019b), § 8, para. 21; Zimmer (2013a), p. 470.

[107]Zimmer (2019b), § 8, para. 222; see as well: CJEU 18.10.2016—C-135/15, BeckRS 2016, 82514 m. Anm. Pfeiffer.

[108]Regulation 1215/2012/EU of the European Parliament and the Council of 12 December 2012 on jurisdiction and the recognition and enforcement of judgments in civil and commercial matters, replacing the Brussels I Regulation.

[109]Is the defendant based outside the EU, due to lacking international norms, the national provisions on local jurisdiction apply, in Germany these are the norms of the ZPO (§§ 12 ff.), Koch (2019), § 1 ArbGG, para. 4.

[110]Zimmer (2019b), § 8, para. 24.

[111]Zimmer (2019b), § 8, para. 24.

[112]Hoek and Hendrickx (2009), p. 45; Krause (2012), p. 760.

[113]Krause (2012), p. 760; Zimmer (2019b), § 8, para. 24.

company agreements since 2005. In that context, it sought the advice of several expert groups,[114] of which one in 2011, developed a specific proposal for a legal framework for voluntary TCAs.[115] The proposal is based upon the precondition that the EU is obliged to take account of the differences in the national systems of industrial relations. Three options for a legal framework were developed by the researchers:

6.3.1 Option One for a Legal Framework in the EU: Uniform Legal Effect in All the Member States

The most far-reaching option would be for the European framework to provide for TCAs to have uniform legal effect in all the Member States.[116] However, given the considerable differences between the different national systems, the problem with this approach is all too evident. The legal effect accorded to European collective agreements by such a directive would result in certain Member States in legal effects previously unknown to those systems. Consequently, bearing in mind in particular the prohibition on EU legal activity established in Article 153(5) TFEU, this option is not viable.[117]

6.3.2 Option Two for a Legal Framework in the EU: Status Contract

A further possibility is that the legal effect of a European collective agreement should depend on the will of the parties to the TCA at issue. In this scenario, the European directive would simply establish a procedural legal framework to be inserted into national law. The legal effect and scope of the transnational collective agreement would be determined according to the will of the parties.[118] The parties could agree that the collective agreement itself produces normative effects or that the employer undertakes to incorporate the relevant worker rights in the individual employment contracts, as is common practice in Scandinavia. This form of agreement has found support amongst legal authors over many decades; they justify this approach by reference to the particular characteristics of the social partners.[119] This flexible approach though comprises a certain risk of legal uncertainty. Moreover, major flexibility with regard to the scope, legal effects and substance of European collective agreements may result in greater pressure on collective agreements

---

[114]In this regard, see the materials and reports uploaded to the European Commission's website https://ec.europa.eu/social/main.jsp?catId=707&langId=en&intPageId=214#navItem-3.

[115]Rodríguez et al. (2011); see in addition: Ales (2018), pp. 3 ff.

[116]Rodríguez et al. (2011), pp. 128 ff.

[117]Zimmer (2013b), p. 258.

[118]Rodríguez et al. (2011), pp. 134 ff.

[119]See Deinert (1999), p. 160; Schiek (2016), para. 914 ff.

concluded under national schemes. Ultimately, this could undermine such national systems.[120] In addition, it is questionable whether such flexibility is at all necessary in relation to European collective agreements. The parties choose voluntarily to engage in collective bargaining and to enter into collective agreements. If the parties wish to avoid the legal effects of a collective agreement, they may choose an alternative form such as a joint declaration. In any event, the relevant European trade union confederation would have to derive its mandate to enter into TCAs directly from the affiliate trade unions holding a mandate at national level.[121]

6.3.3 Option Three for a Legal Framework in the EU: The Same Legal Effect as Collective Agreements Concluded in the Member States

The third possibility is that European TCAs are automatically given the same legal effect as collective agreements concluded in that Member State under national law. Consequently, in terms of their impact on the individual employment relationship, European TCAs would not have the same effect in each Member State. In Germany, the rules of the Tarifvertragsgesetz (Law on Collective Agreements) would apply, whereas in France the provisions of the Code du Travail (Labour Code) would be relevant. In this scenario, the only difference between European TCAs and those concluded under national law would be the parties to the agreement and its content. The legal technique necessary in this regard is known as "adhesion" in certain countries. This signifies that parties at national level would have to implement agreements that they did not negotiate and sign themselves.[122]

This solution appears preferable as it respects the diversity of industrial relations systems and the differences between the legal systems of the Member States. It would avoid the situation that TCAs, regarded as "second class", differ from those concluded in the Member State concerned. In addition, within each Member State, the legal effect of European collective agreements would always be the same and not vary from case to case[123] (as under option two). However, disadvantages could arise in relation to implementation if, e.g. the actors at national level disapproved of the substance of the European agreement and boycotted its transposition.[124] Also in relation to this option, it is essential that sectoral European trade union confederations are given a mandate by the affiliated national trade unions to enter into collective bargaining at European level.[125]

---

[120]Zimmer (2013b), p. 258.

[121]Körtgen (1998), pp. 83 f; Zimmer (2016b), pp. 18 f.

[122]Rodríguez et al. (2011), pp. 138 ff.

[123]A similar view is taken by Deinert (1999), pp. 440 ff. This option is also favoured by the ETUFs and the ETUC, see: ETUC (2016) p. 65.

[124]See also Zimmer (2013b), EuZA, pp. 258 f.

[125]Zimmer (2016b), pp. 18 f; Zimmer (2013b), EuZA, p. 259.

6.3.4   Further Prospects for a Legal Framework for TCAs at European Level

The results of the research explained above, formed the subject of intense discussions with the social partners in the EU during the last years.[126] However, whether the European Commission goes ahead and realizes a legislative proposal is mainly depending on the position of the social partners. Although the European trade union federations (ETUFs) were initially rather reserved as regards the establishment of a legal framework for TCAs at the European level, over time they have become quite open to the idea and are in the meanwhile demanding the establishment of such a legal framework, presenting in 2016 their own proposal for a decision on an optional legal framework for TCAs in Europe.[127] The document is emphasizing "the leading role of the ETUFs in the negotiations of TCAs"; EWCs are to be involved in negotiations with multinational companies, but only the ETUFs are permitted to supply the signature.[128] The optional nature of the proposed legal framework is guaranteed by an "opting-in-clause": the decision containing it only applies if "the bargaining agents declare in writing that the agreement is subject to this decision" (Art. 3 of the proposed document providing a legal frame for TCAs).[129]

The employers' federation Business Europe has opposed consistently the establishment of a legal framework for transnational collective agreements,[130] but also seems to have developed its position on TCAs by the years.[131] By now, Business Europe seems to emphasize, that MNC's might need support when entering into a negotiation procedure with currently unclear legal effects. The organization even entered into a joint project with the ETUC, of which in the Joint Conclusions of the two organizations, TCAs are at least acknowledged as "an important tool for social dialogue that trade unions and multinational companies may make use of, taking into account the specific national circumstances".[132] Nevertheless, the current position of

---

[126]See the materials uploaded to the European Commission's website, https://ec.europa.eu/social/main.jsp?catId=707&langId=en&intPageId=214#navItem-3.

[127]ETUC (2016).

[128]ETUC (2016), p. 61.

[129]ETUC (2016). Building an enabling Environment for voluntary and autonomous Negotiations at transnational Level between Trade Unions and Multinational Companies. Final Report, p. 74.

[130]See the views of Business Europe in relation to the study from 2011, as expressed by Ms Hornung Drauss and recorded in the minutes of the Sixth Meeting of the Expert Group on Transnational Company Agreements on Oct. 11, 2011, p. 7. A rather sceptical view is also taken by the International Organisation of Employers (2007), International Framework Agreements. An Employers' Guide, pp. 10 ff.; although in the fact sheet on IFAs for business from 2013, the IOE takes a neutral position (see p. 3).

[131]International Organisation of Employers (2013), p. 3.

[132]Joint Conclusions of ETUC and Business Europe (2018), in: Building on Experiences: A Win Win Approach to Transnational Industrial Relations in Multinational Companies, Final Report, p. 18.

Business Europe on a legal frame for TCAs in Europe is not quite clear—and the topic was not touched in the joint project.

In any case, an ever-increasing number of companies is entering into transnational agreements, covering many different issues, with industry-wide European trade union federations or with company-level actors such as EWCs. This developing practice is thus creating hard facts and is demanding for legal certainty.

6.3.5 Legal Frame for TCAs at International Level

Unlike at European level, no such discussion about a legal framework for TCAs is taking place at international level. This might be based upon the fact, that international framework agreements are mostly mere minimum standards of working conditions which do not collide with provisions of collective bargaining agreements on national level. The necessity of such a legal framework therefore doesn't seem to be as urgent, as on European level. On the contrary, the participating actors at international level rather emphasized, that the enforceability of agreements rests less on legal enforceability, but is rather a question of trade union strengths.[133] Although with the conclusion of the Bangladesh Accord, the will of the trade union side to conclude agreements which are stronger binding is visible,[134] the actors rather focussed on legally binding dispute resolution mechanism, than on the idea of filing (a classical) lawsuit at court.

At international level, the ILO is the institution in charge of the definition and supervision of international labor standards. However, as customary in international law, ILO-Conventions are binding only for states and not for private actors like transnational companies. The ILO declaration of principles concerning multinational enterprises from 1977 (amended 2000, 2006 and 2017)[135] namely addresses the responsibility of transnational (multinational) companies, but is merely is a non-binding document. Debates at international level are rather conducted on corporate accountability,[136] deriving from human rights due diligence as defined in the UN Guiding Principles on Business and Human Rights.[137] Concerning the ILO, it is demanded, that the institution as a neutral instance should be stronger involved in the process of monitoring, mediation and dispute settlement of IFAs[138] or even move towards a permanent forum for conciliation and binding arbitration for IFAs.[139]

---

[133]Hadwiger (2017), p. 412; Sobczak (2012), pp. 140 f.

[134]Evans (2015), p. 607; Zimmer (2016a), p. 5.

[135]See: ILO (1977, 2017).

[136]For further information: Harrison (2013), pp. 107 ff.; Trebilcock (2015), pp. 93 ff.

[137]UN (2011).

[138]ILO (2016).

[139]Vogt (2019), p. 10.

7 Conclusion

Numerous agreements to protect social standards have been concluded on international level, as well as agreements on European level, relations with the social partners were established. In general, the substance of TCAs has developed, more regulations and procedures concerning implementation are stipulated. New developments can be highlighted with the conclusion of agreements like the Bangladesh Accord on Fire and Building Safety, which contains not just a stronger mechanism of enforcement, but also a legally binding dispute resolution mechanism. This is not just a novelty but will have its impact on the negotiations of further agreements. TCAs might play an important role in solving conflicts within transnational companies and along the value chain,[140] especially if out of court dispute settlement procedures are foreseen. Such mechanisms are especially useful to strengthen adherence to TCAs in countries where due to week legal structures agreed standards will not be enforced by court cases. To summarize, the development of transnational collective agreements can characterized as a step towards the internationalization of industrial relations and towards transnational collective bargaining.

Bibliography

Ales E (2018) Transnational collective agreements: the role of trade unions and employers' associations. A thematic working paper for the annual conference of the European Centre of Expertise (ECE) in the field of labour law, employment and labour market policies: "Perspectives of collective rights in Europe". https://eu.eventscloud.com/file_uploads/185fe09c1a16e079ad008e8927fc6c8a_Ales_Final_EN3.pdf

Blé D (2011) Business commitments in CSR Codes of Conduct and International Framework Agreements: the case of human rights. In: Buhmann K, Roseberry L, Morsing M (eds) Corporate social and human rights responsibilities. Global legal and management perspectives. Palgrave Macmillan, Basingstoke, pp 205–221

Buhmann K, Roseberry L, Morsing M (eds) (2011) Corporate social and human rights responsibilities. Global legal and management perspectives. Palgrave Macmillan, Basingstoke

Carley M (2001) Bargaining at European Level? Joint texts negotiated by EWC, Eurofound Publication. https://www.eurofound.europa.eu/sites/default/files/ef_files/pubdocs/2001/52/en/1/ef0152en.pdf

Däubler W (1997) Der Kampf um einen weltweiten Tarifvertrag. Nomos, Baden-Baden

Däubler W (2016) Einleitung Tarifvertragsgesetz. In: Däubler W (ed) Tarifvertragsgesetz mit Arbeitnehmer-Entsendegesetz. Kommentar, 4th edn. Nomos, Baden-Baden

Daugareilh I (2006) Les accords cadres internationaux: une réponse européenne à la mondialisation de l'économie. In: Descolonges M, Saincy B (eds) Les nouveaux enjeux de la négociation sociale interntionale. La Découverte, Paris, pp 116–129

De Koster P, van den Eynde P (2009) International Framework Agreements on Corporate Social Responsibility: conflict of laws and enforcement. Bus Law Int 10(2), S. 128–155

Deinert O (1999) Der Europäische Kollektivvertrag. Rechtstatsächliche und rechtsdogmatische Grundlagen einer gemeinsamen Kollektivvertragsautonomie. Nomos, Baden Baden

---

[140]Telljohann et al. (2009), p. 8.

Deinert O (2013) Internationales Arbeitsrecht. Deutsches und europäisches Arbeitskollisionsrecht. Mohr Siebeck, Tübingen

Drouin R-C (2015) Freedom of association in International Framework Agreements. In: Trebilcock A, Blackett A (eds) Research handbook on transnational labour law. Edward Elgar, pp 217–229

ETUC (ed) (2016) Building an enabling environment for voluntary and autonomous negotiations at transnational level between trade unions and multinational companies. Final Report, Brussels. https://www.etuc.org/sites/default/files/publication/files/160905_tca_final_report_en_proof_final.pdf

European Commission (2008) The role of transnational company agreements in the context of increasing international integration, SEC 2008, 2155 of 2 July 2008

European Commission and ILO (2018) Database on transnational company agreements: list of all identified transnational company agreements. https://ec.europa.eu/social/main.jsp?catId=978&langId=en

Evans BA (2015) Accord on fire and building safety in Bangladesh: an international response to Bangladesh labour conditions. N C J Int Law (NCJIL) 40(2):597–627

Felkl J (2010) Rechtliche Bedeutung der internationalen Rahmenvereinbarungen. Kovac, Hamburg

Fichter M, Kadire Z, Agtas O (2013) Organization and regulation of employment relations in transnational production and supply networks. Ensuring core labour standards through International Framework Agreements? Friedrich-Ebert-Foundation, Ankara. http://www.fes-tuerkei.org/media/pdf/einzelpublikationen/FES%20Organization%20and%20Regulation%20of%20Employment%20Relations%20in%20Transnational%20Production%20and%20Supply%20Networks.pdf

Fröbel F, Heinrichs J, Kreye O (1979) Die Neue Internationale Arbeitsteilung

Hadwiger F (2015) Global framework agreements: achieving decent work in global supply chains? Int J Labour Res 7:75–94

Hadwiger F (2017) Looking to the future: mediation and arbitration procedures for global framework agreements. Transfer 23(4):409–424

Harrison J (2013) Establishing a meaningful human rights due diligence process for corporations: learning from experience of human rights impact assessment. Impact Assess Project Appraisal 31(2):107–117

Hauch ET (2015) International Framework Agreements. Hintergrund, Rechtsnatur und Justiziabilität. Peter Lang, Frankfurt

Hoek A, Hendrickx F (2009) International private law aspects and dispute settlement related to transnational company agreements. ec.europa.eu/social/BlobServlet?docId=4815&langId=en

Hoffmann J, Hoffmann R, Kirton-Darling J, Rampeltshammer L (2002) The Europeanisation of industrial relations in a global perspective: a literature review, European Foundation for the improvement of living and working conditions. Office for Official Publications of the European Communities, Luxembourg. https://www.eurofound.europa.eu/sites/default/files/ef_files/pubdocs/2002/102/en/1/ef02102en.pdf

Holdcroft J (2015) Transforming supply chain industrial relations. Int J Labour Res (IJLR) 7:95–104

International Council for Commercial Arbitration (2011) ICCA's Guide to the interpretation of the 1958 New York Convention: a handbook for judges. http://www.arbitration-icca.org/media/1/13890217974630/judges_guide_english_composite_final_jan2014.pdf

International Labour Organization (1977) Tripartite declaration of principles concerning multinational enterprises and social policy. Geneva

International Labour Organization (2016) Reports of the Committee on decent work in global supply chains: resolution and conclusions submitted for adoption by the Conference, International Labour Conference 14-1 Provisional Record 105th Session, Geneva, May–June 2016. https://www.ilo.org/wcmsp5/groups/public/%2D%2D-ed_norm/%2D%2D-relconf/documents/meetingdocument/wcms_489115.pdf

International Labour Organization (2017) Tripartite declaration of principles concerning multinational enterprises and social policy, 4th amendment, Geneva. https://www.ilo.org/wcmsp5/groups/.../wcms_101234.pdf

International Organisation of Employers (2007) International Framework Agreements. An employers' guide. Geneva. https://www.ioe-emp.org/index.php?eID=dumpFile&t=f&f=108198&token=638aa6ed75a740810d86f3b927f2ea1f03cab598

International Organisation of Employers (2013) Fact sheet for business: International Framework Agreements (IFAs). Geneva. https://www.ioe-emp.org/index.php?eID=dumpFile&t=f&f=111472&token=aa8d3cac0ec2d67c5ab698498ac187ae0c7c5698

International Transportworkers' Federation (ITF). About the FOC campaign. https://www.itfseafarers.org/FOC_campaign.cfm

Jagodzinski R (2012) Transnational collective bargaining: a literature review. In: Schömann I, Jagodzinski R, Boni G, Clauwaert S, Glassner V, Jaspers T (eds) Transnational collective bargaining at company level. A new component of European industrial relations? ETUI, Brussels, pp. 19–76

Junker A (1992) Internationales Arbeitsrecht im Konzern. Mohr Siebeck, Tübingen

Koch U (2019) Kommentierung Arbeitsgerichtsgesetz. In: Müller-Glöge R, Preis U, Schmidt I (eds) Erfurter Kommentar zum Arbeitsrecht, 19th edn. Beck, München

Kocher E (2014) § 4 Tarifvertragsgesetz (para. 17-133). In: Brecht-Heitzmann H, Kempen OE, Schubert J, Seifert A (eds) TVG. Tarifvertragsgesetz. Kommentar. Bund, Frankfurt

Körtgen A (1998) Der Tarifvertrag im Recht der Europäischen Gemeinschaft: Die Zulässigkeit Europäischer Tarifverträge. Dissertation, Düsseldorf

Krause R (2012) International Framework Agreements as instrument for the legal enforcement of freedom of association and collective bargaining? The German case. Comp Labour Law Policy J (CLLPJ) 33:749–773

Lillie N (2004) Global collective bargaining on flag of convenience shipping. Br J Ind Relat (BJIR) 42(1):47–67

Löwisch M, Rieble V (2017) Tarifvertragsgesetz. Commentary, 4th edn. Vahlen, München

Magnus U (2011) Art 1 – 10 Rom I-VO. In: von Staudinger J (ed) Kommentar zum Bürgerlichen Gesetzbuch: BGB, EGBGB/IPR, Einleitung zur Rom I-VO; Art. 1-10 Rom I-VO (Internationales Vertragsrecht 1). Beck, München

Meißner D, Ritschel A (2012) Europäische Unternehmensvereinbarungen – Chancen für ein kollektives Arbeitsrecht. In: Busch D, Feldhoff K, Nebe K (eds) Übergänge im Arbeitsleben und (Re)Inklusion in den Arbeitsmarkt. Symposium anlässlich des 65. Geburtstages von Prof. Dr. Wolfhard Kohte. Nomos, Baden-Baden, pp 53–72

Miller D (2004) Preparing for the long haul: negotiating international framework agreements in the global textile, garment and footwear sector. Glob Soc Policy 4(2):215–239

Müller T, Platzer H-W, Rüb S (2008) Internationale Rahmenvereinbarungen – Chancen und Grenzen eines neuen Instruments globaler Gewerkschaftspolitik. In: Kurzberichte Nr. 8, Friedrich-Ebert-Stiftung (FES)

Müller T, Platzer H-W, Rüb S (2012) Transnationale Unternehmensvereinbarungen und die Vereinbarungspolitik Europäischer Betriebsräte. WSI-Mitteilungen 6:457–463

Papadakis K (ed) (2008) Cross-border social dialogue and agreements: an emerging global industrial relations framework? ILO-Publication, Geneva

Papadakis K (ed) (2011) Shaping global industrial relations: the impact of international framework agreements. ILO-Publication, Palgrave Macmillan, Basingstoke

Rahmann Z (2014) Accord on fire and building safety in Bangladesh: a breakthrough agreement? Nordic J Working Life Stud (NJWLS) 4(1):69–74

Rodríguez R, Ahlberg K, Davulis T, Fulton L, Gyulavári T, Humblet P, Jaspers T, Miranda J M, Marhold F, Valdés F, Zimmer R (2011) Study on the characteristics and legal effects of agreements between companies and workers' representatives. Investigation for the European Commission (DG Employment, Social Affairs & Inclusion), Brussels. tps://ec.europa.eu/social/main.jsp?catId=707&langId=en&intPageId=214

Royle T, Ortiz L (2009) Dominance effects from local competitors: setting institutional parameters for employment relations in multinational subsidiaries; a case from the Spanish supermarket sector. Br J Ind Relat 47:653–675

Rüb S, Platzer H-W, Müller T (2011) Transnationale Unternehmensvereinbarungen. Edition Sigma, Berlin

Schiek D (2016) Europäische Kollektivvereinbarungen. In: Däubler W (ed) Tarifvertragsgesetz mit Arbeitnehmerentsendegesetz. Kommentar. Nomos, Baden-Baden. Einleitung para, 797–960

Schlachter M (2019) Rom I-VO, Art. 3-9. In: Müller-Glöge R, Preis U, Schmidt I (eds) Erfurter Kommentar zum Arbeitsrecht, 19th edn. Beck, München

Schlachter M, Heuschmid J, Ulber D (2019) Arbeitsvölkerrecht. Mohr Siebeck, Tübingen

Schömann I (2011) The impact of transnational company agreements on social dialogue and industrial relations. In: Papadakis K (ed) Shaping global industrial relations: the impact of international frame work agreements. ILO-Publication, Palgrave Macmillan, Basingstoke, pp 21–37

Schömann I, Jagodzinski R, Boni G, Clauwaert S, Glassner V, Jaspers T (2012) Transnational collective bargaining at company level. A new component of European industrial relations? ETUI, Brussels

Seifert A (2006) Die Schaffung transnationaler Arbeitnehmervertretungen in weltweit tätigen Unternehmen. In: Zeitschrift für ausländisches und internationales Arbeits- und Sozialrecht (ZIAS), vol 3, pp 205–224

Sobczak A (2012) Ensuring the effective implementation of transnational company agreements. Eur J Ind Relat, pp 139–151

Stevis D, Fichter M (2012) International Framework Agreements in the USA: escaping, projecting or globalizing social dialogue? Colorado State University. http://ilera2012.wharton.upenn.edu/RefereedPapers/StevisDimitris%20MichaelFichter%20ILERA.pdf

Telljohann V, da Costa I, Müller T, Rehfeld U, Zimmer R (2009) International framework agreements: a stepping stone towards the internationalization of industrial relations? European Foundation for the improvement of the working and living condition, Dublin

Ter Haar B, Keune M (2014) One step forward or more window-dressing? A legal analysis of recent CSR initiatives in the garment industry in Bangladesh. Int J Comp Labour Law Ind Relat (IJCLLIR) 1:5–25

Thomas MP (2011) Global industrial relations? Framework agreements and the regulation of international labor standards. Labor Stud 36(2):269–287

Thorn K (2019) EGBGB Art. 3–48 mit Rom I-, Rom II- und Rom III-Verordnung. In: Palandt (ed) Bürgerliches Gesetzbuch mit Nebengesetzen. Kommentar, 78th edn. Beck, München

Thüsing G (2010) International Framework Agreements: Rechtliche Grenzen und praktischer Nutzen. Recht der Arbeit (RdA) 63:78–93

Trebilcock A (2015) Due diligence on labour issues – opportunities and limits of the UN Guiding Principles on Business and Human Rights. In: Blackett A, Trebilcock A (eds) Research handbook on transnational labour law, pp 93–107

United Nations (ed) (2011) Guiding principles on business and human rights. Implementing the United Nations "Protect, Respect and Remedy" Framework, New York

United Nations Commission on International Trade Law (2013) UNCITRAL Arbitration Rules. http://www.uncitral.org/pdf/english/texts/arbitration/arb-rules-2013/UNCITRAL-Arbitration-Rules-2013-e.pdf

Vogt J (2019) Gaps in global labour governance: the case of global supply chains. What role for the ILO? Presentation at Global Labour University Conference, 28th March in Berlin

Waddington J (2006) Was leisten Europäische Betriebsräte? WSI-Mitteilungen 10:560–567

Welz C (2011) A qualitative Analysis of International Framework Agreements: implementation and impact. In: Papadakis K (ed) Shaping global industrial relations: the impact of international frame work agreements. ILO-Publication, Palgrave Macmillan, Basingstoke, pp 38–60

Zachert U (2000) Tarifverträge in globalisierter Wirtschaft. NZA 2000:121–124

Zimmer R (2008) Soziale Mindeststandards und ihre Durchsetzungsmechanismen. Sicherung internationaler Mindeststandards durch Verhaltenskodizes? Nomos, Baden-Baden

Zimmer R (2012) Will Corporate Social Responsibility help to improve working conditions? In: Traub-Merz R, Junhua Z (eds) Industrial democracy in China. With additional studies on Germany, South-Korea and Vietnam. Beijing, pp 280–295

Zimmer R (2013a) Kompetenz Europäischer Betriebsräte zum Abschluss europaweiter Kollektivvereinbarungen? Europäische Zeitschrift für Arbeitsrecht (EuZA) 4:459–471

Zimmer R (2013b) Entwicklungsperspektiven transnationaler Kollektivverhandlungen in Europa – Schaffung eines rechtlichen Rahmens für transnationale Kollektivverträge in der Europäischen Union. Europäische Zeitschrift für Arbeitsrecht (EuZA) 2:247–259

Zimmer R (2013c) European Works Councils as participants in Euro-wide collective agreements – analysis from a German perspective. Eur Labour Law J (ELLJ) 4(4):312–327

Zimmer R (2015) EU-Dienstleistungsfreiheit auch für (billig) ausgeflaggte Schiffe. Anmerkung zur EuGH-Entscheidung vom 8.7.2014, C-83/13 (Fonnship). Arbeit und Recht (AuR) 3:103–105

Zimmer R (2016a) Corporate responsibility in the "Bangladesh Accord". Which regulations are transferable to other supply chains? FES-Publication. https://library.fes.de/pdf-files/id-moe/13072.pdf

Zimmer R (2016b) Legitimization: mandate and signatory parties – the trade union side. In: ETUC (ed) Building an enabling environment for voluntary and autonomous negotiations at transnational level between trade unions and multinational companies. Final report, Brussels, pp 18–22. https://www.etuc.org/sites/default/files/publication/files/160905_tca_final_report_en_proof_final.pdf

Zimmer R (2019a) Internationale Arbeitsorganisation (§ 5). In: Schlachter M, Heuschmid J, Ulber D (eds) Arbeitsvölkerrecht. Mohr Siebeck, Tübingen, pp 117–200

Zimmer R (2019b) Internationale Rahmenvereinbarungen (§ 8). In: Schlachter M, Heuschmid J, Ulber D (eds) Arbeitsvölkerrecht. Mohr Siebeck, Tübingen, pp 433–448

Reingard Zimmer is Professor of German, European and International Labour Law at Berlin School of Economics and Law. She is a fully qualified German lawyer (qualified in 2009) and holds a PhD from the University of Bremen. Her topics of research are precarious working conditions, non-discrimination and collective labour law (collective bargaining law, the right to strike (European) works councils), especially concerning cross-border issues. She is also focusing on international social standards of working conditions and the influence of trade & investment agreements.

The ILO Tripartite Declaration of Principles Concerning Multinational Enterprises and Social Policy Revisited: Is There a Need for Its Reform?

Jernej Letnar Černič

Contents

1 Introduction

Ordinary persons around the world have been struggling to have their voices heard about negative impacts of businesses and even alleged corporate human rights violations. They have often in vain attempted to protect their rights in various national and international legal forums. Corporations have often hijacked democratic processes and joined forces with political elites and even at times with organised crimes organisations. Developments in business and human rights have been in recent years advancing very rapidly with many new innovative approaches to responding to the plight of vulnerable persons and groups who have suffered due to the adverse impact of business activities. On the other hand, the Tripartite

I would like to thank Miren Cabada Rodriguez for her assistance in editing this article. All errors remain my own. The author acknowledges that the research for this chapter was financially supported by the Slovenian Research Agency.

J. L. Černič (✉)
Faculty of Government and European Studies, Nova univerza, Ljubljana, Slovenia
e-mail: jernej.letnar@fds.nova-uni.si

© Springer Nature Switzerland AG 2019
M. Bungenberg et al. (eds.), *European Yearbook of International Economic Law 2019*,
European Yearbook of International Economic Law (2020) 10: 193–214,
https://doi.org/10.1007/8165_2019_30, Published online: 17 September 2019

Declaration of Principles concerning Multinational Enterprises and Social Policy of the International Labour Organization (hereinafter the Tripartite Declaration or Declaration) has been one of the early documents in the field of business and human rights.[1]

The Governing Body of International Labour Office has adopted the Tripartite Declaration in November 1978 on its 204th session.[2] It has been later amended three times in November 2000,[3] March 2006[4] and most recently March 2017.[5] Its role has been in the past perhaps overlooked given the challenges concerning the enforcement of the Declaration. However, it should not be underestimated given that it employs unique tripartite approach of International Labour Organization by involving different stakeholders. The introduction of the 2017 version of the Tripartite Declaration attempts to justify its continuing relevance by providing that "the continued prominent role of multinational enterprises in the process of social and economic globalization renders the application of the principles of the MNE Declaration important and necessary in the context of foreign direct investment and trade, and the use of global supply chains."[6] The Declaration has so far not been a star in the global area of business and human rights. This is illustrated by the lack of detailed examination of the Declaration in the literature. More specifically, much has been written in the last decade on different aspects and dimensions in the area business and human rights in terms of books,[7] book chapters and articles.[8] Much of debate has been focused on the UN Guiding Principles on Business and Human Rights[9] and the Business and Human Rights Treaty.[10] However, not much has been surprisingly written on the ILO Declaration, with the exception of a few works.[11]

The International Labour Organization has a long-standing track-record in norm-setting for state obligations to protecting human rights, particularly core labour rights. Its long-standing bet on the tri-partite framework for dialogue on labour

---

[1]International Labour Organization, Tripartite Declaration of Principles concerning Multinational Enterprises and Social Policy (Fifth Edition, March 2017), https://www.ilo.org/wcmsp5/groups/public/%2D%2D-ed_emp/%2D%2D-emp_ent/%2D%2D-multi/documents/publication/wcms_094386.pdf (last accessed 21 January 2019).

[2]ILO, Tripartite Declaration of Principles concerning Multinational Enterprises and Social Policy, Doc. 28197701, OB Vol. LXI, 1978, ser. A, no. 1 (1977).

[3]ILO, Tripartite Declaration of Principles concerning Multinational Enterprises and Social Policy (Third Edition 2001).

[4]ILO, Tripartite Declaration of Principles concerning Multinational Enterprises and Social Policy (Fourth Edition 2006).

[5]ILO, Tripartite Declaration of Principles concerning Multinational Enterprises and Social Policy (Fifth Edition, March 2017).

[6]Ibid., "Introduction", p. 6.

[7]Deva and Bilchitz (2013), Clapham (2006), Jägers (2002), Letnar Černič (2010), Muchlinski (2007), Michalowski (2013), Ruggie (2013) and Álvarez Rubio and Yiannibas (2017).

[8]Ratner (2001), Vásquez (2005), Kinley and Tadaki (2004), Michalowski (2012), Keitner (2008), Dhooge (2007), Scheffer and Kaeb (2011), Lambooy (2014) and Shamir (2004).

[9]Martin Amerson (2012), Bilchitz (2010), Aaronson and Higham (2013), Ruggie (2004, 2013) and Jägers (2011). See also, O'Brien et al. (2016) and de Felice and Graf (2015).

[10]Deva and Bilchitz (2017) and Letnar Černič and Carrillo-Santarelli (2018).

[11]See in detail Letnar Černič (2009), Diller (2002), Morawetz (1991) and Biondi (2015).

issues, including business and workers' enables it to work in the larger business and human rights field. The Director-General of the ILO has observed at the 2018 Business and Human Rights forum that "regarding the responsibility of business to respect, the ILO promotes sustainable enterprises, provides guidance on international labour standards to companies, manages business networks on decent work issues, and participates in international initiatives that enhance due diligence on labour rights".[12] The ILO certainly has the potential to contribute to rights-holders oriented business and human rights fields. Nonetheless, as this article illustrates, it has to adopt more concrete and practical approach and to make available more concrete measures in order to really make the Tripartite Declaration as "a key international reference for collective efforts to ensure that labour rights are protected and respected in the operations of transnational business;. . .."[13] Particularly, it is indispensable to focus more on improving efforts to increase socio-economic livelihoods of workers around the world by insisting on state and corporate obligations.[14]

This chapter therefore revisits the function, role and scope of the ILO Tripartite Declaration of Principles concerning Multinational Enterprises and Social Policy and asks if there is there a need for its reform? It first provides in Sect. 2 a brief historical background and explore its legal nature. Section 3 examines the contents of the revised Tripartite Declaration focusing on labour and/or human rights provisions thereby providing critical account of provisions included or omitted. Section 4, thereafter, describes and critically analyses its implementation tools from promotion to interpretation procedures and provides a critical assessment of their usefulness for rights-holders. Equipped with the knowledge from previous sections, Sect. 5 thereafter provides an overall analysis and assessment of the recent revisions of the ILO Tripartite Declaration outlining both its advantages and disadvantages; places it in the wider context of standard-setting in business and human rights and provides some suggestions how to reform it and to better realize its potential. This chapter, all in all argues, that the ILO Governing Body should rephrase vague and conditional language of the Tripartite Declaration and improve its implementation tools, particularly the interpretation procedures by opening it to individual claimants. In this way, it would emancipate the rights-holders to enforce the core labour rights included in the Declaration against adverse corporate conduct.

---

[12]Remarks by Mr Guy Ryder (Director-General of the ILO), Panel on "Building coherence and reaching scale on human rights due diligence – International organizations' leadership perspectives", United Nations Forum on Business and Human Rights, 27 November 2018.

[13]Ibid., p. 2.

[14]See, for example, Letnar Černič (2018).

2 Historical Backdrop and the Nature of the Tripartite Declaration

The ILO is a specialised international organisation focussing on labour and social security standard settings, which has despite criticism[15] brought about positive change. The Constitution of the ILO has since 1919 built upon ensuring human dignity for individuals in the working process.[16] The Tripartite Declaration was developed as complementary soft-law standard to the existing ILO conventions. Given that it exists already over 42 years, its impact has been hidden and limited.

The Tripartite Declaration is not a binding international legal document as it can be described as a soft-law and quasi-legal document. The Tripartite Declaration itself refers to soft-law nature in its introduction where it explains that the Declaration should be understood as "guidelines for enhancing the positive social and labour effects of the operations and governance of multinational enterprises to achieve decent work for all, a universal goal recognized in the 2030 Agenda for Sustainable Development."[17] The language employed here is notoriously vague as it refers to "guidance", which can hardly resonate in any binding obligations. Its soft-law legal nature conveys that it does not create and impose binding human rights obligations on states and corporations. In spite of its non-binding nature, it has been referred and cited by number of authoritative international documents[18] and soft law documents.[19] Therefore, non-binding and quasi legal soft mechanisms such as the

---

[15]Alston (2004, 2005) and Maupain (2005).

[16]The Preamble of the ILO Constitution notes in second section: "...whereas conditions of labour exist involving such injustice, hardship and privation to large numbers of people as to produce unrest so great that the peace and harmony of the world are imperilled; and an improvement of those conditions is urgently required; as, for example, by the regulation of the hours of work, including the establishment of a maximum working day and week, the regulation of the labour supply, the prevention of unemployment, the provision of an adequate living wage, the protection of the worker against sickness, disease and injury arising out of his employment, the protection of children, young persons and women, provision for old age and injury, protection of the interests of workers when employed in countries other than their own, recognition of the principle of equal remuneration for work of equal value, recognition of the principle of freedom of association, the organization of vocational and technical education and other measures;" ILO, *Constitution of the ILO,* 1 April 1919, http://www.ilo.org/public/english/bureau/leg/download/constitution.pdf.

[17]International Labour Organization, Tripartite Declaration of Principles concerning Multinational Enterprises and Social Policy, Fifth Edition, March 2017. See also Brownlie (1980), pp. 39 and 41.

[18]See, for example, Council of the European Union Conclusions on Sustainable Garment Value Chains, Document 9381/17, 19 May 2017; Council of the European Union Conclusions on Business and Human Rights, Document 10254/16, 20 June 2016; Council of the European Union conclusions on the EU and Responsible Global Value Chains, Document 8833/16, 12 May 2016.

[19]See, for example, OECD Guidelines for Multinational Enterprises (2011 Edition) and UN, Human Rights Council, Report of the Special Representative of the Secretary General on the Issue of Human Rights and Transnational Corporations and Other Business Enterprises, John Ruggie, 'Guiding Principles on Business and Human Rights: Implementing the United Nations "Protect, Respect and Remedy" Framework' ['The Guiding Principles'], UN Doc. A/HRC/17/31, 21 March 2011.

Tripartite Declaration may have binding effect and impacts, particularly when they are translated in domestic law or included in binding international treaties. Moreover, most provisions that are included in the Tripartite Declaration have already been included in binding ILO Conventions or in domestic law and have thereby acquired binding effect at least against states. If they are included also in the legal sources of domestic systems such as national constitutions and statutory legislations, they create binding legal obligations for all natural and legal persons in domestic systems, including corporations. In this way, rights-holders can invoke core labour standards against state authorities and business before domestic courts. For those reasons, the legal nature and scope of Declaration is more long-ranging than it seems from its very cautious and non-binding language. In this way, it could have been used more by the rights-holders in advancing they core labour rights against corporations.

3 The Contents of Tripartite Declaration

The Tripartite Declaration has been divided in six main chapters as follows: Aim and scope, General policies, Employment, Training, Conditions of work and life and Industrial relations.[20] The Declaration starts with setting out its primary objectives and clarifying it scope. It notes the is main aim has been to "encourage the positive contribution which multinational enterprises can make to economic and social progress and the realization of decent work for all".[21] It explains that "this aim will be furthered by appropriate laws and policies, measures and actions adopted by the governments, including in the fields of labour administration and public labour inspection, and by cooperation among the governments and the employers' and workers' organizations of all countries."[22] The Declaration clearly applies to state governments, corporations and individuals.[23] It includes all fundamental labour standards as applicable to states and governments. Its part on general policies refers to core international labour standards, including the ILO Declaration on Fundamental Principles and Rights at Work.[24] Section 10 also refers to the UN Guiding Principles on Business and Human Rights and its tripartite framework of corporate

---

[20]International Labour Organization, Tripartite Declaration of Principles concerning Multinational Enterprises and Social Policy, Fifth Edition, March 2017, pp. 1–16.

[21]International Labour Organization, Tripartite Declaration of Principles concerning Multinational Enterprises and Social Policy, Fifth Edition, March 2017, https://www.ilo.org/wcmsp5/groups/public/%2D%2D-ed_emp/%2D%2D-emp_ent/%2D%2D-multi/documents/publication/wcms_094386.pdf, para. 2.

[22]Ibid. 3.

[23]Ibid., Section 10.

[24]ILO Declaration on Fundamental Principles and Rights at Work, June 18, 1998, 37 I.L.M. 1233 (1998).

responsibility to respect, state duty to protect and access to remedy.[25] Section 11 stipulates that "Multinational enterprises should take fully into account established general policy objectives of the countries in which they operate" and adds that "their activities should be consistent with national law and in harmony with the development priorities and social aims and structure of the country in which they operate. To this effect, consultations should be held between multinational enterprises, the government and, wherever appropriate, the national employers' and workers' organizations concerned."[26] The Declaration, however, despite of referring to the UN Guiding Principles, does not embody the spirit of recent developments in the area of business and human rights, which have concentrated on empowering rights-holders with access to remedy in the case of business-related human rights violations.

Part II on employment includes several references on peremptory human rights obligations. Section 23 calls for the elimination of forced or compulsory labour and urges states to "take effective measures to prevent and eliminate forced labour, to provide to victims protection and access to appropriate and effective remedies, such as compensation and rehabilitation, and to sanction the perpetrators of forced or compulsory labour"[27] and to "develop a national policy and plan of action, in consultation with employers' and workers' organizations."[28] As for corporations, it provides that "Multinational as well as national enterprises should take immediate and effective measures within their own competence to secure the prohibition and elimination of forced or compulsory labour in their operations."[29] As one can see, the language in the above provisions is increasingly conditional, which appears inappropriate, as at least state obligations concerning prohibition of forced or compulsory labour and other core labour standards have been consolidated and accepted at domestic and international levels since many decades.[30] Some commentators have argued that they form part of peremptory norms of international law, which oblige state and non-state actors to comply with them. Further, Section 25 and 26 refer to state and corporate commitments concerning effective abolition of child labour, more particularly minimum age and worst forms of child labour. Section 26 provides that corporations "should respect the minimum age for admission to employment or work in order to secure the effective abolition of child labour in their operations and should take immediate and effective measures within their own competence to secure the prohibition and elimination of the worst forms of child

---

[25]International Labour Organization, Tripartite Declaration of Principles concerning Multinational Enterprises and Social Policy, Fifth Edition, March 2017, Section 10.

[26]Ibid., Section 11.

[27]Ibid., Section 23.

[28]Ibid.

[29]Ibid., Section 25.

[30]See, for example, ILO Convention concerning Forced or Compulsory Labour (ILO No. 29), 39 U.N.T.S. 55, entered into force 1 May 1932; ILO Abolition of Forced Labour Convention (ILO No. 105), 320 U.N.T.S. 291, entered into force 17 January 1959.

labour as a matter of urgency."[31] One can make here similar observations as relating to the compulsory character of the prohibition of forced or compulsory labour. As for non-discrimination, Section 30 provides that "multinational enterprises should be guided by the principle of non-discrimination throughout their operations without prejudice to the measures envisaged in paragraph 18 or to government policies designed to correct historical patterns of discrimination and thereby to extend equality of opportunity and treatment in employment."[32] Non-discrimination is generally accepted in most domestic systems. States have the positive obligation that the non-discrimination principle is followed and complied with also in the private sector in order that equal treatment and equal remuneration of employees are ensured.[33] Moreover, businesses are obliged to introduce non-discrimination rules and policies and to internalize them in their business operations.

The Declarations' section on health and safety includes further provisions on corporate commitments. More specifically, it asks corporations to "maintain the highest standards of safety and health, in conformity with national requirements, bearing in mind their relevant experience within the enterprise as a whole, including any knowledge of special hazards."[34] Such provisions require to be further operationalised if they are not to remain *lex imperfecta*. Another provision, which is already accepted in most domestic systems, is the provision on freedom of association and the right to organize, which notes that "Workers employed by multinational enterprises as well as those employed by national enterprises should, without distinction whatsoever, have the right to establish and, subject only to the rules of the organization concerned, to join organizations of their own choosing without previous authorization. They should also enjoy adequate protection against acts of anti-union discrimination in respect of their employment."[35] Freedom of association is a fundamental civil and political right, which forms a pillar of every functioning constitutional democracy. It is therefore not necessary that the provision uses the conditional verb "should", as such a right has been recognized by well-established international and regional treaties such as the International Covenant on Civil and Political Rights[36] and the European Convention for the Protection of

---

[31] International Labour Organization, Tripartite Declaration of Principles concerning Multinational Enterprises and Social Policy, Section 26.

[32] Ibid., Section 30.

[33] Section 28 provides that "Governments should pursue policies designed to promote equality of opportunity and treatment in employment, with a view to eliminating any discrimination based on race, colour, sex, religion, political opinion, national extraction or social origin", whereas Section 29 stipulates that "Governments should promote equal remuneration for men and women workers for work of equal value."

[34] Ibid., Section 30.

[35] Ibid., Section 48.

[36] International Covenant on Civil and Political Rights, G.A. res. 2200A (XXI), 21 U.N. GAOR Supp. (No. 16) at 52, U.N. Doc. A/6316 (1966), 999 U.N.T.S. 171, entered into force 23 March 1976, Article 22.

Human Rights and Fundamental Freedoms[37] lest to mention its protection in national constitutions. Therefore, such vague language of the Tripartite Declaration is neither understandable nor necessary as binding standards of protections already exist.

The Tripartite Declaration also includes several provisions on access to remedy. States have the primary obligations to ensure that rights-holders enjoy direct access to remedy before judicial, quasi-judicial or non-judicial mechanisms, which are to comply with the principle of fairness, independence, impartiality and transparency. The fairness, independence and quality of domestic judicial systems varies from jurisdiction to jurisdiction, hence regional and international human rights tribunals and other bodies play indispensable role in protecting rights. Nonetheless, corporations carry complementary responsibilities to ensure that voice of rights-holders are fairly heard before impartial tribunal. The Tripartite Declaration states that "Multinational enterprises should use their leverage to encourage their business partners to provide effective means of enabling remediation for abuses of internationally recognized human rights."[38] Such a wording of the provision does not point at the binding language, however it illustrates that transnational corporations are urged to ensure that rights-holders have access to the right to remedy also in their global supply chains as they carry also positive obligations to make sure that remedies are available and efficient. The Tripartite Declaration concerns negative dimension of the access to remedy. For instance, Section 66 stipulates that "Multinational as well as national enterprises should respect the right of the workers whom they employ to have all their grievances processed in a manner consistent with the following provision: any worker who, acting individually or jointly with other workers, considers that he or she has grounds for a grievance should have the right to submit such grievance without suffering any prejudice whatsoever as a result, and to have such grievance examined pursuant to an appropriate procedure."[39] This provision grants workers the right to submit individual and joint complaints. However, such provision is in direct contradiction with the interpretation procedure of the Tripartite Declaration found under its Operational Tools in Annex II, which directly prohibits individual from individual submitting grievances, and allowing them to act only through workers organisations.[40] It appears that the all provisions on access to remedy have been drafted in order to only portray the voluntary nature of the contents of the Tripartite Declaration.

Voluntarism can also be seen in the provisions on industrial disputes. They, for instance, postulate that "Multinational as well as national enterprises jointly with the representatives and organizations of the workers whom they employ should seek to establish voluntary conciliation machinery, appropriate to national conditions, which may include provisions for voluntary arbitration, to assist in the prevention and

---

[37]European Convention for the Protection of Human Rights and Fundamental Freedoms, 213 U.N.T.S. 222, entered into force 3 September 1953, Article 10.

[38]International Labour Organization, Tripartite Declaration of Principles concerning Multinational Enterprises and Social Policy, Fifth Edition, March 2017, Section 65.

[39]Ibid., Section 66.

[40]See Sect. 4.3 of this chapter.

settlement of industrial disputes between employers and workers. The voluntary conciliation machinery should include equal representation of employers and workers."[41] The outstanding question, however, is how can a voluntary system work where the balance of power is so apparent in the favour of businesses as it is in the employment relationships between corporations and workers, particularly in those national environments, which do not have any history and tradition of collective bargaining.

The contents of the Tripartite Declaration therefore leave much to be desired for in terms of the legal nature and scope of its provisions. It is not clearly why it employs such unclear and conditional languages in the provisions, which have been accepted and agreed upon decades ago such as relating to prohibition of forced and compulsory labour and prohibition of child labour. Those provisions oblige both state and non-state actors to follow them and state to provide national mechanisms to enforce them. All in all, the contents of the Tripartite Declaration can be described as more or less binding as most of its provisions have been already translated in binding domestic and international sources of law.

4 Implementation and Enforcement of Declaration

The implementation and enforcement of the Declaration have been a long-standing subject of debate or dispute among different stakeholders. The Tripartite Ad Hoc Working Group on the Follow-up Mechanism of the MNE Declaration has noted in 2012 that the ILO Tripartite Declarations is a "document promoting the adherence of multinational enterprises to economic and social development, based on ILO principles and rights at work, the key responsibilities of governments as well as the pivotal role of dialogue with workers' and employers' organizations."[42] Specifics on implementation and enforcement can be found in Annex II in the Operational tools of the 2017 version Tripartite Declaration. Annex II names three modes of implementation, namely promotion, company-union dialogue and procedure for the examination of disputes concerning the application of the Tripartite Declaration of Principles concerning Multinational Enterprises and Social Policy by means of interpretation of its provisions, as means for the implementation and enforcement of the Tripartite Declaration.[43]

---

[41]International Labour Organization, Tripartite Declaration of Principles concerning Multinational Enterprises and Social Policy, Fifth Edition, March 2017, Section 68.

[42]Report of the Tripartite Ad Hoc Working Group on the Follow-up Mechanism of the MNE Declaration, Governing Body, 313th Session, Geneva, Mar. 2012, GB.313/POL/9 (Rev.), https://www.ilo.org/wcmsp5/groups/public/@ed_norm/@relconf/documents/meetingdocument/wcms_173721.pdf, para. 6.

[43]International Labour Organization, Tripartite Declaration of Principles concerning Multinational Enterprises and Social Policy, Fifth Edition, March 2017, https://www.ilo.org/wcmsp5/groups/public/%2D%2D-ed_emp/%2D%2D-emp_ent/%2D%2D-multi/documents/publication/wcms_094386.pdf, Annex 2, pp. 21–25.

4.1 Promotion

Promotion as a means of implementation is further divided in three sub-means, namely regional follow-up; promotion at the national level by tripartite appointed national focal points; and promotion by the International Labour Office.[44] Promotional measures are aimed at ensuring the preventive dimension of the Tripartite Declaration. The main burden of the responsibility for the promotion of the Tripartite Declaration lies with the Governing Body of the International Labour Office, which "reviews on a regular basis the overall strategy and underlying activities to promote the instrument together with governments, employers' and workers' organizations in all ILO member States."[45]

The first promotional measure, the regional follow-up, envisages drafting "a regional report on the promotion and application of the MNE Declaration in the ILO member States in the region", deriving contents from "inputs received from governments, employers' and workers' organizations in these member States on the basis of a questionnaire and a special session during ILO Regional Meetings provides a tripartite dialogue platform to discuss further promotional activities at the regional level."[46] The reports should be prepared every 4 years and submitted to the ILO Governing body.[47]

The second promotional measures, national focal points, are to provide local context to the implementation of the Tripartite Declaration. National focal points are to actively promote the principles of the MNE Declaration at country level. This could include "raising awareness of principles of the MNE Declaration among government ministries and agencies, multinational enterprises and employers' and workers' organizations; organizing capacity- building events; and developing online information and dialogue platforms in local languages where possible. National focal points with limited resources or capacity could progressively expand their outreach and activities."[48] They were first recommended by the Tripartite Ad Hoc Working Group on the Follow-up Mechanism of the MNE Declaration "to promote the use of the MNE Declaration and its principles, whenever appropriate and meaningful in the national context, and inform the Office of these focal points."[49]

National focal points may serve as a useful tool in the promotion activities. For instance, the ILO reported that Senegal appointed four national contact points for the dissemination activities for promotion and application the Guidelines at the government, workers and business level in 2017. Senegal even introduced the Commission for the Promotion of the ILO MNE Declaration in the High Council of Social Dialogue,

---

[44]Ibid., 1a–1c, pp. 21–22.

[45]Ibid., 21.

[46]Ibid., 21.

[47]Ibid.

[48]Ibid. 21–22.

[49]Report of the Tripartite Ad Hoc Working Group on the Follow-up Mechanism of the MNE Declaration, Governing Body, 313th Session, Geneva, Mar. 2012, GB.313/POL/9 (Rev.), para. 10 (c).

whose president also serves as fourth national focal point.[50] Also, Ivory Coast and Portugal have created National Focal Points,[51] which welcome development, but more than three states will have to introduce localized mechanisms for focal points to gain some ground.

The third subpart of promotion activities includes promotion by the International Labour Office. It is divided in technical assistance and information and guidance. Technical assistance includes "country-level assistance to governments, employers and workers",[52] whereas information and guidance has been described as "free and confidential service of the International Labour Office answers individual questions and also consists of a dedicated website organized by topic where companies, trade unions and others can find information, practical tools and training opportunities and questions and answers to help them put the principles of the MNE Declaration into practice."[53] Such envisaged promotional activity is of programmatic and general nature thereby it may have more medium or long-term impact.

All in all, it is clear that promotional activities are geared towards corporations and governments, whereas rights-holders have been missing from the picture since the last revision. They are aimed at the promotion of the ILO's core labour standards. In doing so, they appear to address potential violations ex ante. It remains to be seen how this approach will affect the effectiveness of the Declaration. What remains certain is that the victims cannot make much use of promotional activities after violations already occurred. Therefore, their added value for rights-holders has been limited.

4.2   Company-Union Dialogue

The second part of the Operational Tools under the Tripartite Declaration include company-union dialogues, which include mostly means of collective bargaining, alternative dispute resolution and mediation. The role of ILO in the Company-union dialogue may take one the three forms: "provide a neutral ground for parties to engage in meaningful dialogue"; "provide input during company–union dialogue as a technical or expert adviser to inform the company–union dialogue", and "facilitate dialogue."[54] Such tools are the result of the advantage of the ILO, which has been

---

[50]ILO, Senegal appoints four national focal points and lays the foundations of a national promotion strategy, 2017, https://www.ilo.org/empent/units/multinational-enterprises/WCMS_616830/lang%2D%2Den/index.htm.

[51]ILO, MNE Declaration, Promotion at the national level/Promotion by tripartite appointed national focal points, https://www.ilo.org/empent/areas/mne-declaration/WCMS_570379/lang%2D%2Den/index.htm.

[52]International Labour Organization, Tripartite Declaration of Principles concerning Multinational Enterprises and Social Policy, Fifth Edition, March 2017, Annex 2, Ibid. 22.

[53]Ibid.

[54]International Labour Organization, Tripartite Declaration of Principles concerning Multinational Enterprises and Social Policy (Fifth Edition, March 2017), Annex II, Company-Union Dialogue, p. 23.

facilitating dialogue between different stakeholders since many decades. The ILO therefore prides itself that as "the global authority on international labour standards, [it] is uniquely placed to support or facilitate such dialogues as part of its overall strategy to promote the uptake of the principles of the MNE Declaration by the various parties addressed therein."[55] The company-union dialogue functions on the basis of negotiations and consensus. More specifically, "where a company and a union voluntarily agree to take advantage of using the facilities of the International Labour Office to meet and talk, without prejudice, the Office will provide a neutral ground for discussion of issues of mutual concern."[56] The dialogue will be based on confidentiality as "[t]he Office and the participants shall maintain strict confidentiality of the dialogue process."[57] The Office aims to draft "in consultation with the secretariats of the Employers' and Workers' groups of the ILO, confidentiality criteria and practices to be considered by the participants in the dialogue process."[58] It is not quite clear why so much emphasis has to be placed on confidentiality, which is not a proper tool for resolving individuals' human rights concerns or even violations that rights-holders may have experienced. However, such developments have been in the line with the trends to make the Tripartite Declaration more in line with expectations of the employers and governments. Nonetheless, the company-union dialogue is an attractive and innovative approach in the implementation process of the Tripartite Declaration. Unfortunately, so far, no data have been published as to how many companies and unions have opted for such ILO assisted dialogue and mediation if any since revision of the Tripartite Declaration. Therefore, it is too early to measure the impact of such a tool in the implementations of the Declaration and assess how effective these dialogues can be for victims. Nonetheless, such an implementation method could certainly be useful in the future particularly if it will be taken seriously by all stakeholders.

4.3 Interpretation Procedure

Annex 2 also provides for a "procedure for the examination of disputes concerning the application of the Tripartite Declaration of Principles concerning Multinational Enterprises and Social Policy by means of interpretation of its provisions (interpretation procedure)".[59] The procedure notes that its aims to "interpret the provisions of the Declaration when needed to resolve a disagreement on their meaning, arising

---

[55]Ibid.

[56]Ibid.

[57]Ibid.

[58]Ibid.

[59]International Labour Organization, Tripartite Declaration of Principles concerning Multinational Enterprises and Social Policy (Fifth Edition, March 2017), Annex II, Interpretation Procedure pp. 24–25. See generally Shin-ichi (2019).

from an actual situation, between parties to whom the Declaration is commended."[60] It is notable that the procedure refers to "disagreement" not to violations. The procedure excludes any other procedures, which have been already started concerning "national law and practice"[61]; "international labour Conventions and Recommendations"[62]; and "matters falling under the freedom of association procedure".[63] The Request of Interpretation may be addressed as a rule "by the government of a member State acting either on its own initiative or at the request of a national organization of employers or workers", "by a national organization of employers or workers, which is representative at the national and/or sectoral level...", and "by an international organization of employers or workers on behalf of a representative national affiliate."[64] *Locus standi* is therefore afforded to the traditional ILO stakeholders, whereas it appears that victims of the direct violations do not have direct access to the interpretation procedure under the 2017 version of the Tripartite Declaration. The procedure ends with a reply. The Annex notes that "[i]n the case of receivable requests the Office shall prepare a draft reply in consultation with the Officers of the Governing Body. All appropriate sources of information shall be used, including government, employers' and workers' sources in the country concerned. The Officers may ask the Office to indicate a period within which the information should be provided"[65] and "[t]he draft reply to a receivable request shall be considered and approved by the Governing Body."[66] The Annex leaves blank what the reply should consist of, including whether it should include findings of violations and recommendations how to remedy them.

The current content and model of the interpretation procedure is therefore a far cry from Section 66 of 2017 version of the Tripartite Declaration, which provided that "...any worker who, acting individually or jointly with other workers, considers that he has grounds for a grievance should have the right to submit such grievance without suffering any prejudice whatsoever as a result, and to have such grievance examined pursuant to an appropriate procedure."[67] Such a provision provides any worker with the right to individually submit a grievance concerning alleged violation of the Declaration, but it is not reflected in the interpretation procedure for enforcement of Declaration. It is therefore not clear why it has been omitted from interpretation version. Even before recent revisions of the Tripartite this provision did not give rise to many complaints nor it has been very efficient. We have noted in 2009 that "[t]he Governing Body has so far delivered decisions in five cases. Two were submitted by a government, and three by international organizations of workers on

---

[60]Ibid., Interpretation Procedure, Section 1.

[61]Interpretation Procedure, Section 2.a.

[62]Interpretation Procedure, Section 2.b.

[63]Interpretation Procedure, Section 2.c.

[64]Interpretation Procedure, Section 5.

[65]Interpretation Procedure, Section 7.

[66]Interpretation Procedure, Section 8.

[67]2006 Tripartite Declaration, 58.

behalf of representative national affiliates."[68] However, even such mechanism did not prove very successful.[69] Therefore we noted in 2009 that "[a]s a result, some commentators consider the ILO Tripartite Declaration to be a failure. There are very legitimate reasons for enforcing the responsibility of corporations for violations of the Tripartite Declaration. At the very least, the Tripartite declaration should provide for a complaints system similar to the OECD NCPs. However, it does not seem likely that many states will want to approve such an extension of the Declaration, and victims are left with a patchwork of international ILO framework which produces inconsistent and conflicting results."[70] It is not clear why such a possibility for victims to enforce their rights was not offered in the 2017 version of Interpretation Tripartite Declaration, as the ILO received and dealt with at least some complaints so far. Nonetheless, it appears that there were pressures from the governments and national organisations of employers to change such a system. Such developments have certainly been unfortunate as they has stripped individuals from being able to voice their grievance under the interpretation procedure. The enforcement mechanisms have therefore been one the largest problems of the Declaration. Biondi observed that "[a] major problem for the success of the MNE Declaration has been the follow-up process, which has proved inadequate to the task. One element of the follow-up was the survey to be conducted globally every four years; this proved to be a negotiating nightmare for the MNE Subcommittee and in the end did not really add to the practical use of the Declaration, even though the language that was eventually negotiated, for example for the 7th Survey, would prove to be very progressive."[71] Strategy on the Implementation Strategy was drafted in 2014 based on 2012 report,[72] however without any substantial success.[73]

What can then be said of the current system? The current interpretation system lacks any added value for victims, who have suffered violations of Tripartite declaration as it does not provide them with fair, impartial, independent and transparent procedure, where they could enforce their rights. They are much better served in turning to domestic courts to protect their labour rights against adverse corporate conduct. Therefore, the interpretation should be reformed in three ways. First, the rights of victims to submit grievances individually should be reinstated, either with opening-up and strengthening interpretation procedure or equipping the National Focal Points with same or similar competences as the National Contact Points have

---

[68]Letnar Černič (2009), p. 31. See Clapham (2006), p. 216; Shin-ichi (2019).

[69]Letnar Černič (2009), p. 31.

[70]*Ibid.*

[71]Biondi (2015), p. 109.

[72]Report of the Tripartite Ad Hoc Working Group on the Follow-up Mechanism of the MNE Declaration, Governing Body, 313th Session, Geneva, Mar. 2012, GB.313/POL/9 (Rev.).

[73]Implementation strategy for the follow-up mechanism of and promotional activities on the Tripartite Declaration of Principles concerning Multinational Enterprises and Social Policy (MNE Declaration), Governing Body, 320th Session, Geneva, Mar. 2014, GB. 320/POL/10. http://www.ilo.org/wcmsp5/groups/public/%2D%2D-ed_norm/%2D%2D-relconf/documents/meetingdocument/wcms_236168.pdf.

under the OECD Guidelines for Multinational Enterprises. Secondly, the interpretation procedure or other enforcement procedure must derive from the fundamental of access to remedy as envisaged by the UN Guiding Principles on Business and Human Rights. Thirdly, the supervision system must be strengthened by complying with fundamental principles of procedural fairness, independence and impartiality. The current system of interpretation procedure therefore only exists for itself and it does not have any practical value for victims of corporate human rights violations not for any other stakeholder for that matter.

5   Assessment of the Declaration and Proposals for Reform

What should be the future role of the Tripartite Declaration in the increasing fragmentation in the area business and human rights? How can it assume greater relevance and gain more recognition in the field of business and human rights than it has had so far? How can it contribute equally also to the advancement of the rights of right-holders? How can it complement and support current debates and points how can the Tripartite Declaration complement to the potential UN Business and Human Rights Treaty?[74]

The Tripartite Declaration includes core labour standards (freedom of association and the effective recognition of the right to collective bargaining,[75] the elimination of all forms of forced and compulsory labour,[76] the effective abolition of child labour[77]; and the elimination of discrimination in respect of employment and occupation[78]) as applicable to business activities. The content of the Declaration therefore follows from the core ILO Conventions; however, its language is conditional. The 2017 Revision of the Tripartite has to some extent modified its content. It has affected mostly those provisions, which have granted individuals protection to the rights. The revised version of the Tripartite Declaration is therefore much to the liking of the business community and government as it employs a very cautious and unclear language. It has almost fully taken up the voluntary approach of the UN

---

[74]Letnar Černič and Carrillo-Santarelli (2018), Deva and Bilchitz (2017), Blackwell and Vander Meulen (2016) and De Schutter (2016).

[75]Freedom of Association and Protection of the Right to Organise Convention (ILO No. 87), 68 U.N.T.S. 17, entered into force 4 July 1950; Right to Organise and Collective Bargaining Convention (ILO No. 98), 96 U.N.T.S. 257, entered into force July 18, 1951.

[76]ILO Convention concerning Forced or Compulsory Labour (ILO No. 29), 39 U.N.T.S. 55, entered into force 1 May 1932; ILO Abolition of Forced Labour Convention (ILO No. 105), 320 U.N.T.S. 291, entered into force 17 January 1959.

[77]ILO, Convention (No. 138) Concerning Minimum Age for Admission to Employment, June 26, 1973, 1015 U.N.T.S. 297 [hereinafter ILO Convention No. 138]; ILO, Convention (No. 182) Concerning the Prohibition and Immediate Action for the Elimination of the Worst Forms of Child Labour, June 17, 1999, 2133 U.N.T.S. 161.

[78]ILO, Convention (No. 100) Concerning Equal Remuneration for Men and Women Workers for Work of Equal Value, June 29, 1951, 165 U.N.T.S. 303; ILO, Convention (No. 111) Concerning Discrimination in Respect of Employment and Occupation, June 25, 1958, 362 U.N.T.S. 31.

Guiding Principles on Business and Human Rights developed by John Ruggie. It has, on the other hand, disregarded more binding initiatives in the area on business and human rights such as the negotiations towards the UN Business and Human Rights Treaty. It seems that such one-sided approach may not be the best in the time of increased efforts to improve victims' access to remedy and to articulate both negative and positive obligations of corporations. The operational tools of the Declaration have been revised in the last revisions and the inclusion of national focal points in the promotional activities is particularly welcome. However, it is not clear how they can contribute to improve victims' access to justice, as their nature has been quite programmatic and vague. Therefore, national focal points should be given competences to hear grievances from individuals or organisations of employees and to provide at least recommendations in terms of violations.

If individuals or victims are not the primary focus of any instrument in business and human rights, then its purpose should be questioned. The Tripartite Declaration also employed a vague—conditional—language, which only refers to voluntary commitments. Given the above, rights holders may show little confidence in the text and mechanisms of the Declaration. Nonetheless, even if it uses conditional language its content is quite unequivocal. It includes standards that are now included not only in many national constitutions, but also in domestic statutes. For those reasons, many of the provisions of Declaration such as the prohibition of forced and compulsory labour[79] and effective abolition of child labour[80] have attained binding status and they indirectly and directly bind all legal subjects in domestic juris-dictions, including corporations. Additionally, core labour standards such as pro-hibitions of forced or compulsory labour standards have attained the status of *ius cogens* or peremptory norms in international law, which do not allow for any derogations. Those core labour standards can therefore be directly enforced in domestic courts. Such a development is welcome given that the interpretation procedure under Declaration has been limited and inefficient.

The Declaration is therefore yet another soft law document, which works parti-cularly well for businesses. Its added value may be the fact that it complements existing ILO conventions and recommendations. In this way, it may, first, supple-ment ILO efforts in clarifying and lifting labour law and social security standards in relation to corporations. Secondly, it may be employed as basic business and human rights document, which serves as a platform for the development of further and specialized ILO standards in the field of business and human rights. The recently adopted ILO Resolution concerning decent work in global supply chains illustrates such trend.[81] It is quite surprising that this ILO Resolution employs more binding language than the Tripartite Declaration itself. Section 10 of the Resolution reads, for

---

[79]International Labour Organization, Tripartite Declaration of Principles concerning Multinational Enterprises and Social Policy, Fifth Edition, March 2017, Section 23–25.

[80]Ibid., Sections 26–27.

[81]ILO, Resolution concerning decent work in global supply chains, 8 June 2016, https://www.ilo.org/ilc/ILCSessions/105/texts-adopted/WCMS_497555/lang%2D%2Den/index.htm.

example as follows "Business has a responsibility to respect labour rights in their operations as laid out in the UN Guiding Principles on Business and Human Rights (UN Guiding Principles), and governments have the duty to implement and enforce national laws and regulations."[82] It further provides that "governments, business and social partners have complementary but different responsibilities in promoting decent work in global supply chains. Business has a responsibility to respect human and labour rights in their supply chains, consistent with the UN Guiding Principles, and to comply with national law wherever they do business."[83] Whereas the ILO Tripartite Declaration can serve as point of departure, one cannot really expect that the ILO Declaration can serve as an effective remedy mechanism in business and human rights, because its contribution to standard-setting is located in designing preventive standards and specific norm setting in the subfield of business and human rights. We have previously noted that

> All in all, the Tripartite declaration has not gained a foothold as a useful tool for enforcing human rights violations by or involving corporations. With more concentration on fundamental labour rights as minimum standards for corporate responsibility, the Tripartite Declaration may gain traction and it could be gradually included in contracts, tenders, codes of conduct and collective bargaining agreements. Even if corporations are not legally bound by the Declaration, however, reference to it in private agreements would suggest consensus that ILO fundamental labour standards should be respected by the multinational enterprises.[84]

The reform of the Declaration should be therefore geared towards enhancing access to justice, making all dealings with the Declaration more transparent and opening up interpretation procedure to more claimants. Further, the enforcement procedure should be more aligned with the specific instances of National Contact Points under the OECD Guidance for Multinational enterprises. National Focal Points under promotional activates of ILO Declaration could be turned in local enforcement activates. The ILO could also do more work in protecting migrants' rights by improving their rights in host states.[85] What role should the Tripartite Declaration play in business and human rights field? We have noted previously that:

> Though the Tripartite Declaration employs indirect methods of enforcement concerning corporate obligations, it has become clear that international initiatives have thus far failed to establish a coherent standard for identifying corporate human rights obligations. And yet, calls for the establishment of a World Court for Human Rights to hear claims against corporations are controversial and highly unlikely to yield results, due to the current real politik of world powers. Therefore, enforcing the Tripartite Declaration is a necessary step for regulation of multinational enterprises in the international arena. The international human rights regime should offer a clear set of minimum standards on human rights obligations of corporations, and corporations and national legal systems should have to comply with and be a fortiori encouraged to exceed minimum standards.[86]

---

[82]Ibid, Section 10.

[83]Ibid, Section 15.

[84]Letnar Černič (2009), p. 33.

[85]Farbenblum and Nolan (2017).

[86]Letnar Černič (2009), p. 34.

The 2017 version of the Tripartite Declaration does not fully contribute to the objective of clarifying standards on corporate accountability for human rights. It shies away from shaping clear and unequivocal provisions on business and labour rights even at instances where they have been already included in other binding ILO conventions or voluntary recommendations. The role of the ILO and its Tripartite Declaration should have been to take leadership in drafting business and human rights standards in the area of minimum labour and social security standards. However, in order to achieve this, the stakeholders and drafters will have to decide what is or what should be the objective and added value of Tripartite Declaration. At the moment, the objectives and contents of the Tripartite Declaration are confusing and unclear. Should it strengthen or water down the existing ILO standards developed and agreed upon in the ILO Convention? Therefore, it is submitted that a Working Group of experts should be established and convened to discuss various options how to move forward and reform the Declaration. Those experts should be gathered from traditional ILO stakeholder groups, but also from the outside, taking advantage of the knowledge of various experts. The reform of the Tripartite Declaration should in our opinion proceed towards sharpening its provisions on core labour standards and strengthening access to remedy for victims of alleged human rights violations. Another dimension to explore would be how to include labour dimension of business and human rights in the debate on the Draft of the potential UN Treaty on Business and Human Rights.

6   Conclusions

The field of business and human rights has recently seen many developments in the creation of national and international binding and soft law standards in order to protect human dignity of rights holders. This article has examined the contents and the implementation tools of the Tripartite Declaration. We have asked in the introduction if there is a need for reform Tripartite Declaration of Principles concerning Multinational Enterprises and Social Policy? We have observed throughout the article that the Tripartite Declaration has followed the core instruments of the ILO, but that it has been characterised by vague and conditional language. At times, such language appears to water down or even undermine already accepted and agreed national and international human rights standards on business and human rights within and outside ILO. Apart from its vague contents, the major drawback of the ILO Declaration has been its very inefficient and programmatic enforcement methods, which do not allow for fair, independent and impartial protections of the human dignity of the rights-holders. Such programmatic enforcement methods often leave victims with no substantial and meaningful recourse to justice in the case of labour or human rights violations by or involving corporations. In spite of high-flying words of ILO officials, the Tripartite Declaration's impact in business and human rights has been marginal at best, particularly in comparison with the rivalling documents such as for example the OECD Guidelines for Multinational Enterprises.

For the Tripartite Declaration to gain recognition and traction in the wider business and human rights community and to at least partially address concerns of victims, the ILO Governing body will have to reform its content by sharpening its language and strengthen its implementation measures by expending the competence of national focal points and allowing them to hear individual complaints concerning the application of the ILO Tripartite Declaration. In the opposite case, the Tripartite Declaration will not improve its presence or even undermine it in the field of business and human rights, which has been recently witnessing so many seminal developments. The reform of the Tripartite Declaration of Principles concerning Multinational Enterprises and Social Policy is therefore more than necessary for its more prominent dissemination and operationalization and in order to effectively protect core labour rights of rights-holders against adverse corporate conduct.

References

Aaronson SA, Higham I (2013) "Re-righting Business". John Ruggie and the struggle to develop to develop international human rights standards for transnational firms. Hum Rights Q 35:333–364

Alston P (2004) Core labour standards and the transformation of international labour rights regime. Eur J Int Law 15:457

Alston P (2005) Facing up to the complexities of the ILO's core labour standards agenda. Eur J Int Law 16:467

Álvarez Rubio JJ, Yiannibas K (eds) (2017) Human rights in business: removal of barriers to access to justice in the European Union. Routledge, Abingdon

Bilchitz D (2010) The Ruggie Framework: an adequate rubric for corporate human rights obligations? Sur – Int J Hum Rights 12:199–229

Biondi A (2015) New life for the ILO Tripartite Declaration on multinational enterprises and social policy. Int J Labour Res 7(1–2):105–116

Blackwell S, Vander Meulen N (2016) Two roads converged: the mutual complementarity of a binding Business and Human Rights Treaty and national action plans on business and human rights. Notre Dame J Int Comp Law 6(1):51–76

Brownlie I (1980) Legal effects of codes of conduct for MNEs: commentary. In: Horn N (ed) Legal problems of codes of conduct for multinational enterprises. Springer, pp 39 and 41

Clapham A (2006) Human rights obligations of non-state actors. Oxford University Press, Oxford

de Felice D, Graf A (2015) The potential of national action plans to implement human rights norms: an early assessment with respect to the UN Guiding Principles on Business and Human Rights. J Hum Rights Pract 7(1):40–71

De Schutter O (2016) Towards a new treaty on business and human rights. Bus Hum Rights J 1(1):41–67

Deva S, Bilchitz D (eds) (2013) Human rights obligations of business: beyond the corporate responsibility to respect. Cambridge University Press, Cambridge

Deva S, Bilchitz D (eds) (2017) Building a treaty on business and human rights: context and contours. Cambridge University Press, Cambridge

Dhooge LJ (2007) A modest proposal to amend the Alien Tort Statute to provide guidance to transnational corporations. UC Davis J Int Law Policy 13(2):119–171

Diller J (2002) ILO Tripartite Declaration of principles concerning multinational enterprises and social policy. Int Leg Mater 41(1):184–201

Farbenblum B, Nolan J (2017) The business of migrant worker recruitment: who has the responsibility and leverage to protect rights? Texas Int Law J 52(1):1–44

Jägers N (2002) Corporate human rights obligations: in search of accountability. Intersentia, Antwerp

Jägers N (2011) UN Guiding Principles on Business and Human Rights: making headway towards real corporate accountability? Netherlands Q Hum Rights 29(2):159–163

Keitner CI (2008) Conceptualizing complicity in Alien Tort cases. Hastings Law J 60:61–104

Kinley D, Tadaki J (2004) From talk to walk: the emergence of human rights responsibilities for corporations at international law. Virginia J Int Law 44(4):931–1023

Lambooy T (2014) Legal aspects of corporate social responsibility. Utrecht J Int Eur Law 30(78): 1–6

Letnar Černič J (2009) Corporate responsibility for human rights: analyzing the ILO Tripartite Declaration of principles concerning multinational enterprises and social policy. Miskolc J Int Law 6(1):24–34

Letnar Černič J (2010) Human rights law and business. Europa Law Publishing, Groningen

Letnar Černič J (2018) Corporate accountability under socio-economic rights (transnational law and governance). Routledge, Oxon

Letnar Černič J, Carrillo-Santarelli N (eds) (2018) The future of business and human rights: theoretical and practical considerations for a UN Treaty. Intersentia, Cambridge

Martin Amerson J (2012) "The End of the Beginning?" A comprehensive look at the business and human rights agenda from a bystander perspective. Fordham J Corporate Financ Law 17: 871–941

Maupain F (2005) Revitalization not retreat: the real potential of the 1998 ILO Declaration for the universal protection of workers' rights. Eur J Int Law 16:439

Michalowski S (2012) No complicity liability for funding gross human rights violations. Berkeley J Int Law 30:451–524

Michalowski S (2013) Corporate accountability in the context of transitional justice. Routledge, New York

Morawetz R (1991) Recent Foreign Direct Investment in Eastern Europe: towards a possible role for the tripartite declaration of principles concerning multinational enterprises and social policy. ILO working papers 71

Muchlinski PT (2007) Multinational enterprises and the law, 2nd edn. Oxford University Press, Oxford

O'Brien CM, Mehra A, Blackwell S, Bloch Poulsen-Hansen C (2016) National action plans: current status and future prospects for a new business and human rights governance tool. Bus Hum Rights J 1(1):117–126

Ratner RS (2001) Corporations and human rights: a theory of legal responsibility. Yale Law J 111: 443–545

Ruggie GJ (2004) Business and human rights: the evolving international agenda. Am J Int Law 101(4):819–840

Ruggie GJ (2013) Just business: multinational corporations and human rights. WW Norton, New York

Scheffer D, Kaeb C (2011) The five levels of CSR compliance: the resiliency of corporate liability under the Alien Tort Statute and the case for a counterattack strategy in compliance theory. Berkeley J Int Law 29(1):334–397

Shamir R (2004) Between self-regulation and the Alien Tort claims act: on the concept of corporate social responsibility. Law Soc Rev 38(4):635–664

Shin-ichi A (2019) Supervision of international labour standards as a means of implementing the guiding principles on business and human rights. Eur Yearb Int Econ Law 10

Vásquez CM (2005) Direct vs indirect obligations of corporations under international law. Columbia J Transl Law 43:927–959

Jernej Letnar Černič is Associate Professor of Human Rights Law at the Faculty of Government and European Studies, Nova univerza, Ljubljana, Slovenia, and Senior Research Fellow at the University Institute of European Studies – IUSE (Turin, Italy). He graduated from University of Ljubljana with the France Prešeren award. He completed his Ph.D. in Human Rights Law in 2009 at the University of Aberdeen. He holds Diploma in Human Rights Law from the European University Institute and Diplome de droit international et de Droit compare des Droits de l'Homme (merit) from René Cassin Institut International des droits de l'homme. His works have been cited in reports by the United Nations, European Parliament and the Council of Europe and in academic studies from around the world.

Part II
Regions

Grading Trump's China Trade Strategy

Steve Charnovitz

Contents

1   Introduction

United States (US) President Donald J. Trump and his Administration have made China their top trade target.[1] Pronouncing US trade with China to be unfair, Trump Administration officials in July 2018 began imposing a 25% tariff on $50 billion of imports from China pursuant to the statutory authority in Section 301 of the Trade Act of 1974.[2] The Section 301 authority provides for negotiations with the target country,[3] and in December 2018, the Administration announced a pause in raising

---

This article is current as of 19 April 2019 and sources from the internet were accessed on this date.

---

[1]To be sure, Trump's fixation on China's economic policies is misplaced as the US has greater interests in securing from China more accommodating policies on regional security and climate change. Cooperation with China is especially vital on climate change to address classic market and government failures.

[2]19 USC § 2415(a)(1).

[3]19 USC § 2465(a).

S. Charnovitz (✉)
George Washington University Law School, Washington, DC, USA
e-mail: scharnovitz@law.gwu.edu

© Springer Nature Switzerland AG 2019   217
M. Bungenberg et al. (eds.), *European Yearbook of International Economic Law 2019*,
European Yearbook of International Economic Law (2020) 10: 217–256,
https://doi.org/10.1007/8165_2019_41, Published online: 5 October 2019

tariffs pending new talks with China.[4] As of mid-April 2019, these China-US negotiations are ongoing, but President Trump has revealed that even if a trade deal with China is achieved, the US tariffs may stay in place for a "substantial period of time."[5]

The Trump Administration justified the original Section 301 actions as an attack on four types of behaviour by the Chinese government: (1) forced technology transfer in China, (2) involuntary licensing requirements in China, (3) technology acquisitions by China in the United States, and (4) cyber and intellectual property theft by China in the United States.[6] After China retaliated against the first tranche of Section 301 tariffs, the Administration, in September 2018, imposed 10% tariffs on $200 billion worth of imports from China.[7]

Besides China, President Trump has hurled criticism at several additional trade targets including the North American Free Trade Agreement (NAFTA), the Trans-Pacific Partnership (TPP), the World Trade Organization (WTO), and the European Union (EU). The competition for pride of place after China has stayed tight, but, as I see it, the Administration's second biggest trade target is the WTO Appellate Body.[8] Trump's Office of the US Trade Representative (USTR) relentlessly attacks the Appellate Body:

> For many years, the WTO Appellate Body repeatedly seized more power for itself – while undermining and disregarding the very rules under which the dispute system was created.[9]

> [The Appellate Body's approach] fails to apply the WTO rules as written and agreed to by the United States and other WTO Members.[10]

> [The] WTO Appellate Body has repeatedly sought to create new obligations not covered in WTO Agreements.[11]

> [E]fforts by the Appellate Body to create new obligations are not legitimate.[12]

> We will not allow the WTO Appellate Body and dispute settlement system to force the United States into a straitjacket of obligations to which we never agreed.[13]

---

[4]USTR, 2019 Trade Policy Agenda and 2018 Annual Report, March 2019, p. 21. Prior to the pause, the Administration had threatened to raise the tariff levels and to impose tariffs on more imports from China.

[5]Davis B, Ballhaus R, Trump says tariffs on Chinese goods will stay on for 'substantial period of time'. Wall Street Journal, 21 March 2019.

[6]USTR, Notice of Determination of Action Pursuant to Section 301, 83 F.R. 14907, 6 April 2018. See Nos. 1, 6, 18 and 20 below. Navarro P, Trump's tariffs are a defense against China's aggression. Wall Street Journal, 21 June 2018, p. A17.

[7]USTR, 2019 Trade Policy Agenda and 2018 Annual Report, March 2019, p. 20.

[8]Nixon S, Trump puts the WTO on the ropes. Wall Street Journal, 11 July 2018. The Appellate Body serves as the WTO's appellate tribunal.

[9]USTR, 2019 Trade Policy Agenda and 2018 Annual Report, March 2019, p. 6.

[10]USTR, 2019 Trade Policy Agenda and 2018 Annual Report, March 2019, p. 26.

[11]USTR, 2019 Trade Policy Agenda and 2018 Annual Report, March 2019, p. 26.

[12]USTR, 2019 Trade Policy Agenda and 2018 Annual Report, March 2019, p. 26.

[13]USTR, 2019 Trade Policy Agenda and 2018 Annual Report, March 2019, p. 27.

In my view, all of these complaints lack validity. Even worse is USTR's absurd complaint that "judicial activism" by the Appellate Body is an "important reason for the failure of the multilateral negotiations" at the WTO.[14] USTR also objects to the Appellate Body's long-time rule allowing an appellator hearing an appeal to continue doing so even if her term expires during the appeal. Abandoning this rule would delay many Appellate Body proceedings, and so there is no small contradiction in the fact that USTR also objects to tardy Appellate Body rulings.

The Trump Administration's twin criticisms of China and the Appellate Body feed off each other. To wit:

[The Appellate Body's] activism had the disastrous effect of making it harder for market-based countries like the United States to push back against unfair trade practices abroad [...].[15]

We will resist efforts by China – or any other country – to hide behind international bureaucracies in an effort to hinder the ability of the United States to take robust actions, when necessary, in response to unfair practices abroad.[16]

China and other WTO Members have put forth proposals that endorse changing the rules of WTO dispute settlement to accommodate and authorize the very WTO Appellate Body actions that the United States has protested.[17]

Instead of constraining market distorting countries like China, the WTO has in some cases given them an unfair advantage over the United States and other market based economies.[18]

Although the United States can readily utilize Section 301 tariffs to sanction China, Section 301 cannot be utilized to sanction the Appellate Body. Instead, USTR has sought to put the WTO appellate court out of business by objecting to the replacement of Appellate Body members when their judicial terms expire. Currently, four of the seven seats on the Appellate Body are vacant as a result of the refusal of the US representative to the WTO Dispute Settlement Body (DSB) to join the consensus needed to commence the appointment process.

Both forms of the Trump Administration's economic aggression are inconsistent with WTO rules. The Section 301 tariffs against China violate Articles I and II of the WTO's General Agreement on Tariffs and Trade (GATT). The refusal by the United States to appoint new judges is inconsistent with the procedural requirement in Article 17.2 of the WTO Dispute Settlement Understanding (DSU) that "Vacancies shall be filled as they arise."[19]

These twin USTR assaults undermine prosperity and the rule of law. The reciprocal trade sanctions between China and the US will reduce economic growth

---

[14]USTR, 2019 Trade Policy Agenda and 2018 Annual Report, March 2019, p. 6.

[15]USTR, 2019 Trade Policy Agenda and 2018 Annual Report, March 2019, p. 6.

[16]USTR, 2018 Trade Policy Agenda and 2017 Annual Report, March 2018, p. 4.

[17]USTR, 2019 Trade Policy Agenda and 2018 Annual Report, March 2019, p. 27.

[18]USTR, 2018 Trade Policy Agenda and 2017 Annual Report, March 2018, p. 2.

[19]Petersmann (2018), p. 187.

in both economies. The US tariff actions are protectionist in practice[20] by inhibiting imports in the short run and by realigning production and supply chains in the long-run (that are a wellspring of China's economic clout). The disruption of the Appellate Body has hindered the ability of countries to secure WTO decisions in a timely fashion so to induce other countries to adhere to their WTO obligations. For the same reasons, these dual assaults can harm the economic interests of the rest of the world, particularly those countries that regularly use WTO dispute settlement. On the other hand, the supply chain disruptions can also shift investment and production from China to third-country beneficiaries.

In parallel to the Trump Administration's trade complaints about China, the Administration has criticized the Paris climate accord for being an "unfair" agreement that would favour China over the United States. In announcing that he would withdraw the US from the Paris Agreement, Trump alleged that the climate accord would allow China to increase its emissions for 13 years even though the United States could not.[21] Back in 2012, Trump had famously declared that "the concept of global warming was created by and for the Chinese in order to make U.S. manufacturing non-competitive."[22]

For climate, trade, and many other fields, US unilateralism is not just a means, but rather is a central part of the Administration's conception of a good world order. As Adam Tooze has noted, "As far as the American trade hawks are concerned, competition within an agreed international order is to be welcomed only so long as the competitors agree to play by America's rules, both economic and geopolitical."[23] Likewise USTR: "The United States will not allow the WTO – or any other multilateral organization – to prevent us from taking actions that are essential to the economic well-being of the American people."[24]

2 Overview of US Complaints About China

Although the Trump Administration has not produced a white paper detailing exactly what it considers China to be doing wrong on trade, one can stitch together a bill of complaint from various statements by President Trump, the White House, USTR, and other parts of the Trump Administration.[25] China is accused of numerous

---

[20]USTR denies that the Trump Administration is engaging in protectionism. Lighthizer, at APEC, says defending U.S. market against unfair trade is not protectionism. World Trade Online, 21 May 2017.

[21]White House, Statement by President Trump on the Paris Climate Accord, 1 June 2017.

[22]https://twitter.com/realdonaldtrump/status/265895292191248385?lang=en.

[23]Tooze (2019).

[24]USTR, 2018 Trade Policy Agenda and 2017 Annual Report, March 2018, p. 2.

[25]For a US private sector analysis, see Business Roundtable, Recommendations for Chinese reforms to address trade and investment barriers, July 2018, https://s3.amazonaws.com/brt.org/archive/letters/BRT%20China%20Priorities.pdf.

examples of "unfair" trade practices and "economic aggression" against the United States.[26] Precisely what renders the named practices "unfair" goes unexplained.

Trump's grievances against China are manifold, but for the purposes of this article can summarized in the following 20 charges[27]:

1. The government of China "is forcing United States companies to transfer technology to Chinese counterparts."[28] "Beijing now requires many American businesses to hand over their trade secrets as the cost of doing business in China."[29]

2. "Chinese industrial policy" seeks to "capture industries of the future" through several means such as public investment and export restraints on critical raw materials.[30] "China's unfair industrial policies, like the 'Made in China 2025' policy initiative, clearly state China's goal of taking away domestic and international market share from foreigners."[31] "Too often, China flouts the rules to achieve industrial policy objectives."[32]

3. China imposes "discriminatory non-tariff barriers."[33] China protects its home market with "high tariffs, non-tariff barriers, and other regulatory hurdles."[34]

4. "China has banned imports of United States agricultural products such as poultry."[35]

5. China uses "market-distorting forces, including subsidies and state-owned enterprises" to promote "excess capacity" and "overproduction of steel and aluminium".[36]

---

[26]White House, What You Need to Know About President Donald J. Trump's Actions Responding to China's Unfair Trade Practices, 6 April 2018; White House, Remarks by President Trump at Signing of a Presidential Memorandum Targeting China's Economic Aggression, 22 March 2018; White House, Statement by the President Regarding Trade with China, 15 June 2018.

[27]If the list were going over 20, this study would have included currency manipulation and weak enforcement of US intellectual property rights.

[28]White House, Statement from the President, 17 September 2018.

[29]White House, Remarks by Vice President Pence to the Hudson Institute on the Administration's Policy Toward China, 4 October 2018.

[30]White House, Office of Trade and Manufacturing Policy, How China's economic aggression threatens the technology and intellectual property of the United States and the world, June 2018, pp. 2, 16.

[31]White House, What You Need to Know About President Donald J. Trump's Actions Responding to China's Unfair Trade Practices, 6 April 2018.

[32]USTR, 2018 USTR Report to Congress on China's WTO compliance, February 2019, p. 8.

[33]White House, President Donald J. Trump is Confronting China's Unfair Trade Policies, 29 May 2018.

[34]White House, Office of Trade and Manufacturing Policy, How China's economic aggression threatens the technology and intellectual property of the United States and the world, June 2018, p. 1.

[35]White House, President Donald J. Trump is Confronting China's Unfair Trade Policies, 29 May 2018.

[36]White House, President Donald J. Trump is Confronting China's Unfair Trade Policies, 29 May 2018; White House, Statement of the United States Regarding China Talks, 31 January 2019.

6. China requires US companies to license intellectual property "at less than economic value."[37]
7. "China disregards many of its WTO's transparency obligations [...]."[38]
8. "China has been a particularly bad actor when it comes to trade remedies."[39]
9. "China is increasingly attempting to force foreign enterprises to localize valuable data or information within China [...]."[40]
10. China imposes "unfair retaliation" against the Trump Administration's Section 301 tariffs.[41] China's retaliation against the Trump Administration's Section 232 steel and aluminium tariffs "appears to be inconsistent with China's [WTO] obligations [...]."[42]
11. China continues to follow a "state-led, mercantilist approach to the economy and trade, despite WTO members' expectations – and China's own representations – that China would transform its economy and pursue the open, market-oriented policies endorsed by the WTO."[43] "WTO membership comes with expectations that an acceding member not only will strictly adhere to WTO rules, but also will support open, market-oriented policies," and "China has failed to comply with these expectations."[44]
12. China exhibits the largest trade "deficit of any country in the history of our world"[45] and the "trade relationship between the United States and China must be much more equitable."[46] "I have great respect and affection for my friend President Xi, but I have made clear that our trade imbalance is just not acceptable."[47]
13. "The United States will request that tariffs and taxes between the two countries [China and US] be reciprocal in nature and value."[48] "China imposes much

---

[37]White House, President Donald J. Trump is Confronting China's Unfair Trade Policies, 29 May 2018.

[38]USTR, 2018 USTR Report to Congress on China's WTO compliance, February 2019, p. 9.

[39]USTR, 2018 USTR Report to Congress on China's WTO compliance, February 2019, p. 8.

[40]White House, Office of Trade and Manufacturing Policy, How China's economic aggression threatens the technology and intellectual property of the United States and the world, June 2018, p. 8.

[41]White House, Statement from President Donald J. Trump on Additional Proposed Section 301 Remedies, 5 April 2018.

[42]WTO, China – Additional Duties on Certain Products from the United States, Request for Establishment of a WTO Panel by the United States, WT/DS558/2, 19 October 2018.

[43]USTR, 2018 USTR Report to Congress on China's WTO compliance, February 2019, p. 2.

[44]USTR, 2018 USTR Report to Congress on China's WTO compliance, February 2019, p. 3.

[45]White House, Remarks by President Trump at Signing of a Presidential Memorandum Targeting China's Economic Aggression, 22 March 2018.

[46]White House, Statement from the President Regarding Trade with China, 18 June 2018.

[47]White House, Remarks by President Trump to the 73rd Session of the United Nations General Assembly, New York, 25 September 2018.

[48]White House, Statement on Steps to Protect Domestic Technology and Intellectual Property from China's Discriminatory and Burdensome Trade Practices, 29 May 2018.

higher tariffs on United States exports than the United States imposes on China."[49] "If they charge us, we charge them the same thing. That's the way it's got to be."[50]

14. Projects in China's Belt and Road Initiative "generally ignore market principles and fail to adhere to internationally accepted best practices in financing, infrastructure development and government procurement."[51]

15. China "has already achieved a leading position in many traditional manufacturing industries" through several methods including "lax and weakly enforced environmental and health and safety standards."[52]

16. China uses a "predatory 'debt trap' model" to "secure and control core global resources globally."[53]

17. "China's policies are contributing to a dramatic misallocation of global resources that leaves everyone – including the Chinese people – poorer than they would be in a world of more efficient markets."[54]

18. "China directs and unfairly facilitates the systematic investment in, and acquisition of, U.S. companies to obtain cutting-edge technologies and intellectual property and generate the transfer of technology to Chinese companies."[55]

19. China uses "corporate governance" law "as a tool to advance China's strategic goals, rather than simply, as is the custom of international rules, to advance the profit-maximizing goals of the enterprise."[56]

20. China seeks to "obtain technology from American companies" by "intellectual property theft" and "cyber theft."[57] "Chinese security agencies have masterminded the wholesale theft of American technology—including cutting

[49]White House, President Donald J. Trump is Confronting China's Unfair Trade Policies, 29 May 2018.

[50]White House, Remarks by President Trump at Signing of a Presidential Memorandum Targeting China's Economic Aggression, 22 March 2018.

[51]USTR, 2018 USTR Report to Congress on China's WTO compliance, February 2019, p. 15.

[52]White House, Office of Trade and Manufacturing Policy, How China's economic aggression threatens the technology and intellectual property of the United States and the world, June 2018, p. 1.

[53]White House, Office of Trade and Manufacturing Policy, How China's economic aggression threatens the technology and intellectual property of the United States and the world, June 2018, p. 1.

[54]White House, Office of Trade and Manufacturing Policy, How China's economic aggression threatens the technology and intellectual property of the United States and the world, June 2018, p. 4.

[55]USTR, Notice of Determination of Action Pursuant to Section 301, 83 F.R. 14907, 6 April 2018.

[56]White House, Office of Trade and Manufacturing Policy, How China's economic aggression threatens the technology and intellectual property of the United States and the world, June 2018, p. 11.

[57]White House, President Donald J. Trump is Confronting China's Unfair Trade Policies, 29 May 2018; Mike Pompeo, Remarks by Secretary Pompeo on America's Economic Revival at Detroit Economic Club, 18 June 2018.

edge military blueprints."[58] "China conducts and supports unauthorized intrusions into, and theft from, the computer networks of U.S. companies to access their sensitive commercial information and trade secrets."[59]

3   Detailed Examination of US Complaints

3.1   *Analytical Methodology*

Part 3 of this article examines the merits of the US complaints about China. Ideally, such an analysis would begin by analysing the veracity of each charge. Here, for reasons of space, such a factual examination is beyond the scope of this article. Yet for a few of the charges, the facts are clear enough to evaluate the validity of the charge.[60] For the rest of the charges, they will be presumed true even though in some instances the Trump Administration has put forward little or no corroborating evidence.

The Trump Administration's denouncement of China diverges from the usual practice in contemporary international relations of assuming good faith and expecting a complaining state to produce evidence for its allegation in an international body or in the court of public opinion. As the WTO Appellate Body has explained, "it is a generally accepted canon of evidence in civil law, common law and, in fact, in most jurisdictions, that the burden of proof rests upon the party, whether complaining or defending, who asserts the affirmative of a particular claim or defence."[61]

For those charges for which the United States has not lodged a complaint at any international fact-finding body, the public could reasonably draw the adverse inference that the claim against China is untrue. That is because if it were true, the Trump Administration would have been eager to vindicate its claim before an independent fact-finding tribunal. Positing an adverse inference from the absence of a formal complaint is especially appropriate in the WTO context because trade law makes use of adverse inferences.

With the top 20 charges now teed up, the study will proceed by analysing each of them. For each charge, the study will report on whether such behaviour by China violates WTO law.[62] The study will also report on whether such behaviour by China is wrongful. A WTO violation is inherently wrongful. Yet, the indicated behaviour

---

[58]White House, Remarks by Vice President Pence to the Hudson Institute on the Administration's Policy Toward China, 4 October 2018.

[59]USTR, Notice of Determination of Action Pursuant to Section 301, 83 F.R. 14907, 6 April 2018.

[60]See below Nos. 8 (Trade remedies), 9 (Data localization), 10 (Retaliation), and 12 (Trade deficit).

[61]United States – *Measure Affecting Imports of Woven Wool Shirts and Blouses from India*, Report of the Appellate Body, WT/DS233/AB/R, p. 14 (adopted 23 May 1997).

[62]When this article states that a measure by China or the United States violates the WTO, that is a prediction of what a WTO tribunal would rule should a well pleaded claim be brought to WTO dispute settlement.

could also be wrongful – for example, for moral or economic reasons – even if the behaviour does not violate WTO law. Next, the study will consider whether WTO negotiations are needed to institute new norms to correct behaviour that is not WTO-illegal. If the WTO is not the right organization to craft such norms, the study will consider whether another international organization would be more suitable. For each charge against China, the study will note and evaluate the response being taken by the Trump Administration to remedy the problem. Finally, if a successful strategy is not currently being pursued, the study will point to a better US strategy.

3.2 The 20 Charges Individually Examined

3.2.1 Forced Technology Transfer

A Chinese government measure to force a US company to "hand over" its technology or trade secrets violates WTO law. Although the WTO Agreement on Trade-Related Intellectual Property Rights (TRIPS) permits compulsory licensing, a taking of foreign technology without compensation could violate TRIPS Articles 26, 28, 36, and 39. A taking of trade secrets could violate TRIPS Article 39.2.

Besides the regular TRIPS rules, China has numerous additional WTO accession obligations that apply only to China. These applicant WTO-plus obligations are found in China's Accession Protocol[63] and Working Party report.[64] Two unique obligations in the Working Party report (paras. 49, 203) prohibit forced technology transfer.[65]

The Trump Administration has not lodged a WTO case against China regarding charge No 1. Instead, the Administration maintains that "Many of the worst actions undertaken by China – such as the numerous informal methods of pressuring U.S. companies to share their technology with Chinese partners – were not captured by China's obligations at the WTO."[66] Count me as sceptical that a government can escape liability under WTO law merely by using informal pressure rather than formal pressure.

In its Section 301 action, USTR contends that "China uses foreign ownership restrictions, such as joint venture requirements and foreign equity limitations, and various administrative review and licensing processes, to require or pressure technology transfer from U.S. companies."[67] Imposing such requirements, limitations,

---

[63]WTO, Protocol of the Accession of the People's Republic of China, WT/L/432, 23 November 2001.

[64]Charnovitz (2008) and Ehring (2014).

[65]WTO, Working Party on the Accession of China, WT/ACC/CHN/49, 1 October 2001.

[66]USTR, 2019 Trade Policy Agenda and 2018 Annual Report, March 2019, p. 7.

[67]USTR, Notice of Determination of Action Pursuant to Section 301, 83 F.R. 14907, 6 April 2018.

and processes is subject to the General Agreement on Trade in Services (GATS) to the extent that it implicates mode 3 commercial presence services. GATS Articles XVI and XVII contain disciplines for China that are supplemented by additional obligations in China's WTO-plus rulebook. Notwithstanding these causes of action, the Trump Administration has failed to lodge a GATS case against China.

In lieu of a legal challenge, the Trump Administration's strategy against forced technology transfer is to impose Section 301 sanctions.[68] By forgoing WTO litigation, which would be the first-best instrument to secure constructive change in China, the Trump Administration is left only with inferior instruments. Even worse, because the Section 301 sanction violates WTO law, the Trump Administration undermines its narrative about China's misbehaviour. If a US sanction is considered to be politically necessary in US politics, then the sanction should have been crafted to be consistent with WTO law and to communicate that China's forced technology transfer is *malum in se*. In addition, the Administration could have championed new WTO negotiations to strengthen the rules against forced technology transfer by making clearer when ostensibly voluntary contracts cross the line into coercion.

3.2.2 Chinese Industrial Policies

Public investment is often carried out via subsidies. An industrial policy using subsidies that cause adverse trade effects on other WTO members violates Article 5 of the WTO Agreement on Subsidies and Countervailing Measures (SCM). In my view, WTO anti-subsidy law may be weaker in practice than it should be because of some regrettable DSB holdings that make it harder to show a financial contribution from a public body and to show a benefit from a subsidy to an enterprise.[69] Nevertheless, WTO subsidy law remains robust. Moreover, in joining the WTO, China took on several stricter obligations regarding industrial policy subsidies as codified in its Protocol (para. 10.2) and Working Party report (paras. 167, 171–2).

Using export restraints violates GATT Article XI. China has already lost two WTO cases (*Raw Materials* and *Rare Earths*) regarding WTO-illegal export restraints. Moreover, China has tougher legal obligations on export restraints than do most (or all) other WTO members.

Thus, depending on the facts, a Chinese industrial policy utilizing subsidies or export restraints could violate WTO rules. Although disturbingly bereft of any legal analysis, the US International Trade Commission (USITC) issued a report in December 2017 holding that China's industrial policies on solar cells "directly contradicted the obligations that China committed to undertake as part of its WTO

---

[68]USTR, Notice of Determination of Action Pursuant to Section 301, 83 F.R. 14907, 6 April 2018.
[69]Ding (2014) and Rovnov (2019).

accession."[70] The Trump Administration was quick to use the USITC report as justification to impose US tariff protection on solar cells, but the Administration did not pursue the cause of action against China suggested by the USITC.

Employing an industrial policy is not inherently wrongful.[71] Indeed, an industrial policy that merely invites private investment in a key industry would neither be wrongful nor a WTO violation. When governments pursue industrial policy, the instrument of subsidy may be appropriate to provide social benefits, particularly in the presence of a market failure. Although the SCM Agreement recognizes the potentially constructive role of subsidies,[72] there remains an unresolved legal tension between domestic policy space and the SCM disciplines that regulate such space.[73]

If governments limited their industrial policies to subsidies, the externalities could be manageable. Yet a common problem with industrial policy is that governments prefer cheaper means that use non-spending instruments such as trade measures. The use of import or export restraints can externalize high net costs on other countries.

The Trump Administration objects to China's pursuit of industrial policies to capture industries of the future, but from my perspective, such pursuit is a lot smarter than the Trump Administration's industrial policies to preserve industries of the past. The Administration's misuse of Section 232 tariffs to increase the capacity utilization of the domestic steel industry is naked industrial policy. Speaking of the effect of those steel tariffs, Trump has bragged that "what's happening with the steel industry is very exciting to me. It's being rebuilt overnight."[74] The Administration's use of Section 201 tariffs to protect the washing machine and solar panel industries is another example of backward-looking industrial policy.[75]

The Administration's claim that it is "unfair"[76] for China to seek to take away domestic and international market share from the United States is facetious at best. Chinese producers have every right to compete to expand their market share just as US producers do. US producers have no vested right to their existing share of the

---

[70]Supplemental Report of the U.S. International Trade Commission Regarding Unforeseen Developments, 28 December 2017, https://solarbuildermag.com/wp-content/uploads/2018/01/ITC_Report_Suniva.pdf.

[71]Charnovitz (1993–94), p. 88.

[72]See, for example, Articles 8 (expired), 25.3, 27.13, 27.14, 29.1.

[73]Meyer (2018), pp. 538–539.

[74]White House, Press Conference by President Trump, 27 September 2018. More recently, Trump declared: "The steel industry is thriving now and it was dead when I came to office." White House, Remarks by President Trump at Signing of Executive Order, "Strengthening Buy-American Preferences for Infrastructure Projects," 31 January 2019.

[75]The import relief to those industries is questionable under US law which requires a path to "positive adjustment" and a showing that the relief will "provide greater economic and social benefits than costs." See 19 USC § 2251(a). Furthermore, the absence of US domestic judicial review of such import relief is in tension with GATT Article X:3(b).

[76]White House, What You Need to Know About President Donald J. Trump's Actions Responding to China's Unfair Trade Practices, 6 April 2018.

domestic market or a foreign market. In a market-based economy, producers have to earn their share every day.

USTR has not lodged a WTO case against China for the illegal use of either industrial subsidies or export restraints.[77] This omission is especially puzzling because, as noted above, USTR argues that "China flouts the rules to achieve industrial policy objectives."[78] So far, the Administration has failed to put forward any response to WTO-illegal subsidies and export restraints by China.

A scheme to utilize Section 301 sanctions against those subsidies would be problematic. Sanctions will be most effective when focused on one outcome and less effective when employed as a Swiss army knife[79] to seek multiple outcomes. The utility of Section 301 sanctions may also depend on whether the target behaviour is itself wrongful as a violation of legal or other norms.

Another problem with the utility of Section 301 sanctions against China for subsidies or export restraints is the fact that China would call attention to the hypocrisy[80] of the U.S. position, since the US government incessantly uses both subsidies and export restraints. Indeed in 2018, Congress and the Trump Administration worked together to strengthen the U.S. Department of Commerce's export control programs with the announced policy purpose of maintaining US leadership in science, technology, engineering and manufacturing.[81]

Establishing better disciplines for the use of industrial policy instruments such as subsidies, export controls, and technical barriers is a matter on which future WTO negotiations should focus. Yet defining proper versus improper industrial policies is quite difficult. For example, the Trump Administration's criticisms of the Made in China 2025 initiative[82] fail to take into account the positive externalities from China's green technology subsidies.

---

[77]A panel against China requested by the Obama Administration was composed at the beginning of the Trump Administration on the subject of China's agricultural support. The cause of action in this case is "support" under the WTO Agreement on Agriculture, not subsidies under the SCM Agreement. Recently, the panel report was released, and the panel found that China was out of compliance with the WTO Agriculture Agreement. China – *Domestic Support for Agricultural Products*, Report of the Panel, WT/DS511/R, circulated 28 February 2019.

[78]USTR, 2018 USTR Report to Congress on China's WTO compliance, February 2019, p. 8.

[79]Kahn (2017).

[80]Bacchus J "Do as I say, not as I do": Trump's sizable China hypocrisy, The Hill, 25 January 2019, https://thehill.com/opinion/finance/426946-do-as-i-say-not-as-i-do-trumps-sizable-china-hypocrisy.

[81]50 USC § 4812.

[82]USTR, Update concerning China's acts, policies and practices related to technology transfer, intellectual property, and innovation, 20 November 2018, p. 8.

3.2.3 Discriminatory or Unjustified Trade Barriers

Non-tariff barriers (NTBs) and regulatory hurdles are neither inherently wrongful nor a violation of WTO law. Yet, they will be a violation of WTO law if they do not meet the stringent conditions in the Agreement on Technical Barriers to Trade (TBT) or the Agreement on the Application of Sanitary and Phytosanitary Measures (SPS). Discriminatory NTBs on products would be a violation of the TBT Agreement if the discrimination is not based on a legitimate regulatory distinction.

Oddly, the Trump Administration has not filed any TBT or SPS cases against China, and so the Administration misses an opportunity to demonstrate unfair and illegal actions by China affecting US exporters. NTBs do appear to be part of the ongoing US trade talks with China, and any deal reached will likely contain some ad hoc concessions by China. Yet by failing to frame the US agenda as seeking to get China to comply with the WTO's regulatory norms, the United States will likely fail to achieve systemic changes in the way that China writes its NTBs.

China's high tariffs are neither WTO-illegal nor wrongful per se. Of course, both China and the United States would be better off if China lowered its tariffs. The best way to secure that win-win outcome is through market access negotiations at the WTO. Unfortunately, USTR under the Trump (and Obama) Administration has not championed a successful conclusion of the WTO Doha Round tariff negotiations.

3.2.4 Agricultural Import Bans

An import ban on agricultural products violates GATT Article XI:1 and is therefore wrongful. Back in August 2017, the Trump Administration lodged a WTO case (DS517) against China regarding tariff-rate quotas on wheat, rice, and corn. The lawsuit alleges that these quotas violate provisions in GATT and in China's accession agreement.[83] In April 2019, the panel found multiple violations of China's accession obligations.

The Trump Administration has failed to lodge a WTO case against any Chinese agricultural import ban such as a ban on US poultry.

3.2.5 Subsidies for Added Industrial Capacity

The use of non-agricultural subsidies to promote capacity is an illegal SCM actionable subsidy if the production or export causes adverse effects on trading partners. A subsidy intended only to raise production distorts markets and is considered wrongful by the trading system, which prioritizes competing producer interests over consumer interests.

---

[83] China – *Tariff Rate Quotas for Certain Agricultural Products, Report of the Panel*, WT/DS517/R, 18 April 2019.

Although the terms "excess capacity" and "overproduction" are intended to be pejorative, the non-legitimacy of such conditions is contestable. In open, market-oriented economies driven by supply and demand, excess capacity and overproduction are normal phenomenon that are corrected by the market. If China produces more steel or aluminium than it will use domestically, such behaviour is not inherently wrong. For any commodity in an open world economy, one would expect that some countries would produce more than they need domestically and other countries would produce less than what they need. The WTO subsidy rules lay out what is legally improper, but that status does not necessarily match any economic concept of irrational or anti-competitive behaviour, or behaviour that externalizes trans-border costs.

If excessive global steel production causes social or employment problems, the most logical solution would be a multilateral commodity agreement negotiated outside of the WTO. The WTO recognizes the legitimacy of commodity agreements (in GATT Article XX(h)). In 2016, the G-20 established a Global Forum on Excess Steel Capacity. Unfortunately, those global talks have been held without transparency so cannot be reported on in this study.

The Trump Administration has not lodged any WTO complaints to challenge China's subsidies that promote excess capacity. For steel, the Administration has responded to Chinese overcapacity by imposing protective tariffs under Section 232 (of the Trade Expansion Act) and by imposing numerous countervailing duties tied to injurious subsidies. Although the US steel tariffs have been effective in raising US capacity utilization, I have not seen any studies of whether the tariffs have reduced China's steelmaking capacity.

3.2.6 Involuntary Licensing Requirements

Requiring US companies to license intellectual property at less than economic value is a WTO violation. To its credit, the Trump Administration has lodged a WTO challenge under TRIPS Articles 3 and 28. Nevertheless, USTR delayed in obtaining the WTO panel until late November 2018, over 15 months after Trump triggered a USTR Section 301 investigation and many months after USTR imposed unilateral sanctions.

This US litigation against China has been poorly executed. The cause of action in the current WTO panel (DS542) is too narrow because USTR neglected to bring licensing claims under paragraph 256 of the China Working Party Report. If China's licensing practices discriminate against the United States, then USTR also failed to bring claims under TRIPS Article 4. If China's licensing practices apply to other countries equally, then USTR missed an opportunity to recruit similarly affected WTO allies to join a case against China. WTO cases with multiple complainants typically do well before WTO tribunals.

3.2.7 Non-transparency

The WTO has two kinds of transparency requirements: domestic and international. The domestic requirements are for publication and disclosure in China for the benefit of domestic and foreign persons. The international requirements are for notification to the WTO for the direct benefit of other WTO Members and the indirect benefit of economic and social actors.

In 2019, USTR publicly reported its findings regarding "China's extremely poor record of adhering to transparency obligations as a WTO member."[84] So far, however, the Administration has filed only one WTO case against China regarding transparency, and that case (DS 517) covers only wheat, grain, rice, and corn. In mid-April 2019, the panel ruled against China.

This timid US litigation strategy is especially self-defeating since the United States was the leading proponent during China's accession negotiations for imposing numerous WTO-plus transparency rules in China's accession agreement that are tougher than the transparency requirements that apply to other WTO Members.[85] The Trump Administration has roundly complained about the terms of China's entry into the WTO,[86] but the Administration has failed to take advantage of the many favourable terms for WTO incumbents (like the US) that provide for numerous WTO causes of action against China. The law of WTO transparency is already extensive, but certainly new WTO negotiations on transparency would be useful, including to universalize China's enhanced transparency obligations.

3.2.8 Improper Trade Remedies

Trade remedies include antidumping, countervailing, and safeguard duties. As noted above, the Trump Administration complains that "China has been a particularly bad actor when it comes to trade remedies."[87] The record shows that in eight WTO cases, China was found to have violated trade remedy rules.[88] None of those eight cases were brought by the Trump Administration, and during the Trump Administration, USTR has not lodged any new trade remedy cases against China. Other than vapidly labelling China a "bad actor," the Trump Administration has not put forward any strategy to address China's misconduct on trade remedies. Whether eight trade

---

[84]USTR, 2018 USTR Report to Congress on China's WTO compliance, February 2019, p. 3.

[85]Yamaoka (2013), pp. 153–156 (taxonomy).

[86]In 2018, USTR declared that "it seems clear that the United States erred in supporting China's entry into the WTO on terms that have proven to be ineffective in securing China's embrace of an open, market-oriented trade regime." USTR, 2017 Report to Congress on China's WTO Compliance, January 2018, p. 2.

[87]USTR, 2018 USTR Report to Congress on China's WTO compliance, February 2019, p. 8.

[88]WTO Cases 427, 483, 454 + 460, 414, 440, 427, 425, 414. Cases are listed in reverse chronological order of final decision. Cases that appear more than once involve follow-on compliance proceedings.

remedy violations by China renders that country a "bad actor" is a matter on which reasonable observers could differ.

No reasonable observer could doubt that the United States is a "bad actor" on trade remedies because the United States has lost an obscene number – currently 49 – WTO trade remedy cases brought against the US.[89] Indeed, the United States is the WTO's most flagrant bad actor on trade remedies because the United States has lost far more trade remedy cases than any other WTO member has.[90] During the Trump Administration, five new trade remedy cases against the US have been assigned to WTO panels.[91] US Secretary of Commerce Wilbur Ross accuses China of "highly protectionist behaviour"[92] without any sense of shame that the WTO-illegal trade remedies administered by the Commerce Department also afford protection.

Ideally, the WTO would carry out negotiations to better discipline improper trade remedies. Unfortunately, trade remedies have been embedded into the protectionist routines of many governments, and so this issue is probably too polarized for WTO legal reform to be achievable.

3.2.9 Data Localization

Data localization, that is, a governmental requirement to store data in the host country, can be one type of digital protectionism.[93] No one disputes that China engages in digital protectionism. Indeed, the Digital Trade Restrictiveness Index finds China to have by far the most restrictive policy for digital trade.[94]

The Trump Administration claims that China forces foreign companies to localize data within China. Data localization is not necessarily wrongful as there may be legitimate regulatory justification including privacy and public security. One recent

---

[89]WTO Cases 534, 523 (under appeal), 505 (under appeal), 437 (under appeal), 488, 471, 464, 429, 437, 436, 449, 422, 404, 382, 379, 402, 383, 302 + 294, 350, 345, 343, 344, 268, 335, 322, 264, 294, 257, 282, 212, 296, 268, 264, 277, 257, 248 + 249 + 251 + 252 + 253 + 254 + 258 + 259, 234, 212, 213, 236, 206, 202, 184, 177 + 178, 179, 166, 136 + 162, 138, 99. Cases are listed in reverse chronological order of final decision. Cases that appear more than once involve follow-on compliance proceedings.

[90]By way of comparison, the EU has lost 11 trade remedy proceedings: WTO Cases 486, 480, 442, 473, 397, 405, 337, 299, 219, 141 (twice).

[91]WTO Cases 436, 533, 534, 539, 536 (order of establishment).

[92]China way more protectionist than US, says Trump official, South China Morning Post, 25 January 2018, https://www.scmp.com/news/china/article/2130520/china-way-more-protection ist-us-says-trump-official.

[93]Aaronson (2018), pp. 10–11.

[94]Ferracane MF et al., Digital Trade Restrictiveness Index. European Centre for International Political Economy, April 2018, pp. 6 (overall conclusion), 54–55 (China's data localization), https://ecipe.org/dte/dte-report.

study found that China's localization measures violate the GATS Agreement.[95] So far, however, the Trump Administration has not lodged any GATS case against China. Other than labelling China a data localizer, the Trump Administration has not laid out any strategy to address China's practices on data localization.

The WTO has a role in policing digital protectionism because the WTO can be an arbiter of when domestic regulation is administered in a reasonable, objective, and impartial manner (see GATS Article VI:1). Nevertheless, WTO rules may not cover data itself,[96] and the disciplines for the regulation of traded digital services may be narrower than the disciplines for regulation of products. At the time that GATS rules were written in the early 1990s, digital protectionism had not yet become an important international concern.

Back in 2001, I advocated WTO negotiations to open up internet market access.[97] Little has been accomplished since then on that problem or the broader problems of digital trade barriers. The WTO's inability to make progress in the intervening years leads me to wonder whether the negotiation of such issues should be pursued in more specialised international fora rather than being reserved for the WTO.

The Trump Administration states that it is "initiating exploratory work on possible future negotiations" on digital trade.[98] So far, however, the Administration's actions on data localization have been feeble.[99] Indeed to date, the Administration failed to propose a set of comprehensive norms to address digital protectionism.

---

[95]Crosby D (2016), Analysis of data localization measures under WTO services trade rules and commitments. E15, March 2016, http://e15initiative.org/wp-content/uploads/2015/09/E15-Policy-Brief-Crosby-Final.pdf.

[96]The WTO law status of digital trade is ambiguous. Data may be a WTO good or a service or both or neither. Many things with value, such as money and real property, are neither a good nor a service. Data may likewise not be a good or a service. Some clarification emerges from WTO legal text and subsequent practice. For example, when data is in an electronic form of something that is a good (like a book), then the electronic book is considered a good. The WTO agreement of 1998 to pledge not to impose customs duties on electronic transmissions (WT/MIN(98)/DEC2, 25 May 1998) may suggest that such transmissions are a good. That various GATS Agreements cover "data processing", "transfers of data", and "data transmission" may suggest that working on data is a service. GATS Article XIV(c)(ii) posits that regulation of the use of personal data is the regulation of a GATS service.

[97]Charnovitz (2001), p. 104.

[98]https://ustr.gov/about-us/policy-offices/press-office/fact-sheets/2018/march/2018-fact-sheet-key-barriers-digital.

[99]USTR, 2019 Trade Policy Agenda and 2018 Annual Report of the President of the United States on the Trade Agreements Program, March 2019, Annual Report, p. 64.

3.2.10 China's Retaliation

China is retaliating against both of the Trump Administration's unilateral tariffs imposed under Sections 232 and 301.[100] Each of these retaliatory actions violate WTO rules (especially GATT Arts. I and II) and, for that reason, the retaliation is wrongful. The Trump Administration has lodged a WTO case against China's Section 232 retaliation (DS 558), but has not brought a case against the Section 301 retaliation.

China commenced its Section 232 retaliation in April 2018, and at that moment, there was a good argument that China (and other countries) had the right to retaliate under WTO safeguard rules against the US steel tariffs that had begun in March 2018.[101] After all, the title of Section 232 is "Safeguarding National Security"[102] and Section 232 authorizes tariffs that are similar to the tariffs that could be employed in a conventional safeguard. Subsequently, however, the Appellate Body interpreted WTO safeguard law in a narrow way that had the effect of cutting out the ground under the argument for the legitimacy of retaliation against Section 232 tariffs.

The threshold question for Section 232 is whether it is a WTO safeguard. The legal case in support of China's retaliation against Section 232 tariffs was that the US tariffs are disguised safeguard tariffs for which an affected country can exercise retaliation rights under GATT Article XIX:3(a). Yet in August 2018, the Appellate Body held that to qualify as a WTO safeguard, a tariff increase "must be designed to prevent or remedy serious injury to the Member's domestic industry caused or threatened by increased imports" of the product.[103] Although Section 232 provides a remedy against imports, the terms of Section 232 do not require either serious injury or increased imports. Because those prerequisites are absent from the statutory text of Section 232, a WTO panel considering such a retaliation case will find that the Section 232 measures are not a safeguard and therefore that China's retaliation is illegal.

Given this subsequent development in WTO jurisprudence, China should withdraw its retaliation. The interposition of subsequent WTO case-law can render illegal a measure that was consistent with WTO law at the time it was instituted. This clarification in WTO law gives USTR a right to claim collateral estoppel from a new and unrelated WTO judicial holding. Ironically, the force of precedent in WTO jurisprudence – a common judicial practice now being opposed by USTR – will grant the United States a win in the ongoing Section 232 disputes at the WTO.

---

[100]Lu Z, Schott, Jeffrey J., How is China retaliating for US national security tariffs on steel and aluminum?. Peterson Institute for International Economics (PIIE), 9 April 2018; Bown CP et al., China's retaliation to Trump's tariffs, PIIE, 22 June 2018.

[101]Charnovitz S, EU can retaliate immediately against Trump's metal tariffs. 2 March 2018, https://worldtradelaw.typepad.com/ielpblog/2018/03/eu-can-retaliate-immediately-against-trumps-metal-tariffs.html.

[102]19 USC § 1862.

[103]WTO, Indonesia – *Safeguard on Certain Iron and Steel Products*, Report of the Appellate Body, WT/DS490, 496 (adopted 27 August 2018), para. 5.60.

China's has also retaliated against the Section 301 tariffs. This retaliation flouts WTO law, particularly GATT Articles I and II and DSU Article 23. (USTR has not brought a WTO case against China for this retaliation.[104]) China's impulse to hit back is understandable, but the tariffs are legally wrongful and China should repeal its retaliation. China's retaliation may also lead to serious environmental consequences from distorting trade.[105]

The Trump Administration responded to China's retaliation against Section 301 tariffs by USTR's decision to impose $200 billion in additional Section 301 tariffs on China. This response shows that China's illegal retaliation was a blunder because it gave the United States an excuse to quadruple down on Section 301 sanctions. The Trump Administration sees itself in a winning position because there are much higher imports from China into the US than from the US into China.

The second tranche of Section 301 tariffs is just as WTO-illegal as the first tranche was. No unilateral tariffs imposed via Section 301 could ever be legal under WTO rules unless imposed as a DSB-authorized suspension of concessions or other obligations (SCOO). To its credit, China lodged a WTO case against the Section 301 tariffs (DS543), but so far, China has held off on securing the appointment of a panel. This delay may be politically connected to the Trump Administration's demand in ongoing US-China bilateral trade talks for China to agree not to bring future WTO challenges against US unilateral enforcement of the prospective China-US deal.

3.2.11 Lack of Market-Oriented Policies

The Trump Administration complains that China's economic policies since joining the WTO have not met the expectations of the United States and other WTO members. According to USTR, "When China acceded to the WTO in 2001, it voluntarily agreed to embrace the WTO's open-market-oriented approach and embed it in its trading system and institutions."[106] Furthermore, "Through China's commitments and representations, WTO members understood that China intended to dismantle existing state-led, mercantilist policies and practices...."[107] These complaints raise the fundamental question of what duty China owes to the WTO regarding China's economic and trade policies.

To analyse this question, one should start with general WTO law. Contrary to the suggestions of the Trump Administration, the WTO does not require its members to adhere to any particular economic or political system. Nowhere does the WTO

---

[104]But consultations are ongoing in DS565.

[105]Sax S, Millions of acres of the Amazon are at risk due to the trade war between the U.S. and China, Pacific Standard, 18 April 2019, https://psmag.com/economics/amazon-could-be-biggest-casualty-of-us-china-trade-war.

[106]USTR, 2018 USTR Report to Congress on China's WTO compliance, February 2019, p. 5.

[107]USTR, 2018 USTR Report to Congress on China's WTO compliance, February 2019, p. 5.

Agreement define the role of the state in relation to the market or civil society. The WTO rule that may come the closest to addressing economic systems is SCM Article 29 (Transformation into a Market Economy), but this provision stops short of requiring a government to effectuate such a transformation. Nor does the WTO constitution contain a provision to expel a Member that renounces market-oriented policies.

Although joining the WTO by accession does not in itself entail any special responsibilities regarding market friendliness, China's accession agreement does cover aspects of its economic system. For example, China reported that it had the objective of establishing and improving the socialist market economy.[108] But China's Accession Agreement does not commit China to adopt "market-oriented" policies and mentions that term only in one sentence wherein China notes that it is "undertaking market-oriented reform in the agricultural sector."[109] China's Accession Agreement does not contain any commitment by China to transform its economy or to abandon mercantilism. The Trump Administration is trying to insinuate rules into China's Accession Agreement that it wishes were there, but are not.

The issue of how broadly to interpret applicant WTO-plus accession obligations has occasionally arisen in WTO dispute settlement. In my view, such obligations should be interpreted narrowly *contra proferentem*. Under this principle, if a provision in a contract is ambiguous, then the tribunal should adopt an interpretation that works against the party who drafted that wording in the contract.

To apply this concept to the WTO, the China Accession Agreement is a contract-like international agreement between the WTO and China drafted by the WTO and agreed to by China. Although the applicant China had a role in accession negotiations, the key documents were drafted by WTO Members (led by the United States) in WTO bodies that did not include China.

In seeking to join the WTO, China made hundreds of detailed accession commitments. To quote a contemporary WTO Secretariat posting, "As a result of this negotiation, China has agreed to undertake a series of important commitments to open and liberalize its regime in order to better integrate in the world economy and offer a more predictable environment for trade and foreign investment in accordance with WTO rules."[110] In my view, China should be held to those "important commitments" which is why this article has expressed disappointment that the Trump Administration has brought only one accession-based complaint against China. Yet, holding China to its own commitments is quite different from asserting that China has failed to keep promises that China in fact did not make.

In my view, the Trump and Obama Administrations should have lodged more cases against China based on China's extraordinary accession commitments. For the

---

[108]WTO, Working Party on the Accession of China, WT/ACC/CHN/49, 1 October 2001, para. 6.

[109]WTO, Working Party on the Accession of China, WT/ACC/CHN/49, 1 October 2001, para. 115.

[110]WTO, WTO Ministerial Conference approves China's Accession, 10 November 2001, https://www.wto.org/english/news_e/pres01_e/pr252_e.htm.

Administration to call China a WTO violator without backing up that assertion in a tribunal of law evidences cowardice if not dishonesty. The best litigation strategy for the US would have been to file a series of cases under each of the WTO agreements. But if the Administration had also chosen to push the envelope by filing a broad case against China for its "state-led, mercantilist approach to the economy and trade,"[111] I would have supported that too.

Disciplining large non-market economies is a difficult challenge for the trading system. Rather than use the WTO, the Obama Administration pursued a flawed geopolitical strategy to craft better rules in the TPP and then to seek to pressure China into adhering to these rules. This strategy was flawed for three reasons: First, the rules achieved in the TPP fall far short of the market economy rules needed to transform the alleged pathologies in China's economy. Second, the idea of refusing to invite China to join the TPP and then seeking to isolate China economically was delusional given China's size as the world's largest trader. Third, the tactic was naive politically in ignoring China's historic sensitivity to rules being foisted on it through unequal treaties. A further flaw in Obama's TPP containment strategy was the failure of his Administration to garner US public support for the TPP project. Notably, all of the leading presidential candidates to succeed Obama opposed Obama's TPP.

Choosing the extent of market-oriented policies is a matter that WTO subsidiarity leaves to governments. While governments need not be clones of each other, there is a role for trade agreements to nudge governments toward best practices in regulation, deregulation, and privatization. In some areas, tight rules may be useful, but in others, governments should be able to retain their diversity and policy space. While internationally-agreed norms play an important role in improving domestic policies, such norms should not seek to displace the role of competition between countries as a way to get governments to lift standards.

3.2.12 High Bilateral Trade Deficit

President Trump has constantly complained about the high US trade deficit with China. In 2018, the bilateral goods deficit was $419 billion, the highest level ever.[112] A bilateral trade deficit in goods is not wrongful per se and is not WTO-illegal. The US trade deficit with China may be more interesting than the US deficit with Chad, but that is only because China is much bigger than Chad, not because the US-China deficit is a meaningful policy target. Although the Trump Administration complains about state-led mercantilism, nothing can be more mercantilist than the demands of the Administration for the bilateral trade balance with China to be "more equitable."[113]

---

[111]USTR, 2018 USTR Report to Congress on China's WTO compliance, February 2019, p. 2.

[112]https://www.census.gov/foreign-trade/balance/c5700.html.

[113]White House, Statement from the President Regarding Trade with China, 18 June 2018.

In general, a higher trade deficit in goods and services wreaks greater negative impact on domestic import-competing industry than a lower trade deficit does. The most meaningful bilateral trade numbers cover both goods and services, and in 2018, that goods and services deficit with China was $379 billion.[114] Thus, undertaking structural economic changes that would lower the $379 billion deficit with China is a good idea.

A US trade deficit with China means that US consumers and producers buy more from China than Chinese consumers and producers buy from the United States. The least coercive way to address this imbalance is for the United States to expand US exports of goods and services to China. By contrast, direct action to reduce US imports from China entails coercion and infringes freedom.

Many targeted policy reforms to expand US exports have been suggested. For example, the US government could reduce its gargantuan budget deficit, which has been expanding under the Trump Administration. A budget deficit pulls in foreign capital that cannot be used to purchase US exports. The US government could make US exports more competitive by reducing production costs stemming from under-investment in infrastructure, underinvestment in Chinese language training, and overregulation of US companies. The US government could also eliminate unnecessary US export controls. Trump's new tariffs on China have had the indirect effect of reducing Chinese demand for high-tech US products such as iPhones. That provides yet another reason to withdraw the Section 301 tariffs.

Unfortunately, the Trump Administration is not pursuing any of those constructive remedies to boost US exports. Instead, the Trump Administration appears to be using two tactics to lower the US trade deficit with China.

First, the President is asking China for a purchase agreement with monetary import targets for US goods.[115] This request is cynical because the Administration on one side of its mouth is demanding that the Chinese government exercise greater management of its trade while on the other side of its mouth, the Administration demands that the Chinese government be more market-oriented and less statist. The request is also problematic for third parties because if China commits to importing more from the US, then China may reduce imports from other WTO member countries. Any quantitative US-China trade agreement may run afoul of Article 11.1(b) of the WTO Safeguards Agreement which forbids arrangements involving "export or import surveillance" when such arrangements afford protection. In addition, should China's government intervene to dictate the origin of goods

---

[114]https://www.bea.gov/system/files/2019-03/trad0119.pdf (BOP basis).

[115]White House, Remarks by President Trump at Signing of a Presidential Memorandum Targeting China's Economic Aggression, 22 March 2018; Sukin G, Mnuchin says China will buy $1.2 trillion in U.S. goods, 22 February 2019, https://www.axios.com/us-china-currency-deal-trump-trade-war-0d1f5de8-26f5-42f1-becd-102f8106b67c.html.

purchased by state-invested or state-owned enterprises, that would violate one of China's accession commitments.[116]

The second tactic is to impose tariffs on China in order to lower imports from China. That result has not clearly happened yet, but with a high enough tariff, it would. One thing that is clear is that most of the Trump Administration's new tariffs against China violate WTO rules. The Section 301 tariffs violate GATT Articles I and II. The Section 232 tariffs violate GATT Articles I and II and are not justified under the national security exception in GATT Article XXI.[117] The Section 201 tariffs on washing machines violate GATT Article XIX because the US government failed to make any determination on "unforeseen developments." The US safeguard on solar panels may also violate GATT Article XIX.

China's high trade surplus with the United States should be subject to WTO tariff negotiations. Unfortunately, the Trump Administration has not shown any interest in the Doha Round or a renamed new trade round. China agreed to lower its tariffs and other barriers as part of its accession negotiations circa 1999, but 20 years later, China should do so again. Likewise, over 25 years after the conclusion of Uruguay Round tariff negotiations, a new round of liberalization by the United States is long overdue.

3.2.13   Unharmonized Tariffs and Taxes

Trump's call for China and US tariffs and taxes to be mirrored or reciprocal is perhaps his most perverse recommendation. For the United States to fail to match China's taxes and tariffs is hardly wrongful. Nor are non-matching taxes and tariffs a violation of WTO rules. Certainly, the US and China could negotiate tariff and tax bindings within the WTO to seek fiscal harmonization. What cannot be done is for China and the US to harmonize higher tariffs and taxes on each other because that would violate the most-favoured-nation (MFN) rule.

The idea that the United States would delegate to China the setting of US tax and tariff levels is fiscally unwise. Allowing China to determine US fiscal policy is also a violation of US constitutional principles of self-government. This deference to China is a surprising recommendation for the Trump Administration which has declared that: "Trade policy, like tax policy, must reflect the wishes, concerns, and priorities of the American people – and should not be dictated by technocrats who are not responsible to Americans. The United States remains an independent nation, and our

---

[116]WTO, Working Party on the Accession of China, WT/ACC/CHN/49, 1 October 2001, para. 46. A measure mandating the importation of goods from a favoured country is a GATT Article I violation.

[117]Charnovitz (2018), pp. 239–240; Pinchis-Paulsen M, Trade multilateralism and national security: Antinomies in the history of the International Trade Organization, 2019, https://papers.ssrn.com/sol3/papers.cfm?abstract_id=3353426.

trade policy will be made here – not in Geneva."[118] Made in Washington except when Trump calls for US taxes and tariffs to be made in Beijing!

The Trump Administration is right in suggesting that China should lower its high tariffs. This is the sort of goal that could properly be addressed in a new round of WTO negotiations. Unfortunately, Trump's USTR (and before it Obama's USTR) failed to press for such negotiations.

If China and the US had a free trade agreement (FTA), then the tariffs of both countries could be harmonized to zero. The goal of joining China in an FTA has never been suggested by the Trump Administration. Indeed, in the negotiations for a new trade agreement between Canada, the United States, and Mexico, the Trump Administration insisted on adding a new provision (Article 32.10) to discourage any North American country from negotiating an FTA with China.[119]

3.2.14 Belt and Road

The Belt and Road Initiative (BRI) is China's major international development investment initiative to expand trade-related foreign infrastructure. BRI is designed not only to expand China's trade, but also to promote development and connectivity to many countries around China. Begun only six years ago, BRI is already having a major economic and political impact. Countries that need to improve their infrastructure are signing on despite misgivings.[120]

Since BRI does not directly involve the United States, the carping at BRI by the Trump Administration can only be the result of envy at the leadership, deep pockets, and administrative prowess shown by China. No question, the Trump Administration has a lot to envy because it is failing to achieve any major infrastructure program abroad or at home. For the Trump Administration, ambitious infrastructure means a wall at the Mexican border and even that ill-advised project is not being achieved.

USTR's complaint that BRI "fails to adhere to internationally accepted best practices in infrastructure development and government procurement"[121] leads to some questions: Do the United Nations Sustainable Development Goals 17.1–17.5 cover best practices in development financing? What are "best practices" in infrastructure development? How much of the success of BRI is owed to the inadequacy of development financing from advanced economies? Such questions are important, but cannot be explored here.

---

[118]USTR, 2019 Trade Policy Agenda and 2018 Annual Report, March 2019, p. 27.

[119]Blanchfield M, Beijing attacks USMCA clause seen as blocking efforts to expand trade with Canada, Mexico. 5 October 2018, https://www.cbc.ca/news/politics/usmca-nafta-china-trade-1.4852269.

[120]Lau S, Italy may be ready to open up four ports to Chinese investment under "Belt and Road Initiative". 19 March 2019, https://www.scmp.com/news/china/diplomacy/article/3002305/italy-may-be-ready-open-four-ports-chinese-investment-under.

[121]USTR, 2018 USTR Report to Congress on China's WTO compliance, February 2019, p. 15.

However well or poorly China follows best practices in development financing, very little of that touches on WTO law. Indeed, subsidies to foreign countries are omitted from coverage in the SCM Agreement. Thus, China's failure to follow best practices in BRI is not wrongful in world trade law. In my view, the best practice mostly missing from BRI is that China has not built a sustainable development dimension into BRI and has not laid out a good plan to conduct environmental impact analysis.[122]

Two respected international legal scholars, Julien Chaisse and Mituso Matsushita, view BRI as a way for China "to export its development model."[123] Certainly, the broad scope of BRI turns it into a transnational issue for which China should engage in negotiations with key governments and international organizations. Based on the scope of BRI, the WTO seems an inapposite forum for such negotiations.

So far, the Trump Administration has not instituted any trade actions specifically against BRI. The main response by the Administration to BRI has been to work with the US Congress to enact a new law to improve US development finance programs.[124] The BUILD Act seeks to reorganize federal agencies with responsibilities for development finance and to expand US funding.[125] The Act takes a step in the right direction of competing with China rather than coercing it.

3.2.15 Lax Environmental Standards

The Trump Administration complains that China's lax environmental standards and weak enforcement of them helps China "dominate traditional manufacturing industries."[126] The theory that lax environmental, health or safety standards can drive national economic success is controversial, and growing evidence shows that a business can enhance its competitiveness by *improving* environmental sustainability.[127] For a government to maintain unjustifiably low environmental standards is wrongful, but such behaviour is not regulated by the WTO.

The WTO did include fishery subsidies as a Doha Round issue, but that issue was a poor fit for the WTO. In general, environmental challenges should be addressed in

---

[122]Murase S, "Belt and Road" from the viewpoint of international law. Unpublished manuscript 2018.

[123]Chaisse and Matsushita (2018), p. 163.

[124]Chatzky and McBride (2019).

[125]Even if the proposed $60 billion level funding level were approved by the US Congress (which seems doubtful), the US government funding would remain substantially less than the Chinese government funding.

[126]White House, Office of Trade and Manufacturing Policy, How China's economic aggression threatens the technology and intellectual property of the United States and the world, June 2018, p. 1.

[127]Esty (2019).

international environmental fora and fishery challenges should be addressed in
international fishery fora. As the eminent environmentalist Konrad von Moltke
pointed out decades ago, an environmental issue migrates to the trading system
only when it is not being successfully managed within the appropriate international
regime.

Many FTAs contain commitments regarding the enforcement of domestic environmental standards. For example, the Comprehensive and Progressive Agreement
for Trans-Pacific Partnership (CPTPP) directs that "a party shall not waive or
otherwise derogate from [...] its environmental laws in a manner that weakens or
reduces the protection afforded in those laws in order to encourage trade or investment between the Parties."[128] At this time, neither China nor the United States is a
party to the CPTPP.[129] To my knowledge, no FTA has regulated the level of
environmental standards (except to incorporate norms in mutually agreed multilateral environmental agreements).

Whether the environmental, health, and safety standards of China and the United
States are set at the right level is a proper matter of mutual interest especially when
standards cover global issues, such as ocean pollution, air pollution, or waste.
Lowering environmental standards can raise trade concerns, but so can the raising
environmental standards. For example in 2018, China imposed a ban on recycled
imports and plans a future ban on rubbish imports.[130] This action directly affects the
US economy because China has been a major destination for US recycling and trash
exports.

3.2.16 Securing Natural Resources

The Trump Administration complains that China uses a predatory debt trap model to
secure natural resources. Depending on the facts as to predation and trapping, this
may be wrongful behaviour. On the other hand, an ungenerous lending practice is
not a WTO violation. Moreover, I am not aware of any pertinent international legal
norms that cover such behaviour other than on tied aid.

Certainly, appropriate sovereign lending terms are a topic ripe for multilateral or
regional negotiations. The World Bank, the United Nations Conference on Trade
and Development (UNCTAD), and the Development Assistance Committee of the

---

[128]Comprehensive and Progressive Agreement for Trans-Pacific Partnership (CPTPP), 3 March
2018, Article 20.3.6.

[129]After the Trump Administration pulled the US out of the TPP, the remaining 11 nations renamed
the Agreement as "Comprehensive and Progressive" and, in true Orwellian fashion, made it less
comprehensive by suspending 22 provisions on investment and intellectual property that had been
championed by the US. Goodman MP, From TPP to CPTPP. CSIS, 8 March 2018, https://www.
csis.org/analysis/tpp-cptpp.

[130]A Chinese ban on rubbish imports is shaking up the global junk trade, The Economist,
29 September 2018, https://www.economist.com/special-report/2018/09/29/a-chinese-ban-on-rub
bish-imports-is-shaking-up-the-global-junk-trade.

Organisation for Economic Co-operation and Development (OECD) could each be an appropriate forum for these discussions. In my view, the WTO would not be the right forum for those issues other than when related to trade governance capacity.

3.2.17 Global Misallocation of Resources

The Trump Administration complains that China is misallocating global resources in a way that leaves everyone poorer. The proper allocation of resources is a key economic function typically left to markets. The Preamble to the WTO Agreement suggests that governments, in their trade relations, should be "allowing for the optimal use of the world's resources in accordance with the objective of sustainable development [. . .]."[131]

Notwithstanding that norm, the WTO has no rules regarding the proper allocation of resources. Adding such an issue to the WTO's agenda would not be a good idea because the WTO's agenda is already overloaded. Moreover, the WTO has performed poorly in negotiating numerous issues much more central to the WTO's mission.

The beauty of markets is that they handle a task like allocating resources through the gainful and voluntary interaction of private actors. Allocation bureaucrats are not needed. The Administration's complaint seems to be that allocation decisions in China are too often being made administratively rather than in the market. Obviously, China could lodge the same complaint against the US given the numerous non-market allocations being imposed by the Trump Administration.

The White House contends that a misallocation of resources can leave the Chinese people poorer than they would be in a world of efficient markets. In defending its economic aggression against China, USTR argues that "the distortions caused by China's non-market system" are bad not only for the United States, but for China too.[132] I agree with both contentions and with USTR's similar claim that reforms in China to pursue an "open, market-oriented approach" will "also benefit China, by placing its economy on a more sustainable path [. . .]."[133] The Trump Administration's insight is supported by the enlightened private sector. For example, Jamie Dimon, in his annual letter to JPMorgan Chase stockholders, recently explained: "We should only expect China to do what is in its own self-interest, but we believe that it should and will agree to some of the United States' trade demands because, ultimately, the changes will create a stronger Chinese economy."[134]

---

[131]Agreement Establishing the World Trade Organization, Preamble, 15 April 1994.

[132]USTR, 2018 USTR Report to Congress on China's WTO compliance, February 2019, p. 6.

[133]USTR, 2018 USTR Report to Congress on China's WTO compliance, February 2019, p. 5.

[134]Annual Report 2018, April 2019, https://reports.jpmorganchase.com/investor-relations/2018/ar-ceo-letters.htm?a=1.

The paradox in this pressure on China to swallow its economic medicine is that given how competitive[135] China now is against the United States with one hand tied behind its back due to distorted allocations, who knows how much more economically powerful China would become once it improves its suboptimal economic policies.

The worst misallocation of resources occurring in the world today is the excessive reliance on energy from fossil fuels. Such behaviour is wrongful in view of what scientists warn about the effects of carbon energy on climate change. The Trump Administration supports "promoting more efficient markets,"[136] but the world's most egregious market inefficiency is the failure to internalize the costs of utilizing carbon energy. Neither China nor the US has appropriate carbon internalization policies.

Instituting carbon charges falls within the wheelhouse of the climate regime. So far, the Paris Agreement has avoided instituting such policy norms. Even if one considers this stance a failure in climate policy (as I do), no one should look to the WTO as a substitute forum for negotiating climate policies such as carbon charges or border adjustments.

3.2.18 China's Acquisitions in US

The Trump Administration complains that China directs and unfairly facilitates investment and acquisition to generate large-scale technology transfer from U.S. companies to Chinese entities. Neither outward foreign investments nor inward foreign investments are intrinsically wrongful in a global economy. Indeed, the movement of capital and technology across borders are normal processes that benefit both capital exporting and capital importing countries.

The WTO is largely silent on the international acquisition of technology, but there is some soft law favouring openness. One WTO agreement calls on governments to "facilitate investment across international frontiers so as to increase the economic growth of all trading partners [...]."[137] Another WTO agreement suggests that developed countries "should provide incentives to enterprises and institutions in their territories for the purpose of promoting and encouraging technology transfer to least developed country Members in order to enable them to create a sound and viable technological base."[138]

The limited international investment law obligations in the WTO need to be read in conjunction with the extensive discretion that remains with national regulators to

---

[135]According to the latest IMF projections, the growth rate for China in 2019 will be 6.3% as compared to the US growth rate of 2.3%. See World Economic Outlook, April 2019.

[136]USTR, 2019 Trade Policy Agenda and 2018 Annual Report of the President of the United States on the Trade Agreements Program, March 2019, p. 2.

[137]WTO Agreement on Trade-Related Investment Measures, Preamble.

[138]TRIPS Article 66.2.

control inward foreign investment and acquisition of domestic enterprises and technologies. WTO rules would permit a government to bar inward foreign investment and foreign acquisition of domestic technology. Barring the importation of capital from one country, but not others, is subject to being examined pursuant to the non-discrimination rules of GATS Article II.

If the Trump Administration wants to bar Chinese entities from making certain investments in the US or transferring technology back to China, then the US government would have prescriptive jurisdiction to enact and enforce national laws to accomplish that objective. Such laws are reviewable under WTO rules, but the United States has nearly complete discretion under the WTO to enforce such laws against China. The TRIPS Agreement regulates the protection of alien intellectual property, but the TRIPS Agreement does not mandate free trade in domestic intellectual property and technology.

The Trump Administration is imposing Section 301 tariffs to punish China's efforts to invest in the United States, to acquire US companies that have cutting-edge technologies, and to transfer such technology back to China.[139] As noted above, the use of Section 301 tariffs violates US obligations in the WTO.

But not only are Section 301 tariffs internationally illegal, they are also grossly inefficient in targeting China's actions in the US. By far, the most effective instrument for the United States to use to regulate China's actions within the US territory is domestic regulation. For a sanctioning addict like the United States to waste sanction-sending resources to achieve a purpose that can be fully achieved under domestic law is feckless. The same point applies in No. 20 below.

The particular domestic law that the United States uses to control foreign investments is notoriously unfair. The regulator is the President and the Committee on Foreign Investment in the United States (CFIUS) who together can review foreign investments affecting national security broadly defined. CFIUS is a committee of federal officials without any public members. In CFIUS proceedings, neither the applicant foreign person nor the domestic counterparty enjoy any rights. Worse yet, the regulator has untrammelled discretion. The closed nature of the process makes it difficult for the public to see how arbitrarily foreign entities are being treated.

Under the Trump Administration, the outrageous CFIUS process has gotten even worse following a new federal law passed by the Congress in 2018 that denies judicial review of the President's findings or actions.[140] The recent ramping up of US regulation of domestic enterprises seeking foreign investment violates market

---

[139]USTR, Notice of Determination of Action Pursuant to Section 301, 83 F.R. 14907, 6 April 2018.
[140]50 USC § 4565(e)(1).

principles[141] and demonstrates the need for new international rules to discipline CFIUS-style regulations.[142]

3.2.19 Corporate Governance Law

The Trump Administration complains that China uses corporate governance law "as a tool to advance China's strategic goals, rather than simply, as is the custom of international rules, to advance the profit-maximizing goals of the enterprise."[143] Of the 20 claims reviewed here, this claim is the most fatuous. As noted above, this article does not attempt to reach the truth as to what is occurring in China. Thus, I will assume that China is using its corporate law to advance China's strategic goals. Corporate law, like any law, exists for the purpose of promoting the public interest.

The Trump Administration claims that there is an international custom or international rule that enterprises should only advance their profit-maximizing goals. No evidence is put forward for that claim and I do not know of any. Certainly, the WTO does not have a rule mandating or suggesting that enterprises should maximize their profits. In the United States, no federal or state law assigns enterprises the duty of maximizing their profits.

In a recent restatement of the basic principles of corporate law around the world, a group of experts explained:

> Contrary to widespread belief, corporate directors generally are not under a legal obligation to maximise profits for their shareholders. This is reflected in the acceptance in nearly all jurisdictions of some version of the business judgment rule, under which disinterested and informed directors have the discretion to act in what they believe to be in the long-term interests of the company as a separate entity, even if it does not entail seeking to maximize short-term shareholder value.[144]

I do not know what the latest trends are in Chinese corporate governance, but contrary to the claim of the Trump White House, if China is seeking to steer companies to pursue goals other than profit maximizing that would not place China out of the comparative mainstream nor diverge from the US approach. If

---

[141] See Joint Statement on Trilateral Meeting of the Trade Ministers of the United States, Japan, and the European Union, Annexed Statement 3, Joint Statement on Market Oriented Conditions, 31 May 2018 ("The Ministers noted the following elements or indications that signal that market conditions exist for businesses and industries: [. . .] (2) decisions of enterprises on investments are freely determined and made in response to market signals;. . ."), https://ustr.gov/about-us/policy-offices/press-office/press-releases/2018/may/joint-statement-trilateral-meeting.

[142] Klein JX, It's not just the U.S.: Around the world, doors are shutting on Chinese investment. South China Morning Post, 13 September 2018, https://www.politico.com/story/2018/09/13/china-us-investment-788834.

[143] White House, Office of Trade and Manufacturing Policy, How China's economic aggression threatens the technology and intellectual property of the United States and the world, June 2018, p. 11.

[144] The modern corporation, Statement on company law, October 2016, https://papers.ssrn.com/sol3/papers.cfm?abstract_id=2848833.

instead of leaving corporate goals up to each company, China were to task its corporations to pursue sustainability and decent work and to refrain from corruption, such corporate law would not appear to impose any harm on the US economy.

3.2.20 Cyber and Intellectual Property Theft

The Trump Administration complains that China's government engages in "theft" of American technology. Such theft is illegal under U.S. law. Rather than improving enforcement of federal law, however, the Trump Administration in July 2018 imposed Section 301 tariffs on China to counter the thefts. Finally, in an apparent afterthought, the Administration began stepping up high-profile domestic enforcement actions against Chinese entities.[145]

A proposition that either theft and espionage violates WTO law seems doubtful, but I reserve judgment. No doubt exists that a Section 301 tariff against theft and espionage violates WTO law. Using the Section 301 instrument is especially paradoxical for a purpose for which straightforward penalties such as US criminal prosecutions are available. Whether US criminal law provides sufficient deterrence against perpetrators beyond the reach of US courts is a matter that should be considered. Some analysts have suggested that indicting wrongdoers is not sufficient, and that non-tariff sanctions against the responsible Chinese perpetrators are needed.[146]

The analysis above of Trump's top 20 gripes about China's trade practices is summarized in Table 1 starting on the next page.

3.3 Overall Findings

One of the most dangerous trade fallacies propounded by the Trump Administration is that its aggressive trade actions against China will "ensure that the costs of China's non-market economic system are borne by China, and not by the United States."[147] Nothing can be further from reality. U.S. tariffs are paid by importers within the United States with the costs ultimately borne by either US domestic purchasers of imports or foreign exporters. A recent empirical study suggests that in this current episode, the costs are being borne by US consumers rather than Chinese

---

[145]Yap, C-W, U.S. weaponizes its criminal courts in fight against China and Huawei, Wall Street Journal, 17 January 2019.

[146]Barfield C, New China intellectual property indictments: A step forward and a cop-out. AEI, 7 January 2018, http://www.aei.org/publication/new-china-intellectual-property-indictments-a-step-forward-and-a-cop-out/.

[147]USTR, 2018 USTR Report to Congress on China's WTO compliance, February 2019, p. 25.

Table 1 Key aspects of Trump's top 20 complaints about China's behaviour

Complaint	Is behaviour wrongful?	Does this behaviour violate WTO?	Did Trump lodge WTO case?	Are new WTO negotiations necessary?	Are negotiations outside the WTO necessary?
1. Forced technology transfer	Yes	Yes	No	No, but could be useful	No
2. Chinese industrial policies	Depends on the facts	Yes, depending on the facts	No	No, but could be useful	No
3. Non-tariff barriers and high tariffs	Yes, if unjustifiable or discriminatory	Yes, if unjustifiable or discriminatory	No	Yes, for tariffs	No
4. Agricultural import bans	Yes	Yes	No	No	No
5. Subsidies for added industrial capacity	Yes, if no other policy purpose	Yes	No	No, but could be useful	No, but could be useful
6. Involuntary licensing requirements	Yes	Yes	Yes	No, but could be useful	No
7. Disregard of transparency obligations	Yes	Yes	Yes	No, but could be useful	No, but could be useful
8. Improper trade remedies	Yes	Yes	No	Yes	No
9. Data localization	Yes, depending on the facts	Yes, depending on the facts	No	Yes	Yes
10. China's tariff retaliation	Yes	Yes	Yes for §232 No for §301	No	No
11. Lack of market-oriented policies	No	Maybe depending on future legal interpretation	No	Yes	Yes, in some regimes
12. High bilateral trade deficit	No, but it is not optimal	No	No	Yes	No

				No, not for harmonization in itself	
13. Unharmonized tariffs and taxes	No	No	No	No	No
14. Belt and Road	No	No	No	No	Yes in some regimes
15. Unjustifiably lax environmental standards	Yes	No	No	No	Yes, in environmental regimes
16. Securing natural resources	Depends on the facts	No	No	No	Yes
17. Global misallocation of resources	Yes	No	No	No	Yes, in the climate regime
18. China's acquisitions in US	Not in general	No	No	No	This issue amenable to national law, but more international cooperation could be useful
19. Corporate governance law	No	No	No	No	No
20. Cyber and intellectual property theft	Yes	Not generally	No	No	This problem amenable to national law, but more international cooperation would be useful

exporters.[148] While China may suffer some lost sales to the United States, the US economy definitely suffers harm. One analyst has recently predicted that "because China exports to Americans dwarf our exports to them, trade restrictions can inflict disproportionate harm to China's economy."[149] This argument errs by looking only at the export side of the trade transaction and not looking at the harm caused by US tariffs to Americans.

Besides being a double-edged weapon, US tariffs obscure the normative message that the United States should be communicating about China's misbehaviour. Instead, the US tariffs themselves become the message and China focuses its attention to how to defend itself from the assault by retaliating against the sender country and by shifting exports to third countries. In the US public arena, the processes to choose US tariff targets and award exemptions to lawyered-up importers absorb most of the media's attention. This cybernetic failure renders the tariffs an incoherent and defective strategy for transforming China.

As the Trump Administration will learn, the ad hoc nature of the Section 301 sanctions will make them difficult to remove in a negotiation with China. Because the sanctions are normless, a perfectionist-protectionist coalition is sure to rise up to fight against tariff removal. Both groups in the coalition will argue that the Administration should not be a patsy to empty promises by China.

The Trump Administration's most serious normative failure is to engage China through power rather than law. The narrative is oddly disjunctive. The Trump's Administrations anti-China rhetoric often sounds in law. For example, USTR explained that "Unfortunately, China has a poor record when it comes to complying with WTO rules and observing the fundamental principles on which the WTO agreements are based."[150] The White House declared that Trump "is following through on his pledge to take action to ensure that China finally plays by the rules."[151] Trump himself has referred to China's "illicit trade practices" and to its "misconduct."[152] Given these assertions, the Administration's multiple failures to bring legal complaints is a non-sequitur.

The Administration has been remarkably candid as to why it has not invoked WTO dispute settlement:

> China has no fear of WTO dispute settlement, even as it continues to embrace a state-led mercantilist approach to the economy and trade [. . .].[153]

---

[148]Fajgelbaum PD et al., The return to protectionism. 10 March 2019, http://www.econ.ucla.edu/pfajgelbaum/RTP.pdf.

[149]Porter R, Trump's big trade opening, Wall Street Journal, 14 March 2019.

[150]USTR, 2018 USTR Report to Congress on China's WTO compliance, February 2019, p. 8.

[151]White House, What You Need to Know About President Donald J. Trump's Actions Responding to China's Unfair Trade Practices, 6 April 2018.

[152]White House, Statement from President Donald J. Trump on Additional Proposed Section 301 Remedies, 5 April 2018.

[153]USTR, 2019 Trade Policy Agenda and 2018 Annual Report, March 2019, p. 26.

No matter how many cases are brought at the WTO, China can always find a way to engage in market-distorting practices.[154]

Any suggestion that the United States or other WTO members could address the numerous problems outlined in this [USTR] report solely by relying on the WTO dispute settlement mechanism is naïve in theory, and likely to prove downright harmful in practice.[155]

While the WTO dispute settlement process is of only limited value in dealing with China's non-market practices, the Chinese government is eager to draw upon the judicial activists at the WTO to protect its economic system.[156]

USTR provides no evidence to back up these claims and I am not aware of any. Whether or not China fears WTO dispute settlement, the government of China's failure to comply after losing a WTO case would seem to be no worse than the US government's failure to comply.

Instead, the Administration's true concern may be that continued compliance by China will put the spotlight on persistent non-compliance by the United States, especially on trade remedy violations. For the Trump Administration, WTO dispute settlement is a problem not a solution. That is why zeroing out the WTO Appellate Body is a higher priority for USTR than lodging cases against China. Moreover, if there will not be an Appellate Body after 2019, why bother bringing new legal cases against China?

By failing to make legal arguments against China, the Trump Administration dilutes whatever normativity may exist for persuading the world of its claim that China is not playing by the rules. Many WTO experts agree that the Administration has missed an opportunity to file WTO cases against China.[157] In the current trade war against China, the most notorious rule-breaker is the United States which is ignoring its DSU Article 23 obligation to use the WTO dispute system rather than Section 301 and is ignoring its obligation not to impose unilateral tariffs on China.

The Trump Administration's myopia regarding the benefits of challenging China's actions as a violation of WTO rules is strangely shared by others who are quick to point out what China is doing wrong. The most maddening advocacy comes from the U.S.-China Economic and Security Review Commission, an advisory group established by Congress in 2000. In its most recent report (the 2018 report which is its 16th annual report) the taxpayer-funded Commission floats the idea that USTR should bring a "*non*-violation" case against China at the WTO.[158] Besides missing the key point that China is *violating* the WTO, a non-violation case is difficult to win and hardly worth the effort as any resulting award is unenforceable due to DSU Article 26.1.

---

[154]USTR, 2018 USTR Report to Congress on China's WTO compliance, February 2019, p. 10.

[155]USTR, 2018 USTR Report to Congress on China's WTO compliance, February 2019, p. 23.

[156]USTR, 2019 Trade Policy Agenda and 2018 Annual Report, March 2019, p. 26.

[157]For example, see Schoenbaum and Chow (2019), pp. 190–192.

[158]U.S.-China Economic and Security Review Commission, 2018 Report to Congress, November 2018, p. 22.

In pointing out the obvious normative failures in the Trump Administration's strategy, I am certainly not suggesting that China always faithfully executes WTO law. Rather, my point is that the best way, and perhaps the only way, to get China to act more responsibly is to inculcate international legal norms into China's national trade practices. The Trump Administration's strategy to use coercion rather than reason to change China's behaviour may seem pragmatic and realist to Trump's team, but nothing could be more naive than to imagine that weapons that hurt the United States as much as (or more than) they hurt China will succeed in enabling the United States to dictate to China what China's economic policies will be.

As explained above, the US strategy of bilateral bargaining with China in the shadow of US tariffs suffers the pathology of displacing law with power. Another dimension of the pathology is the displacement of the multilateral WTO negotiating forum with secretive US-China bilateral talks. Other than No. 12 above, all of the US complaints about China reflect systemic issues that affect the WTO membership as a whole. Should China pledge to reduce state control, the ensuing policies can externalize benefits to all WTO members, not just the US. But there is also a danger of reaching exclusive US-China arrangements that would externalize costs on other WTO members.[159]

4 Conclusion

This study dissects America's top 20 charges against Chinese trade-related misbehaviour. The study finds that at least half of the charges (Nos. 1–10) violate WTO rules. Of those 10, the Trump Administration has brought claims against only three of them (Nos. 6, 7, and 10).

China should be held to the international rule of law, but so should the United States. The US tariffs being imposed against China under the Sections 201, 232, and 301 schemes violate international trade law, and this US misbehaviour in the WTO obscures misbehaviour by China. The US Section 301 tariffs have been imposed in response to five types of alleged misbehaviour by China (Nos. 1, 6, 10, 18, and 20). The Section 201 and 232 tariffs are not predicated on China's misbehaviour.

Table 1 above reveals notable surprising features of the US trade war against China: Six of the US claims are for types of behaviour that are not inherently wrongful in a diverse world economy and that are not a WTO violation (Nos. 11, 12, 13, 14, 18, and 19). Four types raise policy issues that are more properly considered outside of the WTO and for which better international cooperation is needed (Nos. 14–17.) Two of the types (Nos. 18, 20) relate to China's activities within the prescriptive jurisdiction of the United States for which the Trump

---

[159]Bown CP, Why the US needs allies in a trade war against China, Harvard Business Review Digital, 11 December 2018, https://hbr.org/2018/12/why-the-u-s-needs-allies-in-a-trade-war-against-china.

Administration has tightened up domestic regulation and enforcement. Yet, the Trump Administration is also using Section 301 sanctions against those two types. The use of Section 301 sanctions for Chinese investment (No. 18) is especially perverse as China owes no duty to the US until US regulators prescribe what movements of capital and technology are prohibited.

Two of the claims (Nos. 12 and 18) ascribe to China's government full responsibility for actions that occur in large part in China's private sector. Seeking to make China's government accountable for private sector behaviour is consistent with the Trump Administration's assumptions as to the limited extent of market conditions in China. That logic is circular, however, because to achieve the changes that the Administration seeks in at least five claims (Nos. 1, 12, 17, 18, 19), the Chinese government will need to expand its control of private economic actors.

Seven of the US claims raise systemic issues for which WTO law is said to be inadequate to govern problems related to large non-market economies (Nos. 1, 2, 5, 7, 8, 9, 11). Yet the Trump Administration has not promoted WTO negotiations for any of these issues. Instead, the most USTR has done is to co-author a Joint Scoping Paper with the EU and Japan regarding the need for stronger rules on industrial subsidies, state-owned enterprises, the definition of a public body, and the identification of market-oriented conditions.[160]

If there are to be new international norms to govern the competition between market and non-market economies, the norms and standards have to be based on competitive neutrality principles that apply to all countries and economic systems equally. USTR can pontificate that China "continues to embrace a state-led mercantilist approach to the economy and trade that is fundamentally incompatible with the open, market-based approach envisioned and followed by other WTO members."[161] Nevertheless, to many observers, the Trump Administration's trade policies also look state-led, mercantilist, closed, and non-market based. This is especially true of the industrial policies for steel, aluminum, and washing machines, the calculated selection of beneficiaries of Section 301 tariffs, the blocking of China's inward investment into the United States, and Trump's recent expansion of Buy-American requirements.[162]

Decrying state capitalism is easy rhetorically, but when governments meet together to write rules, a granular approach is needed to unpack complex terms such as "state-led," "mercantilist," "open," and "market-based." How does an international regulator objectively determine when those indicated conditions exist? Are government policies to provide public goods state-led? Should steel

---

[160]See Joint Statement on Trilateral Meeting of the Trade Ministers of the United States, Japan, and the European Union, Annexed Statement 3, Joint Statement on Market Oriented Conditions, 31 May 2018.

[161]USTR, 2019 Trade Policy Agenda and 2018 Annual Report, March 2019, p. 26.

[162]Hoe S et al., Trump's new Executive Order requires additional Buy American preferences for infrastructure projects. Covington, 7 February 2019, https://www.insidegovernmentcontracts.com/2019/02/trumps-new-executive-order-requires-additional-buy-american-preferences-infrastructure-projects/.

"overcapacity" be addressed by market or non-market approaches? Will market-based policies be sufficient to address market failure? What strategies are needed to control the pathologies of government failure?[163] What rules should guide industrial policies in "open" economies? Should the SCM Agreement be expanded to cover implicit downstream subsidies? Anyone seeking to devise a code of fair competition between market and nonmarket economies will need to think through difficult questions such as these.

The existential challenge facing the OECD countries is not low-cost imports from China, but rather how to maintain an attractive development model for the rest of the world. The key advantage for the United States, Europe, and Japan is the jointly-shared embedded commitment to rule of law, democratic institutions, free markets, effective regulatory structures, and international cooperation.

The tragedy of the Trump Administration's economic aggression against China is its willingness to cast those principles aside in order to elicit ad hoc Chinese concessions. Whether or not the Chinese government agrees to alter some domestic policies, Trump's narcissistic economic war against China will erode the public's appreciation for the benefits of rule of law and international cooperation. By contrast, other than China's blunder in retaliating against the Section 301 tariffs, China has shown itself to be a WTO supporter that will not cave into US efforts to return the trading system to the law of the jungle.[164] China was among the many governments that brought a WTO case against the Section 232 tariffs, and the recent WTO panel report in the Russia – *Traffic in Transit* case makes a win by the Section 232 plaintiffs much more likely.[165]

The Administration's efforts to shut down the Appellate Body may make it impossible for the United States to prosecute cases against China in the WTO dispute system. This is puzzling at a time when Trump himself is bragging that because of his policies, "we're doing better even with WTO. We're winning cases all of a sudden because they know my attitude."[166] Of course, the US cannot win WTO cases against China unless USTR is willing to do the heavy lifting to prepare and prosecute such cases.

By holding the Appellate Body hostage, the Trump Administration is apparently seeking to pressure other WTO members to agree to a change in DSU rules that would increase the likelihood of Appellate Body rulings against China as defendant

---

[163]Charnovitz (2010).

[164]Deng C, China defends WTO record as trade fight looms. Wall Street Journal, 28 June 2018 (discussing China's White Paper). Taking note of China's pro-legalization stance, USTR has complained that "It is very troubling to see that China believes that giving more authority to the Appellate Body would be in China's interest." USTR, 2019 Trade Policy Agenda and 2018 Annual Report, March 2019, p. 27.

[165]Baschuk B, WTO defies Trump with historic ruling on national security, 5 April 2019, https://www.bloomberg.com/news/articles/2019-04-05/wto-defies-trump-with-historic-first-ruling-on-national-security.

[166]Trump claims U.S. winning more cases thanks to this trade policies, World Trade Online, 22 March 2019.

and, at the same time, decrease the likelihood of rulings against the United States as defendant. Failing that first-best outcome, the revealed preference of USTR seems to be to turn off WTO enforcement in order to preserve "policy space"[167] for the US to impose WTO-illegal Section 301 and trade remedy tariffs against China. Rather than being viewed as a valuable public good, the judicial independence of the Appellate Body is despised by the Trump Administration as a restriction on US sovereignty.[168]

Although US unilateral power may still be strong enough to humble China, the projection of US power cannot be the sole basis on which to lead the world. Addressing the global problems of the twenty-first century—particularly climate, health, and cyberspace—will require more intensive intergovernmental cooperation buttressed by an effective international legal system.[169] The Trump Administration's rejection of global governance on trade, climate, and other important areas of law is a misstep of major consequence. Unlike the state of play when America rejected the League of Nations a century ago, this time there is a record of accomplishment by the multilateral system.

For its overall strategy to reform China and provide US global leadership on trade, I give the Trump Administration a generous grade of "D". The best features are the WTO cases lodged against Nos. 6, 7, and 10 and the exemplary case studies demonstrating how *not* to carry out trade policy. Three of Trump's complaints against China (Nos. 2, 3, and 8) expose the double standards in US protectionism. Five of the US complaints (Nos. 11, 14, 15, 16, 17) concern complex international problems for which the Administration has offered neither thoughtful ideas nor political leadership. The rest of Trump's trade strategy suffers for being poor lawyering (Nos. 1–11), mercantilist (No. 12), WTO-illegal (Nos. 1, 6, 10, 13, 18, and 20), or nonsense (Nos. 13, 19).

References

Aaronson S (2018) What are we talking about when we talk about digital protectionism? World Trade Review online, 6 Aug 2018. https://www.cambridge.org/core/journals/world-trade-review/article/what-are-we-talking-about-when-we-talk-about-digital-protectionism/F0C763191DE948D484C489798863E77B

Chaisse J, Matsushita M (2018) China's 'Belt and Road' initiative: mapping the world trade normative and strategic dimensions. J World Trade 52(1):163–186

Charnovitz S (1993–94) Designing American industrial policy: general versus sectoral approaches. Stanford Law Policy Rev 5:78–92

Charnovitz S (2001) The WTO and the rights of the individual. Intereconomics Rev Eur Econ Policy 36(2):98–108. https://archive.intereconomics.eu/year/2001/2/

---

[167]USTR, 2019 Trade Policy Agenda and 2018 Annual Report, March 2019, p. 27.

[168]Patrick SM, Trump's search for absolute sovereignty could destroy the WTO, World Policy Review, 25 March 2019, https://www.cfr.org/blog/trumps-search-absolute-sovereignty-could-destroy-wto.

[169]Haas (2019), p. 29.

Charnovitz S (2008) Mapping the law of WTO accession. In: Janow ME, Donaldson V, Yanovich A (eds) The WTO: governance, dispute settlement and developing countries. Juris Publishing, Huntington, pp 855–920

Charnovitz S (2010) Addressing government failure through international financial law. J Int Econ Law 13(3):743–761

Charnovitz S (2018) How American rejectionism undermines international economic law. Trade Law Dev 10(2):226–269

Chatzky A, McBride J (2019) China's massive belt and road initiative. Council on Foreign Relations, New York

Ding R (2014) "Public Body" or not: Chinese state-owned enterprise. J World Trade 48(1):167–190

Ehring L (2014) Nature and status of WTO accession commitments: "WTO-Plus" obligations and their relationship to other parts of the WTO Agreement. In: Cremona M, Hilpold P, Lavranos N, Schneider SS, Ziegler AR (eds) Reflections on the constitutionalisation of international economic law, Liber Amicorum for Ernst-Ulrich Petersmann. Martinus Nijhoff, Leiden, pp 337–361

Esty DC (ed) (2019) The labyrinth of sustainability. Anthem Press, New York

Haas R (2019) How a world order ends. Foreign Aff 98(1):22–30

Kahn R (2017) Have sanctions become the Swiss army knife of U.S. foreign policy? Council on Foreign Relations, New York. https://www.cfr.org/blog/have-sanctions-become-swiss-army-knife-us-foreign-policy

Meyer T (2018) Free trade, fair trade, and selective enforcement. Columbia Law Rev 118(2):491–566

Petersmann EU (2018) The 2018 trade wars as a threat to the world trading system and constitutional democracies. Trade Law Dev 10(2):179–225

Rovnov Y (2019) The life and death of a non-recurring subsidy: the role of change in ownership of subsidy recipient. J World Trade 53(2):211–228

Schoenbaum TJ, Chow DCK (2019) The perils of economic nationalism and a proposed pathway to trade harmony. Stanford Law Policy Rev 30:115–195

Tooze A (2019) Is this the end of the American century? Lond Rev Books 41(7). https://www.lrb.co.uk/v41/n07/adam-tooze/is-this-the-end-of-the-american-century

Yamaoka T (2013) Analysis of China's accession commitments in the WTO: new taxonomy of more and less stringent commitments, and the struggle for mitigation by China. J World Trade 47(1):105–158

Steve Charnovitz teaches on the Law Faculty of the George Washington University. He is a member of the Council on Foreign Relations, the American Law Institute, and the Bar of the Supreme Court of the United States.

The Renegotiation of NAFTA: The "Most Advanced" Free Trade Agreement?

Jean-Michel Marcoux

Contents

1 Introduction

The plans to modernize the international rules regulating trade between Canada, Mexico and the United States have been disrupted by the trade policy of the US administration. Given that the North American Free Trade Agreement (NAFTA) has been governing regional trade between the three States since 1994,[1] the content of

---

[1] North American Free Trade Agreement (NAFTA), signed 17 December 1992, entered into force 1 January 1994.

J.-M. Marcoux (✉)
McGill University, Faculty of Law, Montreal, QC, Canada
e-mail: jean-michel.marcoux@mail.mcgill.ca

© Springer Nature Switzerland AG 2019
M. Bungenberg et al. (eds.), *European Yearbook of International Economic Law 2019*,
European Yearbook of International Economic Law (2020) 10: 257–284,
https://doi.org/10.1007/8165_2019_42, Published online: 31 July 2019

the agreement was ripped for an update.[2] The participation of the three Parties in the negotiations of the Trans-Pacific Partnership Agreement (TPP) allowed the elaboration of modern rules that would have been applicable to their trade relationship.[3] However, shortly after his investigation in January 2017, President Trump decided to withdraw from TPP.[4] In light of his often-repeated criticism of NAFTA as being the "worst trade deal ever made",[5] it was clear that NAFTA was heading toward a tumultuous renegotiation.

The events that led to the signature of the United States–Canada–Mexico Agreement (USMCA) unfolded over more than a year and a half.[6] By a letter sent on 18 May 2017, the United States Trade Representative (USTR) formally notified the Congress of President Trump's intent "to initiate negotiations with Canada and Mexico regarding modernization of the North American Free Trade Agreement".[7] Ninety days after this notification, the negotiations began with a first round that was held in Washington.[8] After several rounds, the dynamics of the elaboration of USMCA were marked by a crucial change. On 27 August 2018, the negotiators of Mexico and the United States announced that they had reached an agreement on specific issues, leading the US administration to notify the Congress of its intent to sign a free trade agreement with Mexico within 90 days.[9] When reporting the notification to the Congress, the USTR nevertheless emphasized that Canada could join the agreement in the meantime. On 30 September 2018, the Canadian Foreign Affairs Minister and the USTR announced that they had reached an agreement.[10]

---

[2]See Leblond and Fabian (2017), Bergstein and de Bole (2017), p. 3; Ortiz-Mena (2017), p. 30; Schott and Cimino-Isaacs (2017).

[3]Trans-Pacific Partnership Agreement (TPP), signed 4 February 2016.

[4]Withdrawal of the United States from the Trans-Pacific Partnership Negotiations and Agreement, 23 January 2017, Fed Reg Vol 82 No 15, p. 8497.

[5]For example, in his remarks that followed the conclusion of USMCA negotiations, President Trump mentioned the following: "I have long contended that NAFTA was perhaps the worst trade deal ever made". See White House, Remarks by President Trump on the United States–Mexico–Canada Agreement, 1 October 2018, https://www.whitehouse.gov/briefings-statements/remarks-president-trump-united-states-mexico-canada-agreement/ (last accessed 22 May 2019).

[6]United States–Mexico–Canada Agreement (USMCA), signed 30 November 2018.

[7]USTR, Letter to Congressional Leadership, 18 May 2017, https://ustr.gov/sites/default/files/files/Press/Releases/NAFTA%20Notification.pdf (last accessed 22 May 2019).

[8]See USTR, Press Release, Opening Statement of USTR Robert Lighthizer at the First Round of NAFTA Renegotiations, 16 August 2017, https://ustr.gov/about-us/policy-offices/press-office/press-releases/2017/august/opening-statement-ustr-robert-0 (last accessed 22 May 2019).

[9]USTR, Press Release, USTR Statement on Trade Negotiations with Mexico and Canada, 31 August 2018, https://ustr.gov/about-us/policy-offices/press-office/press-releases/2018/august/ustr-statement-trade-negotiations (last accessed 22 May 2019).

[10]USTR, Press Release, Joint Statement from United States Trade Representative Robert Lighthizer and Canadian Foreign Affairs Minister Chrystia Freeland, 30 September 2018, https://ustr.gov/about-us/policy-offices/press-office/press-releases/2018/september/joint-statement-united-states (last accessed 22 May 2019).

What had evolved as two distinct bilateral negotiations ultimately concluded with the signature of USMCA on 30 November 2018.[11]

One aspect that is particularly important to consider from a legal perspective is the advancement for the broader free trade regime provided by the provisions of USMCA. After reaching an agreement with Mexico, the USTR referred to it as "the most advanced and high-standard trade agreement in the world".[12] Likewise, President Trump claimed that USMCA was a highly innovative agreement. In his remarks that were pronounced the day after the conclusion of the negotiations, he depicted USMCA as "the most advanced trade deal in the world with ambitious provisions [in several areas] where the United States has a strong competitive advantage".[13]

Major changes can be noted when comparing NAFTA and USMCA. One must nevertheless question whether the text of USMCA constitutes a genuine advancement for the free trade regime, broadly considered. Of course, the level of advancement characterizing a free trade agreement depends upon whose interests are advanced in the agreement.[14] It is nevertheless worth noting that the claims made by the US administration do not solely relate to the advancement of US interests. Rather, what is suggested by the statements of the USTR and President Trump is that USMCA is nothing less than the most advanced trade agreement worldwide. Such a characterization requires a thorough contextual analysis of the provisions included in USMCA. In light of the political and legal context underlying the renegotiation process, how can differences between NAFTA and USMCA be explained?

This article suggests that, although the USMCA negotiations allowed modernizing the content of NAFTA and addressing more progressive objectives, the majority of the changes included in the agreement constitute a reflection of the context in which the renegotiation occurred and are hardly reconcilable with the consideration of USMCA as the most advanced trade agreement. The article proceeds in two steps. First, it addresses the political and legal context in which the USMCA negotiations took place. From a political perspective, the renegotiation of NAFTA occurred in a very tense context, marked by an insistence by the United States to reduce bilateral trade deficits and a reliance on tariffs as a negotiation tool. Moreover, several trade disputes that arose during the span of the negotiations and previous free trade agreements constitute important components of the legal landscape in which the

---

[11]Global Affairs Canada, News Release, Canada Signs New Trade Agreement with United States and Mexico, 30 November 2018, https://www.canada.ca/en/global-affairs/news/2018/11/canada-signs-new-trade-agreement-with-united-states-and-mexico.html (last accessed 22 May 2019).

[12]USTR, Press Release, USTR Statement on Trade Negotiations with Mexico and Canada, 31 August 2018, https://ustr.gov/about-us/policy-offices/press-office/press-releases/2018/august/ustr-statement-trade-negotiations (last accessed 22 May 2019).

[13]White House, Remarks by President Trump on the United States–Mexico–Canada Agreement, 1 October 2018, https://www.whitehouse.gov/briefings-statements/remarks-president-trump-united-states-mexico-canada-agreement/ (last accessed 22 May 2019).

[14]Some authors have already suggested that USMCA reflects US interests. See Puig (2019), p. 57; Perezcano Diaz (2019), pp. 9–10; Lilly (2019), p. 17.

renegotiation occurred. Second, the article focuses on specific provisions that contrast with NAFTA. Whilst major changes have undoubtedly been included in USMCA, the text of the agreement is in line with a bilateral approach that can potentially restrict trade and partially draws from the language found in previous agreements.

2   The Political and Legal Context

In order to assess whether the text of USMCA constitutes a genuine advancement in contrast to other free trade agreements, it is worth focusing on key aspects of the political and legal landscape in which the negotiations took place. Although the formal intent of the Parties was to proceed with a modernization of NAFTA, several statements and official documents demonstrate a political context characterized by the US administration's insistence to address bilateral trade deficits and the imposition of tariffs as a negotiation tool. Trade disputes were also ongoing during the USMCA negotiations, either under NAFTA or the World Trade Organization (WTO). As far as free trade agreements are concerned, the Parties had all participated in the negotiations of treaties since the adoption of NAFTA.

2.1   Political Discourse

One important component of the context in which the USMCA negotiations occurred relates to the political discourse of the negotiating Parties. Several statements and official documents intended to frame the renegotiation of NAFTA as a way to merely "modernize" the free trade agreement. As mentioned above, the letter that was sent by the USTR to notify the Congress of the President Trump's intent to renegotiate NAFTA explicitly referred to the modernization of the agreement.[15] Similarly, after the first round of negotiation, the three Parties issued a trilateral statement that referred to the "renegotiation and modernization" of NAFTA.[16] Even if the Parties considered the renegotiation as reflecting a commitment to an ambitious outcome, the statement referred to "the importance of updating the rules governing the world's largest free trade area", as well as "an accelerated and comprehensive

---

[15]USTR, Letter to Congressional Leadership, 18 May 2017, https://ustr.gov/sites/default/files/files/Press/Releases/NAFTA%20Notification.pdf (last accessed 22 May 2019).

[16]Global Affairs Canada, News Release, Trilateral Statement on the Conclusion of NAFTA Round One, 21 August 2017, https://www.canada.ca/en/global-affairs/news/2017/08/trilateral_statementontheconclusionofnaftaroundone.html (last accessed 22 May 2019).

negotiation process that will upgrade our agreement and establish 21st century standards".[17]

Other aspects of the political discourse nevertheless hinted toward different objectives. For the United States, the idea of modernizing NAFTA was strongly linked to efforts at reducing bilateral trade deficits with its trading partners.[18] For example, in the Summary of the Objectives for the NAFTA Renegotiation that was circulated in July 2017, the USTR emphasized that "[s]ince the deal came into force in 1994, trade deficits have exploded, thousands of factories have closed, and millions of Americans have found themselves stranded, no longer able to utilize the skills for which they have been trained".[19] It also provided that "the new NAFTA will be modernized to reflect 21st century standards and will reflect a fairer deal, *addressing America's persistent trade imbalances in North America*".[20] Improving trade balance and reducing trade deficit were even listed as the very first objective provided in the summary.[21] Similarly, in his opening statement at the first round of the renegotiation, the USTR maintained that "the huge trade deficits, the lost manufacturing jobs, the businesses that have closed or moved because of incentives – intended or not – in the current agreement" could not be ignored.[22] Taken as a whole, the rhetoric and proposals of the US administration can be considered as an example of a "populist trade policy".[23]

By contrast, the other negotiating Parties focused on avoiding a trade agreement that would be less favourable than NAFTA.[24] For example, a speech provided by the Canadian Foreign Affairs Minister 2 days before the first round of negotiations adopted a decidedly defensive approach. After identifying the aim to modernize NAFTA as the first core objective of Canada, she recalled that Canadians "pursue

---

[17]Global Affairs Canada, News Release, Trilateral Statement on the Conclusion of NAFTA Round One, 21 August 2017, https://www.canada.ca/en/global-affairs/news/2017/08/trilateral_statementontheconclusionofnaftaroundone.html (last accessed 22 May 2019).

[18]See Bergsten (2017), p. 13; Ortiz-Mena (2017), p. 24; Hufbauer and Jung (2017), p. 50.

[19]USTR, Summary of Objectives for the NAFTA Renegotiation, 17 July 2017, https://ustr.gov/sites/default/files/files/Press/Releases/NAFTAObjectives.pdf (last accessed 22 May 2019), p. 2.

[20]USTR, Summary of Objectives for the NAFTA Renegotiation, 17 July 2017, https://ustr.gov/sites/default/files/files/Press/Releases/NAFTAObjectives.pdf (last accessed 22 May 2019), p. 3 (emphasis added).

[21]USTR, Summary of Objectives for the NAFTA Renegotiation, 17 July 2017, https://ustr.gov/sites/default/files/files/Press/Releases/NAFTAObjectives.pdf (last accessed 22 May 2019), p. 4.

[22]USTR, Press Release, Opening Statement of USTR Robert Lighthizer at the First Round of NAFTA Renegotiations, 16 August 2017, https://ustr.gov/about-us/policy-offices/press-office/press-releases/2017/august/opening-statement-ustr-robert-0 (last accessed 22 May 2019).

[23]Lester and Manak (2018), p. 160.

[24]Although the examples provided in this paragraph concern Canada, Mexico's participation in the negotiation primarily amounted to a reaction to US demands. See Perezcano Diaz (2019), p. 9. For other analyses of the Mexican perspective, see Bergstein and de Bole (2017), p. 8; Ortiz-Mena (2017), p. 24; Crespo (2018), pp. 973–979.

trade, free and fair, knowing it's not a zero-sum-game".[25] Echoes of this defensive approach were also found in a news release published by Global Affairs Canada at the moment of the signature of USMCA, which mentioned that "Canada succeeded in preserving key elements of the original NAFTA, including the cultural exemption and the use of binational panels to resolve disputes on duties".[26]

During the negotiation process, the US administration imposed tariffs on steel and aluminum products by relying on Section 232 of the Trade Expansion Act of 1962.[27] In two proclamations adopted on 8 March 2018, President Trump decided to impose a 10% ad valorem tariff on aluminum articles and a 25% ad valorem tariff on steel articles imported from all States as of 23 March 2018, except from Canada and Mexico.[28] At that time, President Trump considered both States as presenting "a special case" and determined that the more appropriate means to address his concerns was to continue ongoing discussions.[29] On 22 March 2018, President Trump subsequently expanded the exemption to products from other States and determined that the tariffs will be effective for the exempted States on 1 May 2018, unless otherwise determined by a future proclamation.[30] Although aluminum and steel products imported from some States were still exempted from these tariffs beyond this deadline, President Trump later confirmed that the tariffs shall be effective for Canadian and Mexican products on 1 June 2018.[31]

The proclamations from President Trump emphasized that the decision to impose tariffs on aluminum and steel products was justified by the US Secretary of Commerce's findings that the importation of these products occurred "in such quantities and under such circumstances as to threaten to impair the national security of the

---

[25]Global Affairs Canada, Address by Foreign Affairs Minister on the Modernization of the North American Free Trade Agreement (NAFTA), 14 August 2017, https://www.canada.ca/en/global-affairs/news/2017/08/address_by_foreignaffairsministeronthemodernizationofthenorthame.html (last accessed 22 May 2019).

[26]Global Affairs Canada, News Release, Canada Signs New Trade Agreement with United States and Mexico, 30 November 2018, https://www.canada.ca/en/global-affairs/news/2018/11/canada-signs-new-trade-agreement-with-united-states-and-mexico.html (last accessed 22 May 2019).

[27]19 USC § 1862.

[28]Adjusting Imports of Aluminum into the United States (Proclamation 9704), 8 March 2018, Fed Reg Vol 83 No 51, p. 11619, para 7; Adjusting Imports of Steel into the United States (Proclamation 9705), 8 March 2018, Fed Reg Vol 83 No 51, p. 11625, para 8.

[29]Adjusting Imports of Aluminum into the United States (Proclamation 9,704), 8 March 2018, Fed Reg Vol 83 No 51, p. 11619, para 9; Adjusting Imports of Steel into the United States (Proclamation 9705), 8 March 2018, Fed Reg Vol 83 No 51, p. 11625, para 10.

[30]Adjusting Imports of Aluminum into the United States (Proclamation 9710), 22 March 2018, Fed Reg Vol 83 No 60, p. 13355, paras 4 and 11; Adjusting Imports of Steel into the United States (Proclamation 9711), 22 March 2018, Fed Reg Vol 83 No 60, p. 13361, paras 4 and 11.

[31]Adjusting Imports of Aluminum into the United States (Proclamation 9739), 30 April 2018, Fed Reg Vol 83 No 88, p. 20677, para 6; Adjusting Imports of Steel into the United States (Proclamation 9740), 30 April 2018, Fed Reg Vol 83 No 88, p. 20683, para 7.

United States".[32] However, shortly after the conclusion of the USMCA negotiations, President Trump explicitly referred to tariffs as a negotiation tool.[33] In remarks formulated on 1 October 2018, he mentioned the following:

> By the way, without tariffs, we wouldn't be talking about a deal, just for those babies out there that keep talking about tariffs. That includes Congress – 'Oh, please don't charge tariffs.' Without tariffs, we wouldn't be standing here. I can tell you, Bob [the USTR] and all these folks would not be standing here right now. *And we are totally prepared to do that if they don't negotiate.*[34]

Later during the same remarks, when asked whether there had been discussions to eliminate retaliatory tariffs imposed by Canada and Mexico on US producers, President Trump mentioned that the United States was "using tariffs very successfully to negotiate".[35] Even after the conclusion of the negotiations, the tariffs on aluminum and steel products imported from Canada and Mexico were still imposed by the United States.[36]

President Trump also threatened to impose tariffs on automobiles and auto parts during the negotiation process. On 23 May 2018, he instructed the US Secretary of Commerce to initiate an investigation to "determine whether imports of automobiles, including SUVs, vans and light trucks, and automotive parts into the United States threaten to impair the national security".[37] Once again, despite their justification as a way to address national security issues, President Trump openly admitted using these potential tariffs as a negotiation tool:

---

[32] Adjusting Imports of Aluminum into the United States (Proclamation 9704), 8 March 2018, Fed Reg Vol 83 No 51, p. 11619, para 4; Adjusting Imports of Steel into the United States (Proclamation 9705), 8 March 2018, Fed Reg Vol 83 No 51, p. 11625, para 5.

[33] See Galbraith (2018a), p. 513; Galbraith (2019), p. 151.

[34] White House, Remarks by President Trump on the United States–Mexico–Canada Agreement, 1 October 2018, https://www.whitehouse.gov/briefings-statements/remarks-president-trump-united-states-mexico-canada-agreement/ (last accessed 22 May 2019) (emphasis added).

[35] White House, Remarks by President Trump on the United States–Mexico–Canada Agreement, 1 October 2018, https://www.whitehouse.gov/briefings-statements/remarks-president-trump-united-states-mexico-canada-agreement/ (last accessed 22 May 2019).

[36] On 17 May 2019, two joint statements were signed by the United States with Canada and Mexico to remove the tariffs and related retaliatory measures. See USTR, Press Release, United States Announces Deal with Canada and Mexico to Lift Retaliatory Tariffs, 17 May 2019, https://ustr.gov/about-us/policy-offices/press-office/press-releases/2019/may/united-states-announces-deal-canada-and (last accessed 22 May 2019).

[37] US Department of Commerce, Press Release, US Department of Commerce Initiates Section 232 Investigation into Auto Imports, 23 May 2018, https://www.commerce.gov/news/press-releases/2018/05/us-department-commerce-initiates-section-232-investigation-auto-imports (last accessed 22 May 2019). See also Galbraith (2018b), p. 756.

> Look, Canada has been ripping us off for a long time. And now, they've got to treat us fairly.
> I don't want to do anything bad to Canada. I can; all I have to do is tax their cars. It would be
> devastating. . . . But we want to make a fair deal. I do use that *as a leverage in negotiating*.[38]

Another interesting point regarding the concerns of the US administration about bilateral trade deficits and the use of tariffs as a negotiating tool is that they were not strictly limited to Canada and Mexico. These broader concerns were articulated by President Trump in his remarks following the conclusion of the USMCA negotiations. After mentioning that doing business with the United States constituted a "privilege",[39] he made the following remarks:

> And I'm not talking about Mexico, Canada – I'm talking about everybody. Everybody. It's a
> privilege for China to do business with us. It's a privilege for the European Union, who has
> treated us very badly – but that's coming along – to do business with us. Japan, every
> country – It's a privilege for them to come in and attack the piggy bank.[40]

One should thus not be surprised to see that some provisions of USMCA were developed as a model for future negotiations with other US trading partners.

2.2   Trade Disputes

In addition to the political discourse, the USMCA negotiations were punctuated by the arising of trade disputes. Between 18 May 2017 and 30 November 2018, not less than 17 international dispute settlement proceedings were initiated between the negotiating Parties under the auspices of the WTO or the applicable provisions of NAFTA. Although the trade disputes do not appear to have been extensively considered in statements made by the negotiators, it is clear that they constitute an integral part of the legal context in which the negotiations were held.

At the WTO, the United States submitted a (second) complaint against Canada with respect to the sale of wine in grocery stores in October 2017.[41] According to the United States, several measures adopted by the province of British Columbia were inconsistent with Article III:4 of the General Agreement on Tariffs and Trade (GATT). Likewise, Canada requested consultations with the United States regarding countervailing and antidumping measures on softwood lumber products in

---

[38]White House, Remarks by President Trump in Press Gaggle Aboard Air Force One, 7 September 2018, https://www.whitehouse.gov/briefings-statements/remarks-president-trump-press-gaggle-aboard-air-force-one/ (last access 22 May 2019) (emphasis added).

[39]White House, Remarks by President Trump on the United States–Mexico–Canada Agreement, 1 October 2018, https://www.whitehouse.gov/briefings-statements/remarks-president-trump-united-states-mexico-canada-agreement/ (last accessed 22 May 2019).

[40]White House, Remarks by President Trump on the United States–Mexico–Canada Agreement, 1 October 2018, https://www.whitehouse.gov/briefings-statements/remarks-president-trump-united-states-mexico-canada-agreement/ (last accessed 22 May 2019).

[41]Request for Consultations by the United States, *Canada–Measures Governing the Sale of Wine in Grocery Stores (Second Complaint)*, WT/DS531/1, 2 October 2017.

November 2017.[42] Less than 2 months later, it also submitted an additional request focusing on systemic trade remedies measures adopted by the United States.[43]

The tariffs that were imposed by the United States on steel and aluminum products imported from Canada and Mexico led to another set of requests for consultations. In June 2018, Canada and Mexico both submitted requests for consultations and argued that the tariffs were inconsistent with several provisions of GATT and the Agreement on Safeguards.[44] These requests were quickly followed by other requests for consultations submitted by the United States.[45] The latter challenged "additional duties measures" that were adopted by Canada and Mexico regarding products imported from the United States.[46] According to the requests for consultations, these measures were inconsistent with Article I:I GATT (as well as Article II:1 GATT in the case of the request for consultations with Canada).

Several determinations made by the United States regarding countervailing and antidumping duties were also challenged by Canada and Mexico under Chapter 19 NAFTA.[47] Three panel reviews related to softwood lumber products from Canada were requested and were still active at the time of the signature of USMCA.[48] Four other requests related to civil aircrafts and uncoated groundwood paper were made by Canada,[49] but they were terminated after the United State International Trade Commission (USITC) found that the respective industries in the United States were not materially injured or threatened with material injury by the imports of these

---

[42]Request for Consultations by Canada, *United States–Countervailing Measures on Softwood Lumber from Canada*, WT/DS533/1, 30 November 2017; Request for Consultations by Canada, *United States–Anti-Dumping Measures Applying Differential Pricing Methodology to Softwood Lumber from Canada*, WT/DS534/1, 30 November 2017. For the latter, a panel report was circulated on 9 April 2019. See Report of the Panel, *United States–Anti-Dumping Measures Applying Differential Pricing Methodology to Softwood Lumber from Canada*, WT/DS534/R, 9 April 2019.

[43]Request for Consultations by Canada, *United States–Certain Systemic Trade Remedies Measures*, WT/DS535/1, 10 January 2018.

[44]Request for Consultations by Canada, *United States–Certain Measures on Steel and Aluminum Products*, WT/DS550/1, 6 June 2018; Request for Consultations by Mexico, *United States–Certain Measures on Steel and Aluminum Products*, WT/DS551/1, 7 June 2018.

[45]Request for Consultations by the United States, *Canada–Additional Duties on Certain Products from the United States*, WT/DS557/1, 19 July 2018; Request for Consultations by the United States, *Mexico–Additional Duties on Certain Products from the United States*, WT/DS560/1, 19 July 2018. See also Galbraith (2018b), pp. 755–756.

[46]Request for Consultations by the United States, *Canada–Additional Duties on Certain Products from the United States*, WT/DS557/1, 19 July 2018; Request for Consultations by the United States, *Mexico–Additional Duties on Certain Products from the United States*, WT/DS560/1, 19 July 2018.

[47]For information on these disputes see NAFTA Secretariat, Status Report of Panel Proceedings, https://www.nafta-sec-alena.org/Home/Dispute-Settlement/Status-Report-of-Panel-Proceedings (last accessed 22 May 2019).

[48]Panel Review Numbers USA-CDA-2017-1904-02, USA-CDA-2017-1904-03 and USA-CDA-2018-1904-03.

[49]Panel Review Numbers USA-CDA-2018-1904-01, USA-CDA-2018-1904-02, USA-CDA-2018-1904-05 and USA-CDA-2018-1904-06.

products.[50] Mexico also requested a panel review regarding antidumping duties imposed on large residential washers[51] and circular welded non-alloy steel pipes (although the latter was terminated by joint consent of the Parties).[52]

2.3 Recent Free Trade Agreements

Another important aspect of the context underlying the renegotiation of NAFTA pertains to the evolution of free trade agreements since the initial treaty between Canada, Mexico and the United States. When compared to the text of NAFTA, it is plain that USMCA addresses several concerns that were not taken into consideration in the early 1990s. However, a more accurate yardstick to assess the "advanced" character of USMCA should be found in recent regional free trade agreements.[53]

One of these agreements is the Comprehensive and Economic Trade Agreement (CETA), which was signed by Canada and the European Union on 30 October 2016.[54] In addition to the issues that are typically included in free trade agreements, the content of CETA includes entire chapters on mutual recognition of professional qualifications, domestic regulation, international maritime transport services, electronic commerce, regulatory cooperation, sustainable development, labour, environment and transparency, among others. CETA provisionally entered into force on 21 September 2017, slightly more than a month after the beginning of the NAFTA renegotiation.

Notwithstanding that President Trump instructed the USTR to withdraw from TPP, the text of this agreement constitutes an integral part of the legal context in which USMCA was negotiated. On 8 March 2018, when the 11 remaining States signed the Comprehensive and Progressive Trans-Pacific Partnership (CPTPP), they decided to incorporate the provisions of TPP, with some limited exceptions.[55] Article 2 CPTPP provides that the Parties have decided to suspend the application of specific provisions that are listed in the Annex to the agreement. As a result, the text of TPP that was incorporated into CPTPP covers 30 chapters, including

---

[50]100- to 150-Seat Large Civil Aircraft from Canada (Determinations), 13 February 2018, Fed Reg Vol 83 No 34, p. 7218; Uncoated Groundwood Paper from Canada (Determinations), 24 September 2018, Fed Reg Vol 83 No 188, p. 48863.

[51]Panel Review Number USA-MEX-2018-1904-04.

[52]Panel Review Number USA-MEX-2018-1904-01.

[53]For example, CETA and/or TPP have been considered as good templates to upgrade NAFTA. See Leblond and Fabian (2017), p. 2; Bergstein and de Bole (2017), p. 6; Ortiz-Mena (2017), p. 30; Dobson et al. (2017), pp. 37 and 48; Esty and Salzman (2017), pp. 135–136; Lester et al. (2019), pp. 69–74.

[54]Comprehensive and Economic Trade Agreement (CETA), signed 30 October 2016, provisionally entered into force 21 September 2017.

[55]Comprehensive and Progressive Agreement for Trans-Pacific Partnership (CPTPP), signed 8 March 2018, entered into force 30 December 2018.

electronic commerce, labour, environment, cooperation and capacity building, competitiveness and business facilitation, development, small and medium-sized enterprises, regulatory coherence as well as transparency and anti-corruption.

The European Union and Mexico also reached an agreement in principle pertaining to the trade part of a modernized EU-Mexico Global Agreement on 23 April 2018.[56] After having started in May 2016, the negotiations of this agreement were still ongoing after the signature of USMCA.[57] According to the index included in the agreement in principle, the negotiating Parties had already reached an agreement on 19 items. The final EU-Mexico agreement is thus supposed to include provisions specifically addressing animal welfare and antimicrobial resistance, sustainable development, transparency, good regulatory practice, small and medium enterprises and anti-corruption, among others.

Most importantly, some of these agreements were considered by the negotiating Parties as a useful starting point to renegotiate NAFTA. For example, when listing the objectives of Canada, the Foreign Affairs Minister maintained that a revised NAFTA had to be more "progressive".[58] In this regard, she mentioned that Canadian negotiators had to be informed by the content of CETA, which she considered as "the most progressive trade deal in history".[59] With respect to the United States, it would have been incoherent for the US administration to explicitly rely upon the content of TPP as a basis to negotiate USMCA when considering President Trump's assertion that bilateral agreements are better suited to serve US interests.[60] However, the USITC extensively referred to the text of TPP when it conducted its analysis of the likely impact of USMCA on the US economy. It thus acknowledged that the text of USMCA builds on the language found in TPP with respect to digital trade, investment, labour, environment and anti-corruption, among others.[61] Even if the report was completed after the signature of the agreement, the fact that US agencies have acknowledged the strong link between USMCA and TPP confirms that the

---

[56]New EU–Mexico Agreement: The Agreement in Principle, 23 April 2018, http://trade.ec.europa.eu/doclib/docs/2018/april/tradoc_156791.pdf (last accessed 22 May 2019).

[57]European Commission, Countries and Regions: Mexico, http://ec.europa.eu/trade/policy/countries-and-regions/countries/mexico/ (last accessed 22 May 2019).

[58]Global Affairs Canada, Address by Foreign Affairs Minister on the Modernization of the North American Free Trade Agreement (NAFTA), 14 August 2017, https://www.canada.ca/en/global-affairs/news/2017/08/address_by_foreignaffairsministeronthemodernizationofthenorthame.html (last accessed 22 May 2019).

[59]Global Affairs Canada, Address by Foreign Affairs Minister on the Modernization of the North American Free Trade Agreement (NAFTA), 14 August 2017, https://www.canada.ca/en/global-affairs/news/2017/08/address_by_foreignaffairsministeronthemodernizationofthenorthame.html (last accessed 22 May 2019).

[60]Withdrawal of the United States from the Trans-Pacific Partnership Negotiations and Agreement, 23 January 2017, Fed Reg Vol 82 No 15, p. 8497.

[61]USITC, US–Mexico–Canada Trade Agreement: Likely Impact on the US Economy and on Specific Industry Sectors, April 2019, https://www.usitc.gov/publications/332/pub4889.pdf (last accessed 22 May 2019), pp. 172, 198, 217, 251–252 and 255.

latter was a relevant part of the legal context underlying the renegotiation of NAFTA.

The statements and official documents mentioned above are far from constituting an exhaustive list. They nevertheless allow concluding that the Parties to NAFTA entered into the renegotiation of the agreement amidst a very particular political and legal context. The intent to reduce bilateral trade deficits by the United States, the use of tariffs as a negotiating tool and ongoing trade disputes between the Parties have all potentially tainted the discussions between the negotiating Parties. Furthermore, negotiators could rely on the text of previous free trade agreements that already included important innovations in comparison to the initial text of NAFTA. The consideration of USMCA as the "most advanced" agreement must thus be assessed against this broader context.

3 Exploring Differences Between NAFTA and USMCA

Having highlighted the political and legal context in which the NAFTA renegotiation took place, it becomes possible to examine major changes included in USMCA. Of course, some provisions constitute genuine advancements that are intended to increase free trade and to address progressive objectives. However, this section demonstrates that several changes included in USMCA reflect either a bilateral approach that can potentially restrict trade or a partial reproduction of provisions found in previous free trade agreements.

To be clear, an exhaustive list of items that are not included in NAFTA and appear in USMCA is beyond the scope of this analysis. It is nevertheless possible to focus on some major changes with a view to highlighting the limits of USMCA with respect to its ability at advancing free trade. It must also be noted that the aim of this section is not to identify the first occurrence of the major changes included in USMCA by assessing a plurality of free trade agreements. Here, additions to the original text of NAFTA are analyzed in light of recently signed free trade agreements by the negotiating Parties in order to demonstrate that these provisions can be found elsewhere. It is in this regard that TPP (and CETA, to a lesser extent) offers a particularly interesting yardstick to complete the analysis.[62]

---

[62]For a side-by-side comparison of USMCA, NAFTA and TPP, see Stewart and Stewart, The United States–Mexico–Canada Agreement (USMCA) of 2018, the North American Free Trade Agreement (NAFTA) Text, and the Trans-Pacific Partnership (TPP) Text Side-by-Side, http://www.stewartlaw.com/PracticeAreas/USMCASidebySide (last accessed 22 May 2019).

3.1 Rules of Origin

The focus of the US administration on the reduction of bilateral trade deficits has implied several efforts to incentivize the sourcing of goods and materials from the United States and North America.[63] Given that they encompass requirements that products must meet in order to be considered as originating from the territories of the Parties and to benefit from the applicable preferential tariff treatment, the rules of origins included in Chapter 4 USMCA constitute a useful tool to achieve this objective. In addition to changes that borrow from the language of TPP, the bulk of the modifications included in this chapter are primarily geared toward the creation of incentives to protect the production of specific goods in the United States.

Some provisions of Chapter 4 USMCA echo the language that was originally found in NAFTA. For example, the calculation method of the regional value content that is provided at Article 4.5 USMCA builds on the methods found at Article 402 NAFTA. However, the negotiating Parties also updated the language of this chapter by adopting provisions that are closer to Chapter 3 TPP. Examples are reflected in the language regarding wholly obtained or produced goods,[64] the treatment of recovered materials used in the production of a remanufactured good,[65] the value of materials used in production,[66] adjustments to the value of materials,[67] accumulation,[68] packaging materials,[69] as well as transit and transshipment,[70] among others.

Some of the most drastic changes included in USMCA can be found in Annex 4-B, which includes a list of requirements applicable to specific goods that are produced from materials not originating from the territories of the Parties. Whereas an exhaustive list of requirements that differ from NAFTA cannot be covered here, the product-specific rules of origins pertaining to the automotive sector are particularly noteworthy.[71] These requirements are included in a separate appendix to Annex 4-B, entitled Provisions Related to Product-Specific Rules of Origins for Automotive Goods.

---

[63]USTR, Summary of Objectives for the NAFTA Renegotiation, 17 July 2017, https://ustr.gov/sites/default/files/files/Press/Releases/NAFTAObjectives.pdf (last accessed 22 May 2019), p. 6. See also Lester and Manak (2018), p. 161; McDaniel (2019), p. 4; Lilly (2019), pp. 15–16.

[64]Article 4.3 USMCA; Article 3.3 TPP.

[65]Article 4.4 USMCA; Article 3.4 TPP.

[66]Article 4.6 USMCA; Article 3.7 TPP.

[67]Article 4.7 USMCA; Article 3.8 TPP.

[68]Article 4.11 USMCA; Article 3.10 TPP.

[69]Articles 4.15-4.16 USMCA; Articles 3.14-3.15 TPP.

[70]Article 4.18 USMCA; Article 3.18 TPP.

[71]Article 4.10 USMCA specifically refers to the Appendix to Annex 4-B for additional provisions that apply to the automotive goods. Less detailed provisions on the automotive sector are also included in Appendix 1, Annex 3-D TPP.

The main requirements imposed on the automotive sector through this appendix are threefold. First, the appendix sets requirements for regional value content for autos and automobile parts. With respect to passenger vehicles and light trucks, the regional value content requirement will gradually rise to 75% by 1 January 2023 or 3 years after the entry into force of USMCA, whichever comes the later.[72] The requirements for parts of passenger vehicles and light trucks vary between 65 and 85%, depending upon the parts and the calculation method.[73] A regional value content of 70% will also be gradually required by 1 January 2027 or 7 years after the entry into force of the agreement for heavy trucks,[74] whilst their parts are subject to requirements varying between 60 and 80%.[75]

Second, Article 6 of the appendix to Annex 4-B USMCA adds a requirement pertaining to steel and aluminum used for the production of passenger vehicles, light trucks and heavy trucks. In order for these vehicles to be considered as originating from the territories of the Parties, at least 70% of the producers' purchases of steel and aluminum must be of originating goods.

Third, the same appendix imposes requirements regarding "labour value content", which consists in a combination of expenditures pertaining to high-wage material and manufacturing, technology and assembly. As far as passenger vehicles are concerned, producers must certify that their production meets a requirement of labor value content of 40% as of 1 January 2023 or 3 years after the entry into force of the agreement, whichever comes the later.[76] This requirement amounts to 45% for light and heavy trucks.[77]

In contrast to product-specific rules of origin, the increase of the de minimis thresholds that allow considering a good produced from non-originating materials as an originating good contributes to a deeper trade relationship between the Parties. Even if a good does not meet the tariff classification change that is required in Annex 4-B or a requirement regarding regional value content, Article 4.12 USMCA provides that it can still be considered as an originating good if the value of all non-originating materials is not more than 10% of its transaction value or its total cost.[78] Whereas the de minimis thresholds provided under NAFTA amounted only to 7%,[79] an increase to 10% has already been agreed between the Parties to TPP.[80]

---

[72] Annex 4-B, Appendix, Article 3(1)(d) USMCA.

[73] Annex 4-B, Appendix, Articles 3(2)(d), 3(4)(d) and 3(5)(d) USMCA.

[74] Annex 4-B, Appendix, Article 4(1)(c) USMCA.

[75] Annex 4-B, Appendix, Articles 4(2)(c) and 4(3)(c) USMCA.

[76] Annex 4-B, Appendix, Article 7(1)(d) USMCA.

[77] Annex 4-B, Appendix, Article 7(2) USMCA.

[78] Some exceptions are nevertheless imposed in Annex 4-A USMCA.

[79] Article 405 NAFTA.

[80] Article 3.11(1) TPP.

3.2 Agriculture

When listing the objectives for the renegotiation of NAFTA, the Office of the USTR has explicitly referred to expanding competitive market opportunities to US agricultural goods with a view to making them equivalent to the opportunities afforded to foreign exports into the United States.[81] Even if some changes brought to USMCA allow achieving this objective, Chapter 3 USMCA generally reflects a focus on bilateral trade relationships and extensively replicates the language of TPP.

As far as its provisions are concerned, Chapter 3 USMCA results from a blend of NAFTA and TPP. For example, the provisions pertaining to the Committee on Agricultural Trade build on the text of both agreements.[82] However, the language that does not appear in the original text of NAFTA is largely inspired by the text of TPP. Examples of these provisions relate to export restrictions for food security purposes[83] and agricultural special safeguards.[84] Moreover, both agreements explicitly cover trade of products of modern biotechnology and the inadvertent low level presence of biotechnology products in a shipment,[85] as well as the establishment of a working group to specifically address matters related to products of modern biotechnology in agriculture.[86]

Beyond the articles included in the main text of Chapter 3 USMCA, additional provisions have been negotiated by the United States through bilateral annexes with each of the other Parties. In addition to tariff rate quotas agreed between Canada and the United States for specific products (i.e. dairy, poultry, egg and sugar products),[87] Annex 3-A USMCA addresses matters of agricultural trade between both States. Several improvements regarding market access are thus included in Annex 3-A USMCA and relate to dairy products, wheat and sugar, among others.[88] With respect to Mexico and the United States, Annex 3-B USMCA includes specific provisions mostly regarding sugar. However, in contrast to Annex 3-A, the provisions negotiated between Mexico and the United States do not seem to establish additional market opportunities. For example, Annex 3-B allows both States to consider that a good is not originating under specific circumstances, thus allowing the Party to refuse to provide the applicable preferential tariff treatment under the agreement.[89]

---

[81] USTR, Summary of Objectives for the NAFTA Renegotiation, 17 July 2017, https://ustr.gov/sites/default/files/files/Press/Releases/NAFTAObjectives.pdf (last accessed 22 May 2019), p. 4.

[82] Article 3.7 USMCA; Article 706 NAFTA; Article 2.25 TPP.

[83] Article 3.5 USMCA; Article 2.24 TPP.

[84] Article 3.9 USMCA; Article 2.26 TPP.

[85] Articles 3.14-3.15 USMCA; Article 2.27 TPP.

[86] Article 3.16 USMCA; Article 2.27(9) TPP.

[87] Annex 2-B, Appendix 2, Section B USMCA.

[88] Annex 3-A, Articles 3.A.3-3.A.5 USMCA.

[89] Annex 3-B paras 5–6 USMCA.

3.3   Digital Trade

One of the obvious changes regarding the way businesses conduct trade since the negotiations of NAFTA is the advent of the Internet. The inclusion of a chapter addressing digital trade appeared as inevitable and constitutes an undeniable novelty of USMCA in comparison to its predecessor. However, a closer analysis of the text suggests that the bulk of USMCA Chapter 19 builds on the corresponding text in other free trade agreements.

For example, the USMCA and TPP chapters are both intended to apply "to measures adopted or maintained by a Party that affect trade by electronic means".[90] Without precluding a Party to impose internal charges on a digital product transmitted electronically, they provide that a Party shall not impose customs duties regarding the importation or the exportation of such a product.[91] Among the more specific obligations included in these agreements, both agreements address the non-discriminatory treatment of digital products,[92] the protection of personal information,[93] the cross-border transfer of information by electronic means,[94] as well as the inclusion of an obligation for Parties not to require the use or the location of computing facilities in its own territory as a condition for conducting business.[95]

Two provisions are included in USMCA without explicit prior language in TPP or CETA. Article 19.17 relates to interactive computer services and must be read with Annex 19-A, which provides a specific regime of application for Mexico. Article 19.18 focuses on an increasingly relevant matter, namely open government data. Despite its novel character, this provision does not impose any concrete obligations on States. Rather, it merely mentions that the Parties "recognize that facilitating public access to and use of government information fosters economic and social development, competitiveness, and innovation".[96] It also provides that Parties "shall endeavor" to ensure that the information is in a machine-readable and open format, and to cooperate to expand access to government information.[97]

3.4   Investment

One area in which USMCA clearly fails to provide the most advanced model for free trade agreements relates to the protection of foreign investment. Even if important

---

[90] Article 19.2(2) USMCA; Article 14.2(2) TPP.

[91] Article 19.3 USMCA; Article 14.3 TPP. See also Article 16.3 CETA.

[92] Article 19.4 USMCA; Article 14.4 TPP.

[93] Article 19.8 USMCA; Article 14.8 TPP. See also Article 16.4 CETA.

[94] Article 19.11 USMCA; Article 14.11 TPP.

[95] Article 19.12 USMCA; Article 14.13 TPP.

[96] Article 19.18(1) USMCA.

[97] Article 19.18(2)-(3) USMCA.

changes are included in contrast to Chapter 11 NAFTA, the substantive rules in Chapter 14 USMCA do not reach further than what can be found in other free trade and international investment agreements. Moreover, the unequal access to investment arbitration for investors depending upon their State of origin is consistent with the conception of international trade through bilateral relations that has been noted in other USMCA chapters.

Without addressing all the changes that were made to the substantive rules of the investment chapter, it is worth noting that multiple clarifications pertaining to the scope of protections granted to foreign investments in USMCA closely follow the language of Chapter 9 TPP. For example, USMCA provides a definition of the obligation for States to accord "fair and equitable treatment" to investment, with the explicit exclusion of a measure that is inconsistent with an investor's expectations as a violation of the minimum standard of treatment.[98] The provision regarding expropriation also builds on previous investment treaties by including the language mentioned in a separate annex that clarifies the scope of indirect expropriation.[99] The language of TPP is also considerably reproduced in USMCA provisions regarding the scope of the chapter,[100] the treatment of investments in case of armed conflict or civil strife,[101] transfers,[102] performance requirements[103] and denial of benefits,[104] among others.

Recent international investment agreements also include provisions that reach beyond the traditional protection of investment, thus allowing to advance other concerns articulated by various stakeholders. Interestingly, the provision on corporate social responsibility is more detailed in USMCA than in TPP. Article 14.17 USMCA refers to the Organisation for Economic Co-operation and Development Guidelines for Multinational Enterprises. However, other international investment agreements include a reference to this instrument.[105] Regarding the inclusion of legitimate public welfare objectives among the factors to consider when determining the existence of "like circumstances" for the purposes of national treatment and the most-favored-nation treatment,[106] similar concerns are also included in other international investment agreements.[107]

---

[98]Articles 14.6(2)(a) and 14.6(4) USMCA; Articles 9.6(2)(a) and 9.6(4) TPP.

[99]Article 14.8 and Annex 14-B USMCA; Article 9.8 and Annex 9-B TPP; Article 8.12 and Annex 8-A CETA.

[100]Article 14.2 USMCA; Article 9.2 TPP.

[101]Article 14.7 USMCA; Article 9.7 TPP.

[102]Article 14.9 USMCA; Article 9.9 TPP.

[103]Article 14.10 USMCA; Article 9.10 TPP.

[104]Article 14.14 USMCA; Article 9.15 TPP.

[105]See e.g. Agreement on Encouragement and Reciprocal Protection of Investments between the Kingdom of the Netherlands and the United Arab Emirates, signed 23 November 2013, Article 2(3).

[106]Articles 14.4(4) and 14.5(4) USMCA.

[107]See e.g. Agreement between the Slovak Republic and the Islamic Republic of Iran for the Promotion and Reciprocal Protection of Investments, signed 19 January 2016, entered into force 30 August 2017, Article 4(3)-(4). See also Article 9.4 fn 14 TPP.

Most importantly, some agreements encompass stronger efforts than those made during the negotiations of USMCA to address progressive objectives in the specific context of investment. For example, Article 8.9 CETA includes a provision that reaffirms the right of States to regulate and that excludes the typical phrase "otherwise consistent with this Chapter" found in several investment agreements.[108] CETA also explicitly impedes an investor from submitting a claim to arbitration if the related investment was made through fraudulent misrepresentation, concealment, corruption or conduct amounting to an abuse of process.[109]

A significant distinction between USMCA and NAFTA stems in the reduction of international adjudication with respect to investment. Chapter 11 NAFTA allows an investor from any Party to submit a claim to investor-State dispute settlement. Even if Annex 14-C USMCA provides that the Parties consent to the submission of a claim to arbitration under Chapter 11 NAFTA for 3 years after the termination of NAFTA,[110] the other annexes included in Chapter 14 USMCA operate in a drastically different manner that cannot be found in recently signed free trade agreements.

Beyond these "Legacy Investment Claims and Pending Claims", Annex 14-D USMCA limits the use of investor-State dispute settlement to investment relationships between Mexico and the United States,[111] with less standards that can be used as a legal basis for a claim. Article 14-D.3(1) USMCA thus provides that a claimant can only submit a claim to arbitration that the respondent State has breached its obligations regarding national treatment or the most-favored-nation treatment (both with the exception of the establishment or the acquisition of an investment), or direct expropriation. These claims are also subject to a requirement to exhaust domestic remedies.[112] The other obligations included in Chapter 14 can only form the basis of a claim related to investment matters between Mexico and the United States if the claimant or an enterprises that it owns or controls is a party to a government contract or engaged in specific activities in covered sectors (i.e. oil and natural gas controlled by a national authority, power generation services, telecommunication services, transportation services as well as ownership and management of infrastructures).[113]

In addition to the unequal relationship established between the Parties regarding investment dispute settlement, some important innovations developed in other free trade agreements have been excluded from Chapter 14 USMCA. In this regard, the procedures included in USMCA sharply contrast with efforts spearheaded by the European Commission to establish an investment court system in CETA[114] and in

---

[108]Article 14.16 USMCA; Article 9.16 TPP.

[109]Article 8.18(3) CETA.

[110]Annex 14-C paras 1 and 3 USMCA.

[111]The incorporation of Chapter 9 TPP in CPTPP allows investor-State dispute settlement for investment relationships between Canada and Mexico.

[112]Article 14-D.5(1)(b) USMCA.

[113]Annex 14-E paras 2(a)(i)(A), 2(b)(i)(A) and 6(b) USMCA.

[114]Articles 8.27-8.28 CETA.

the eventual agreement with Mexico.[115] Even the reference in TPP with respect to the potential development of an appellate mechanism for reviewing awards rendered by investor-State dispute settlement tribunals is excluded from the text of USMCA.[116]

3.5 Progressive Objectives

In addition to progressive objectives that are included amidst provisions on investment protection, the renegotiation of NAFTA has led to the inclusion of entire chapters and specific provisions addressing progressive objectives that reach beyond trade in goods, services and investment. Given that these chapters and provisions integrate important concerns that are not explicitly taken into consideration in NAFTA, they constitute notable changes. Whereas some provisions are genuinely unprecedented, others only partially replicate rules included in other free trade agreements.

The inclusion of a chapter on environment into the text of the agreement has been mentioned in the objectives of the Office of the USTR.[117] Whilst ensuring that it is subject to the general dispute settlement mechanism adopted under USMCA, this approach is not unprecedented. With some notable exceptions,[118] most of Chapter 24 USMCA reflects the content of Chapter 20 TPP. For example, both agreements include an obligation to ensure high levels of environmental protection at the domestic level[119] and to effectively enforce environmental laws.[120] Provisions pertaining to multilateral environmental agreements,[121] the protection of the ozone layer,[122] the protection of the marine environment from ship pollution,[123] voluntary mechanisms to enhance environmental performance,[124] trade and biodiversity,[125]

---

[115]New EU–Mexico Agreement: The Agreement in Principle, 23 April 2018, http://trade.ec.europa.eu/doclib/docs/2018/april/tradoc_156791.pdf (last accessed 22 May 2019), p. 11.

[116]Article 9.23(11) TPP.

[117]USTR, Summary of Objectives for the NAFTA Renegotiation, 17 July 2017, https://ustr.gov/sites/default/files/files/Press/Releases/NAFTAObjectives.pdf (last accessed 22 May 2019), p. 13.

[118]For example, see Article 24.7 USMCA (Environmental Impact Assessment); Article 24.11 USMCA (Air Quality); Article 24.12 USMCA (Marine Litter); Article 24.23 USMCA (Sustainable Forest Management and Trade).

[119]Article 24.3(2) USMCA; Article 20.3(3) TPP.

[120]Article 24.4(1) USMCA; Article 20.3(4) TPP.

[121]Article 24.8 USMCA; Article 20.4 TPP.

[122]Article 24.9 USMCA; Article 20.5 TPP.

[123]Article 24.10 USMCA; Article 20.6 TPP.

[124]Article 24.14 USMCA; Article 20.11 TPP.

[125]Article 24.15 USMCA; Article 20.13 TPP.

invasive alien species,[126] conservation and trade,[127] as well as environmental goods and services[128] are all included in both agreements. In addition to the various procedures pertaining to cooperation and consultation, USMCA and TPP both allow Parties to ultimately request the establishment of a panel according to their respective dispute settlement chapter.[129]

Similar provisions between USMCA and TPP can also be noted with respect to labour. Instead of the original side agreement accompanying NAFTA, both agreements include a chapter that specifically focuses on labour.[130] For example, the agreements imply that Parties affirm their obligations as members of the International Labour Organization (ILO), including those encompassed in the ILO Declaration on Fundamental Principles and Rights at Work and its Follow-up.[131] Moreover, USMCA and TPP include the same list of labour rights that must be adopted and maintained by each Party in its domestic legislation,[132] the same non-derogation clause[133] and a similar provision on public awareness and procedural guarantees,[134] among others. With respect to the implementation of these obligations, both agreements address issues of cooperation,[135] the establishment of a Labour Council,[136] the designation of a contact point,[137] as well as the request of consultations and the establishment of a panel to resolve any matters arising under these chapters.[138]

In addition to provisions reflecting the content of TPP, Chapter 23 USMCA nevertheless reaches beyond previously adopted free trade agreements. Whereas TPP only requires Parties to "discourage" the importation of goods produced by forced or compulsory labour,[139] Article 23.6 USMCA provides that the Parties shall "prohibit" the importation of these goods. Other USMCA provisions that are absent from TPP include Article 23.7 (Violence Against Workers), Article 23.8 (Migrant

---

[126]Article 24.16 USMCA; Article 20.14 TPP.

[127]Article 24.22 USMCA; Article 20.17 TPP.

[128]Article 24.24 USMCA; Article 20.18 TPP.

[129]Article 24.32 USMCA; Article 20.23 TPP.

[130]Chapter 23 USMCA; Chapter 19 TPP.

[131]Article 23.2(1) USMCA; Article 19.2(1) TPP.

[132]Article 23.3 USMCA; Article 19.3 TPP. Both agreements include a footnote providing that the obligations set out in these articles refer only to the ILO Declaration on Fundamental Principles and Rights at Work and its Follow-Up rather than specific ILO conventions.

[133]Article 23.4 USMCA; Article 19.4 TPP.

[134]Article 23.10 USMCA; Article 19.8 TPP.

[135]Articles 23.12-23.13 USMCA; Articles 19.10-19.11 TPP.

[136]Article 23.14 USMCA; Article 19.12 TPP.

[137]Article 23.15 USMCA; Article 19.13 TPP.

[138]Article 23.17(8) USMCA; Article 19.15(12) TPP.

[139]Article 19.6 TPP.

Workers),[140] Article 23.9 (Discrimination in the Workplace) and Annex 23-A (Worker Representation in Collective Bargaining in Mexico).

The inclusion of an entire chapter on anticorruption constitutes an important difference from NAFTA. Once again, despite its novel character, Chapter 27 USMCA reproduces to a great extent the content of Chapter 26 TPP. For example, both agreements include a provision in which the Parties affirm their resolve to eliminate bribery and corruption in international trade and investment, as well as their adherence to international anticorruption instruments.[141] Replicated language is also included in provisions regarding the adoption of measures to combat corruption,[142] the promotion of integrity among public officials,[143] the participation of the private sector and civil society[144] and the enforcement of anticorruption laws.[145] An addition regarding facilitation payments was nevertheless added in Article 27.3(8) USMCA, without being included in TPP.

Cultural industries are considered in a separate provision of Chapter 32 USMCA. After reproducing the same definitions as the ones included in NAFTA,[146] Article 32.6(2) USMCA mentions that this agreement does not apply to Canadian measures regarding a cultural industry, except under limited circumstances. Reciprocally, Article 32.6(3) USMCA provides that Mexico and the United States can adopt or maintain similar measures with respect to Canadian goods, services and content. The same article also allows a Party to take a measure that has an equivalent commercial effect in response to an action by another Party under the other paragraphs of Article 32.6.[147]

One innovation regarding progressive objectives found in USMCA concerns references to Indigenous Peoples' rights in the text of the agreement. Among the exceptions included in Chapter 32 USMCA, Article 32.5 provides the following:

> Provided that such measures are not used as a means of arbitrary or unjustified discrimina-
> tion against persons of the other Parties or as a disguised restriction on trade in goods,
> services and investments, this Agreement does not preclude a Party from adopting
> or maintaining a measure it deems necessary to fulfill its legal obligations to [I]ndigenous
> [P]eoples.

Moreover, some of the provisions included in Chapter 24 USMCA that are not included in Chapter 20 TPP refer to Indigenous Peoples.[148]

These provisions are undoubtedly welcome when comparing USMCA to NAFTA. However, other relevant provisions addressing progressive objectives in

---

[140]However, a reference to "migrant workers" is included in Article 23.3(2)(c) CETA.

[141]Article 27.2(2) USMCA; Article 26.6(1) TPP.

[142]Article 27.3 USMCA; Article 26.7 TPP.

[143]Article 27.4 USMCA; Article 26.8 TPP.

[144]Article 27.5 USMCA; Article 26.10 TPP.

[145]Article 27.6 USMCA; Article 26.9 TPP.

[146]Article 2107 NAFTA.

[147]Article 32.6(4) USMCA.

[148]Articles 24.2(4), 24.17(1), 24.23 and footnote 15 USMCA.

free trade agreements are not included in USMCA. For example, with respect to environmental protection, USMCA does not refer to a low emissions economy transition.[149] In light of the recent amendment of the free trade agreement between Canada and Chile,[150] more detailed provisions on trade and gender could have also been added to the text of USMCA.

3.6 State-Owned Enterprises and Designated Monopolies

Some limited aspects pertaining to State-owned enterprises and designated monopolies have been included in Chapter 15 NAFTA, alongside with issues regarding competition policy. Even if a specific chapter on this matter suggests an important innovation from the original agreement, the disciplines included in USMCA have initially been crafted in the context of TPP.

In fact, almost each provision of Chapter 22 USMCA is a reflection of the language found in Chapter 17 TPP. For example, the language of the scope of the two chapters are highly similar.[151] Other similarities between USMCA and TPP include provisions on delegated authority,[152] non-discriminatory treatment when State-owned enterprises and designated monopolies engage in commercial activities,[153] courts and administrative bodies[154] and transparency,[155] among others. Whereas the prohibition of some specific forms of non-commercial assistance is new,[156] TPP also includes a provision disciplining non-commercial assistance to State-owned enterprises that can cause adverse effects to the interests of another Party or injury to a domestic industry.[157] Finally, the notions of adverse effect and injury are developed in similar terms in both agreements.[158]

---

[149] Article 20.15 TPP.

[150] Agreement to Amend, in Respect of Investment and Trade and Gender, the Free Trade Agreement between the Government of Canada and the Government of the Republic of Chile, done at Santiago on 5 December 1996, signed 5 June 2017, entered into force 5 February 2019, Appendix II.

[151] Article 22.2 USMCA; Article 17.2 TPP.

[152] Article 22.3 USMCA; Article 17.3 TPP.

[153] Article 22.4 USMCA; Article 17.4 TPP.

[154] Article 22.5 USMCA; Article 17.5 TPP.

[155] Article 22.10 USMCA; Article 17.10 TPP.

[156] Article 22.6(1)-(3) USMCA.

[157] Article 22.6(4)-(7) USMCA; Article 17.6 TPP.

[158] Articles 22.7 and 22.8 USMCA; Articles 17.7 and 17.8 TPP.

3.7 Non-Market Economies

The inclusion of an entire chapter that focuses on macroeconomic policies and exchange rate matters, as well as a provision on negotiations with non-market economies, are novel when compared to the text of other free trade agreements signed by the Parties. Even if they constitute an important change in contrast to NAFTA, the extent to which these provisions genuinely advance free trade remains questionable.

Chapter 33 USMCA specifically includes macroeconomic policies and exchange rates in the text of the agreement. According to Article 33.2 USMCA, the Parties "affirm" the fundamental character of market-determined exchange rates and "recognize the importance" of macroeconomic stability. More specifically, Article 33.4(1) USMCA mentions that

> [e]ach Party confirms that it is bound under the IMF Article of Agreement to avoid manipulating exchange rates or the international monetary system in order to prevent effective balance of payments adjustments or to gain an unfair competitive advantage.

In addition to including similarities with a joint declaration that was adopted in parallel to TPP,[159] the language used in these provisions does not constitute clearly enforceable obligations. Beyond the general weakness of the provisions' terms, Article 33.8(1) USMCA provides that a Party can use the dispute settlement procedure only to submit a claim that another Party has failed to meet its obligations pertaining to transparency and reporting "in a recurring and persistent manner".

Most importantly, the provisions related to negotiations of a free trade agreement with a "non-market economy" can seriously restrict trade between the Parties to USMCA. In addition to obliging a Party to provide the full text of such an agreement prior to its signature with the non-market country,[160] Article 32.10(5) USMCA provides that "[e]ntry by a Party into a free trade agreement with a non-market country will allow the other Parties to terminate this Agreement on six months' notice and replace this agreement with an agreement as between them". Even if the novel character of this provision is unquestionable, including a provision that threatens to exclude a Party from an agreement if it seeks to negotiate a free trade agreement with a third party is in stark contrast with the idea that USMCA is the "most advanced" trade agreement.

---

[159]Joint Declaration of the Macroeconomic Policy Authorities of Trans-Pacific Partnership Countries, 5 November 2015.
[160]Article 32.10(4) USMCA.

3.8 Dispute Settlement

Some changes between NAFTA and USMCA specifically concern the settlement of disputes between the Parties. Even if binational reviews for domestic trade remedies determinations and a general dispute settlement chapter have been kept in the final text of the agreement, the language of USMCA sometimes combines the provisions found in NAFTA with those included in the TPP.

Despite the avowed intent of the US administration to eliminate Chapter 19 NAFTA,[161] Chapter 10 USMCA preserves a dispute settlement mechanism that specifically concerns trade remedies. With respect to antidumping and countervailing duties, it echoes the text of TPP by recalling the rights and obligations of each Party under Article VI GATT, the Antidumping Agreement and the SMC Agreement.[162] As far as dispute settlement is concerned, Section D of Chapter 10 USMCA largely reproduces the language of Chapter 19 NAFTA. It thus includes provisions on the retention of antidumping and countervailing duties law,[163] the review of statutory amendments[164] and the binational panel review of final determinations,[165] among others. The annexes governing the review and dispute settlement related to trade remedies also reproduce the corresponding annexes of NAFTA.[166] Interestingly, the preservation of the dispute settlement mechanism is accompanied by new provisions on cooperation regarding "duty evasion" of antidumping, countervailing and safeguard duties.[167]

With respect to the general dispute settlement mechanism established in Chapter 31 USMCA, some provisions reiterate the terms that were adopted in NAFTA. For example, Article 31.1 USMCA echoes the original language regarding cooperation.[168] The role of the Free Trade Commission related to the resolution of a dispute further to consultations,[169] the establishment of a roster of panelists,[170] the panel composition for a specific dispute,[171] as well as the section on domestic

---

[161]USTR, Summary of Objectives for the NAFTA Renegotiation, 17 July 2017, https://ustr.gov/sites/default/files/files/Press/Releases/NAFTAObjectives.pdf (last accessed 22 May 2019), p 14. See also Lester and Manak (2018), p. 166.

[162]Article 10.5 USMCA; Article 6.8 TPP.

[163]Article 10.10 USMCA; Article 1902 NAFTA.

[164]Article 10.11 USMCA; Article 1903 NAFTA.

[165]Article 10.12 USMCA; Article 1904 NAFTA.

[166]Annexes 10-B.1, 10-B.2, 10-B.3 and 10-B.4 USMCA; Annexes 1901.2, 1903.2, 1904.13 and 1905.6 NAFTA.

[167]Chapter 10, Section C USMCA.

[168]Article 31.1 USMCA; Article 2003 NAFTA.

[169]Article 31.5(1)-(5) USMCA; Article 2007 NAFTA.

[170]Article 31.8 USMCA; Article 2009 NAFTA. However, Article 31.8(1) USMCA provides that the roster shall "remain in effect for a minimum of three years or until the Parties constitute a new roster".

[171]Article 31.9 USMCA; Article 2011 NAFTA.

proceedings and private commercial dispute settlement[172] are also relatively close to the provisions from the original NAFTA.

Even with these provisions largely inspired by NAFTA, Chapter 31 USMCA extensively follows the model of TPP. USMCA and TPP thus include similar provisions pertaining to the scope of dispute settlement,[173] the choice of forum,[174] consultations,[175] the voluntary use of alternative methods of dispute resolution,[176] terms of reference,[177] the rules of procedures for panels,[178] the functions of panels,[179] third party participation,[180] and the role of experts,[181] among others. Moreover, the requirements regarding panel reports provided at Article 31.17 USMCA appear as a shorter version of Articles 28.17 and 28.18 TPP. As far as the establishment of the panel[182] and the non-implementation of the final report are concerned,[183] USMCA combines the language of NAFTA and TPP.

3.9 Final Provisions and Side Letters

Finally, some general provisions included in USMCA and side letters differ from the language of the original text in NAFTA. Whereas these provisions are unprecedented, they seem to be driven by the focus on bilateral trade deficits of the US administration or to result from the trade disputes underlying the negotiations.

One of the final provisions included in USMCA without having a counterpart in NAFTA relates to "review and term extension". According to Article 34.7(1) USMCA, the agreement will terminate 16 years after its entry into force, "unless each Party confirms it wishes to continue this agreement for a new 16-year term". A joint review by the Free Trade Commission of the operation of USMCA is scheduled on the sixth anniversary of its entry into force.[184] It is during this joint review that each Party is expected to confirm its will to extend the term of the agreement for another 16 years.[185] It is plain that the inclusion of a review and term extension provision adds some

---

[172]Chapter 31, Section B USMCA; Chapter 20, Section C NAFTA.

[173]Article 31.2 USMCA; Article 28.3 TPP.

[174]Article 31.3 USMCA; Article 28.4 TPP.

[175]Article 31.4 USMCA; Article 28.5 TPP.

[176]Article 31.5(6)-(9) USMCA; Article 28.6 TPP.

[177]Article 31.7 USMCA; Article 28.8 TPP.

[178]Article 31.11 USMCA; Article 28.13 TPP.

[179]Article 31.13 USMCA; Article 28.12 TPP.

[180]Article 31.14 USMCA; Article 28.14 TPP.

[181]Article 31.15 USMCA; Article 28.15 TPP.

[182]Article 31.6 USMCA; Article 2008 NAFTA; Article 28.7 TPP.

[183]Article 31.19 USMCA; Article 2019 NAFTA; Article 28.20 TPP.

[184]Article 34.7(2) USMCA.

[185]Article 34.7(3) USMCA.

uncertainty regarding the future of the agreement and could potentially restrict trade. Considering the extent to which the US administration's focus on bilateral trade deficits has influenced the negotiation process, one can presume that these concerns might play a similar role in an eventual review of the agreement.

In addition to the text of USMCA, the Parties have negotiated 14 side letters that are all dated from 30 November 2018.[186] To the extent that they address issues that have led to trade disputes between the negotiating Parties, these letters reflect the context in which the negotiations occurred. For example, Canada and Mexico have been able to reach separate agreements with the United States regarding the exclusion of their automobiles from potential tariffs pursuant to Section 232 of the Trade Expansion Act.[187] Other letters entail that Canada and Mexico will be excluded from future measures taken by the United States under the same legislation for at least 60 days after their imposition.[188] In another side letter between Canada and the United States, Canada has agreed to modify the measures adopted by the province of British Columbia with respect to the sale of wine in grocery stores.[189] Whilst the solutions found in these letters can be somehow encouraging, it must also be noted that they constitute more a way to preserve trade between the Parties than a means to advance free trade itself.[190]

4 Conclusion

Important modifications included in USMCA in comparison to NAFTA are better explained through a contextual analysis that reaches beyond the text of the agreement. By taking into consideration the political and legal landscape, this article demonstrates that major changes extensively reflect the broader context in which the

---

[186]USTR, Agreement between the United States of America, the United Mexican States and Canada Text, https://ustr.gov/trade-agreements/free-trade-agreements/united-states-mexico-canada-agreement/agreement-between (last accessed 22 May 2019).

[187]Side Letter Text on 232 CA–US Response, 30 November 2018, https://ustr.gov/sites/default/files/files/agreements/FTA/USMCA/Text/Side_Letter_Text_on_232_CA-US_Response.pdf (last accessed 22 May 2019); MX–US Side Letter on 232, 30 November 2018, https://ustr.gov/sites/default/files/files/agreements/FTA/USMCA/Text/MX-US_Side_Letter_on_232.pdf (last accessed 22 May 2018); MX–US Side Letter on 232 Dispute Settlement, 30 November 2018, https://ustr.gov/sites/default/files/files/agreements/FTA/USMCA/Text/MX-US_Side_Letter_on_232_Dispute_Settlement.pdf (last accessed 22 May 2019).

[188]CA–US Side Letter on 232 Process, 30 November 2018, https://ustr.gov/sites/default/files/files/agreements/FTA/USMCA/Text/CA-US_Side_Letter_on_232_Process.pdf (last accessed 22 May 2019); MX–US Side Letter on 232 Process, 30 November 2018, https://ustr.gov/sites/default/files/files/agreements/FTA/USMCA/Text/MX-US_Side_Letter_on_232_Process.pdf (last accessed 22 May 2019).

[189]CA–US Side Letter on Wine, 30 November 2018, https://ustr.gov/sites/default/files/files/agreements/FTA/USMCA/Text/CA-US_Side_Letter_on_Wine.pdf (last accessed 22 May 2019).

[190]Perezcano Diaz (2019), p. 10.

renegotiation of NAFTA occurred. Since the United States announced its intent to renegotiate the agreement, the political discourse shifted from a will to modernize NAFTA to a clear intention to counter bilateral trade deficits and to use tariffs as a negotiating tool. The negotiations also occurred amidst several trade disputes and a plurality of recent free trade agreements. Unquestionably, some new provisions appear as genuine innovations that can foster more progressive free trade. However, the overwhelming majority of changes included in USMCA denote a bilateral approach that sometimes restricts trade, or a partial reproduction of provisions found in recent free trade agreements. These changes can hardly be reconcilable with the idea that USMCA is the "most advanced" free trade agreement.

In itself, determining that claims from the US administration according to which USMCA is the most advanced free trade agreement constitute an exaggeration is not very surprising. The extent to which the political and legal context in which the renegotiation of NAFTA was held is reflected in the text of USMCA is nevertheless striking. It would have been particularly difficult to reach an innovative agreement that genuinely advances the free trade regime in this context. At best, from the perspective of Canada and Mexico, the text of USMCA results from a successful reliance on the content of previous free trade agreements with a view to avoiding a less favourable deal than NAFTA. At worst, the approach adopted by the US administration can be considered as an attempt at purposely restricting trade to reduce bilateral deficits and denying the pre-existing language on which USMCA relies.

Acknowledgements The author is grateful to the Editors of the European Yearbook of International Economic Law and acknowledges the financial support of the Postdoctoral Fellowship of the Social Sciences and Humanities Research Council of Canada.

References

Bergsten CF (2017) The US agenda: trade balances and the NAFTA renegotiation. In: Bergsten CF, de Bolle M (eds) A path forward for NAFTA. PIIE Briefing 17-2. Peterson Institute for International Economics, Washington, pp 13–23

Bergsten CF, de Bolle M (2017) Overview. In: Bergsten CF, de Bolle M (eds) A path forward for NAFTA. PIIE Briefing 17-2. Peterson Institute for International Economics, Washington, pp 3–12

Crespo CS (2018) A Mexican outlook on NAFTA, TPP and their renegotiation: investment arbitration's transparency and international supervision at peril? Houst J Int Law 40 (3):937–1002

Dobson W et al (2017) NAFTA modernization: a Canadian perspective. In: Bergsten CF, de Bolle M (eds) A path forward for NAFTA. PIIE Briefing 17-2. Peterson Institute for International Economics, Washington, pp 36–49

Esty DC, Salzman J (2017) Rethinking NAFTA: deepening the commitment to sustainable development. In: Bergsten CF, de Bolle M (eds) A path forward for NAFTA. PIIE Briefing 17-2. Peterson Institute for International Economics, Washington, pp 125–139

Galbraith J (2018a) Developments relating to US trade negotiations–KORUS, NAFTA, and trade promotion authority. Am J Int Law 112(3):510–513

Galbraith J (2018b) Tariff-based disputes continue to characterize trump administration trade policies. Am J Int Law 112(4):751–759

Galbraith J (2019) NAFTA is renegotiated and signed by the United States. Am J Int Law 113 (1):150–159

Hufbauer GC, Jung E (2017) NAFTA renegotiation: US offensive and defensive interests vis-à-vis Canada. In: Bergsten CF, de Bolle M (eds) A path forward for NAFTA. PIIE Briefing 17-2. Peterson Institute for International Economics, Washington, pp 50–68

Leblond P, Fabian J (2017) Modernizing NAFTA: a new deal for the North American economy in the twenty-first century. CIGI Papers No 123

Lester S, Manak I (2018) The rise of populist nationalism and the renegotiation of NAFTA. J Int Econ Law 21:151–169

Lester S et al (2019) Access to trade justice: fixing NAFTA's flawed State-to-State dispute settlement process. World Trade Rev 18(1):63–79

Lilly M (2019) A Canadian perspective on the future of North America's economic relationship. In: Lilly M (ed) The future of North America's economic relationship: from NAFTA to the new Canada–United States–Mexico Agreement and beyond. CIGI Special Report, pp 15–20

McDaniel C (2019) A US perspective on the future of North America's economic relationship. In: Lilly M (ed) The future of North America's economic relationship: from NAFTA to the new Canada–United States–Mexico Agreement and beyond. CIGI Special Report, pp 3–6

Ortiz-Mena A (2017) Toward a positive NAFTA renegotiation: a Mexican perspective. In: Bergsten CF, de Bolle M (eds) A path forward for NAFTA. PIIE Briefing 17-2. Peterson Institute for International Economics, Washington, pp 24–35

Perezcano Diaz H (2019) Trade in North America: a Mexican perspective on the future of North America's economic relationship. In: Lilly M (ed) The future of North America's economic relationship: from NAFTA to the new Canada–United States–Mexico Agreement and beyond. CIGI Special Report, pp 7–14

Puig S (2019) Can international trade law recover? The United States–Mexico–Canada Agreement: a glimpse into the geoeconomic world order. AJIL Unbound 113:56–60

Schott JJ, Cimino-Isaacs C (2017) Updating the North American Free Trade Agreement. In: Bergsten CF, de Bolle M (eds) A path forward for NAFTA. PIIE Briefing 17-2. Peterson Institute for International Economics, Washington, pp 69–90

Jean-Michel Marcoux is a Postdoctoral Fellow at McGill University, Faculty of Law. He holds a PhD in Law (University of Victoria), an MA in International Studies (Institut québécois des hautes études internationales) and a BA in Public Affairs and International Relations (Université Laval). Interested in international economic law and international relations theory, he has published a dozen articles and chapters in peer-reviewed journals and collections of essays. He is also the author of *International Investment Law and Globalization: Foreign Investment, Responsibilities and Intergovernmental Organizations* (Routledge, 2018).

EU Free Trade Agreements as an Instrument of Promoting the Rule of Law in Third Countries: A Framework Paper

Maryna Rabinovych

Contents

1 Introduction

The "crisis of the liberal international order" and the "overlapping crises" in the EU, increasingly discussed in the literature, seem to share a crucial characteristic: both involve a significant degree of normative contestation.[1] Internationally, the foundations of liberal democracy and the rule of law are contested by emerging powers (e.g. Russia, China)[2]; in the EU, there is no agreement on how to counter the decline of democracy and safeguard the rule of law in Central and Eastern European (CEE)

---

[1]Duncombe and Dunne (2018), pp. 25–26; Hooghe and Marks (2016), pp. 2–4.
[2]Duncombe and Dunne (2018), pp. 28–29.

M. Rabinovych (✉)
University of Hamburg, Hamburg, Germany
e-mail: m-rabinovych@europa-kolleg-hamburg.de

© Springer Nature Switzerland AG 2019
M. Bungenberg et al. (eds.), *European Yearbook of International Economic Law 2019*,
European Yearbook of International Economic Law (2020) 10: 285–314,
https://doi.org/10.1007/8165_2019_31, Published online: 17 September 2019

countries.[3] These developments call for reassessing the EU's approach towards the external promotion of values it is founded on.[4] Notwithstanding the fact that the rule of law represents a "guiding principle" of EU external action (Article 21(1) TEU) and its foreign policy objective (Article 21(2)(b) TEU), there is no consensus as regards the meaning of this notion.[5] Subsequently, the EU lacks clear strategies that would allow it to assess partner countries' progress in the rule of law domain and evaluate the effectiveness of various policy and legal instruments it uses to promote the rule of law (e.g. political dialogue, the imposition of contractual obligations, financial and technical assistance).[6] Thus, an effort to strengthen the normative role the EU seeks to play externally may benefit from an insight into both the conceptual foundations of EU external rule of law promotion and the patchwork of instruments the EU uses to exercise it.

Notably, the empowerment of the EU as an external rule of law promoter may also win from the reconsideration of the interplay between various policies, strategies and instruments the EU utilizes to promote the rule of law. In line with the EU's strong emphasis on the consistency of its external policies in the Treaty of Lisbon,[7] the abovementioned effort also requires a fresh look at the rule of law effects of instruments, not immediately directed at the promotion of the rule of law. Against this background, this article aims to explore EU FTAs[8] with third countries as an instrument of promoting the rule of law.

The rationale for concentrating on FTAs is twofold. First, due to the deadlock of the WTO Doha Round, the EU shifted to pursuing the ambitious "deep" bi- and plurilateral trade liberalization agenda.[9] The FTAs negotiated and concluded by the EU in the recent decade, go far beyond trade in goods and encompass various disciplines, such as trade in services, administrative and technical cooperation, sustainable development, public procurement and competition.[10] Such "deep" agreements inevitably exert profound impact on domestic legal systems that have not yet been addressed in scholarship either independently or with regard to the rule of law in partner countries.[11] Secondly, since the creation of "cooperative regional orders", stipulated in the 2016 EU Global Strategy (EUGS), is directed *inter alia* to "reaping" the economic gains, "deep" trade liberalization represents an instrument of the EU's

---

[3]See, for instance: Cianetti et al. (2018) and Sheppele and Pech (2018).

[4]Consolidated version of the Treaty on European Union. OJ 2012 C326, Article 2 [TEU or TEU (L)].

[5]Pech (2012/2013), p. 7.

[6]Ibid, pp. 14–21.

[7]TEU, Article 21(3).

[8]For the purposes of this paper, the notion "Free Trade Agreement" refers to any reciprocal agreement between the EU and a third state or a group of states that includes a trade-liberalization component.

[9]Commission's Communication "Global Europe: Competing in the World", COM(2006)567 final.

[10]Araujo (2016), p. 2.

[11]Ibid, p. 4.

"order-building".[12] Furthermore, given the uncontested nature of "economic prosperity" as a goal of EU cooperation with third countries, the potential of the rule of law promotion through trade liberalization requires particular attention in the normative contestation era.

This paper is structured as follows. First, it will operationalize the concept of the rule of law for the purposes of this study. The analysis of the foundational ("framework") foreign policy and legal aspects of the EU's rule of law promotion through FTAs will follow. It will encompass the interplay between economic and normative objectives in the EU external action, the nature of EU power in external trade relations, its bargaining power in trade negotiations as well as legal bases for EU FTAs, capable of promoting the rule of law, and major disciplines that can serve as an instrument of promoting it. Based on the above, the paper will distinguish Stabilization and Association Agreements (SAAs) with Western Balkans, Association Agreements (AAs) with Eastern Neighbours and EU-CARIFORUM Economic Partnership Agreement (CEPA) as the ones, possessing the strongest potential to influence the rule of law in partner countries, due to the EUs' high bargaining power and "deep" nature of the Agreements. Thirdly, the paper will explore rule of law standards, embedded into administrative cooperation and public procurement-related chapters of the above-mentioned agreements. The choice of these two categories of FTA chapters is explained by two considerations. First, the paper seeks to illustrate that different types of FTA chapters (i.e. cooperation-related, "deep disciplines") can represent the source of rule of law standards. Second, respective chapters are included into all three categories of FTAs in question and, thus, allow for a comparative approach. The paper will conclude with emphasizing the rule of law promotion potential of EU FTAs with third countries and the need to synergize their rule of law effects with further EU rule of law promotion instruments.

2 The Rule of Law in EU External Relations Law

2.1 The Rule of Law as a Fundamental Value of the EU

Characterized by both its structural and aspirational nature, "the rule of law already manifests itself in the very existence of the Union and its predecessors".[13] Addressing the European Economic Community (EEC) as a "phenomenon of law", the first EEC Commission President Walter Hallstein coined the understanding of a European supranational legal Community (*Rechtsgemeinschaft*).[14] Importantly,

---

[12]A Global Strategy for the European Union's Foreign and Security Policy "Shared Vision, Common Action: A Stronger Europe", https://europa.eu/globalstrategy/en/global-strategy-for eign-and-security-policy-european-union (last accessed 8 February 2019).

[13]Larik (2016), p. 220.

[14]Hallstein (1979), pp. 51–53.

Hallstein conceptualized the Community as *Rechtsgemeinschaft* in four senses: as a creation of law (*Rechtsschöpfung*), a source of law (*Rechtsquelle*), as legal order (*Rechtsordnung*) and legal policy (*Rechtspolitik*).[15] In turn, ensuring the functioning of the multidimensional *Rechtsgemeinschaft* would require a strong *Rechtstaat* or the rule of law. Since the concepts of *Rechtsgemeinschaft, Rechtstaat* and the rule of law significantly differ in their substance,[16] the referral by the European Court of Justice (ECJ) to the former EC as a "*Community based on the rule of law*" in its landmark *Les Verts* judgment brought about a crucial conceptual disarray.[17] Nevertheless, the analysis of this judgment, allows capturing the ECJ's early understanding of the concept. First, the Court implicitly addressed the rule of law as a "*positive good in itself*".[18] Secondly, since the judgment refers to the Treaty as the "*Constitutional Charter*", the rule of law can consequently be regarded as the Community's constitutional principle to be upheld by courts at both the supranational and national level.[19] Thirdly, the Court approached the rule of law from a formal standpoint, limiting its substance to the Union's institutions and the Member States being subject to the rules, contained in the Treaties.[20]

The Treaty of Maastricht [TEU(M)] was the first EU primary law document to formalize the rule of law without either pointing to its role in Community legal order or defining it.[21] The Treaty of Amsterdam [TEU(A)] mentioned the rule of law among the founding principles of the EU and made it part of the criteria for membership in the EU and the objectives of the CFSP.[22] As opposed to Article 6 (1) of the TEU(A), Article 2 of the Treaty of Lisbon [TEU(L)] referred to the rule of law as one of the common values the Union is founded on, rather than its founding principle. Apart from the terminological change, the TEU(L) promoted the consolidation of functions the rule of law plays in the EU legal order. Articles 3(1) and 13 (1) TEU(L) provide for the institutions' "value-promoting mandate", according to which the rule of law shall be understood as an objective of the institutions' action. Similar to the previous versions of the Founding Treaties, Article 49 of the TEU (L) also mentions the rule of law among the criteria for EU membership. Furthermore, the TEU made safeguarding the Union's values as one of the objectives of EU external action.[23] Notwithstanding the above, the TEU(L) did not shed light on the substance of the rule of law.

---

[15]Ibid.

[16]Pech (2009), pp. 22–47.

[17]CJEU, Case 294/83 Partiécologiste "Les Verts" v European Parliament, ECLI:EU:C:1986:166, para 23.

[18]Ibid.

[19]Ibid.

[20]Ibid.

[21]Treaty on European Union. OJ 1992 C191, Preamble.

[22]Treaty of Amsterdam amending the Treaty on European Union, the Treaties establishing the European Communities and certain related acts. OJ 1997 C 340, Articles 6(1), 49 and 11(1).

[23]TEU, Article 21(2)(b).

2.2 Consensual Components of the Rule of Law

Despite the open-endedness of the rule of law concept in EU primary law, in its 2014 Rule of Law Framework, adopted in response to the rule of law crises in Poland and Hungary, the Commission applied the consensual approach to the rule of law.[24] Given the consensual nature of the rule of law components, distinguished in the Venice Commission's Rule of Law Checklist[25] that was referenced by the European Commission in its 2014 Rule of Law Framework, this paper will base its operationalization of the rule of law on these documents and secondary sources. The validity of such approach can be substantiated by the fact that the EU emphasizes that it promotes values "that inspired its own creation"[26] and, consequently, the substance of the "export version" shall follow the "domestic" one. Based on the above, this paper will focus on six rule of law standards, namely: legality; legal certainty; independence and impartiality of public authorities; authorities' accountability and transparency; equality and non-discrimination and the relationship between international and domestic law.

The principle of legality lies at the heart of the rule of law. The Rule of Law Checklist introduces for major dimensions of legality: the features of laws and legal systems, institutions, procedures and law enforcement.[27] In legal theory, the first dimension of legality is linked to the principle of supremacy of law (e.g. "absolute supremacy or predominance of regular law as opposed to arbitrary power"[28]). According to the Venice Commission, the institutional dimension of legality refers to the separation of powers between authorities, their compliance with laws and limitedness of the law-making authorities of the executive.[29] In procedural terms, the legality principle is connected to transparent, accountable and inclusive law-making procedures and transparent and accountable procedures of applying exceptions in emergency situations.[30] Finally, the law enforcement aspect of the concept deals with the authorities' duty to implement the law.[31]

Pursuant to the Rule of Law Checklist, the legal certainty requirement encompasses the accessibility of laws, regulations and court decisions; the foreseeability of laws; stability of laws; their prospective nature, as well as the "*nullum crimen sine*

---

[24]Commission's Communication "A New EU Framework to Strengthen the Rule of Law", COM (2014) 158 final/2.

[25]European Commission for Democracy through Law (2016) Rule of Law Checklist. Study No 711/2013, https://www.venice.coe.int/webforms/documents/default.aspx?pdffile=CDL-AD(2016) 007-e (last accessed 8 February 2019).

[26]TEU, Article 21(1).

[27]European Commission for Democracy through Law (2016), pp. 11–14.

[28]Dicey (1985), p. 202.

[29]Ibid.

[30]Ibid.

[31]Ibid.

lege" ("no crime without the law"), "*nulla poena sine lege*" ("no punishment without the law") and *res judicata* principles (obligatory nature of the judicial decision).[32]

The above analysis of the principle of legality reveals the importance of institutions' compliance with the legislation that stems *inter alia* from the proper delineation of powers between different institutions.[33] The Checklist refers to the appropriate distribution of powers between institutions as a component of the "enabling environment" for the rule of law, referring solely to the independence and impartiality of the judiciary.[34] Nevertheless, since the rule of law includes the prevention of abuse (misuse) of powers by all the institutions,[35] an independent and impartial judiciary can be hardly viewed as a *panacea* for ensuring the leading role of law in a society. Thus, for the purpose of this paper I suggest extending the principles of independence and impartiality to a non-exhaustive range of public authorities. Based on the Checklist's definition of judicial independence, the independence of a public body means its freedom from external pressures, political influence or manipulation by the bodies, belonging to the different branches of power or the same branch.[36] In turn, the impartiality requirement is intertwined with the requirements of authorities' independence, equality and non-discrimination and is investigated based on the public perceptions thereof, the public perceptions of corruption, and the application of anti-corruption measures to public bodies.[37]

Ensuring institutions' compliance with laws and preventing their abuse of powers requires public accountability and transparency in their functioning.[38] According to Madalina Busuioc, public accountability can be understood as a three-component relationship between an actor (a public authority) and a forum (society).[39] These components include an actor providing a forum with information regarding its activities; the debate between the actor and the forum; and, finally, the forum's power to sanction an actor.[40] Thus, the key indicators of accountability include the legal basis for an accountability relationship; an institution's obligation to provide an accountability forum with information regarding its activities; an obligation to engage in the debating phase; and finally the sanctioning power of an accountability forum.[41] The EU's understanding of transparency encompasses (but is not limited to) the transparency of decision-making procedures of public bodies,[42] the right to

---

[32]Ibid, pp. 15–17.

[33]Ibid, p. 11.

[34]Ibid, p. 20.

[35]Ibid, p. 11.

[36]Ibid, p. 20.

[37]Ibid. See also: Council of Europe Committee of Ministers (1994) Recommendation No R (94) 12 on the independence, efficiency and role of judges.

[38]Bovens (2007), p. 182.

[39]Busuioc (2013), p. 32.

[40]Ibid.

[41]Ibid.

[42]Karageorgou (2014), p. 2.

access documents of EU institutions,[43] "precision, clarity and transparency" in transposing directives into Member States' law[44] and "the duty to give reasons for legislative and administrative acts".[45]

Located at the crossroads between democracy, the rule of law and human rights, the principles of equality and non-discrimination play a crucial role in the EU legal order.[46] According to the Venice Commission, the constitutional stipulation of the equality principle is essential for a state's adherence to the rule of law.[47] Alongside the constitutional status of the non-discrimination principle, its observance requires clear definitions of what constitutes direct and indirect discrimination and the substantiation of possible deviation from the non-discrimination imperative.[48] Finally, the principle of non-discrimination implies the accessibility of judicial review.[49]

Finally, the Checklist's dimension of legality related to laws and their features encompasses "the relationship between international law and domestic law" requirement, focusing solely on a state's observance of international human rights law obligations.[50] Article 3(5) TEU stipulates, however, that

> in its relations with the wider world, the Union shall contribute....to the strict observance and the development of international law, including respect for the principles of the United Nations Charter.

Given the expansive nature of this commitment, this paper views "the relationship between international law and domestic law" as a self-standing aspect of EU's rule of law promotion agenda. For the purposes of this paper, "the relationship between international law and domestic law" refers to partner countries' observance of a wide variety of international law standards, ranging from the principles of the UN Charter to WTO law.

---

[43]Council and European Parliament Regulation (EC) No 1049/2001 regarding public access to European Parliament, Council and the Commission documents. OJ 2001 L 45.

[44]CJEU, Case C-417/99 Commission v. Spain, ECLI:EU:C:2001:445, para. 40.

[45]Consolidated version of the Treaty on the Functioning of the European Union. OJ 2012 C326, Article 296 (TFEU).

[46]TEU, Articles 2 and 3(2).

[47]European Commission for Democracy through Law (2016), p. 18.

[48]Ibid, p. 18.

[49]Ibid, p. 18.

[50]Ibid, p. 12.

3   Political and Legal Framework of the EU Rule of Law Promotion Through FTAs

3.1   Foreign Policy Objectives

Article 21(2) TEU provides for a broad range of objectives the EU shall pursue in its external action. According to Joris Larik,

> objectives play an important role in the case law of the Court of Justice of the European Union, not least, given its hallmark teleological approach, and in discussions about the finalité of European integration.[51]

Pursuant to Article 21(2)(a) TEU,

> the Union shall define and pursue common policies and actions, and shall work for a high degree of cooperation in all fields of international relations in order to safeguard its values, fundamental values, independence and security.

Article 21(2)(b) TEU grants the consolidation and support of democracy, the rule of law, human rights and the principles of international law the status of an objective of EU external action, immediately pointing to the normative aspiration behind it. The normative dimension of EU external action is also manifested in Article 3(5) TEU that obliges the Union to contribute to the promotion of its values, peace, the protection of human rights, especially the rights of the child and the "strict observance and development of international law". Both Articles 3(5) and 21(2) TEU postulate economic objectives the EU shall pursue externally, such as the encouragement of "the integration of all countries into the world economy...".[52]

The analysis of the normative and economic objectives of the EU's external action yields three important questions: How shall the EU balance self-interest and values in its external economic policy? How shall the EU balance the different objectives, stipulated in Article 21(2) TEU in a case of conflict between them? How can normative objectives be embedded into EU FTAs? Answering the first question, I would like to emphasize that the EUGS is the first EU foreign policy strategy to refer to the Union's self-interest, acknowledging limits, imposed on the EU by its own capabilities and the intractability of others.[53] Trying to reconcile its "turn to Realpolitik"[54] with normative aspirations, the EUGS stated that values represent a part of EU self-interest and introduced the concept of "principled pragmatism".[55] According to Ana Juncos,

---

[51]Larik (2016), p. 5.

[52]TEU, Article 21(2)(e).

[53]A Global Strategy for the European Union's Foreign and Security Policy "Shared Vision, Common Action: A Stronger Europe".

[54]Biscop (2016), p. 1.

[55]A Global Strategy for the European Union's Foreign and Security Policy "Shared Vision, Common Action: A Stronger Europe".

> principled pragmatism implies that the EU should act in accordance with universal values (liberal ones in this case), but then follow a pragmatic approach which denies the moral imperatives of those universal categories.[56]

Following her argument, this concept would

> generate more criticisms of self-interest, selectivity and double standards,. . .eroding its [the Union's] identity as a normative actor.[57]

Nevertheless, the problem of balancing self-interest and values, and divergent objectives of the EU's external action shall not be viewed as "an either-or choice", because the relationship between them can be far more complex. In some cases, the only solution is a trade-off, benefiting either interest or values, or, alternatively, prioritizing one value (objective) for the sake of another. Moreover, an example of the Union's promotion of environmental and labour standards through FTAs demonstrates that self-interest (benefits of trade liberalization) may not contradict both economic (promotion of free trade) and normative (environmental and social protection) objectives. However, as it can be illustrated by the EU's history of selective and politicized application of "essential elements" clauses,[58] the interplay between the EU's self-interest and values, and between its economic and normative objectives is highly context-dependent.

Ideally, the EU's effort to utilize FTAs as an instrument of promoting the rule of law would serve three objectives under Article 21(2) TEU: "safeguarding its values, fundamental interests. . ." (a); encouragement of the integration of all countries into the world economy (e) and consolidation of the rule of law (b). Moreover, since both increased integration of developing countries into the world economy and upholding of the rule of law are part of the Agenda 2030,[59] the use of FTAs as an instrument of rule of law promotion follows the EU's aspiration to

> foster the sustainable economic, social and environmental development of developing countries, with the primary aim of eradicating poverty.[60]

The EU external action demonstrates the complex context-dependent interplay between self-interest and aspirations toward normative actorness, and various objectives the EU seeks to pursue externally. In an ideal case, FTAs may represent instruments that synergize the components of EU self-interest and economic, normative and development objectives of its external action.

---

[56]Juncos (2017), p. 5.

[57]Ibid.

[58]Hachez (2015), p. 18.

[59]UN General Assembly Resolution "Transforming Our World: the 2030 Agenda for Sustainable Development", 25 September 2015, A/RES/70/1.

[60]TEU, Article 21(2)(d).

3.2   EU Power and Norm Diffusion

At first glance, EU's external promotion of its fundamental values is attributed to the EU's normative power.[61] According to the founder of the Normative Power Europe (NPE) concept Ian Manners,

> the central component of normative power Europe is that it exists as being different to pre-existing political forms and that this particular difference pre-disposes it to act in a normative way.[62]

Based on its normative power, the EU applies a range of norms diffusion avenues, such as norm contagion, informational diffusion, overt diffusion, procedural diffusion, transference and cultural filter.[63] Since procedural diffusion and transference involve the use of remunerative instruments, the key critique of Manners' NPE concept is that

> the EU normative power was not primarily exercised through persuasion and normative justification, but through a skillful application of political and economic conditionality[64]

or

> it is only through the unique and rich combination of stick and carrots that are present in the accession process that the EU can exert the strongest normative influence on its partners.[65]

Thus, the diffusion of EU norms is to a significant extent driven by economic aspects of EU power (Market Power Europe (MPE)[66] and EU as a Trade Power[67]). Both concepts assume that the key driver behind the EU's power is that it represents one of the world's largest markets and trade players.[68] According to the founder of the MPE Chad Damro, market size supports the externalization of the EU's internal rules in two major ways, namely, creating material incentives for governments to coordinate their regulatory standards with the ones of the large market and, second, influencing their perceptions regarding the outcomes of adopting the respective standards.[69] Subsequently, the size and scope of the Internal Market serve as a foundation for EU's "power through trade" that, according to Sophie Meunier and Kalypso Nicolaïdis, enables the EU to use its market strategically and utilize FTAs as a

---

[61]Manners (2002).

[62]Ibid, p. 242.

[63]Ibid.

[64]Aggestam (2013), p. 464.

[65]Haukkala (2011), p. 47.

[66]Damro (2012).

[67]Meunier and Nicolaïdis (2006).

[68]European Commission (2018) The EU's position in world trade in figures, http://www.europarl.europa.eu/news/en/headlines/economy/20180703STO07132/the-eu-s-position-in-world-trade-in-figures-infographic (last accessed 8 February 2019).

[69]Damro (2012), p. 687.

means to diffuse its influence, values and norms.[70] Moreover, since the implementation of the last generation of "deep" trade arrangements requires long-term multi-level cooperation, functional cooperation represents a crucial avenue of EU norms' diffusion to partner countries.[71]

To conclude, the EU's aspiration to use its FTAs with third countries as an instrument of achieving non-trade objectives (e.g. the rule of law promotion) is consonant with the Union's normative power. However, its ability to do so is to a significant extent determined by its "power through trade" that relies on the MPE.

3.3   Who Is the Counterpart? EU Bargaining Power in Trade Negotiations

In discussing the political prerequisites behind the EU's promotion of the rule of law through trade, it is not sufficient to limit oneself to an insight into the types of power the EU relies on in its external trade relations. To understand the circumstances, under which the EU can promote the rule of law through FTAs, one shall take into account parties' relative abilities to influence each other (bargaining powers). For the purposes of this paper, I distinguish four major properties of the EU's counterparts that affect the Union's ability to use FTAs as an instrument of promoting the rule of law.

3.3.1   Economic Characteristics

From the neorealist perspective, economic resources and capabilities of a state, frequently linked to market size, constitute the key factor to determine a state's bargaining power in trade negotiations.[72] Thus, as a general rule, a large and economic powerful state will have more leverage in bilateral trade negotiations with the EU, than a small and economically weak one. In their study of asymmetries in trade negotiations, Diana Tussie and Marcelo Saguier point to the relational nature of the market power and argue that market size does not matter as much in trade negotiations as the economy's dependence on imports and exports does.[73] According to Albert Hirschman, a small country's vulnerability in its relations with a larger country or a trading block is determined by its exports' and/or imports' and/or orientation on this larger country.[74] Thus, the understanding of an economic dimension of a country's bargaining power shall consider its economic interests and

---

[70]Meunier and Nicolaïdis (2006).

[71]Freyburg et al. (2011).

[72]Tussie and Saguier (2013), p. 3.

[73]Ibid, p. 14.

[74]Hirschmann (1980), p. 25.

preferences in geographical and sector-related terms, rather than solely market size-related data.

Furthermore, the analysis of a counterpart's bargaining power in its relations with the EU requires the consideration of a state and prospects of its integration into global markets, such as its membership and role in particular regional integration initiatives. Pursuant to Jens Lamprecht, participation in negotiating coalitions is a crucial factor, increasing a state's bargaining power.[75] The impact of this factor, however, strongly depends on a number of participants, the economic power of the coalition and the degree of its cohesion.[76]

Thus, EU bargaining power in trade negotiations is impacted by the economic characteristics of its counterpart, such as its resources and capabilities, exports/imports orientation, and its role in trade blocks.

3.3.2 Development Aid/Aid Dependency

Given the importance of "carrots and sticks" for the diffusion of EU norms and the EU's aspiration towards a more "development-friendly" trade policy,[77] a counterpart's interest in irrevocable development aid is highly likely to increase the EU's leverage in negotiating the non-trade objectives as part of FTAs. This statement can be substantiated by the evolution of references to human rights and other fundamental values in the EU's trade and cooperation agreements with African, Caribbean and Pacific (ACP) countries. According to Christopher Clapham,

> the renegotiations of the Convention, from Lome II onwards essentially consisted in the EC telling the ACP states how much aid they were going to get, and the ACP complaining that it was not enough.[78]

While not discussing whether money can actually generate a successful legal reform,[79] it can doubtlessly constitute a factor that allows the Union to insert non-trade objectives into respective FTAs.

3.3.3 Political Regime (and the Interplay of Economic and Political Factors)

Since the pursuit of non-trade objectives that may be included into EU FTAs with third countries might impact political regimes of the latter, a counterpart's existing

---

[75]Lamprecht (2014), p. 47.

[76]Ibid.

[77]European Commission (2018) Trade and Development in a Nutshell, http://ec.europa.eu/trade/policy/countries-and-regions/development/ (last accessed 8 February 2018).

[78]Clapham (1996), p. 101.

[79]For the criticism of externally funded legal reforms, see: Erbeznik (2011).

political regime and its vision of the future may exert decisive impact on its readiness to accept the rule of law-related obligations.

Starting from the extreme case, it has to be mentioned that for authoritarian regimes, the costs of accepting genuine external value-promotion efforts would be too high.[80] In such cases, a regime's economic strength and interest in aid, on the one hand, as well as the EU's strategy vis-à-vis a country/region and its economic interests, on the other, will determine the design of rule of law-related obligations, included in the respective trade deals. For instance, since the EU is a major export and import as well as development cooperation partner for Southern Neighbourhood countries, and the region is strategically important for the Union's security, the EU tries to pursue limited rule of law promotion in the region, in general, through trade.[81]

The situation, however, looks different, if a Union's counterpart is an economically powerful authoritarian regime. Overall, the EU's trade relationships with economically powerful, yet undemocratic regimes (e.g. China, Russia, the Gulf Cooperation Council (GCC) countries) are characterized with the lack of trade liberalization arrangements.[82] The reasons behind such *status quo* may include geopolitical issues, parties' inability to reach consensus as regards tariff concessions within particular sectors, and, not least, their divergent views on values. An insight into the 2016 New EU Strategy on China demonstrates that in its relations with big powers that contest Western values the EU prefers to emphasize mutual economic interests and those aspects of the rule of law that are immediately linked to trade (e.g. transparency of customs cooperation).[83]

The third combination refers to the EU's trade with economically powerful and democratic actors, such as Canada, Japan or South Korea. In such cases, parties' commitments to democracy, human rights and the rule of law tend to be reaffirmed in the preamble to the respective FTAs.[84] The symmetry of power relations between the parties determines regulatory convergence efforts they undertake with regard to "deep disciplines" chapters, rather than the unilateral transfer of EU norms.[85]

Finally, the unilateral transfer of EU norms is peculiar for the Union's relationships with young democracies that depend on it in terms of exports, imports and development aid.

---

[80]On the challenges of EU external democratization efforts in authoritarian regimes, see: Risse and Babayan (2015).

[81]Wetzel (2015).

[82]European Commission (2018) Trade and Development in a Nutshell, http://ec.europa.eu/trade/policy/countries-and-regions/development/ (last accessed 8 February 2018).

[83]European Commission's and High Representative's Joint Communication "Elements for a New EU Strategy for China", JOIN(2016) 30 final.

[84]See, for instance: Comprehensive Economic and Trade Agreement (CETA) between Canada, of the one part, and the European Union and its Member States, of the other part. OJ 2017 L11, Preamble.

[85]Araujo (2014), pp. 279–280.

3.3.4 Integration Aspirations and EU Strategic Interests

Ultimately, a counterpart's aspirations to join the EU or achieve profound economic integration with it may shape the parties' bargaining powers in trade negotiations. The comparison of the EU's leverage in the enlargement and ENP context demonstrates that it is to a great extent depends on "membership perspective", included into the framework of EU's relations with a third state.[86] However, the case of "associated neighbourhood" proves that a countries' official aspiration to join the EU, which is not substantiated by the perspective of membership, may add value to the Union's bargaining power.[87]

Moreover, the extent and nature of the EU's strategic interests in a country or region can also influence the bargaining power of the EU and its counterpart. In view of the increasingly unstable international order and the interest-driven nature of the EUGS, security and stability-related interests of the Union come to the forefront.

The present analysis demonstrates that the EU has the strongest bargaining power in trade negotiations with young democracies, for which it is a major export, import and development cooperation partner. Moreover, the EU's bargaining power is reinforced by respective countries' membership or integration aspirations. The above combination of factors, allowing for the EU's pursuit of non-trade objectives through FTAs, can be illustrated by three categories of EU's international agreements: SAAs with Western Balkans, AAs with Eastern Neighbourhood Partners and CEPA.[88] Naturally, given the Western Balkans' aspiration to join the EU eventually, the envisaged scale of legislative approximation and the long-term nature of the EU's stabilization and development engagement with the region,[89] the EU has strong bargaining power vis-à-vis the region. Despite the fact the AAs with Eastern Neighbours do not envisage future membership, "associated neighbourhood" aspires to achieve an in-depth political and market integration with the EU and thus orients its markets towards the Union.[90] Finally, the incorporation of political goals into the EU-ACP relationship dates back to the Lomé IV Convention. Ever since, the EU represents an important trade and development cooperation partner for the region.[91] The subsequent legal analysis will, however, only focus on CEPA, since it is the only EPA that goes beyond trade liberalization also incorporating "deep disciplines".[92]

---

[86]Schimelfennig and Sedelmeier (2004), p. 669.

[87]Petrov et al. (2015), pp. 1–4.

[88]While this paper focuses on these three groups of agreements, further EU FTAs can be strategically used by the EU to promote the rule of law, provided that it possesses the necessary bargaining power.

[89]For an overview of the EU's democratization efforts in the Western Balkans over the period from 1994 to 2010, see: Grimm and Mathis (2017).

[90]Petrov et al. (2015), pp. 1–4.

[91]Fourth ACP-EEC Lomé Convention signed at Lomé on 15 December 1989. OJ 1991 L 229, Article 5.

[92]For the reasons behind the trade liberalization-only focus of the other EU EPAs with ACP countries, see: Gammage (2017), pp. 158–178.

3.4   Legal Basis

The key legal basis for EU FTAs with third countries is the Common Commercial Policy (CCP).[93] Along with the overarching foreign policy objectives of the EU, stipulated by Article 21(2) TEU, the CCP aims to contribute to

> the harmonious development of world trade, the progressive abolition of restrictions on international trade and on foreign direct investment, and the lowering of customs and other barriers.[94]

The understanding of the importance of extending general objectives of the EU external action to the CCP would not be complete without referring to the legal value of Article 21(2) TEU. According to Vivian Kube, the analysis of the EU's human rights-related objectives, stipulated in Article 21(2)(b) TEU, testifies to the EU's adoption and constitutionalization of its extraterritorial human rights responsibility.[95] This statement was reaffirmed by the CJEU in *Opinion 2/15* on the EU's competence to conclude the so-called "new generation" of trade agreements.[96] In particular, the CJEU stipulated that the EU is obliged to integrate the respective general objectives and principles into the CCP.[97] This finding would, presumably, have several implications on the EU's external value-promotion, such as the focus on the role of values in the CCP and EU external action and the consolidation of the EU's concept of extraterritorial human rights responsibility.[98]

According to Article 3(1)(e) TFEU, the CCP belongs to the exclusive competences of the EU. Notably, the Treaties do not directly link the EU's right to conclude international agreements with the exclusive nature of its competences. Thus, Article 3(2) TFEU provides for the EU's exclusive competence to conclude an international agreement, when

> its conclusion is provided for in a legislative act of the Union or is necessary to enable the Union to exercise its internal competence, or in so far as its conclusion may affect common rules or alter their scope.[99]

Article 216 TFEU distinguishes four set of circumstances, under which the Union possesses the respective right

> ("when the Treaties so provide", "where the conclusion of an agreement is necessary in order to achieve, within the framework of the Union's policies, one of the objectives referred to in the Treaties", where the conclusion of the agreement is "provided for in a legally binding act" or "is likely to affect common rules or alter their scope").

---

[93]TFEU, Articles 206 and 207.

[94]TFEU, Article 206.

[95]Kube (2016), p. 15.

[96]CJEU, Opinion 2/15, ECLI:EU:C:2017:376.

[97]Ibid, para 142.

[98]Kube (2016), p. 29.

[99]TFEU, Article 3(2).

Referring to the rules and procedures, contained in Article 218 TFEU, Article 207 TFEU grants the EU an explicit competence to conclude international agreements, thus, representing the first circumstance, mentioned by Articles 3(2) and 216 TFEU. However, since many of the EU FTAs go beyond one are of cooperation, they tend to be founded on several legal bases.[100] The algorithm for choosing substantive legal basis (bases) for respective decisions is provided for in Article 208(9) TFEU. Moreover, since FTAs frequently include areas, falling within the scope of shared competences and competences of the Member States, the vast majority of EU agreements, involving trade liberalization arrangements are "mixed" agreements.[101] In this view, it is essential to briefly refer to the legal basis behind each category of agreements under study.

In case of

> agreements. . .establishing an association involving reciprocal rights and obligations, common action and special procedure,

such as the SAAs with Western Balkans and the AAs with Eastern Neighbours, Article 217 TFEU shall apply.[102] Furthermore, since both SAAs with Western Balkans and AAs with Eastern Neighbours encompass a broad range of cooperation domains that go beyond the exclusive competencies of the Union (e.g. political cooperation, cooperation related to freedom, justice and security), they are concluded as "mixed" agreements.[103] The legal basis for the Union's conclusion of international agreements related to development cooperation (such as CEPA) is represented by Article 208 TFEU, according to which

> The Union may conclude with third countries and competent international organizations any agreement helping to achieve the objectives referred to in Article 21 of the Treaty on European Union and in Article 208 of this Treaty.[104]

However, according to paragraph 2 of Article 209(2) TFEU, the above rule shall apply without prejudice to Member States' competence to conclude international agreements. Similar to the SAAs with Western Balkans and AAs with Eastern Neighbours, CEPA is a "mixed" agreement.[105]

---

[100]EUR-LEX (n.d). International Agreements and the EU's External Competences, https://eur-lex.europa.eu/legal-content/EN/TXT/?uri=LEGISSUM%3Aai0034 (last accessed 09 February 2019).

[101]Ibid.

[102]For an in-detail discussion regarding the "split" legal basis of the EU-Ukraine AA, see: Van der Loo (2016), pp. 166–175.

[103]See, for instance: Stabilization and Association Agreement between the European Communities and their Member States, of the one part, and the Republic of Albania, of the other part. OJ L 2009 107/66, (EU-Albania SAA); Association Agreement between the European Union and its Member States, of the one part, and Ukraine, of the other part. OJ 2014 L 161/3 (EU-Ukraine AA).

[104]TFEU, Article 208.

[105]Economic Partnership Agreement between the CARIFORUM States, of the one part, and the European Community and its Member States of the other part. OJ 2008 L 289/173 (CEPA).

3.5 Disciplines That Contain Rule of Law Obligations

Alongside the bargaining power-related prerequisites behind the rule of law promotion through FTAs, an important factor that makes it possible is the "deep" nature of respective agreements.[106] The tangential overview of the scope of SAAs with Western Balkans, the AAs with Eastern Neighbours allows for distinguishing four major categories of provisions, capable of promoting the rule of law. They include the liberalization of capital movement and financial services; administrative and technical cooperation with the EU, and trade facilitation; "deep disciplines" (e.g. public procurement, competition, IP rights, sustainable development) and "Transparency" chapters, contained in the EU's DCFTAs with Eastern Neighbours. The emphasis on the above disciplines is without prejudice to the rule of law standards that may be included on a case-by-case basis into other chapters of FTAs.

In contemporary development economics theory, financial liberalization and the development of markets for financial services represents an important "juncture" between law, trade and development.[107] All three categories of FTAs under study include chapters, dedicated to the circulation of capital and financial services.[108] Aiming to promote stabilization of partner countries' financial systems for the purposes of intensifying international trade and foreign direct investment (FDI), these provisions tend to stipulate legality, legal certainty, transparency and equality and non-discrimination standards as well as refer to the relationship between domestic and international law.[109] The intertwined nature of legal certainty, transparency and equality and non-discrimination requirements as regards financial rules can be illustrated by Article 127 of the EU-Ukraine AA and Article 105 of the CEPA that oblige the Parties to ensure "effective and transparent" regulation in the financial services sector. Moreover, the capital liberalization and financial services-related chapters under all these categories of FTAs in question obligate the Parties to adhere to relevant provisions of GATS, thus, touching upon the relationship between domestic and international law. Given the fact that an in-depth insight into the interplay between financial liberalization and the rule of law would require additional expertise in the domain of finances, this paper will not consider the rule of law promotion through FTAs' provisions regarding the liberalization of capital circulation and financial services.

Secondly, legality, legal certainty, equality and non-discrimination, and transparency standards and the observance of relevant international law form an essential part of FTAs' provisions on administrative and technical cooperation. This paper will utilize the case of administrative cooperation provisions across all three

---

[106]Araujo (2014), p. 279.

[107]On the "junctures" between law, trade and development and the "augmented" Washington Consensus: Rodrik (2006), p. 978.

[108]See, for instance: EU-Albania SAA, Chapter IV; EU-Ukraine AA, Chapter 7; CEPA, Chapter 5, Section 5.

[109]Ibid.

categories of agreements under study and refer to the DCFTAs' chapters on "Customs and Trade Facilitation" to illustrate the rule of law standards and regulatory mechanisms, utilized by the Union to promote them in the abovementioned domain.

Thirdly, an important source of the rule of law standards in FTAs in question is represented by "deep disciplines", such as public procurement, competition, sustainable development and IP rights. Typically, "deep disciplines" chapters envisage a significant degree of approximating partner countries' legislation to the relevant EU rules and ensuring the independence and impartiality of relevant institutions, so that EU companies' access to partner countries' markets is not restricted through discriminatory practices.[110] This paper will use the case of "Public procurement" chapters of the EU's SAAs with Western Balkans, DCFTAs with "associated" Eastern Neighbours and the CEPA to acquire an insight into the substance of respective rule of law requirements and the regulatory mechanisms the EU utilizes to promote them.

Finally, the EU's DCFTAs with "associated" Eastern Neighbours are marked by the inclusion of separate chapters, encompassing various aspects of transparency of the Parties' trade policy. In my earlier paper on the EU's rule of law promotion through DCFTAs in the "associated Neighbourhood" I demonstrated that these chapters imply partner countries' observance of numerous rule of law standards, such as legality, legal certainty (with a focus on foreseeability and predictability of regulations) and equality and non-discrimination.[111] Moreover, the "Transparency" chapters stipulate that

> each party shall establish or maintain judicial, arbitral or administrative tribunals or procedures for the purpose of the prompt review and, where warranted, correction of administrative action relating to matters, covered by the Titles V and IV ("Trade and Trade-related matters") respectively[112],

thus emphasizing authorities' independence and impartiality.

4 Legal Mechanisms of EU Rule of Law Promotion Through FTAs

4.1 Administrative Cooperation

In EU law terms, the core of administrative cooperation between the EU and Member States is comprised by the notion of the European Administrative Space (EAS), wherein "increasingly integrated administrations jointly exercise powers,

---

[110]See, for instance: EU-Ukraine AA, Article 148, Article 50.

[111]Rabinovych (2017).

[112]EU-Ukraine AA, Article 286.

delegated to the EU in a system of shared sovereignty".[113] Alternatively, the EAS can be defined as a "harmonized synthesis of values", shaped by EU institutions and Member States' administrations.[114] The literature on the EAS distinguishes the following values, it is founded on: stability and the enforcement of the democratic rule of law; sustainable and environment-friendly economic development; increase of the role of national administrations; reliability, transparency and democratic nature of the administration and the multilevel enforcement of "good governance".[115] According to Sandra Lavenex, an important aspect of the external differentiated integration deals with third countries' contribution to the EAS through their participation in the EU's regulatory bodies (e.g. European Environment Agency (EEA), European Medicine Agency (EMA) and administrative cooperation with them.[116] The above demonstrates that administrative cooperation with the EU presupposes the observance of the rule of law principle, in general, and the principles of transparency and procedural legality, in particular. The EU's trade relations with Western Balkans, Eastern Neighbourhood and CARIFORUM involve three sources of regulations regarding administrative cooperation: respective FTAs; Customs Cooperation and Mutual Administrative Assistance Agreements and DCFTAs' "Customs and Trade Facilitation" chapters.

4.1.1 Administrative Cooperation *Stricto Sensu*

An insight into the administrative cooperation provisions, contained in each of the three categories of FTAs in question enables one to distinguish several ways in which it can be linked to the umbrella rule of law concept. First, the exercise of the administrative cooperation *stricto sensu* requires the third state's adherence to the principles shaping the EAS.[117] Secondly, a party's failure to provide administrative cooperation and/or report customs-related irregularities or fraud can result in the temporary suspension of preferential treatment.[118] For the purposes of administrative cooperation in the narrow sense, customs irregularities or fraud refer to the different breaches of the principles of legality and legal certainty in the domain of customs, such as, for instance, an authorities' failure to verify the origin of a product or the miscommunication of the results of such verification.[119] Furthermore, the

---

[113]Hofmann (2008), p. 662.

[114]Torma (2011), p. 149.

[115]Torma (2011), pp. 148–156.

[116]Lavenex (2015), pp. 842–845.

[117]Lavenex (2015), pp. 836–838.

[118]See, for instance: Stabilization and Association Agreement between the European Union and the European Atomic Energy Community, of the one part, and Kosovo, of the other part. Official Journal of the European Union L 71, 16.3.2016, Article 48(4) (EU-Kosovo SAA); EU-Ukraine AA, Article 37; CEPA, Article 20.

[119]Ibid.

conventional formulations of breaches in the administrative cooperation domain (e.g. "a repeated refusal or undue delay in carrying out/communicating the results of the subsequent verification of the proof of origin")[120] are testimony to the administrative cooperation-related provisions' emphasis on transparency standards. The key instruments, used by FTAs to promote a partner countries' customs administrations' compliance with legality, legal certainty and transparency standards encompass the imposition of basic standards as well as legislative approximation or cooperation obligations,[121] consultations with the association bodies in case of alleged breaches[122] and sanctioning mechanisms.[123]

4.1.2 Customs Cooperation and Mutual Administrative Assistance Agreements/Protocols

The EU's Customs Cooperation and Mutual Administrative Assistance Agreements tend to be based on respective FTAs and frequently exist as protocols to them.[124]

Similar to the FTAs' provisions on administrative cooperation *stricto sensu*, Customs Cooperation and Mutual Administrative Assistance Agreements/Protocols emphasize the observance of the legality dimension of the rule of law in the domain of customs.[125] For instance, respective Protocol attached to the EU-Kosovo SAA aim to

> ensure the correct application of the customs legislation, in particular by preventing, investigating the breaches and combating breaches of such legislation.[126]

Furthermore, the Protocols uphold the legal certainty and transparency dimensions of the rule of law by obliging requested authorities to provide the applicant authorities with all relevant information regarding the matters of their competence.[127] Since the completeness and relevance of provided information is estimated according to its suitability for ensuring correct application of customs legislation by the applicant party, respective cooperation obligations are also directed to promoting authorities' compliance with legislation and its appropriate enforcement (that are part to the legality standard).[128] As well as the FTAs' chapters on administrative

---

[120]EU-Ukraine AA, Article 37(3); CEPA, Article 20(3)(b).

[121]EU-Kosovo SAA, Article 104; EU-Ukraine AA, Article 36; CEPA, Article 20(1).

[122]EU-Kosovo SAA, Article 136(4), sentence 2; EU-Ukraine AA, Article 37(4)(a); CEPA, Article 20(5).

[123]EU-Ukraine AA, Article 37(2); CEPA, Art. 20(2).

[124]See: EU-Kosovo SAA, Protocol IV; EU-Ukraine AA, Protocol II; CEPA, Protocol II.

[125]EU-Kosovo SAA, Protocol IV, Article 2(1); EU-Ukraine AA, Protocol II, Article 2(1); CEPA, Protocol II. Article 2(1).

[126]EU-Kosovo SAA, Protocol IV, Article 2(1).

[127]EU-Kosovo SAA, Protocol IV, Article 3(1); EU-Ukraine AA, Protocol II, Article 3(1); CEPA, Protocol II. Article 3(1).

[128]Ibid.

cooperation *stricto sensu*, the Protocols do not create the obligations for the Parties to adhere to the particular international law norms. Nevertheless, they still touch upon the relationship between international and domestic law by distinguishing cases in which the assistance can be refused (e.g. if it is likely to prejudice the sovereignty, public policy, security or other essential interests of the Parties).[129]

Ultimately, the Customs Cooperation and Mutual Administrative Assistance Agreements/Protocols illustrate the promotion of legality, legal certainty and transparency dimensions of the rule of law in the customs domain through the imposition of in-detail cooperation-related obligations.[130]

4.1.3 "Customs and Trade Facilitation" Chapters of the DCFTAs

Alongside the provisions regarding administrative cooperation *stricto sensu* and the Protocols/Agreements on Mutual Administrative Assistance on Customs Matters, the EU's DCFTAs with "associated" Eastern Neighbours include chapters on "Customs and Trade Facilitation",[131] worth consideration from the standpoint of the promotion of the rule of law. As defined by the WTO, trade facilitation encompasses the "simplification, modernization and harmonization of export and import processes".[132] According to the DCFTAs, the relevant legislation, procedures and efforts, directed towards raising the administrations' capacity shall be aimed to

> fulfill the objectives of effective control and support facilitation of legitimate trade, as a matter of principle.[133]

In this regard, the concept of "legitimate trade" deserves particular attention. Despite having been used in the DCFTAs and beyond (e.g. the proposal for the EU-Vietnam FTA),[134] this concept remains undefined. However, the teleological analysis of "Customs and Trade Facilitation" chapters of the DCFTAs demonstrates that it is to a significant extent connected to the umbrella rule of law principle. For instance,

---

[129]EU-Kosovo SAA, Protocol IV, Article 9; EU-Ukraine AA, Protocol II, Article 9; CEPA, Protocol II. Article 9.

[130]EU-Kosovo SAA, Protocol IV, Article 7; EU-Ukraine AA, Protocol II, Article 7; CEPA, Protocol II. Article 7.

[131]EU-Ukraine AA, Part IV, Chapter 5; Association Agreement between the European Union and the Atomic Energy Community and their Member States, of the one part, and the Republic of Moldova, of the other part. OJ 2014 L260, Part IV, Chapter 5 (EU-Moldova AA); Association Agreement between the European Union and the Atomic Energy Community and their Member States, of the one part, and Georgia, of the other part. OJ 2014 L 261/4, Part IV, Chapter 5 (EU-Georgia AA).

[132]World Trade Organization (2017) Trade Facilitation, https://www.wto.org/english/tratop_e/tradfa_e/tradfa_e.htm (last accessed 10 February 2019).

[133]See, for instance: EU-Moldova AA, Article 192.

[134]European Commission (2018) EU-Vietnam Free Trade Agreement, Chapter 4, Article 4(1)(2), http://trade.ec.europa.eu/doclib/docs/2018/september/tradoc_157349.pdf (last accessed 10 February 2019).

according to Article 193(1)(a) of the EU-Moldova DCFTA, the protection and facilitation of legitimate trade requires *inter alia* "effective enforcement of, and compliance with, legislative requirements".

Moreover, meeting these requirements means compliance with a range of the rule of law-inspired standards, such as transparency, non-discrimination and the uniform application of legislation. Additionally, according to Andreas Heinemann, trade can be qualified as "legitimate" if it is free from barriers, arising from a party's (parties') non-compliance with the international antitrust and IP rights protection standards.[135]

Following their "legitimate trade" objective, DCFTAs' "Customs and Trade Facilitation" chapters introduce a range of rule of law standards, such as legality (comprehensiveness of legislation; authorities' compliance with the legislation),[136] legal certainty (stability and predictability of the legal framework; proportionality; the uniform application of laws and regulations)[137] and authorities' accountability and transparency of their operation.[138] In addition, the principle of non-discrimination is reaffirmed by the Parties' commitment

> "to avoid unnecessary or discriminatory burdens on economic operators" and "to ensure the non-discriminatory administration of requirements and procedures applicable to imports, exports and the good in transit."[139]

Notably, the "Customs and Trade Facilitation" chapters oblige the Parties to the DCFTAs

> to provide effective, prompt and non-discriminatory procedures, guaranteeing the right of appeal against customs and other authorities' administrative actions, rulings and decisions, affecting the goods submitted to the citizens[140]

Moreover, the provision underlines the need for accessible appeal procedures (also to SMEs) and ensuring reasonable costs for such access, thus, contributing to the Parties' observance of an individual's right to fair trial (Article 47 CFR) and the right to good administration (Article 44 CFR).[141]

Finally, the "Customs and Trade Facilitation" chapters of the DCFTAs promote the mutually intertwined rule of law standards through a rich toolbox that includes the imposition of basic standards,[142] obligations regarding cooperation[143] and legislative approximation[144] and the referral to the Parties' commitments under the

---

[135]Heinemann (2007), p. 262.

[136]See, for instance: EU-Moldova AA, Article 193(1).

[137]Ibid, Article 193(1), Article 194(a).

[138]Ibid, Article 194(a), Article 193(2)(e).

[139]Ibid, Article 193(1)(b), Article 193(2)(g).

[140]Ibid, Article 193(2)(c).

[141]Ibid, Articles 194–195; Charter of Fundamental Rights of the European Union. OJ 2012 C326, Article 47, 44.

[142]EU-Moldova AA, Article 193(1).

[143]Ibid, Article 197.

[144]Ibid, Article 201.

international law (e.g. the Agreement on Customs Valuation and numerous World Customs Organization (WCO) documents).[145] Similar to the DCFTAs' "Transparency" chapters, their norms on customs and trade facilitation are marked by the comprehensiveness of rule of law standards and diversity of tools the EU utilizes to promote them.[146]

4.2 Public Procurement

According to the Commission's Directorate General (DG) Growth, a considerable part of public investment is spent via public procurement, accounting for 2 trillion EUR a year or 14% of the EU's GDP.[147] The most recent EU Public Procurement Strategy emphasizes the improvement of access to public procurement markets through encouraging partner countries to join the plurilateral Agreement on Government Procurement (GPA) and including public procurement chapters into FTAs.[148] Moreover, following the trend of expanding the role of non-trade objectives in FTAs,[149] the Strategy stipulates the EU's effort to make public procurement innovative, green and social.[150] The document also points to the observance of particular dimensions of the rule of law in the public domain (e.g. legality, transparency).[151]

The foundational principles of the award of public contracts in the EU are set out in Directive 2014/24/EU.[152] According to its preamble, the award of public contracts by the Member States' authorities or on their behalf shall comply with the principles of the TFEU, such as the free movement of goods, freedom of establishment and the freedom to provide services, and the principles, derived thereof (equal treatment, non-discrimination, mutual recognition and transparency).[153] Apart from presupposing compliance with the TFEU (legality), the above principles immediately refer to two dimensions of the rule of law: equality and non-discrimination as well as transparency. Given the EU's effort to promote third states' joining the

---

[145]Ibid, Article 193(1)(h).

[146]Rabinovych (2017).

[147]European Commission (n.d) Public Procurement, https://ec.europa.eu/growth/single-market/public-procurement_en (last accessed 10 February 2019).

[148]Commission's Communication "Making Public Procurement work in and for Europe", COM (2017)572 final.

[149]Araujo (2016), p. 4.

[150]Commission's Communication "Making Public Procurement work in and for Europe", COM (2017)572 final, pp. 5 and 10.

[151]Ibid.

[152]European Parliament and Council Directive 2014/24/EU on public procurement and repealing Directive 2014/18/EC. OJ 2014 L94.

[153]Ibid, p. 1 of the Preamble.

GPA,[154] its cooperation with third states in this domain touches upon the relationship between domestic and international law. In turn, the GPA itself is to a significant extent a rule of law-oriented document that promotes legal certainty, transparency, equality and non-discrimination as well as the authorities' independence and impartiality.[155] This statement can be exemplified by Article VIII GPA that limits the conditions for participation in procurement to those, "essential to ensure that a supplier has the legal and financial capacities and the commercial and technical abilities to undertake the relevant procurement" (equality and non-discrimination and transparency standards) or Article XVIII GPA that obliges the parties to "provide timely, effective, transparent and non-discriminatory administrative or judicial review", including the right to appeal.

4.2.1 SAAs with Western Balkans

Moving on with the analysis of specific agreements, it is worth mentioning that even the most recent EU's SAAs with Western Balkans do not include separate chapters on "deep disciplines". The key source of public procurement standards for candidate countries is, therefore, constituted by the *acquis*, specified in the SAAs' legislative approximation provisions.[156] An insight into three key directives that are to be transplanted into the domestic legislation of candidate countries (Directive 2014/24/EU; Directive 2014/23/EU; Directive 89/665/EC) demonstrates that, similar to the GPA, they encompass provisions, attributable to the legality, legal certainty, equality and non-discrimination, transparency and authorities' independence and impartiality rule of law standards.[157] Let me illustrate this statement by referring to the Council's Directive 89/665/EC that focuses on the application of review procedures to the award of public supply and public work contracts.[158] Pursuant to Article 1 of the Directive 89/665/EC, Member States bear an obligation to ensure the possibility of the review of contracting authorities' decisions, as rapidly as possible, on the basis of the respective decisions' infringing Community law in the field of public procurement or national rules implementing that law. Furthermore, the

---

[154]European Commission (n.d) Public Procurement, https://ec.europa.eu/growth/single-market/public-procurement_en (last accessed 10 February 2019).

[155]WTO (2014) Revised Agreement on Government Procurement (GPA), https://www.wto.org/english/docs_e/legal_e/rev-gpr-94_01_e.htm (last accessed 10 February 2019).

[156]EU-Albania SAA, Article 70, Article 74.

[157]See: European Parliament and Council Directive 2014/24/EU on public procurement and repealing Directive 2014/18/EC. OJ 2014 L94, Preamble (pp. 1, 2, 45, 52, 58, 59, 61, 107), Section 2, Article 76 etc.; European Parliament and Council Directive 2014/23/EU on the award of concession contracts. OJ 2014 L94, Preamble (pp. 4, 6, 33, 53, 61), Article 3, Article 15 etc.; Council Directive 89/665/EEC on the coordination of the laws, regulations and administrative provisions relating to the application of review procedures to the award of public supply and public works contracts. OJ 1989 L 395.

[158]Council Directive 89/665/EEC.

Directive obliges Member States to ensure the effectiveness of the enforcement of decisions by bodies, responsible for the review procedure.[159] Notably, Directive 89/665/EC provides for the extension of Member States' judicial independence requirement to administrative bodies, responsible for considering the claims in question.[160] According to Article 2(8) of Directive 89/665/EC,

> the independent body shall take its decisions following a procedure in which both sides are heard, and these decisions shall, by means determined by each Member State, be legally binding.

Additionally, given the limitedness of subjects, capable of submitting a claim under Directive 89/665/EC, p. 122 of the preamble to the Directive 2014/24/EU grants "citizens, concerned stakeholders, organized or not, and other persons and bodies" an opportunity to indicate the possible violations of the Directive 2014/24/EU, without directly referring to their right to judicial review. The above demonstrates that the fulfillment of Candidate Countries' legislative approximation obligations is tightly intertwined with the observance of the rule of law standards.

4.2.2 DCFTAs with Eastern Neighbours

Given the market integration *finalité* of the EU's DCFTAs with Eastern Neighbours, the scope of legislative approximation, envisaged by the DCFTAs, is virtually analogous to the SAAs.[161] However, the "integration without membership" model[162] of the EU-"associated neighborhood" relationships determines the fact that the DCFTAs combine legislative approximation with two novel instruments of the rule of law promotion: the imposition of basic standards and market access conditionality.

The "basic standards", included in the "Public Procurement" chapters of the EU's DCFTAs with Eastern Neighbours contribute to equality and non-discrimination, transparency and impartiality dimensions of the rule of law.[163] The interconnectedness of these dimensions of the rule of law can be exemplified by Article 151(5) of the EU-Ukraine AA that stipulates that

> the impartiality shall be ensured especially by the non-discriminatory description of the subject-matter of the contract, equal access for all economic operators, appropriate time-limits and a transparent and objective approach.

Furthermore, contracting entities are expressly prohibited to impose conditions that result in "*direct or indirect discrimination against the economic operators of the other Party*". The judicial review-related basic standards under the respective

---

[159]Ibid, Article 7.

[160]Ibid, Article 2(8).

[161]Van der Loo (2016), p. 304.

[162]Petrov et al. (2015).

[163]See, for instance: EU-Ukraine AA, Article 151(2)(5)(8)(11)(12).

chapters of the DCFTAs tend to mirror the provisions of the Directive 89/665/EC, considered above.[164]

According to Gillaume Van der Loo, the central novelty of the DCFTAs is represented by market access conditionality, immediately connected to legislative approximation.[165] Thus, the decision to proceed with the subsequent phase of market opening is to be made based on the Association Committee's in Trade Configuration assessment of both the quality of adopted legislation and its implementation.[166] Following the last phase of the gradual approximation, the Parties shall consider the complete mutual liberalization of public procurement markets.[167] Additionally, the legislative approximation process under the DCFTAs is reinforced by its dynamic nature and the partner countries' obligation to "take due account" of the CJEU case law and implemented measures.[168]

Thus, by comparison with the SAAs, the "Public Procurement" chapters of the EU's DCFTAs with Eastern Neighbours offer a more sophisticated mechanism of promoting the rule of law, reflecting the Union's being cautious about the "opening up its public procurement market for a third country with a less developed economy and economic capacity than the EEA country".[169]

4.2.3 CEPA

An important peculiarity of the EU's EPAs with ACP countries as compared to the SAAs with Western Balkans and other AAs is that they provide for various degrees of cooperation between the Union and its partner countries.[170] Consequently, the CEPA is a single trade liberalization agreement between the EU and a group of ACP countries that contains "deep disciplines".[171]

The objective-related clause of the CEPA links "transparent competitive tendering" to economic development, putting particular emphasis on the need to take into account the "special situation of the economies of CARIFORUM states".[172] Notably, the GPA stresses "special consideration to the development, financial and trade needs and circumstances of developing and least developed countries", offering preference programmes and longer transitional periods before market

---

[164]EU-Ukraine AA, Article 151(15).

[165]Van der Loo (2016), p. 308.

[166]EU-Ukraine AA, Article 154(2).

[167]Ibid, Article 154(4).

[168]Ibid, Article 153.

[169]Van der Loo (2016), p. 308.

[170]European Commission (n.d) Economic Partnership Agreements, http://ec.europa.eu/trade/pol icy/countries-and-regions/development/economic-partnerships/ (last accessed 11 February 2019).

[171]For the reasons behind the trade liberalization-only focus of the other EU EPAs with ACP countries, see: Gammage (2017), pp. 158–178.

[172]CEPA, Article 165.

liberalization.[173] The application of the above preferences is, however, only possible, if the transparency and non-discrimination dimensions of the rule of law are observed.[174] The "Public Procurement" chapter of CEPA also emphasizes the above rule of law principles, viewing the intra-region liberalization of public procurements as a part to the EU effort to promote regional integration of the CARIFORUM countries.[175] In this view, CEPA utilizes the GPA and UNCITRAL Model Law—inspired "basic standards" to promote transparency, equality and non-discrimination and impartiality dimensions of the rule of law.[176] The scope of respective "basic standards" is close to those, included into the DCFTAs. The intertwined nature of the rule of law components under the respective standards can be illustrated by the referral to Article 179(1) of the Agreement, according to which

> the parties and the Signatory CARIFORUM States shall provide transparent, timely, impartial and effective procedures enabling suppliers to challenge domestic measures implementing this Chapter in the context of procurements in which they have, or have had, a legitimate commercial interest.

Similar to the GPA, relevant acts of the *acquis communautaire* and "Public Procurement" chapters of the EU's DCFTAs with "associated" Eastern Neighbours, CEPA promotes the transparency, equality and non-discrimination dimensions of the rule of law as well as judicial independence and impartiality.

5 Conclusion

Despite its "contested" nature, the rule of law tends to be high on the political agenda of the EU's cooperation with third states. This paper demonstrated that, relying on the combination of its normative, market and trade powers, the EU can utilize its FTAs with third countries as an instrument to promote the rule of law. In international trade negotiations, the EU's ability to promote non-trade objectives depends on the relationship between the parties' bargaining powers, shaped by their economic power and export/import orientation, values, strategic interests and foreign policy objectives. The combination of a relatively small size of a counterpart's market, its exports/imports orientation on the EU, interest in development aid, democratic aspirations and directedness at political/market integration with the EU is most beneficial for the Union to channel the promotion of values and non-trade objectives through FTAs.

Focusing on three categories of EU FTAs (SAAs with Western Balkans, DCFTAs with Eastern Neighbours and CEPA), the analysis showed that the above

---

[173]GPA, Article 5.

[174]Ibid.

[175]CEPA, Article 182.

[176]CEPA, Articles 167–182. For the comparative analysis of GPA, UNCITRAL and CEPA public procurement rules.

agreements refer to numerous aspects of the rule of law, such as legality, legal certainty, transparency, equality and non-discrimination and the relationship between domestic and international law. The most detailed regulation of rule of law requirements partner countries need to fulfil with regard to administrative cooperation and trade facilitation as well as acquiring access to the EU public procurement market are contained in the EU's DCFTAs with Eastern Neighbours. Furthermore, while the SAAs with Western Balkans tend to promote the components of the rule of law through legislative approximation, the DCFTAs with Eastern Neighbours are marked by the multiplicity and intertwined nature of respective regulatory mechanisms. They include *inter alia* the combination of gradual and dynamic legislative approximation with market access conditionality, basic standards and the recourse to international law. Resonating with the theory of "democracy promotion through functional cooperation", an insight into all three agreements revealed the potential of instrumentalizing administrative cooperation, trade facilitation and "deep disciplines"-related chapters of FTAs for the purposes of the rule of law promotion and institution-building. Finally, as illustrated by the public procurement-related provisions of the GPA and EU-CARIFORUM EPA, the trade-development nexus can be used to promote partner countries' observance of the rule of law standards in specific cooperation domain.

Thus, the EU's "power through trade", the scope of rule of law standards in existing FTAs and continuous evolution of mechanisms, used to ensure partner countries' compliance with their rule of law-related obligations determine the yet insufficiently explored potential of the EU's promotion of the rule of law and other non-trade objectives through FTAs. In this view, it might be beneficial for future research to focus on the interplay between FTAs and other legal instruments the EU uses to promote the rule of law in third countries.

References

Aggestam E (2013) Global norms and European power. In: Jorgensen E et al (eds) Routledge handbook on the European Union and international institutions. Palgrave McMillan, Basingstoke

Araujo B (2014) The EU's deep trade agenda: stumbling block or stepping stone towards multilateral liberalization? In: Herrmann C, Krajewski M, Terhechte J (eds) European yearbook of international economic law 2014. Springer, Berlin

Araujo B (2016) The EU deep trade agenda: law and policy. Oxford University Press, Oxford

Biscop S (2016) The EU global strategy: Realpolitik with European characteristics. Egmont Institute Security Policy Brief 75

Bovens M (2007) Public accountability. In: Ferlie E et al (eds) The Oxford handbook of public management. Oxford University Press, Oxford

Busuioc E (2013) European agencies: law and practices of accountability. Oxford University Press, Oxford

Cianetti L, Dawson J, Hanley S (2018) Rethinking "democratic backsliding" in Central and Eastern Europe: looking beyond Hungary and Poland. East Eur Polit 34(3):243–256

Clapham C (1996) Africa and the international system: the politics of state survival. Cambridge University Press, Cambridge

Damro C (2012) Market power Europe. J Eur Public Policy 19(5):682–699

Dicey A (1985) Introduction to the study of the law of the Constitution, 10th edn. Springer, Berlin

Duncombe C, Dunne T (2018) After liberal world order. Int Aff 94:25–42

Erbeznik K (2011) Money can't buy you law: the effects of foreign aid on the rule of law in developing countries. Indiana J Glob Leg Stud 18:873–900

Freyburg T, Lavenex S, Schimmelfennig F, Skripka T, Wetzel A (2011) Democracy promotion through functional cooperation? The case of the European Neighbourhood Policy. Democratization 18(4):1026–1054

Gammage C (2017) North-South regional trade agreements as legal regimes. A critical assessment of the EU-SADC Economic Partnership Agreement. Edward Elgar, Cheltenham

Grimm S, Mathis O (2017) Democratization via aid? The European Union's democracy promotion in the Western Balkans 1994–2010. Eur Union Polit 19(1)

Hachez N (2015) "Essential Elements" clauses in EU trade agreements: making trade work in a way that helps human rights. Leuven Centre for Global Governance Studies No 158. https://ghum. kuleuven.be/ggs/publications/working_papers/2015/158hachez. Last accessed 8 Feb 2019

Hallstein W (1979) Die Europäische Gemeinschaft. ECON, Munich

Haukkala H (2011) The European Union as regional normative hegemon: the case of European Neighbourhood Policy. In: Whitman R (ed) Normative power Europe: empirical and theoretical perspectives. Springer, Berlin, pp 1601–1622

Heinemann A (2007) International antitrust and intellectual property. In: Heath C, Sanders A (eds) Intellectual property and free trade agreements. Bloomsbury, Oxford, pp 261–283

Hirschmann A (1980) National power and the structure of foreign trade. University of California Press, Cambridge

Hofmann CH (2008) Mapping the European administrative space. West Eur Polit 31(4):662–676

Hooghe L, Marks G (2016) Europe's crises and political contestation. Paper presented at the Conference, "Theory Meets Crisis", pp 2–4, Robert Schuman Center, EUI. http://www. euengage.eu/wp-content/uploads/2016/05/Hooghe-Marks-Europes-Crises-and-Political-Contes tation.pdf. Last accessed 8 Feb 2019

Juncos A (2017) Resilience as a new European foreign policy paradigm: a pragmatist turn? Eur Secur 26(1):1–18

Karageorgou V (2014) Transparency as an evolving principle of EU law: regulative contours and implications. Rights2Info. https://www.right2info.org/resources/publications/eu-karageorgou-vasiliki-transparency-principle-as-an-evolving-principle-of-eu-law. Last accessed 8 Feb 2019

Kube V (2016) The European Union's external human rights commitment: what is the legal value of Art. 21 TEU? EUI Law 2016/10. http://cadmus.eui.eu/handle/1814/40426. Last accessed 8 Feb 2019

Lamprecht J (2014) Bargaining power in multilateral trade negotiations: Canada and Japan in the Uruguay Round and Doha Development Agenda. London School of Economics. http://etheses. lse.ac.uk/903/1/Lamprecht_Bargaining_power_multilateral_trade_negotiations.pdf.   Last accessed 8 Feb 2019

Larik L (2016) Foreign policy objectives in European constitutional law. Oxford University Press, Oxford

Lavenex S (2015) The external face of differentiated integration: third country participation in EU sectoral bodies. J Eur Public Policy 22(6):836–853

Manners I (2002) Normative power Europe: a contradiction in terms? J Common Mark Stud 40 (2):235–258

Meunier S, Nicolaïdis K (2006) The European Union as a conflicted trade power. J Eur Public Policy 13(6):906–925

Pech L (2009) The rule of law as a constitutional principle of the European Union. Jean Monnet Working Paper Series 4, pp 22–47. https://papers.ssrn.com/sol3/papers.cfm?abstract_ id=1463242. Last accessed 8 Feb 2019

Pech L (2012/2013) Rule of law as a guiding principle of the European Union's external action. CLEER Working Papers 2012/2013. https://www.asser.nl/upload/documents/2102012_33322cleer2012-3web.pdf. Last accessed 8 Feb 2019

Petrov R, Van der Loo G, Van Elsuwege P (2015) The EU-Ukraine Association Agreement: a new instrument of integration without membership. Kyiv-Mohyla Law Polit J (1):1–15

Rabinovych M (2017) The rule of law promotion through trade in the "Associated Neighbourhood". Polish Yearb Int Law. XXXVII:71–101

Risse T, Babayan N (2015) Democracy promotion and the challenge of illiberal regional powers: introduction to the special issue. Democratization 22:381–399

Rodrik D (2006) Goodbye Washington Consensus, Hello Washington Confusion? A review of the World Bank's economic growth in the 1990s: learning from a decade of reform. J Econ Lit XLIV:973–987

Schimelfennig F, Sedelmeier U (2004) Governance by conditionality: EU rule transfer to the candidate countries of Central and Eastern Europe. J Eur Public Policy 11(4):669–687

Sheppele K, Pech L (2018) What is rule of law backsliding? Verfassungsblog. https://verfassungsblog.de/what-is-rule-of-law-backsliding/. Last accessed 8 Feb 2019

Torma A (2011) The European Administrative Space (EAS). Eur Integr Stud 9(1):149–161

Tussie D, Saguier M (2013) The sweep of asymmetric trade negotiations: introduction and overview. In: Bilal S et al (eds) Asymmetric trade negotiations. Ashgate, Farnham

Van der Loo G (2016) The EU-Ukraine Association Agreement and deep and comprehensive free trade area: a new legal instrument for integration without membership. Brill, Nijhof

Wetzel A (2015) The substance of EU democracy promotion: introduction and conceptual framework. In: Wetzel A, Orbie J (eds) The substance of EU democracy promotion: concepts and cases. Palgrave McMillan, London

Maryna Rabinovych LL.M (Hamburg) is a PhD Candidate at the University of Hamburg and Global Community Manager at the Ukraine Democracy Initiative (University of Sydney). Her research interests include EU external relations law, EU trade law, trade and development nexus in the EU, Agenda 2030 and its implementation by the EU. Ms. Rabinovych held visiting positions at the Universities of Thessaloniki (2016/2017) and Vienna (2018). She holds an LL. B from Odessa National University and an LL.M in EU law from the University of Hamburg.

Challenges to International Investment Law Within the European Union

Luke Tattersall

Contents

1 Introduction

The past year has given rise to a number of developments effecting international investment law within the European Union. These events, when taken together, threaten the equilibrium of the current regime for resolving investor-State disputes within the EU. The following chapter considers the two most prominent of these developments; setting out what has occurred, the effects upon investment law within Europe and what the position is likely to be going forward. The first of these developments concerns the decision of the Court of Justice of the European Union which recently held that intra-EU investor-State arbitration clauses are contrary to EU law, with the effect that the clauses, the proceedings themselves and any subsequent awards are to be deemed invalid. This ruling is now binding on the courts of all European Member States. The second development comes as the European Commission has held that payments made by States to satisfy awards rendered by investor-State tribunals, be it in the context of intra-EU disputes or disputes concerning investors whose host State is outside the European Union, are in breach of the rules on EU State aid. Together these developments have the potential

L. Tattersall (✉)
Essex Court Chambers, London, UK
e-mail: LTattersall@essexcourt.net

© Springer Nature Switzerland AG 2019
M. Bungenberg et al. (eds.), *European Yearbook of International Economic Law 2019*,
European Yearbook of International Economic Law (2020) 10: 315–338,
https://doi.org/10.1007/8165_2019_44, Published online: 9 October 2019

to undermine the entire regime of investment protection within the European Union and threaten investment relations globally, as non-EU States begin to question whether their investors will continue to enjoy the same levels of protection afforded to the investors of Member States situated outside of the EU.

2 The *Achmea* Decision

In March 2018 the Grand Chamber of the Court of Justice of the European Union (the "CJEU") heard a preliminary reference from the German Federal Supreme Court in relation to an arbitral award that had been rendered in *Achmea v Slovak Republic*.[1] The Slovak Republic had brought an application in Germany to set aside the award made by a tribunal administered under the UNCITRAL rules and seated in Frankfurt. The arbitration had been commenced under the Netherlands-Slovakia BIT. The basis of the set aside application was that the tribunal lacked jurisdiction to hear the claim on the grounds that the investor-State arbitration clause was in breach of EU law. The Slovak Republic sought to argue that the arbitration clause was in breach of the Treaty of the Functioning of the European Union, specifically Articles 18 (non-discrimination on the grounds of nationality); 267 (the CJEU's jurisdiction to give rulings on the interpretation and application of EU law); and 344 (the exclusive jurisdiction of the EU to resolve matters concerning the interpretation of EU law). The thrust of the Slovak Republic's case was that investor-State arbitration breaches EU law as claims may require the tribunal to consider points of European law for which tribunals are not considered a competent court of the European Union.

Having considered the submissions of both parties, the CJEU found in favour of the Slovak Republic, holding that the arbitration clause contained in the BIT was in violation of EU law for the reasons outlined above.[2] The court explained that in cases involving intra-EU BITs, the domestic law of the respondent State will include EU law by virtue of being a Member State, and as a result an arbitration clause has the effect of removing disputes which have the potential to raise issues of EU law from the European court system.[3] The court noted that as the tribunal was not a court of a Member State, it had no power to make preliminary references to the CJEU, as domestic courts of Member States can.[4] The court also took issue with the fact that arbitral awards are final, subject only to limited review.[5] As a result, the CJEU found that the TFEU precluded the investor-State arbitration clause contained in the Netherlands-Slovakia BIT, as it undermined "*not only the principle of mutual trust between the Member States but also the preservation of the particular nature of the*

---

[1]*Achmea v Slovak Republic* UNCITRAL, PCA Case No. 2008-13 (December 2012).

[2]*Slovak Republic v Achmea* C-284/16 (6 March 2018).

[3]*Slovak Republic v Achmea* C-284/16 (6 March 2018) at [56].

[4]*Slovak Republic v Achmea* C-284/16 (6 March 2018) at [46]–[49].

[5]*Slovak Republic v Achmea* C-284/16 (6 March 2018) at [51]–[53].

law established by the Treaties", which accordingly has "*an adverse effect on the autonomy of EU law*".[6]

Interestingly, the preliminary reference from the German courts required the CJEU only to examine the clause contained in the Netherlands-Slovakia BIT, yet the court took the opportunity to find against investor-State arbitration clauses contained in BITs more generally.[7] As a result, the CJEU's ruling in *Achmea* represents a significant challenge to the international investment regime within the European Union and has the potential to undermine more than 200 intra-EU BITS which are currently in force between Member States. The CJEU's decision is in many respects surprising as all of the previous entities which had considered the claim that investor-State arbitration is contrary to EU law had come down firmly against the proposition. For instance, the Higher Regional Court of Germany concluded that the arbitration provisions were compatible with EU law, as had the EU's Advocate General—Melchior Wathelet—in his Opinion delivered on 19 September 2017.[8] The Advocate General's Opinion is long, well-reasoned and goes into detail in respect to each of the points raised in opposition to investor-State arbitration. AG Wathelet noted that the question before the European Courts was one of "*fundamental importance*" in light of the number of intra-EU BITs currently in force.[9] Wathelet was of the view that "*the risk which, according to the Commission, intra-EU BITs represent to the uniformity and effectiveness of EU law is greatly exaggerated*".[10] In supporting this argument, he noted that out of a significant number of investment claims that had been decided, only one example could be cited of an award which was inconsistent with EU law.[11]

The Advocate General sought to highlight a number of difficulties with the arguments of those States which advanced the view that BITs are contrary to EU law. First, the AG split the States into two groups, those who were in favour of investor-State arbitration and those who considered it to be a breach of EU law. Of the latter group, he said that "*it is surprising. . .that, in the second group, which maintains that intra-EU BITs are incompatible with the EU and FEU Treaties, only the Italian Republic has terminated its intra-EU BITs. . .whereas the other Member States in that group maintain them in force. . .thus allowing their own investors to benefit from them. In effect, a large number of investment arbitrations have been launched by investors from those Member States and are often brought against another Member State in the same group*".[12] The second difficulty arose in relation to the European Commission's stance on investor-State arbitration. Wathelet

---

[6]*Slovak Republic v Achmea* C-284/16 (6 March 2018) at [58]–[62].

[7]*Slovak Republic v Achmea* C-284/16 (6 March 2018) at [60].

[8]Opinion of Advocate General Wathelet C-284/16 (19 September 2017); Higher Regional Court of Frankfurt 18 December 2014.

[9]Opinion of Advocate General Wathelet C-284/16 (19 September 2017) at [3].

[10]Opinion of Advocate General Wathelet C-284/16 (19 September 2017) at [44].

[11]Opinion of Advocate General Wathelet C-284/16 (19 September 2017) at [44]–[46].

[12]Opinion of Advocate General Wathelet C-284/16 (19 September 2017) at [37].

summarised the position, saying *"the Commission's argument is also striking"* as *"for a very long time, the argument of the EU institutions, including the Commission, was that, far from being incompatible with EU law, BITs were instruments necessary to prepare for the accession to the Union of the countries of Central and Eastern Europe"*.[13] Wathelet explained that *"the Association Agreements between the Union and candidate countries contained provisions for the conclusion of BITs between Member States and candidate countries"*.[14] As a result, the Advocate General found it hard to accept the argument that all intra-EU investor-State arbitration clauses were, and always had been, contrary to EU law since the time of the Member's accession to the European Union. Awards would be invalid on the basis that the arbitration clauses had been void *ab initio*. The European Commission responded by submitting that whilst States were encouraged to form BITs in order to facilitate their accession to the European Union, that upon joining, the arbitration agreements contained within the BITs became void on account of being contrary to EU law.[15] This argument was given little weight as Wathelet highlighted that had that been the case, *"why did the accession treaties not provide for the termination of those agreements"* upon membership to the Union.[16]

The Advocate General also recognised a more fundamental point, which is that arbitration provisions contained in BITs are there to give effect to the protections enshrined in the investment treaties which the relevant States have signed, without which such protections would largely be rendered futile. The AG described the arbitration provisions as *"creat[ing] a forum in which the investor may bring an action against the State in order to rely on the rights conferred on him, in public international law, by the BIT, a possibility that would not be open to him without that article"*.[17] He went on to state that it is uncertain whether *"an individual would be able to rely on the provisions of an international treaty before the national courts, since those courts automatically exclude that possibility on the ground that treaties do not create rights and obligations between States,...[and] do not guarantee individuals the possibility of relying on the provisions of the treaties"*.[18] The AG therefore concluded that *"far from expressing lack of trust in other Member State's legal systems"*, investor-State arbitration *"is the only means of giving full practical effect to the BITs by creating a specialised forum where investors may rely on the rights conferred on them by the BITs"*.[19]

This reasoning is buttressed by the fact that the various entities of the European Union have not previously found that international arbitration in respect of other, non-investment, disputes in which questions of EU law may arise is contrary to EU

---

[13]Opinion of Advocate General Wathelet C-284/16 (19 September 2017) at [40].

[14]Opinion of Advocate General Wathelet C-284/16 (19 September 2017) at [40].

[15]Opinion of Advocate General Wathelet C-284/16 (19 September 2017) at [41].

[16]Opinion of Advocate General Wathelet C-284/16 (19 September 2017) at [41].

[17]Opinion of Advocate General Wathelet C-284/16 (19 September 2017) at [264].

[18]Opinion of Advocate General Wathelet C-284/16 (19 September 2017) at [265].

[19]Opinion of Advocate General Wathelet C-284/16 (19 September 2017) at [266].

law by undermining the autonomy of the Union's legal system. To this, the AG said[20]:

> If international arbitration does not undermine the allocation of powers fixed by the EU and FEU Treaties and, accordingly, the autonomy of the EU legal system, even where the State is a party to the arbitral proceedings, I think that the same must apply in the case of international arbitration between investors and States, all the more so because the inevitable presence of the State implies greater transparency. ...If the Commission's logic were followed, any arbitration would be liable to undermine the allocation of powers fixed by the EU and FEU Treaties and, accordingly, the autonomy of the EU legal system.
>
> Nor am I able to see how the arbitral proceedings at issue...would breach the principle of mutual trust, since those proceedings took place only with the consent of the Member States concerned and Achmea's freely expressed choice to use the facility which the Member States offered it.

The likelihood that European law will be applied correctly, or that failures will be detected, is in fact greater in respect to investor-State disputes than in international arbitrations more generally, as any subsequent measures which the State takes on account of the award can be challenged under the relevant provisions of the TFEU if contrary to EU law, whereas the subsequent actions of an individual are not open to the same redress. The CJEU in *Achmea* sought to address this point, but failed to engage in a detailed analysis. The court accepted that points of EU law have the potential to arise in international arbitration and that this does not violate EU law. The court sought to justify the distinction by explaining that "*[investment] arbitration proceedings...are different from commercial arbitration proceedings. While the latter originate in the freely expressed wishes of the parties, the former derive from a treaty by which Member States agree to remove from the jurisdiction of their own courts...disputes which may concern the application or interpretation of EU law*".[21] However, this distinction does not withstand scrutiny. The European Union's concern is that questions of EU law are being dealt with outside the courts of the Member States. The fact that international arbitration arises by virtue of the consent of two parties, whereas investment arbitration arises by virtue of States accepting that investors can bring claims against them, does nothing to alleviate the EU's primary concern. In both instances the process of dispute resolution has come about by way of consent. Within an investor-State context, States do not bring claims against investors – the system is one sided in that only investors may initiate claims. By commencing arbitration under the relevant provisions of an investment treaty the party is accepting the State's offer to arbitrate. Arbitration is unique in the sense that it can only occur if both parties to the dispute have consented to its use. The notion that international arbitration ensures the proper application of EU law whereas investment arbitration does not cannot be sustained upon the grounds on which the CJEU has sought to frame the argument. Similarly, outside of the ICSID regime, which the court chose not to comment upon, both international and investment

---

[20]Opinion of Advocate General Wathelet C-284/16 (19 September 2017) at [259].

[21]*Slovak Republic v Achmea* C-284/16 (6 March 2018).

arbitration awards are subject to the same process of appeal and enforcement through the domestic laws of the relevant State and the New York Convention. The chance for the domestic courts of Member States to police the application of EU law is therefore identical regardless of which form of arbitration is in issue. The EU's stance that investment arbitration is in breach of EU law therefore appears to present itself more as a policy rather than as a *de jure* application of European law.

Having considered the difficulties faced by the applicant States' arguments, the AG addressed the Articles which the Slovak Republic claimed the arbitration clause was in breach of. Wathelet ultimately held that Articles 18, 267 and 344 of the TFEU should not be interpreted to preclude the use of investor-State arbitration in intra-EU BITs concluded before accession to the European Union, with the effect that investors would remain entitled to bring claims and have awards enforced accordingly.[22] It is perhaps surprising therefore that the CJEU proceeded to find that intra-EU investment arbitration clauses are nevertheless in breach of EU law, with the effect that such provisions are deemed invalid from the date of accession to the European Union, without any reference being made to the Advocate General's Opinion.

2.1 Investment Tribunals' Response to Achmea

As a result of the *Achmea* decision, a significant number of tribunals hearing investor-State claims have had to deal with the ramifications as States seek to argue that the tribunals lack jurisdiction to hear the claims. Of note is the award in *Masdar v Spain*[23] which was handed down on 16 May 2018, in which Spain was ordered to pay EUR 64.5 million to Masdar for breaching the FET provisions in the Energy Charter Treaty (the "ECT"). Following the *Achmea* decision, Spain submitted an application challenging the jurisdiction of the tribunal. In response, the tribunal held that the *Achmea* decision applies only to bilateral investment treaties, and thus has "*no bearing*" upon disputes brought under the ECT, which is distinct as being a multilateral framework agreement.[24] The tribunal considered that the CJEU's decision was of "*limited application*", as it was addressed to the Netherlands-Slovakia BIT and, taken at its highest, only to bilateral investment agreements more generally.[25]

The tribunal noted that the Advocate General in his opinion had expressly drawn a distinction between bilateral investment treaties and the ECT.[26] The tribunal was of

---

[22]Opinion of Advocate General Wathelet C-284/16 (19 September 2017).

[23]*Masdar v Spain* ICSID Case No. ARB/14/1 (16 May 2018).

[24]*Masdar v Spain* ICSID Case No. ARB/14/1 (16 May 2018) at [678], [683].

[25]*Masdar v Spain* ICSID Case No. ARB/14/1 (16 May 2018) at [679].

[26]See Opinion of Advocate General Wathelet C-284/16 (19 September 2017) at [43]: "*All the Member States and the Union have ratified the Energy Charter Treaty...That multilateral*

the view that the CJEU could have addressed the ECT or like agreements in its judgment had it wanted to make its findings applicable to arbitrations under the treaty. However, since the judgment omitted any reference, the tribunal concluded that "*the Achmea Judgment has no bearing upon the present case*".[27]

Building upon the award in *Masdar v Spain*, and also concerned with the ECT, is the recent decision of *Vattenfall v Germany* handed down in August 2018.[28] The case concerned an ICSID claim brought by a Swedish energy company against the Republic of Germany. The tribunal rejected Germany's contention that it lacked jurisdiction as a result of the decision in *Achmea*, agreeing with the tribunal in *Masdar v Spain* that *Achmea* concerned a bilateral investment treaty and was silent as to its effects with respect to the Energy Charter Treaty, under which Vattenfall had commenced the arbitration.

The European Commission argued in *Vattenfall* that EU law was part of the "*relevant rules of international law applicable…between the parties*" that must be taken into account when interpreting the treaty.[29] It was accepted that the rules of international law should be taken into account, but not at the expense of the ordinary meaning of the treaty's text. The tribunal found that it "*remains unclear*" what was established in *Achmea* as the court held that agreements "*such as*" the Netherlands-Slovakia BIT were incompatible with EU law, but said nothing of multilateral agreements.[30] The tribunal therefore felt that it was "*an open question whether the same considerations necessarily apply to the ECT*".[31] As a result it was held that EU law did not need to be taken into account when interpreting the arbitration clause. In any event, if EU law fell to be considered, it would not justify an interpretation that so "*radically departed*" from the ordinary meaning of the clause.[32]

The tribunal found nothing to indicate that intra-EU claims were prohibited under the text of the ECT. In fact, the ECT expressly contemplates the possibility of arbitration against an EU Member State by an investor of "*another Contracting Party*", and the tribunal saw no basis to read "*another*" as referring only to non-EU States.[33] The tribunal also considered that there was a "*simpler and clearer*" way of resolving the matter, as Article 16 of the ECT provided that where other international

---

treaty…*operates even between Member States, since it was concluded not as an agreement between the Union and its Member States…all the Contracting Parties participate on an equal footing….if no EU institution and no Member State sought an opinion from the Court on the compatibility of that treaty…that is because none of them had the slightest suspicion that it might be incompatible.*"

[27]*Masdar v Spain* ICSID Case No. ARB/14/1 (16 May 2018) at [678].

[28]*Vattenfall v Germany* ICSID Case No. ARB/12/12 (31 August 2018).

[29]Under Article 31(3)(c) of the Vienna Convention on the Law of Treaties: "*There shall be taken into account, together with the context: any relevant rules of international law applicable in the relations between the parties.*"

[30]*Vattenfall v Germany* ICSID Case No. ARB/12/12 (31 August 2018) at [161].

[31]*Vattenfall v Germany* ICSID Case No. ARB/12/12 (31 August 2018) at [161].

[32]*Vattenfall v Germany* ICSID Case No. ARB/12/12 (31 August 2018) at [167].

[33]*Vattenfall v Germany* ICSID Case No. ARB/12/12 (31 August 2018) at [171], [189].

agreements bore upon the same subject matter, parties could not derogate from the ECT in circumstances where the provisions under the ECT were more favourable to the investor.[34] The tribunal doubted whether the EU treaties "*concerned*" the same subject-matter as the ECT, but noted that if they did, Article 16 would apply.[35] As Article 26 permitting arbitration was more favourable to investors than the CJEU's judgment prohibiting arbitration, Article 16 would result in the arbitration clause prevailing. The tribunal explained that, "*while the ordinary meaning of Article 26 was already clear, Article 16 confirms beyond doubt that [Germany's] proposed reading...is untenable*".[36]

The tribunal formed the view that if the European Commission or EU Member States considered the ECT to be incompatible with EU law, they must "*take the necessary action to remedy that situation*"; but that it is not for tribunals to "*redraft the treaty*".[37] Germany contended that any award made by the tribunal would be contrary to EU law and therefore unenforceable. While the tribunal agreed that it had a duty to render enforceable awards, its primary duty was to resolve investor-State disputes arising out of the treaty provisions.[38] In the tribunal's view, any subsequent questions of enforceability were a distinct matter and should not be dispositive of the question of jurisdiction.

This line of reasoning is swiftly becoming entrenched, as in *Greentech v Spain*, which was handed down in November 2018, the tribunal adopted the reasoning of the tribunals in *Masdar* and *Vattenfall*, concluding that the *Achmea* decision was "*irrelevant to [Spain's] jurisdictional objection*" as its application was limited to the Netherlands-Slovakia BIT or to bilateral investment treaties, but did not apply to multilateral treaties such as the ECT.[39]

A further post-*Achmea* decision of significant consequence can be seen in the award of *UP & CD Holdings v Hungary*[40] which was handed down in October 2018. The arbitration had been commenced under the France-Hungary BIT and adminis-tered by ICSID. In that case, the tribunal found that the CJEU's ruling was inappli-cable as its jurisdiction derived from the ICSID Convention, which the tribunal considered placed it in a "*public international law context and not in a national or regional context*".[41] The tribunal held that the *Achmea* decision was premised on the fact that Germany was the seat of the arbitration and thus German law would apply to any review of the validity of the award. Whilst the arbitration in *UP & CD Holdings* was seated in England, the courts would not be permitted to review the validity of the award as Article 54 of the ICSID Convention requires awards to be enforced in the

---

[34]*Vattenfall v Germany* ICSID Case No. ARB/12/12 (31 August 2018) at [192].

[35]*Vattenfall v Germany* ICSID Case No. ARB/12/12 (31 August 2018) at [194].

[36]*Vattenfall v Germany* ICSID Case No. ARB/12/12 (31 August 2018) at [196].

[37]*Vattenfall v Germany* ICSID Case No. ARB/12/12 (31 August 2018) at [208].

[38]*Vattenfall v Germany* ICSID Case No. ARB/12/12 (31 August 2018) at [230]ff.

[39]*Greentech v Spain* SCC Case No. 2015/150 (November 2018) at [195].

[40]*UP & CD Holdings v Hungary* ICSID Case No. ARB/13/35 (October 2018).

[41]*UP & CD Holdings v Hungary* ICSID Case No. ARB/13/35 (October 2018) at [253].

territories of signatory States as if they were a judgement of the courts of that State.[42] Further, ICSID awards are only open to challenge through the annulment procedures contained in Article 52 of the ICSID Convention which occurs by way of an international *ad hoc* committee, meaning that the awards are never subject to review by national courts.[43] In essence, the tribunal sought to insulate all ICSID investment arbitrations from the effects of the CJEU's ruling.

The tribunal also considered that *Achmea "cannot be understood or interpreted as creating or supporting an argument that, by its accession to the EU, Hungary was no longer bound by the ICSID Convention"*.[44] Hungary had not withdrawn from the ICSID Convention, nor was there any implied withdrawal.[45] The *Achmea* decision did not have the effect of Hungary retroactively withdrawing its consent to arbitrate when it acceded to the EU, and, even if it had, the 20-year survival clause in Article 12(2) precluded any *"implicit termination"* of the arbitration clause contained in the BIT.[46] The tribunal therefore decided that there was no ground to disturb the finding that it had jurisdiction to determine the dispute.[47]

Similarly, in *Marfin Investment Group v Cyprus*, heard in July 2018, Cyprus sought to rely on the *Achmea* judgment to argue that the BIT's arbitration clause was invalid under EU law.[48] The tribunal, relying heavily upon the reasoning in *EURAM v. Slovak Republic*, found that the TFEU and BIT were not concerned with the same subject matter and therefore Articles 30 and 59 of the VCLT relating to successive treaties and the implied termination of treaties were irrelevant. As for the argument that the treaty was incompatible with EU law which was to take precedence, the tribunal chose to focus upon a plain reading of the text of the ICSID Convention under which the arbitration was administered. The tribunal concluded that the Convention granted it jurisdiction, noting that when both parties have given their consent to arbitrate *"no party may withdraw that consent unilaterally"*.[49] Cyprus's offer to arbitrate contained in the BIT was viewed as solidifying its willingness to take part in arbitral proceedings and to satisfy any awards that may be made. The tribunal therefore held that *"the principle of legal certainty entitles investors to legitimately rely upon a State's written consent to arbitrate disputes as long as that consent has not been withdrawn through the proper procedures"* contained in the treaty.[50] As a result, the tribunal held that there can be no implied termination of the BIT to the detriment of investors who had legitimately relied upon the treaty's arbitration clause. As the TFEU and the BIT did not concern the same subject matter

---

[42]*UP & CD Holdings v Hungary* ICSID Case No. ARB/13/35 (October 2018) at [256].

[43]*UP & CD Holdings v Hungary* ICSID Case No. ARB/13/35 (October 2018) at [255].

[44]*UP & CD Holdings v Hungary* ICSID Case No. ARB/13/35 (October 2018) at [258].

[45]*UP & CD Holdings v Hungary* ICSID Case No. ARB/13/35 (October 2018) at [258]–[260].

[46]*UP & CD Holdings v Hungary* ICSID Case No. ARB/13/35 (October 2018) at [264]–[265].

[47]*UP & CD Holdings v Hungary* ICSID Case No. ARB/13/35 (October 2018) at [266].

[48]*Marfin Investment Group v Cyprus* ICSID Case No. ARB/13/27 (July 2018).

[49]*Marfin Investment Group v Cyprus* ICSID Case No. ARB/13/27 (July 2018) at [592].

[50]*Marfin Investment Group v Cyprus* ICSID Case No. ARB/13/27 (July 2018) at [593].

the rules of treaty interpretation effecting implied termination and precedent of conflicting agreements did not fall to be considered.

Cyprus further sought to argue that any award would be unenforceable as the courts of Member States would find that the tribunal had no jurisdiction to hear claims under the BIT. The tribunal considered that whilst this *"may well be correct"* its jurisdiction was not to be determined by the *"national rules governing the enforceability of arbitral awards."* It would be for national courts *"to draw the necessary consequences from the Achmea judgment and their national laws with respect to the enforceability of this Award"*.[51]

The consensus of the publicly available awards made in relation to the *Achmea* judgment is that, for the time being, tribunals appear to have insulated claims arising under both the ICSID Convention and any multilateral investment agreements (including free trade and mega-regional agreements) from the effects of *Achmea*, leaving only intra-EU BITs at the mercy of the CJEU's ruling. This is largely as a result of the court's judgment being framed in broad terms and failing to draw distinctions between the various forms of treaties under which investment protections can arise. However, it may be that in response to the jurisprudence cited above, certain organs of the European Union will be minded in the near future to publish a clarification, expressly stating which forms of treaty and arbitration regimes the judgment applies to. However, until then, tribunals appear to have crafted a safe harbour from the storm.

2.2   *Domestic Court Decisions Concerning Achmea*

Whilst a significant and increasing number of tribunals are having to grapple with the effects of *Achmea* as States seek to oust jurisdiction in intra-EU disputes, it is not only arbitrators who are facing difficulties. State parties are also seeking redress in the domestic courts of States in an attempt to resist enforcement of awards rendered in intra-EU investment disputes. So far, the most notable decision has been that of the German Federal Supreme Court, who are responsible for first submitting the preliminary reference to the CJEU, thereby sparking the *Achmea* decision. It is perhaps unsurprising therefore that the German Federal Court followed the ruling of the CJEU, finding that no arbitration agreement had existed between the parties.[52] Notably, the German court held that Slovakia's offer to arbitrate investor-State disputes under the Netherlands-Slovakia BIT was rendered inapplicable when Slovakia became a member of the European Union in May 2004, at which point the offer was in breach of EU law which takes supremacy. The court noted that, pursuant to section 1059(2)(1)(a) of the German Code of Civil Procedure, any arbitral award may be set aside if the arbitration agreement is invalid. The court found that this

---

[51]*Marfin Investment Group v Cyprus* ICSID Case No. ARB/13/27 (July 2018) at [596].
[52]German Federal Supreme Court, 31 October 2018.

set-aside power was not limited exclusively to situations in which an agreement existed but was invalid, but also extended to situations where an arbitration agreement was *ex post facto* non-existent. The court reasoned that, absent the CJEU's decision, the arbitration clause would be read as a unilateral offer to arbitrate and an agreement would be formed when the investor initiated proceedings thereby accepting the offer. However, pursuant to Article 8(6) of the BIT, the law of the respondent State was part of the law applicable to the dispute. The court held that as Achmea initiated proceedings after Slovakia had become a member of the European Union, European law was applicable to the dispute, being part of Slovakia's domestic law. The German court agreed that the arbitration clause endangered the autonomy of the Union's legal system and was incompatible with the principles of mutual trust and cooperation under EU law. The court added that, in cases of conflict, EU law prevailed over any other international agreement concluded by Member States of the European Union.

Interestingly, the German court found that the Slovak Republic had not induced Achmea to invest on the basis of the arbitration clause, however, this reasoning is difficult to accept when one considers that investment arbitration exists to assure investors that they can have recourse to an impartial third-party system to resolve their disputes, without which many investors, particularly in less developed nations, would likely be reluctant to invest without further assurances.

It is possible that by relying upon Article 1059 of the German Code of Civil Procedure, the Federal Supreme Court has opened the door to refusing the recognition and enforcement of non-ICSID awards rendered in intra-EU BIT claims outside of Germany. This is because the wording of Article 1059 closely mirrors that of Article 5(1)(a) of the New York Convention. Hence the court's reasoning could easily be transposed to situations where the courts of other Member States are confronted with requests for the recognition and enforcement of intra-EU BIT awards under the New York Convention. However, the same reasoning cannot apply to the enforcement of ICSID awards, as their enforcement is governed by Article 53 of the ICSID Convention.[53]

The courts of Germany are not the only domestic courts to rule on the effects of *Achmea*. The Svea Court of Appeal in Stockholm, Sweden has had to consider two set-aside applications relating to investor-State awards which are being challenged in respect to the tribunal's jurisdiction following the CJEU's ruling.[54] The first set-aside application pertains to an award issued in *PL Holdings v Poland*, which was commenced under the Luxemburg-Poland BIT.[55] In the *PL Holdings* application both parties submitted expert reports on the role of EU law in determining the

---

[53] Article 53(1) sets out that: "The award shall be binding on the parties and shall not be subject to any appeal or to any other remedy except those provided for in this Convention. Each party shall abide by and comply with the terms of the award except to the extent that enforcement shall have been stayed pursuant to the relevant provisions of this Convention."

[54] Svea Court of Appeal, Case No T 8538-17; Case No T 12033-17.

[55] *PL Holdings v Poland* SCC Case No. V 2-14/163 (June 2017).

scope of the arbitration agreement. Notably, Poland submitted an expert opinion of a former judge on the CJEU. In this instance, the Svea Court of Appeal went to great lengths to find that the arbitration was not invalid based upon jurisdictional argument that the arbitration agreement contained in the BIT was contrary to EU law. Instead, the court chose to interpret the CJEU's judgment as having the following effects:

> [T]he CJEU's ruling does not mean that an arbitration agreement between an investor and a Member State in a specific case violates the TFEU. To the contrary – where there is joint expression of party autonomy– there is no impediment against arbitration, provided that fundamental EU regulations can be considered within the limited review available to the Member States' court systems, and, when appropriate, can be made subject of a request to the CJEU for a preliminary ruling.... .i.e. as regards Swedish courts, the review of whether an arbitral award is invalid or challengeable in accordance with the SAA.

> The conclusion from the Achmea ruling is therefore that articles 267 and 344 TFEU would not as such preclude Poland and PL Holdings from entering into an arbitration agreement and participating in arbitral proceedings regarding an investment-related dispute.

The argument that so long as both parties have consented to the arbitration and that the final award can be subject to some form of review within the domestic court system in the place of enforcement, and that the domestic courts will be able to submit questions of EU law to the CJEU by way of preliminary reference, offers an interesting line of reasoning, which, in time, may form the basis for the courts of the Member States to permit investor-State awards to be upheld by relying upon this inventive interpretation of the CJEU's decision in *Achmea*. The second set-aside application brought before the Stockholm courts concerns an award issued in *Novenergia v Spain* which was commenced under the Energy Charter Treaty.[56] In both set-aside applications the Svea Court of Appeal stayed the enforcement of the awards pending the outcome of any subsequent challenges. Had the Svea courts chosen to follow the lines of jurisprudence developed by arbitral tribunals thus far they may have been minded to find that the *PL Holdings* award should be set-aside on the basis that it was initiated under the BIT whereas the *Novenergia* award could be upheld given that it was initiated under the ECT. However, it is interesting to note that the courts did not take this approach, perhaps considering the distinction drawn between BITs and other treaties containing investment provisions to be overly contrived. Instead, the courts have sought to chart a new path by relying upon what are largely novel arguments with respect to how the decision in *Achmea* should be applied. It is likely that parties engaged in *Achmea*-based jurisdictional challenges before both tribunal and domestic courts will seek to rely upon the judgment as providing a persuasive example of how the higher courts of an EU Member State have chosen to interpret and apply *Achmea*. Notably, the CJEU has not yet issued national courts with any guidance as to how investors should seek to rely upon the

---

[56]*Novenergia v Spain* SCC Case No. 2015/063 (February 2018).

protections under the investment treaties if the arbitration clauses are held to be invalid.[57]

2.3   Member States' Reactions to Achmea

On 17 January 2019 the 28 Member States of the Union released a joint statement entitled a declaration on the legal consequences of *Achmea* to investment protection within the EU.[58] In this, the Member States declared that the law of the Union takes precedence over all BITs concluded between Member States and that the arbitration clauses are contrary to EU law. As a result, it was held that all investor-State tribunals lack jurisdiction as no valid offer to arbitrate exists between the States party to the underlying treaties.

In respect to the issue of how investors ought to protect their investments in other EU States, the declaration holds that all Member States are *"obliged to provide remedies sufficient to ensure the effective legal protection of investors' rights under Union law".*[59] This entails that the Member States consider the current EU regime of investment provisions suitable to provide protection. However, the States were also clearly alert to the fact that the sparse framework of investment protection under EU law is not comparable to the body of jurisprudence that has built up around the protections granted by the majority of bilateral investment treaties *vis-à-vis* the FET, MFN, national treatment, security and expropriation standards (etc.). It was declared therefore that the Member States along with the Commission *"will intensify discussions without undue delay with the aim of better ensuring complete, strong and effective protection of investments within the European Union"*, indicating that the Union intends to create a body of protection standards akin to those found in international investment law which will apply to all intra-EU investors but will operate under the exclusive competence of the Union as a matter of EU law.[60] Such a scheme would have the intended consequence of removing any investment matters from the purview of arbitration and seating them firmly within the jurisdiction of the courts of Member States.

---

[57]Although, it should be noted that the European Commission has put out an extensive document detailing how investors may seek to protect their investments under provisions of EU law within the courts of the Member States, yet nothing has been said as to how the parties can rely upon the specific protections granted under investment treaties (such as expropriation and fair and equitable treatment, for example). See https://eur-lex.europa.eu/legal-content/EN/TXT/?uri=COM:2018:0547:FIN (last accessed May 2019).

[58]*Declaration of the Member States On the Legal Consequences of Achmea* (https://ec.europa.eu/info/publications/190117-bilateral-investment-treaties_en) (last accessed May 2019).

[59]*Declaration of the Member States On the Legal Consequences of Achmea*, p. 2.

[60]*Declaration of the Member States On the Legal Consequences of Achmea*, p. 3.

Going forward, the 28 Member States declared that they would "*inform*" investment tribunals of the "*legal consequences*" of *Achmea* in all pending proceedings.[61] They will also request the courts of Member States to set aside awards where applicable and to refuse their enforcement. It was declared that Member States would "*inform the investor community*" that no new intra-EU arbitrations should be initiated in the future.[62] With respect to these declarations, whilst they are termed as proclamations, Member States in fact have limited powers to facilitate their intended effects. States can inform investment tribunals of what they perceive the intended effects of a judgment of another court are, however, ultimately it is for the tribunal itself to review the treaty, the relevant principles of public international law and any other authorities to determine the issues according. As can be seen, investment tribunals are already fully aware of the stance that the Court of Justice, the European Commission and the majority of Member States are taking with respect to the issue of jurisdiction following *Achmea*, therefore informing tribunals of the legal consequences in practice adds very little. Similarly, requesting the courts of Member States not to enforce awards and to set them aside where possible is sometime that Member States are already doing in a large number of intra-EU proceedings in cases where awards have been rendered in favour of investors. Requesting the courts to take a course of action simply means that the respondent-State will appear with the goal of resisting enforcement, there is nothing monumental behind this declaration, it will still remain open to the courts of all Member States to review the relevant BIT, the applicable law, the arbitral rules and any other international obligations which the States have signed up to, for example the ICSID and New York Conventions, in determining whether the awards ought to be enforced. As for informing the investor community that no new intra-EU arbitrations should be commenced, the investment community, or at least their legal representatives, will be aware of the effects of *Achmea*, and Member States can do nothing to prevent investors from initiating claims under the relevant treaties. Therefore, whilst the declarations may appear stark at first instance, upon inspection they are in practice merely political statements of intent.

The declarations which are likely to have more wide ranging effects are those in which the Member States agreed, in light of *Achmea*, to "*terminate all bilateral investment treaties concluded between them by means of a plurilateral treaty or, where. . .more expedient, bilaterally*".[63] It was also held that Member States will make "*best efforts*" to ratify and approve plurilateral or bilateral treaties terminating their existing stock of EU-BITs by no later than 6th December 2019. This represents a significant undertaking on the part of the Member States, under which they have sided with the Commission in agreeing to hand over exclusive competence of investment matters between themselves to the European Union. Further, the tight deadline of 6th December, which gives Member States less than 12 months to

---

[61] *Declaration of the Member States On the Legal Consequences of Achmea*, p. 3.

[62] *Declaration of the Member States On the Legal Consequences of Achmea*, p. 3.

[63] *Declaration of the Member States On the Legal Consequences of Achmea*, p. 4.

facilitate the removal of treaty-based investment protection from Europe, represents a hasty and arguably lofty goal. However, given that all 28 Member States are agreed that there should be no intra-EU bilateral investment treaties it does, theoretically, remain open to them to facilitate this transition within the time frame in light of a unanimous consensus. It is somewhat concerning that this statement has been made without any guidance being given to investors with regards to what their rights will be in the intervening period and how long any hang-over period will be in which investors are permitted to bring claims.

Little has been said by the European Commission or the Member States with respect to the effects of sunset or survival clauses contained in the relevant treaties. Ordinarily, such clauses would result in the protection standards under the treaty being extended for years, and in some cases decades, following a treaty's termination. The declaration briefly mentions that the Member States consider the survival clauses found in intra-EU BITs to be inapplicable. However, the answer as to their applicability is of course a far more nuanced question and will no doubt result in a significant number of arbitral proceedings being brought to determine the effects of these clauses, which differ from treaty to treaty. Theoretically it remains open to Member States to seek to terminate their bilateral investment treaties by way of a two-stage process in which they would first seek to amend the terms of the survival clauses and then seek to engage the termination provisions. This approach was adopted successfully by the Czech Republic in 2010 to terminate BITs with Denmark, Slovenia, Malta and Italy.[64] However, it would remain open to investors to seek to challenge this method before a tribunal.

With respect to awards which have been made in favour of investors in intra-EU proceedings, the Member States have agreed that those which can no longer be annulled or set aside and which have voluntarily been complied with or enforced prior to the *Achmea* judgment should not be challenged. This is a relatively meek concession given that the Member States will have already paid the award, or be in the process of paying, and any route to resisting enforcement has already been waived. What this declaration likely refers to is the European Commission's stance on classifying awards paid in intra-EU investment disputes as illegal State aid. However, despite the declarations made by the Member States, the Commission is still pursuing this line of argument against a number of awards, and as the declaration was not on behalf of the Commission it is not binding upon it, and therefore carries little weight in reassuring investors who have had awards satisfied by Member States.

Of particular interest is the approach of Member States to the issues arising from the Energy Charter Treaty, which, as discussed above, tribunals have sought to insulate on the basis that it is not a bilateral investment treaty. Whilst the Member States are agreed with respect to what should happen to the intra-EU BITs, they do not speak with one voice concerning the ECT. 21 of the Member States have

---

[64]"*Czech Republic Terminates Investment Treaties In Such a Way As To Cast Doubt on Residual Legal Protection For Existing Investments*" (Investment Arbitration Reporter, 1 February 2011).

declared that the *Achmea* judgment applies with equal force to both BITs and the ECT. The States explained that the investor-State arbitration clause contained in the ECT, as currently interpreted by tribunals, is incompatible with EU law and will have to be disapplied. Whilst 21 of the Member States intend for *Achmea* to apply with equal force to arbitrations initiated under the ECT, they recognise that the awards handed down by tribunals are likely to carry significant weight, and thus have declared that they, along with the Commission, will "*discuss without undue delay whether any additional steps are necessary to draw all the consequences from the Achmea judgment in relation to the intra-EU application of the Energy Charter Treaty*".[65] It is likely, therefore, that if investment tribunals continue to shield ECT claims from the CJEU's ruling, that the Member States and the Union will need to amend the ECT to remove investment arbitration as the means of dispute resolution with respect to intra-EU claims. However, it is likely that any such amendments would take time and prove more challenging that the plurilateral amendments being considered in respect to the intra-EU BITs. In contrast, Sweden, Finland, Slovenia, Malta, Luxembourg and Hungary have dissented with the majority, and instead consider that *Achmea* is silent as to the effects of the investor-State arbitration clause found in the ECT and thus that it is of no effect to pending and prospective claims under the treaty. It is clear that this disagreement alone has the potential to stall any attempts made to remove investor-State arbitration from intra-EU disputes commenced under the ECT.

Investors who have initiated or are considering initiating intra-EU investment proceedings under BITs currently face a significant degree of uncertainty as the Member States have failed to clarify what will happen to awards obtained by investors. All that has been said is that the Member States will discuss, when drafting the plurilateral treaty to terminate the stock of intra-EU BITs, the "*practical arrangements, in conformity with Union law, for such arbitral awards and settlements. This is without prejudice to the lack of jurisdiction of arbitral tribunals in pending intra-EU cases*".[66] This statement is interesting as it upholds the fact that States consider that investment tribunals lack jurisdiction to hear claims, yet puts on hold the issue of what will become of any awards made by those tribunals. If a tribunal lacks jurisdiction then its award is invalid and unenforceable. However, it appears that the Member States are envisaging a more diplomatic solution in which potentially some compensation or settlement will be reached in respect to those awards made in the intervening period. As is evident, the Member States' pronouncements thus far have been extremely vague, resulting in a situation in which investors are left in the dark as to the sustainability of their claims, the protection of their investments and the enforceability of any awards, giving rise to a highly unsatisfactory situation. This is particularly acute in light of the fact that investors were in large part enticed to invest in other European jurisdictions secure in the knowledge that their investments would attract the protections set out in the treaties

---

[65]*Declaration of the Member States On the Legal Consequences of Achmea*, p. 4.

[66]*Declaration of the Member States On the Legal Consequences of Achmea*, p. 4.

and that a third party system for resolving disputes would be available with awards being easily enforced in the courts of all Member States.

A tribunal in the recent award of *Eskosol S.P.A. v Italy*, handed down in May 2019 and arising under the ECT, addressed the Member States' pronouncement for the purposes of deciding a jurisdictional challenge brought by Italy.[67] With respect to this the tribunal found that the pronouncements drawn from the CJEU's judgment in *Achmea* "*have gone far beyond the actual holding in the Achmea Judgment*". They expressed concern in relation to the fact that whilst the Member States' pronouncements are set out in definitive terms, it remains "*far from clear whether the Achmea Judgment stands for the proposition that 'all investor–State arbitration clauses contained in bilateral investment treaties...are contrary to Union law' or simply those with a provision such as Article 8 of the Achmea BIT*".[68] The tribunal noted that even if, assuming *arguendo*, the *Achmea* decision does have the effect of rendering all intra-EU BIT arbitration clauses invalid, it does not address the ECT or render the arbitration provisions of the ECT invalid, particularly in light of the fact that the European Union is a signatory to the ECT. With respect to this point the tribunal drew support from the six Member States who have thus far refused to conclude on the application of EU law to the ECT.

It should be noted that whilst the Member States' announced that all intra-EU arbitration agreements should be deemed invalid under both EU law, and under general principles of international law, no explanation or analysis was given for why this conclusion is correct. The tribunal voiced concerns that the Member States "*made no reference to any international law analysis*" and that there was no attempt to "*work through, for example, the impact of the numerous VCLT provisions*" which the tribunal had engaged with.[69] It was therefore concluded that the pronouncement serves only as a "*means of information*" and that it does not have the effect of either permitting a retroactive termination of pending arbitrations nor does it represent a shared understanding of the Member States at the time they entered into investment treaties, instead it is only to be seen as an "*offer of a new understanding*" when going forward.[70]

3 Awards in Breach of State Aid

In addition to the threats posed to investment arbitration by the judgment in *Achmea* are the growing number of decisions which seek to classify awards rendered in favour of investors as a form of illegal State aid in breach of EU law. This approach has serious ramifications for the longevity of investment arbitration in Europe if

---

[67] *Eskosol S.P.A. v Italy* (2019) ICSID Case No. ARB/15/50, see paras [207]–[227].

[68] *Eskosol S.P.A. v Italy* (2019) ICSID Case No. ARB/15/50 at [213].

[69] *Eskosol S.P.A. v Italy* (2019) ICSID Case No. ARB/15/50 at [216].

[70] *Eskosol S.P.A. v Italy* (2019) ICSID Case No. ARB/15/50 at [223], [226], [227].

awards made in favour of investors cannot be satisfied by States without breaching their other international obligations.

This issue has arisen as a result of two decisions of the European Commission. The first was issued in March 2015 in relation to the *Micula v Romania* award rendered by a tribunal in December 2014.[71] The tribunal granted an award in favour of the investor and ordered Romania to pay approximately EUR € 82 million in damages. The European Commission initiated an investigation in relation to the sums due to be paid by Romania. It concluded that if such sums were paid, it would constitute a breach of the EU's rules on State aid. In particular, Article 107(1) of the TFEU, which provides that[72]:

> aid granted by a Member State or through state resources in any form whatsoever which distorts or threatens to distort competition by favouring certain undertakings or the production of certain goods shall, in so far as it affects trade between Member States, be incompatible with the internal market.

Therefore, a measure constitutes State aid if the following four cumulative conditions are met: (1) the measure must confer a selective economic advantage upon an undertaking; (2) the measure must be imputable to the State and financed through State resources; (3) the measure must distort or threaten to distort competition; and (4) the measure must have the potential to affect trade between Member States. The European Commission found that the implementation or execution of the award would grant the claimant an economic advantage not otherwise available on the market. Perhaps most surprisingly, the Commission ruled that "*the presence of an advantage is...not precluded by the fact that the payment of the compensation awarded to the complainants by the Tribunal through the implementation or execution of the Award entails a payment of compensation for damages*".[73] This reasoning was premised upon a legalistic reading of the CJEU's former jurisprudence on the rules governing State aid.

However, it became apparent that the European Commission's primary goal was to reiterate to all States and investors that its general line regarding intra-EU BITs was to be upheld. It rationalised its findings in relation to State aid by stating[74]:

> In the present case, the compensation has been awarded to the claimants on the basis of an intra-EU BIT which the Commission considers invalid as of Romania's accession to the Union. The Commission has consistently taken the view that intra-EU BITs, such as the BIT upon which the claimants base their claim, are contrary to Union law since they are incompatible with provisions of the Union Treaties and should therefore be considered invalid. The Commission has repeatedly made this view known to the Member States, including the Member States in question.

It is clear from this section of the Commission's decision that its reasoning for finding that investor-State awards rendered by tribunals are contrary to the rules on

---

[71]*Micula & Ors v Romania* (ICSID Case No. ARB/05/20 – 11 December 2014).

[72]Commission Decision (EU) 2015/1470 (30 March 2015) at [79].

[73]Commission Decision (EU) 2015/1470 (30 March 2015) at [100].

[74]Commission Decision (EU) 2015/1470 (30 March 2015) at [102].

State aid is in fact part of a campaign to end all intra-EU investor-State arbitrations and to return exclusive competence back to the institutions of the European Union. The remaining elements of the test set down under Article 107 TFEU were easily satisfied in the Commission's ruling. The award is made only to the claimants and is thereby selective and the award is paid out by a State party and is thereby financed by State resources. Crucially, the Commission's decision has the potential to effect all awards paid out by European Member States. With regard to the future of awards, the Commission's decision is currently being challenged by the investors and a case is now pending before the CJEU.

The second case in which the European Commission has sought to apply its position vis-à-vis arbitral awards breaching State aid rules is *Eiser Infrastructure Ltd v Spain*,[75] which involved an award handed down in May 2017 concerning an investor-State arbitration heard under the ICSID regime. The tribunal awarded the investors a sum of EUR € 128 million to be paid by Spain for breaches of the Energy Charter Treaty. As with the award in *Micula*, the European Commission reviewed the decision to determine whether if, in the event Spain satisfied the award, they would be in breach of the EU rules on State aid. The Commission's findings were published in November 2017.[76] The Commission outlined that a number of investors had initiated arbitrations against Spain on the basis of the ECT.[77] It noted that the majority of these claims had been brought by investors of fellow Member States and ruled that "*the Commission considers that any provision for investor-State arbitration between two Member States is contrary to Union Law*".[78] It went on to outline a significant number of provisions under European law which it considered that investor-State arbitration was in breach of.[79] The Commission sought to point out that the conflict with European law concerns "*both substance and enforcement*". As to substance, the Commission said that EU law provides for a "*complete set of rules on investment protection*" and that "*Member States are hence not competent to conclude bilateral or multilateral agreements between themselves, because by doing so, they may affect common rules or alter their scope*".[80] This is the crux of the European Union's opposition against international investment agreements and their requisite dispute provisions – that they disrupt the exclusive competence of the EU.

With specific respect to the adjudication process of investor-State arbitration, the Commission thought that as two sets of rules concerning investment protection are

---

[75]*Eiser Infrastructure Ltd v Spain* (ICSID Case No. ARB/13/36 – 4 May 2017).

[76]Commission Decision (EU) State aid SA.40348 (2015/NN) (10 November 2017).

[77]Commission Decision (EU) State aid SA.40348 (2015/NN) (10 November 2017) at [159].

[78]Commission Decision (EU) State aid SA.40348 (2015/NN) (10 November 2017) at [160].

[79]Commission Decision (EU) State aid SA.40348 (2015/NN) (10 November 2017) see [161]; "*Article 19(1) TEU, the principles of the freedom of establishment, the freedom to provide services and the free movement of capital, as established by the Treaties (in particular Articles 49, 52, 56, and 63 TFEU), as well as Articles 64(2), 65(1), 66, 75, 107, 108,215, 267 and Article 344 TFEU, and the general principles of Union law of primacy, unity and effectiveness of Union law, of mutual trust and of legal certainty*".

[80]Commission Decision (EU) State aid SA.40348 (2015/NN) (10 November 2017) at [161].

potentially applicable and which "*are not identical in content and are applied by different adjudicators*" there is a risk of conflicts between investment treaties and EU law.[81] The Commission found that investor-State tribunals had to apply EU law which it said was applicable both as a matter of international law and as the domestic law of the host State. However, as the tribunals are not a court of a Member State and cannot make references to the CJEU, they are purportedly in breach of EU law. Unsurprisingly, the Commission felt that "*the resulting treaty conflict is to be solved. . .on the basis of the principle of primacy in favour of Union law*".[82]

In respect to the award rendered in *Eiser & ors v Spain*, the Commission found that "*any compensation which an Arbitration Tribunal were to grant to an investor. . .would constitute in and of itself State aid*" adding that "*the Arbitration Tribunals are not competent to authorise the granting of State Aid. That is an exclusive competence of the Commission*".[83] It concluded by stating that if tribunals were to "*award compensation. . .or were to do so in future*" it would amount to a breach of EU law by the Member State.[84] The remedies for illegal State aid require the Member State to recover all of the sums paid to the entities in question along with interest for the period in which they were in possession of the funds.

In short, the European Union's attack on investment agreements, and by association, investor-State arbitration, represents a worrying in-road into the current system of treaty protections granted to investors. Distinct from the problems arising from *Achmea*, which, for the moment, seem to be falling short of effecting ICSID and multilateral investment agreements, the Commission's rulings in relation to the awards of *Micula* and *Eiser* represent a perforation into the effective application of the ICSID Convention within the EU, which has until now operated almost seamlessly for the past 50 years.

The problems created by the EU's approach to investor-State awards constituting a breach of State aid is having to be dealt with by domestic courts in instances where investors are seeking to enforce awards against State assets. The latest difficulties have been dealt with by the English Court of Appeal in *Micula v Romania v European Commission*[85] in which judgment was handed down in July 2018. The investors in *Micula* were attempting to enforce an ICSID award in the English courts against Romania. The court was asked to determine whether by failing to enforce the award, the United Kingdom would be in breach of its international obligations under the ICSID Convention, and conversely, if the English courts did enforce the award, would the UK be in breach of its obligations under the law of the European Union. The case represents an archetypal example of the sorts of situation which will continue to arise as the European Union seeks to dismantle international investment

---

[81]Commission Decision (EU) State aid SA.40348 (2015/NN) (10 November 2017) at [162].

[82]Commission Decision (EU) State aid SA.40348 (2015/NN) (10 November 2017) at [163].

[83]Commission Decision (EU) State aid SA.40348 (2015/NN) (10 November 2017) at [165].

[84]Commission Decision (EU) State aid SA.40348 (2015/NN) (10 November 2017) at [165].

[85]*Micula v Romania v European Commission* [2018] EWCA Civ 1801.

agreements in a piecemeal fashion both by way of *Achmea* and through the European Commission's attack on State aid.

The English courts were acutely aware of these difficulties and sort to chart a path of least resistance, ensuring that the United Kingdom would not, for the time being, be in breach of any of its immediate international obligations. The court described whether the UK would be in breach of its pre-accession obligations under the ICSID Convention if it acted contrary to the EU Commission's findings as *"very difficult and sensitive questions"*.[86] The court went on to find that[87]:

> It would be wrong, in my view, even to embark on addressing those questions unless there is plainly no alternative to doing so and as a last resort. Both UK law and EU law have a variety of methods available for avoiding conflict and those methods need to be exhausted before a court entertains the possibility that it is not required...to apply EU law. As Lord Mance wisely counselled..."the recipe for avoiding any problem is that all concerned should act with mutual respect and with caution in areas where member states' constitutional identity is or may be engaged." The power of a member state to implement its pre-existing obligations under international treaties may be seen as an aspect of its constitutional identity.

The Court of Appeal's resolution came about as a result of the current uncertainty created by the EU Commission's decisions on State aid. The decision in *Micula* is currently on appeal to the Grand Chamber of the CJEU and is due to be heard in 2019. Accordingly, the Court of Appeal found that[88]:

> In the present case the methods available for avoiding conflict have not been exhausted, not least because it is not yet apparent whether there is an irreconcilable conflict between EU law as interpreted by the European courts and the UK's international obligation under the ICSID Convention to enforce the Award. In particular, there would be no such conflict if the GCEU (or the CJEU on an appeal) were to annul the Commission Decision or were otherwise to interpret Article 351 in a way which is consistent with the UK giving priority to its obligation under the ICSID Convention.

The court therefore decided that the point has *"not yet been reached at which the UK is in breach of its obligations under the ICSID Convention if it does not take immediate steps to facilitate execution of the Award"*.[89] It was therefore open to the court to grant a stay of execution pending the outcome of the proceedings in the European courts, after which a decision will need to be made regarding how to reconcile the UK's obligations under EU law with its obligations under the ICSID Convention. However, this problem is not unique to the United Kingdom. All of the Member States of the European Union who are also party to the ICSID Convention will need to grapple with how to rectify these competing obligations. It is hoped that the CJEU will be alert to these problems and will provide much needed clarity in its judgment on the Commission's rulings on State aid. As is apparent from the Court of Appeal's decision, unlike the *Achmea* judgment which has been limited to intra-EU

---

[86]*Micula v Romania v European Commission* [2018] EWCA Civ 1801 at [268].

[87]*Micula v Romania v European Commission* [2018] EWCA Civ 1801 at [268].

[88]*Micula v Romania v European Commission* [2018] EWCA Civ 1801 at [269].

[89]*Micula v Romania v European Commission* [2018] EWCA Civ 1801 at [270].

BITs and does not affect ICSID or multilateral agreements, the Commission's rulings on State aid affects *all* awards paid by Member States, even in cases where the enforcement procedures are under the ICSID Convention. When one considers the result of the two-pronged attack on international investment agreements, it soon becomes clear that there is now no space in which intra-EU investment treaties are immune from the EU's regulatory control.

4 Concluding Remarks

The two developments discussed in this chapter have to be viewed in the wider context of what the EU is attempting to achieve. Investment agreements encourage States to branch out and form independent international relations. The EU wishes to facilitate a transition to a system in which the EU has exclusive competence over investment agreements with non-EU States on behalf of Member States. To further this goal the Commission has sought to advance on two fronts against the system of investment protection within the EU. The intended effects of *Achmea* were that all investor-State arbitration clauses were to be read as being in breach of EU law and thus investors had no jurisdiction to bring claims against Member States. However, as is evidenced from the most recent decisions, tribunals have sought to capitalise upon the lack of precision and ambiguity in the *Achmea* judgment in an attempt to insulate the jurisdiction of tribunals to hear claims brought by investors.

This has taken the form that all non-BIT agreements, that is to say all multilateral agreements, FTAs and regional agreements (etc.) containing investment provisions are, for the moment, safe from the effects of *Achmea*. Similarly, a number of tribunals have held that all investment arbitrations administered under the ICSID Convention, whether they relate to BITs or multilateral agreements, are to continue unhindered as the reasoning contained in the CJEU's judgment does not apply to ICSID proceedings on account of the fact that awards are not subject to review by national courts. These are all, admittedly, technical readings which exploit the failings of the Court of Justice to be precise in respect to which forms of investment treaties the judgment applies to, but nevertheless the awards appear to be on a strong legal footing, finding support in the rules of treaty interpretation and the wider principles of public international law.

Therefore, the only agreements which appear to fall foul of the ruling in *Achmea* are those contained in intra-EU bilateral investment treaties administered under an arbitral body other than ICSID and to which the rules on enforcement under the ICSID Convention do not apply. As is immediately apparent, this is likely to be only a very small number of disputes, with the consequence that despite the initially broad ranging ramifications of *Achmea*, its effects in practice have largely been diminished through the resourceful interpretation of a number of tribunals. However, it is likely that in due course, if given the opportunity, the Court of Justice will no doubt seek to remedy its initial omissions by specifying which sorts of investment agreements contain clauses contrary to EU law. Such guidance is likely to bring into conflict the

ICSID Convention with the treaties of the European Union, a conflict to which domestic courts will no doubt be forced to become the *de facto* final adjudicators. In the meantime, it is interesting to note that the CJEU have ruled that arbitration clauses in bilateral investment treaties are invalid, yet have not proposed how investors should go about enforcing their rights under the relevant treaties, thereby leaving a significant number of intra-EU investors in a state of legal uncertainty as to the safety of their investments made within the European Internal Market.

Whilst it can be said that the ingenuity of tribunals has stemmed the tide of the effects of *Achmea*, the same cannot be said for the EU's drive towards classifying awards paid out by Member States as being in breach of the rules of State aid. This issue is currently before the Court of Justice and its decision will undoubtedly have significant ramifications upon the future viability of international investment protection within the European Union. Unlike the effects of *Achmea* which are limited to intra-EU disputes, and which only effect bilateral, non-ICSID BITs, the effects of the Commission's stance on State aid are far more wide ranging.

If satisfying an award to an investor amounts to State aid that will include all awards issued under multilateral and other investment agreements and all awards made under the ICSID Convention. Similarly, there exists scope to apply the Commission's ruling to awards other than those made in intra-EU disputes. If an investor based in the EU, but from a non-EU State, brings a claim against a Member State and that Member State satisfies the award, if the investor supplies goods or services within the EU then that will be classified as illegal State aid in breach of EU rules. The outcome will be that the entire sum paid in satisfaction of the award, along with interest for the period that the investor has been in possession of the sum, will need to be recovered by the Member State. Whilst the European Commission's rulings currently only apply to the specific awards which they have investigated, the rulings themselves form authoritative guidance on the laws to be applied by all States, and grant EU Member States a strong foothold with which to resist satisfying future awards.

As a result, non-EU States which have investment treaties with EU States will no doubt be considering whether those agreement have, or are soon to become, one sided, with EU investors being able to enforce awards obtained against non-EU States whilst their own investors based in the EU face a host of problems in a region in which investment protection is being dismantled in a piecemeal fashion. In light of the fact that ICSID awards may no longer be effectively executed automatically within the EU, or that, if executed, the States will be required to take steps to recover the sums, investors may start to reconsider whether EU Member States are the appropriate place for the recognition and enforcement of ICSID awards. Investors may instead begin to seek enforcement against State owned assets in other jurisdictions through subsidiary and parent companies, provided that those corporate entities of the investor do not also supply goods and services to EU Member States. As is evident from these concerns, and the recent experiences of the English and Swedish courts, domestic courts will undoubtedly face increasing questions as to the compatibility of EU law set against States' other international obligations in protecting foreign investors. The Court of Justice will be advised to keep these considerations in mind when ruling on both arbitration clauses and State aid in the future, as it is insufficient to rule that the current investment regime is in breach of EU law, without addressing how these conflicts and the protection of investments should be resolved in practice.

For the time being, all that is clear is that the EU has expressly communicated its intention to dismantle the current patchwork of investment agreements signed by Member States, with a view to investment protection becoming an exclusive competence of the European Union on behalf of all its Members. However, in light of how adeptly investment tribunals and domestic courts have sought off the effects of *Achmea*, facilitating this view of an exclusive EU investment regime is unlikely to come to fruition in the near future. Until then, investment law in Europe faces what are sure to be interesting and uncertain times.

Luke Tattersall is a barrister practising at Essex Court Chambers in London. He primarily practises in the areas of investment treaty arbitration, international commercial arbitration and public international law.

Part III
Institutions

Rule of Law in International Monetary and Financial Law: Reviving Old Spectres

Marcin J. Menkes

Contents

1 Introduction: Law and Economic Growth

The tenth anniversary of the Lehman Brothers insolvency brought as an array of occasional conferences and papers, mostly discussing "what have we learned" and "are we better prepared" for next economic downturn.[1] Depending on the author's view, some warn against inherent instability and short-sightedness of untamed financial markets,[2] others believe that regulators misdiagnosed the crisis,[3] and

---

The author thanks the Kosciuszko Foundation for the support of research at Cornell University and Prof. Markus Krajewski for comments and suggestions.

---

[1] See for instance: Ball (2018), Kress et al. (2018), Andrews (2018), Mayer (2018), Demirgüç-Kunt (2018) and Meeks and Velu (2018).

[2] Wetzer (2018) and Coyle (2018).

[3] Skeel (2018).

M. J. Menkes (✉)
Warsaw School of Economics, Warsaw, Poland
e-mail: marcin.menkes@sgh.waw.pl

© Springer Nature Switzerland AG 2019
M. Bungenberg et al. (eds.), *European Yearbook of International Economic Law 2019*,
European Yearbook of International Economic Law (2020) 10: 341–360,
https://doi.org/10.1007/8165_2019_32, Published online: 7 September 2019

again others hint to the possibility of a regulatory overreach.[4] Given the populism waves sweeping liberal democracies which resulted inter alia in the legitimacy crisis of international economic law, currently the pendulum swings towards regulation which should allow sustainable and more fair economic growth. The Rule of Law (RoL) thus became the new buzzword.

However, whether paying lip service to RoL, like a recent paper by the International Monetary Fund (IMF) Assistant General Counsel,[5] or reflecting true conviction about its usefulness to improve law, authors tend to picture it as a new value in international economic law. At best cyclical nature of regulation and deregulation is acknowledged. And yet, it is precisely international financial cooperation, where the relationship between law and economics (finance) has been tested.

Historically, economic relations were mostly shaped under the predominant influence of ever-evolving economic theories. In the post-WWII period, these stretched from modernization to dependency theory, from economic growth theories to welfare theories of development, from feminist theories of development to sustainable development.[6] Rules of economics translated into economic laws. However, as the factors and conditions of economic growth remain unclear despite decades of economic research, primacy in shaping the economic environment occasionally was given to non-economic considerations. This was case, for instance, when Part IV on "Trade and Development" was added to the GATT in 1965, or the adoption of the UNCTAD Generalized System of Preferences (GSP) in 1968, or comprehensive debt forgiveness-restructuring programmes of the Paris Club (est. 1956) and London Club (est. 1976).

The same shift of paradigm can also be traced in Law and Development (L&D),[7] as Latin American and African states struggled with structural barriers inherited from colonisation (at least that was the dependency narrative). Although L&D movement seemed irrevocably discredited by the early 1970s, interest in this period was renewed following the end of the Cold War. After the collapse of the USSR, a number of states embarked upon a somewhat similar path of transformation and structural reforms. Reports of L&D's death have been greatly exaggerated, arguably, due to U.S. historic myopia—lack of acknowledgment of earlier similar attempts.[8]

---

[4]J Langford, A decade after the 2008 crisis: Grudge-holding taxpayers and regulatory risks, Washington Examiner, 25 September 2018, https://washex.am/2EsHOuU; Taking stock on 10th anniversary of Lehman Brothers' collapse, China Daily, 19 September 2018, https://bit.ly/2SRKPc7.

[5]Liu (2018). Despite the usual disclaimer concerning attribution of author's views, given the current interest in the RoL in international law paper seems like a publicity stunt. It does not address the substance of RoL and most certainly does not suggest any commitment on the IMF side to apply the respective norms in its practice.

[6]Davis and Trebilcock (1999).

[7]Pes (2007).

[8]Tamanaha (1995) and Cao (1997).

Accordingly, after pioneering research in 1980,[9] academia found an ever-greater interest in L&D[10] from 1992 onwards. Eventually the notion of new Law and Development emerged.[11]

Obviously the most well-known embodiments of law vs. economics bate remains the so-called Washington Consensus (or rather its reception by the IMF) and, in terms of acknowledging the interdependence of macroeconomics and micro-development, the Comprehensive Development Framework (CDF) of the World Bank.[12] Presented by World Bank President James Wolfensohn, the CDF was supposed to be a vehicle for a "holistic view of development" that included a better balance in policymaking (highlighting various elements of governance, e.g., RoL) and emphasizing the partnership of government with other actors, including the private sector.[13] In the 1990s, the World Bank alone reported 330 Rule of Law projects, including US$2.9 billion in expenditures.[14] Although initially it seemed as if all the stakeholders thought of the RoL in the same manner, the more they looked into it the more RoL wasn't there. It turned out to be yet another reincarnation of the equilibrium between the law and economic development.

Current interest in the Rule of Law in International Economic Law (IEL) due to, inter alia, the post-crisis restructuring of the world economy and current legitimacy crisis, should thus be perceived as a cyclical rebalancing rather than a breaking point. Neglecting these lessons not only will lead to the same result, but risks undermining the very RoL, so crucial to Western legal civilization.

2   Law and Development as Predecessor of RoL

Law and Development (L&D) studies can be traced back to Max Weber's works on the relationship between the society, law and development, or even to Marx and Engels.[15] However, as American academia did not acknowledge this heritage, the field, in its narrow sense, grew in the 1950s and thrived in the 1960s. At this time, it was an effort by a relatively small group of liberal lawyers at development agencies

---

[9]Gardner (1982). It is worth noting that the 'imperial law' became a coined expression of the ahistorical reading of Law and Development, as if the movement started in and by the U.S. in the 1960s. One could trace, however, its roots back to the post-War modernisation efforts and beginnings of decolonisation.

[10]Carty (1992), Faundez (1997) and McAuslan and Thome (1997).

[11]Trubek and Santos (2006).

[12]In parallel the field of law and finance developed, analysing the influence of law and institutional set-up on financial markets. It started with the seminal paper La Porta et al. (1996). For current dilemmas, see: Cottier et al. (2012). For a general overview of development in the field, see: Engelen (2003).

[13]For a critical analysis of the CDF's achievements, failures and challenges it creates for both the World Bank and the world's poorest, see: Blake (2000).

[14]Trubek and Santos (2006) and Chua (1998).

[15]Cao (1997), Chantal (2008) and Lange (2005).

(such as USAID and the Peace Corps), foundations (Ford Foundation,[16] the Rockefeller Foundation) and universities (Harvard, Yale, Stanford, Wisconsin) in the US and Europe,[17] who believed that the development of societies is linear and state-driven. Arguably the pensée unique culminated with Fukuyama's End of History.[18] It implied the active engagement of the state in the economy, from planning and active industrial policies, to state-ownership of strategic enterprises, to measures enhancing industrialisation and import-substitution (in developing states). Benefits of development, including freedom and democracy, were supposed to spillover from institutional reforms and economic growth.

Development was equated with progress (some claimed that it was merely a euphemism), and so law could transform society, which in turn granted lawyers the privileged position of social engineers.[19] In light of the greater goods—democracy and freedom—the focus on growth and even the imposition of a certain normative solution seemed as justified interim measures. Not accidently, 1958 symbolizes the birth of the modern public choice theory[20] and 1960 is the symbolic beginning of the new institutional economics, and law and economics, focusing on social and legal rules.[21]

Thus defined, progress was to be achieved in the least costly manner through a culturalist approach and a utilitarian understanding of law—education of new legal professionals[22] and the transplanting of a Western, and Western-friendly, normative framework. It is estimated that US public and private legal assistance reached US$15 million in Africa and 5 million in both Asia and Latin America.[23]

Law and development attempted to transfer four legal concepts[24]:

- case studies and a Socratic approach to teaching methodology,
- a basic American model for legal education,
- the American perception of lawyers as "problem-solvers and social engineering" professionals,
- a non-formal, even instrumental, jurisprudential view of law.

Yet, without understanding of local languages, culture, politics or laws, not only was the formalist approach of one-size-fits-all reforms rejected by the supposed beneficiaries, but alongside the decolonisation process there was a growing sense that this Eurocentrism (Western-centrism) was yet further evidence of neoliberal tendencies and a show of hubris.

---

[16]J. Gardner, quoted here on several occasions, was a Ford Foundation employee.

[17]But not international organisations. Neither the World Bank nor regional banks contributed towards the Law and Development programs.

[18]Fukuyama (1992).

[19]Merryman (1977).

[20]Black (1958).

[21]Coase (1960).

[22]Burg (1977).

[23]Gardner (1982), p. 8.

[24]Gardner (1982), p. 4.

Although the L&D movement was relatively small and short-lived and had little impact on development policies at the time, it did put the issue of how law and legal reforms relate to "development" on the intellectual agenda.[25] The scale of its failure was, however, well reflected by the Brazilian case in which the instrumental approach to law during the "interim period", before the economy was boosted and democracy cherished, strengthened authoritarian tendencies instead.[26] Eventually, even research in the field was abandoned in the 1970s,[27] just as Western societies started to doubt the state's capacity to be an economic operator, and the newly independent states forged their theory of the right to development within the New International Economic Order.[28]

3   From Synergies of Human Rights and Free-Market Movements to the RoL

When considering why the L&D experiences were initially superseded, one has to bear in mind the fundamental transformation of the international financial paradigm in the 1990s.

Faced with the Mundell-Fleming trilemma,[29] the architects of the original Bretton Woods framework opted for monetary autonomy of states and managed exchange rates at the cost of renouncing free international capital flows. Thus, the established embedded liberalism allowed semi-free international trade while leaving to governments enough space to shield domestic economies from global shocks.[30]

By contrast, since the 1980s, ever-greater scepticism with respect to public involvement in the economy led to the development of New Public Management—a managerial approach to public administration, oriented towards markets and consumers.[31] The 1990s witnessed ever-stronger globalisation, the dynamic development of the "Asian Tigers" (but also a major financial crisis), and the countries that gained autonomy after the USSR collapsed joined the race to tap international capital markets. The end of the Cold War appeared to be ultimate proof of the market economy's superiority over the

---

[25]Trubek (2003).

[26]Gardner (1982), pp. 35–52 and 231–235.

[27]Galanter and Trubek (1974).

[28]UN GA Resolution *Declaration for the Establishment of a New International Economic Order* (A/RES/S-6/3201), as well as Programme *of Action and a Charter of Economic Rights and Duties of States* (A/RES/29/3281). Sacerdoti (2011).

[29]Also called the impossible trinity: out of three desirable monetary policy goals—exchange rate stability, free movement of capital, autonomous monetary policy—only two are achievable at one time.

[30]The concept of the embedded liberalism largely based on theoretical work of Karl Polanyi, The Great Transformation (1944). The post-war idea was to "re-embed" economy within society and social expectations, Rawi and Ruggie (2009).

[31]Supernat (2004).

centrally planned, which strengthened market-led tendencies to further liberalise international capital flows.[32] Deregulation dominated the thinking about law and economics independently of political divisions.[33] Accordingly, we witnessed "a triple shift, from state to market, from internal to export-led growth, and from official capital flows to private foreign investment",[34] with the resulting market pressure to foster business climate by enhancing the legal framework.

In those new conditions, two trends that paved the way for the Rule of Law movement, can be identified. On the one hand, the human rights movement, as reflected under Principle VII of the Helsinki Final Act (the so-called Third Basket of the Conference on Security and Cooperation in Europe (CSCE) and a predecessor to the Organisation for Security and Co-operation in Europe (OSCE) Human Dimension). The process focused not only on substantive rights but also on the institutional and procedural effectiveness of safeguarding them.

On the other hand, the new sets of ideas dominated economic thinking. These are typically, and often imprecisely, referred to as the Washington Consensus. The unfortunate term coined by English economist John Williamson in a conference on restructuring Latin American debts as a form of financial assistance in recognition of their reform efforts, included, inter alia, liberalisation of foreign direct investment (FDI), deregulation and privatisation and legal security of property rights.[35] International financial institutions, including the IMF and the World Bank, which were still looking for new identity after the fall of the Bretton Woods order, thus became involved in championing international investment flows in a stable legal framework.

The new structural reform packages for supposed assistance recipients thus acquired the good-governance label.[36] As defined by the World Bank, governance consisted of: form/structure of political order, process of governing, and government capacity to design and realise policies.[37] "Governments in the 1970s relied on this rationale to rush into unwise policies [of compensating for market failure] and investments, although their own policy interventions often were responsible for market failures, and the investments did not yield adequate returns".[38] Allegedly,

---

[32]Whereas it is difficult to identify a single reason for the failure of the original Bretton Woods formula, one has to acknowledge the role of private capital markets. Establishment of Euromarkets (which rapidly expanded in the late 1960s and 1970s) and then recycling of petrodollars (in the 1970s) had to undermine either state monetary autonomy or the IMF par-value system. Eventually states dismantled the latter.

[33]It is sufficient to note that deregulation was supported both by Republican presidents, including Ronald Reagan and Richard Nixon, and Democrats such as Jimmy Carter and Bill Clinton.

[34]Trubek (2003), p. 9.

[35]Not only was it far from acknowledging some form of liberal homogeneity in Western thinking about economics, and even further from neo-colonial conspiracy behind international investment flows, but even during this conference Williamson observed that the notion of consensus was too optimistic, as relatively homogenous groups of participating economists struggled to agree even on very basic issues, Williamson (2008).

[36]Campbell (2000) and Bevir (2011).

[37]World Bank, *Governance and development*, Report No. 10650 (1992), pp. 3–4. Coopération Internationale "Le développement: pour un débat politique" Dourdan, France 2000.

[38]World Bank, *Governance and development*, Report No. 10650 (1992), p. 6.

this justified greater engagement of the Bretton Woods organisations in institution-building: "[b]y its function, the Bank is intimately involved in this broad reform process, and governments are turning to it more and more to assist them in addressing a broader range of economic management issues, including the legal framework",[39] despite concerns stemming from limitations of World Banks mandate to intervene in domestic matters.[40] The capture of governance by the Bretton Woods organisations was accentuated by the ever-greater importance of markets as partners of governments and the birth of hybrid public-private administration.[41]

Hence, questioning the state-led economy and then even state managerial capacities eventually in the 1990s undercut the legitimacy of public actions. The challenge was willingly addressed through governance both championed and managed by international financial institutions. By 1994s accountability, adequate legal framework and transparency were already considered as important criteria for receiving financial assistance.[42] As the Rule of Law became the ambition for both free-market and Human Rights advocates, some even argued that, unlike the Williamsons proposal,[43] there was actually global consensus on the desirability of the RoL.[44]

During this initial period of RoL euphoria, a common approach seemed to include[45]:

- neo-formalism,
- a focus on the administration of justice (rather than legal education),
- an emphasis on contract and property,

  but mostly,

- belief in a universal model of RoL, somewhat surprising in light of the Law and Development lesson.

---

[39]World Bank, *Governance and development*, Report No. 10650 (1992), p. 8.

[40]'In undertaking such work, the World Bank faces some inherent limitations: (...) the Bank's legal mandate clearly delimits its areas of concern. (...) the Bank is rightly concerned with financial and economic accountability, but political accountability is (...) outside its mandate (...) With regard to the legal framework for development, the Bank's concern is with its procedural and institutional aspects. The substantive elements of such a framework have political connotations that may sometimes lie outside the Bank's mandate', World Bank, *Governance and development*, Report No. 10650 (1992), pp. 50–51. On the World Bank see below Sect. 3.

[41]When considering the development of international economic governance, one should recognise the significance of the alleged break of the transmission mechanism between the US government and administration due to, *inter alia*, administrative capture, Steward (1975) and Mashaw (2005).

[42]World Bank, *Governance—the World Bank's experience*, Report No. 13134, Washington 1994.

[43]See footnote 35 above.

[44]At the same time, such arguments point towards a particular convergence between the market approach and the conservative approach to human rights (property rights, fair treatment of foreign investors, strong police, and law and order) rather than the liberal one (FET, human rights, and substantive content), Carothers (2009).

[45]Trubek and Santos (2006), pp. 12–13.

It was only after acknowledgment of some self-contradictory elements of this programme that theoretical works began to distinguish between various concepts of the Rule of Law.

4   The Rule of Law and the World Bank

Both Bretton Woods organisations' approach to the Rule of Law can be traced back to their adherence to the good governance principles.[46] Defining governance in its non-political aspects, a former WB General Counsel, Ibrahim Shihata, explained the meaning of

> *good order* . . . not in the sense of maintaining the status quo by the force of the state (law and order) but in the sense of having a system, based on abstract rules which are actually applied and functioning institutions which ensure the appropriate application of such rules. This system of rules and institutions is reflected in the concept of *the rule of law*. . . often expressed in the familiar phrase of a *government of law and not of men* (emphasis as in the original).[47]

As for the Rule of Law *per se*, is was to be understood as: a set of rules actually in force and known in advance. Rules should be matched with a mechanism ensuring the proper application thereof, but also allowing for departure from them according to established procedures. Conflicts of the rules must be resolved through binding decisions of an independent judicial or arbitral body, Finally, once the rules no longer serve their purpose, there is an established procedures for their amendment.[48]

This formal approach was modified by the subsequent General Counsel, Ko-Yung Tung. In accordance with a 2002 statement, the Rule of Law prevails where

> the government itself is bound by the law, every person in society is treated equally under the law, the human rights dignity of each individual is recognised and protected by law, and justice is accessible to all. The Rule of Law requires transparent legislation, fair laws, predictable enforcement, and accountable governments to maintain order, promote private sector growth, fight poverty, and have legitimacy[49].

Currently the RoL constitutes one of six dimensions of governance (alongside voice and accountability, political stability and absence of violence/terrorism, government effectiveness, regulatory quality and control of corruption).[50] The Rule of Law implies that[51]: the government itself is bound by the law, that every person in society

---

[46]Which does not mean that there were no internal divisions. See analysis of the tension within the WB favouring different approaches to the rule of law: Santos (2006).

[47]Shihata (1991), pp. 53–96.

[48]Shihata (1991), p. 85.

[49]Some contested such a reading, suggesting that it may be still limited to formal aspects, even if Tung's definition remains 'ambiguous' from a legal positivist perspective, Barron (2005).

[50]World Bank, *Worldwide Governance Indicators*, http://bit.ly/2iY2WuB.

[51]World Bank, *Legal and Judicial Reform: Strategic Directions*, Legal Vice Presidency World Bank 2002.

is treated equally under the law and that the human dignity of each individual is recognized and protected by law, while justice is accessible to everyone.

It is reflected by the RoL indices, which capture:

> perceptions of the extent to which agents have confidence in and abide by the rules of society, and in particular the quality of contract enforcement, property rights, the police, and the courts, as well as the likelihood of crime and violence.[52]

In order to safeguard achievement of these goals several elements are indispensable, namely: transparent and equitable laws, legal empowerment and security in one's rights, enforceable contracts, basic security of one's person and property and access to justice.[53]

The World Bank's RoL index includes multiple elements, defined and quantified by other organisation, with different geographical and substantial scope. From the IIL perspective, those with the broadest reach (so-called representative sources) can be grouped within following categories[54]:

– Physical protection and security from crime (Full Protection and Security)

- Crime costs for EIU, WEI,
- Police reliability services for WEI, GWP,
- Sense of security in general for IPD;

– Fair and Equitable Treatment

- Fairness of judicial process, for EIU,
- Equal treatment of foreigners before the law for IPD,
- Enforceability of (private) contracts, for EIU, IPD, WMO,
- Enforceability of public-private contracts IPD,
- Speediness of judicial process for EIU, IPD,
- Judicial independence, for WEI, IPD,
- Efficiency of the Legal Framework for Challenging Regulations for WEI,
- Reliability of judicial process (in general) for GWP;

– Property protection, expropriation, compensation

- Confiscation/expropriation, Intellectual property rights protection, Private property protection for EIU, IPD, WMO,
- IPR protection, Property Rights for WEI, HER, IPD.

---

[52]World Bank, *Rule of Law*, http://bit.ly/2kedX02.

[53]World Bank, *Legal and Judicial Reform: Strategic Directions*, Legal Vice Presidency World Bank 2002.

[54]EIU—Economist Intelligence Unit Riskwire & Democracy Index, GWP—Gallup World Poll, HWR—Heritage Foundation Index of Economic Freedom, IPD—Institutional Profiles Database, WEI—World Economic Forum Global Competitiveness Report, WMO—Global Insight Business Conditions and Risk Indicators.

Accordingly, unlike the focus on legal training in the case of Law & Development, here attention shifts towards the judiciary and dispute settlement. Hence, the WB takes a three-prong approach based on: (1) judicial reform—independence, judicial training, court administration and case management, corruption, appointment of judges, quality of criminal justice, accountability of government, (2) legal reform—context dependent, (3) access to justice.[55]

Finally, the World Bank recognises the significance, in its subsidiary capacity, of arbitration and ADR, even though bypassing courts or other formal dispute resolution systems was recognised as a problem.[56]

5 The Rule of Law and the International Monetary Fund

Whereas the financial nature of the World Bank mandate appears to legitimise and strengthen its Law and Development/RoL conditionality, as they are framed as instruments fostering economic growth of a beneficiary state, the IMF seems reticent to step ahead in governance conditionality, even though it is not subject to the same political statutory limitations.

The IMF's interest in governance is defined by the goal of sound and efficient management of public and private resources.[57] The goal was formally adopted in 1996, as the IMF "has found that a much broader range of institutional reforms is needed if countries are to establish and maintain private sector confidence and thereby lay the basis for sustained growth",[58] even though at the time the Fund was still "feeling its way regarding the approach to governance".[59] Subsequently, the importance of the good governance principle for the public trust in its government, market integrity, competition, and endangers economic development were acknowledged on numerous accounts.[60]

Good governance, in turn, includes the Rule of Law principle.[61] Among various aspects of governance, the IMF held that "improving the management of public

---

[55]World Bank, *Legal and Judicial Reform: Strategic Directions*, Legal Vice Presidency World Bank 2002.

[56]EBRD/BIICL, *The Importance of the Rule of Law and Respect for Contractual Rights in Transition Countries*, World Bank 2003.

[57]IMF, *Review of the Fund's Experience in the Governance Issues*, IMF 2001, p. 11.

[58]IMF, *Partnership for Sustainable Global Growth Interim Committee Declaration*, IMF 1996.

[59]IMF, *Review of the Fund's Experience in the Governance Issues*, IMF 2001, p. 3.

[60]IMF, *The IMF and Good Governance. Factsheet*, IMF 2016. Also, statements by former Managing Directors of the IMF: M. Camdessus, *Old Battle and New Challenges: a Perspective on Latin America*, speech at the Europe-Latin American Convention, Bordeaux, October 20, 1997; H. Köhler, *Building Shared Prosperity in the Americas*, speech at the Special Summit of Americas, Monterrey, January 12, 2004.

[61]IMF, *Partnership for Sustainable Global Growth Interim Committee Declaration*, IMF 1996; IMF, *Good Governance. The IMF's Role*, Washington 1997.

resources" and "supporting the development and maintenance of a transparent and stable economic and regulatory environment conducive to efficient private sector activities" are particularly relevant to its mandate.[62] The second element includes price systems, exchange and trade regimes, banking regulation.[63] In areas, where the Fund acknowledged it has rather limited expertise—public enterprise reform, civil service reform, property rights, contract enforcement, and procurement practices—it is to cooperate with other institutions, notably with the World Bank.

After several years of searching for an exact meaning, by 2001 the Fund already believed that "a global consensus has emerged on the importance of good governance for key dimensions of economic performance, including growth, poverty reduction, resilient economic and financial systems, and the effectiveness of aid and private capital inflows".[64] At the same time, the IMF acknowledged the importance of leadership of international financial institutions, notably through annual meetings of the Fund and the World Bank. Expanding its governance toolkit (which in 1996 consisted mainly of surveillance, financial programs and technical assistance), the Fund used the following means for promoting good governance: data dissemination, reports on observance of standards and codes, fiscal transparency, monetary and financial policy transparency, financial sector assessment programs, guidelines on misreporting, safeguards on the use of fund resources, monitoring use of debt relief for poverty reduction, internal governance.

In terms of legal and judicial system reform, the IMF undertook actions including[65]: the approval of regulations governing the functioning of an arbitration court, enactment of a new commercial code, enactment of foreign investment law, adoption/revision of labour code, implementation of an effective law on bankruptcy, preparation/implementation of a strategy for breaking up or dismantling monopolies, and reviewing forest concession contracts and cancellation of concessions in violation of regulations.

Without official IMF methodology, we remain, however, limited to documents published under its auspices subject to the usual disclaimer concerning attribution of such views.

In one such study we thus find a reference to numerous measures used by other institutions, including points of reference for the World Bank. Variables include[66]: BERI/DRI index of contract enforceability, DRI/EIU index of costs of crime, FHNT/PRS rule of law index, property protection WCY/WDR index, law and order HR

---

[62]IMF, *The Role of the IMF in Governance Issues: Guidance Note (Approved by the IMF Executive Board, July 25, 1997)*, IMF 1997.

[63]Thus indirectly, the norms adopted by the Basle Committee on Banking Supervision (BCBS), *inter alia*, on transparency, reporting and supervision became an important element of international financial institutions' understanding of the Rule of Law.

[64]IMF, *Review of the Fund's Experience in the Governance Issues*, IMF 2001, p. 5.

[65]IMF, *Review of the Fund's Experience in the Governance Issues*, IMF 2001, p. 10.

[66]BERI—Business Environment Risk Intelligence, DRI—Standard & Poor's DRI, FHNT—Freedom House, GCS—Global Competitiveness Survey, HF—Heritage Foundation, PRS—Political Risk Services, WCY—World Competitiveness Report, WDR—World Development Report.

index, reliability of the judiciary according to GCS/WCY/WDR index, as well as the CEER/ICRG index (discussed in relation to EBRD).[67] We thus observe circular reference of one organisation referring to data of two (several) others, among which there are further cross-references, which may result in overemphasis of certain factors over others.

6   The Rule of Law and the European Bank for Reconstruction and Development

Compared to both Bretton Woods organisations, the European Bank for Reconstruction and Development (ERBD) is a much younger initiative. Its constitutive agreement was signed in Paris in 1990 and entered into force in March 1991. This time gap was, however, more than a number. Whereas the World Bank could not consider or get involved in political matters,[68] the EBRD, founded after the fall of the Iron Curtain and with a surge of new optimism with respect to multilateralism,[69] acquired an explicit political mandate.

The European bank was established to

> ... foster the transition towards open market-oriented economies and to promote private and entrepreneurial initiative in the Central and Eastern European countries committed to and applying the principles of multiparty democracy, pluralism and market economics (Article 1).

Since the Peter the Great, Russia perceived western neighbours as a source of inspiration, know-how and investments. Despite ebbs and flows of socio-economic cooperation, even the Russian Revolution of 1917 did not bring the exchanges to a halt. It was only after the World War II that both Cold War blocs started to perceive respective economic systems as mortal enemies in a struggle for survival, hence any political/economic preaching was vehemently rebuffed. With the rise of the EBRD the West was yet again perceived as a source of capital and technology.[70]

The Board of Directors had to give substance to its political mandate. Accordingly, the Board acknowledged in a memorandum the link between economic development and democracy and the Rule of Law.[71] Since the political element

---

[67]Fredriksson and Mani (2002), p. 23. The study uses measures from Kaufmann et al. (1999), p. 30 (and another IMF Working Paper by the same authors, quoted below).

[68]IBRD Articles of Agreement, Article IV(10): The Bank and its officers shall not interfere in the political affairs of any member; nor shall they be influenced in their decisions by the political character of the member or members concerned. Only economic considerations shall be relevant to their decisions, and these considerations shall be weighed impartially in order to achieve the purposes stated in Article. The IMF statute does not contain similar provision.

[69]Notably, short-lived, the reactivation of the UN Security Council.

[70]Grzybowski (1990), p. 284.

[71]EBRD, *Procedures to implement the Political Aspects of the Mandate of the European Bank for Reconstruction and Development*, EBRD 2013.

was "novel" to it, the Bank reached for the experience of other international organisations, notably the Council of Europe. It also referred to the European Convention on Human Rights (ECHR), the Helsinki Final Act and the CSCE Charter of Paris, as well as to the works of the Commission on Human Rights.

Given the above-mentioned two approaches to the RoL, i.e., market-oriented or Human Rights, it is important to stress the EBRD's adherence to the latter. Its conditionality includes environmental and political (including RoL) criteria.

When comparing the political components of EBRD conditionality with the Bretton Woods political-risk assessments ("assumptions underlying loans"), some stressed that it can play two functions.[72] First, policy-related conditions play a quasi-securitisation function, as in the IMF case. Second, they may be used to encourage particular attitudes, as in the case of World Bank loans. And yet, despite its broad mandate, the EBRD may actually be less involved in politically-sensitive issues than its Bretton Woods siblings.[73]

The EBRD declares its defining values as: transition, environmental and social sustainability, gender equality, transparency and integrity, and compliance (focusing on business ethics). I did not come across any quantification or assessment of the Rule of Law as an official decision of the EBRD. Papers published by the Bank's officers also contain the disclaimer concerning the nature of the presented views. In just one instance, the RoL constituted one of three pillars of judicial efficiency (alongside an index of the effectiveness of corporate and bankruptcy law in transition economies and survey data on the ability of the legal system to protect private property rights and enforce contracts). Whereas the two other measures were constructed or conducted by the Bank itself, the Rule of Law index is based on the reports by the Central European Economic Review (CEER).

CEER is a part of the European branch of the *Wall Street Journal*.[74] Its Rule of Law index is, in turn, based on a survey of business analysts in Europe and the U.S. Conducted since 1995, the questionnaire requests a rating for 27 Central and Easter European transition economies. I did not find the constituent variables of the index. However, as stressed in the World Bank's paper, the CEER shows a strong correlation with the International Country Risk Guide (ICRG).[75]

The ICRG comprises 22 variables classified in three categories: political, financial, and economic risks. The political risk rating includes 12 variables: Government Stability, Socioeconomic conditions, Investment Profile (i.e., investment risk factors

---

[72]Linarelli (2014), pp. 402–408.

[73]Linarelli (2014), p. 404.

[74]Kaufmann et al. (1999), p. 31. The CEER index is also included in the World Bank's RoL index. However, due to its narrow geographical scope, it is classified as a 'non-representative source' and so it was not mentioned above.

[75]As the authors of the ICRG, the PRS Group states that the methodology is 'used consistently by researchers at the IMF, and has been acclaimed in such publications as *Barron's*, *The Economist*, and *The Wall Street Journal*, PRS, *International Country Risk Guide (ICRG)*, http://bit.ly/2j8MLy0. In fact, in another publication under EBRD auspices, the author indirectly based his research on the ICRG, Dietrich (2002), pp. 57–61.

not covered elsewhere), Internal Conflict, External Conflict, Corruption, Military in Politics, Religious Tensions, Law and Order, Ethnic Tensions, Democratic Account-ability, and Bureaucracy Quality.

Whereas fighting corruption and crime seem to belong to the Rule of Law *sensu stricto* from the international financial institutions perspective, the most common components are: Law (up to three points for the strength and impartiality of the legal system), Order (three points for general observance of law), Democratic account-ability (six points on a scale stretching from alternating democracies to autarchy) and bureaucracy quality as a stabiliser of political changes (four points). Accordingly, strictly legal elements constitute 13 out of the 100-point scale of political risks.[76] This means that the legal components of the Rule of Law index that indirectly shape the EBRD thinking (and influence the IBRD) remain rather limited.

7   Conclusions

Predictability and enforceability of law, crucial factors of investment risks and availability of capital, have major significance for economic growth and stability. Accordingly, international monetary and financial organisation have long been interested in shaping the relationship between law and economic development.

In the paper, I have discussed the approach to the Rule of Law by some of the most important international monetary and financial organisations (the IBRD, the IMF, the EBRD). Obviously it is also considered an element of good governance by many other institutions, including the African Development Bank, whose definition of governance implied fostering legal and judicial reform including law reform, judicial reform and the legal framework for private sector development, the Asian Development Bank—the RoL as a dominant element of predictability, i.e., one of four pillars of governance, the Inter-American Development Bank and the Organi-zation for Economic Development and Cooperation.[77]

While thinking of international monetary organisations, one also cannot ignore the particular relevance of the Rule of Law as a guarantee of the autonomy of central banks from the executive and current political expectations.[78] This is true both at the international plane, notably the European Central Bank is bound by the RoL principle as are all other organs of the European Union,[79] and domestically.[80] This

---

[76]PRS, *International Country Risk Guide Methodology*, http://bit.ly/2iY6o8i.

[77]IMF, *Review of the Fund's Experience in the Governance Issues*, IMF 2001, pp. 45, 46, 51, 53.

[78]Central banks' autonomy and reliance on markets was true at least for the Victorian period and from the 1980s until the global financial crisis. Not so much in the original Bretton Woods period, C. Goodhart, *The Changing Role of Central Banks*, BIS Working Papers No 326 (2010).

[79]Christodoulou (2005), pp. 183–184.

[80]J. Sanusi, *Central banking authority, economic stability and the rule of law*, Paper presented by Dr Joseph O Sanusi, Governor of the Central Bank of Nigeria, at the Ninth Annual Harvard International Development Conference, Boston, 4 April 2003, http://bit.ly/2jME1y8.

does not prevent third-party control, whether by the Court of Justice of the EU or the IMF, and good practices and guidelines for exercising the central bank's mandate, most importantly rules adopted by the Basle Committee on Banking Supervision. At the same time, the Rule of Law may also limit central bank powers, as reflected in the fascinating *Gauweiler* case concerning the ECB's Outright Monetary Transaction programme, adopted to save the Eurozone, and challenged before the CJEU by the German Federal Constitutional Court.[81] The OMT allowed the ECB to buy EMU government bonds on the secondary market, which—according to the Federal Court—violated the prohibition of monetary financing (Article 123 TFEU).[82]

Yet, despite decades of research and empirical experiments, the relationship eludes quantification. In an ever-changing social context, it is highly unlikely to find a single institutional formula. This partly explains why leading Rule of Law international advocates use complex indices, outsourcing certain variables from other indices that partly overlap, thus amplifying the magnitude of same components while ignoring others. For instance, a hybrid RoL Index presented by a "nonpartisan, non-profit think-tank", the Center for Financial Stability, consists of five variables: Protection of Property Rights, Burden of Government Regulation, Efficiency of Legal Framework in Settling of Disputes, Efficacy of Corporate Boards, and Strength of Investor Protections.[83] Here, however, the first four elements are quantified by the *Global Competitiveness Report* and the last is taken from the World Bank/International Finance Corporation's *Doing Business*. Similar incidents of overlap were indicated above. Accordingly, even though we are not any closer to

---

[81] CJEU, Case C-62/14, *Gauweiler,* ECLI:EU:C:2015:400. For analysis of the case and its supremacy in EU law aspects, see: Fabbrini (2016).

[82] BVerfG, Order of the Second Senate of 14 January 2014—2 BvR 2728/13, paras. 84—87: "the prohibition of monetary financing of the budget enshrined in Art. 123 TFEU also includes a prohibition of bypassing (a). The OMT Decision is likely to violate this prohibition as well (b).

a) Art. 123 TFEU and Art. 21.1. ESCB Statute forbid the purchase of government bonds "directly" from the emitting Member States, i.e. the purchase on the primary market. This prohibition is, however, not limited to this interdiction, but is an expression of a broader prohibition of monetary financing of the budget (. . .) Union law recognises the legal concept of bypassing as do the national legal systems. It is ultimately based on the principle of effectiveness ("effet utile") and has repeatedly been alluded to in the Court of Justice's jurisprudence (. . .)

b) Also in the present context, the Court of Justice has (in the Pringle case) largely focused on the objective pursued by the provision for the interpretation of Art. 125 TFEU (. . .) and thus conducted a teleological interpretation. It seems obvious that this must also apply to the interpretation of Art. 123 TFEU, and that the prohibition of the purchase of government bonds directly from the issuing Member States may not be circumvented by functionally equivalent measures. (. . .)

c) In addition to the above-mentioned aspects (. . .) the following aspects – at least when taken together – also indicate that the OMT Decision aims at a circumvention of Art. 123 TFEU and violates the prohibition of monetary financing of the budget: The willingness to participate in a debt cut with regard to the purchased bonds (aa), the increased risk of such a debt cut regarding the purchased government bonds (bb), the option to keep the purchased government bonds to maturity (cc), the interference with the price formation on the market (dd), and the encouragement of market participants to purchase the bonds in question on the primary market (ee).", https://bit.ly/1JNSayy.

[83] CFS, *CFS 2012-2013 Rule of Law Index (RLI)*, http://bit.ly/2j8Xk3Z.

finding the perfect equilibrium between the Rule of Law and investment flows, several conclusions can be drawn.

After more than two decades of significant financial assistance and restraint (through conditionality) aimed at fostering the Rule of Law, it seems clear, as should have been already seen after the failure of the Law and Development projects, that any legal and judicial reform must be context-dependent. Whether in the form of multilevel constitutionalism, global administrative law or other,[84] socio-cultural factors in accordance with regional preferences must be acknowledged in the structure and substance of law. As proved on numerous occasions, replication of the same structures in a different environment does not entail the same results,[85] as culture must be perceived as both the object of and a predetermining factor of law.[86]

This does not mean, however, that there is no common normative denominator necessary, if international economic cooperation is to be sustained, restructured and strengthened. The formal approach to the Rule of Law constitutes a minimum threshold for any community. Which substantive elements are to be included in this normative core is yet to be discussed. However, as already noted, approaches to the RoL formulated by various international stakeholders largely overlap, not only between different financial organisations but also across international investment, monetary, and financial law. This raises at least doubts as to the normative justification behind the separation doctrine between those fields. The following has to be acknowledged at least: First, efficiency of international economic laws requires a more streamlined approach. Otherwise objectives of investment, on the one hand, and monetary and financial law, on the other hand, either contradict one another, or we witness multiplication of the same functions performed by several bodies. Second, the stability of the system in light of the legitimacy crisis requires internalisation of social externalities, as shown above in respect of the Law & Development and embedded liberalism. This, again, due to the risk of regulatory arbitrage, requires greater convergence between legal regimes. Alternatively we are most likely to continue witnessing current practices best exemplified by the so-called carbon leakage phenomena, Third, international investment law standards appear to provide a good basis for a broader reflection of the role of the Rule of Law in international economic law as they can be found, at least implicitly, in other areas of IEL.[87] However, if RoL reform is to serve the goals stated at the outset of this paper, the future debate must be inclusive with respect to the interest crucial for its legitimacy. Otherwise, any definition will not be worth the paper it is written on.

---

[84]For a comprehensive comparison between various approach to such global constitutionalism, see: Petersmann (2012).

[85]Connelly (2000).

[86]M. Menkes, *Culture: the Creator and the Creation of International Investment Law*, paper at the European Society of International Law and International Law Association conference 'UNESCO World Heritage Between Education And Economy. A Legal Analysis', Ravenna, October 27–28, 2016.

[87]See the works of the International Law Association committee on the Rule of Law and International Investment Law, Conference Report, Sydney 2018, https://bit.ly/2N4ZxL5.

References

Andrews E (2018) Ten years after the financial meltdown: what have we learned? Insights by Stanford Business, Stanford Business Graduate School. https://stanford.io/2A4I9Rs

Ball L (2018) The Fed and Lehman Brothers: setting the record straight on a financial disaster. Cambridge University Press

Barron G (2005) The World Bank & the rule of law reforms. Working Paper Series No. 05-70, Development Studies Institute LSE

Bevir M (2011) Governance as theory, practice, and dilemma. In: Bevir M (ed) The SAGE handbook of governance

Black D (1958) The theory of committees and elections. Cambridge University Press

Blake R (2000) The World Bank's draft comprehensive development framework and the micro-paradigm of law and development. Yale Hum Rights Dev J 3(1):159–189

Burg E (1977) Law and development: a review of the literature and a critique of 'scholars in self-estrangement'. Am J Comp Law 25:492–530

Campbell B (2000) Gouvernance: un concept apolitique?, Séminaire d'été du Haut Conseil de la Coopération Internationale "Le développement: pour un débat politique" Dourdan, France

Cao L (1997) Book review: 'law and economic development: a new beginning?'. Texas Int Law J 32:545–559

Carothers T (2009) Rule of law temptations. Fletcher Forum World Aff 31(1):49–61

Carty A (1992) Law and development. Dartmouth

Chantal T (2008) Re-reading weber in law and development: a critical intellectual history of "good governance" reform. Cornell Law Faculty Publications. Paper 118

Christodoulou P (2005) The issue of the democratic legitimacy of the Eurosystem: a sketch. In: ECB, legal aspects of the European System of Central Banks, ECB, pp 179–188

Chua AL (1998) Markets, democracy, and ethnicity: toward a new paradigm for law and development. Yale Law J 108:1–108

Coase R (1960) The problem of social cost. J Law Econ 3:1–44

Connelly J (2000) Captive University. The Sovietization of East German, Czech, and Polish Higher Education, 1945–1956. The University of North Carolina Press

Cottier T, Jackson JH, Lastra RM (2012) International law in financial regulation and monetary affairs. Oxford University Press

Coyle D (2018) 10 years after the failure of Lehman Brothers: a wasted crisis? The Forum Network. https://bit.ly/2S5c2YP

Davis K, Trebilcock M (1999) What role do legal institutions play in development? paper for the IMF Conference on Second Generation Reforms, November 8–9

Demirgüç-Kunt A (2018) Ten years after Lehman: where are we now? The World Bank. All about finance. https://bit.ly/2R3FbpW

Dietrich M (2002) Three foundations of the rule of law: education, advocacy and judicial reform. In: EBRD, Law in transition. Ten years of legal transition, EBRD

Engelen PJ (2003) Law and finance state of the art. Ekonomia nr 9:118–131

Fabbrini F (2016) The European Court of Justice, the European Central Bank and the supremacy of European law: introduction. In: Fabbrini F (ed) The European Court of Justice, the European Central Bank and the supremacy of EU law. Maastricht Journal of European & Comparative Law Special Issue 23(1)

Faundez J (1997) Good governance and law: legal and institutional reform in developing countries. St. Martin's Press

Fredriksson P, Mani M (2002) The rule of law and the pattern of environmental protection. IMF Working Paper WP/02/49, IMF

Fukuyama F (1992) The end of history and the last man. Free Press

Galanter M, Trubek D (1974) Scholars in self-estrangement: some reflections on the crisis in law and development studies in the united states. Wisconsin Law Rev 1062(4):1062–1102

Gardner J (1982) Legal imperialism: American lawyers and foreign aid in Latin America, University of Wisconsin Press 1980 and its review. Mich Law Rev 80:957–959

Grzybowski K (1990) The council for mutual economic assistance and the European community. AJIL 84:284

Kaufmann D, Kraay A, Zoido-Lobató P (1999) Aggregating governance indicators. IMF Policy Research Working Paper 2 195, IMF

Kress J, McCoy P, Schwarcz D (2018) Regulating entities and activities: complementary approaches to nonbank systemic risk. Southern California Law Review (forthcoming)

La Porta R, Lopez-de-Silanes F, Shleifer A, Vishny RW (1996) Law and finance. NBER Working Paper, no. W5661

Lange M (2005) The rule of law and development: a Weberian Framework of states and state-society relations. In: Lange M, Rueschemeyer D (eds) States and development. Political evolution and institutional change. Palgrave Macmillan, New York

Linarelli J (2014) The European Bank for reconstruction and development and the post-cold war era. Univ Pa J Int Law 16(3):402–408

Liu Y (2018) The rule of law in the International Monetary Fund: past, present and future. AIIB Yearb Int Law

Mashaw J (2005) Structuring a 'dense complexity': accountability and the project of administrative law, Issues in legal scholarship article 4. Berkeley Electronic Press

Mayer (2018) Lehman's lessons, ten years on. The British Academy. https://bit.ly/2Es9Kiv

McAuslan P, Thome J (1997) Law, governance, and the development of the market: practical problems and possible solutions. Julio Faundez

Meeks G, Velu C (2018) Ten years from the crash: time to row back on financial regulation and compliance? LSE US Centre, American Policy and Politics Blog. https://bit.ly/2QCOWMv

Merryman J (1977) Comparative and social change: on the origins, style, decline & revival of the law and development movement. Am J Comp Law 25:457–483

Pes L (2007) Diritto e sviluppo neoliberale: il dibattito sul new law and development. Politica del diritto 4:611–638

Petersmann EU (2012) International economic law in the 21st century. Constitutional pluralism and multilevel governance of interdependent public goods. Bloomsbury, Oxford

Rawi A, Ruggie J (2009) The principles of embedded liberalism: social legitimacy and global capitalism. In: Moss D, Cisternino J (eds) New perspectives on regulation. Harvard Business School, Cambridge, pp 151–162

Sacerdoti G (2011) Nascita, affermazione e scomparsa del Nuovo Ordine Economico Internazionale: un bilancio trant'anni dopo. In: Ligustro A, Sacerdoti G (eds) Problemi e tendenze del diritto internazionale dell'economia. Editoriale Scientifica, pp 127–153

Santos A (2006) The World Bank's uses of the 'rule of law' promise in economic development. In: Trubek D, Santos A (eds) The new law and economic development: a critical appraisal. Cambridge University Press, pp 253–300. http://ssrn.com/abstract=2034333

Shihata I (1991) The World Bank and 'governance' issues in its borrowing members. In: Shihata I (ed) The World Bank in a changing world, vol I

Skeel D (2018) History credits Lehman Brothers' collapse for the 2008 financial crisis. Here's why that narrative is wrong. Brookings Institute, Series on Financial Markets and Regulation. https://brook.gs/2xVjFrY

Steward R (1975) The reformation of American administrative law. Harv Law Rev 88:1667

Supernat J (2004) Administracja publiczna w świetle koncepcji New Public Management, Uniwersytet Wrocławski. http://bit.ly/1w0Wq5a

Tamanaha B (1995) The lessons of law-and-development studies. Am J Int Law 89(2):470–486

Trubek D (2003) The "rule of law" in development assistance: past, present, and future. Global Legal Studies Center University of Wisconsin Law School. https://bit.ly/2EyFPGh

Trubek D, Santos A (2006) The new law and economic development: a critical appraisal. Cambridge University Press

Wetzer T (2018) Ten years after the financial crisis: 'we are safer, but not as safe as we should and could be'. Oxford University Faculty of Law. Business Law Blog. https://bit.ly/2USuaqw

Williamson J (2008) A short history of the Washington Consensus. In: Serra N, Stiglitz JE (eds) The Washington Consensus reconsidered. Oxford University Press

Marcin J. Menkes is an associate professor at the Warsaw School of Economics, where he directs the Post-graduate studies of Law & Economics of the Securities Market. He is a lawyer admitted to Warsaw Bar Association and holds dr. habil. from the Jagiellonian University. He is also graduate of Ph.D. studies in economics (Warsaw School of Economics).

The Appellate Body of the WTO: An International Court by Another Name

Fernando Dias Simões

Contents

1   From an Afterthought to the 'Heart' of the WTO Dispute Settlement System

Within the sphere of activity of the World Trade Organization (WTO), dispute resolution has been the primary focus of attention.[1] This is comprehensible in light of the dispute settlement system's 'central' role in 'providing security and predictability to the multilateral trading system'.[2] On top of this structure lies the Appellate Body, a standing body composed of seven members, three of whom serve on any one case, in rotation.[3] Members of the Appellate Body should be 'broadly representative of membership in the WTO'[4] and, especially, be persons of recognized authority, with demonstrated expertise in law, international trade and the subject

---

[1]Weiler (2002), p. 177.

[2]WTO, Understanding on Rules and Procedures Governing the Settlement of Disputes (hereafter 'DSU'), article 3.2, <https://www.wto.org/english/docs_e/legal_e/28-dsu.pdf>.

[3]DSU, art. 17.1. The Dispute Settlement Body formally set up the Appellate Body in its Decision of 10 February 1995 on the Establishment of the Appellate Body—WT/DSB/1, of 19 June 1995 (henceforth 'Decision of the DSB of 10 February 1995').

[4]DSU, art. 17.3.

F. D. Simões (✉)
Chinese University of Hong Kong, Hong Kong, PR China
e-mail: fdiassimoes@cuhk.edu.hk

© Springer Nature Switzerland AG 2019   361
M. Bungenberg et al. (eds.), *European Yearbook of International Economic Law 2019*,
European Yearbook of International Economic Law (2020) 10: 361–388,
https://doi.org/10.1007/8165_2019_33, Published online: 2 August 2019

matter of the covered agreements generally, and unaffiliated with any government.[5] Their mandate is to hear appeals from panel cases, limited to issues of law covered in the panel report and legal interpretations developed by the panel.[6] Members are appointed on a 4-year term, renewable once.[7]

The idea of creating an Appellate Body was an afterthought in the Uruguay Round negotiations.[8] Few expected the Appellate Body to receive many cases[9] or to play a central role in WTO dispute settlement system.[10] Accordingly, membership of the newly created adjudicatory body was devised as a part-time position. The assumption of a limited, sporadic caseload soon proved inaccurate. The Appellate Body has always had a lot on its plate.[11] In the early years every panel report was appealed.[12] The last two decades witnessed a steady flow of cases, against the expectations of the founders of the system.[13] This high caseload became more of a rule than an exception.[14] The formidable increase in the number of cases was accompanied by a growth in the complexity, novelty, and sophistication of the claims.[15] Over the last two decades the WTO dispute settlement system became 'a judicial branch in full evolution (...) entertaining hundreds of claims and producing a vast jurisprudential acquis.'[16] It has been described as 'prolific',[17] 'one of the most actively used international dispute settlement mechanisms in the world',[18] 'the most effective international tribunal for settling disputes',[19] 'the most active and productive dispute settlement system in the entire field of public international law',[20] the

---

[5]DSU, art. 17.3.

[6]DSU, arts. 17.1 and 17.6.

[7]DSU, art. 17.2.

[8]Van den Bossche (2006), p. 297. See also Elsig (2017). One official who was involved in the negotiations described this unexpected outcome as follows: 'I couldn't believe it myself. Why had the US accepted the creation of the Appellate Body?'—Elsig and Eckhardt (2015), p. 20.

[9]Shaffer et al. (2016), pp. 243–244; Von Bogdandy and Venzke (2014), p. 88; VanGrasstek (2013), p. 241. According to the chairman of the WTO dispute settlement negotiations and first chairman of the Appellate Body, the late Julio Lacarte, many member states believed that panels would continue to be the 'backbone' of WTO dispute settlement and that the Appellate Body would be called upon 'infrequently'—see Graham (2017), p. 114.

[10]Graham (2016), p. 3; Graham (2017), p. 113.

[11]Mavroidis (2008), p. 367.

[12]VanGrasstek (2013), p. 242.

[13]Ehlermann (2004), p. 503; Hughes (2005b), p. 26; Azevêdo (2014), p. 2; Hughes (2008), p. 494.

[14]Hughes (2008), p. 494; Hughes (2009), p. 282.

[15]Azevêdo (2014), p. 2; VanGrasstek (2013), p. 242; Wha Chang (2017), p. 105.

[16]Howse (2016), p. 10.

[17]Van den Bossche (2003), p. 3; Van den Bossche and Zdouc (2013), p. 157; de Baere et al. (2016), p. 773.

[18]Huber and Tereposky (2017), p. 546.

[19]Matsushita (2012), p. 510.

[20]Palmeter (2008), p. 854.

'busiest forum litigating State-to-State disputes'[21] and even the 'busiest international dispute settlement system in history'.[22] As a matter of fact, Appellate Body members decide more disputes per year than judges of the International Court of Justice.[23] In the words of Howse, the Appellate Body is 'a formidable engine of global economic governance, probably the most active and productive of all international courts not only in the number and range of its decisions but also in the number of disputes that its jurisprudential guidance has helped to settle, often out of the courtroom.'[24] The Appellate Body has definitely grown from an 'afterthought' to a 'centerpiece',[25] becoming the 'heart' of the WTO dispute settlement system.[26]

The WTO dispute settlement mechanism has been by and large considered a success.[27] The growing number and complexity of the WTO caseload can be said to reflect the consolidation of the system.[28] The Appellate Body, in particular, has been labeled 'a notable success'[29] and even 'conspicuously successful'.[30] This probably explains why proposals specifically targeted at reforming the Appellate Body are not frequent.[31] However, the intensification of political tensions on a global scale following the election of Donald Trump as President of the United States of America also reverberates within the international trading system. The Appellate Body, and the WTO's dispute settlement mechanism as a whole, is currently under grave threat. Several procedural and substantive objections to Appellate Body practice voiced by the Obama administration are being taken to a new, unprecedented level by the Trump administration.[32] The United States' obstruction of the appointment or reappointment of various members has reduced the number of current Appellate Body members to three. While some cases can still be heard by the remaining three judges, this will only make it more difficult to meet deadlines, aggravating the current backlog.[33] In addition, some cases in which one of the three members took part in an earlier stage could not be decided due to conflict of interest issues.[34] To

---

[21]Mavroidis (2013), p. 103; Hoekman and Mavroidis (2007), p. 82.

[22]Bacchus (2002), p. 1026.

[23]Petersmann (1999), p. 241; WTO, Committee on Budget, Finance and Administration (2004), p. 4.

[24]Howse (2016), p. 75.

[25]Van den Bossche (2006), p. 292.

[26]Von Bogdandy and Venzke (2014), p. 88.

[27]Van Den Bossche (2009), p. 113; Yanovich (2007), p. 248; Davey (2008), p. 409; Matsushita (2008), pp. 505 and 523; Matsushita (2012), p. 510; Hughes (2006), p. 193.

[28]Ehlermann (2016), p. 29.

[29]Davey (2014), p. 690.

[30]Crawford and McIntyre (2012), p. 190.

[31]Miyagawa (2007), p. 278.

[32]See Condon (2018); Gantz (2018), pp. 3 ff; Shaffer et al. (2017a); Kuijper (2017); Marquet (2018); Payosova et al. (2018).

[33]Art. 17.5 of the DSU requires reports to be issued in no more than 90 days after appeal.

[34]Art. 17.3 of the DSU specifies that members 'shall not participate in the consideration of any disputes that would create a direct or indirect conflict of interest'.

make matters even worse, on 10 December 2019 two of the current members (Ujal Singh Bhatia and Thomas Graham) will finish their terms.[35] If they are not replaced, the Appellate Body will fall below the minimum number of three required by the DSU.[36]

It is still unclear whether the Trump administration is keen on ultimately abolishing the WTO's dispute settlement system or merely using its paralysis as a bargaining chip to persuade other WTO members to share its concerns and agree on potential solutions.[37] What is beyond doubt is that this deadlock is putting enormous pressure on a body that has been under significant stress since its inception. In addition, by using the Appellate Body as a 'trump card' for reform of the whole system, the United States is politicizing the appointment process,[38] fragilizing the independence of its members.[39] Several solutions have been put forward to solve this stalemate in the short and even longer term, as part of a broader process of reform of the dispute settlement mechanism.[40] While not offering any suggestions to address the current impasse, this chapter invites WTO member states to reflect about the role that the Appellate Body plays as an international tribunal and whether its original features still serve its mandate. The current deadlock offers a unique opportunity to shift the mind-set and institutional philosophy underpinning the Appellate Body: WTO membership should start treating the Appellate Body as a real court, and its members as true judges.

2 'On-Call' Judges

Appellate Body members are required to 'be available at all times and on short notice' and 'stay abreast of dispute settlement activities and other relevant activities of the WTO.'[41] This requirement finds no parallel in the statutes of the International Court of Justice,[42] the International Criminal Court[43] or the International Tribunal

---

[35]WTO, 'Appellate Body Members', <https://www.wto.org/english/tratop_e/dispu_e/ab_members_descrp_e.htm>.

[36]DSU, art. 17.1.

[37]Gantz (2018), p. 2.

[38]Shaffer et al. (2017a), p. 5; Condon (2018), p. 551.

[39]Sacerdoti (2017a), p. 123; Shaffer et al. (2017a), p. 5.

[40]See, e.g., Payosova et al. (2018), Andersen et al. (2017), Bacchus (2018) and Raina (2018).

[41]DSU, article 17.3.

[42]The Statute of the International Court of Justice provides that its members 'shall be bound, unless they are on leave or prevented from attending by illness or other serious reasons duly explained to the President, to hold themselves permanently at the disposal of the Court.' This results from the fact that the court is permanently in session, except during the judicial vacations and periodic leave—Statute of the International Court of Justice, art. 23, <http://www.icj-cij.org/en/statute>.

[43]Rome Statute of the International Criminal Court, <https://www.icc-cpi.int/resourcelibrary/official-journal/rome-statute.aspx>.

for the Law of the Sea[44] because it is plain to see that judges in these adjudicatory bodies should be 'available' for work and keep themselves acquainted with the applicable law.[45] Taking into account that Appellate Body members were not expected to work full-time, the creators of the Appellate Body found it necessary to guarantee they would be readily available for WTO work.[46] The regime contained in the DSU is complemented by the Decision of the Dispute Settlement Body of 10 February 1995,[47] which regulates the operation of the Appellate Body in greater detail. As regard the conditions of employment of its members, the Decision starts by recalling that, pursuant to the DSU, Appellate Body members 'shall be available at all times and on short notice'. According to the Decision, '[t]he first part of this clause suggests that members of the Appellate Body have a priority working relationship with the WTO. The second part of the clause suggests that members may have other activities.'[48] The Decision further adds:

> The contractual basis of members of the Appellate Body should reflect the overriding concern that candidates are of a high enough calibre to ensure the integrity and authority of decisions taken by the Appellate Body. The requirement that high-calibre members be available at all times could be met, on a flexible basis, by offering Appellate Body members contracts based on a monthly retainer plus a fee for actual days worked. This contractual arrangement could also lead to a wider range of candidates being available, since members could continue to pursue other activities where they were resident. This arrangement could be kept under review by the DSB, and considered at the latest at the first Ministerial Conference, to determine whether a move to full-time employment was warranted.[49]

These provisions are supplemented by the Working Procedures for Appellate Review,[50] which set out the duties and responsibilities of members of the Appellate Body. During his/her term, a member of the Appellate Body 'shall not accept any employment nor pursue any professional activity that is inconsistent with his/her duties and responsibilities.'[51] An *a contrario* reading of this provision confirms that members of the Appellate Body are allowed to pursue other professional activities as long as they are compatible with their work for the Appellate Body[52] and do not

---

[44]Statute of the International Tribunal for the Law of the Sea, <https://www.itlos.org/fileadmin/itlos/documents/basic_texts/statute_en.pdf>.

[45]Van den Bossch (2005), p. 66; Van den Bossche (2006), p. 297.

[46]Van den Bossch (2005), p. 66; Van den Bossche (2006), p. 297.

[47]Decision of the DSB of 10 February 1995. See also Preparatory Committee for the World Trade Organization, Sub-Committee on Institutional, Procedural and Legal Matters, Establishment of the Appellate Body: Recommendations by the Preparatory Committee to the WTO approved on 6 December, PC/IPL/13, of 8 December 1994.

[48]Decision of the DSB of 10 February 1995, para 10.

[49]Decision of the DSB of 10 February 1995, para 11. Footnotes omitted.

[50]WTO, Working Procedures for Appellate Review (WT/AB/WP/6), of 16 August 2010.

[51]WTO, Working Procedures for Appellate Review, art. 2(2).

[52]Walter (2006), p. 450.

prevent them from serving on a case on short notice.[53] To this end, Appellate Body members shall keep the Secretariat informed of their whereabouts at all times.[54]

The creators of the Appellate Body did not consider a part-time status to be incompatible with the objective of luring candidates 'of a high enough calibre'.[55] A permanent institution operated with part-time adjudicators is not totally unusual in the international arena.[56] In fact, while some international courts and tribunals employ their adjudicators on a full-time basis, others opt for a part-time regime.[57] The latter option has been frequently adopted as way to deal more efficiently with variable caseloads.[58] Because its members are appointed on a part-time basis, the Appellate Body can be said to be a quasi-permanent, standing tribunal,[59] or, at least, its members can be said to be semi-permanent.[60]

The existing regulatory framework reflects the expectations of the creators of the Appellate Body in 1995. Under the General Agreement on Tariffs and Trade, dispute settlement had almost always been a 'part-time affair'.[61] Naturally, member states could not possibly guess how many cases would be filed and how many would get to the appeal stage of the newly created appellate review mechanism.[62] In their minds, Appellate Body members would be called upon sporadically to hear a few cases per year,[63] operating like a 'safety net of last resort' that would be activated only to correct egregious decisions by panels.[64] Since the Appellate Body's caseload would be low, it did not seem reasonable to retain its members full-time.[65] The first members were recruited based on this assumption,[66] and during some years this decision proved sensible as the number of appeals did not justify any changes to their regime.[67]

---

[53]Steger and Hainsworth (1998), p. 207.

[54]WTO, Working Procedures for Appellate Review, art. 2(4).

[55]Van den Bossch (2005), p. 67; Van den Bossche (2006), p. 299.

[56]Sacerdoti (2006a), p. 43; Sacerdoti (2006b), p. 59.

[57]Terris et al. (2007), p. 53.

[58]Mackenzie and Sands (2003), p. 283.

[59]Steger (1996), p. 325; Steger and Hainsworth (1998), p. 203.

[60]Wofford (2000), pp. 564 and 591; Conti (2011), p. 65.

[61]Jackson (1998), p. 173.

[62]Lowenfeld (2008), p. 179.

[63]Terris et al. (2007), p. 106; Shaffer et al. (2016), pp. 245–246; Graham (2016), pp. 3–4.

[64]Terris et al. (2007), p. 106.

[65]United Nations Conference on Trade and Development (2003b), p. 5; Hughes (2009), p. 282; Sacerdoti (2006a), p. 43; Sacerdoti (2006b), p. 59; Venzke (2012), p. 193; Van den Bossche and Zdouc (2013), p. 232, fn. 421; Van den Bossche (2006), p. 299.

[66]Bernal et al. (1998), p. 879.

[67]Ehlermann (2004), p. 503.

Since Appellate Body members were appointed on a part-time basis, they were not expected to reside in Geneva, where Appellate Body proceedings take place,[68] and normally they do not.[69] Members travel from their home locations whenever they have to decide an appeal.[70] Furthermore, as mentioned above, Appellate Body members are allowed to initiate or continue other professional commitments. The original members of the Appellate Body accepted their mandate on this assumption.[71] Many Appellate Body members work simultaneously as scholars, practising lawyers, or arbitrators.[72] Still, pursuant to the Working Procedures for Appellate Review, such activities should not be inconsistent with their duties and responsibilities as Appellate Body members.[73] While the rules do not clarify what 'activities' would be 'inconsistent', it seems clear that the exercise of functions as lawyer or consultant in WTO matters would be excluded.[74] On the other hand, this provision should not be confused with the circumstances that disqualify Appellate Body members from hearing a specific case.[75]

The fact that Appellate Body members may pursue other professional activities leads some to express concern about potential conflicts of interests.[76] The DSU provides that Appellate Body members shall not participate in the consideration of any disputes that would create a direct or indirect conflict of interest.[77] This injunction is developed in the Rules of Conduct for the Understanding on Rules and Procedures Governing the Settlement of Disputes.[78] Whenever selected to hear

---

[68]Bernal et al. (1998), p. 875; Petersmann (1998), p. 39; Hudec (1999), p. 28; United Nations Conference on Trade and Development (2003b), p. 5; Hughes (2005a), p. 84; Mavroidis and Van der Borght (2006), p. 206; Lowenfeld (2008), p. 179; Van den Bossche and Zdouc (2013), p. 232; Steger (2015), p. 454; Pauwelyn (2015), pp. 790–791.

[69]Donaldson (2005), p. 1288, fn. 60; Petersmann (1998), p. 28; United Nations Conference on Trade and Development (2003b), p. 5; Hughes (2005a), p. 84; Mavroidis and Van der Borght (2006), p. 206; Lowenfeld (2008), p. 179; Van den Bossche and Zdouc (2013), p. 232; Steger (2015), p. 454; Pauwelyn (2015), pp. 790–791.

[70]United Nations Conference on Trade and Development (2003b), p. 5.

[71]Bernal et al. (1998), p. 875.

[72]Hughes (2005a), p. 84; Hughes (2009), p. 282; Pauwelyn (2015), pp. 790–791; Graham (2016), p. 4; Amerasinghe (2009), p. 520; WTO (2017), p. 33; Graham (2013), p. 4; Hughes (2008), p. 494.

[73]WTO, Working Procedures for Appellate Review, art. 2(2).

[74]Mavroidis and Van der Borght (2006), p. 207.

[75]Mavroidis and Van der Borght (2006), p. 207, fn. 24.

[76]Nader (1994), p. A12; Shell (1995), p. 850, fn. 99.

[77]DSU, art. 17.3.

[78]WTO, Rules of Conduct for the Understanding on Rules and Procedures Governing the Settlement of Disputes (WT/AB/WP/6), annex II, of 16 August 2010. According to the preamble, the goal of the Rules of Conduct is to strengthen the operation of the DSU by rules of conduct 'designed to maintain the integrity, impartiality and confidentiality of proceedings conducted under the DSU thereby enhancing confidence in the new dispute settlement mechanism'. In an annex, the Rules contain an illustrative list of information to be disclosed, which includes 'professional interests (e.g. a past or present relationship with private clients, or any interests the person may have in domestic or international proceedings, and their implications, where these involve issues similar to

an appeal, members of the Appellate Body are also required to sign a disclosure form.[79] However, this document does not exclude particular activities, offering only very broad hints about what kind of professional activities may (and may not) be performed by Appellate Body members.[80] Even though concerns about potential conflicts of interests in WTO dispute settlement are rare, and mostly limited to the panel system,[81] the possibility of cumulating different activities raises questions as to which activities are admissible.[82] Such doubts do not make sense in a full-time regime, which by nature excludes any other activities, whether conflicting or not.[83]

Members of the Appellate Body, like other part-time adjudicators, are not subject to the same restrictions regarding external activities as full-time judges.[84] The Burgh House Principles on the Independence of the International Judiciary,[85] a scholarly attempt to distil general principles on judicial independence and impartiality in international courts and tribunals, recognise that each institution is unique.[86] Thus, the applicability of the principles might vary depending on whether adjudicators

---

those addressed in the dispute in question)'. On the Rules, see Marceau (1998); Renouf (2005), pp. 120–127; Donaldson (2005), pp. 1307–1308.

[79]See WTO, Working Procedures for Appellate Review, art. 9(1), and WTO, Rules of Conduct for the Understanding on Rules and Procedures Governing the Settlement of Disputes, article VI:4(b)(i). The disclosure form reads: 'I have read the Understanding on Rules and Procedures Governing the Settlement of Disputes (DSU) and the Rules of Conduct for the DSU. I understand my continuing duty, while participating in the dispute settlement mechanism, and until such time as the Dispute Settlement Body (DSB) makes a decision on adoption of a report relating to the proceeding or notes its settlement, to disclose herewith and in future any information likely to affect my independence or impartiality, or which could give rise to justifiable doubts as to the integrity and impartiality of the dispute settlement mechanism; and to respect my obligations regarding the confidentiality of dispute settlement proceedings.'—Annex 3 to the Working Procedures for Appellate Review.

[80]Mavroidis and Van der Borght (2006), p. 207.

[81]Mackenzie and Sands (2003), p. 281; Davey (2003), pp. 180–181; Pauwelyn (2015), p. 780, fn. 120.

[82]Mackenzie and Sands (2003), p. 283.

[83]As stated by the United States in its 2009 proposal to move members of the Appellate Body into a full-time regime, '[a]nother problem with the part-time status of Appellate Body members is that it allows for, and may even require, Appellate Body members to engage in other paid employment. Attempting to retain other employment while being an Appellate Body member raises the possibility of conflicts of interest; it is not in the interests of WTO Members to increase the possibility of an inadvertent conflict of interest presenting itself in the course, or after conclusion, of an appeal.'—see Dispute Settlement Body, Improvements for the WTO Appellate Body—Proposal by the United States, WT/DSB/W/398, of 16 January 2009, p. 2.

[84]Mackenzie and Sands (2003), p. 283.

[85]The Principles were drafted between 2002 and 2004 by the International Law Association (ILA) Study Group on the Practice and Procedure of International Tribunals in collaboration with the Project on International Courts and Tribunals and the Centre on International Courts and Tribunals, University College of London. The Principles are published as an annex to Sands et al. (2005), pp. 251 ff.

[86]Sands et al. (2005), p. 249.

serve on a full-time or part-time basis.[87] Each adjudicatory body should ponder on the application of the Burgh House Principles taking into account its specific circumstances.[88] As regards extra-judicial activities, the Principles state that '[j] udges shall not engage in any extra-judicial activity that is incompatible with their judicial function or the efficient and timely functioning of the court of which they are members, or that may affect or may reasonably appear to affect their independence or impartiality.'[89]

In similar fashion, the International Bar Association's Minimum Standards of Judicial Independence,[90] adopted in 1982, provide that part-time judges 'should be appointed only with proper safeguards.'[91] The Montreal Universal Declaration on the Independence of Justice (Montreal Declaration),[92] from 1983, states that '[t]he appointment of temporary judges and the appointment of judges for probationary periods is inconsistent with judicial independence. Where such appointments exist, they shall be phased out gradually.'[93] However, an explanatory note clarifies that this provision is not intended to exclude part-time judges.[94] Still, where such practice exists, 'proper safeguards shall be laid down to ensure impartiality and avoid conflict of interests.'[95] While other major non-binding instruments are silent on the question of part-time adjudicators, some make it clear that their provisions apply, to the extent possible, to all individuals exercising judicial functions.[96]

There is no universal standard of independence and impartiality. As emphasized in the Burgh House Principles on the Independence of the International Judiciary, each institution is unique.[97] Still, the appointment of part-time adjudicators may tend

---

[87]The preamble to the Burgh House Principles on the Independence of the International Judiciary notes that 'each court or tribunal has its own characteristics and functions and that in certain instances judges serve on a part-time basis or as ad hoc or ad litem judges (. . .)'. Therefore, the Principles 'shall apply primarily to standing international courts and tribunals (. . .) and to full-time judges. The Principles should also be applied as appropriate to judges ad hoc, judges ad litem and part-time judges, to international arbitral proceedings and to other exercises of international judicial power.'—Burgh House Principles on the Independence of the International Judiciary. See also Sands et al. (2005), p. 249.

[88]Sands et al. (2005), p. 249.

[89]Burgh House Principles on the Independence of the International Judiciary, art. 8(1).

[90]International Bar Association's Minimum Standards of Judicial Independence, <https://www. ibanet.org/Document/Default.aspx?DocumentUid=bb019013-52b1-427c-ad25-a6409b49fe29>.

[91]International Bar Association's Minimum Standards of Judicial Independence, §25.

[92]Montreal Universal Declaration on the Independence of Justice, unanimously adopted at the final plenary session of the First World Conference on the Independence of Justice held at Montreal (Quebec, Canada) on 10 June 1983, <https://www.icj.org/wp-content/uploads/2016/02/Montreal-Declaration.pdf>.

[93]Montreal Universal Declaration on the Independence of Justice, §2.20.

[94]Montreal Universal Declaration on the Independence of Justice, §2.20.

[95]Montreal Universal Declaration on the Independence of Justice, §2.20.

[96]Olbourne (2003), p. 123.

[97]Sands et al. (2005), p. 249.

to indicate a lack of independence.[98] The increasing resort by courts and tribunals to part-time adjudicators makes it harder to allay fears of bias, whether actual or merely apparent.[99] The international judiciary, in particular, is debilitated by the fact that a great part of the adjudicative process is still conducted by part-time or ad hoc judges.[100]

The creators of the WTO dispute settlement system did not seem to be as concerned with potential conflicts of interests as to require members to forego any other professional activities and devote their activity exclusively to the Appellate Body. Still, because some member states were not exactly happy with this option[101] the Dispute Settlement Body promised to keep a move into a full-time regime open to discussion in the future.[102]

3   A Court by Any Other Name

More than two decades after its creation, the Appellate Body retains the original structure, with members still being appointed (at least formally) on a part-time basis.[103] At first, some expressed doubts about who would accept taking such an appointment and committing to be 'available at all times and on short notice.'[104] This problem did not emerge, as the Appellate Body was always able to attract high-level professionals. Naturally, the reputation associated with the position contributes to this.[105] Yet, the fact is that Appellate Body members continue to be paid on a part-time basis even though their workload frequently equates to a full-time position.[106] The remuneration conditions designed at the inception of the Appellate Body clearly do not match the present reality.[107] The part-time arrangement may actually narrow down the pool of potential candidates.[108] This disconnect between original

---

[98]Crawford and McIntyre (2012), p. 198.

[99]Brown (2003), p. 96.

[100]Crawford and McIntyre (2012), p. 191.

[101]Van den Bossche (2006), p. 300.

[102]Decision of the DSB of 10 February 1995, para 11.

[103]Graham (2016), p. 4.

[104]Lowenfeld (1994), p. 484.

[105]Hughes (2008), p. 495; Hughes (2005b), p. 31.

[106]Steger (2004), p. 45; Office of the United States Trade Representative, WTO Appoint US Trade Scholar to WTO Appellate Body, 7 November 2003, <https://ustr.gov/archive/Document_Library/ Press_Releases/2003/November/WTO_Appoints_US_Trade_Scholar_to_WTO_Appellate_Body. html>; Office of the United States Trade Representative, U.S. Proposes WTO Appellate Body Reforms (2009), <https://ustr.gov/about-us/policy-offices/press-office/press-releases/2009/janu ary/us-proposes-wto-appellate-body-reforms>.

[107]Hughes (2008), p. 495.

[108]Office of the United States Trade Representative, U.S. Proposes WTO Appellate Body Reforms (2009).

expectations and present-day demands puts the future of the Appellate Body, and of the WTO dispute settlement system more broadly, in risk.[109] In the words of Hughes[110]:

> The WTO membership has been extremely fortunate thus far to have had dedicated Appellate Body members willing to serve the system on a part-time basis and at a moment's notice under the demanding circumstances of a 90-day timeline. The question is whether the good fortune thus enjoyed by the WTO membership will continue. In my view, there is a risk that the pool of those interested and willing to serve on the Appellate Body will grow increasingly smaller, and that even those who accept to serve will find it increasingly difficult to devote the considerable time needed at home and in Geneva to carry out the demanding work with the necessary attention.

Potential candidates consider a position at the Appellate Body after pondering on many factors which go beyond remuneration conditions. These are not, however, negligible. Accepting an appointment as member of the Appellate Body is a commitment that, like any other professional activity, has its perks and downsides, requiring an overall assessment. From the side of the 'employer', a similar all-rounded evaluation is necessary on what conditions should be offered. A move towards a full-time regime should not be based merely on budgetary concerns.[111] Beyond the more mundane remuneration questions, there is a fundamental reason why Appellate Body members should be promoted to a full-time status—and that is to acknowledge the work they do and dignify the position they occupy.

The founders of the Appellate Body did not wish to give it too much 'institutional clout'.[112] This is demonstrated by the fact that, among the 27 provisions of the Dispute Settlement Understanding, only one—article 17—focuses exclusively on the Appellate Body.[113] Furthermore, this provision is extremely cautious in its terminology.[114] While the use of the term 'appellate' brings to mind judicial landscapes,[115] the founders of the WTO decided not to call the 'Dispute Settlement Body' a court[116] or 'tribunal'.[117] They did not refer to adjudicators as 'judges' either: at the Panel level, the dispute is reviewed by 'panelists',[118] and at the Appellate

---

[109]Hughes (2008), p. 494.

[110]Hughes (2008), pp. 494–495.

[111]Dispute Settlement Body, Minutes of the Meeting held in the Centre William Rappard on 12 March 2001, WT/DSB/M/101, of 8 May 2001, p. 25, para 119.

[112]Mavroidis and Van der Borght (2006), p. 206.

[113]Mavroidis and Van der Borght (2006), p. 206.

[114]Messenger (2016a), p. 129.

[115]Messenger (2016b), p. 54, fn. 42.

[116]Weiler (2002), p. 190; Hughes (2008), p. 491; Ghias (2006), p. 542; Terris et al. (2007), p. 270, fn. 7; Elsig and Pollack (2014), p. 402; Shaffer et al. (2016), pp. 237 and 246; Messenger (2016b), p. 54; Shaffer et al. (2017b), p. 280; Messenger (2016a), p. 129; McRae (2004), p. 7.

[117]Messenger (2016a), p. 129; Montana I Mora (1993), p. 144; Messenger (2016b), p. 54.

[118]Ghias (2006), p. 542.

Body level, by 'persons who comprise the Appellate Body membership'.[119] Panels and Appellate Body have no fixed bench per se.[120] They issue 'reports' which are subject to adoption by the Dispute Settlement Body, not 'judgements'.[121] Its 'rules of procedure' are called 'working rules'.[122] Its 'registrar' is known as 'chief administrator'.[123] This is unusual terminology, to say the least.

In the words of former Appellate Body member Peter Van den Bossch, '[t]he decision to establish a standing Appellate Body was certainly not the reflection of a grand design to create a strong, authoritative court that would be at the epicentre of the new WTO dispute settlement system.'[124] The use of discreet, understated nomenclature reflects the views and limited expectations of the negotiators at the time. WTO members clearly avoided the use of the word 'court', opting for the 'unappealing, technical, non-descriptive term' Appellate Body.[125] They also circumvented the use of the word 'judge',[126] probably to tone down the judicialization of dispute settlement that the creation of the Appellate Body entailed.[127] The use of this alternative terminology reveals an attempt at discursive control.[128] More than a question of semantics, such vocabulary suggests a veiled purpose: to reduce the authority of the Appellate Body,[129] maintaining a 'façade of ultimate political control over dispute settlement',[130] probably in an attempt to overcome the reluctance of states to commit to international adjudication.[131] According to Weiler, the use of this 'non-judicial nomenclature'[132] 'serves for the internal legitimacy of the construct to pretend' that the Appellate Body is not a court.[133] The problem is that avoiding the use of the word 'court' ends up diminishing the external legitimacy of the WTO in general and the Appellate Body in particular.[134]

---

[119]Petersmann (2014), p. 659; Ghias (2006), p. 542; Terris et al. (2007), p. 270, fn. 7; Elsig and Pollack (2014), p. 402; Shaffer et al. (2017b), p. 246; Messenger (2016b), p. 54; Shaffer et al. (2017b), p. 280; Hughes (2008), p. 491.

[120]Ghias (2006), p. 542.

[121]Ghias (2006), p. 542; Terris et al. (2007), p. 270, fn. 7; Elsig and Pollack (2014), p. 402; Messenger (2016b), p. 54; Kolsky Lewis (2006), p. 911; McRae (2004), p. 7; Hughes (2008), p. 491.

[122]Terris et al. (2007), p. 270, fn. 7.

[123]Terris et al. (2007), p. 270, fn. 7.

[124]Van den Bossch (2005), p. 67; Van den Bossche (2006), pp. 294 and 300.

[125]Van den Bossch (2005), p. 65; Van den Bossche (2006), p. 294.

[126]Van den Bossch (2005), p. 65; Van den Bossche (2006), p. 294.

[127]Mavroidis et al. (2010), p. 1024, fn. 1.

[128]See Elsig and Pollack (2014), p. 402.

[129]Shaffer et al. (2016), p. 237.

[130]Shany (2014), p. 146, fn. 40.

[131]Montana I Mora (1993), p. 144.

[132]Kolsky Lewis (2006), p. 911.

[133]Weiler (2002), p. 190.

[134]Weiler (2002), p. 190.

Terminology aside, in practice the Appellate Body resembles a court.[135] Among the institutions involved in dispute settlement at the WTO, one can distinguish between political institutions, such as the Dispute Settlement Body, and judicial-type institutions, such as the ad hoc panels and the Appellate Body.[136] The creation of the Appellate Body was a clear move towards 'legalism'[137] and a 'significant step toward the creation of an international legal tribunal on trade'.[138] The 'standing' nature of the Appellate Body demonstrates the idea of creating a body that bears resemblance to a judicial institution.[139] While some of its characteristics distance it from other judicial settlement processes, there are clear suggestions that the goal was to create a juridical process.[140] The founders of the Appellate Body 'deliberately stopped short of creating a court per se.'[141] Weiler quotes state delegations that expressed some incredulity when they realized they had 'created a court' and adds: '[t]hey are right. That is exactly what the Appellate Body is.'[142]

The Appellate Body has a clear judicial physiognomy.[143] It was designed to adjudicate disputes in a court-like manner,[144] not just enable negotiations.[145] In a broad sense, the concept of court covers any institution that performs a court-like function, and that is exactly what the Appellate Body does, even if it does not formally decide appeals.[146] In practice, the Appellate Body has become an independent court,[147] not just the enforcement wing of the WTO.[148] Authors refer to it using a myriad of designations with a judicial flavor: 'judicial-type institution',[149] 'judicial body',[150] 'judicial organ',[151] 'judicial power',[152] 'international court',[153]

---

[135] Shaffer et al. (2017b), p. 277.

[136] Sacerdoti (2006b), p. 67; United Nations Conference on Trade and Development (2003a), p. 49; Van den Bossche and Zdouc (2013), p. 205.

[137] Young (1995), p. 403; Montana I Mora (1993), p. 151; Elsig and Eckhardt (2015), p. 14.

[138] Dillon Jr. (1995), p. 379.

[139] Charnovitz (2015), p. 99; Montana I Mora (1993), p. 144; Baudenbacher (2004), p. 394.

[140] McRae (2004), p. 7.

[141] Ghias (2006), p. 542.

[142] Weiler (2002), p. 191.

[143] Janow (2008), pp. 250 and 255; Montana I Mora (1993), p. 144; Sacerdoti (2006b), p. 52; Romano (1999), p. 719.

[144] Ghias (2006), p. 542.

[145] Litvak (1995), p. 583.

[146] Von Bogdandy and Venzke (2013), p. 162, fn 1.

[147] Howse (2016), p. 12.

[148] Howse (2016), p. 12.

[149] United Nations Conference on Trade and Development (2003a), p. 49.

[150] Reitz (1996), p. 583.

[151] Kelly (2002), pp. 353–354.

[152] Howse (2003), p. 11.

[153] Ghias (2006), p. 553.

'independent judicial tribunal',[154] 'high court',[155] 'standing, high-order tribunal',[156] 'appellate court',[157] 'the second instance WTO court',[158] 'the mighty court of world trade',[159] the 'world trade court',[160] 'supercourt',[161] 'court of last resort',[162] 'last instance court',[163] 'the highest appeals court for the rules of global trade',[164] 'the supreme court of the WTO',[165] the 'supreme custodian of WTO Law'.[166] In some aspects the Appellate Body even resembles a traditional constitutional court.[167]

The Appellate Body is frequently labelled a 'quasi-judicial' institution.[168] The prefix is employed because its decisions are not legally binding as they need to be approved by the Dispute Settlement Body.[169] Even though the Appellate Body cannot be qualified as a truly judicial system, there is no doubt that it performs a quasi-judicial function.[170] It is actually closer to a judicial institution than ad hoc panels.[171] Still, it can be said that both bodies 'fall within the province of judicial settlement.'[172] The use of the term 'quasi-judicial' has become commonplace despite the fact that, in practice, the Appellate Body has the main features of true courts.[173] This designation is outdated and undercuts the perception of the Appellate Body as an independent institution, weakening its authority.[174]

Notwithstanding the official nomenclature, members of the Appellate Body have clearly seen themselves as judges.[175] From the beginning, members of the Appellate Body have been exercising their function as members of the international judiciary

---

[154]Howse (2003), p. 11.

[155]Shoyer and Forton (1998), p. 740; Weiler (2002), p. 188.

[156]Broude (2004), p. 133.

[157]Shaffer et al. (2016), p. 238; Ghias (2006), p. 535; Ehlermann (2004), p. 500.

[158]Mavroidis (2013), p. 107.

[159]Porges (2003), p. 141.

[160]Ehlermann (2004), p. 599; Van den Bossch (2005), p. 64; Van den Bossche (2006), p. 289; Ragosta et al. (2003), p. 697.

[161]Evans (2000), p. 47.

[162]Kolsky Lewis (2006), p. 911.

[163]Mavroidis et al. (2010), p. 881.

[164]Graham (2013), p. 2.

[165]Lawrence (2007), p. 7; Abi-Saab (2005), p. 10.

[166]Vermulst and Graafsma (2002), p. 43, fn. 89.

[167]Gaffney (1999), p. 1191.

[168]Steger (2002), p. 482; Smith (2003), p. 66; Ehlermann (2003), p. 470; Hughes (2008), p. 491.

[169]Ehlermann (2003), pp. 470 and 478; Graham (2017), p. 113; Graham (2016), p. 3; Petersmann (2007), p. 87.

[170]Ehlermann (2003), p. 479; Petersmann (2007), p. 87.

[171]Ehring (2008), p. 1029.

[172]Gaffney (1999), p. 1182.

[173]Ruiz Fabri (2009), p. 155.

[174]Hughes (2008), p. 492.

[175]Ehlermann (2004), p. 500; Kolsky Lewis (2006), p. 911; Venzke (2013), p. 249.

comparable, for instance, to the judges of the International Court of Justice.[176] They have been applying the law as judicial bodies do, and even following prior decisions of the Appellate Body itself.[177] Appellate Body members are increasingly more comfortable in the exercise of their judicial function,[178] and many authors refer to them as 'judges'.[179] In fact, that word describes better what they do—they decide cases.[180]

The creation of the Appellate Body was a clear step towards the judicialization of dispute settlement at the WTO.[181] Even though some aspects of its structure could in theory diminish its normative authority, in practice this has not happened.[182] It can be said that the level of judicialization attained by the Appellate Body surpassed expectations, and it is now established as a true international court.[183] Regardless of discussions about the precise nature of the Appellate Body, the fact is that 'it looks like a court, it works much like a court, and one litigates as in a court.'[184]

The dispute settlement mechanism is time and again described as the 'jewel in the crown' of the WTO.[185] It has been portrayed as 'unique (...) as a matter of international law juridical activity, and (...) probably unique in all of world history'[186] and 'arguably the most authoritative judicial institution at the multilateral level in world politics'.[187] In the words of Hughes, '[t]he WTO dispute settlement system is THE success story of the WTO.'[188] Owing to this success, the WTO dispute resolution system is often advanced as a model for other areas of international law.[189] The Appellate Body, in particular, has been suggested as a prototype for other areas of international public law,[190] namely investment treaty arbitration.[191]

---

[176]Van Damme (2010), p. 606; Van Damme (2009), pp. 7 and 156 ff; Abi-Saab (2006), pp. 455–456; Mitchell (2007), p. 829; Ghias (2006), p. 542; McRae (2004), p. 7.

[177]McRae (2004), p. 7.

[178]Van Damme (2009), p. 210.

[179]See, e.g., Kelly (2002), pp. 353 and 369; Esserman and Howse (2003), *passim*; Wofford (2000), p. 567; Mavroidis (2014), p. 243; Mavroidis (2013), p. 103; Mavroidis (2009), *passim*; Mavroidis (2008), *passim*.

[180]Bacchus (2002), p. 1024; Graham (2013), pp. 2 and 11; Graham (2017), p. 113; Graham (2016), p. 3.

[181]Baudenbacher (2004), p. 394; Gaffney (1999), p. 1182.

[182]Shaffer et al. (2016), p. 246.

[183]Terris et al. (2007), p. 106.

[184]Evans and de Tarso Pereira (2005), p. 266.

[185]See, e.g., Broude (2004), p. 343; Ostry (2000), p. 108; Sacerdoti (2017b), p. 147; Footer (2006), p. 1; Elsig and Eckhardt (2015), p. 14; Ragosta et al. (2003), p. 697; Wolff (1998), p. 951.

[186]Jackson (2007), p. 31.

[187]Shaffer et al. (2016), p. 238.

[188]Hughes (2007), p. 186.

[189]See, for example, Petersmann (1999), p. 241.

[190]Zimmermann (2005), p. 36.

[191]See, e.g., Mann et al. (2004), p. 14; Laird (2016), p. 115; Howse (2016), p. 77; Huber and Tereposky (2017), p. 591; Katz (2016), p. 163; McRae (2010), p. 376.

The most recent example of the Appellate Body as a model for 'judicializing' other fields is the recent European Union's proposal to replace investor-state arbitration with a two-level international tribunal.[192] According to Howse, '[l]arger than the current life of the WTO "institution", the Appellate Body, as this move suggests, may well have come of age as a true court of world trade.'[193]

The Appellate Body was an afterthought designed to review a few cases per year. However, its activity expanded beyond the most optimistic expectations. The current number and complexity of its caseload calls for an upgrading of its structure.[194] Its founders should reflect about the role that the Appellate Body currently plays as an international tribunal and whether its original features still serve its mandate.[195] Thus far, member states seem to have failed to assume the consequences that flow from a move towards a more 'legal', judicialized mechanism of dispute resolution.[196] Greater legalization and judicialization of international trade dispute settlement naturally carries additional costs.[197]

The Appellate Body stands at the apex of the WTO dispute settlement system[198]—it is a court in all but name.[199] In the realm of international law, adjudicative bodies are named incoherently—sometimes they are 'courts', others they are 'tribunals'.[200] It has been suggested that the Appellate Body should change its official title to the 'World Trade Court'.[201] Weiler prefers the official name of 'International Court of Economic Justice', to be known colloquially as 'World Trade Court.'[202] In the international law sphere the difference between the concepts of 'judge', 'arbitrator', and 'panellist' also remains unclear.[203] Some believe that Appellate Body members should be appointed on a full-time basis and adopt the formal title of 'judges' of the 'World Trade Court'.[204]

---

[192]Sacerdoti (2017b), p. 147. See European Commission (2015): '[t]he judges would have very high technical and legal qualifications, comparable to those required for the members of permanent international courts such as the International Court of Justice and the WTO Appellate Body. (...) The members of the Appeal Tribunal under TTIP would be subject to: stringent qualifications comparable to those required for the members of permanent international courts such as the International Court of Justice and the WTO Appellate Body; strict ethical requirements; a remuneration system based on that of the WTO Appellate Body (a monthly retainer fee and fees for days worked)'.

[193]Howse (2016), p. 77.

[194]Schoenbaum (1998), p. 658.

[195]Steger (2004), p. 45.

[196]Dunoff (2002), p. 198.

[197]Shaffer (2009), p. 169.

[198]Smith (2003), p. 66.

[199]Van den Bossch (2005), p. 64; Van den Bossche (2006), p. 289; Weiler (2002), p. 191.

[200]Gal-Or (2008), p. 57.

[201]Taniguchi (2009), p. 21.

[202]Weiler (2002), p. 190.

[203]Gal-Or (2008), p. 58. See Vagts (1996).

[204]Taniguchi (2009), p. 21.

More important than the official title of Appellate Body members are the conditions that support the exercise of their adjudicative function. The increased participation of member states in the WTO dispute settlement system denotes a growing acceptance of its authority. Its reputation and credibility has been established over more than two decades, producing an impressive corpus of jurisprudence. The foremost challenge facing the WTO dispute settlement system is to ensure it remains effective.[205] This question includes dealing with an ever-increasing, evermore complex workload. In practice, Appellate Body members resemble a career-based judiciary.[206] The growing caseload is incompatible with short deadlines and the part-time status of adjudicators.[207] Since the two first elements seem to be unchangeable, member states should seriously consider the overall impact of the latter in the operation of the system, changing the appointment of Appellate Body members to full-time.[208]

Further than facilitating the management of its heavy caseload, the main reason to convert Appellate Body membership into a full-time appointment is be to bring the Appellate Body closer to a court-like institution.[209] The judicial features of the WTO dispute settlement mechanism have been praised as one of its key triumphs.[210] While the expression 'quasi-judicial' is commonly applied to describe the process, in practice and in substance, it is a judicial one.[211] It is therefore time to move from quasi-judges to real judges, who deliver justice full-time.

4   Final Remarks

Judging is an intense process that benefits from a full-time commitment and thus it is preferable to appoint adjudicators on a full-time basis.[212] This is the model followed by the European Commission' project for a Multilateral Investment Court.[213] The European Commission believes that ensuring the independence of the future court calls for the full time employment of adjudicators.[214] In a paper prepared for the first meeting of the United Nations Commission on International Trade Law (UNCITRAL) Working Group III (Investor-State Dispute Settlement Reform) in November 2017, the European Commission stated[215]:

---

[205]Davey (2014), p. 693.

[206]Renouf (2005), pp. 116–117.

[207]Mavroidis (2008), p. 367.

[208]Mavroidis (2008), p. 367.

[209]Suami (2009), p. 182.

[210]Porges (2003), p. 141.

[211]McRae (2004), p. 8.

[212]Wald (2008), p. 683.

[213]See European Commission (2016).

[214]European Commission (2017a), p. 2.

[215]European Commission (2017b), p. 3, para 7.

Permanent adjudicatory bodies offer a number of advantages (. . .). These advantages operate in multiple and overlapping ways. Permanent bodies, by their very permanency, deliver predictability and consistency and manage the fact that multiple disputes arise, since they can elaborate and refine the understanding of a particular set of norms over time and ensure their effective and consistent application. This is particular relevant when the norms are relatively indeterminate. When appointing adjudicators in a permanent setting, thought is given to a long-term approach. States have an interest that public actions can be taken and at the same time individual interests protected and they know that the balance between these interests is to be maintained in the long term. Permanent bodies with full-time adjudicators also free the adjudicators from the need to be remunerated from other sources and typically provide some form of tenure. This prevents the adjudicators from coming under pressure to take short-term considerations into account and ensures that there are no concerns as to their impartiality.

When the WTO dispute settlement system was created, governments knew they were granting substantial powers to the new institution, and prudently committed to review their arrangement soon after the beginning of its operation.[216] The idea of moving Appellate Body members to a full-time regime has been floated on several occasions, but has never gathered consensus. Some authors, while acknowledging that the current regime occasionally poses difficulties, do not see such move as absolutely necessary, arguing that the Appellate Body has been managing its workload satisfactorily despite operating part-time.[217] The members of the WTO seem to prefer to retain the *status quo* for as long as possible.[218] The key concern seems to be to 'do no harm' to the existing system.[219] Proposals for reform of the dispute settlement system depend to a large extent on members' views about the proper legal nature of the system, and how to strike a balance between 'judicial' and 'diplomatic' dimensions.[220] Reforming the current structure and philosophy of the Appellate Body has thus far proven to be unachievable. Member states seem to feel more comfortable developing the system in a cautious manner, without any drastic changes.[221] Taking into account the consensus rule and the considerable support for the current system, it will not be easy to build consensus on any major proposal for reform.[222]

Sacerdoti has proclaimed that the WTO dispute settlement system 'stands out as a new chapter in the evolution of international justice.'[223] The Appellate Body, in particular, is praised as an 'authoritative international tribunal'[224] and even a 'unique

---

[216]Hudec (1999), p. 3. 'This arrangement could be kept under review by the DSB, and considered at the latest at the first Ministerial Conference, to determine whether a move to full-time employment was warranted.'—Decision of the DSB of 10 February 1995, para 11.

[217]Hughes (2006), p. 218.

[218]Ehlermann (2004), p. 503.

[219]Sutherland et al. (2004), p. 56, para 254.

[220]Evans and de Tarso Pereira (2005), p. 267.

[221]Petersmann (2007), p. 40.

[222]Bernauer et al. (2012), p. 502.

[223]Sacerdoti (2006a), p. 55; Sacerdoti (2006b), p. 71.

[224]Hudec (1998), p. 120; Shaffer et al. (2016), p. 237.

and unprecedented institution in international trade'.[225] It is, to borrow from the work of Ehring, 'the official face of justice in the multilateral trading system'.[226] From the start, member states knew that the success of the WTO would depend, to a large extent, on the proper composition of the Appellate Body.[227] It may be argued that the Appellate Body was not designed to operate in the same way as traditional judicial institutions, which would explain the use of an alternative, almost exotic nomenclature. However, the fact is that in practice it operates like a court, with parties and adjudicators behaving in a judicial fashion. The Appellate Body needs to be adjusted to the new reality of how the system is currently being used by the members of the WTO.[228] In a word, the Appellate Body needs a reality check.

The remarkable work conducted over the last decades by Appellate Body members makes them worthy of being called judges.[229] Changing their formal designation to 'judges' would enhance their prestige among lawyers and society at large but also boost their self-esteem.[230] Even more so, moving them towards a full-time regime would contribute to highlight the importance of the appointment.[231] Appellate Body membership is a key piece in the engine of WTO dispute settlement, and the conditions of employment should reflect the importance and responsibility of the position.[232] WTO member states should reflect on whether it still makes sense, more than two decades after the inception of the Appellate Body, to treat such a paramount assignment as a part-time occupation. It is time to promote Appellate Body members to a full-time status, enhancing the gravitas of the position and reinforcing public perceptions of authority and legitimacy.

References

Abi-Saab G (2005) The WTO dispute settlement and general international law. In: Yerxa R, Wilson B (eds) Key issues in WTO dispute settlement: the first ten years. Cambridge University Press, Cambridge, pp 7–12

Abi-Saab G (2006) The Appellate Body and Treaty Interpretation. In: Sacerdoti G, Yanovich A, Bohanes J (eds) The WTO at ten: the contribution of the dispute settlement system. Cambridge University Press, Cambridge, pp 453–464

Amerasinghe C (2009) Jurisdiction of specific international tribunals. Martinus Nijhoof, Leiden

Andersen S, Friedbacher T, Lau C, Lockhart N, Remy J, Sandford I (2017) Using Arbitration under Article 25 of the DSU to ensure the availability of appeals. Centre for Trade and Economic

---

[225]Chen (1995), p. 1329.

[226]Ehring (2008), p. 1029.

[227]Decision of the DSB of 10 February 1995, para 4.

[228]Wha Chang (2017), p. 105.

[229]Matsushita (2015), p. 549.

[230]Matsushita (2015), p. 549.

[231]Janow (2008), p. 252.

[232]Steger (2004), p. 46.

Integration Working Paper 2017-17. https://repository.graduateinstitute.ch/record/295745/files/CTEI-2017-17-.pdf

Azevêdo R (2014) Director-General of the WTO, Speech to the Dispute Settlement Body on 26 September 2014. In: Dispute Settlement Body, Minutes of Meeting held in the Centre William Rappard on 26 September 2014, WT/DSB/M/350, of 21 November 2014, pp 2–10

Bacchus J (2002) Table talk: around the table of the Appellate Body of the World Trade Organization. Vanderbilt J Transl Law 35(4):1021–1039

Bacchus J (2018) Might unmakes right: the American assault on the rule of law in World Trade. Centre for International Governance Innovation, CIGI Paper 173. https://www.cigionline.org/sites/default/files/documents/Paper%20no.173.pdf

Baudenbacher C (2004) Judicialization: can the European model be exported to other parts of the world? Texas Int Law J 39(2):381–399

Bernal R, Steger D, Stoler A (1998) Key procedural issues: resources. Int Lawyer 32(3):871–881

Bernauer T, Elsig M, Paywelyn J (2012) Dispute settlement mechanism – analysis and problems. In: Narlikar A, Daunton M, Stern R (eds) The Oxford handbook on the World Trade Organization. Oxford University Press, Oxford, pp 485–506

Broude T (2004) International governance in the WTO: judicial boundaries and political capitulation. Cameron May, London

Brown C (2003) The evolution and application of rules concerning independence of the international judiciary. Law Pract Int Courts Tribunals 2(1):63–96

Charnovitz S (2015) The path of World Trade Law in the 21st century. World Publishing, Singapore

Chen J (1995) Going bananas: how the WTO can heal the split in the global banana trade dispute. Fordham Law Rev 63(4):1283–1335

Condon B (2018) Captain America and the tarnishing of the crown: the feud between the WTO Appellate Body and the USA. J World Trade 52(4):535–556

Conti J (2011) Between law and diplomacy: the social contexts of disputing at the World Trade Organization. Stanford University Press, Stanford

Crawford J, McIntyre J (2012) The independence and impartiality of the 'International Judiciary'. In: Shetreet S, Forsyth C (eds) The culture of judicial independence: conceptual foundations and practical challenges. Martinus Nijhoff, Leiden, pp 189–214

Davey W (2003) The case for a WTO Permanent Panel Body. J Int Econ Law 6(1):177–186

Davey W (2008) Expediting the panel process in WTO dispute settlement. In: Janow M, Donaldson V, Janovich A (eds) The WTO: governance, dispute settlement and developing countries. Juris Publishing, New York, pp 409–470

Davey W (2014) The WTO and rules-based dispute settlement: historical evolution, operational success, and future challenges. J Int Econ Law 17(3):679–700

de Baere G, Chané A, Wouters J (2016) International courts as keepers of the rule of law: achievements, challenges, and opportunities. Int Law Polit 48(3):715–793

Dillon T Jr (1995) The World Trade Organization: a new legal order for world trade? Mich J Int Law 16(2):349–402

Donaldson V (2005) The Appellate Body: institutional and procedural aspects. In: Macrory P, Appleton A, Plummer M (eds) The World Trade Organization: legal, economic and political analysis, vol I. Springer, New York, pp 1277–1339

Dunoff J (2002) The WTO's legitimacy crisis: reflections on the law and politics of WTO dispute resolution. Am Rev Int Arbitration 13:197–208

Ehlermann C (2003) Experiences from the WTO Appellate Body. Texas Int Law J 38(3):469–488

Ehlermann C (2004) Six years on the bench of the "World Trade Court". In: Ortino F, Petersmann E (eds) The WTO dispute settlement system, 1995–2003. The Hague, Kluwer Law International, pp 499–530

Ehlermann C (2016) The dispute settlement system of the WTO: a bright picture with a few dark spots. In: Chaisse J, Lin T (eds) International economic law and governance: essays in honour of Mitsuo Matsushita. Oxford University Press, Oxford, pp 26–29

Ehring L (2008) Public access to dispute settlement hearings in the World Trade Organization. J Int Econ Law 11(4):1021–1034

Elsig M (2017) Legalization in context: the design of the WTO's dispute settlement system. Br J Polit Int Relat 19(2):304–319

Elsig M, Eckhardt J (2015) The creation of the multilateral trade court: design and experiential learning. World Trade Rev 14(1):13–32

Elsig M, Pollack M (2014) Agents, trustees, and international courts: the politics of judicial appointment at the World Trade Organization. Eur J Int Relat 20(2):391–415

Esserman S, Howse R (2003) The WTO on trial. Foreign Aff 82(1):130–140

European Commission (2015) Reading guide to the draft text on Investment Protection and Investment Court System in the Transatlantic Trade and Investment Partnership (TTIP), 16 September 2015. http://trade.ec.europa.eu/doclib/press/index.cfm?id=1365

European Commission (2016) The Multilateral Investment Court project. http://trade.ec.europa.eu/doclib/press/index.cfm?id=1608

European Commission (2017a) Recommendation for a council decision authorising the opening of negotiations for a convention establishing a multilateral court for the settlement of investment disputes, COM(2017) 493 final, 13 September 2017

European Commission (2017b) The identification and consideration of concerns as regards investor to state dispute settlement, 20 November 2017. http://trade.ec.europa.eu/doclib/docs/2017/november/tradoc_156402.pdf

Evans G (2000) Lawmaking under the trade constitution: a study in legislating by the World Trade Organization. Kluwer Law International, The Hague

Evans D, de Tarso Pereira C (2005) DSU review: a view from the inside. In: Yerxa R, Wilson B (eds) Key issues in WTO dispute settlement: the first ten years. Cambridge University Press, Cambridge, pp 251–268

Footer M (2006) An institutional and normative analysis of the World Trade Organization. Martinus Nijhoff, Leiden

Gaffney J (1999) Due process in the World Trade Organization: the need for procedural justice in the dispute settlement system. Am Univ Int Law Rev 14(4):1173–1221

Gal-Or N (2008) The concept of appeal in international dispute settlement. Eur J Int Law 19(1):43–65

Gantz D (2018) An existential threat to WTO dispute settlement: blocking appointment of Appellate Body Members by the United States. Arizona Legal Studies, discussion Paper no. 18-26. https://papers.ssrn.com/sol3/papers.cfm?abstract_id=3216633

Ghias S (2006) International judicial lawmaking: a theoretical and political analysis of the WTO Appellate Body. Berkley J Int Law 24(2):534–553

Graham T (2013) It sure looks different from the inside: deciding international disputes at the WTO. Maurice A. Deane School of Law, Hofstra University, Philip J. Shapiro Endowed International Visiting Scholar Lecture. http://scholarlycommons.law.hofstra.edu/lectures_shapiro/2

Graham T (2016) Speaking up: the state of the Appellate Body. Special lecture hosted by the World Trade Institute of the University of Bern, the University of Geneva Law School and the Graduate Institute of International and Development Studies, Geneva, 22 November 2016. https://www.wto.org/english/news_e/news16_e/ab_22nov16_e.pdf

Graham T (2017) Farewell speech on 22 November 2016 – speaking up: the state of the Appellate Body. In: World Trade Organization, Appellate Body Annual Report for 2016, WT/AB/27, 16 May 2017, pp 112–117

Hoekman B, Mavroidis P (2007) The World Trade Organization: law, economics, and politics. Routledge, Abingdon

Howse R (2003) The most dangerous branch? WTO Appellate Body Jurisprudence on the nature and limits of the judicial power. In: Cottier T, Mavroidis P (eds) The role of the judge in International Trade Regulation: experience and lessons from the WTO. University of Michigan Press, Ann Arbor, pp 11–41

Howse R (2016) The World Trade Organization 20 years on: global governance by judiciary. Eur J Int Law 27(1):9–77

Huber M, Tereposky G (2017) The WTO Appellate Body: viability as a model for an investor-state dispute settlement appellate mechanism. ICSID Rev 32(3):545–594

Hudec R (1998) The role of the GATT Secretariat in the evolution of the WTO dispute settlement procedure. In: Bhagwati J, Hirsch M (eds) The Uruguay round and beyond: essays in honour of Arthur Dunkel. Springer, Berlin, pp 101–120

Hudec R (1999) The new WTO dispute settlement procedure: an overview of the first three years. Minn J Glob Trade 8(1):1–53

Hughes V (2005a) Special challenges at the appellate stage: a case study. In: Yerxa R, Wilson B (eds) Key issues in WTO dispute settlement: the first ten years. Cambridge University Press, Cambridge, pp 80–87

Hughes V (2005b) WTO dispute settlement: an overview. In: Mitchell A (ed) Challenges and prospects for the WTO. Cameron May, London, pp 23–53

Hughes V (2006) The WTO dispute settlement system – from initiating proceedings to ensuring implementation: what needs improvement? In: Sacerdoti G, Yanovich A, Bohanes J (eds) The WTO at ten: the contribution of the dispute settlement system. Cambridge University Press, Cambridge, pp 193–234

Hughes V (2007) Accomplishments of the WTO dispute settlement mechanism. In: Taniguchi Y, Yanovich A, Bohanes J (eds) The WTO in the twenty-first century: dispute settlement, negotiations, and regionalism in Asia. Cambridge University Press, Cambridge, pp 185–211

Hughes V (2008) The strengths, weaknesses, and future of WTO appellate review. In: Janow M, Donaldson V, Janovich A (eds) The WTO: governance, dispute settlement and developing countries. Juris Publishing, New York, pp 471–504

Hughes V (2009) The institutional dimension. In: Bethlehem D, McRae D, Neufeld R, Van Damme I (eds) The Oxford handbook of international trade law. Oxford University Press, Oxford, pp 269–297

Jackson J (1998) Designing and implementing effective dispute settlement procedures: WTO dispute settlement, appraisal and prospects. In: Krueger A (ed) The WTO as an international organization. University of Chicago Press, Chicago, pp 161–180

Jackson J (2007) The WTO dispute settlement system after ten years: the first decade's promises and challenges. In: Taniguchi Y, Yanovich A, Bohanes J (eds) The WTO in the twenty-first century: dispute settlement, negotiations, and regionalism in Asia. Cambridge University Press, Cambridge, pp 23–37

Janow M (2008) Reflections on serving on the appellate body. Loyola Univ Chic Int Law Rev 6 (1):249–258

Katz R (2016) Modeling an International Investment Court after the World Trade Organization dispute settlement body. Harv Negotiation Law Rev 22:163–188

Kelly JP (2002) Judicial activism at the World Trade Organization: developing principles of self-restraint. Northwest J Int Law Bus 22(3):353–388

Kolsky Lewis M (2006) The lack of dissent in WTO dispute settlement. J Int Econ Law 9 (4):895–931

Kuijper P (2017) The US attack on the WTO Appellate Body, ACIL Research Paper 2017-29. https://papers.ssrn.com/sol3/papers.cfm?abstract_id=3076399

Laird I (2016) TPP and ISDS: the challenge from Europe and the proposed TTIP Investment Court. Canada-United States Law J 40(1):106–125

Lawrence R (2007) The United States and the WTO dispute settlement system, Council on Foreign Relations, Council Special Report no 25. https://www.cfr.org/report/united-states-and-wto-dispute-settlement-system

Litvak U (1995) Regional integration and the dispute resolution system of the World Trade Organization after the Uruguay Round: a proposal for the future. Univ Miami Inter-American Law Rev 26(3):561–610

Lowenfeld A (1994) Remedies along with rights: institutional reform in the new GATT. Am J Int Law 88(3):477–488

Lowenfeld A (2008) International economic law, 2nd edn. Oxford University Press, Oxford

Mackenzie R, Sands P (2003) International Courts and Tribunals and the independence of the international judge. Harv Int Law J 44(1):271–285

Mann H, Cosbey A, Peterson L, von Moltke K (2004) Comments on ICSID Discussion Paper, "Possible Improvements of the Framework for ICSID Arbitration", International Institute for Sustainable Development. https://iisd.org/pdf/2004/investment_icsid_response.pdf

Marceau G (1998) Rules on ethics for the new World Trade Organization dispute settlement mechanism: the rules of conduct for the understanding on rules and procedures governing the settlement of disputes. J World Trade 32(3):57–97

Marquet C (2018) Crisis at the Appellate Body: towards more or less consent in WTO adjudication?. Society of International Economic Law (SIEL), Sixth Biennial Global Conference. https://papers.ssrn.com/sol3/papers.cfm?abstract_id=3220525

Matsushita M (2008) A review of major WTO jurisprudence. In: Janow M, Donaldson V, Janovich A (eds) The WTO: governance, dispute settlement and developing countries. Juris Publishing, New York, pp 505–524

Matsushita M (2012) The dispute settlement mechanism at the WTO: the Appellate Body – assessment and problems. In: Narlikar A, Daunton M, Stern R (eds) The Oxford handbook on the World Trade Organization. Oxford University Press, Oxford, pp 507–534

Matsushita M (2015) Reflections on the functioning of the Appellate Body. In: Marceau G (ed) A history of law and lawyers in the GATT/WTO: the development of the rule of law in the multilateral trading system. Cambridge University Press, Cambridge, pp 547–558

Mavroidis P (2008) Legal eagles? The WTO Appellate Body's first ten years. In: Janow M, Donaldson V, Janovich A (eds) The WTO: governance, dispute settlement and developing countries. Juris Publishing, New York, pp 345–368

Mavroidis P (2009) Licence to adjudicate: a critical evaluation of the work of the WTO Appellate Body so far. In: Hartigan J (ed) Trade dispute and the dispute settlement understanding of the WTO: an interdisciplinary assessment. Emerald, Bingley, pp 73–90

Mavroidis P (2013) Selecting the WTO judges. In: Huerta-Goldman J, Romanetti A, Stirnimann F (eds) WTO litigation, investment arbitration, and commercial arbitration. Alphen an den Rijn, Kluwer Law International, pp 103–114

Mavroidis P (2014) Justice is coming (…from behind closed doors: the WTO judges). In: Cremona M, Hilpold P, Lavranos N, Schneider S, Ziegler A (eds) Reflections on the constitutionalisation of international economic law. Martinus Nijhoff, Leiden, pp 243–252

Mavroidis P, Van der Borght K (2006) Impartiality, independence and the WTO Appellate Body. In: Georgiev D, van der Borght K (eds) Reform and development of the WTO dispute settlement system. Cameron May, London, pp 201–224

Mavroidis P, Bermann G, Wu M (2010) The law of the World Trade Organization (WTO): documents, cases and analysis. West, St. Paul

McRae D (2004) What is the future of WTO dispute settlement? J Int Econ Law 7(1):3–21

McRae D (2010) The WTO Appellate Body: a model for an ICSID appeals facility? J Int Dispute Settlement 1(2):371–387

Messenger G (2016a) The development of international law and the role of causal language. Oxf J Leg Stud 36(1):110–134

Messenger G (2016b) The development of World Trade Organization law: examining change in international law. Oxford University Press, Oxford

Mitchell A (2007) The legal basis for using principles in WTO disputes. J Int Econ Law 10 (4):795–835

Miyagawa M (2007) Japan's perspectives on the present dispute settlement understanding negotiations. In: Taniguchi Y, Yanovich A, Bohanes J (eds) The WTO in the twenty-first century: dispute settlement, negotiations, and regionalism in Asia. Cambridge University Press, Cambridge, pp 267–281

Montana I Mora M (1993) A GATT with teeth: law wins over politics in the resolution of international trade disputes. Columbia J Transl Law 31(1):103–180

Nader R (1994) WTO means rule by unaccountable tribunals. Wall Street Journal, 17 August 1994, A12

Olbourne B (2003) Independence and impartiality: international standards for national judges and courts. Law Pract Int Courts Tribunals 2(1):97–126

Ostry S (2000) Looking back to look forward: the multilateral trading system after 50 years. In: World Trade Organization Secretariat, From GATT to the WTO: the multilateral trading system in the new millennium. Kluwer Law International, The Hague, pp 97–112

Palmeter D (2008) The WTO dispute settlement system in the next ten years. In: Janow M, Donaldson V, Janovich A (eds) The WTO: governance, dispute settlement and developing countries. Juris Publishing, New York, pp 845–854

Pauwelyn J (2015) The rule of law without the rule of lawyers? Why investment arbitrators are from Mars, Trade Adjudicators from Venus. Am J Int Law 109(4):761–805

Payosova T, Hufbauer G, Schott J (2018) The dispute settlement crisis in the World Trade Organization: causes and cures. Peterson Institute for International Economics. https://piie.com/publications/policy-briefs/dispute-settlement-crisis-world-trade-organization-causes-and-cures

Petersmann E (1998) How to promote the international rule of law? Contributions by the World Trade Organization appellate review system. J Int Econ Law 1(1):25–48

Petersmann E (1999) Dispute settlement in international economic law – lessons for strengthening international dispute settlement in non-economic areas. J Int Econ Law 2(2):189–248

Petersmann E (2007) WTO dispute settlement practice 1995–2005: lessons from the past and future challenges. In: Taniguchi Y, Yanovich A, Bohanes J (eds) The WTO in the twenty-first century: dispute settlement, negotiations, and regionalism in Asia. Cambridge University Press, Cambridge, pp 38–97

Petersmann E (2014) Need for a new philosophy of international economic law and adjudication. J Int Econ Law 17(3):639–669

Porges A (2003) Settling WTO disputes: what do litigation models tell us. Ohio State J Dispute Resolution 19(1):141–184

Ragosta J, Joneja N, Zeldovich M (2003) WTO dispute settlement: the system is flawed and must be fixed. Int Lawyer 37(3):697–752

Raina A (2018) Meditations in an emergency: the Appellate Body deadlock – what it is, why it is a problem, and what to do about it. Glob Trade Customs J 13(9):376–386

Reitz C (1996) Enforcement of the general agreement on tariffs and trade. Univ Pa J Int Law 17(2):555–603

Renouf Y (2005) Challenges in applying codes of ethics in a small professional community: the example of the WTO rules of conduct for the understanding on rules and procedures governing the settlement of disputes. In: De Cooker C (ed) Accountability, investigation and due process in international organizations. Martinus Nijhoff, Leiden, pp 111–127

Romano C (1999) The proliferation of international judicial bodies: the pieces of the puzzle. N Y Univ J Int Law Polit 31(4):709–751

Ruiz Fabri H (2009) Dispute settlement in the WTO: on the trail of a court. In: Charnovitz S, Steger D, Van den Bossche P (eds) Law in the service of human dignity: essays in honour of Florentino Feliciano. Cambridge University Press, Cambridge, pp 136–158

Sacerdoti G (2006a) The dispute settlement system of the WTO in action: a perspective on the first ten years. In: Sacerdoti G, Yanovich A, Bohanes J (eds) The WTO at ten: the contribution of the dispute settlement system. Cambridge University Press, Cambridge, pp 35–57

Sacerdoti G (2006b) The dispute settlement system of the WTO: structure and function in the perspective of the first 10 years. Law Pract Int Courts Tribunals 5(1):49–75

Sacerdoti G (2017a) The future of the WTO dispute settlement system: confronting challenges to consolidate a success story. In: Braga C, Hoekman B (eds) Future of the global trade order, 2nd edn. European University Institute, Florence, pp 123–146

Sacerdoti G (2017b) The WTO dispute settlement system: consolidating success and confronting new challenges. In: Elsig M, Hoekman B, Pauwelyn J (eds) Assessing the World Trade Organization: fit for purpose? Cambridge University Press, Cambridge, pp 147–174

Sands P, McLachlan C, Mackenzie R (2005) The Burgh House principles on the independence of the international judiciary. Law Pract Int Courts Tribunals 4:247–260

Schoenbaum T (1998) WTO dispute settlement: praise and suggestions for reform. Int Comp Law Q 47(3):647–658

Shaffer G (2009) Developing country use of the WTO dispute settlement system: why its matters, the barriers posed. In: Hartigan J (ed) Trade dispute and the dispute settlement understanding of the WTO: an interdisciplinary assessment. Emerald, Bingley, pp 167–190

Shaffer G, Elsig M, Puig S (2016) The extensive (but fragile) authority of the WTO Appellate Body. Law Contemp Probl 79(1):237–273

Shaffer G, Elsig M, Pollack M (2017a) U.S. threats to the WTO Appellate Body. Legal Studies Research Paper Series no. 2017-63. https://ssrn.com/abstract=3087524

Shaffer G, Elsig M, Puig S (2017b) The law and politics of WTO dispute settlement. In: Sandholtz W, Whytock C (eds) Research handbook on the politics of international law. Edward Elgar, Cheltenham, pp 269–305

Shany Y (2014) Assessing the effectiveness of international courts. Oxford University Press, Oxford

Shell G (1995) Trade legalism and international relations theory: an analysis of the World Trade Organization. Duke Law J 44(5):829–927

Shoyer A, Forton H (1998) Performance of the System II: panel adjudication, comments. Int Lawyer 32(3):737–745

Smith J (2003) WTO dispute settlement: the politics of procedure in Appellate Body rulings. World Trade Rev 2(1):65–100

Steger D (1996) WTO dispute settlement: revitalization of multilateralism after the Uruguay Round. Leiden J Int Law 9(2):319–335

Steger D (2002) The Appellate Body and its contribution to WTO dispute settlement. In: Kennedy D, Southwick J (eds) The political economy of international trade law – essays in honor of Robert E. Hudec. Cambridge University Press, Cambridge, pp 482–495

Steger D (2004) Improvements and reforms of the WTO Appellate Body. In: Ortino F, Petersmann E (eds) The WTO dispute settlement system, 1995–2003. The Hague, Kluwer Law International, pp 41–49

Steger D (2015) The founding of the Appellate Body. In: Marceau G (ed) A history of law and lawyers in the GATT/WTO: the development of the rule of law in the multilateral trading system. Cambridge University Press, Cambridge, pp 447–465

Steger D, Hainsworth S (1998) World Trade Organization dispute settlement: the first three years. J Int Econ Law 1(2):199–226

Suami T (2009) Regional integration in East Asia and its legalization: can law contribute to the progress of integration in East Asia? In: Nakamura T (ed) East Asian regionalism from a legal perspective: current features and a vision for the future. Routledge, Abingdon, pp 169–189

Sutherland P, Bhagwati J, Botchwey K, FitzGerald N, Hamada K, Jackson J, Lafer C, de Montbrial T (2004) Report by the Consultative Board to the Director-General Supachai Panitchpakdi: the future of the WTO – addressing institutional challenges in the new millennium. World Trade Organization, Geneva

Taniguchi Y (2009) The WTO dispute settlement as seen by a proceduralist. Cornell Int Law J 42 (1):1–21

Terris D, Romano C, Swigart L (2007) The international judge: an introduction to the men and women who decide the world's cases. University Press of New England, Hanover

United Nations Conference on Trade and Development (2003a) Dispute settlement: World Trade Organization. 3.1 Overview, p. 52 (2003). http://unctad.org/en/docs/edmmisc232add11_en.pdf

United Nations Conference on Trade and Development (2003b) Dispute settlement. World Trade Organization. 3.3 Appellate Review, UNCTAD/EDM/Misc.232/Add.17. http://unctad.org/en/docs/edmmisc232add17_en.pdf

Vagts D (1996) The international legal profession: a need for more governance? Am J Int Law 90 (2):250–261

Van Damme I (2009) Treaty interpretation by the WTO Appellate Body. Oxford University Press, Oxford

Van Damme I (2010) Treaty interpretation by the WTO Appellate Body. Eur J Int Law 21 (3):605–648

Van den Bossch P (2005) The making of the 'World Trade Court': the origins and development of the Appellate Body of the World Trade Organization. In: Yerxa R, Wilson B (eds) Key issues in WTO dispute settlement: the first ten years. Cambridge University Press, Cambridge, pp 63–79

Van den Bossche P (2003) The Doha Development Round negotiations on the dispute settlement understanding. Institute for International Law of the University of Leuven, Working Paper No 47. https://www.law.kuleuven.be/iir/nl/onderzoek/working-papers/WP47e.pdf

Van den Bossche P (2006) From afterthought to centrepiece: the WTO Appellate Body and its rise to prominence in the World Trading System. In: Sacerdoti G, Yanovich A, Bohanes J (eds) The WTO at ten: the contribution of the dispute settlement system. Cambridge University Press, Cambridge, pp 289–325

Van Den Bossche P (2009) Reform of the WTO dispute settlement system: what to expect from the Doha Development Round? In: Charnovitz S, Steger D, Van den Bossche P (eds) Law in the service of human dignity: essays in honour of Florentino Feliciano. Cambridge University Press, Cambridge, pp 103–126

Van den Bossche P, Zdouc W (2013) The law and policy of the World Trade Organization: text, cases and materials, 3rd edn. Cambridge University Press, Cambridge

VanGrasstek C (2013) The history and future of the World Trade Organization. World Trade Organization, Geneva

Venzke I (2012) Making general exceptions: the spell of precedents in developing Article XX GATT into standards for domestic regulatory policy. In: von Bogdandy A, Venzke I (eds) International judicial lawmaking: on public authority and democratic legitimation in global governance. Springer, Berlin, pp 179–214

Venzke I (2013) Antinomies and change in international dispute settlement: an exercise in comparative procedural law. In: Wolfrum R, Gätzschmann I (eds) International dispute settlement: room for innovations? Springer, Heidelberg, pp 235–269

Vermulst E, Graafsma F (2002) WTO disputes: anti-dumping, subsidies and safeguards. Cameron May, London

Von Bogdandy A, Venzke I (2013) International courts as lawmakers. In: Wolfrum R, Gätzschmann I (eds) International dispute settlement: room for innovations? Springer, Heidelberg, pp 161–213

Von Bogdandy A, Venzke I (2014) In whose name? A public law theory of international adjudication. Oxford University Press, Oxford

Wald P (2008) An outsider's look at the WTO Appellate Body. In: Janow M, Donaldson V, Janovich A (eds) The WTO: governance, dispute settlement and developing countries. Juris Publishing, New York, pp 671–694

Walter C (2006) Article 17 DSU. In: Wolfrum R, Stoll P, Kaiser K (eds) WTO – institutions and dispute settlement. Martinus Nijhoff, Leiden, pp 447–473

Weiler J (2002) The rule of lawyers and the ethos of diplomats: reflections on the internal and external legitimacy of WTO dispute resolution. Am Rev Int Arbitration 13:177–196

Wha Chang S (2017) Farewell Speech on 26 September 2016. In: World Trade Organization, Appellate Body Annual Report for 2016, WT/AB/27, of 16 May 2017, pp 105–111

Wofford C (2000) A greener future at the WTO: the refinement of WTO jurisprudence on environmental exceptions to GATT. Harv Environ Law Rev 24(2):563–592

Wolff A (1998) Reflections on WTO dispute settlement. Int Lawyer 32(3):951–958

World Trade Organization, Committee on Budget, Finance and Administration (2004) Letter from the Chairman of the Appellate Body (WT/BFA/W/109), of 18 March 2004
World Trade Organization (2017) A handbook on the WTO dispute settlement system, 2nd edn. Cambridge University Press, Cambridge
Yanovich A (2007) The evolving WTO dispute settlement system. In: Taniguchi Y, Yanovich A, Bohanes J (eds) The WTO in the twenty-first century: dispute settlement, negotiations, and regionalism in Asia. Cambridge University Press, Cambridge, pp 248–258
Young M (1995) Dispute resolution in the Uruguay Round: lawyers triumph over diplomats. Int Lawyer 29(2):389–409
Zimmermann T (2005) WTO dispute settlement at ten: evolution, experiences, and evaluation. Aussenwirtschaft 60:27–61

Fernando Dias Simões is Associate Professor at the Faculty of Law of the Chinese University of Hong Kong (CUHK). He holds a PhD from the University of Santiago de Compostela (Spain), an LLM from the University of Glasgow (United Kingdom) and a Bachelor degree from the University of Coimbra (Portugal). Professor Dias Simões also teaches regularly at the Summer Law Institute (Beijing) and at the Institute of International Studies, Ramkhamhaeng University, Bangkok. He is Senior Research Fellow at the University Institute of European Studies (Italy); Member of the Scientific Committee and Senior Research Associate at gLAWcal—Global Law Initiatives for Sustainable Development (United Kingdom); member of the Asia WTO Research Network (AWRN); and Rapporteur for the Oxford International Organizations—OXIO (Oxford University Press and Manchester International Law Centre). His research interests include international arbitration, comparative law, and consumer law.

Overview of WTO Jurisprudence in 2017

Kholofelo Kugler, Faith Pittet, and Saweria Mwangi

Contents

K. Kugler (✉)
Advisory Centre on WTO Law, Geneva, Switzerland
e-mail: Kholofelo.Kugler@acwl.ch

F. Pittet
Tutwa Consulting Group, Johannesburg, South Africa
e-mail: faith.tigere@tutwaconsulting.com

S. Mwangi
World Trade Organization, Geneva, Switzerland
e-mail: saweria.mwangi@wto.org

© Springer Nature Switzerland AG 2019   389
M. Bungenberg et al. (eds.), *European Yearbook of International Economic Law 2019*,
European Yearbook of International Economic Law (2020) 10: 389–432,
https://doi.org/10.1007/8165_2019_46, Published online: 20 November 2019

1 Introduction

This contribution to the European Yearbook of International Economic Law follows the format of the previous editions that provided a summary of all WTO Panel and Appellate Body reports issued during the previous year. This year's article features nine diverse disputes[1] that were adopted by the Dispute Settlement Body (DSB) in the year 2017. The disputes were diverse in their subject matter, as well as litigants. This article provides summaries of the disputes according to the order in which the DSB adopted them. In cases where the panel report was appealed, the article includes a discussion of the relevant panel findings and Appellate Body report. The article discusses the following disputes, in order of their adoption the panel report in *Canada – Welded Pipe*; the Appellate Body report in *Russia – Pigs (EU)*; the panel reports in *EU – Poultry Meat (China)* and *China – Cellulose Pulp*; the Appellate Body Reports in *US – Anti-Dumping Methodologies (China)*, *EU – Fatty Alcohols (Indonesia)*, and *Indonesia – Import Licensing Regimes*; and the panel report in *Indonesia – Chicken*.[2]

As usual, trade remedies disputes, particularly disputes related to anti-dumping measures featured heavily in 2017. This group of anti-dumping cases included the anti-dumping methodologies of the United States (US). The only other "rules-area" dispute adopted in 2017 was another instalment in the never-ending saga between the US and the European Union (EU) in their Boeing/Airbus aircraft subsidies disputes. This one related to tax incentives provided by the US state of Washington to encourage large civil aircraft manufactures to locate their production facilities there.[3] The dispute settlement adjudicators also made key findings under

---

[1] All the panels established under a single dispute are counted as one dispute and not as individual disputes based on their DS numbers.

[2] The panel reports were discussed in the previous Volume of this Yearbook. Although the panel and Appellate Body Reports of *US – Tax Incentives* were adopted in 2017, this dispute was reported in the previous Volume of this Yearbook.

[3] These are the panel and Appellate Body Reports of *US -Tax Incentives*.

non-trade remedies agreements. In particular, we saw important jurisprudential developments made under the Agreement on Sanitary and Phytosanitary Measures (SPS Agreement); a discreet issue under the Agreement on Agriculture; and compensation negotiations under Article XXVII of the General Agreement on Tariffs and Trade 1994 (GATT 1994).

2 Canada: Welded Pipe (Panel Report)

Chinese Taipei initiated this dispute in early 2015. In late 2016, the panel issued its report. This section describes the key elements of the panel's findings.

2.1 Facts of the Case

In this dispute, Chinese Taipei challenged the provisional and definitive antidumping measures applied by Canada on imports of certain Carbon Steel Welded Pipe (CSWP) from its territory. It also challenged certain provisions of Canada's Special Import Measures Act (SIMA) and the Special Import Measures Regulations (SIMR).

Chinese Taipei raised various claims under the Agreement on Implementation of Article VI of the General Agreement on Tariffs and Trade 1994 or the Anti-Dumping Agreement (ADA) and the GATT 1994. Regarding the treatment of exporters with a *de minimis* (less than 2%) dumping margin, it invoked Articles 1, 5.8, 6.10, 7.1(ii), 7.5 and 9.2[4] and Article VI:2 of the GATT 1994. In respect of the treatment of non-dumped imports and "other factors", it raised claims under Articles 3.1, 3.2, 3.4, 3.5, and 3.7. With respect to the dumping determination and the determination of the duty rate for "all other exporters" it invoked Article 6.8 and Annex II, paragraph 7. Regarding the treatment of new product types to be exported by cooperating producers, it invoked Articles 9.3, 2.2, 6.10, 6.8 and Annex II. Chinese Taipei also raised consequential claims under Article 1 of the ADA and Article VI of the GATT 1994.[5]

Chinese Taipei further raised "as such" claims in respect of the provisions of SIMA and SIMR. It specifically raised claims under Articles 1, 5.8, 7.1(ii), 7.5 and 9.2 of the ADA and Article VI:2 of the GATT 1994 in respect of the SIMA and Articles 3.1, 3.2, 3.4, 3.5, and 3.7 in respect of the SIMR. It also raised consequential claims in respect of its "as such" claims. It alleged that Canada violated Article XVI:4 of the WTO Agreement, Article 18.4 and, consequently, Article 1 of the ADA and Article VI of the GATT 1994.[6]

---

[4]All provisions in this dispute refer to the ADA unless otherwise mentioned.

[5]Panel Report, *Canada – Welded Pipe*, para. 3.1.

[6]Panel Report, *Canada – Welded Pipe*, paras. 3.2–3.3.

Chinese Taipei's main bone of contention in this dispute was that Canada did not terminate its anti-dumping investigation after the Canada Border Services Agency (CBSA) had made a finding of *de minimis* anti-dumping margins. This article will thus focus on these claims.

2.2 Salient Legal Findings

2.2.1 Article 5.8 of the ADA: Immediate Termination

Chinese Taipei submitted that Canada violated Article 5.8 by failing to terminate the investigation in respect of two Chinese Taipei exporters for which the CBSA had determined *de minimis* final margins of dumping. Pursuant the second sentence of this provision, WTO Members (Members) are required to immediately terminate an anti-dumping investigation if they determine that, inter alia, that the margin of dumping is *de minimis*. Chinese Taipei's arguments were mainly based on the Appellate Body's finding in *Mexico – Anti-Dumping Measures on Rice* that "margin of dumping" in Article 5.8, second sentence, refers to the individual dumping margin of an exporter, rather than a country-wide dumping margin.[7]

The panel recalled that this issue was addressed by both the panel and Appellate Body in *Mexico– Anti-Dumping Measures on Rice* and agreed with Chinese Taipei's view. The panel confirmed that Article 6.10 provides the general rule of calculating an individual dumping margin for each known exporter or producer. Thus the "investigation" can be terminated with respect to each individual producer/exporter. Thus the "margin of dumping" that triggers the immediate termination of the investigation should be understood as the dumping margin established for each individual producer/exporter and not a countrywide dumping margin.[8]

Canada argued that there are cogent reasons to depart from *Mexico– Anti-Dumping Measures on Rice* because of the reference to a countrywide dumping margin in Article 3.3, the redundancy of part of Article 9.4, and the alleged inconsistent treatment of *de minimis* exporter under Article 9.5.[9]

The panel confirmed that, in line with previous jurisprudence, Article 5.8, second sentence, requires the immediate termination of an investigation with respect to producers/exporters that have individual *de minimis* dumping margins.

The panel thus *concluded* that Canada failed to establish cogent reasons to depart from previous findings.[10]

---

[7]Panel Report, *Canada – Welded Pipe*, paras. 3.2–3.3. Chinese Taipei refers to Appellate Body Report, *Mexico – Anti-Dumping Measures on Rice*, paras. 216–221.

[8]Panel Report, *Canada – Welded Pipe*, paras. 7.21–7.22.

[9]Panel Report, *Canada – Welded Pipe*, para. 7.22.

[10]Panel Report, *Canada – Welded Pipe*, para. 7.37.

2.2.2   Article 6.10 of the ADA: Multiple Margins of Dumping

Chinese Taipei further claimed that Canada acted inconsistently with Article 6.10, first sentence, which requires investigating authorities to determine an individual dumping margin for each known producer/exporter of the product under investigation. According to Chinese Taipei, the CBSA determined two dumping margins for each exporter i.e. a company specific one for the purposes of Article 2 and a countrywide one for the purposes of Article 5.8. Chinese Taipei's main concern was that the countrywide margin was used to determine the termination of the investigation under Article 5.8, second sentence.[11]

The panel *rejected* Chinese Taipei's assertions because it saw no factual or legal basis for this claim. The panel further found that nothing in the text of Article 6.10, first sentence, precludes an investigating authority from determining a countrywide dumping margin in addition to an exporter-specific margin.[12]

2.2.3   Article 7.1(ii) of the ADA: Provisional Measures on Imports

Chinese Taipei further claimed that Canada violated Article 7.1(ii) by imposing provisional measures on imports from a Chinese Taipei exporter with a preliminary margin of dumping below the *de minims* threshold established in Article 5.8.[13] This provision stipulates that provisional measures may be applied only if a preliminary affirmative dumping and injury determination has been made.

The panel *rejected* Chinese Taipei's claim for two reasons. *First,* it found that a "preliminary affirmative determination" should be made in respect of individual exporters and not on a countrywide basis, if provisional duties are to be applied on exporter-specific dumping margins. *Second,* the term "dumping" in the context of Article 7.1(ii) does not contain the notion of *de minimis* dumping but refers to all instances of dumping.[14]

2.2.4   Additional Claims Under Articles 1, 7.5, and 9.2 of the ADA, and Article VI:2 of the GATT 1994

Chinese Taipei argued that exporters with final *de minimis* dumping margins do not constitute "sources found to be dumped" within the meaning of Article 9.2, first sentence. This provision is the non-discrimination obligation on the ADA and stipulates that anti-dumping duties must be collected on imports of products from all sources found to be dumped and causing injury, unless a price undertaking has

---

[11]Panel Report, *Canada – Welded Pipe*, paras. 7.39–7.40.
[12]Panel Report, *Canada – Welded Pipe*, paras. 7.43–7.45.
[13]Panel Report, *Canada – Welded Pipe*, para. 7.46.
[14]Panel Report, *Canada – Welded Pipe*, paras. 7.64–7.66.

been accepted. Further, Chinese Taipei argued that Article 9.2 applies equally to the imposition of provisional measures by virtue of Article 7.5. Therefore, exporters with final *de minimis* dumping margins do not qualify as "sources found to be dumped" within the meaning of Article 9.2, first sentence, and the imposition of definitive anti-dumping duties on those exporters is inconsistent with that provision and Article 7.5. Moreover, Chinese Taipei argued that Canada violated Article VI:2, first sentence, of the GATT 1994 by imposing provisional and final anti-dumping duties, respectively, on imports from exporters with preliminary and final *de minimis* dumping margins. According to Chinese Taipei, the existence of *de minimis* dumping margins means that there was no dumping to offset or prevent as required under Article VI:2 of the GATT 1994. Chinese Taipei further argued that this led to a consequent violation of Article 1 of the ADA, which requires Members to apply anti-dumping measures only under, inter alia, the circumstances provided for in Article VI of the GATT 1994.[15]

The panel recalled that its findings under Article 5.8, second sentence, only applied to final *de minimis* dumping margins. Thus, exporters with final *de minimis* dumping margins should not have been treated as "sources found to be dumped" for the purpose of imposing a duty under Article 9.2. Once the final determinations of *de minimis* dumping margins were made, the investigation should have been terminated immediately and no anti-dumping duties should have been applied on those products. Subsequently, the panel upheld Chinese Taipei's claim under Article 9.2 and affirmed the consequential claims under Article 1 and Article VI:2 of the GATT 1994. Furthermore, the panel recalled that it rejected Chinese Taipei's claim under Article 7.1(ii) and found that at the preliminary determination stage, the CBSA was entitled to treat the exporter as a "source found to be dumped". Therefore, no immediate termination under Article 5.8 was required.

The panel thus *concluded* that there was no basis to conclude that the imposition of provisional measures on imports from that exporter was inconsistent with Articles 1 or 7.5 or Article VI:2 of the GATT 1994.[16]

2.2.5   Article 3 of the ADA: The Treatment of Imports from Exporters with *de minimis* Margins of Dumping for Determining Injury

Chinese Taipei considered that the Canadian International Trade Tribunal's (CITT) decision to treat imports from Chinese Taipei exporters with final *de minimis* dumping margins as "dumped imports" was inconsistent with Articles 3.1, 3.2, 3.4, 3.5, and 3.7. Article 3 and its various subparagraphs require the investigating authority to demonstrate that "dumped imports" are causing material injury to a domestic industry. Thus, Chinese Taipei contended that the CBSA's injury and causation determination were inconsistent with those provisions as imports from

---

[15]Panel Report, *Canada – Welded Pipe*, paras. 7.73–7.74.

[16]Panel Report, *Canada – Welded Pipe*, paras. 7.76–7.77.

the *de minimis* exporters may not be considered as "dumped" within the meaning of Article 3 and should have been excluded from CBSA's injury analysis.[17]

The panel followed the finding of the panel in *EC–Salmon (Norway)* that imports from an exporter with a *de minimis* dumping margin may not be treated as "dumped" for the purposes of the injury analysis.[18] The panel found that the application of Article 5.8 implies that there is no "legally cognizable dumping" by an exporter with a final *de minimis* dumping margin. Thus, imports from that exporter cannot be considered "dumped imports" for the purposes of the injury analysis under Article 3.

Consequently, the panel *concluded* that Canada had violated Articles 3.1, 3.2, 3.4, 3.5, and 3.7 by treating imports from two Chinese Taipei exporters with final *de minimis* dumping margins as "dumped imports" in the CITT's analysis and injury and causation final determinations.[19]

2.3 Observations

This case provides some clarity regarding Article 5.8 of the ADA, which stipulates that an investigating authority must terminate an investigation where it finds a dumping margin less than 2% or lower (*de minimis*). However, this provision does not specify whether the dumping margin is "countrywide" or "exporter-specific". Relevant to the analysis of Article 5.8 is Article 6.10, which states that an investigating authority must, as a rule, determine an individual margin of dumping for each known exporter or producer of the product under investigation.

The panel in this case followed previous jurisprudence, particularly *Mexico – Beef and Rice* to clarify that Article 5.8 requires the authorities to terminate an anti-dumping investigation in respect of *individual exporters/producers* who were found to have a *de minimis* dumping margin. This provides some legal and commercial certainty to companies who are under investigation but have been found to have a *de minimis* dumping margin. Investigating authorities are obliged to exclude those companies from the investigation and not lump them in the countrywide dumping margin.

---

[17]Panel Report, *Canada – Welded Pipe*, paras. 7.78–7.79.

[18]Panel Report, *Canada – Welded Pipe*, para. 7.83, referring to Panel Report, *EC – Salmon (Norway)*, para. 7.628.

[19]Panel Report, *Canada – Welded Pipe*, paras. 7.83, 7.87–7.89.

3   Russia: Pigs (EU) (Appellate Body Report)

This dispute was initiated by the EU in June 2014 and the panel report was circulated in August 2016. In early 2017, the Appellate Body issued its report. This section describes the key elements of the Appellate Body's findings.

3.1   Facts of the Case

This dispute concerns African swine fever (ASF), which is a highly contagious haemorrhagic disease that affects pigs, warthogs, European wild boar, and American wild pigs. Severe cases of ASF are characterised by high fever, loss of appetite, respiratory distress, diarrhoea, haemorrhages in the skin and internal organs, and death in 2–10 days on average. Mortality rates may be as high as 100%.[20] According to the World Organization for Animal Health (OIE), ASF is highly contagious between sick and healthy animals and can remain viable for 3–6 months in uncooked pork products. It is highly resistant to low temperatures but can be inactivated by heat. The OIE's Technical Disease Card of April 2013 indicates that ASF is enzootic in most Sub-Saharan Countries. In Europe, it has been successfully eradicated from the Iberian Peninsula but is still found in Sardinia in Italy. It has most recently appeared in the Caucus and Russia.[21]

The EU challenges certain Russian measures adopting, maintaining, or applying an import ban on live pigs and their genetic material, pork, and certain other pig products. According to the EU, these measures prevent the importation of these product from the EU into Russia.[22] The measures comprise the "EU-wide ban" on the importation of live pigs and pig products from the EU to Russian and the country-specific bans on imports from Estonia, Latvia, Lithuania, and Poland of certain heat-treated and non-heated treated pig products.[23] These measures were put into effect by certain letters and administrative notices issued by the Russian Federal Service for Veterinary and Phytosanitary Supervision (FSVPS).[24] These measures were notified to the WTO. The EU alleged that the EU-wide ban was constructed from various letters, official instructions, announcements, and practices.[25] It thus sought the panel to review this measure as such and as applied, *de jure* and *de facto*, and insofar as it is written or unwritten.[26]

---

[20]Panel Report, *Russia – Pigs (EU)*, para. 2.1.

[21]Panel Report, *Russia – Pigs (EU)*, paras. 2.4, 2.6.

[22]EU's panel request, p. 1.

[23]Panel Report, *Russia – Pigs (EU)*, para. 7.37.

[24]Panel Report, *Russia – Pigs (EU)*, section 7.3.5 Table 2.

[25]Panel Report, *Russia – Pigs (EU)*, para. 7.60.

[26]Panel Report, *Russia – Pigs (EU)*, para. 2.9.

Before the panel, the EU claimed that Russia's measures are inconsistent with Articles 2.2, 2.3, 3.1, 3.2, 3.3, 5.1, 5.2, 5.3, 5.4, 5.5, 5.6, 5.7, 6.1, 6.2, 6.3, 7, 8, Annex B(1), (2), (5), (6), and Annex C(1)(a), (b), (c) of the SPS Agreement. The panel found that Russia acted inconsistently with Articles 2.2, 3.1, 3.2, 5.1, 5.2, 5.3, 5.6, 6.1, and 8, and Annexes C(1)(a) and C(1)(c) of the same agreement.

On appeal, Russia challenged certain threshold issues decided by the panel and the panel's findings under Articles 6.1 and 6.3 of the SPS Agreement. The EU challenged the panel's findings under Article 6.2 of the same agreement.

3.2 Salient Legal Findings

3.2.1 Threshold Issue: Whether the Panel Erred in Attributing the EU-Wide Ban to Russia

Russia appealed the panel's finding that the EU-wide ban is a measure attributable to Russia. Russia challenged the panel's findings on two grounds. *First*, that the panel erroneously attributed to the Russian government the content of the bilateral veterinary certificates that facilitated the export of the products at issue from the EU to Russia. Russia argues that while it is authorised by its domestic law to require veterinary certificates to import these products, the specific condition that the EU must be free from ASF is not established in Russian SPS legislation. *Second*, Russia alleges that the panel failed to recognize the sequencing inherent in the bilateral veterinary certificates – the EU must first issue a valid certificate before Russia can recognise its validity and allow the products access to its market.[27] Only the first argument is addressed below.

The Appellate Body recalled its findings in *US – Corrosion-Resistant Steel Sunset Review* that any act of omission attributable to a Member can be a measure of that Member for dispute settlement purposes.[28] The Appellate Body found that the panel focused on the fact that it is Russia not the EU that requires the bilateral veterinary certificates for the importation of the products at issue into its territory. These certificates are a part of a broader Russian regulatory framework governing the importation of products into Russia and it is the Russian authorities that enforce this requirement by rejecting products that do not satisfy it.

Thus, the Appellate Body *upheld* the panel's findings and concluded that these actions taken together constitute a composite measure that the EU refers to as an "EU-wide ban", which constitutes a measure attributable to Russia.[29]

---

[27] Appellate Body Report, *Russia – Pigs (EU)*, para. 5.15.

[28] Appellate Body Report, *Russia – Pigs (EU)*, para. 5.17, referring to Appellate Body Report, *US – Corrosion-Resistant Steel Sunset* Review, para. 81.

[29] Appellate Body Report, *Russia – Pigs (EU)*, paras. 5.18–5.20, 5.22–5.23.

3.2.2 Whether the Panel Erred in Finding That Russia's Terms of Accession to the WTO Did Not Limit Its Assessment of the EU-Wide Ban

According to Russia, the panel erred in its finding that the EU-wide ban is attributable to it because the terms of its accession commitments in paragraphs 892 and 893 of its Working Party Report shield the measure from further scrutiny under the SPS Agreement. Russia claims that the "validity" of the bilateral veterinary certificates must be given "full legal effect" by requiring a finding that the actions that Russia took to comply with the certificates' requirements render them WTO-consistent. Russia's argument is twofold. *First*, it submits that the commitment in its Working Party Report that the bilateral veterinary certificates "would remain valid" constitutes a commitment during Russia's accession that only certificates used to import the products at issue are those agreed to by Russia and the EU. *Second*, Russia posits that in order to ensure the "full legal effect" of the bilateral veterinary certificates, it must, in acting in accordance with those certificates, be found to have acted consistently with its WTO obligations.[30]

The Appellate Body interpreted Russia's commitments in its Working Party Report as an undertaking that addresses which certificate would remain in effect, until amended or replaced, in the relations between Russian and other Members. In effect, Russia accepted that, where a bilateral veterinary certificate exists, it is the certificate and not the Customs Union common certificate that would be considered valid. The Appellate Body distinguished between the bilateral veterinary certificates, which require, inter alia, certain factual attestations regarding the disease status of the exporting country and the WTO-consistency of the actions of the importing country. The Appellate Body highlighted that the WTO-consistency of the bilateral veterinary certificates themselves is not at issue. Rather, whether a particular SPS measure i.e. the EU-wide ban, which was adopted on the basis of the ASF status of the EU, is consistent with Russia's obligations under Article 6 of the SPS Agreement.[31]

The Appellate Body recalled its findings in *India – Agricultural Products* and found that the obligation under Article 6 is not static – it requires SPS measures to be adjusted over time to reflect the SPS characteristics of the relevant areas. The Appellate Body did not consider that the commitment set out in Russia's Working Party Report can be understood to be an obligation that holds Russia or any other Member captive to the terms of the bilateral veterinary certificates if acting according to them would result in WTO inconsistency. Russia is also not obliged to choose between violating the terms of its Working Party Report and other obligations under WTO law. According to the Appellate Body, all provisions of the WTO covered agreements must be read in a way that gives meaning to all of them, harmoniously.

---

[30] Appellate Body Report, *Russia – Pigs (EU)*, paras. 5.24, 5.27.

[31] Appellate Body Report, *Russia – Pigs (EU)*, para. 5.32. All provisions in this dispute refer to the SPS Agreement unless otherwise mentioned.

Russia and other Members agreed that the bilateral certificates would remain in effect until the Customs Union common certificate was agreed upon. However, this does not absolve the Members concerned from acting in good faith and making the necessary amendments to the certificates to ensure that they are consistent with WTO law, including the SPS Agreement.[32]

The Appellate Body consequently *upheld* the panel's finding that Russia's terms of accession to the WTO did not limit the panel's assessment of the EU's claims regarding the EU-wide ban.[33]

3.2.3 Findings Under Article 6 of the SPS Agreement

Whether the Panel Erred in Its Findings Under Article 6.3 of the SPS Agreement

Russia challenged the panel's findings under Article 6.3 because it considered that the panel made an error in its interpretation by failing to find that this provision: (1) requires panels to take into account the scientific and technical evidence relied upon by the *importing* Member, in accordance with that Member's appropriate level of sanitary or phytosanitary protection. Russia challenged that the EU provided it with the necessary evidence to demonstrate that areas within Lithuania, Poland, Latvia, and Estonia, and the EU as a whole, are ASF free and that those areas were likely to remain ASF free; and (2) contemplates a "reasonable period of time" for an importing Member to evaluate and verify the evidence provided by an exporting Member. As a result, the panel erroneously found that as at 11 September 2014, the EU had provided Russia with sufficient evidence that parts of Estonia are, and are likely to remain, ASF free.[34]

The Appellate Body explained that Article 6.3 addresses the situation where an *exporting* Member claims that areas within its territory are pest-or disease-free or of low pest or disease prevalence. Pursuant to the first sentence of this provision, an exporting Member must provide the necessary evidence to support its claim. This evidence must be of a nature, quantity, and quality sufficient for an objective determination by the importing Member as to the pest or disease status of the areas in question. Article 6.3, second sentence, adds that the exporting Member must give the importing Member reasonable access to the areas covered by its claim for the importing Member to conduct inspections and tests. The Appellate Body recalled that the importing Member's determination of the pest or disease status of an area is addressed by Article 6.2, second sentence, and forms part of that Member's assessment of the SPS characteristics of that area within the meaning of Article 6.1.

---

[32]Appellate Body Report, *Russia – Pigs (EU)*, paras. 5.33–5.34, quoting Appellate Body Report, *India – Agricultural Products*, para. 5.132.

[33]Appellate Body Report, *Russia – Pigs (EU)*, paras. 5.35–5.36.

[34]Appellate Body Report, *Russia – Pigs (EU)*, paras. 5.39–5.41.

Thus, Article 6.3 does not contain any obligations for the *importing* Member, rather the *exporting* Member.[35]

The Appellate Body found that when an exporting Member makes a claim under Article 6.3, the importing Member *must* review the evidence provided by the exporting Member. The importing Member *may* also rely upon data collected through on-site visits and other relevant information acquired from other sources, including international organisations. While the Appellate Body found that the panel could have articulated its task under Article 6.3 clearer (i.e. to determine if the information provided by the EU to Russia was sufficient to make an objective assessment of the risk), the Appellate Body *found* that the panel did not err in finding that Article 6.3 does not require consideration of the evidence relied upon by the *importing Member*.[36]

Further, the Appellate Body found that while the importing Member's evaluation of the evidence for the purposes of assessing the SPS characteristics of a particular area cannot be performed instantly, that period of time is not left to that Member's unfettered discretion. Annex C(1)(a) of the SPS Agreement requires Members to ensure that inspecting procedures are undertaken and completed without undue delay. What constitutes an appropriate period of time, however, must be assessed on a case-by-case basis and will depend on, among other things, the nature and complexity of the procedure at hand.[37] However, these obligations are covered by Article 6.1 and Article 6.2, second sentence, and not Article 6.3. The panel considered that the period of time provided to the Russian authorities to assess the evidence provided by the EU was not appropriate.[38]

The Appellate Body thus *upheld* the panel's findings that, as at 11 September 2014, the EU had provided the necessary evidence to objectively demonstrate to Russia that the areas within Estonia, Latvia, Lithuania, and Poland, as well as those in the rest of the EU, were ASF free and that the ASF-free areas in all the areas except for Latvia would likely remain so.[39]

Whether the Panel Erred in Its Findings Under Article 6.1 of the SPS Agreement

Russia argued that the panel, in finding that an importing Member can be found to have failed to adapt its measures to the SPS characteristics of the areas within the exporting Member's territory even when the exporting Member, had failed to provide the necessary evidence pursuant to Article 6.3. Russia contented that this

---

[35] Appellate Body Report, *Russia – Pigs (EU)*, paras. 5.61–5.64.

[36] Appellate Body Report, *Russia – Pigs (EU)*, paras. 5.72–5.75.

[37] Appellate Body Report, *Russia – Pigs (EU)*, paras. 5.80–5.81.

[38] Appellate Body Report, *Russia – Pigs (EU)*, paras. 5.86, 5.87.

[39] Appellate Body Report, *Russia – Pigs (EU)*, paras. 5.87–5.88.

interpretative error led to the panel's view that the ban on the imports at issue from Latvia is inconsistent with Article 6.1.[40]

The Appellate Body explained that the relationship between Article 6.1 and 6.3 were addressed by the panel and Appellate Body in *India – Agricultural Products*. The Appellate Body in that case found that all the provisions of Article 6 must be read together. The Appellate Body explained that when the importing Member has received a request from an exporting Member to recognise an area within its territory as disease-free, the exporting Member will be able to establish that the importing Member failed to comply with its obligations under Article 6.1 and 6.2 only if that exporting Member can also establish that it took the steps under Article 6.3.[41] However, situations exist in which even in the absence of such objective demonstration by an exporting Member, an importing Member may still be found to have violated Article 6.1. For example, (1) where an importing Member's regulatory regime precludes the recognition of the concept of pest- and disease-free areas; and (2) pest-or disease-free areas and areas of low pest or disease prevalence are only a subset of the SPS characteristics that may call for the adaptation of an SPS measure.[42]

The Appellate Body considered that a panel should conduct a case-by-case evaluation before reaching its conclusion as to the relationship between the exporting Member's compliance with Article 6.3 and the alleged breach of Article 6.1 by the importing Member. In the current case, the Appellate Body found that the potential implications of a finding that the EU has not complied with Article 6.3 for an analysis of Russia's obligations under Article 6.1 arise in connection with the panel's finding relating to the likelihood that the areas in Latvia would remain ASF free.[43]

In this case, once the panel had found that the EU had failed to provide the necessary evidence to objectively demonstrate that the ASF-free areas in Latvia would remain so, the panel should have considered the implications of that finding on Russia's obligations under Article 6.1. However, the panel did not do so. It, instead, moved on to assess whether Russia had adapted its measure to the SPS characteristics of the relevant areas, including those in Latvia, pursuant to Article 6.1. In doing so, the panel did not attach any significance to its finding that the EU failed to comply with its obligation under Article 6.3. The Appellate Body thus *found* that the panel erred in finding that Russia failed to adapt the ban on imports of the products at issue from Latvia to the ASF-free areas within Latvia.[44]

Consequently, the Appellate Body *modified* the panel's findings to the effect that the EU failed to demonstrate that Russia did not adapt the ban on imports of the products at issue from Latvia to the SPS characteristics of Latvia. However, given

---

[40]Appellate Body Report, *Russia – Pigs (EU)*, para. 5.89.

[41]Appellate Body Report, *India – Agricultural Products*, para. 5.156.

[42]Appellate Body Report, *India – Agricultural Products*, para. 5.157.

[43]Appellate Body Report, *Russia – Pigs (EU)*, paras. 5.97, 5.100.

[44]Appellate Body Report, *Russia – Pigs (EU)*, para. 5.103.

the panel's finding that the Russia failed to adapt its ban on imports to the products at issue to the SPS characteristics within Russia, the panel's conclusion that this measure is inconsistent with Article 6.1 stands.[45]

Whether the Panel Erred in Its Findings Under Article 6.2 of the SPS Agreement

The EU requested the Appellate Body to reverse the panel's conclusions that Russia recognises the concepts of pest- or disease-free areas and areas of low pest or disease prevalence in respect of ASF. Therefore, the EU-wide ban and the country-specific bans on the importation of the product at issue from the affected EU member states are not inconsistent with Russia's obligation under Article 6.2. The EU further requested the Appellate Body to complete the legal analysis and find that Russia failed to comply with its obligation under Article 6.2 to recognise the concept of regionalisation in respect of ASF.[46]

The Appellate Body noted that Article 6.2 does not prescribe how a Member must recognise the concept of pest- or disease-free areas or low pest or disease prevalence. These concepts will often be embodied in a Member's regulatory framework or manifests itself in practice. It considered that making a determination pursuant to Article 6.2 requires the importing Member to take specific steps for the determination of pest- or disease-free areas or areas of low pest of disease prevalence. In fact, Article 6.2 is an obligation to render operational these concepts.[47]

The Appellate Body disagreed with the panel that Article 6.2 establishes a less stringent obligation in comparison to Article 6.1 by requiring merely the acknowledgement of the concept of regionalisation by way of "abstract ideas". It also considered that the panel erred in deeming itself precluded from taking account its analysis under Article 6.2 specific instances of recognition or non-recognition of the concept of regionalisation.

The Appellate Body thus *reversed* the panel's finding that Russia recognises the concept of pest- or disease-free areas and areas of low pest or disease prevalence in respect of ASF and that, therefore, the EU-wide ban and ban in the import of the products at issue from the four EU member states are not consistent with Article 6.2 of the SPS Agreement. The Appellate Body did not complete the legal analysis because it lacked panel findings as to whether there are elements of Russia's SPS regulatory framework, and Russia's administrative practice, that suggest that Russia recognises these concepts.[48]

---

[45] Appellate Body Report, *Russia – Pigs (EU)*, para. 5.108.

[46] Appellate Body Report, *Russia – Pigs (EU)*, para. 5.109.

[47] Appellate Body Report, *Russia – Pigs (EU)*, paras. 5.125–5.127.

[48] Appellate Body Report, *Russia – Pigs (EU)*, para. 5.152.

3.3 Observations

The Appellate Body has confirmed and further developed its findings in *India – Agricultural Products* in respect of the concept of regionalisation. Clearly, the obligation on the importing Member to regionalise under Article 6.1 applies to regions in the exporting Member as well as regions in the importing Member's own territory.

Further, the obligations imposed on importing countries are under Article 6.1 and 6.2 of the SPS Agreement, while the exporting country is obliged to comply with Article 6.3. However, there are instances when an importing Member can claim that it cannot comply with its obligations under the former provisions because the exporting Member did not comply with its obligations under Article 6.3. However, a panel must provide adequate explanation for a finding upholding this claim made by the importing Member. In this dispute, the Appellate Body found that the panel did not comply and modified the panel's finding without providing further guidance as to what type of missing information from the exporting Member would preclude the importing Member from complying with its obligations under Article 6.

The Appellate Body has also clarified that the obligation to recognise the concepts of pest- and disease-free areas and areas of low pest and disease prevalence is not merely abstract and must be enshrined in the importing Member's regulatory regime or applied in practice.

4 European Union: Poultry Meat (China) (Panel Report)

This dispute was initiated by China in June 2015 and the panel report was circulated in March 2017. This section describes the key elements of the panel's findings.

4.1 Facts of the Case

This dispute concerns the EU's modification of its tariff concessions on certain poultry products pursuant to negotiations held under Article XXVIII of the GATT 1994.

The EU initiated two different tariff negotiation exercises. The First Modification Package was initiated in 2006 and covered three tariff lines. The Second Modification Package was initiated in 2009 and covered seven tariff lines. In both negotiation exercises, the EU notified its intention to modify its tariff concessions under Article XXVIII of the GATT 1994. However, it only entered into negotiations with Brazil and Thailand, which it considered to have the requisite legal interest to participate in the negotiations. The EU reached an agreement with those two Members in which the EU replaced its previous tariff concessions on the poultry products concerned with tariff rate quotas (TRQs). Between 2003 and 2008, the EU also applied several SPS measures. China's poultry imports to the EU were negligible when the EU initiated the modifications.

Subsequent to a relaxation of the EU SPS measures in 2008, imports of poultry products from China into the EU increased significantly under two tariff lines at issue. The increase occurred during the EU's negotiations with Brazil and Thailand under the Second Modification Package. China challenged the EU's poultry measures claiming that they are inconsistent with Articles I.1, II.1, XIII, and XXVIII of the GATT 1994.[49]

4.2 Salient Legal Findings

4.2.1 Article XXVIII:1 of the GATT 1994

China argued that the EU violated Article XXVIII:1 of the GATT 1994[50] by failing to recognize China as a Member with a principal or substantial supplying interest for purposes of the negotiations under Article XXVIII. In addition, China argued that the EU's SPS measures restricting its poultry imports over the reference periods had constituted "discriminatory quantitative restrictions". As a result, the EU breached the provision by failing to determine which Members held a principal or substantial supplying interest.

The panel *concluded* that China failed to demonstrate that the EU violated Article XXVIII:1 by not recognising that China held a principle or substantial supplying interest in the First and Second Modification Packages.[51] The panel held that the rules applicable to the determination of which Members hold a supplying interest under Article XXVIII should be interpreted in a way that strikes a balance between the several competing objectives that find expression in the text of the *Ad Note* to Article XXVIII:1 (*Ad Note*).[52] The panel found that the SPS measures in place over the reference periods selected by the EU did not constitute "discriminatory quantitative restrictions" within the meaning of the *Ad Note*. In addition, the panel found that the EU was under no legal obligation to re-determine which Members held a principal or substantial supplying interest based on the latest available import data for 2009–2011.[53]

---

[49]This section does not discuss the arguments and findings under Articles I, XIII:1 and XIII:4 of the GATT 1994.

[50]All provisions in this dispute refer to the GATT 1994 unless otherwise mentioned.

[51]Panel Report, *EU – Poultry Meat (China)*, para 7.236.

[52]Panel Report, *EU – Poultry Meat (China)*, para 7.216.

[53]Panel Report, *EU – Poultry Meat (China)*, para 7.235.

4.2.2 Article XXVIII:2 of the GATT 1994 and Understanding on the Interpretation of Article XXVIII

China claimed that the TRQs negotiated in the two packages are inconsistent with Article XXVIII:2 read with paragraph 6 of the *Understanding on the Interpretation of Article XXVIII* (*Understanding*). China argued that the TRQs do not maintain "a general level of reciprocal and mutually advantageous concessions not less favourable to trade", within the meaning of Article XXVIII:2. As such, China argued that the TRQs did not reflect "future trade prospects" calculated in accordance with paragraph 6 of the *Understanding*.

The panel held that the *Ad Note* suggests that, when calculating the amount of the compensation for the purpose of Article XXVIII:2 and paragraph 6 of the *Understanding*, there is no requirement to make allowance for each and every measure that may have restricted the importation of the products concerned under that concession, but only for those measures that constitute "discriminatory quantitative restrictions". In addition, the panel held that that the EU was not obliged to calculate the total amount of the TRQs on the basis of import levels over the 3 years preceding the conclusion of the Article XXVIII negotiations.[54] Consequently, the panel *rejected* China's claims that the EU had acted inconsistently with Article XXVIII:2 by failing to calculate future trade prospects.

4.2.3 Article XIII:2 of the GATT 1994

China argued that by allocating the vast majority of the TRQs to Brazil and Thailand, the EU had acted inconsistently with Article XIII: 2(d) and the *chapeau* of Article XIII: 2. China claimed it had a substantial interest in supplying poultry meat to the EU.

The panel found that China had demonstrated that its increased ability to export poultry products following the relaxation of the SPS measures was a "special factor". Therefore, it held that the EU breached Article XIII:2(d) by failing to take this "special factor" into account when it determined which countries had a "substantial interest" in supplying the products.

Moreover, the panel ruled that China failed to justify its arguments that the EU had acted inconsistently with the *chapeau* of Article XIII:2 by determining the TRQ shares allocated to "all others" on the basis of actual share of imports into the EU, rather than on the basis of an estimate of what import shares would have been in the absence of the SPS measures restricting poultry imports from China.[55] Therefore, the panel found that the EU had not acted inconsistently with the *chapeau* of Article XIII:2.

---

[54]Panel Report, *EU – Poultry Meat (China)*, para 7.277.

[55]Panel Report, *EU – Poultry Meat (China)*, para 8.1

4.2.4 Article II of the GATT 1994

China argued that the EU's application of the higher out-of-quota tariff rates arising from the two Modification Packages violated Article II:1 because those rates exceeded the bound rates previously recorded in the EU Schedule of Concessions (Schedule). In addition, China argued that since the changes have not been translated into the EU's Schedule through the certification procedure, they have no legal effect to replace the existing bound duties. Hence according to China, the absence of certification means that the bound rates that existed in the EU Schedule prior to the completion of the Article XXVIII negotiations remain unchanged, and that the EU's application of the higher out-of-quota tariff rates violates Article II:1.

The panel noted that the higher out-of-quota tariffs arising from the two Modification Packages were notified to all Members. However, those changes have not yet been incorporated into the EU Schedule by means of certification.[56] The panel found that certification was *not a legal requirement* to be fulfilled in order to modify concessions before a Member can proceed to implement the changes agreed upon in Article XXVIII negotiations. As a result, the panel *rejected* China's claims that the EU violated Article II by giving effect to the modifications arising from the Article XXVIII negotiations prior to the changes being reflected in the authentic text of its Schedule through certification.[57]

4.3 Observations

This panel decision provides direction and clarity on Members' obligations when they are modifying their tariff commitments. The panel clearly explains the concepts of substantial and legal interest and the effect of notification of modifications of Members' Schedules, among other issues. Moreover, the panel also sheds some light on the obligations under Article XIII:2 of which Members may not be aware during their Schedule modification exercise. Members that previously did not have the necessary right to negotiate because of low trade volumes should be considered when apportioning TRQs. Finally, the panel provided clarity by stating that the certification of modifications of a Member's Schedule is not a legal requirement for those modifications to have a legal effect. While a Member modifying its Schedule might need to compensate certain Members, it does not require Member agreement to apply its new goods Schedules. This means that Members may apply Schedule modifications that have not been certified. This could be relevant, e.g., to the United Kingdom's Brexit negotiations.

---

[56]Panel Report, *EU – Poultry Meat (China)*, para 7.500.
[57]Panel Report, *EU – Poultry Meat (China)*, paras 7.751–7.552.

5 China: Anti-dumping Measures on Imports of Cellulose Pulp from Canada, (Panel Report)

Canada initiated this dispute in February 2015. The panel issued its report in December 2016. This section discusses the main findings of the panel.

5.1 Facts of the Case

The dispute revolves around the anti-dumping measures imposed by Ministry of Commerce of the People's Republic of China (MOFCOM) on imports of cellulose pulp originating from Canada, US and Brazil. MOFCOM conducted anti-dumping investigations on imports of cellulose from Brazil, Canada, and the US. It found that imports of cellulose from the investigated countries including Canada were dumped and had caused material injury to the Chinese domestic industry. Thereafter, MOFCOM applied an anti-dumping measure in the form of *ad valorem* duties. Canada challenged MOFCOM's determination of injury in the anti-dumping investigation and argued that the measure was inconsistent with Articles 3.1 to 3.5 of the ADA. Consequently, the measure was also inconsistent with Article 1 of the ADA and Article VI of the GATT 1994.

5.2 Salient Legal Findings

5.2.1 Articles 3.1 and 3.2 of the ADA: Volume of Dumped Imports

Canada argued that in order to consider whether an increase in the absolute volume of the dumped imports is "significant", MOFCOM had to examine the factual circumstances surrounding that increase.[58]

At the outset, the panel explained that Article 3.1 of the ADA[59] stipulates that an injury determination must be based on positive evidence and involve an examination of both the volume of the dumped imports and the effect of those imports on the domestic market for "like" products and the impact of these imports on domestic producers of these products. Further, Article 3.2, first sentence, requires that, in respect of the volume of the dumped imports, the investigating authorities must consider whether there has been a significant increase in those imports in either absolute or relative terms to the production or consumption of the importing Member. The panel stressed that even a significant increase in the volume of dumped imports may not alone suffice to demonstrate that dumped imports are causing

---

[58]Panel report, *China – Cellulose Pulp*, para. 7.31.

[59]All provisions in this dispute refer to the ADA unless otherwise mentioned.

material injury. The impact of those imports and of any increase in those imports over the period of investigation (POI) on the condition of the domestic industry must be considered.[60]

The panel found that, in the light of its interpretation of Article 3.2, second sentence, the Final Determination indicated that MOFCOM adequately took into account whether there was a significant in increase in the volume of the dumping imports in both absolute and relative terms.[61] The panel further rejected Canada's argument that MOFCOM failed to provide a reasoned and adequate explanation of how MOFCOM's reference to the share of dumped imports in total imports support its conclusion that the volume of dumped imports had increased in absolute terms. The panel found that, pursuant to Article 3.2, the investigating authority is required to *consider*, not to *determine*, whether there was a significant increase in dumped imports in absolute terms. As there is no requirement to make a determination, there would be no obligation under Article 3.2 to provide a reasoned and adequate explanation. Whether an increase in dumped imports supports a demonstration that dumped imports cause material injury under Article 3.5 requires an explanation to also be consistent with Article 3.1.[62]

The panel thus *concluded* that Canada did not demonstrate the MOFCOM's consideration of the volume of dumped imports was not consistent with Articles 3.1 and 3.2.[63]

5.2.2   Articles 3.1 and 3.2 of the ADA: Price Effects

Canada asserted that MOFCOM's injury determination was based on a flawed consideration of the effect of dumped imports on the prices of the domestic like product, and thus inconsistent with Articles 3.1 and 3.2.[64]

In reaching its conclusions, the panel considered five issues. Specifically, MOFCOM's consideration of: (1) parallel price trends; (2) the fact that dumped imports were sold at higher prices than the domestic like product; (3) trends relating to the dumped imports' market share; (4) certain business information; and (5) evidence and factors collectively.[65]

The panel *concluded* that MOFCOM's consideration of price effects was inconsistent with Articles 3.1 and 3.2 for the following reasons. While MOFCOM

---

[60]Panel Report, *China- Cellulose Pulp*, paras. 7.34–7.36.

[61]Panel Report, *China- Cellulose Pulp*, paras. 7.48–7.51.

[62]Panel Report, *China- Cellulose Pulp*, para. 7.55.

[63]Panel Report, *China- Cellulose Pulp*, para. 7.56.

[64]Panel Report, *China- Cellulose Pulp,* para. 7.57.

[65]The factors are as follows: (a) intense price competition between dumped imports and domestic like product; (b) a dramatic 43% increase in the dumped import volume; (c) a drastic decline in domestic like product prices; (d) parallel price trends; (e) pricing documents and meeting minutes; and (f) significant dumping margins. See, Panel Report, *China- Cellulose Pulp*, para. 7.109.

reasonably found parallel trends between dumped import and domestic like product prices, it failed to explain the role of those price trends and the decline of domestic like product prices and how the changes in the prices and volume of the dumped imports affect the domestic like product prices. Moreover, MOFCOM failed to provide an adequate explanation of its consideration of price depression given the undisputed fact that the prices of the dumped imports were higher than those of the domestic like product during the latter part of the POI. In addition, the panel found that Canada failed to demonstrate that MOFCOM acted inconsistently with Articles 3.1 and 3.2 in (1) considering changes in the market share of dumped imports in its consideration of price effects; and (2) just because MOFCOM took into account pricing documents and meeting minutes in its consideration of price effects.[66]

5.2.3 Articles 3.1 and 3.4 of the ADA: Impact of Dumped Imports

Canada claimed that MOFCOM's examination of the impact of the dumped imports on the domestic industry was inconsistent with Articles 3.1 and 3.4 as MOFCOM failed to objectively examine the domestic industry's market share and also failed to properly analyse and interpret data relating to factors that showed an improvement in the state of the domestic industry.[67]

The panel *concluded* that Canada failed to demonstrate a violation of Article 3.1 and 3.4 with respect to both indicators.[68]

5.2.4 Articles 3.1 and 3.5 of the ADA: Causation and Examination of Other Factors

Relating to causal link between dumped imports and material injury to the domestic market, Canada claimed that MOFOCM's demonstration was inconsistent with Articles 3.1 and 3.5. Specifically, Canada argued that MOFCOM failed to objectively examine several "other factors" allegedly causing injury to the domestic industry at the same time as the dumped imports. Specifically, (1) changes in cotton and Viscose Staple Fibre (VSF) prices; (2) domestic industry overexpansion, overproduction, and inventory build-up; (3) non-dumped imports; and (4) shortage of cotton linter.[69]

The panel reiterated that the ADA required the demonstration of a causal link between the dumped imports and the material injury. This could be achieved through the effects test and an examination of the relevant evidence before the authorities. The panel highlighted three elements to determine injury must be (1) known to the

---

[66]Panel Report, *China- Cellulose Pulp,* paras. 7.81, 7.88, 7.100, 7.108, 7.112.

[67]Panel Report, *China- Cellulose Pulp,* para. 7.113.

[68]Panel Report, *China- Cellulose Pulp,* paras. 7.126 and 7.138.

[69]Panel Report, *China- Cellulose pulp,* para. 7.139.

investigating authority; (2) a factor other than dumped imports; and (3) injuring the domestic industry at the same time as the dumped imports.[70] There is no guidance or methodology to determine these requirements.

The panel *concluded* that MOFCOM had failed to establish a causal link between the dumped imports and the material injury.[71] It considered this finding sufficient to conclude that China violated Articles 3.1 and 3.5. Nonetheless, the panel continued to examine Canada's non-attribution claims as "it may provide some useful guidance in the context of implementation of any DSB recommendation in this dispute".[72]

Regarding the non-attribution claims, the panel *concluded* that China acted inconsistently with Articles 3.1 and 3.5. Concretely, the panel found that, inter alia, MOFCOM failed to conduct a proper non-attribution analysis with respect to: the effects of cotton and VSF prices and failed to ensure that any injury caused by cotton and VSF prices were not attributed to the dumped imports, overcapacity, overexpansion, and inventory build-up, non-dumped imports, and the shortage of cotton linter.[73]

5.3 Observations

The case reiterates some of the important nuances in determining injury when looking at the anti-dumping requirements. The case particularly focuses on the following anti-dumping requirements, (1) the volume of imports, (2) price effects, (3) impact, and (4) causation. The panel emphasises that even if the requirements are met on paper, it does not necessarily mean that there is material injury. For example, on the issue of the volume, the panel stressed the fact that an increase in volume did not necessarily mean that there was material injury to the domestic industry. The panel also emphasised that parties did not have to determine an increase in the imports but rather take it into consideration when measuring the injury with an emphasis on the word *consideration*. This means that, determining an increase itself is not crucial to injury but rather considering the impact that such an increase has had on domestic industry will help to determine injury.

In addition, the panel also clarified that the effects test conducted in anti-dumping cases to establish a causal link between dumped imports and the material injury was a flexible test. There was no guidance or strict methodology applied to the requirements of the test. Thus, all anti-dumping cases must be evaluated on a case by case basis.

[70]Panel Report, *China- Cellulose pulp*, para. 7.141.

[71]Panel Report, *China- Cellulose pulp*, para. 7.151.

[72]Panel Report, *China- Cellulose pulp*, para. 7.152.

[73]Panel Report, *China- Cellulose pulp*, paras. 7.172, 7.185, 7.193, 7.202.

6   US: Certain Methodologies and Their Application to Anti-dumping Proceedings Involving China, (Appellate Body Report)

The US initiated this dispute in 2014. The Panel Report was circulated in 2016 and appealed by China in the same year. The Appellate Body circulated its Report in May 2017. This section addresses the Appellate Body's main findings.

6.1   Facts of the Case

The dispute revolved around certain methodologies used by the US Department of Commerce (USDOC) in their anti-dumping proceedings against Chinese imports. Before the panel, the Chinese challenged three methodologies used by the USDOC including: (1) the weighted average-to-transaction (W-T) methodology, (2) its treatment of multiple exporters from a non-market economy (NME) as a single NME-wide entity (Single Rate Presumption); and (3) the manner in which it determined anti-dumping duty rates for NME-wide entities and the level of such duty rates (AFA Norm).[74]

The panel found that with respect to the W-T methodology, the US had acted inconsistently with Article 2.4.2 of the ADA.[75] Regarding the USDOC's use of zeroing, the panel found that the measure was inconsistent with Article 9.3. Regarding the Single Rate Presumption, the panel found the measure to be inconsistent with Articles 6.10 and 9.2 and exercised judicial economy regarding China's claims under the second sentence of Article 9.4. Finally, concerning the AFA Norm, the panel found that China had not demonstrated that it constitutes a norm of general and prospective application and, consequently, there was no need to examine whether the AFA Norm fell within the panel's terms of reference or to address China's "as such" claims under Article 6.8 and paragraph 7 of Annex II. Consequently, the panel exercised judicial economy in relation to China's "as applied" claims under Articles 6.1, 6.8, 9.4, and Annex II paragraphs 1 and 7 in the light of the findings of inconsistency under Articles 6.10 and 9.2.[76]

On appeal, regarding the USDOC's application of the Nails test[77] in the Oil Country Tubular Goods (OCTG), Coated Paper, and Steel Cylinders investigations,

---

[74]Appellate Body Report, *US – Anti-Dumping Methodologies (China)*, para 1.2.

[75]All provisions in this dispute refer to the ADA unless otherwise mentioned.

[76]Panel Report, *US – Anti-Dumping Methodologies (China)*, para 1.6.d.

[77]This test consisted of two sequential stages the USDOC would apply after receiving an allegation of "targeted dumping" by a domestic industry petitioner identifying an "alleged target". First, the standard deviation test to find a pattern of export prices that differed among different purchasers, regions or periods. Second, the "price gap test" to establish whether the differences found under standard deviation test were significant. Under both stages, the USDOC conducted its initial

China argued that the panel erred in its interpretation and application of Articles 2.4.2 and 17.6(i) in finding that China has not established that the US acted inconsistently with these provisions by reason of the first[78] and third[79] alleged quantitative flaws with the Nails test and in relation to the USDOC's use of W-A export prices under the Nails test. Further, China challenged the panel's interpretation of Article 2.4.2 by suggesting that the comparison methodologies may be combined to establish dumping margins. Moreover, in respect of the AFA Norm, China challenged the panel's finding that China did not establish that the AFA Norm is a rule of general and prospective application and asked the Appellate Body to complete the analysis and find that the AFA Norm is a rule of general and prospective application that can be challenged "as such". If the Appellate Body can find the AFA Norm to be challengeable "as such", to complete the legal analysis and find this measure to be inconsistent with Article 6.8 and paragraph 7 of Annex II of the ADA.[80]

6.2 Salient Legal Findings

6.2.1 Articles 2.4.2 and 17.6(i) of the ADA

China challenged the application of the Nails test and the W-T methodology in the three challenged investigations. Particularly, (1) the first and third alleged quantitative flaws with the Nails test; (2) China's claim pertaining to certain qualitative factors in determining whether prices differ "significantly"; (3) the USDOC's use of weighted-average export prices to establish the existence of a "pattern"; and (4) the panel erred in suggesting that an investigating authority may combine comparison methodologies to establish dumping margins.[81]

Article 2.4.2, first sentence, provides for two symmetrical comparison methodologies that must be normally used by investigating authorities to establish dumping margins: (1) the weighted average-to-weighted average (W-W) methodology, where dumping margins are established by comparing the weighted average normal value with a weighted average of prices of all comparable export transactions; and (2) the

---

analysis on a model basis, which each model assigned a control number (CONNUM). The USDOC would exclusively examine the CONNUMs that were sold to both the alleged target and the non-targets. The price gap test also involved a two-step process: (1) the USDOC would calculate on a COONUM-specific basis the alleged target price gap; (2) if all CONNUMs where the alleged target price gap was wider than the W-A non-target price gap exceeded 5% of the total volume of the sales to the alleged target, the USDOC would conclude that the exporter passed the price gap test. See, Appellate Body Report, *US – Anti-Dumping Methodologies (China)*, paras. 5.6–5.8.

[78]The standard deviation test.

[79]Price gap test.

[80]Appellate Body Report, *US – Anti-Dumping Methodologies (China)*, paras. 4.1–4.2.

[81]Panel Report, *US – Anti-Dumping Methodologies (China)*, para. 5.2.

transaction-to-transaction (T-T) methodology, where the normal value and export transactions are compared on a transaction-specific basis. Article 2.4.2, second sentence, provides for an asymmetrical comparison methodology i.e. the W-T methodology in which the weighted average normal value is compared to prices of individual export transaction. This methodology may only be used if (1) the authorities find a pattern of export prices which differ significantly among differed purchasers, regions or time periods; and (2) an explanation is provided as to why these differences cannot be taken into account by using the symmetrical comparison methodologies. The function of the second sentence is to identify "targeted dumping" and address it appropriately.[82]

Applying the Nails test in the investigations, the USDOC found that the existence of patterns of export prices which differed significantly among different purchasers in the Coated Paper investigation and among different periods in the Steel Cylinders and OCTG investigations. The USDOC then examined the different between the dumping margins using the W-W methodology (without zeroing) and those using the W-T methodology (with zeroing). The USDOC concluded that there were differences between the dumping margins that showed that the W-W methodology concealed the differences in price patters between the targeted and non-targeted groups by averaging low-priced sales to the targeted group with high-priced sales to the non-targeted group. Consequently, the USDOC applied the W-T methodology to all export transactions of the Chinese exporters involved in the three investigations.[83]

In respect of China's first claim, the Appellate Body *found* that China failed to establish that the panel erred in its interpretation or application of Article 2.4.2, second sentence.[84]

Regarding the first alleged quantitative flaw, the Appellate Body found that a large number of export prices may fall below the one standard deviation threshold where the distribution of the export prices is not normal or single-peaked and symmetrical comparison does not preclude an investigating authority from finding that the export prices to the target differ significantly from the other export prices and form a "pattern". Regarding the third alleged quantitative flaw, the panel considered that this flaw rests on the assumption that in the three challenged investigations, the alleged target price gap was based on prices located at the tail end of the distribution of the export price data and the weighted non-target price was based on the prices located nearer to the peak of that distribution. However, China failed to show that this assumption was factually correct.[85]

Pursuant to Article 17.6(i), first sentence, the Appellate Body explained that in assessing the facts of the matter, the panel must determine whether the investigating authority's establishment of the facts was proper and whether their evaluation of

---

[82]Appellate Body Report, *US – Anti-Dumping Methodologies (China)*, para. 5.4.

[83]Appellate Body Report, *US – Anti-Dumping Methodologies (China)*, para. 5.9.

[84]Appellate Body Report, *US – Anti-Dumping Methodologies (China)*, paras. 5.31, 5.45.

[85]Appellate Body Report, *US – Anti-Dumping Methodologies (China)*, paras. 5.31, 5.45.

those facts was biased and objective. A claim under this provision is not merely subsidiary to a claim that a panel erred in its application of a WTO provision. The Appellate Body has previously cautioned that it will not interfere lightly with a panel's exercise of its discretion under this provision. Thus, an appellant must persuade the Appellate Body with sufficient compelling reasons why it should disturb a panel's assessment of the facts.[86]

In the light of the above legal standard, the Appellate Body *upheld* the panel's findings that China had not established that the US acted inconsistently with Article 2.4.4 in the three investigations because of the alleged qualitative issues with the Nails test.[87]

In its second claim, China alleged that the panel erred in its interpretation and application of Article 2.4.2, second sentence, by failing to recognise that investigating authorities must consider objective market factors in determining whether relevant pricing difference are "significant".[88]

The Appellate Body relied on its findings in *US – Washing Machines*.[89] It *upheld* the panel's finding that the USDOC was not required to consider the reasons for the differences in export prices forming the relevant pattern to determine whether those differences were qualitatively different within the meaning of the pattern clause of Article 2.4.2. Consequently, the Appellate Body found that China failed to establish that the US acted inconsistently with Article 2.4.4 in the three investigations because of the alleged qualitative issues with the Nails test.[90]

The Appellate Body turned to China's third claim on the panel's examination of the USDOC's use of weighted-average export prices to determine a "pattern" within the meaning of Article 2.4.2, second sentence.[91]

The Appellate Body *found* that the panel did not err in its interpretation and application of Article 2.4.2, second sentence, when examining the USDOC's use of purchaser or time period averages under the Nails test.[92] This is because the panel correctly found that China did not establish that the US acted inconsistently with Article 2.4.2, second sentence, in the three investigations by establishing the relevant pattern on the basis of averages as opposed to individual export transaction prices.[93] In addition, it confirmed the panel's finding that China did not establish that the US acted inconsistently with Article 17.6(i) because it did not advance any argument that is distinct from its arguments under Article 2.4.2 and thus failed to demonstrate

---

[86]Appellate Body Report, *US – Anti-Dumping Methodologies (China)*, para. 5.47, quoting Appellate Body Report, *EC – Tube or Pipe Fittings*, para. 125 (quoting Appellate Body Report, *EC – Bed Linen (Article 21.5 – India)*, paras. 169, 170.

[87]Appellate Body Report, *US – Anti-Dumping Methodologies (China)*, para. 5.49.

[88]Appellate Body Report, *US – Anti-Dumping Methodologies (China)*, para. 5.50.

[89]Appellate Body Report, *US – Anti-Dumping Methodologies (China)*, paras. 5.57–5.62.

[90]Appellate Body Report, *US – Anti-Dumping Methodologies (China)*, para. 5.71.

[91]Appellate Body Report, *US – Anti-Dumping Methodologies (China)*, paras. 5.72–5.73.

[92]Appellate Body Report, *US – Anti-Dumping Methodologies (China)*, para. 5.101.

[93]Appellate Body Report, *US – Anti-Dumping Methodologies (China)*, paras. 5.95–5.96.

that the panel failed to comply with Article 17.6(i). In conclusion, the Appellate Body *upheld* the panel's findings that China has not established that the US acted inconsistently with Article 2.4.2, second sentence, in the challenged investigations by determining the existence of a pattern or the basis of average prices instead of individual export transaction prices.[94]

Finally, regarding China's fourth claim, the Appellate Body *declared* the panel's findings *moot* to the extent that they are based on the erroneous understanding that Article 2.4.2 permits the combining of comparison methodologies to establish dumping margins. The Appellate Body referred to its findings in *US – Washing Machines*[95] and considered that Article 2.4.2, second sentence, permits an investigating authority to establish dumping margins by applying the W-T only to pattern transactions. This provision does not permit the combining of comparison methodologies.[96]

6.2.2   Article 6.8 and Paragraph 7 of Annex II of the ADA

China requested the Appellate Body (1) to find that the AFA Norm can be challenged "as such"; and (2) to find that the AFA Norm is inconsistent with Article 6.8 and of Annex II, paragraph 7.[97]

The Appellate Body observed that the distinction between "as such" and "as applied" measures is an analytical tool to facilitate the understanding of the challenged measure. Measures need not fit squarely within one of the categories to be susceptible to a WTO challenge.[98] The Appellate Body further explained that in an "as such" challenge, a complaining party must clearly establish that the rule or norm is attributable to the responding Member; the precise content of the rule or norm; and that the rule or norm has general and prospective application.[99] Only the latter element was discussed in the appeal.

The Appellate Body *reversed* the panel's findings. It found that the panel erred in concluding China did not demonstrate that the AFA Norm has prospective application. By requiring "certainty" of future application, the panel's examination of the prospective nature of the AFA Norm is inconsistent with the legal standard for establishing the prospective application of a rule or norm.[100]

---

[94]Appellate Body Report, *US – Anti-Dumping Methodologies (China)*, paras. 5.95–5.96, 5.100–5.101.

[95]Appellate Body Report, *US – Washing Machines*, paras. 5.124, 5.129.

[96]Appellate Body Report, *US – Anti-Dumping Methodologies (China)*, paras. 5.107–5.108.

[97]Appellate Body Report, *US – Anti-Dumping Methodologies (China)*, para. 5.111.

[98]Appellate Body Report, *US – Anti-Dumping Methodologies (China)*, para. 5.124, quoting Appellate Body Reports, *US – Continued Zeroing*, para. 179; *Argentina – Import Measures*, para. 5.102.

[99]Appellate Body Report, *US – Anti-Dumping Methodologies (China)*, para. 5.127, quoting Appellate Body Reports, *US – Zeroing (EC)*, para. 198; *Argentina – Import Measures*, para. 5.104.

[100]Appellate Body Report, *US – Anti-Dumping Methodologies (China)*, paras. 5.142–5.143.

The Appellate Body completed the analysis and found that the AFA Norm has general application because it affects an unidentified number of economic operators.[101] It further has prospective application as it reflects USDOC policy, provides administrative guidance for future action, and generates expectations among economic operators. It will thus continue to be used in the future. The Appellate Body thus *found* that the AFA Norm is a rule or norm of general and prospective application and can be challenged "as such".[102] However, the Appellate Body refused to complete the analysis on whether the AFA Norm is inconsistent with Article 6.8 and paragraph 7 of Annex II. The Appellate Body considered that there were no findings of inconsistency with these provisions by the panel and insufficient undisputed facts on the panel record for it to evaluate the process the USDOC undertakes for its selection of which "facts available" reasonable replace the missing "necessary information" in order to arrive at an accurate determination.[103]

6.3   Observations

This case provides more clarity in respect of the USDOC's dumping margin calculation methodologies, especially in respect of China and other NMEs. The Appellate Body ruled against the USDOC on three important aspects: (1) the use of the Nails test to use the exceptional method in Article 2.4.2 of the ADA to justify the W-T methodology in dumping margins calculations; (2) the treatment of multiple companies in a non-market economy as a single NME-wide entity; and (3) the USDOC's policy of using adverse facts available for this type of entity. Nevertheless, some aspects of the Appellate Body's decision, for example, giving the green light to the use of average prices in identifying patterns, could open the door to increased use of the exceptional method under this provision.

However, given the Appellate Body's findings in the dispute between Korea and the US in *US – Washing Machines*, several of the Appellate Body's findings on targeted dumping and zeroing in this case were unsurprising. While this case is far from being the nail in the coffin of more than 20 years of WTO zeroing disputes, the Appellate Body's findings could have the (un)intended consequence of opening the lid of targeted dumping and trigger disputes on how and when Members can calculate dumping margins using the exceptional method.[104]

---

[101] Appellate Body Report, *US – Anti-Dumping Methodologies (China)*, paras. 5.152. 5.156.

[102] Appellate Body Report, *US – Anti-Dumping Methodologies (China)*, paras. 5.163–5.164.

[103] Appellate Body Report, *US – Anti-Dumping Methodologies (China)*, paras. 5.178–5.179.

[104] See, Prusa and Vermulst (2019), pp. 1–2.

7   European Union: Anti-dumping Measures on Imports of Certain Fatty Alcohols from Indonesia, (Appellate Body Report)

This case was originally brought before the panel by Indonesia in 2013. The panel issued its decision on the matter in 2016. The decision was appealed, and the Appellate Body issued its Report in September 2017. This section focuses on the findings of the Appellate Body.

7.1   Facts of the Case

The dispute concerns the definitive and provisional anti-dumping measures applied by the EU on imports of certain fatty alcohols and their blends from Indonesia. Fatty alcohols are intermediary products mainly used as inputs to produce surfactants, which are used to produce detergents and household cleaning and personal care products.

Before the panel, Indonesia challenged three of the EU measures. *First*, Indonesia alleged that the EU investigating authorities had failed to make a fair comparison between the export price and the normal value. As such, the EU authorities had made an improper deduction for a factor that did not affect the price comparability.[105] *Second*, Indonesia alleged that the EU had failed to properly conduct a non-attribution analysis. *Third*, Indonesia argued that the EU had failed to disclose information to the Indonesian companies under investigation the results of the verification visits.

The panel found that Indonesia had failed to prove that the EU authorities had violated Articles 2.3, 2.4, 3.1 and 3.5 of the ADA.[106] As such, Indonesia failed to demonstrate that the EU had acted inconsistently with Articles 2.3, 3.1 and 3.5. Concerning Article 6.7, the panel found in Indonesia's favour and ruled that the EU had failed to disclose results of the on-spot investigations to the Indonesian companies under investigation.

Indonesia and the EU each appealed the panel's decision. Indonesia principally required the Appellate Body to consider whether the panel correctly applied and interpreted Article 2.4. The EU's main point of contention was whether the panel correctly applied Article 6.7.

---

[105]Appellate Body Report, *EU- Fatty Alcohols (Indonesia)*, para. 4.1.a.

[106]All provisions in this dispute refer to the ADA unless otherwise mentioned.

7.1.1 Improper Adjustment of Export Prices: Articles 2.3 and 2.4 of the ADA

In relation to the adjustment of the export price, the EU authorities established that Indonesian companies had paid a mark-up of sales to a related company following a sale and purchase agreement between them. In addition, the EU established that the mark-up paid had no corresponding price component on the domestic side. Consequently, the EU investigating authorities characterised the mark-up as commission paid in respect of export sales to the EU and treated it as a difference affecting price comparability for which a downward adjustment to the export price was warranted.[107]

In its claim under Article 2.4, Indonesia clarified that its argument was that the EU authorities should not have made any adjustment to the export price in relation to the mark-up, and not that the EU authorities erred "because the amount of the adjustment was improper",[108] as underscored in the panel report. Indonesia argued that the downward adjustment to the export price was inconsistent with Article 2.4. It contended that (1) the existence of a single economic entity precluded the EU authorities from making an allowance for the mark-up; (2) the allowance resulted in an asymmetrical comparison with the normal value; and (3) the different outcomes for the Indonesian producers demonstrate that the EU authorities' analysis was arbitrary.[109]

Article 2.4 requires investigating authorities to ensure a fair comparison between the export price and the normal value and, to this end, to make due allowance, or adjustments, for differences affecting price comparability. As such, the Appellate Body had to consider not just the comparison between the export price and the normal value but rather the means to ensure that the comparison was fair.[110] The Appellate Body emphasised the need to make due allowances in specific circumstances to be made in each case, on its merits, for *differences which affect price comparability*. These differences include the conditions and terms of sale, taxation, levels of trade, quantities, physical characteristics, and any other differences which are also demonstrated to affect price comparability.

Consequently, the Appellate Body agreed with the panel's decision that the EU authorities had a sufficient evidentiary basis for establishing that the mark-up paid in connection with export sales to the EU was a difference affecting price comparability under Article 2.4.[111] Moreover, the Appellate Body confirmed that the related trading company did not form part of the Indonesian producer company and as a result, the two companies did not constitute a single economic entity. In addition, an analysis of the Sale and Purchase Agreement indicated that the relationship between

---

[107]Appellate Body Report, *EU- Fatty Alcohols (Indonesia)*, para. 5.5.

[108]Appellate Body Report, *EU- Fatty Alcohols (Indonesia)*, para. 5.14.

[109]Appellate Body Report, *EU- Fatty Alcohols (Indonesia)*, para. 5. 29.

[110]Appellate Body Report, *EU- Fatty Alcohols (Indonesia)*, para. 5.19.

[111]Appellate Body Report, *EU- Fatty Alcohols (Indonesia)*, para. 6.3.

the Producer company and the related company was "similar to those of an agent working on a commission basis".[112] In the end, the mark-up constituted a difference which affected the price comparability.

Therefore, the Appellate Body *upheld* the panel's finding that Indonesia had not demonstrated that the EU authorities acted inconsistently with Article 2.4 by treating the mark-up paid by the Indonesian producer to its related entity as a difference affecting price comparability, and, therefore, making a downward adjustment to the export price.[113]

7.1.2   Failure to Disclose Information: Article 6.7 of the ADA

The EU appealed the panel's finding that the EU authorities failed to make available or disclose the results of the on-the-spot verifications to Indonesian producers pursuant to Article 6.7. In particular, the EU challenged the panel's interpretation of Article 6.7 as imposing an obligation to provide information. The EU argued that the term "results" in this provision refers specifically to information related to "essential facts" as underscored in Article 6.9.

The Appellate Body reaffirmed the panel's decision and expressed that Article 6.7 requires that when on-the-spot verifications are conducted, investigated firms must be provided with the results or the outcomes of the verification process. The scope of these verifications and the ensuing "results" to be communicated to the investigated firms vary from case-to-case.[114] Such disclosure is not limited to essential facts and may include the "questions posed by the investigating authorities, the responses thereto, the scope of the advance notice, and the collection of any additional evidence during the on-the-spot investigations". The disclosure of the "results" of these verifications must enable the investigated firms to effectively defend their interests in the remaining stages of the anti-dumping investigation.[115]

7.2   *Observations*

This decision touches on the much-contended use of transfer pricing between related companies in different jurisdictions. In addition to reducing tax and tariff liability between two related companies, transfer pricing can also be used to manipulate prices for purposes of reducing anti-dumping duty liability. The Appellate Body in this decision, following its findings in *US – Hot-Rolled Steel*, confirmed that, for the purposes of Article 2.4 of the ADA, "the focus of the investigating authority's

---

[112]Appellate Body Report, *EU- Fatty Alcohols (Indonesia)*, para. 5.57.

[113]Appellate Body Report, *EU- Fatty Alcohols (Indonesia)*, para. 5.115.

[114]Appellate Body Report, *EU- Fatty Alcohols (Indonesia)*, para. 5.149.

[115]Appellate Body Report, *EU- Fatty Alcohols (Indonesia)*, para. 5.164.

assessment is not on the nature of the relationship between related companies *per se*, but rather on whether that relationship can be demonstrated to be a factor that impacts the prices of the relevant transactions."[116]

After finding that Indonesia failed to demonstrate the alleged errors in the panel's interpretation of Article 2.4, the Appellate Body was careful to mention that its findings are not to be construed to mean that the nature and degree of affiliation between related companies is irrelevant to whether any allowances should be made to ensure a fair comparison between the normal value and the export price. It also mentioned that it does not rule, in the abstract, on circumstances in which an inquiry into the nature of the relationship between the companies will be sufficient or determinative of whether allowances should be allowed pursuant to Article 2.4 of the ADA.[117]

8 Indonesia: Chicken (Panel Report)

Brazil initiated this dispute in October 2015 and the panel issued its report in October 2017. This section focusses on the main findings of the panel.

8.1 Facts of the Case

Brazil challenged Indonesia's measures on imports of certain chicken meat and chicken products, which it claimed had a combined effect of a general prohibition on importation. These measures are: (1) a restriction on importation of chicken meat cut into pieces; (2) the authorisation of food imports only when the domestic food supply in Indonesia is considered "insufficient" by the government; (3) subjecting the effective importation of essential and strategic goods to the discretion of the Minister of Trade, who could prohibit and/or restrict their importation and prices; (4) limitation on the importation of chicken meat and chicken products to certain intended uses; (5) Indonesia's refusal to examine and approve the Health Certificates for poultry products proposed by Brazil since 2009; (6) Indonesia's import licensing regime; and (7) Indonesia's regulations regarding *halal* slaughtering and labelling requirements for imported chicken meat and products.

Brazil challenged the measures under Articles III:4 and XI:1 of the GATT 1994, Article 4.2 of the Agreement on Agriculture, Article 1.3 of the Import Licensing Agreement and Article 8 and Annex C of the SPS Agreement.[118]

---

[116] Appellate Body Report, *EU- Fatty Alcohols (Indonesia),* para 5.40.

[117] Appellate Body Report, *EU- Fatty Alcohols (Indonesia),* para 5.45.

[118] Panel Report, *Indonesia – Chicken,* para. 3.1.

8.2   Preliminary Matters: Panel's Jurisdiction over Amended Measures Adopted After Panel Establishment

In line with the Appellate Body jurisprudence, the panel considered that it only had jurisdiction over subsequent changes, if and to the extent that, the measures at issue remained in essence the same as those identified in the panel request.[119] The panel considered that Brazil's Panel Request included "any amendments, replacements, related measures, or implementing measures" and was therefore broad enough to cover such changes. Further, the panel considered that the subsequent legal instruments amended the challenged legal instruments, and the scope, subject matter and structure was identical. Thus, the subsequent legal instruments were replacements of the preceding legal instruments. The panel considered each of the measures at issue at the time of panel establishment and their subsequent amendments and concluded that the essence remained the same and therefore properly within the scope of the proceedings.

8.3   Salient Legal Findings

8.3.1   Article XI: 1 of GATT 1994: Positive List Requirement

Indonesia's regulations did not include chicken meat and products among products for which import licences could be issued. This, Brazil submitted, violated Article XI:1 of the GATT 1994.[120]

The panel set out the test for inconsistency with Article XI:1 as: whether the measure was a prohibition or restriction; and whether it was made effective through quotas, import or export licences or other measures. The panel recalled the definition of the term "prohibition" to be a "legal ban on the trade or importation of a specified commodity".[121] It found that the positive list requirement was a legal ban made effective through a licence, hence a violation under Article XI:1.

Indonesia sought to justify this measure under Article XX(d) of the GATT 1994, on the basis that the measure was necessary to secure compliance with Indonesia's laws and regulations dealing with *halal* requirements, and deceptive practices and customs enforcement relating to *halal*. The panel initially examined the relationship between the inconsistent measure and the relevant laws or regulations, through a

---

[119]Panel Report, *Indonesia – Chicken*, para. 7.84, referring to the Appellate Body Report, *Chile – Price Band System*, paras.135–139.

[120]Panel Report, *Indonesia – Chicken*, para. 7.113.

[121]Panel Report, *Indonesia – Chicken*, para. 7.116, referring to the Appellate Body Reports, *China – Raw Materials*, para. 319; and *Argentina – Import Measures*, para. 5.217.

scrutiny of the design of the measures sought to be justified.[122] The panel accepted that the ban worked towards the objective of ensuring *halalness* of products in Indonesia, thus it was designed to secure compliance with the *halal* requirements under Indonesian law.

The panel then recalled that the necessity test entails "an in-depth, holistic analysis" of the relationship between the measure and the objective it pursues.[123] The panel agreed with the parties that *halalness* is of great importance to the Indonesian population. While agreeing that the measure eliminates the risk of non-*halal* chicken cuts being passed off as *halal*, the panel concluded that the measure also banned the importation of *halal* chicken cuts and was counterproductive to the stated objective. Regarding trade-restrictiveness of the measure, the panel observed that while the Indonesian measure banned the importation of chicken cuts, it allowed for importation of whole chicken carcasses. Brazil suggested that a viable less trade-restrictive alternative would be application of *halal* certification, which already existed under Indonesian law, to chicken cuts. The panel therefore concluded that the Indonesian measure did not meet the necessity test.

8.3.2   Intended Use Requirement

Indonesia limited the sale of imported frozen chicken to hotels, restaurants, catering and industries; and the sale of processed products to "modern markets".[124] Brazil challenged this measure under Articles XI:1 and III:4 of the GATT 1994, and Article 4.2 of the Agreement on Agriculture.

Article XI:1 of the GATT 1994

The panel found that the measure amounted to a *de jure* restriction as importers were only allowed to import upon committing to not sell chicken meat in modern markets, and chicken meat and processed chicken in traditional markets. This restriction was made effective through an import licence.[125]

Indonesia sought to justify this measure under Article XX(b) of the GATT 1994 on the basis that it sought to protect human health. The panel agreed with Indonesia that the process of freezing and thawing increases microbial growth, which poses a health risk. The measure prevented the sale of processed chicken products in

---

[122]Panel Report, *Indonesia – Chicken*, para. 7.127, referring to the Appellate Body Report, *Argentina – Financial Services*, para. 6.203.

[123]Panel Report, *Indonesia – Chicken*, para. 7.135-6, referring to the Appellate Body Reports, *Colombia – Textiles*, para. 5.70; *Argentina – Financial Services*, para. 6.204; and *EC – Seal Products*, para. 5.169.

[124]The panel understood "modern markets", unlike traditional markets, to *usually* have had cold storage.

[125]Panel Report, *Indonesia – Chicken*, paras. 7.200–7.201.

traditional markets, which did not have freezing facilities. Thus, the panel found that the measure eliminated risks arising from thawing and was "not incapable" of achieving the intended objective.[126] In undertaking the necessity analysis, the panel considered the protection of human health to be an interest of high importance. The panel then observed that while the measure contributed to the objective by reducing risks arising from thawing, it also prevented safe chicken from being sold in the market, hence did not make any contribution in this regard. The measure prohibited access to traditional markets and was thus highly trade restrictive. The panel further considered that a reasonably available alternative would be implementation of the cold-storage requirement (which was already in Indonesian law, but limited to frozen and chilled chicken – not chicken products) to the sale of imported chicken meat and products in traditional markets, where such markets have cold storage.[127]

Indonesia also sought to justify its measure under Article XX(d) on the basis that it ensured compliance with its consumer protection law because consumers mistook thawed chicken for fresh chicken. The panel agreed that the measure was designed to secure compliance with Indonesian consumer protection laws. However, the panel concluded that the level of contribution to the intended objective was not substantial because the sanctions applied to the importer and not the seller, who would be more predisposed to deceptive practices. The panel found that an available alternative would be restricting the sale of previously frozen meat in cold storage.[128]

Thus, the panel *concluded* that the measures were neither justified under Article XX(b) nor (d).[129]

Article III:4 of GATT 1994

Brazil claimed that while the requirement that frozen and chilled chicken be stored in cold storage applied to both imported and domestic products, the fact that this requirement did not apply to fresh chicken was inconsistent with Article III:4 of the GATT 1994, because the nature of transportation of imported chicken requires it to be frozen.

In assessing likeness (between frozen chicken thawing at tropical temperatures and fresh chicken), the panel relied on the Appellate Body's jurisprudence in *EC – Asbestos*, and considered the health risk associated with thawing chicken at tropical

---

[126]Panel Report, *Indonesia – Chicken*, para. 7.222.

[127]Panel Report, *Indonesia – Chicken*, paras. 7.238–7.239.

[128]Panel Report, *Indonesia – Chicken*, para. 7.257.

[129]Having found violations under Article XI:1 of the GATT 1994, the panel exercised judicial economy and did not undertake analysis under the Agreement on Agriculture. (Panel Report, *Indonesia – Chicken*, para. 7.263).

temperatures to present a difference in the physical properties of the products at issue that indicated non-likeness.[130]

Additionally, Brazil submitted that enforcement of the intended use requirements was stricter for imported products than for domestically produced products, contrary to Article III:4. The panel presumed likeness because the distinction in enforcement was based on origin. The panel further found that competitive disadvantage resulted from the enforcement of the intended end use requirement for three reasons. *First*, unlike domestic producers, importers who breached the cold storage requirement faced punitive action.[131] *Second*, the intended use requirement bound importers to only distribute chicken to specific users.[132] *Third*, importers were required to submit distribution plans and weekly distribution reports while domestic distributers were required to submit a sales report every 3 months, which the panel found resulted in a competitive disadvantage for imports.[133]

Indonesia sought to justify these measures under Article XX(b) and (d) of the GATT 1994 based on the health risks posed by improperly thawed chicken and protection of consumers. Noting that these arguments did not explain the difference in treatment, the panel found that Indonesia had not established its *prima facie* case to justify the inconsistent measures.[134]

8.3.3   Article 1.3 of the Import Licensing Agreement: Positive List and Intended Use Requirements

The panel found that, contrary to Brazil's arguments, the positive list requirement limits products which can be imported, while the intended use requirement is a substantive requirement that importers commit to when applying for import approvals. For this reason, the panel considered that these requirements are import licensing rules and are therefore not covered under the Import Licensing Agreement.[135]

---

[130]Panel Report, *Indonesia – Chicken*, para. 7.317. The panel further observed that the health risk associated with improperly thawed chicken may affect a consumer's choice between buying such a thawed chicken and buying a fresh one. None of the parties had submitted on this issue, hence the panel did not further make a finding on it. (Panel Report, *Indonesia – Chicken*, para. 7.318).

[131]Panel Report, *Indonesia – Chicken*, para. 7.326.

[132]Panel Report, *Indonesia – Chicken*, para. 7.327.

[133]Panel Report, *Indonesia – Chicken*, para. 7.329.

[134]Panel Report, *Indonesia – Chicken*, para. 7.329.

[135]Panel Report, *Indonesia – Chicken*, para. 7.360.

8.3.4   Article XI:1 of the GATT 1994: Application Windows, Validity Periods and Fixed Licence Terms

Brazil challenged the joint operation of Indonesia's application window (time in the year during which importers may apply for import licence recommendations and approvals), validity periods (period of time during which importers may use such recommendations and approvals) and fixed licence terms (limitations on the possibility of importers to modify certain aspects of import recommendations and approvals, which forced importers to have all the details of transactions in advance of importation) under Article XI:1 of the GATT 1994.

The design of the Indonesian import licensing regime in respect to application windows and validity periods resulted in importers not having access to the Indonesian market for at least 4 weeks of each import period, which the panel concluded amounted to a restriction in market access contrary to Article XI:1.[136] However, the panel observed that Indonesia subsequently amended its legislation, eliminated the application windows, and extended its validity periods. The panel found that the initially challenged measures, while inconsistent, had expired and therefore did not make recommendations in their respect. Additionally, it found that Brazil did not dispense with its burden of proof that the new measures were inconsistent with Article XI:1.[137]

Brazil also challenged the fixed licence terms which precluded importers from varying their imports after obtaining import approvals. The panel concluded these fixed terms had a limiting effect within the meaning of Article XI:1 on the imports because importers could not modify their ports of entry or quantity of product after obtaining approvals.[138]

Indonesia sought to justify these measures under Article XX(d) of the GATT 1994 on the basis that the measures allow the allocation of human resources to ensure compliance with its laws and regulations.[139] The panel agreed with Indonesia that appropriate human resources management at the time of importation is necessary for the proper enforcement of customs laws and regulations and accepted the argument that the challenged measures are not incapable of securing compliance with Indonesia's laws and regulations.[140] In its necessity analysis, the panel acknowledged the importance of complying with Indonesia's laws and regulations. However, the panel considered the level of contribution to the objective to be limited because the information collected by Indonesia was not meaningful enough. The panel noted the measures were heavily trade restrictive as they had the effect of distorting trade flows, and accepted Brazil's alternative measure which entailed the use of monthly arrival plans to allocate human resources to ensure compliance with

---

[136]Panel Report, *Indonesia – Chicken*, para. 7.373.

[137]Panel Report, *Indonesia – Chicken*, paras. 7.438–7.447.

[138]Panel Report, *Indonesia – Chicken*, para. 7.396.

[139]Panel Report, *Indonesia – Chicken*, para. 7.403.

[140]Panel Report, *Indonesia – Chicken*, paras. 7.416–7.419.

Indonesia's laws and regulations as less trade restrictive than the challenged measures, and therefore rejected Indonesia's defence.[141]

8.3.5 Article 8 and Annex C(1)(a) of the SPS Agreement: Undue Delay in the Approval of the Veterinary Health Certificate

Brazil submitted that Indonesia had caused an undue delay regarding the approval of a veterinary certificate for the importation of poultry. The parties did not contest that the veterinary certificate is an SPS approval procedure subject to Annex C of the SPS Agreement.[142] However, Indonesia justified the delayed approval on the basis that Brazil had not submitted its *halal* compliance information. Borrowing from the findings of the panel in *Russia – Pigs (EU),* the panel found that the delay was unjustified, as it was not SPS related and was not information necessary to check and ensure fulfilment of sanitary requirements.[143]

8.4 Comments

In this dispute the relevance of non-product related characteristics in likeness analysis resurfaced, with the panel accepting that health risks could impact the physical characteristics of the products at issue. While the parties had not submitted on the impact of health risks on consumer behaviour, the panel observed that such risks could further affect consumer choice.

Additionally, in undertaking the necessity analysis under Article XX of the GATT 1994, the panel in this dispute considered alternatives which had not been put forward by the respondent. In supporting this approach, the panel indicated that while it was mindful of its role not to advance either party's claim or defence, the Appellate Body has also held that where a defence or rebuttal of a defence has been made, a panel may rule on the defence relying on arguments advanced by the parties or developing its own reasoning. On this basis, the panel examined alternatives which were on the panel record (introduced with regard to other measures at issue).

---

[141]Panel Report, *Indonesia – Chicken*, para. 7.426. Having found violations of Article XI:1 of the GATT 1994, the panel exercised judicial economy regarding the claims under the Agreement on Agriculture and the Import Licensing Agreement.

[142]Panel Report, *Indonesia – Chicken*, para. 7.517.

[143]Panel Report, *Indonesia – Chicken*, paras. 7.528, 7.531.

9 Indonesia: Import Licensing Regimes (Appellate Body Report)

This dispute was brought by New Zealand and the US in March 2015 and decided by a panel in August 2016. Indonesia appealed against certain findings of the panel and the Appellate Body issued its Report in November 2017. This section discusses the salient findings made by the Appellate Body.

9.1 Facts of the Case

New Zealand and the US challenged Indonesia's import licensing regimes for horticultural products and animal products.

These measures included: (1) limited periods to apply for import approvals and limited validity periods for horticultural and animal products; (2) periodic and fixed import approval terms for horticultural and animal products; (3) the requirement that registered importers import at least 80% of the quantity of each type of product specified on their import approvals for horticultural and animal products; (4) importation of horticultural products can only take place prior to, during and after the harvest season, within a certain time period established by the Indonesian authorities; (5) the requirement that importers must own their storage facilities with sufficient capacity to hold the full quantity requested on their Import Application; (6) the requirement that importers of horticultural products limit their use to industrial processes or trade to distributors respectively; (7) maintenance of a reference price for chilies, fresh shallots and beef for consumption, pursuant to which importation is suspended when the domestic market price falls below the pre-established reference price; (8) the requirement that all imported fresh horticultural products have been harvested less than 6 months prior to importation; (9) Indonesia's import licensing regime for horticultural products; (10) prohibition on importation of certain animals and animal products, except in "emergency circumstances"; (11) the requirement that importers of animal products would limit their use to scientific purposes, distribution to catering establishments and sale in modern markets; (12) the requirement that importers of beef absorb local beef; (13) import licensing regime for animals and animal products as a whole; and (14) contingency of importation of horticultural products, animals and animal products upon the sufficiency of domestic supply for consumption and/or government food reserves.[144]

New Zealand and the US challenged the consistency of Indonesia's measures with Articles XI:1 and III:4 of the GATT 1994, Article 4.2 of the Agreement on Agriculture and Articles 2.2(a) and 3.2 of the Import Licensing Agreement before the panel.

---

[144]Panel Report, *Indonesia – Import Licensing Regimes*, paras. 2.4–2.66.

The panel found that Indonesia's measures were inconsistent with Article XI:1 of the GATT 1994 and were not justified under Article XX. The panel exercised judicial economy and did not make findings with respect to the rest of the claims.

9.2   Salient Legal Findings

9.2.1   Order of Analysis: Panel's Decision to Commence with Article XI:1 of the GATT 1994

Indonesia submitted that Article 4.2 of the Agreement on Agriculture applies to the exclusion of Article XI:1 of the GATT 1994. The Appellate Body drew from its previous findings and found that pursuant to Article 21.1 of the Agreement on Agriculture,[145] this Agreement only prevails where there is a conflict between its provisions and provisions of other WTO agreements.[146] The Appellate Body further found that Article 4.2 of the Agreement on Agriculture and Article XI:1 of the GATT 1994 are not in conflict, but rather the obligations arising therefrom are cumulative.[147]

Further, Indonesia submitted that the panel ought to have commenced its analysis with Article 4.2 of the Agreement on Agriculture. The Appellate Body recalled its findings in *Canada – Renewable Energy/Canada – Feed-in Tariff Program*, where it considered that while issues of sequencing may become relevant to a logical consideration of claims under different agreements, nothing in the provisions at issue indicated that there was an obligatory sequence of analysis to be followed.[148] The Appellate Body further recalled that Articles 4.2 of the Agreement on Agriculture and Article XI:1 of the GATT 1994 provided similar obligations with similar justifications, and therefore there was no prejudice in the panel's order of analysis.

---

[145] Article 21.1 of the Agreement on Agriculture states as follows: "The provision of GATT 1994 and of other Multilateral Trade Agreements in Annex 1A to the WTO Agreement shall apply subject to the provisions of this Agreement."

[146] Appellate Body Report, *Indonesia – Import Licensing Regimes*, paras. 5.9–5.12, referring to the Appellate Body Reports, *EC – Export Subsidies on Sugar*, para. 221; and *EC – Bananas III*, para. 155.

[147] Appellate Body Report, *Indonesia – Import Licensing Regimes*, para. 5.15.

[148] Appellate Body Report, *Indonesia – Import Licensing Regimes*, para. 5.22, referring to the Appellate Body Reports, *Canada – Renewable Energy / Canada – Feed-in Tariff Program*, paras. 5.8 and 5.5.

9.2.2 Burden of Proof: Footnote 1 to Article 4.2 of the Agreement on Agriculture

Indonesia submitted that, by virtue of footnote 1 to Article 4.2 of the Agreement on Agriculture, the complainants had the obligation to demonstrate that challenged measures fall within the scope of that provision. According to Indonesia, this burden includes demonstrating that the challenged measures are not exempted under Article XX of the GATT 1994.[149]

The Appellate Body rejected Indonesia's proposed interpretation and found that a respondent seeking to justify their measures under Article XX would be required to demonstrate that on the basis of such justification, the challenged measures do not fall within the scope of Article 4.2.[150]

It therefore *upheld* the Panel's findings in this regard.

9.2.3 Operation of Article XI:2(c) of the GATT 1994 Regarding Agricultural Measures

Indonesia challenged the panel's findings that by virtue of Article 4.2 of the Agreement on Agriculture, Article XI:2(c) of the GATT 1994 had been rendered "inoperative" and therefore Indonesia could not use the latter provision to exclude the challenged measures.[151]

The Appellate Body observed that while Article 4.2 of the Agreement on Agriculture prohibits quantitative import restrictions, these are allowed under Article XI:2(c). In order to resolve this textual conflict, the Appellate Body referred to Article 21.1 of the Agreement of Agriculture, and concluded that Article 4.2 of that agreement prevailed. On this basis, the Appellate Body concluded that Indonesia could not rely on Article XI:2(c) in order to justify its import restrictions.[152]

The Appellate Body therefore *upheld* the panel's findings.

---

[149]Appellate Body Report, *Indonesia – Import Licensing Regimes*, para. 5.44. Article 4.2 of the Agreement on Agriculture provides as follows "Members shall not maintain, resort to, or revert to any measures of the kind which have been required to be converted into ordinary customs duties[1], except as otherwise provided for in Article 5 and Annex 5." Footnote 1 states that "[t]hese measures include quantitative import restrictions, variable import levies, minimum import prices, discretionary import licensing, non-tariff measures maintained through state-trading enterprises, voluntary export restraints, and similar border measures other than ordinary customs duties, whether or not the measures are maintained under country-specific derogations from the provisions of GATT 1947, but not measures maintained under balance-of-payments provisions or under other general, non-agriculture-specific provisions of GATT 1994 or of the other Multilateral Trade Agreements in Annex 1A to the WTO Agreement."

[150]Appellate Body Report, *Indonesia – Import Licensing Regimes*, para. 5.46.

[151]Appellate Body Report, *Indonesia – Import Licensing Regimes*, para. 5.65, referring to the Panel Report, *Indonesia – Import Licensing Regimes*, para. 7.60.

[152]Appellate Body Report, *Indonesia – Import Licensing Regimes*, paras. 5.80–5.81.

9.2.4 The Panel's Analysis Under Article XX of the GATT 1994

Indonesia took issue with the fact that in assessing nine of Indonesia's measures, the panel assessed the requirements of the *chapeau* of Article XX of the GATT without first examining whether the measures were provisionally justified under this Article.[153] The Appellate Body recalled its previous jurisprudence that analysis under Article XX should commence with the specific paragraphs invoked (for provisional justification) followed by assessment under the *chapeau*. However, it stated that depending on the specific facts of the case, a panel may be able to analyse the requirements of the *chapeau* even when the sequence of analysis has not been followed.[154] That said, the Appellate Body declined to rule on Indonesia's claim on appeal for the reason that it was of no legal effect.[155]

9.3 Observations

In this dispute the Appellate Body clarified the relationship between Article XI:2 (c) of the GATT 1994 and Article 4.2 of the Agreement on Agriculture. Noting that footnote 1 to Article 4.2 provides that measures prohibited under Article 4.2 do not include non-agriculture specific provisions of GATT 1994, the Appellate Body observed that Article XI:2(c) is agriculture specific. Thus, Members cannot rely on Article XI:2(c) of GATT 1994 to justify their quantitative restrictions on agricultural products, and would in that case be in violation of Article 4.2 of the Agreement on Agriculture.

Reference

Prusa T, Vermulst E (2019) *United States – certain methodologies and their application to anti-dumping proceedings involving China*: nails in the coffin of unfair dumping margin calculation methodologies. World Trade Review 18:287–307. 1–2

Kholofelo Kugler is Counsel at the Advisory Centre on WTO Law (ACWL) where she provides legal advice on international trade law issues, litigates at the WTO, and conducts training on various WTO law topics. She is also a visiting Research Fellow at the Law School of the University of the Witwatersrand. She holds a Bachelor's in Economics and International Politics (UNISA), an LL.B degree, *cum laude* (Wits), and a Master's in International Law and Economics, *summa cum laude* (University of Bern, Switzerland).

---

[153] Appellate Body Report, *Indonesia – Import Licensing Regimes*, para. 5.86.

[154] Appellate Body Report, *Indonesia – Import Licensing Regimes*, para. 5.100.

[155] Appellate Body Report, *Indonesia – Import Licensing Regimes*, para. 5.103.

Faith Pittet is a consultant in international trade law issues, competition and investments. She holds an LLB (Wits), Postgraduate Diploma in International Law (Wits) and LLM (UniBe).

Saweria Mwangi holds a Master of Laws in International Economic Law from the University of Barcelona.

Part IV
Book Reviews

Irmgard Marboe, Calculation of Compensation and Damages in International Investment Law, 2nd Edition

Oxford University Press, 2017, ISBN 9780198749936

Eleni Methymaki

Contents

Irmgard Marboe's second edition of *Calculation of Compensation and Damages in International Investment Law* is a timely update of a seminal work in a field that is subject to dynamics of constant change. Valuation of damages and compensation has been acquiring increasing significance in international law and adjudication for some time, and will continue to do so, as the recent judgment of the International Court of Justice in the case concerning *Certain Activities Carried out by Nicaragua in the Border Area* (Costa Rica *v* Nicaragua) demonstrated.[1] The judgment of the Court in this case revealed many of the complexities with which international judges and arbitrators have to deal in these type of proceedings.

Marboe's book addresses the topic from the perspective of international investment law, in which valuation of both compensation for lawful expropriation and reparations for wrongful acts are crucial. Private parties resorting to judicial settlement of their investment disputes with host States resolve to commit time and resources to what is often lengthy and expensive proceedings because, ultimately, they seek compensation for the damage (allegedly) suffered (2). Certainty and precision in the assessment of compensation and damages have multiple benefits (2, 4–5). As a recent study on remedies in investment arbitration illustrated,

---

[1] *Certain Activities carried out by Nicaragua in the Border Area* (Costa Rica *v*. Nicaragua), Compensation Owed by the Republic of Nicaragua to the Republic of Costa Rica, Judgment of 2 February 2018.

E. Methymaki (✉)
University of Oxford, St. Catherine's College, Oxford, UK
e-mail: eleni.methymaki@law.ox.ac.uk

© Springer Nature Switzerland AG 2019
M. Bungenberg et al. (eds.), *European Yearbook of International Economic Law 2019*,
European Yearbook of International Economic Law (2020) 10: 435–438,
https://doi.org/10.1007/8165_2019_34, Published online: 31 July 2019

however, investment tribunals when awarding compensation to investors for the breach of protection standards in investment treaties, other than expropriation, often rush into an 'imperfect application' of the principles enunciated by the Permanent Court of International Justice in the *Chorzow Factory* case.[2] This tends to obscure both the fact that, contrary to expropriation provisions, other protection standards most often do not contain an explicit obligation to provide compensation in case of breach,[3] as well as the difference between compensation for lawful expropriation and reparation for the breach of other treaty standards, being essentially reparation for an internationally wrongful act (also at 80).[4]

In her second chapter, Marboe exposes these differences in the meaning of the terms 'compensation' and 'damages' (10–19), as well as their different functions (19–36), which albeit not clear-cut have, or at least should have, a bearing on the selection of the appropriate valuation method (15, 18, 36–41, 82–83). In case of compensation for lawful expropriation, the applicable standard is generally accepted to approximate the 'fair market value' of the investment, which has to be determined through an objective-abstract valuation (40). Contrariwise, the relevant standard for wrongful conduct is 'full reparation', which has to be determined through subjective-concrete valuation (38, 40, 55).

Following that (Chapter 3), the analysis goes into the various elements relevant to calculation. The lawfulness or unlawfulness of expropriation, lost profits, factors potentially reducing compensation or damages, selection of the valuation date, and equitable considerations are discussed. Three points are particularly insightful: first, as Marboe observes, the standard of compensation as a requirement for lawful expropriation is a rather challenging issue, significantly influencing the selection of a suitable valuation method (45–46). Second, when calculating damages for the breach of contracts, special caution is required so that 'double counting' (leading to double recovery for the investor) is avoided (107–109). Third, choosing the appropriate valuation date is according to Marboe one of the most important differences between an objective-abstract and a subjective-concrete valuation approach (153, also 410).

Chapter 4 discusses the internationally applicable principles for the valuation of economic assets. In an accessible manner, Marboe explains that a prerequisite for the application of any valuation approach is the identification of the 'basis of valuation' (173, 408), which is a 'legal question' (173) and depends on 'the purpose of valuation' (at 174). Marboe distinguishes between the 'basis of valuation' for the calculation of compensation for lawful expropriation ('value in exchange') requiring objective-abstract valuation (most times calculated on the basis of the 'fair market

---

[2]Desierto (2017), p. 410.

[3]Desierto (2017), p. 445.

[4]According to the ILC Articles on the Responsibility of States for Internationally Wrongful Acts, Yearbook of the International Law Commission (2001), vol. II (Part Two), annexed to GA Res 56/83, 12 December 2001, Article 31 'full reparation for the injury caused' is one of the consequences of an internationally wrongful act.

value') and that for the calculation of damages for wrongful conduct ('value to the holder'), which requires subjective-concrete valuation to arrive to 'full reparation' (and should be performed on bases 'other than market value') (175–176, also 408–410). In Chapter 5, then, the various valuation approaches (the market value approach, the income approach and the asset-based/cost approach) used in international practice are analysed in detail in view of their application by international courts and tribunals. This chapter includes a whole new section on moral damages, which since the first edition seem to have a bigger role to play in investment arbitration. Chapter 6 gives an overview of the intricacies involved in the award of interest by arbitral tribunals, which is again (or at least should be) informed by the distinction between compensation for expropriation and reparation for wrongful conduct.

Overall, Marboe concludes that investment lawyers and arbitral tribunals have in recent years engaged more deeply with quantification and economic principles in valuation proceedings (407). In her opinion, to achieve a swift and accurate outcome to the proceedings it is key that issues relating to valuation are not reserved for the late stages, but are resolved early, especially when it comes to choosing the appropriate basis and standard of valuation as well as the valuation date (415). This second edition, apart from including a fully updated bibliography, also benefits from an inventory of all jurisprudential developments with significance for the topic since 2008 (in the form of tables, 417ff). These tables very helpfully complement the ones found in the work by Ripinski and Williams, which cover previous years.[5]

From a practitioner's perspective, Marboe's second edition will continue to be a point of reference, notwithstanding the increase of scholarly studies in the field, for there have been many since the publication of the first edition in 2009. As Marboe's analysis illustrates, the primary difficulty in calculating compensation and damages in investment arbitration (as in international commercial arbitration) is selecting both the basis of valuation and the most appropriate method on which calculations are to be performed. Challenges relating to the determination of the value of the investment (for 'value is a relative concept', 25 and 173, and 'valuation of assets always contains a certain amount of uncertainty and imprecision', 153), considerations of fairness vis-à-vis the method elected by the parties in an investment contract, among others, frame the discussions and the reasoning of arbitrators. Although today calculation of compensation and damages is performed on much safer and established grounds, some uncertainty remains; thus a thorough compilation and critical analysis of the relevant case law proves invaluable. As Marboe's analysis shows a variety of valuation models is used by different tribunals operating under different treaty and arbitration regimes and for different types of disputes. Perhaps the single most crucial point she makes is the impact that the distinction between compensation for lawful expropriation and reparation for treaty and contract breaches has for valuation proceedings; this difference and its importance is reinforced time and again throughout the book.

---

[5]Ripinsky and Williams (2008), pp. 406ff.

The field of remedies and valuation of compensation is one in which many actors interact and influence one another: the parties with their choices when the investment relationship is established; arbitrators and counsel during the proceedings; experts that assist the tribunal in establishing matters of domestic law and economics. This second edition, incorporating all latest developments in the practice of arbitral tribunals, is undoubtedly a very useful resource for any practitioner and academic in the field of investment arbitration and beyond. On top of this (and perhaps more importantly), by bringing to the fore the complexities and diverse practice in this area, this second edition of Marboe's book sounds a loud call for the further study of this aspect of dispute settlement also from the perspective of general international law and with respect to inter-State disputes, where it currently constitutes (to say the least) murky waters.

References

Desierto DA (2017) The outer limits of adequate reparations for breaches of non-expropriation investment treaty provisions: choice and proportionality in Chorzów. Columbia J Transnatl Law 55(2):395–456

Ripinsky S, Williams K (2008) Damages in international investment law. British Institute for International and Comparative Law, London

Eleni Methymaki is a DPhil in Law candidate at the University of Oxford, her research focusing on the role of domestic law in international adjudication. She is a Greek lawyer and has studied law at the University of Glasgow (LL.M. res.), the National and Kapodistrian University of Athens (LL. B.; LL.M.) and Freie Universitaet Berlin. She holds an LL.M. with specialization in international law from the University of Cambridge. Before joining Oxford, Eleni was a research associate for international law at the University of Glasgow, School of Law (2016–2018).

Duncan French and Louis J. Kotzé (Eds.), Sustainable Development Goals – Law, Theory and Implementation

Edward Elgar, 2018, ISBN 9781786438751

Winfried Huck

The 17 Sustainable Development Goals (SDGs) and their related 169 targets were set by a resolution of the United Nations (UN) on 25 September 2015 titled "Transforming our world: the 2030 Agenda for Sustainable Development". Leaders of the Member States went to New York in September 2015, not to celebrate the UN's 70th birthday but to conclude unanimously in favour of the blue planet we all inhabit and for those, in particular, whose living conditions remain poor. Inequality, as a natural phenomenon e.g. in landlocked developed countries or as a human caused phenomenon provoked through corruption and violence causes poverty, hunger, and blatant forms of discrimination.[1] Enormous disparities of opportunities can be detected throughout the world where wealth and (corporate) power, quite often deprive cultures and people from their natural rights. Globally, gender inequality remains a key challenge, in particular for women and girls. The survival of many societies, and of the biological support systems of the planet, seems in times of climate change at risk. The SDGs, entered into force on 1 January 2016, are

---

[1]The Landlocked Developing Countries (LLDCs) are among the poorest countries in the world. Their positive economic performance was mainly driven by the boom in minerals and energy demand up to mid-2008. Of the 20 lowest-ranked countries in the human development index (2010) 10 were LLDCs. UNOHRLLS, UN LLDC Factsheet, 2011, http://unohrlls.org/UserFiles/File/UN_LLDCs_Factsheet.pdf (last accessed 6 February 2019). See further UNCTAD: "In recognition of the special development needs of LLDCs, the international community adopted the Vienna Programme of Action (VPoA) for these countries for the decade 2014–2024. The overarching goal of the VPoA is to help the LLDCs achieve sustainable and inclusive growth and to eradicate poverty." https://unctad.org/en/Pages/ALDC/Landlocked%20Developing%20Countries/UN-recognition-of-the-problems-of-land-locked-developing-countries.aspx (last accessed 6 February 2019).

W. Huck (✉)
Ostfalia University of Applied Sciences, Brunswick European Law School (BELS),
Wolfenbüttel, Germany
e-mail: w.huck@ostfalia.de

© Springer Nature Switzerland AG 2019
M. Bungenberg et al. (eds.), *European Yearbook of International Economic Law 2019*,
European Yearbook of International Economic Law (2020) 10: 439–444,
https://doi.org/10.1007/8165_2019_35, Published online: 31 July 2019

described by the UN as integrated and indivisible and are balancing three dimensions of sustainable development: the economic, social and environmental.

Duncan French/Louis J. Kotzé have edited one of the first books about the SDGs concerning Law, Theory and Implementation, embarking on an academic voyage through different areas of normativity. There is a vast amount of literature across many disciplines that deal with the concepts of sustainability and sustainable development. It is therefore helpful to distinguish between the fields of law in general and books regarding sustainable development as such (*Schrijver*; *Sachs*) or those that are more and less connected to policy (*Kanie/Biermann*; *Kamau, Chasek, O'Connor*), trade (*Bonanomi*), economics (*Sen; Daly*), indicators (*Merry; Davis, Fisher et al.*), or decisions of International Courts and Tribunals (*Cordonier Segger/ Weeramantry*).

As even this roughly sketched background suggests it is not an easy undertaking to pin down the SDGs from a normative perspective. It is useful therefore that *Duncan French/Louis J. Kotzé* arrive, not only with their gripping and wide ranging in-depth reflections of the multi-layered and complex issues surrounding the SDGs but also with the offer of lucid interpretations and thought provoking meta-theoretical approaches. Within states the willingness to engage with the SDGs on the political agenda and to implement them domestically appears to be growing.[2] Likewise the EU has stated intent to integrate the SDGs in their internal and external policies. This shift in policy clearly underlines the urgent demand for this book. Although the book does not cover all of the 17 Goals the focus lies on the most pressing issues, like water, environment, human rights, gender, rule of law, and global partnerships.

In terms of structure *Duncan French/Louis J. Kotzé*'s anthology is divided into two parts and is accompanied by a masterly introduction in which the vast scenery of SDGs are interwoven with international law. The book is comprised of 12 chapters including the introduction, with contributions from well-known academics mostly from UK but also South Africa, Germany, Ireland, the Netherlands, and Finland. It is laudable that the editors have pointed out three fields where further work and reflection on the SDGs will be needed in the future. Firstly, a lawyerly approach would be helpful to understand the current lack of legal status enjoyed by the goals. Indeed such a critique could enable an understanding of how to give legal effect to the SDGs. Secondly, the SDGs raise questions concerning outdated notions of rights and responsibilities and the corresponding ambivalent role of civil society, which in practice rarely has significant influence on states and in the global political process. Thirdly, while the process of implementing the SDGs is essentially interdisciplinary

---

[2]See for example https://sustainabledevelopment.un.org/memberstates (last accessed 6 February 2019).

Italy: Istituto nazionale di statistica (ISTAT), Rapporto SDGs 2018. Informazioni statistiche per l'Agenda 2030 in Italia. Prime analisi, 2018.

Germany: Bundesregierung, Deutsche Nachhaltigkeitsstrategie—Aktualisierung 2018, BT-Drs. 19/5700, p. 40.

in nature it is up to lawyers to bring the necessary structure, clarity of language, and a focus of implementation.

The first part of the book, made up of five chapters, is dedicated to the general themes of the SDGs.

Sam Adelman analyses the SDGs ("The Sustainable Development Goals, anthropocentrism and neoliberalism") from a meta theoretical point of view; while contrasting them with the outcome of the Brundtland Commission, defining development as the needs of the present without compromising the ability of future generations to meet their own needs.

The Goals continue the neoliberal sustainability myth that economic growth and respecting environmental constraints are mutually compatible. The SDGs are in *Adelman's* view an "incarnation of a neoliberal form of green capitalism".

His existential critique of the SDGs is helpful in demonstrating an alternative to the harmonious rose tinted view of the global goals, which jeopardises long-term social justice and environmental protection In his view it is out of question that endless economic growth is sustainable if it breaches biophysical limits and planetary boundaries and ignores the rupture of the Earth system in the Anthropocene. *Adelman* castigates in particular the Washington consensus as a crucial turning point of neoliberalism which promotes dogmatic market fundamentalism and senseless eternal economic growth. He fears that by 2030 any global poverty reduction would represent only a pyrrhic victory as it will be at the cost of ecological destruction, species extinction, and growing injustice.

Louis J. Kotzé interrogates the SDGs ("The Sustainable Development Goals: An Existential Critique alongside three New-millennial Analytical Paradigms") on the background of the Anthropocene, planetary boundaries theory, and Earth system governance theory. *Kotzé* demands a radical change. In a normative sense the SDG are non-binding legal norms but grounded in international law and made consistent with existing binding international agreements and other soft law instruments. Like *Adelman*, *Kotzé* is sceptical about the concept of growth, which will not only prevent harm, but will exacerbate negative changes. For *Kotzé* it is time for political, legal, and governance action avoiding at the same time delaying discussion while regarding the SDGs as rhetorically ambitious but simultaneously destructive to the planetary inherent boundaries.

In her chapter *Lynda M. Collins* ("Sustainable Development Goals and human rights: challenges and opportunities") scrutinises the relationship between human rights and the global goals. She starts with a friendly tone, considering that the SDG have arguably become the primary unifying narrative among global actors, and there is no denying the SDG have already succeeded in catching the world's attention and holding it. But beneath the explicit endorsement of Human Rights in the SDGs the omission of the United Nations Declaration on the Rights of Indigenous People cannot be overlooked. Many SDG's are weaker than their Human Rights counterparts. The suggestion is that it is not merely a slight and meaningless shift of linguistic approach. The move from the requirement for all states "to respect, protect and fulfil human rights" to respect, protect and (only) "promote" human rights in the global agenda; this represents a watering down of obligation and arguably translates into less efforts for implementing the goals and could lead as a consequence to a legislative gap in the transformation of SDGs including Human Rights in the Member States. Therefore *Collins* underlines that "it will be important to ensure that civil and political rights are not neglected in the roll-out of the SDGs". *Graham Long* ("Underpinning Commitments of the Sustainable Development Goals: indivisibility, universality, leaving no one behind") deconstructs the goals down to their inner system of normative principles. The SDGs represent a new model for how to govern; in particular governing through goals must expose the underlying normative principles, which are crucial to the process in particular how such governance might operate and find success. The term normative principle is used by *Long* for three reasons: first to denote that the principles are action guiding, second, to note that the connection of SDGs with wider currents of moral and political aspects, and third to highlight the evolving status of sustainable development as a "norm" in international politics. *Long* discusses the SDG's in the three senses of normativity reaching out to wider questions in the political theory of sustainable development, Cosmopolitanism, and global justice and concludes that his contribution might be taken as a defence of the SDGs.

The final chapter of the first part is dedicated to areas beyond national jurisdiction, often referred to as the global commons. Those areas are protected by legal obligation of states to avoid environmental harm resulting from activities within their jurisdiction or control. In this essay *Nadia Sánchez Castillo-Winckels* ("How the Sustainable Development Goals promote a new conception of ocean commons governance") analyses one of the most current and pressing problems in international law, how the high seas and its resources including the deep seabed, in international law known as the Area, and its resources are governed and how the SDGs relate to it. Even when those SDG's may not be legally binding in the strict sense of the word, they are deeply rooted in international law and called on states to fulfil their legally binding obligations of the resolution. The mere spatial scope of application of SDG 14 remains quite amazing. The oceans cover nearly ¾ of the Earth's surface area. Preventing and significantly reducing marine pollution of all kinds, including marine debris pollution and plastic garbage are the target of SDG 14. *Castillo-Winckels* advocates the potential of enhancing public access to information and participation in institutions to manage these resources. Here SDG 16 acts in a supportive role for SDG 14 in order to prevent the oceans from unsustainable fishing practices, exploitation of the seabed mineral, which could threaten to hasten the oceans rate of ecological decline.

In the second part of the book a selective analysis of particular goals is offered. *Karen Morrow* (Gender and the Sustainable Development Goals) examines the coverage in the SDGs of gender issues shedding light on the legacy of the millennium development goals. The selection of indicators to measure the SDGs is a core concern. It depends on the constitution and on the understanding of the specific rule of law principle whether there is a real chance that a selected indicator or target could fulfil the proper function. To centre a regime on indicators could highlight other problems, like the current flow of development in the information and communication technology sector. Other systematic problems like lack of quality control, patchy coverage, delays in the access to new technologies must be discussed. Quoting Hillary Clinton, who said that "the rights of women and girls is a great unfinished business of the 21st century", *Morrow* concludes that gender equality remains at best work in progress and civil society engagement is integral to progressing it.

Owen McIntyre writes about ("International water Law and SDG 6: mutually reinforcing paradigms") the increasingly pressing problem of reliable access (or lack thereof) to adequate fresh water supplies in the context of growing water scarcity and global warming as a result of climate change. A growing world population leads to the estimation that the requirements for water will, by 2030, be nearly double those in 2005 and will exceed the current water supply by 40%. Implementation is complicated by the need for SDG 6 to be reconciled with pre-existing legal frameworks surrounding water and sanitation. Water stress as a phenomenon affects states and their populations, of course, but also established patterns of agricultural production and the broader ecosystem. Water must be recognized as one of the most valuable natural resources and international water law has an important role to play to promote equitable transboundary water resources management. In this respect SDG 6 appears to be a crucial part of current and future international effective hydro-diplomacy.

Helmut Philipp Aust and Anél du Plessis interrogate "Good urban governance as a global aspiration: on the potential and limits of SDG 11". They recognize that SDG 11 is unique in encouraging cities and communities to see themselves as global actors and therefore broadening the understanding of good urban governance. *Aust/ du Plessis* consider that the underlying message of the SDG 11 is that globalization is a driving force for the growth of the cities, and it facilitates the influence of the city over larger geographical areas. Although a standardized metrics for its inherent objectives is missing, how is good urban government to be measured, it is widely understood that poverty remains one of the key causes hindering the development of cities.

The chapter from *Werner Scholtz* and *Michelle Barnard* deals with "The environment and the Sustainable Development Goals: 'We are on a Road to Nowhere'" considering the environmental cluster of the goals dealing with climate (SDG 13), water resources (SDG 6), and marine (SDG 14) and the biodiversity (SDG 15). They present a vivid discussion as to whether the SDGs are a normative contribution to international law. *Scholtz/Barnard* argue that the SDGs do have a normative value and potentially contribute to international law. This normative weight may serve to evolve the SDG norms into customary international law. Although the criticism that the goals fail to create new international rules is not unfounded, it should be added that a teleological interpretation of the SDGs indicates myriad references to existing international law—not least Human Rights and international environmental law.

Niko Soininen reflects about SDG 16 and the rule of law including the access to justice in his essay about "Torn by (un)certainty – can there be peace between rule of law and other Sustainable Development Goals?". *Soininen* opts for a classical discussion of the rule of law by looking at the formal, procedural, and substantive theoretical aspects of this fundamental principle. One key challenge with all the rule of law theories is that they impose certainty on an uncertain social and ecological world. Uncertainty, here, is at the very least is provided by the unknowns of e.g. new technology and gaps in scientific knowledge. The clash between such legal certainty and social ecological uncertainty may be the single greatest obstacle to effectively achieving environmental goals such as those contained in the SDGs. From my point of view, I think *Soininen* is perfectly right when he argues that "placing less emphasis on the substantive and the formal, and more on the procedural is the best combination of all the rule of law worlds for the SDGs".

In the final contribution, *Nathan Cooper* and *Duncan French* look at the cooperation in development and SDG 17 ("SDG 17: partnerships for the goals – cooperation within the context of a voluntarist framework"). This chapter reflects on how SDG 17 operates in the context of ongoing debates regarding the normative divide between obligation and voluntarism, between legally binding solidarity and weaker optional variations. The lack of SDG institutionalisation means the intensity of promotion of the goals is limited and so it seems obvious that a way must be found to treat the goals in a more formalised and normative way. Civil society must, therefore, have a meaningful role to play in the future in order to prevent the fulfilment of the SDGS from halting if normative uncertainty and the absence of a rights-based approach is allowed to continue. Thus, the normative framework is not only useful it is essential to facilitate the global agenda for the future and for the betterment of all.

This book convinces with a multifaceted theoretical approach combining detailed and critical arguments, which will be needed in the upcoming debates regarding the implementation of the SDGs. The Sustainable Development Goals - Law, Theory and Implementation from *Duncan French/Louis J. Kotzé* delivers an excellent resource for academics, postgraduate students, governments, and all participants organized in the global partnerships for the process of implementation of the SDGs, which will influence the further discussion.

Winfried Huck is Professor for economic law with a specialisation in international and European economic law at the Brunswick European Law School, Germany, where he is currently the dean. He is Professor at the Chinese-German Institute for postgraduate studies (CDHK) at the Tongji University in Shanghai as well and since 2015 Miembro corresponsal de la Sociedad Cubana de Derecho Constitucional y Administrativo de la Unión Nacional de Juristas de Cuba.

Armin Steinbach, EU Liability and International Economic Law

Hart Publishing, 2017, ISBN 9781509901593

Jens Hillebrand Pohl

Contents

Over the 10 years since the Lisbon Treaty, the European Union has increasingly entered into international trade and investment agreements. These are agreements under international law, but they also form part of EU law within the framework of EU competences. As affirmed by the European Court of Justice, Union liability for the breach of EU law is essential to ensure the law's full effectiveness. This leads to the question of whether an individual can hold the EU liable under EU law for violations of international economic law. The book under review, a revised doctoral dissertation by Armin Steinbach, addresses this matter, and in so doing, puts forward a framework within which the conditions for liability can be fruitfully analysed.

Steinbach's conceptual approach throughout is to strive for a common framework linking together the EU liability regimes with respect to international trade law and international investment law. As the author rightly points out, however, the divergent traditional role of the individual in each respective area of international economic law is reflected in the heterogeneous design of dispute resolution at the international level and in a lack of coherence in the recognition and enforcement of EU liability. As befits a scholar with dual doctoral degrees in law and economics, he does not question, however, the overarching utility of the international economic law 'narrative'. When looking at the similarities and differences of the relevant substantive law, the link between international trade law and international investment law is, at times, far from obvious. On the other hand the economic case for a common analytical framework certainly remains more robust. Even those who find the juxtaposition of international trade law and international investment law issues relating to EU liability less compelling will appreciate the systematic approach underpinning the author's line of argumentation.

J. H. Pohl (✉)
Maastricht University, Maastricht, The Netherlands
e-mail: jens.pohl@maastrichtuniversity.nl

© Springer Nature Switzerland AG 2019   445
M. Bungenberg et al. (eds.), *European Yearbook of International Economic Law 2019*,
European Yearbook of International Economic Law (2020) 10: 445–450,
https://doi.org/10.1007/8165_2019_36, Published online: 7 September 2019

The book is divided into three parts. The first part, covering more than half of the volume, concerns the question of whether the EU can be held liable under EU law for failure to comply with rulings by the adjudicative bodies of the World Trade Organisation (WTO) even though WTO rules do not have direct effect in the EU legal order. It is followed by a part devoted to the economic analysis of liability for WTO violations aimed at the conclusions of the previous section. The third part deals with EU liability issues with respect to international investment treaties and concerns, not the question of *whether* the EU can be held liable, but rather the criteria pursuant to which such liability can be attributed to the EU, as opposed to its Member States.

The departure point of Steinbach's analysis is the consistent jurisprudence of the Court of Justice of the European Union (CJEU) rejecting EU liability for WTO breaches due to the lack of direct effect of WTO rules and of rulings by the WTO Dispute Settlement Body (DSB). While DSB rulings are binding as a matter of international law, they are also binding as a matter of EU law by virtue of Article 216 (2) of the Treaty on the Functioning of the European Union (TFEU). Yet, that is not to say that such rulings have direct effect, permitting an individual to invoke the rights derived from such a ruling directly before the courts of the EU. The reason for this can be traced to the fact that, although DSB rulings are binding as a matter of EU law, they are entirely binding only insofar as concerns their objective (the 'whether' to comply), while leaving the losing party a certain space to manoeuvre with respect to the time period within which to bring itself into compliance (the 'when' to comply) and a certain degree of freedom in the choice of means to bring about compliance (the 'how' to comply). It follows that granting DSB rulings direct effect would be tantamount to denying the EU, as a losing party, the policy space it is entitled to under WTO law in order to decide when and how to comply with the ruling.

In the main part of his analysis, Steinbach questions the consistency of linking EU liability to the direct effect of WTO rules and rulings in the EU legal order. While the policy-space argument may validly justify denying the availability of an action for annulment directed against a WTO non-compliant EU measure, it does not necessarily explain why an action for damages under Article 340 TFEU could not succeed, given the different objectives of the two remedies. To make his argument, the author embarks on a systematic and detailed review of the criteria for Article 340 liability developed in caselaw based on the *Schöppenstedt* and *Bergaderm* cases. As to the first criterion—the existence of violation of a 'norm intended to protect individual rights' (*Schutznorm*)—Steinbach proposes an application by analogy of the *Francovich* doctrine, which relates to Member States' liability to individuals for failing to implement EU law, to decouple this criterion from the concept of direct effect. Looking in turn at each of the *Francovich* pillars, he argues that the *effet utile* principle can be applied to the primary law obligation in Article 216(2) TFEU recognizing the binding character of international agreements, with the individual being seen as an 'instrument' for making that article more effective—mirroring the *Francovich* Court's arguments vis-à-vis what today is Article 288 TFEU. Turning next to the second and third pillars, the author identifies a ground for legal redress in the objective duty of implementation under Article 216(2) TFEU and the possible existence of subjective protection of individual interests in DSB rulings, while also pointing to Article 4(3) of the Treaty on European Union as further ground for sustaining EU liability.

The next stepping stone in the analysis is to justify the analogous application of *Francovich*. Here the caselaw of *parallélisme nécessaire*, derived from *Brasserie du Pêcheur*, tells us that the conditions under which a Member State may incur liability for damage caused to individuals by a breach of EU law cannot, in the absence of particular justification, differ from those governing the liability of the EU in like circumstances. Hence, the author argues, if *Francovich* can be applied to Member States' liability as a matter of EU law for violations of WTO law, then the EU's own liability under Article 340 TFEU may not be different (absent particular justification). Furthermore, applying the same principle of parallelism confirms that indirect or secondary protection of individual interests would be sufficient. Since WTO rules aim at safeguarding security and predictability in the trading environment, this benefits—at least indirectly (as a 'reflex')—individual traders, even if the primary purpose of WTO rules is to regulate trade between WTO Members. Provided that a 'normative minimum' can be clearly discernible in DSB rulings, Steinbach concludes that sufficiently specific individual rights can be identified meeting the requirements developed in caselaw for Member State liability under EU law, which, by means of parallel application, should also apply to the EU's own liability under Article 340 TFEU.

The effect of the analysis in this part is to expose a lack of consistency between, on the one hand, the current line of CJEU cases denying liability under EU law for WTO breaches and, on the other hand, the preponderance of caselaw dealing with EU and Member State liability for EU law breaches in general. This part of the analysis is concluded by arguing that the 'sufficiently serious breach' criterion of the *Schöppenstedt* formula might provide the necessary reassurances that the EU legislator preserves a margin of manoeuvre for itself against judicial intervention, thus obviating the need to retain the direct-effect criterion for liability. A comparison is also made with the CJEU caselaw on fundamental rights to examine whether such rights may provide alternative *Schutznormen*, with the impression being conveyed that the *Francovich* analogy provides the more solid argument—or, what is equivalent, a more severe blow to the consistency of the current restrictive caselaw.

Viewed in isolation, the reasoning indeed appears robust from an EU law perspective. Perhaps less so from a WTO law perspective, because the WTO system of remedies is designed to provide only prospective, not retrospective, relief. Although good reasons have been put forward why this system of remedies is insufficient and should be amended,[1] it nonetheless remains in place. Allowing an action for damages against the EU for a WTO breach that would not give rise to corresponding remedies under WTO law is not a straightforward matter. It could also potentially alter the effect of WTO law and result in an asymmetric enforcement of

---

[1] See e.g. Bronckers and Baetens (2013).

WTO rules that would be stricter than the WTO regime requires. It would have been interesting to know the author's perspective had this and related issues been discussed in the book.

Having demonstrated that the CJEU's current failure to recognize liability for WTO breaches cannot be justified for reasons of systemic coherence of the law, the author next turns to examining the matter normatively from an economic perspective. Applying the framework of institutional economics, Steinbach concludes that the recognition of liability would force the EU legislator to internalise the costs for companies of the EU's WTO non-compliance. These 'economic' costs would then translate into 'political' costs, since WTO non-compliance—which would have negative economic consequences for the EU, as EU liability would be established by the CJEU—would also result in more significant, negative political consequences than is currently the case. As such, EU liability would ensure that the costs of WTO non-compliance were integrated in a cost-benefit analysis at the level of the legislator, which is not sure to happen when the costs are entirely externalised to individual traders and not necessarily taken into consideration at the political level. However, the author also argues that another type problem might arise in the event of EU liability for WTO non-compliance: since the EU legislator has an *ex ante* information deficit as to whether its legislative measures will be found WTO incompatible and whether this would give rise to liability in an individual case, there is a risk that the legislator would be 'over-deterred' for fear of political cost, leading to legislative paralysis. This, however, would be the case only to the extent losses are overcompensated, i.e. where damages granted exceed social welfare losses resulting from the WTO breach. To overcome this problem and find an equilibrium between inefficiencies due to under-compensation (today's situation) and inefficiencies due to overcompensation, Steinbach suggests that the 'sufficiently serious breach' condition of the *Schöppenstedt* formula might serve this very purpose and provide the CJEU with the discretion required to avoid overcompensation.

In the last part of the book, the author looks at the question of the EU's liability under international investment agreements. Acknowledging that broad-based investment treaties with the EU as a party would have to be mixed agreements—and, one might add post-Opinion 2/15, also treaties stipulating ISDS—the issue of breaches of such treaties triggers the question of attribution of liability and the related choice of respondent. This part provides a detailed description of the discrepancy between attribution of liability on the international plane and the internal allocation of financial responsibility within the EU, as well as of the relevance of the latter to the former. The author points out an important weakness of the current internal financial responsibility regime established under Regulation 912/2014 in the asymmetric ability of the EU and Member States to enforce internal liability claims among themselves. While the Regulation provides a basis for enforcement vis-à-vis Member States, the latter only has recourse to the general remedies available under the Treaties, which are not well-adapted for such claims. The author concludes that in practice, Member States would probably enforce their claims by deducting the equivalent amounts from their Member contributions to the EU.

Since the book was published in 2017, Opinion 2/15 and the recent *Achmea* ruling (Case C-284/16) have radically reshaped the landscape of EU liability for investment treaty breaches. While the issues analysed in the book remain relevant, they are in part overshadowed by other fundamental issues relating to the book's overall question of whether the EU can be held liable for breaches of international economic law. The *Achmea* ruling puts into question to what extent an investment arbitration award rendered against a Member State is enforceable as a matter of EU law for reasons of the autonomy of the EU legal order. Certainly, that would not appear to be the case with respect to the enforcement of an arbitral award rendered under an intra-EU bilateral investment treaty, but it might also be problematic with respect to other investment arbitral awards. With Opinion 1/17, delivered on 30 April 2019, the issue of whether the EU's own investment treaties may be equally problematic in this respect has now been determined.

In this context, the conclusions under part 1 of the book may potentially offer interesting applications for investment treaties. It is understandable if this did not occur to the author, but it could have been interesting to explore whether the Article 340 TFEU liability foreseen for breaches of WTO law could be relevant as an alternative means of enforcing investment protections under international investment agreements concluded by the EU. Given the EU's lack of competence to enter into ISDS clauses, as affirmed in Opinion 2/15, the prospect of relying on Article 340 TFEU would open the possibility of EU-only international investment agreements in the field of direct investments. Knowing whether Article 340 TFEU could be viewed as a workable alternative to ISDS would then be valuable. Such a solution might also have the capacity of bypassing the *problématique* surrounding ISDS and the autonomy of the EU legal order.

Reference

Bronckers M, Baetens F (2013) Reconsidering financial remedies in WTO dispute settlement. J Int Econ Law 16(2):281–311

Jens Hillebrand Pohl is a lecturer and doctoral researcher in International Economic Law at the Faculty of Law, Maastricht University. He is a New York attorney and an Irish and English solicitor and holds an LL.M. from Harvard Law School.

Robert Howse, Hélène Ruiz-Fabri, Geir Ulfstein, Michelle Q. Zang, (Eds.), The Legitimacy of International Trade Courts and Tribunals

Cambridge University Press, 2018, ISBN 9781108424479

Gianpaolo Maria Ruotolo

Contents

The issue of the legitimacy of international law, of its institutions,[1] and of its dispute settlement systems[2] has always been paramount to international law scholars.

Since the second half of the 1990s, in particular, the attention of scholars— stimulated by the proliferation of international tribunals, by their success, and by the consequent increased fragmentation of the international legal order—has focused especially on the latter.

Much of this attention, mainly thanks to the success of the World Trade Organization (WTO), has concerned the international trade law sector.[3] In recent years, this attention has been further focused by the crisis that is affecting international systems of adjudication in general, and those in trade matters in particular, a crisis caused both by the rise of sovereigntist movements in many States[4] and by certain intrinsic limits that characterize the systems themselves.[5]

Despite this, trade relations continue to represent the most frequent form of international intercourse between States, and therefore the analysis of both their regulation and the connected dispute resolution mechanisms may offer a privileged observatory of certain general trends of the international legal order as a whole. This

---

[1]For references see. Meyer (2009); Yasuaki (2010); Wolfrum and Röben (2009).

[2]Specifically on the legitimacy of international tribunals see von Bogdandy (2013); Dothan (2013).

[3]Among others see, also for further bibliographical references, Bonzon (2014); Cass (2005).

[4]Voeten (2017).

[5]Pauwelyn and Hamilton (2018).

G. M. Ruotolo (✉)
University of Foggia, Foggia, Italy
e-mail: gianpaolo.ruotolo@unifg.it

© Springer Nature Switzerland AG 2019   451
M. Bungenberg et al. (eds.), *European Yearbook of International Economic Law 2019*,
European Yearbook of International Economic Law (2020) 10: 451–456,
https://doi.org/10.1007/8165_2019_37, Published online: 31 July 2019

in turn could lead to the verification, among other things, of the level of effectiveness of the principle of multilateralism and of the respect for the international rule of law.[6]

We must therefore welcome a volume like the one reviewed here, which gathers works of leading scholars and practitioners, as it may be of interest for a multiplicity of readers.

The volume was originally intended as a tool for specialists, and was conceived as a work of great scientific rigour which aims to dogmatically frame the complex legal issues it faces; first and foremost of these the "legitimacy of International Trade Courts and Tribunals" which gives the volume its title. However, thanks to its linear style, and the sparing use of technicalities, it could also be of interest to less experienced readers (such as under- and post-graduate law students) who wish to engage with an accessible but non-superficial account of the international trade Courts and Tribunals and the impact of these on the international legal order more generally.

The Introduction, jointly written by the Editors, along with the expected job of providing the context for the individual chapters, each one relating to a specific "Court or Tribunal"[7] or to some appealing cross-cutting issues,[8] opens with an affirmation that every international trade law expert would surely subscribe to: "at first glance, the legal system in international trade is *confusing*".[9]

The book raises the matter of how 'confusing' the international trading regime can be in order to address the matter of legitimacy and how it can be both hampered and concealed by that complexity.

The huge number of existing trade agreements and the frequent overlap in their application—also due to the absence of rules aimed at settling the conflicts of both law and jurisdiction that they generate—does indeed make for a particularly complex regulatory system, which has been accused of lacking legitimacy.

Now, the "L" word has been used with many meanings, not only merely non-coincident, but also sometimes even completely conflicting. In addition to the more classical distinction between a sociological perspective and a more strictly normative one, legitimacy can even be seen "as opposed to legality (. . .), to indicate a judgement based on values different from those of conformity with the law. These values include moral principles such as the safeguarding of human life and dignity. "Legitimate" indicates a perception of acceptability in light of these values. There are also other ways of looking at legitimacy such as the notion put forward by

---

[6]On this see Weiler (2018).

[7]The volume examines 11 different trade adjudication bodies, 9 international and 2 domestic, some of which had previously received little attention in doctrine: the WTO adjudicating bodies, the EU Court of justice, the EFTA Court, the US Court of international trade, the federal Courts of Canada, MERCOSUR, the Andean Court of justice, the Economic Court of the CIS, the COMESA Court of Justice, the WAEMU Court of Justice, the ASEAN trade dispute settlement mechanism.

[8]These are: formal independence, judicial interaction, access to trade tribunals, justice in the WTO context.

[9]See page 3 of the reviewed book. Emphasis added.

Thomas M. Franck. He proposes that legitimacy be verified in light of correspondence with certain "indicators"".[10]

Also, this volume can be included in the line of studies aimed at constructing models for assessing the legitimacy of international adjudication systems[11]: to this end, and with specific regard to the international trade regime, it identifies a number of "indicators", which are used both to scan the specific profiles of each Court examined, and as "symptomatic figures" of the existence of such legitimacy, and of its "degree" of legitimacy.

The work identifies, among these indicators, the independence of the judging body (and the related mechanisms for choosing the judges); the rules of procedure applied during the dispute; the fact-finding and burden of proof mechanisms used therein; the legal approach followed in the interpretation of the cases examined by each dispute resolution body; the interaction between the different mechanisms, in particular with reference to the possibilities and aspects of forum shopping (and the mechanisms for resolving jurisdiction conflicts); the relations with domestic courts and, in a broader sense, with domestic legal systems; the issue of relevance and *locus standi* of individuals before the international trade Courts and Tribunals.

The domestic aspect is dealt with, in particular, by the analysis of Marceau and Malacrida, and Kuijper. They engage with the classic and yet complex issue of the absence of direct effects of WTO rules and rulings in national legal orders confirming how the role of private parties in international trade dispute settlement systems impacts on the latter's effectiveness and legitimacy (see also, even if in a more doubtful tone, the work of Fauchald, pp. 454 ff.), as commercial operators, and not States, are ultimately the recipients of the rules for the liberalization of international trade.

It is precisely the analysis of this role that constitutes, in my opinion, the main cross-cutting theme of the volume: the inadequacy of the domestic jurisdictional instruments that could be triggered by private individuals to protect their international trade agreements connected prerogatives, has led to—since the mid-1990s and essentially as a consequence of the implementation of WTO obligations—the flourishing of internal administrative procedures by which the same individuals could at least trigger, and subsequently lobby, the activation, by their own State, of international trade disputes settlement mechanisms.

Examples include Section 301 of the U.S. Trade Act (on the US legal system in connection with international trade rules see the work of Pogue, p. 199), or the EU Trade Barriers Regulation (TBR), or even more specific provisions such as those on anti-dumping measures (see Kuijper, p. 127).

The overall context outlined by the volume highlights how the legal positions of individuals are also benefiting from various forms of protection provided by

---

[10]Treves (2009). Franck proposes determinacy, symbolic validation, coherence and adherence as those indicators; see Franck (1995), pp. 30 ff.

[11]In the same sense see also Grossman et al. (2018), which adopt a less sectorial scope than the volume reviewed here.

international law, which allows them to participate in inter-State litigation proceedings or to directly activate other international dispute resolution mechanisms.

These forms can be grouped into two distinct models.

The first involves a kind of indirect, and in any case not particularly effective, role of the private parties, as in the case of their participation as *amici curiae*, in purely inter-State disputes, which they are not allowed to activate (see Malacrida and Marceau, pp. 30 ff).

The second provides instead for the direct participation of individuals in trade disputes: in some cases, indeed, international law recognizes their right to action, even without the consent of the State, which they belong to, in order to autonomously convene before an international *forum* the States possibly responsible for violations of international trade obligations. The volume examines the case of the Andean Court of justice (Villamizar, p. 255) and of the Comesa Court of Justice (Gathi, pp. 314 ff.), as well as the ECJ (widely studied by Kuijper).

In a more strictly methodological perspective—and we come to what I believe is the other main theme of the book—of great interest is the somehow comparative approach that permeates every paper, an approach explored explicitly by Fauchald (pp. 454 ff.), but which perhaps represents the true "soul" of the entire investigation.

Indeed, the volume is not limited to comparing the different mechanisms of trade dispute settlement systems (and the fact that the analysis of each specific "Court and Tribunal" follows the same model makes it possible for the reader to undertake independently further comparisons and parallels) but necessarily requires a comparison of and between the different legal sensitivities of the various authors, even though all international lawyers.

This places the book, albeit not explicitly (and without the authors taking any position on the matter) within the ongoing scholarly debate on the opportunity of a comparative approach to the study of contemporary international law, the so-called Comparative International Law (CIL),[12] an approach that some see as an inescapable tool for dealing with the complexities of modern international law.[13]

In short: the volume is a valuable tool for those who wish to understand, in a non-superficial way, the international mechanisms of adjudication in trade matters, both in terms of their concrete functioning and of their dogmatic classification, also by being part of the debate currently taking place within the scientific community of international lawyers.

One of its main achievements is indeed that its scientifically rigorous approach allows for comparison across the separate chapters.

This makes it not only a tool for understanding the current international trading system, but also an excellent starting point for further reflections that could be conducted, as well as (and this even if the book has a rigidly theoretical framework), a useful tool for international trade practitioners.

In the end, the volume highlights how many factors (not only legal but also, and perhaps above all, political) can impact on legitimacy of international systems for

---

[12] Roberts (2017a, b); El Boudouhi (2017), pp. 981 ff.

[13] Arcari and Palchetti (2018).

settling disputes in trade issues and, therefore, on their appeal on States: the latter, certainly, will be more and more influenced, as it already is, by local, regional and global attitudes towards international courts and, for this reason closes with a question: "will we see a reversal in the recent rise of the regional and global judiciary?".

The answer will surely be influenced by the resilience of the studied mechanisms to the recent emergence of sovereign movements in many Countries, resilience which needs to be based on a renewed awareness of the centrality of the legal regulation of international trade in order to avoid the excess of discretion, when not a real arbitrariness, of the States, through that function of "gentle civilization of Nations"[14] which is proper to international law.

References

Arcari M, Palchetti P (2018) Doctrinal thoughts on a doctrinal approach to the problem of diversity in International Law. Revisiting Anthea Roberts' Is International Law International? and Comparative International Law. Questions of International Law. www.qil-qdi.org

Bonzon Y (2014) Public participation and legitimacy in the WTO. Cambridge University Press, Cambridge

Cass DZ (2005) The constitutionalization of the World Trade Organization: legitimacy, democracy, and community in the International Trading System. Oxford University Press, Oxford

Dothan S (2013) How international courts enhance their legitimacy. Theor Inq Law 14(2):455–478

El Boudouhi S (2017) Le droit international comparé. Mythe ou realité? Revue Générale de Droit International Public

Franck TM (1995) Fairness in international law and institutions. Oxford University Press, Oxford

Grossman N, Cohen HG, Follesdal A, Ulfstein E (eds) (2018) Legitimacy and international courts. Cambridge University Press, Cambridge

Koskenniemi M (2001) The gentle civilizer of nations. The rise and fall of international law 1870–1960. Cambridge University Press, Cambridge

Meyer LH (ed) (2009) Legitimacy, justice and public international law. Cambridge

Pauwelyn J, Hamilton R (2018) Exit from international tribunals. J Int Dispute Settlement 9 (4):679–690

Roberts A (2017a) Is international law international? Oxford University Press, Oxford

Roberts A (ed) (2017b) Comparative international law. Oxford University Press, Oxford

Treves T (2009) Aspects of legitimacy of decisions of International Courts and Tribunals. In: Wolfrum R, Röben V (eds) Legitimacy in international law. Springer, Heidelberg

Voeten E (2017) Liberalism, populism, and the backlash against international courts. https://global. upenn.edu/sites/default/files/voetenpaper.original.pdf. Last accessed 28 Mar 2019

von Bogdandy A (2013) The democratic legitimacy of international courts: a conceptual framework. Theor Inq Law 14(2):361–379

Weiler JH (2018) Black lies, white lies and some uncomfortable truths in and of the International Trading System. Eur J Int Law 29(2):339–345

Wolfrum R, Röben V (eds) (2009) Legitimacy in international law. Springer, Heidelberg

Yasuaki O (2010) A transcivilizational perspective on international law, in collected courses of the Hague Academy of International Law. Martinus Nijhoff, Leiden

---

[14]See Koskenniemi (2001).

Gianpaolo Maria Ruotolo is Professor of European Union Law and International Law at the University of Foggia. He's an Italian lawyer authorized to practice before higher Courts, currently enrolled in the special register of full-time university professors, and obtained his PhD in international law at the University of Naples "Federico II". He has been visiting associate fellow at the Dickson Poon School of Law at King's College London and at the Institute of Advanced Legal Study (IALS) of the University of London. He is Member of the Italian Society of International Law and of the European Union (SIDI) in which he coordinates the Group of interest in international and EU law and new technologies (www.netilaw.eu), of the European Society of International Law (ESIL), of the International Law Association (ILA), of the Association of Public Comparative and European Law, within which he is the National Coordinator of the European Union Law section, and the Internet Society (ISOC); of the Interuniversity Center on the Law of International Economic Organizations (CIDOIE) established by the Universities of Genoa, Milan-State, Milan-Bocconi, Turin, Eastern Piedmont and Valle d'Aosta and of the International Economic Law Interest Group at the University of Goettingen. He has held teaching positions in Masters and PhD courses in many Universities, as well as in UNESCO, UNICRI (United Nations Interregional Crime and Justice Research Institute) and has been a consultant to private and public entities, and of the Italian Ministry of the Interior for the International School of Higher Education for the Prevention and Contrast of Organized Crime. Author of two books and many articles in the field of international and European law, many of which can be found at the address gianpaolomariaruotolo.academia.edu.

Valentina Vadi, Proportionality, Reasonableness and Standards of Review in International Investment Law and Arbitration

Edward Elgar, 2018, ISBN 9781785368578

Marcin J. Menkes

Contents

Valentina Vadi, professor at Lancaster University Law School, is a prolific author[1] who skilfully combines different fields of international law with international investment law (IIL). Her books cover the interplay of IIL with public health[2] or cultural heritage.[3] Vadi's "well-established reputation in studies of the interaction of other fields of law with international investment law" is acknowledged on the back cover of the book by the one and only Prof. M. Sornarajah. This time, she invites us for yet another[4] legal cross-country journey. *Proportionality, Reasonableness and Standards of Review in International Investment Law and Arbitration* is an attempt to subject these institutions, oft-quoted but frequently lacking adequate methodological rigour, to systematic analysis. The topic of the book presents a daunting task even for such a well-established author to tackle in as much as it attempts to consider the

---

Unless otherwise stated, all references are to the reviewed book and chapters therein.

---

[1]More than 80 articles in the world's top journals (in less than 10 years), including the Harvard International Law Journal, the Vanderbilt Journal of Transnational Law, the Stanford Journal of International Law, the Columbia Human Rights Review, the European Journal of International Law, and the Journal of International Economic Law.

[2]Vadi (2013).

[3]Vadi (2014).

[4]Vadi (2015).

M. J. Menkes (✉)
Warsaw School of Economics, Warsaw, Poland
e-mail: marcin.menkes@sgh.waw.pl

© Springer Nature Switzerland AG 2019   457
M. Bungenberg et al. (eds.), *European Yearbook of International Economic Law 2019*,
European Yearbook of International Economic Law (2020) 10: 457–462,
https://doi.org/10.1007/8165_2019_38, Published online: 7 September 2019

matter in a concise yet carefully structured manner. Vadi's approach aims to do this mostly by synthesising the substantive analysis of even more renowned colleagues. As a result, the reader may be inspired by the spectrum of problems and yet somewhat puzzled about the central questions behind these problems; thus the more fundamental question of who should reach for this book and how they read it is raised.

The book consists of three parts and conclusions. The first part includes general characteristics of IIL as a field of international law (Ch. 1) and a general introduction to the migration of constitutional ideas from domestic legal orders to international investment law and arbitration (Ch. 2). The second part consists of three chapters (3–5) dealing with the three substantive areas signalled in its title. Chapter 6 maps the interactions between all three elements, followed by the conclusions. The first thing that strikes one about this book is that three substantive matters of utter complexity, together with fundamental methodological considerations, and even general characteristics of IIL (altogether six chapters followed by conclusions) are squeezed into less than 300 pages. Within this restricted space—thanks to a combination of international law, theory of law, and comparative constitutional law methodologies (p. xx)—the author tackles the interactions between IIL and various axiological orders, proportionality in different legal fields, reasonableness in various legal fields, standards of review generally in international law and specifically in IIL (pp. xviii-xix). The substantive part is followed by 30 pages of tightly scripted bibliography (i.e., over 10% of the actual contents) and the entire book is very well structured, which could reflect a rare virtue of brevity. Nevertheless a large bibliography requires substantial synthesis to be truly admired in this regard Vadi is not always successful.

These quantitative observations should be secondary to the qualitative assessment. Yet, in this particular case, this "formal analysis" gives us insight into the methodology, which had a fundamental impact on the substance. Below, I point out just a few examples where entire paragraphs consist exclusively of opinions and normative findings of other scholars. Although some of these are not very controversial (e.g., proportionality reflects the human yearning for aesthetic beauty) an independent formulation thereof would require proof. This would obviously multiply the page-count to thousands. Instead, the author chooses to meticulously acknowledge a reference for each opinion, each observation, every conclusion, and almost each sentence. Rather than synthesising a number of references (indicated in a single or several footnotes), Vadi leads the reader through a series of other works. Almost each bibliographic note constitutes a sign prescribing the itinerary. To be clear, I appreciate original contribution to the debate in a form of much interesting and much needed, even if somewhat fragile, narrative. However, acknowledgment of the particular mix of density and mode of using references was important to my reading of the book and its conclusions.

Obviously any message needs to begin somehow. To this extent, Chapter 2 on the *Migration of constitutional ideas to international investment law and arbitration* would have seemed to be the substantively justified place to open the book. Whereas IIL academics and practitioners with a background in public international law risk unconsciously falling into public-law thinking to discover normative contents of proportionality, reasonableness, and standard of review, Vadi challenges us to pause before taking this first step. IIL is more than public law (the relationship between foreign investor and the host-state) it is also international (home-host state relations). Since "constitutional ideas vary from jurisdiction to jurisdiction, reflecting the preferences of society . . . it would be problematic to automatically transpose the experience of any particular jurisdiction to the international level" (p. 33). Accordingly, one should not confuse migration of constitutional ideas, which "implies a distance and/or an invisible boundary between the source of given concepts (. . .) and their destination" and constitutionalism, which is "conceptual movements or doctrinal project (. . .)which conceiv[e] public law as a field of knowledge that transcends the dichotomy between the national and the international" (p. 35). But constitutionalism also entails legal risks, including blurring the constitutional-international law distinction, misusing constitutional ideas for purposes undermining constitutional goals, and undermining IIL by adopting a constitutional interpretative lens (pp. 37–38). Against this background, we can analyse that the migration of constitutional ideas through "legal transplants (. . .) would only be legitimate if such concepts were general principles of law or reflected customary international law" (p. 33). Alternatively, migration can occur through cross-judging (i.e., precedents *de facto*), or the coalescence of general principles. Also, in the latter context, one should be wary of mechanical transposition of concepts (p. 44), without a proper understanding of their normative context and significance, as well as a "narrow inquiry, which at best attaches special weight and at worst confines the scope of the review to a single, specific legal system" (quoted after A. Borda, p. 45).

For some reason, perhaps out of an urge to accentuate the book's place within IIL *sensu strice*, the author instead of starting with the subject of Chapter 2 started with a general introduction to IIL instead, hence, Chapter 1 on *International investment law as a field of international law*. In 30 pages, Vadi rushes through the failures of multilateralism and success of bilateralism in IIL, provides a general overview of contents of investment treaties, introduces investment arbitration, discusses the current legitimacy problem as well as different conceptualisations of investment treaty arbitration. Now, given the ambitious nature of this scientific endeavour, arguably not intended for readers fully unfamiliar with the field, the book could do without it. On the other hand, if this part was intended as a crash course in IIL, it would require great attention from the reader to trace the kaleidoscope of hugely important topics, changing every 3–5 pages. With certain interesting substantive considerations hidden among the array of most elementary issues, it is likely that more advanced readers will accidently skip through the value-added bits, which in turn will probably not be fully appreciated by the more scrupulous novice reader. The part on different conceptualisations of investment law (1.5) is a prime example of that. It starts with the all-too obvious public v. private and domestic v. international debate. Subsequently, the author jumps to a meta-analysis of heuristic models "far from having a purely theoretical character" (p. 18), then back to introductory issues, which again are followed by a brief yet meaningful paragraph (1.5.4).

Against this backdrop, Part II focuses on the three substantive areas of the book.

First, it addresses proportionality with its "aesthetic qualities [as] there is something good—certainly something beautiful—in the very idea of things being properly aligned" (quoted after Poole, p. 62). It is deemed to "express objectivity, harmony and justice in legal reasoning" (quote after Tsakyrakis, p. 62) and as a "heuristic device provid[es] a simple, structured and manageable method to adjudicate conflicting values" (quote after Tsakyrakis, p. 62). Chapter 3 opens with a crash course on proportionality: mapping the methodological scope of the problem through various instrumental and theological approaches (p. 54) with an epistemological topping of two sentences (p. 55, top), then structuring a three-part proportionality test (p. 55), then moving to fundamental questions concerning the possibly illusory nature of proportionality creating a mirage rather than order of normative concepts (pp. 55–56). Altogether, a little over one page of text based on 10 difficult bibliographic references. This upbeat pace continues over the subsequent 70 pages dealing with eight problems, followed by conclusions. We thus have five sequential introductory/interim parts to the actual topic (besides the first, also a general overview of the literature on origins and structure of proportionality; functions and advantages; perils; reference to EU law and international trade law), followed by two parts dealing directly with actual proportionality in IIL and then back to the level of general principles of law. The notion of proportionality is tied to mathematical concepts of proportionality and the Renaissance take on the golden section (p. 57). After several very basic observations—compared to the earlier considerations— we're invited to look at the "historical trajectories" of the concept, from Babylonian code of Hammurabi, to Plato and Aristotle, to Greek and Roman law, to medieval law (pp. 58–59), to proportionality becoming "an element of a globalised, common constitutional grammar" in the nineteenth century (quoted after Rautenbach, p. 59). Before the end of the historical introduction to proportionality (part 3.1), we learn, *inter alia*, about "how proportionality works in practice" (four-phase review at pp. 60–61, to be distinguished from the three-part test at p. 55). Undeniably, all these issues are important for a proper understanding of the daunting task at hand (notably the pros and cons of proportionality, respectively, parts 3.2 and 3.3). However, while diving into yet more huge topics of proportionality in EU and GATT-WTO law (3.4–3.5), taking 34 out of the chapter's 74 pages, I could not help but wonder when we would actually get to the gist of the matter?

The core parts are *Proportionality in International Investment Law and Arbitration* (part 3.6) and *Critical Assessment* (3.7). The first seemingly understandable statement is that "the section [3.6] does not purport to be exhaustive (. . .) [it] discusses selected awards that have used the concept of proportionality *expressis verbis*. [. . .] The implicit use of all of the various elements of proportionality without identifying or naming it would give rise to a number of distinct hermeneutical concerns" (footnote 257 on p. 89). Having acknowledged the reasons for restricting the substantive scope of the analysis, one is faced with the most fundamental question—what was the methodology behind the positive choices? Proportionality is traced in investment awards concerning expropriation (3.6.1), FET and Full Protection (3.6.2), non-discrimination (3.6.3), non-precluded measures and exception clauses (3.6.4), and compensation (3.6.5) and procedural matters (3.6.6). In one case, we have up to six pages (3.6.1) where, with one exception, no award occupies more than a single paragraph; at other times the review of arbitral awards consists of one page covering 1–2 rulings (3.6.5–3.6.6). To be clear, a synthesized approach is to be most appreciated in writings on IIL—it is not a problem to multiply the contents with extensive quotes in order to reveal a certain order in the arbitral mosaic. However, the chapter is not an analysis of tribunals' approach to proportionality but a (random?) collection of one-sentence summaries of awards. This limits the possibility of drawing broader conclusions upon this basis (even though the author extrapolates such observations to general patterns without quantitative support for such claims, pp. 105–106) and even later in the book, where the alleged conclusions are repeated or reiterated, they are actually attributed to other scholars (footnote 415 on p. 113).

In the subsequent *Critical Analysis* (3.7) the advancements of the proportionality principle in investment arbitration are compared against the reception thereof by the dispute-settlement bodies of the EU and the WTO. Vadi asks whether proportionality fits with IIL (p. 107), and whether migration is useful and/or desirable. These seem to be purely rhetorical questions, as in the very next sentence the author introduces three factors behind the limited relevance of proportionality (p. 107) and then again addresses those factors with a set of three challenges (p. 114), concluding that proportionality is "useful and desirable in legal systems with constitutional density (. . .) may not be so desirable and/or useful in legal systems that lack constitutional or quasi-constitutional features" (pp. 116–117). This shortage of normative grounds could be compensated, if proportionality was a general principle of law (3.8). Even assuming that we're reading a presentation of scientific research in reversed order with respect to the analysis, the framing of the questions largely predetermines the results.

In light of the above questions concerning the (implicit) methodology, it needs to be stressed that the conclusions of the chapter deserve careful reading. Vadi does synthesize the multidimensional challenge that such a "constitutional transplant" creates. There are possible advantages to this approach; however, there are also numerous perils on such a path.

Observations made with respect to the *Proportionality* chapter could be repeated in two subsequent substantive areas (with a more optimistic outlook with respect to the full embrace of reasonableness).

Taken together, the book *prima facie* creates an impression of bringing order to an ambiguous, complex area, where different legal norms, orders, and philosophies influence each other. Yet, this eclectic method of small steps—from the conclusion of one renowned scholar to another—raises the question as to the extent the choice was made intentionally. Why are the dots connected in this particular order? How would the final image change if we replaced certain scholars with others (perhaps less known and thus requiring critical analysis rather than relying on their "brand")? Obviously, the author humbly considers the book a voice in the discussion and not the guide to the problems at hand (NB. the author explicitly declares that she is not advocating in favour or against proportionality or reasonableness, p. 266). But it is more than the usual caveat. Because of the particular methodology of a linear, single-thread narrative, the emerging view could fundamentally change with a minor alteration of any part.

Vadi's book charts the development of IIL and as such it certainly can inspire the reader to look at the problem at hand from new angles and to broaden one's perception. At the same time, it is important to know what one is reaching for, and this volume does not provide actual analysis, rather it offers a particular reading. As such it might be better titled: *An Advanced Reader's Guide to Proportionality, Reasonableness and Standards of Review in International Investment Law and Arbitration.*

References

Vadi V (2013) Public Health in International Investment Law and Arbitration. Routledge, London
Vadi V (2014) Cultural Heritage in International Investment Law and Arbitration. Cambridge University Press, Cambridge
Vadi V (2015) Analogies in International Investment Law and Arbitration. Cambridge University Press, Cambridge

Marcin J. Menkes   is an associate professor at the Warsaw School of Economics, where he directs the Post-graduate studies of Law & Economics of the Securities Market and Law & Economics for Corporate Counsels. He is a lawyer admitted to Warsaw Bar Association and holds dr. habil. from the Jagiellonian University. He is also graduate of Ph.D. studies in economics (Warsaw School of Economics).

Stephan Griller, Walter Obwexer, and Erich Vranes (Eds.), Mega-Regionals Trade Agreements: CETA, TTIP, and TiSA – New Orientations for EU External Economic Relations

Oxford University Press, 2017, ISBN 9780198808893

Maria Laura Marceddu

Mega-Regionals Trade Agreements: CETA, TTIP, and TiSA – New Orientations for EU External Economic Relations is a book about how three mega-regional agreements (CETA, TTIP, and TiSA) impact on, shape, and re-orient the EU's external relations and, more broadly, the international economic order.

Although the volume focuses predominantly on CETA and on the available information and negotiating materials of TTIP and TiSA several contributors also consider the Trans-Pacific Agreement, and other EU FTAs, such as the EU agreements with Singapore and Vietnam. The book has three main parts. The first sets the scene and contextualizes the issue of mega-regional economic instruments within the EU's external relations. The second part expands on selected issues, covering key areas on which these agreements might have an impact, such as trade, investment, intellectual property, data protection, financial services, and environmental and labour standards. The third part considers the challenges posed by these agreements, both in terms of economic development and global governance.

The book traces the origins of the mega-regional agreements to various limitations of the WTO system, although there is some disagreement and differing emphasis among the authors on the particular causal links. In the opening article, Stephan Griller, Walter Obwexer, and Erich Vranes argue that the stalemate of the Doha Round, along with outdated services regulations and the lack of measures to tackle non-trade barriers effectively, made the WTO an inadequate multilateral setting for negotiating regulatory issues. They claim it is as a result of these factors that states have been drawn towards regional initiatives. However, Ernst-Ulrich

M. L. Marceddu (✉)
King's College London, London, UK
e-mail: maria.marceddu@kcl.ac.uk

© Springer Nature Switzerland AG 2019   463
M. Bungenberg et al. (eds.), *European Yearbook of International Economic Law 2019*,
European Yearbook of International Economic Law (2020) 10: 463–468,
https://doi.org/10.1007/8165_2019_39, Published online: 31 July 2019

Petersmann claims in his article that the primary factor behind mega-regional agreements is to be found more in the limits of the WTO consensus-based negotiations and the single-undertaking approach rather than specific failings associated with the Doha Round, since the latter has not impeded the successful conclusion of other agreements. According to Petersmann, mega-regional agreements are symptomatic of the disagreement among the 164 WTO Members about political, legal, and judicial methodologies in WTO governance, as illustrated by politically motivated refusals to appoint Appellate Body judges since 2016 and the inconclusive negotiations about improvements of the WTO Dispute Settlement Understanding. In his view, mega-regional FTAs are the political responses to governance failures in WTO practices, and emphasise the need to review how 'principles of justice' should guide and limit trade regulation and adjudication inside and outside the WTO.

The limitations of the WTO system and the fragmentation of international economic law are recurrent themes in several of the articles. Christoph Ohler, for example, emphasizes that the WTO, as well as other international regulatory institutions, have proven to be inadequate forums for handling the relations between trade and regulatory issues in the context of financial services. Against this backdrop, CETA and the TTIP draft promisingly appear to fill the gaps. Ohler welcomes the inclusion of a chapter on regulatory cooperation in the TTIP, and he observes that CETA's approach is particularly interesting when it comes to the 'prudential carve-out', i.e. the right of prudential regulation for the proper functioning of individual institutions (such as consumers, bank customers, securities firms, and insurance companies) and the financial market as a whole. Going beyond the prescriptions of the GATS, CETA develops further high-level principles for the application of this carve-out, among which is explicit reference to international prudential commitments that are common to the parties. Despite these positive contributions, Ohler ultimately maintains that to overcome the persistent mutual distrust among states in relation to financial services and to recognize the regulations of other trading partners, a multilateral approach remains preferable to bilateral interactions.

Erich Vranes warns against the constraints these renewed bilateral and plurilateral settings pose to today's economic relations, with a particular focus on the trade disciplines envisaged in these agreements. In his view, these mega-regionals are a clear attempt to go beyond the corpus of WTO trade rules, and they all represent what have been called 'WTO-plus' agreements. In principle, he acknowledges that CETA and TTIP might be praised for surpassing WTO law through, inter alia, rules on regulatory cooperation, in terms of both their substance and their depth of commitments when trade in goods and services is at stake. In practice, however, some fundamental issues have remained unclear, such as the interplay between market access and non-discrimination disciplines in the field of services. Even more alarming, the regulatory cooperation established under the CETA and TTIP projects introduces rules that are meant to be non-binding. Therefore, the success of this soft approach risks being undermined by and made heavily reliant on political will and political contingencies. For these reasons, Vranes argues that mega-regionals have ended up looking like 'WTO-minus' agreements, with detrimental effects that increase the fragmentation of the WTO system. In Vranes's view, a truly multilateral setting would be more desirable than bilateral or plurilateral negotiations.

That multilateralism is the ideal setting even from an economic perspective is further emphasized by Christoph Moser. While recognizing that negative effects from these mega-regionals agreements are quite unlikely, he nonetheless claims that these agreements might cause trade diversion, especially for those non-participating countries geographically close to, and integrated with, the EU and its partners.

Beyond the repercussions these agreements might have on the cohesion of the international economic order as a whole, decentralized plurilateral negotiations hold the potential to undermine the WTO system itself, or to water down EU policies. In relation to the latter, two contributors insist on the negative impact mega-regionals might have on certain EU policies. Walter Berka deals with the deep Atlantic divide regarding data protection. In his view, the transatlantic agreement is particularly problematic and tends to exacerbate the divergences between the approaches of the US and the EU. On the EU side of the Atlantic, data protection operates through an overarching framework: Data protection is a human right, which everybody (regardless of their origins) can rely on; and the processing of data is generally prohibited. The US, by contrast, has traditionally opted for a piecemeal approach, with data protection operating only in favour of US citizens, and data processing allowed unless expressly prohibited by US law. Unsurprisingly, the EU's view is that personal data can be shared only with those countries that display adequate levels of protection of privacy. From the US standpoint, however, data protection amounts to a trade barrier against economic interests. Bridging the two approaches looks difficult, if not impossible, and Berka wonders whether the successful story of EU data protection will continue or whether data protection will cede ground to competing economic interests. While the latter does not appear manifest in CETA, the TiSA proposal appears to emphasize the free flow of information more than it does data protection, thereby raising questions on the desirability of new international rules for data protection, even for the EU.

The other contributor to warn against the watering down of EU policies triggered by these comprehensive FTAs is Lorand Bartels' article on human rights, labour standards, and environmental standards. In relation to CETA, Bartels observes that the agreement combines traditional elements with new ones. Substantive standards on labour and the environment belong to the former category, as the way they are drafted in CETA is broadly in line with recent EU and Canadian agreements. When it comes to the novel elements, Bartels finds it particularly interesting that the implementation of relevant standards has somehow been watered down. In his view, this is particularly notable in the clause on human rights in the 2016 EU–Canada Strategic Partnership Agreement, which cross-refers to CETA and provides for the termination, but not the suspension, of the agreement in the case of human rights' violations by either signatory. While the clause aligns with Canadian practice, from an EU standpoint the clause marks an important shift in EU practice, which has traditionally been anchored in a 1995 policy that permits the partial or full suspension of an agreement in case of human rights' violations.

Despite recognizing the presence of certain limitations, the volume takes the view that these mega-regionals agreements offer, in principle, an opportunity to rethink the rules currently governing the international economic order, and possibly to address some of the existing problems. Many contributors emphasize, however, that the considerable expectations placed on these agreements are ultimately frustrated, particularly by CETA. This sense of frustration is particularly acute when intellectual property and investment issues are at stake. Tomas Cottier, for example, recognizes in his article that the new standards developed under CETA and the TPP agreement are likely to benefit other WTO members through the most-favoured nation clause included in the TRIPS agreement. However, these mega-regionals lack the audacity to properly overcome existing problems, especially when it comes to the interactions between IP and other FTA chapters, and they overlook the potential overlaps and conflict of norms to which those who are parties to more than one preferential agreement are exposed.

In their contribution, Christian Tietje and Kevin Crow point out that the reform carried out in the investment chapters of these comprehensive FTAs is not substantial, or at least is not as innovative as is sometimes claimed. Although acknowledging certain welcome clarifications in its wording, the authors observe that these clarifications remain limited merely to codifying the existing practice of arbitral tribunals, which is particularly noticeable in the EU–Vietnam FTA, rather than truly engaging in any call for reform. While the changes introduced by recently negotiated mega-regionals have indeed played a part in addressing the problems related to arbitrators' interpretations, they are inadequate when it comes to addressing the structural problems long affecting the investment regime. The elephant in the room is, in fact, the asymmetry of the investment system, which assigns only rights to investors and only obligations to states. Against this backdrop, the proposed reforms lack focus, as they do not change the functioning of the system. In Tietje and Crow's view, what is needed to this end is a considerable reform in the investment system's structure through the introduction of counterclaims by states against investors, which would redress the regime's asymmetry. By the same token, Verena Madner's article questions why foreign investors are to be granted special rights in highly developed judicial systems like the European and the Canadian ones. This is, in her view, symptomatic of broader power asymmetries within the EU's trade policy, in respect of which the political debate over the values reflected in these agreements and their distributional effects is often overshadowed by rhetorical promises, or else entirely disregarded. Trade, in her view, is not an end in itself, but a tool to benefit people and should serve to enhance values such as transparency and sustainability.

Beyond the legal and economic questions, things are further complicated by the controversial distribution of competences these agreements entail for EU competences. Stefan Mayr has extensively examined the impact these agreements have on the fundamentals of the EU order, and on the complex relationship between the EU and its Member States, as well as between EU institutions themselves. Issues that have proven particularly contentious are competence and mixity. Based on Opinion 2/15 (pending at the time when Mayr's article was written), Mayr rightly predicted the mixity of CETA, even though he emphasizes that mixity remains a 'second best solution' to the effective representation of EU interests at international level. It is not clear what will happen with TTIP, since the negotiations have been put on hold. As regards TiSA, Mayr suggests that it should fall under the Common Commercial Policy, even though the question of mixity is likely to arise again in the area of transport—as confirmed by Opinion 2/15.[1] In respect of competence, Mayr submits that the establishment of an investor–state dispute settlement mechanism, as envisaged in CETA and TTIP, might conflict with EU law. As Stefan Griller notes in his article, the imbalanced advantages for investors at dispute settlement level are likely to raise further problems in terms of the permissibility of the creation of international tribunals whose rulings might impact on EU law. While the establishment of these tribunals is not in principle incompatible with EU law (as articulated by the CJEU in its Opinion 2/13[2]), the CJEU will ultimately clarify the extent of this compatibility as requested by Belgium.[3]

Doubts about the investor–state dispute settlement system are also expressed by Stephan W Schill. The low level of judicialization in inter-state dispute settlement, characteristic of both CETA and TPP, minimizes the negative effects on WTO dispute settlement; thereby preserving WTO authority, shrugging off the risk of conflicts, and avoiding fragmentation. However, when it comes to investor–state dispute settlement Schill seems rather sceptical. He recognizes that CETA and TPP have attempted to address some of the concerns raised against ISDS by, for example, increasing transparency, providing for a joint interpretative mechanism, imposing ethical rules on the adjudicators, and adopting more detailed language. The promising effects of this reformed ISDS falter upon encountering the starkly divergent positions of the EU and the US when it comes to its constitutional structure. While both players agree on the need to preserve a regulatory space and tighter state control, their positions diverge regarding the nature of structural change. The US (at least prior to the Trump administration) prefers to reform ISDS, whereas the EU is more inclined towards its proper institutionalization, advancing the idea of creating an international investment court. In Schill's view such a court should be presented less as a solution to a problem and more as a means to shape the future institutional infrastructure of the global economy in line with constitutional values, like the principle of democracy, the concept of the rule of law, and the protection of fundamental and human rights.

The uncertainty surrounding the allocation of EU competences within external relations arguably accentuates the apprehension of EU citizens, who are already increasingly estranged from the multi-level decision-making system of the EU. In this respect, several contributors have hailed transparency as instrumental to enhancing the legitimacy of the EU. Sonja Puntscher Riekmann emphasizes that secrecy of negotiations is harmful to citizens, who feel largely ignored within FTA negotiations. In her view, relaunching the debate on EU representative democracy is the

---

[1] Opinion 2/15, *EU–Singapore FTA* [2017] ECLI:EU:C:2017:376, para 168.
[2] Opinion 2/13, *ECHR II* [2014] ECLI:EU:C:2014:2454, para 182.
[3] Opinion 1/17, *EU–Canada CET Agreement* [2019] ECLI:EU:C:2019:341.

way for the EU organs to regain public trust and to demonstrate they are genuinely representing the European interests in international forums, albeit the process might take years to be completed.

Despite transparency being ever more linked to legitimacy, Panagiotis Delimatsis postulates that the intention in the EU treaties to implement transparency in practice is not always fulfilled, as shown by the negotiations of CETA and TiSA. Different considerations pertain to the TTIP negotiations, whose transparency records are quite unique and are likely to mark the beginning of a new period in international negotiations. The significant turn towards greater transparency within the trans-atlantic negotiations is indeed praiseworthy, especially in respect to the release of documents like the negotiating directives issued by the Council and the negotiating text proposed from the EU Commission to the US. In Delimatsis's view, early involvement and diffusion of information are crucial to enhance accountability and legitimacy, even though these practices need to be developed and implemented consistently for the agreements due to enter into force in the very near future.

As a whole, this volume is a milestone in the study of recent mega-regionals agreements and their impacts on several legal fields. In today's changing landscape, the book will be a fundamental resource for lawyers, economists, policymakers, government officials, and scholars from various disciplines. It addresses critical topics clearly and comprehensively, and the articles engage readers to navigate the present intricacies of the international economic order.

Maria Laura Marceddu is visiting lecturer in international investment law at King's College London. She has recently been elected executive treasurer of the Society of International Economic Law (2018), where she also serves as the coordinator of the investment law network. Maria Laura comes with an interdisciplinary background that combines International Relations and Legal expertise. She holds a BA (*Laurea Triennale*) in Political Sciences, a MA (*Laurea Specialisitica*) in International Relations (magna cum laude) at LUISS University of Rome, and a PhD in Law Research at King's College London.

Constantine Michalopoulous, Aid, Trade and Development. 50 Years of Globalization (Palgrave Macmillan, 2017, ISBN 9783319658605)/Clair Gammage, North-South Regional Trade Agreements as Legal Regimes. A Critical Assessment of the EU-SADC Economic Partnership Agreement (Edward Elgar, 2017, ISBN 9781784719616)

Maryna Rabinovych

Contents

The post-World War II era has been marked by the multi-dimensional globalization, leading to the expansion and sophistication of political and economic interdependencies between the developed and developing countries. Not surprisingly, the expansion of global trade, investment and aid flows and the proliferation of respective international law and governance structures have been accompanied by intense policy and scholarly debate that, in turn, has been shaping crucial turns in the trade and aid policies of major powers.[1] With an ambitious task to "trace the evolution of thinking and practice of developed and developing country policies on trade and foreign aid" over the period from the 1960s to modern days, Constantine Michalopoulous narrates it as a story of uncertainty, ambitious hypotheses, trials, errors, and the correction of mistakes. Interestingly, the author declines a strictly chronological approach in favour of looking at turning points in the history of development cooperation, such as the 1973 oil crisis, the debt crisis and the debates on debt relief in 1980s, the inception of the WTO, the challenge of aiding post-Soviet countries following the Union's dissolution and the Greek crisis. While providing an

---

[1]For a meta-study on the evolution of the relationship between trade and aid policy, see: Suwa-Eisenmann and Verdier (2007).

M. Rabinovych (✉)
University of Hamburg, Hamburg, Germany
e-mail: m-rabinovych@europa-kolleg-hamburg.de

© Springer Nature Switzerland AG 2019   469
M. Bungenberg et al. (eds.), *European Yearbook of International Economic Law 2019*,
European Yearbook of International Economic Law (2020) 10: 469–476,
https://doi.org/10.1007/8165_2019_40, Published online: 7 September 2019

in-depth account of ideas, shocks, and various actors' policy reactions that shaped modern development economics, Michalopoulous, however, acknowledges the open-endedness of many conceptual economic questions, such as the interplay between trade liberalization and economic growth/poverty reduction, the redistributive effects of trade liberalization and the determination of aid effectiveness. As such, "*Aid, Trade and Development*" contributes to voluminous literature, directed to explaining the factors of development, by arguing that "both aid and trade can benefit development, but whether they actually do depends very much on coherent supportive policies in both developed and developing countries" (p. 4). More specifically, it falls within the research strand that studies the nexus between trade liberalization (market openness) and development (economic growth, poverty alleviation).[2] Simultaneously resonating with the 1977 Brandt Commission's Report "North-South: A Programme for Survival"[3] and modern focus on policy coherence in the global governance for sustainable development,[4] the contribution, however, does not touch upon the modern institutional and legal explanations of development (reflected *inter alia* in New Institutional Economics and governance paradigms of international development).[5]

This is one of the key reasons why it is worth starting to read "North-South Regional Trade Agreements as Legal Regimes..." by Clair Gammage just after turning over the last page of "Aid, Trade and Development". Conceptualizing the EU's Economic Partnership Agreements (EPAs) with African countries as development-oriented "region-to-region spaces, integrated through law" (p. 3), Gammage dedicates significant attention to law as a medium of development. To deconstruct the EU's relationships with African, Caribbean, and Pacific countries (ACPs), she refers to multiple norms, contained in GATT and WTO Agreements, EU Treaties, and secondary law, as well as the jurisprudence of the Dispute Settlement Body, and explains their implications for using EPAs as engines for development. Second, the book by Gammage can be a useful follow-up to reading "*Aid, Trade and Development...*", because it takes us from the global to the regional level of analysis and allows for imaginative application of analytical concepts and policy insights from the former to a single case study of the EPA between the EU and the South African Development Community. Third, in discipline-related terms, "North-South Regional Trade Agreements as Legal Regimes..." takes us from international to EU studies by explaining the nuances of the relationship between market and normative aspects of power Europe in EU-ACP relationships and elaborating on role of EU law norms as a means of constructing interregional legal regimes. Hence, the contribution lies at the crossroads of a number of research

---

[2]Van den Berg and Lewer (2015).

[3]See: Independent Commission on International Development Issues (1980). North-South: a Programme or Survival, 1980. https://idl-bnc-idrc.dspacedirect.org/handle/10625/5357 (last accessed 2 November 2018).

[4]See, for instance: Forster and Stokke (2013).

[5]See: Davis and Trebilcock (2008).

strands, such as EU studies, foreign policy, and EU external relations law, and, more broadly, the dynamics of North-South trade liberalization,[6] New Regionalism,[7] as well as the interplay between law and development.[8]

Although the contributions in question conduct analysis at different levels and belong to divergent research strands, they share several crucial themes. First, both texts look at non-trade objectives of multi-, regional and bilateral trade policies, thus, supplementing emerging literature on the interplay between trade and non-trade objectives and the latter's enforceability under the WTO and EU law. Encompassing *inter alia* sustainable development and climate governance, corruption and good governance, human rights and labour standards, non-trade objectives become increasingly debated with respect to (1) the legal framing and enforceability of non-trade objectives in multi- and bilateral trade agreements and (2) the implications of the expansion of non-trade objectives for global and regional trade governance.[9] Whereas Gammage extensively engages with both themes in her analysis of the EU-SADC EPA, Michalopoulous emphasizes the importance of understanding macroeconomic links between trade, the non-trade development agenda, and aid. Second, both Michalopoulous and Gammage explore the interlinkages between donors' foreign policy, security, trade and development objectives, engaging with the literature on the interfaces between the market and normative rationales behind the non-trade agenda in modern trade liberalization. To exemplify the triumph of self-interest in the trade-aid nexus, Michalopoulous referred to the rise of impediments to access to developed country markets (especially, in the domains of developing countries' export interest, such as agriculture and textile) following the implementation of Uruguay Round Agreements and the limited scope of Generalized Schemes of Preferences (GSP). Similarly, Gammage is quite frank, when criticizing adverse in-depth interdependencies, created by the Lome partnership and, later on, accusing the Union of consciously taking an insufficient account of political and economic realities in Caribbean counties, when pushing for the EPA with CARIFORUM (Caribbean Forum). Expectedly, both Gammage and Michalopoulous touched upon the theme of "winners" and "losers" of trade and aid at the global and regional levels respectively and highlighted the reasons thereof, stemming from both developed and developing countries. For instance, Gammage connected insignificant developmental effects of the EU-SADC EPA both to the deficiencies in framing the EPA (especially, its institutional arrangements), and the flourishing political economy of neopatrimonialism in the SADC. Based on his experiences in East Asia and the former USSR countries, Michalopoulous underlined the importance of developing countries' commitment to policy reforms that frequently go in line with North-South trade liberalization. Third, reflecting on the ways to boost the effectiveness of trade and aid policies, the authors point to the

---

[6] Gilbert et al. (2015) and Manger and Schadlen (2014).
[7] Hettne et al. (2016).
[8] Davis and Trebilcock (2008) and Krever (2011).
[9] Milewicz et al. (2018).

importance of coherence between trade, aid, and all other developed countries' policies that may affect developing countries, hence, contributing to the research on policy coherence in international and EU development cooperation. In this respect, it is worth highlighting brilliant examples of incoherence between trade and aid policies, used by Michalopolous, such as the U.S' simultaneous support of Sri Lankan textile exports and imposition of quantitative restrictions thereto in the late 1990s, and Gammage's critical discussion of coherence challenges, accompanying the implementation of "deep" and ambitious EU-CARIFORUM EPA.

While both books share common themes ("non-trade objectives", "self-interest vs development objectives", winners and losers from trade and aid and policy coherence), each of the books in question bears unique emphases, features, added value and approach to the narrative. Hence, the key trait that differentiates "*Aid, Trade and Development*" from most of "Development Economics" titles is its focus on linkages between different-scale policy challenges (e.g., oil shocks of 1973, the dissolution of the USSR or the bank crisis in Thailand in 1997), the evolution of development policy paradigms at the multi- and bilateral levels and he consequences of such changes. For instance, Michalopolous provides an in-detail explanation of the connections between the genesis and peculiarities of the debt crisis of the early 1980s, the IMF's and World Bank's immediate policy responses to it and the introduction of the "Washington Consensus" as the world's first comprehensive strategy that links aid, trade, and development. Second, in each case the author makes a particular effort to display the relevant domestic policies of developing countries, emphasizing the need for coherence between aid and trade policies of developed countries, on the one hand, and respective policies of developing countries, on the other hand. Such nexus is of special visibility in the excellently written chapter on Greek crisis that discusses policy reactions at the national, European, and international (IMF, World Bank) levels. Furthermore, the added value of the contribution is its detailed analysis of ideas' and policies' failures and lessons learnt. For example, discussing the early years of the "Washington Consensus" and Structural Adjustment Programs (SAPs), Michalopoulous pays particular attention to unveiling the reasons for the failure of early SAPs in Sub-Saharan Africa (such as the lack of country-specific approaches and local ownership) and the steps the World Bank took to counter these issues. An in-depth focus on developed and developing countries' policies' design, and an account of country-specific factors and local ownership is also contained in the discussion on the nexus between trade liberalization and poverty alleviation (in Vietnam, Mauritius, Zambia and Zimbabwe). Another important reason why "*Aid, Trade and Development*" deserves a reader's attention is its "*The Twilight of Liberalism?*" chapter that discusses modern challenges to globalization, trade and aid, such as the rise of anti-globalization populism, anti-immigration sentiments and protectionist movements in the USA and Europe, the death of the WTO Doha Round and the weakening of international aid effectiveness commitments since the 2011 High-Level Meeting in Busan. Noting that nowadays "the developed world is starting to look ominously inward" (p. 301), Michalopoulous, nonetheless, encourages the international community to mobilize itself around two crucial tasks: development of the social protection systems for those, "left behind" by globalization processes and continuing to support developing countries' efforts to achieve the Sustainable Development Goals (SDGs) (p. 333)

As opposed to the work by Michalopolous, that does not apply a particular theoretical lens to the problematic of trade, aid, and development, the work by Clair Gammage is distinguished by its elaborate interdisciplinary nature and the elegancy of its theoretical approach. Arguing that the modern international economic order is characterized both by increased integration and fragmentation, Gammage emphasizes the significance of regionalism as a trade strategy and, more broadly, "the form of social interaction". Based on the insights from both rationalist and constructivist schools of international political economy (IPE) and Habermasian discourse theory of law, the monograph suggests concentrating on the modern shift to inter-regionalism or, in other words, the creation of "region-to-region spaces, integrated through law" that also represent discursive spaces for deliberation (p. 3). The value of such an approach lies in the fact that it enables a researcher to deconstruct interregional relationships and reveal power asymmetries therein through the analysis of legal norms that serve as a medium of integration for the respective inter-regional space. While Gammage concentrates on a single case study of the EU-SADC EPA (also drawing some insights from the EU-CARIFORUM EPA), the theoretical framework she uses can be extrapolated to other regional trade agreements, not even necessarily North-South ones. Such extrapolation will evidently make sense, since the studies of politics and law of EU's regional trade agreements (RTAs), and the dynamics of the EU's global role remain highly disintegrated,[10] largely due to the lacking conceptualization of RTAs as relatively self-standing *legal regimes*. Next, while Michalopoulous traces the interplay between trade, aid, and development from the macroeconomic and development policy perspectives, Gammage analyses a large corpus of the WTO and EU legal acts and jurisprudence to find out whether sustainable development represents a "justiciable legal norm" in the context of international trade. Initially suspecting a shift toward recognizing sustainable development a norm of legal nature on international and EU level, Gammage further points to "vague, imprecise and ambiguous language" of development concepts, depriving them of legal normativity (p. 135). Hence, in her discussion, Gammage is extremely critical about the added value of trade-sustainable development nexus in EU RTAs, thus, detaching herself from an array of recent contributions, emphasizing the positive role of EU RTAs in promoting sustainable development and good environmental governance. Besides a novel interdisciplinary theoretical framework and an in-depth legal analysis of sustainable development concept as embedded into modern international trade, the work by Gammage is distinctive due to the author's in-depth knowledge of the South African domestic context and the dynamics of regional integration. While the EU promotes "regime-boosting regionalism" as a panacea for growth and development in the ACP region, Clair Gammage convincingly demonstrated how the "spaghetti bowl" of

---

[10]For an example of a study, lying at the crossroads of the above research strands, see: Araujo (2016).

regional integration projects, coupled with neo-patrimonial nature of domestic politics actually impedes economic development in the South. Moreover, the author's in-depth understanding of the region is reflected in her analysis of the SADC countries' positions in the negotiations of the EU-SADC EPA, and comparative insights into the challenges of implementing EU-SADC and EU-CARIFORUM EPA. Hence, Gammage manages to demonstrate the reasons why the vast majority of the EPAs deviate from the EU's original ambitions, and advocates for meaningful implementation of existing EPAs for the sake of future widening of the EU-ACP trade and development relationship.

Notwithstanding multiple advantages and profound insights, offered by both of the contributions under review, several critical points are to be raised with respect to each of them. While in *"North-South Regional Trade Agreements as Legal Regimes. . ."* Clair Gammage introduces an impressive interdisciplinary theoretical framework for the research of inter-regionalism; her conclusions offer an insufficient linkage between her framework and the case of EU-SADC EPA. Furthermore, I found it surprising that, positioning her research as based on a single case study of the EU-SADC EPA, Gammage extensively utilized evidence from the negotiation and implementation of the EU-CARIFORUM EPA and drew multiple parallels between the EU-SADC and EU-CARIFORUM EPA. Given the fact that EU-SADC EPA is a "goods-only" EPA and the EU-CARIFORUM EPA encompasses services and numerous "deep disciplines", the comparison between them is highly relevant in view of the author's aspiration to explore EPAs as legal regimes, but requires preliminary clarification in the introductory part and a stronger comparative focus. Finally, to my mind, *"North-South Regional Trade Agreements as Legal Regimes. . ."* would also benefit from a more detailed discussion of the findings' implications particularly to North-South relationships, and the opportunities and challenges of extrapolating theoretical framework/findings of the research to further cases of North-South trade and development cooperation. As regards *"Aid, Trade and Development. . ."*, it seems that the book could have benefited from adding a law and governance dimension to the trade-aid nexus debate, and a more integrated debate on "supporting policies" of developed and developing countries, capable of reinforcing the synergies between aid and trade. In terms of audience for these books both *"Aid, Trade and Development. . ."* and *"North-South Regional Trade Agreements as Legal Regimes. . ."* are most suited to those with a good preliminary understanding of key concepts, stemming from development economics, political science and legal studies.

Exploring multiple inter-linkages between international trade and aid, law and development, regionalism and globalization, both books portray the evolution of trade and aid as an uneven path of harsh challenges, sophisticated policy solutions, and continuous search for lessons to be learnt from policy practice. Therefore, the interfaces between the above concepts and their reflections in developed and developing countries' policies represent an exciting domain for further research, especially under the "twilight of liberalism". Well-written, coherent and thought-provoking, *"Aid, Trade and Development. . ."* and *"North-South Regional Trade Agreements as Legal Regimes. . ."* will be of interest for both scholars and practitioners of development cooperation.

References

Araujo D (2016) The EU deep trade agenda: law and policy. OUP, Oxford

Davis KE, Trebilcock M (2008) The relationship between law and development: optimists vs sceptics. Am J Comp Law 56(4):895–946

Forster J, Stokke O (eds) (2013) Policy coherence in development cooperation. Routledge, London

Gilbert J, Beladi H, Oladi R (2015) North-south trade liberalization and economic welfare. Rev Dev Econ 19(4):1006–1117

Hettne B, Sunkel O, Inotai A (2016) Globalism and new regionalism. Palgrave Macmillan, London

Krever T (2011) The legal turn and the late development theory: the rule of law and the World Bank's development model. Harv Int Law J 52(1):288–319

Manger MS, Schadlen KC (2014) Political trade dependence and North-South trade agreements. Int Stud Q 58(1):79–91

Milewicz K, Hollway J, Peacock C (2018) Beyond trade. The expanding scope of the nontrade agenda in trade agreements. J Conflict Resolution 62(4):743–773

Suwa-Eisenmann A, Verdier T (2007) Aid and trade. Oxf Rev Econ Policy 23(3):481–507

Van den Berg H, Lewer J (2015) International trade and economic growth. Routledge, New York

Maryna Rabinovych LL.M (Hamburg) is a PhD Candidate at the University of Hamburg and Global Community Manager at the Ukraine Democracy Initiative (University of Sydney). Her research interests include EU external relations law, EU trade law, trade and development nexus in the EU, Agenda 2030 and its implementation by the EU.Ms. Rabinovych held visiting positions at the Universities of Thessaloniki (2016/2017) and Vienna (2018). She holds an LL. B from Odessa National University and an LL.M in EU law from the University of Hamburg.

Printed by Printforce, the Netherlands